CRITICAL ACCLAIM FOR THE BERKELEY GUIDES

"[The Berkeley Guides are] brimming with useful information for the low-budget traveler — material delivered in a fresh, funny, and often irreverent way." —*The Philadelphia Inquirer*

"...hip, blunt and lively....these Cal students boogie down and tell you where to sleep in a cowboy bunkhouse, get a tattoo and eat cheap meals cooked by aspiring chefs." —*Atlanta Journal Constitution*

"...Harvard hasn't yet met 'On the Loose's' pledge to plant two trees in Costa Rica for every one felled to print its books—a promise that, given the true grit of these guides, might well mean a big new forest in Central America." —*Newsweek*

"[The Berkeley Guides] offer straight dirt on everything from hostels to look for and beaches to avoid to museums least likely to attract your parents...they're fresher than Harvard's Let's Go series." —*Seventeen*

"The books are full of often-amusing tips written in a youth-tinged conversational style." —*The Orlando Sentinel*

"So well-organized and well-written that I'm almost willing to forgive the recycled paper and soy-based ink." —*P.J. O'Rourke*

"These guys go to great lengths to point out safe attractions and routes for women traveling alone, minorities and gays. If only this kind of caution weren't necessary. But I'm glad someone finally thought of it."

—*Sassy*

"The very-hip Berkeley Guides look like a sure-fire hit for students and adventurous travelers of all ages. This is real budget travel stuff, with the emphasis on meeting new places head on, up close and personal....this series is going to go places." —*The Hartford Courant*

"The guides make for fun and/or enlightening reading."

—*The Los Angeles Times*

"The new On the Loose guides are more comprehensive, informative and witty than Let's Go ." —*Glamour*

the BERKELEY guides

THE BUDGET TRAVELER'S HANDBOOK

SAN FRANCISCO

ON THE LOOSE **1995**

WRITTEN BY BERKELEY STUDENTS IN COOPERATION WITH THE
ASSOCIATED STUDENTS OF THE UNIVERSITY OF CALIFORNIA

SAN FRANCISCO ON THE LOOSE

Editors: Nicole Harb, Elda Tsou
Editorial Coordinators: Laura Comay Bloch, Sharron S. Wood
Executive Editor: Scott McNeely
Creative Director: Fabrizio La Rocca
Cartographer: David Lindroth, Inc.; Eureka Cartography
Text Design: Tigist Getachew
Cover Design and Illustration: Rico Lins

SPECIAL SALES

Contents

PRESENTING
AN INDEPENDENT
APPROACH TO
TRAVEL.

If you have independent ideas about travel, we specialize in putting you exactly where you want to be. And with over 100 offices worldwide, we'll take care of you when you're there. So when it's time to plan your trip, call us at 1.800.777.0112.

New York: 212-477-7166
Washington DC: 202-887-0912
Philadelphia: 215-382-2928
Boston: 617-266-6014
Los Angeles: 213-934-8722
San Francisco: 415-391-8407

STA
STA TRAVEL
We've been there

Thanks to You

Lots of people helped us put together the _Berkeley Guide to San Francisco._ Some are listed below, but many others, whom our writers met briefly on buses, in cafés, and in clubs, also helped out. We would like you to help us update this book and give us feedback. Drop us a line—a postcard, a scrawled note on some toilet paper, whatever—and we'll be happy to acknowledge your contribution below. Our address is 515 Eshleman Hall, University of California, Berkeley, CA 94720.

Special thanks go to Chris Barton, San Francisco; Laura Boatman, Tilden Regional Park; Brian Callanan, Berkeley; Robin Haglund, Albany; Rad Hall, Pacifica; Charles Hendricks and Diana Giese, Castro Valley; Michael Huff, San Francisco; Wendy Jameson and Greg Chin, Berkeley; Rich Jepsen, Olympic Circle Sailing Club; Dan Kotin, Berkeley; Karmela Lejarde, Washington, D.C.; Carlos Luna, Berkeley; Sean McFarland, San Francisco; Rob Middleton, San Francisco; Ohana, Golden Gate Women's Soccer League; Jeffrey B. Roth, Los Angeles; Laura Schultz, San Francisco; James Silliman, Anthony Chabot Regional Park; Jim Stanley, San Francisco; Armando Ugarte, Berkeley; Melissa Wahl, Columbus, OH; Mike Westphal and Ryan Martin, Butano State Park.

Berkeley Bios

Behind every restaurant blurb, lodging review, and introduction in this book lurks a student writer. After years of living in San Francisco and the East Bay, the writers had plenty of ideas about how to have a great time here for next to nothing. They spent the summer sizing up all their favorite places and dozens of unknown, out-of-the-way joints to bring you the very best ways to live in and explore the Bay Area on a budget.

The Writers

Move over, Norm Peterson: After writing for the Berkeley Guides, **Carmen Aguirre** may have a few things to teach you. Updating the Shopping chapter was a return to familiar territory for her, but working on the After Dark section demanded that she learn some essential tools for her new vocation as a bar fly—how to play "My Life is Worse than Yours," how to think up a story pathetic enough to be offered one "on the house," and (the all important) how to get kicked out of a bar without picking up your tab. In an attempt to make this knowledge useful, Carmen has been talking about approaching the university with a proposal for a class in which she can teach her newly acquired skills. She's managed to compile quite an extensive reading list so far, mostly with books by Charles Bukowski.

Kelly Green, a four-year resident of San Francisco, ventured into the Bay Area restaurant and café scene on assignment for the Berkeley Guides and emerged wired beyond belief and salivating uncontrollably. Kelly scouted Palo Alto looking for the Cheapest Sushi in the World (she found it), wandered slack-jawed through Berkeley's Gourmet Ghetto looking for the Perfect Slice of Pizza (she found that, too), and trod along the streets of Tiburon, looking for the Perfect View of the City (on a clear day you can almost see the people in the Transamerica building). Other adventures included the search for the Perfect Sourdough, the Perfect Cuppa Joe, and the Best Pad Thai. Her various missions accomplished, Kelly returned home exhausted, overfed, and completely addicted to caffeine. She's now considering counseling to help her adjust to three meals and two cups of coffee a day.

Timothy McIntyre, without a car and not old enough to rent one, learned to improvise: He traveled by foot, bus, train, subway, taxi, ferry, and cable car to update the Where to Sleep chapter and part of the Exploring chapter and is now in the market for a new pair of shoes. He would like to thank the San Francisco MUNI operator who let him ride free that one time when he was caught without any cash—if it were not for her, he would still be wandering around the Haight trying to get home. A junior at Cal, he gets much practice in perfecting the art of bullshitting from his English and political science classes. His next project will be to try to prove that Boris Yeltsin is really the reincarnation of William Wordsworth.

After two years as an editor at the Berkeley Guides, **Lisa Roth** did not harbor romantic notions of travel writing. Still, determined to share her enthusiasm for the city she calls home, Lisa bravely trooped through the parks and neighborhoods of San Francisco, updating the Outdoor Activities chapter and part of the Exploring chapter. Some of Lisa's favorite San Francisco rituals are welcoming the morning with a cup of Pasqua coffee, soaking up outdoor theater and concerts in Dolores Park or Stern Grove, hamming it up at the Bay to Breakers race, playing soccer in the Festival of the Babes, dancing in the streets on Freedom Day, and watching the fog roll in.

Berkeley Guides editorial coordinator and closet travel writer **Sharron S. Wood** likes to complicate her life by taking on Bay Area writing assignments in her "spare time." The editors of this book were surprised when she volunteered to update the Basics chapter, which required that she spend three weeks talking to veg heads about plans for the upcoming Whole Life Expo and hounding BART officials about planned extension projects. Other writers return from abroad to tell of the villagers they met in southern Mexico; Sharron speaks fondly of an employee at the Berkeley TRiP store that gave her buckets of pamphlets on Bay Area bus systems. Other writers reminisce about evenings spent drinking in Irish pubs; Sharron waxes nostalgic about the evening she called 20 car-rental companies to ask about their age requirements. Still, how many people do you know who can tell you exactly how much it costs to park in each of the Bay Area airport parking lots?

The Editors

When **Nicole Harb** left her hometown of L.A. and headed up to Berkeley five years ago, she didn't know the Northern/Southern California rivalry existed. Surprised to find that the majority of the state does not have blond hair or silicone implants, and that the sky is actually blue instead of brownish-gray, Nicole soon defected to the Bay Area. After a harried summer editing the San Francisco and California guides, though, the sights, sounds, and smells of Berkeley's Telegraph Avenue were finally getting old. So she took off for Spain to visit old friends, relax on the beach, and drink plenty of red wine. She plans to stay until her skin turns brown, she goes to a party down a red dirt road, and Joni Mitchell manages to make her miss California.

Having acquired a particular fondness for hot springs from editing so many reviews lauding their virtues, **Elda Tsou** has determined to systematically hunt down each one to experience their miraculous properties for herself. After a summer of consuming unhealthy quantities of green licorice and espresso (for inspiration), she is relieved to be ensconced once again in the safety of academia for her last year, pondering Great Thoughts like whether the Wife of Bath from *The Canterbury Tales* was really a lesbian.

We'd also like to thank some of the writers of *The Berkeley Guide to California 1995*, whose work appears in this book: **Julie Feinstein, Terence Priester,** and **Zak Smith**. Moonlighting Berkeley Guides editors and writers **Jessica Blatt, Loretta Johnson, Emily Miller,** and **Ada Vassilovski** also contributed to the Food chapter. In addition, thanks go to the Random House folks who helped us with cartography, page design, and production: Bob Blake, Ellen Browne, Denise DeGennaro, Janet Foley, Tigist Getachew, Fabrizio La Rocca, and Linda Schmidt.

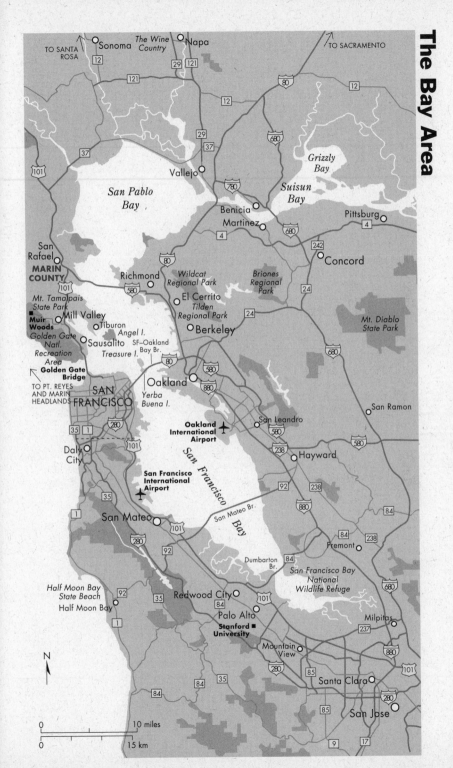

The Bay Area

BASICS

By Sharron Wood

Sometimes it's wonderful to drift through the city without thinking, letting Zen adventures come your way. But there are other times when you need to have a clue about things, whether it's how to get from San Francisco's Sunset district to downtown Oakland, where to look for this weekend's live music offerings, when next year's San Francisco Book Festival will take place, or what organizations exist to help women in trouble. Below are some basic facts to help you survive and keep your sanity in the Bay Area. For more comprehensive listings, let your fingers do the walking through the Pacific Bell yellow pages; the Local Access pages, in the front of the book, can help you with everything from choosing seats for a concert to finding the nearest park with a swimming pool.

Getting In, Out, and Around

San Francisco has one of the most comprehensive public transportation systems of any U.S. city, making it easy for commuters and travelers to get around without contributing to traffic jams. Enviro-friendly public transportation is almost hip here, and cycling, the ultimate in green commuting, also has an avid following. Although many Bay Area cities, and San Francisco in particular, are seriously lacking in bike lanes, BART and CalTrain (*see below*) let you bring your bike along for the long haul. For the lowdown on public transit, order the *Regional Transit Guide* ($4.95), an excellent resource listing transportation agencies, lines, and frequency. Send a check for $5.30 to MTC/Regional Transit Guide, 101 8th St., Oakland 94607.

BY CAR

No, it's not L.A., but no one's going to mistake Bay Area driving for a relaxing spin down a country back road. Common frustrations include, among other things, high tolls on the Golden Gate Bridge, traffic jams at any time of the day or night, and a notable lack of places to leave the damn car once you've arrived at your destination. For degree-of-difficulty bonus points, go straight to San Francisco: If you learned to drive just about anywhere else, the combination of hills and traffic should present a formidable challenge to your driving skills—not to mention your car's brakes and transmission.

You wouldn't be the first to shudder as you sit at a stoplight on a steep San Francisco hill in a temperamental stick shift, staring in the rearview mirror at the car you expect to cream as soon as you lift your foot off the brake.

North of the Golden Gate Bridge lie Marin County and the Wine Country; to the south are San Francisco and the South Bay Peninsula (including Palo Alto); and on the east side of the bay lie Berkeley and Oakland. A network of freeways helps you move your vehicle from one town to another. The most beautiful highway, **Route 1** (a.k.a. the Pacific Coast Highway), runs north–south along the coast, right over the Golden Gate Bridge. Renowned for stunning views and treacherous curves, Route 1 provides an excellent opportunity to look into the great, pounding nothingness of the Pacific and ponder your insignificance. Although it extends almost the entire length of California, Route 1 is so narrow and winding that you shouldn't drive it if you're in a hurry. As the highway enters San Francisco from the south, it becomes 19th Avenue, then Park Presidio Boulevard, and then the Golden Gate Bridge. On the bridge, it merges with the north–south U.S. 101, eventually splitting from that road and heading back toward the coast at the Stinson Beach/Route 1 exit in Marin County.

Running parallel to Route 1, but a ways inland, **U.S. 101** also whisks you from the South Bay through the city and over the Golden Gate Bridge into Marin County. Avoid the leg of 101 that runs along the Peninsula between San Francisco and Palo Alto, unless you're a traffic fetishist. Instead, take the meandering **I–280,** accurately called "The World's Most Beautiful Freeway." This route is a bit longer mile-wise, but at least your car will be moving the entire time. You'll pass verdant hills, a sparkling reservoir, and exquisite vista points. On U.S. 101 the trip from San Francisco to Palo Alto takes about 45 minutes in good conditions, up to 1 hour 15 minutes in traffic. On I–280, count on 50 minutes to an hour at any time of day.

In the East Bay, all the freeways are miserable. From San Francisco, **I–80** carries you east across the **Bay Bridge** to Berkeley and continues northeast toward Sacramento and Lake Tahoe. It could use a few more lanes for optimal traffic flow, but there's no avoiding it if you're heading east. The trip from San Francisco to Berkeley takes about 20 minutes in optimal conditions, closer to 45 minutes during rush hour. For a truly bleak driving experience, veer south at the eastern end of the Bay Bridge toward Oakland on the north–south **I–880.** It brings new meaning to the term industrial blight. This is, however, *the* East Bay corridor, taking you to such thrilling suburban destinations as Hayward, Fremont, and eventually San Jose. It also runs to the Bay Area's two southern bridges, the **San Mateo Bridge,** connecting Hayward and San Mateo, and the **Dumbarton Bridge** farther south, which links Fremont and Palo Alto. Running parallel to I–880 between Oakland and Hayward (at which point it veers off to the east), **I–580** has a small but avid cult following. The cute little hills, the green bushes, the rows of windmills by Livermore—all seem to inspire affection.

RENTAL CARS Because of the dearth of parking, the excellent public transportation, and the high insurance rates in much of the Bay Area, many residents have chosen to forgo car ownership entirely. But for those times that you're seized by the urge to meander up the coast, a rental car can be a great convenience.

Your best bet is always to rent at one of the region's airports. Although the cheapest rates are available only to those who can present a plane ticket, even residents can save as much as $15 a day over the rates at downtown rental franchises. If you absolutely can't make it to the airport, almost all the rental car agencies have pick-up and drop-off spots in downtown San Francisco, within five or six blocks of Union Square. The cheapest rates at these agencies vary quite a bit, depending on who's running a special deal. No matter where you pick up your car, you'll always pay a heavy surcharge (starting at about $25) if you don't return it to the same spot.

Small, independent agencies generally have cheaper daily rates than the national chains, but they usually impose mileage charges. A typical weekday price for a subcompact at an independent company is $18–$30, with a limit of 50–100 miles a day. **Flat Rate Rent-A-Car** (830 Huntington Ave., San Bruno, near SFO, tel. 415/583–9232) rents cars for a rock-bottom $16 a day with 75 free miles, but their restriction on taking the car more than 100 miles from the city could put a crimp in your travel plans. The national companies (Avis, Hertz, Budget, etc.) usually offer unlimited mileage, so if you're planning on going far, they may end up being cheaper. If you call around, you should be able to find a subcompact car for about $30 a day on weekdays, $25 on weekends. At press time, **Alamo** (tel. 800/327–9633) at the Oakland Airport offered the cheapest rates of any big company in the Bay Area. They charge an extra $20 a day if you're under 25, but many companies won't rent to you at all until you reach the quarter-century mark. (The 21-to-24 set does best at **Enterprise**, tel. 800/325–8007, which charges only $8 extra per day.)

Unfortunately, all Bay Area companies require a credit card for deposit purposes. The upside to this restriction is that some cards—American Express, for example—provide liability and damage insurance as a service for card members. Make sure to check with your credit card company before paying for the rental agency's insurance policy. A final note: As with airline tickets, you'll always pay less if you reserve in advance.

PARKING Welcome to the Bay Area—hope you left your car behind. If you ever find a parking space, it may be on the side of a sheer precipice. Should you succeed in the hideous task of parallel parking on a slope that looks like the north face of Everest, remember to curb your wheels, set the emergency brake, and, if you're in a stick shift, leave the car in gear.

If you've circled Union Square for half an hour and are ready to dump your car any place it fits, think again. The city issues 2.4 million parking tickets a year—and the number is only expected to increase.

If this all seems too much for you, there are plenty of parking lots and garages that offer parking by the hour or by the day. Pay close attention to rates, as they can get quite steep, especially around prime tourist country like San Francisco's Fisherman's Wharf. In the Union Square area, the large **Sutter-Stockton Garage** (444 Stockton St., tel. 415/982–7275) charges a graduated rate—$3 for three hours, $8 for five hours, and $18 for 24 hours. The cheapest lot near Fisherman's Wharf ($2 an hour) is on the Embarcadero at Jefferson Street. Parking in the East Bay is less difficult, though finding places near the U.C. Berkeley campus isn't exactly fun. At **Sather Gate Garage** (2450 Durant Ave., just west of Telegraph Ave.), the rate is $1 an hour for the first two hours, $1.50 for each hour thereafter. The daily rate is $10. For all-day parking, the lot next to Berkeley Arts (2590 Durant Ave.) is a better deal; $6 lets you park from 8 AM to 7 PM.

BRIDGE TOLLS Toll on the **Golden Gate Bridge** (tel. 415/921–5858) is $3, collected as you travel south into San Francisco. Discount ticket books are available at the bridge, Westamerica banks, Safeway stores, and some gas stations. For $20 you get eight crossings, for $40 16 crossings. There is no toll 5–9 AM and 4–6 PM weekdays for cars carrying at least three passengers.

All of the state bridges, including the **Bay Bridge, San Mateo/Hayward Bridge, Dumbarton Bridge,** and **Richmond Bridge,** have the same toll ($1), collected in the westbound or northbound direction. A discount booklet, good for four months from purchase, is available at Safeway and Lucky stores, as well as at the bridges. For $34 you get 40 crossings. Carpoolers (three or more people in a car) cross free 5–10 AM and 3–6 PM weekdays.

Since carpoolers don't pay tolls and often get to ride in special lanes on Bay Area bridges, commuters are often grateful for the chance to pick up a couple of passengers for the drive over the bridge. Wily types who lack cars head to **Park and Ride** locations—or to the Emeryville bus nexus (cnr Yerba Buena and San Pablo Aves.) or the North Berkeley BART station in the East Bay—and hitch a ride into the city. For more info on sharing a ride, call **Rides for Bay Area Commuters** at 800/755–POOL, **Berkeley TRiP** at 510/644–POOL, or **Solano Commuter Information** at 800/53–KMUTE. Give them your commute information, and within a few days they'll give you a list of commuters who live and work near you and want to share a ride.

BY BUS

Despite all the griping about graffiti and rising fares, Bay Area bus systems do provide excellent coverage of most towns. If you'll be using both BART and buses on a regular basis, look into **BART Plus** passes, good for a fixed amount of BART travel and unlimited rides on AC Transit, MUNI, and SamTrans, among others (*see* BART, *below*). The bus companies listed below all have wheelchair-accessible buses for some routes; call for specifics.

MUNI San Francisco's main bus and streetcar service covers the city with 91 lines. Buses run as often as every five minutes in certain well-traveled parts of town, though frequent

An estimated 95% of San Francisco's addresses lie within three blocks of a MUNI stop.

breakdowns and delays gum up the works considerably. Between 1 AM and 5 AM, the Owl service offers just 9 lines that run every 30 minutes. Should you be stranded someplace within the city, anxious to get elsewhere but unsure of how to do it, call 415/673–MUNI weekdays 7–5 or weekends 9–5 and an operator will tell you exactly which bus(es) to use. If you lose something on board, call 415/923–6168.

The adult fare is $1, the youth, senior, and disabled fare 35¢. MUNI eliminated transfers in 1993, but brought them back in 1994 after commuters gave them an earful. Now your fare gets you a free transfer good for at least an hour. **Passport** passes allow unlimited access to MUNI (including cable cars) for one day ($6), three days ($10), or one week ($15). You can buy a one-day pass from the driver when you board; three-day and one-week passes are available from a number of locations, including the visitor information booth at the Powell and Market cable car turnaround and the Tix booth at Union Square. But if you're going to be using the system regularly, you're better off getting a **Fast Pass,** which allows you unlimited travel on MUNI buses, light-rail vehicles, and cable cars, and on BART within the city. The $35 adult pass, good for one calendar month, is available from any Safeway grocery store in San Francisco, as well as many liquor stores and check-cashing places. The $8 youth, senior, and disabled pass can be purchased at City Hall.

➤ **CABLE CARS** • San Francisco's cable cars were the world's first large-scale mechanized street transportation. Developer Andrew Hallidie drove the first run on August 2, 1873. In 1964, the cable cars were declared a National Historic Landmark, the first moving entity to receive that honor. If you can handle throngs of tourists, the cable cars are actually pretty groovy; you should take one at least once, if only to feel like you're in a Rice-A-Roni commercial. They run at a pace straight out of the early 1900s (the cables that propel the cars move at 9½ mph), so if you're Type A, take the bus. Fare is $2, though many discount passes (*see above*) allow you to ride for free. For great views, take the Hyde and Powell line, which travels from Fisherman's Wharf to Powell and Market streets downtown. Along the way, you'll get a gander at Alcatraz and pass right by Lombard Street, the crookedest street in the world. Unfortunately, the wait to get on at the Hyde Street turnaround can be over an hour.

In Maya Angelou's autobiography, I Know Why the Caged Bird Sings, she professes to be the first African-American hired on the San Francisco streetcars. But the job didn't come easy—it took almost a month of persistence before she was the one saying "Step forward in the car, please."

AC TRANSIT With over 100 lines, AC Transit (tel. 510/839–2882) covers the East Bay from north of Richmond to south of Fremont. For personalized trip planning and the hours of various lines, call 800/559–INFO weekdays 7–6 or weekends 9–5. Stop by the **Berkeley TRiP Commute Store** (2033 Center St., tel. 510/644–7665) or the AC Transit office (1600 Franklin St., Oakland) for schedules and an excellent map of all routes. Maps are also sporadically available on the buses. The fare for adults and youth is $1.10, for seniors and the disabled 55¢. Transfers (25¢) are good for at least an hour. Monthly passes run $40 for adults, $21 for youth, and $7 for seniors and the disabled. Books of 10 tickets cost $9 for adults (blue) and $4.50 for youth, seniors, and the disabled (yellow).

Certain lines (those designated by letters rather than numbers) cross the Bay Bridge to San Francisco's **Transbay Terminal** (1st and Mission Sts.). Most run from dawn to dusk, but the F and T lines operate until 2 AM and the N runs all night. Fare to San Francisco is $2.20 for adults ($1.10 youth, seniors, and disabled). Monthly transbay passes cost $75.

GOLDEN GATE TRANSIT Golden Gate Transit (tel. 415/453–2100 in Marin, 415/332–6600 in S.F., 707/544–1323 in Sonoma) provides excellent service almost everywhere in the North Bay. Buses connect San Francisco with Sausalito, Mill Valley, Tiburon, San Rafael, Novato, Rohnert Park, and Santa Rosa every half-hour during the week. Most buses run weekdays only, from dawn to dusk, but some routes (including those numbered 10, 20, 30, etc.) run on weekends and go as late as 4 AM. Unfortunately, no buses travel from San Francisco directly up Route 1 to coastal destinations like Stinson Beach and Point Reyes. On weekends, though, you can take Bus 20 or Bus 50 from San Francisco to San Rafael, then transfer to Bus 65, which stops in Inverness, Point Reyes, Olema, and Stinson Beach. Rates range from $1.10 to $4, depending on how far you're going. Booklets of 20 tickets at a 25% discount can be purchased from drivers; at the **San Rafael Transit Center** (850 Tamalpais St., at 3rd St.); at the **Larkspur Ferry Terminal** (101 E. Sir Francis Drake Blvd., Larkspur); and at many bookstores, gas stations, and grocery stores.

SAMTRANS South of the city, SamTrans (tel. 800/660–4BUS) runs buses regularly throughout San Mateo County. They leave from the Daly City BART station, downtown San Francisco, and San Francisco International Airport (*see* By Plane, *below*), and go as far south as Palo Alto and the Stanford Shopping Center. Bus 1L travels from Daly City BART along the coast to Half Moon Bay (85¢) about five times daily on weekends. Most other buses run weekdays only, though some heavily trafficked routes are covered all week; call SamTrans for help planning your trip. Fares are 85¢–$2 for adults, 35¢–$1 for youth, and 25¢–$2 for seniors and the disabled. No transfers are issued. Monthly passes cost $29 for adults ($51 for a long-distance route pass), $13 for youth, and $10 for seniors and the disabled.

GREYHOUND Greyhound (tel. 800/231–2222) travels to and from Bay Area cities all day, every day, but it's more useful for long distances than for local jaunts. If you're *sans* auto and need to get to Tahoe (about $20), they're the folks to call. Other popular destinations include Santa Cruz (2–4 hrs, $9.60), L.A. (11–12 hrs, $46.50), and Seattle (20–26 hrs, $69). In San Francisco, Greyhound operates out of the **Transbay Terminal** (1st and Mission Sts., tel. 415/495–1569), where quite a few MUNI lines (*see above*) begin. The terminal is not the safest place, so you may want to plan your arrival for daytime. You'll find Greyhound on the terminal's third floor. In the East Bay, the Greyhound office is in **Oakland** (2103 San Pablo Ave., tel. 510/834–3213), in the South Bay in **San Jose** (70 Almaden Ave., tel. 408/295–4151), and in Marin County in downtown **San Rafael** (850 Tamalpais St., at 3rd St., tel. 415/453–0795).

GREEN TORTOISE Green Tortoise Travel (494 Broadway, San Francisco 94133, tel. 415/285–2441) is *the* cheap, fun alternative to humdrum bus travel. Only on Green Tortoise does your journey to Seattle (24 hrs, $49 one-way) feature a cookout ($3) and skinny-dipping. Buses come equipped with sleeping pads, kitchens, and stereos to make the ride enjoyable. Regularly scheduled runs also go from the Bay Area to L.A. (12 hrs, $30), Eugene (17 hrs, $39), and Portland (20 hrs, $39). Plus—get this—they'll stop almost anywhere else on I–5 for an additional $10. All fares are for one-way travel and must be paid in cash, traveler's checks, or money orders. Make reservations before you show up at their pick-up point in San Francisco (1st and Natoma Sts.) or Berkeley (Berkeley Marina, across from the bait shop).

BY TRAIN AND SUBWAY

BART Relatively clean and quiet, **Bay Area Rapid Transit** (tel. 415/992–2278 or 510/465–BART; lost and found 510/464–7090), better known as BART, is a smooth subway system that's better at moving you from one town to another than getting you around town. Its four lines serve San Francisco, Daly City, and the East Bay from Richmond to Fremont and out to Concord. An extension to Colma, southwest of Daly City, should be completed by late 1995. All BART stations and trains are wheelchair accessible.

BART runs daily until 1:30 AM (though stations close as soon as the last train goes through, which may be as early as midnight). Service starts up again at 4 AM on weekdays, 6 AM on Saturday, and 8 AM on Sunday. Expect trains every 15–20 minutes; schedules are available at the stations, or you can call ahead to plan your journey. A special Sunday route called the "Sunday Double-Header Express" runs from around noon to 5 PM and stops at the MacArthur, 12th Street, Embarcadero, Powell Street, Civic Center, 24th Street, and Daly City stations only.

➤ **FARES AND DISCOUNTS** • BART has recently been making a lot of noise about raising fares, so don't be surprised if you're charged slightly more than the prices listed here. The cost of a ticket ranges from 80¢ to $3, depending on the length of the journey. For example, a 15-minute ride from San Francisco's Embarcadero Station to Oakland's MacArthur Station costs $1.60; a ride from Concord to the Oakland Coliseum takes 52 minutes and costs $2. From downtown San Francisco to Berkeley (20–25 min) you'll pay $1.80. BART is seriously lacking in discounted fares. Adults can purchase a "discount" ticket that gets them $32 worth of rides for $30—big whoop. Seniors, children under 12, and the disabled get a much better deal: a $16 ticket for $1.60.

BART also sells two passes that, though they don't save you money on BART itself, give you a discount on local bus systems. With the **BART Plus** ticket, you buy $15–$50 of BART rides, and for an added flat fee ($11–$13) get unlimited rides on MUNI, AC Transit, SamTrans, BART Express, the County Connection, Dumbarton local service, Martinez Link, Santa Clara County Transit local service, and Union City Transit. BART Plus tickets are issued for half-month periods, but should you not use all your BART credit in time, you have a five-day grace period. The **Premium BART Plus** ticket ($36, $42, or $47) provides $14 of BART fare, unlimited rides on the systems listed above, and privileges on several additional systems (Vallejo Transit, some Golden Gate Transit zones, Dumbarton Express), depending on how much money you fork over.

➤ **BIKES ON BART** • Bearers of BART bicycle permits ($3 for three years) can bring their bikes onto trains. Bikes are allowed only in the last car, and generally during non-commute hours only, though sometimes in the non-commute direction during peak times. Call 415/464–7133 for more info, or 415/456–7135 for a permit application. A free one-day bike permit, available one time only, can be obtained on the spot at BART stations when you show ID. Most stations have bike lockers; call 415/464–7136 for details.

CALTRAIN CalTrain (tel. 800/660–4BUS) offers regular service from San Francisco (4th and Townsend Sts., and 22nd St. at Pennsylvania Ave.) to downtown San Jose (65 Cahill St.) on double-decker trains. A one-way trip costs $4.50 and takes 1½ hours; trains leave hourly between 5 AM and 10 PM, more frequently during commute times. Along the way, the trains stop at a number of Peninsula cities, including Burlingame, Palo Alto, Mountain View, and Santa Clara. If your bike folds up, you can bring it on the train with you; if it doesn't, you'll need a free permit (pick up applications at any CalTrain office).

AMTRAK Several Amtrak (tel. 800/USA–RAIL) lines, including the *Zephyr* from Chicago via Denver, the *Coast Starlight* from San Diego or Seattle, and the *Capitol* from Sacramento and the San Joaquin Valley, stop at the three East Bay stations: Richmond (16th St. and Macdonald Ave., adjoining Richmond BART), Berkeley (3rd St. and University Ave.—you can board, but you can't buy tickets) and Emeryville (5885 Landregan St.). From the Emeryville station, you can catch a connecting Amtrak bus that will drop you at 4th and Townsend streets (the CalTrain station) in San Francisco. Fares vary according to the time of year and other factors; a Bay Area–Seattle round-trip (24 hrs) runs $88–$176, while Bay Area–Los Angeles round-trips (12 hrs) are $68–$154.

BY TAXI

You can usually hail a cab in San Francisco, but sometimes they are inexplicably scarce. Most residents phone. All taxis are metered, but you may be able to negotiate a flat rate to the airport. **Veteran's Cab** (tel. 415/552–1300) in San Francisco charges a base fee of $1.70, 30¢ every ⅙ mile thereafter, and 30¢ for every minute of waiting time or traffic delay. **Yellow Cab** (tel. 415/626–2345) charges the same. In the East Bay, both **Friendly Cab** (tel. 510/536–3000) and **Yellow Cab** (tel. 510/841–8294) offer competitively priced service ($2 base fee, $2 a mile) within Oakland, to Berkeley ($12–$15), and to San Francisco ($25–$30). Don't forget to tip the driver (15% is typical).

BY FERRY

If you're sick of Bay Area traffic, or just in the mood for a change of pace, pack a thermos of coffee and a warm jacket and hop on one of the commuter ferries from San Francisco to Marin County or the East Bay. The ferries are comparable to other forms of transport in speed, and you can drink your morning java in peace while taking in a lovely view.

GOLDEN GATE FERRY Golden Gate Ferry (tel. 415/332–6600) crosses the bay between Marin County and the **San Francisco Ferry Terminal** (on the Embarcadero, at the bottom of Market St.). Ferries run from about 7 AM to 8 PM. The 30-minute journey from San Francisco to the **Sausalito Ferry Dock** (south end of Bridgeway) costs $4.25; the 50-minute trip to the **Larkspur Ferry Terminal** (101 E. Sir Francis Drake Blvd.) is $2.50, $4.25 weekends. Tickets include free transfers for Golden Gate Transit buses (*see* By Bus, *above*).

RED AND WHITE FLEET The fleet (tel. 415/546–BOAT or 800/229–2784) leaves from Pier 43½ at Fisherman's Wharf for the Sausalito Ferry Dock (south end of Bridgeway). Fare is $5.50 ($2.75 children), and the trip takes 15–30 minutes. The fleet also runs commuter services to Tiburon ($5.50) and Vallejo ($7.50) and excursion trips to Angel Island ($9), Alcatraz ($5.75), and Marine World/Africa U.S.A ($36, including bus shuttle and park admission). A number of these ferries leave from Pier 41; call for details.

OAKLAND/ALAMEDA FERRY The Oakland/Alameda Ferry (tel. 510/522–3300), also known as the **Blue and Gold Fleet,** leaves from Jack London Square in Oakland or the Alameda Ferry Dock (2990 Main St.) and arrives at the San Francisco Ferry Building 30 minutes later; the ferry then continues to Pier 39 at Fisherman's Wharf. Ferries begin running from the East Bay at 6 AM on weekdays, 10 AM on weekends and holidays, and leave on their last run at 7:55 PM. One-way adult fare is $3.50; seniors, military, and the disabled pay $2.50; and children under 12 pay $1.50. Buy tickets on board the ferry. Parking at the Alameda and Oakland terminals is free. Ferry stubs serve as transfers to MUNI and AC Transit.

BY PLANE

SAN FRANCISCO INTERNATIONAL AIRPORT San Francisco International (tel. 415/876–7809), the big cheese of Northern California airports, lies about 10 miles south of San Francisco on U.S. 101 (take the San Francisco International exit, not the Airport Road exit). All the major domestic airlines and many international ones fly to SFO, as it's called; contact individual carriers for specific flight information. The airport has two **currency exchange** offices, both in the International Terminal. Here you'll also find **baggage storage** (near the Air France ticket desk, tel. 415/877–0422), open 7 AM–11 PM. Charges are based on the size of the luggage; an average bag runs $3.50 per day. There are also lockers available (15 by 24 inches, 31 inches deep) that cost $1 for 24 hours, $2 for every day after that.

Until BART finally extends its service to the airport (sometime around 2002), the best public transit to SFO is **SamTrans Buses 7B** and **7F** (*see* By Bus, *above*). Both lines travel between the airport and San Francisco's Transbay Terminal (board in front at Mission and Fremont Sts.) and can also drop you along Mission Street, within two blocks of any of the downtown BART/MUNI stations. The buses run every half-hour from about 5:45 AM to 1:15 AM. Express Bus 7F costs $1.75 and takes 35 minutes; you're restricted to one small carry-on bag. Bus 7B costs 85¢, takes 55 minutes, and has no luggage restrictions. Bus 7F will also tote you from Palo Alto, near the Stanford Shopping Center, to the airport. Another option is to take a private shuttle (*see box, below*). If you can't bear to relinquish your car, parking (tel. 415/877–0227) is $1 the first hour, $3 for two hours, and $16 for the day in the short-term lot. Long-term parking is $9 a day, but this lot tends to fill up during peak travel times, especially three-day weekends. Call the above number and listen to their recording on availability before you set out.

OAKLAND INTERNATIONAL AIRPORT Oakland International (1 Airport Dr., off Hegenberger Rd., tel. 510/577–4000) is a smallish airport, easily accessible by public transportation from points throughout the Bay Area, and less hectic and crowded than SFO. It's often much cheaper to fly into here, particularly on **Southwest** (tel. 800/435–9792), which has over 80 flights in and out of Oakland, many of which go to Los Angeles. With Southwest's Friends Fly Free program, two people can fly round-trip to Los Angeles for a total of $144 on selected flights; reservations for these fares should be made well in advance. Short-term parking (tel. 510/633–2571) is 85¢ for a half hour or $17 per day; long-term parking runs $1.65 an hour, $8.25 daily; "economy" rates (in lots farther away) are $1.65 an hour, $6.60 all day.

For $2, the **Air-Bart Shuttle** (tel. 510/562–7700) runs every 15 minutes (Mon.–Sat. 6:05 AM–midnight, Sun. 8:30 AM–midnight) between the airport and the Coliseum BART station in Oakland, allowing you to connect to all destinations served by BART. AC Transit **Bus 58** also runs between the airport and Jack London Square, stopping at Lake Merritt and near the Coliseum BART station along the way. Another option is an airport shuttle (*see box, below*). A taxi to downtown Berkeley costs about $30–$35.

SAN JOSE INTERNATIONAL AIRPORT Fourteen carriers, most notably **American Airlines** (tel. 800/433–7300), fly into San Jose International Airport (1661 Airport Blvd., off I–880 near U.S. 101, tel. 408/277–4759). The airport is served by San Jose Light Rail, Santa Clara County Transit, and various private shuttles (*see box, below*). Short-term parking runs 75¢ per half hour and $15 per day; long-term is $8 per day.

Bay Area Directory

LOW-COST MEDICAL AID

The post-college years can be tough on your health in any number of ways, but one of the biggest threats is lack of insurance. You've graduated from Mom and Dad's coverage, you no longer get to use the university health services, and chances are you don't have a full-time job with benefits to take up the slack. Suddenly the new contact lenses and the checkup at the dentist become a real problem. That's when you turn to the clinic. The health clinics listed below are all either free or low-cost. Many use a "sliding scale": The higher your income, the higher your fees. If your income is low enough, services are sometimes free. Many clinics also accept Medi-Cal and Medicare.

Airport Shuttles

Can't find a friend to take you to the airport for that 5 AM flight? No worry—just call an airport shuttle, one of the Bay Area's favorite ways to ride (and the biggest thing to happen to vans since the 1970s). If you call about a day in advance, shuttles will pick you up at your doorstep at any time of day or night and whisk you to the airport. Fare from San Francisco to SFO runs a mere $10–$11; expect to pay roughly $20 from Oakland to SFO, and about the same from downtown San Francisco to the Oakland airport. There's often a reduced rate for pickup of two or more people. If you get on the shuttle at a major hotel, rather than at your home, you could save up to $10.

The king of airport service is Super Shuttle (tel. 415/558–8500), serving SFO from San Francisco and the Peninsula. You can hardly take a drive on U.S. 101 without seeing one of their blue vans speeding some anxious vacationers to their flight. If big companies turn you off, try the reliable Quake City (tel. 415/255–4899). It's employee-owned, it costs a dollar less than Super Shuttle, and its friendly drivers can be counted on to provide some pleasant chit-chat during the trip.

In addition, Yellow Shuttle Service (tel. 415/282–7433) and Airport Connection (tel. 510/841–0150) run from most Bay Area cities to SFO, Oakland International, and San Jose International. The Bay Porter Express (tel. 415/467–1800) runs from the East Bay and South Bay to SFO, Oakland, and San Jose; and from San Francisco to Oakland. The Marin Airporter (tel. 415/461–4222) will take you from Marin County to SFO.

Whether publicly funded or privately supported, all clinics are in constant financial straits because of the limited amount of money our country puts toward affordable health care. Sadly, they often have to cut back on services and staff—or close altogether—when funds dry up. Always call the clinic first to make sure they're still there, and to see if you should make an appointment or just show up. All provide quality care and try to operate as efficiently as possible, but long waits are not uncommon. Bring a book and try to be thankful that the clinic exists at all.

Clinics don't always make you prove how much money you make, which helps when you're truly strapped for cash; but try to be a good socialist and give according to your ability.

For medical information 24 hours a day, you can call Alta Bates Medical Center's **Audio Health Library** (tel. 800/322–1322), where you'll have access to information on over 400 health-related topics. The audio library is designed to help you make informed decisions about your health. The service can also refer you to a private practitioner or clinic in your area, should you need one. When you need any advice, testing, or treatment having to do with AIDS, let your first call be to the **San Francisco AIDS Hotline** (tel. 415/863–AIDS). They have the most up-to-date information on programs to help those who are infected, as well as comprehensive listings of free or low-cost HIV testing sites in every city. For affordable family planning services, **Planned Parenthood** has many locations around the Bay Area that administer pregnancy tests and gynecological exams; prescribe birth control; perform abortions; treat sexually transmitted diseases (STDs); and offer free, anonymous AIDS tests. Look in the yellow pages under "Family Planning" or the white pages under "Planned Parenthood."

The following codes are used below to indicate services provided: DEN—dentistry; EYE—optometry; GM—general medicine; GYN—gynecology and family planning; OB—perinatal care; PED—pediatrics; STD—sexually transmitted disease treatment.

SAN FRANCISCO The **San Francisco Department of Public Health** has eight sliding-fee health centers throughout the city, with services including GM, GYN, PED, STD, and HIV testing and referrals. Call the Health Department's main office (tel. 415/554–2500) for the one nearest you.

Buena Vista Women's Services. Cost: sliding. Services: GM, GYN, OB, STD. *2000 Van Ness Ave., #406, near Jackson St., tel. 415/771–5000.*

Haight-Ashbury Free Medical Clinic. Cost: free, donations requested. Services: GM, GYN, STD; HIV programs. *558 Clayton St., at Haight St., tel. 415/487–5632.*

Mission Neighborhood Health Center. Cost: sliding. Services: DEN, GM, GYN, PED. *240 Shotwell St., at 16th St., tel. 415/552–3870.*

North East Medical Services. Cost: sliding. Services: DEN, EYE, GM, GYN, PED, STD. *1520 Stockton St., btw Green and Union Sts., tel. 415/391–9686.*

San Francisco City Clinic. Cost: sliding. Services: GYN, STD. *356 7th St., btw. Folsom and Harrison Sts., tel. 415/487–5500.*

South of Market Health Center. Cost: sliding. Services: DEN, GM, GYN, OB, PED, STD. *551 Minna St., btw 6th and 7th Sts., tel. 415/626–2951.*

UCSF Eye Clinic. Cost: sliding. Services: EYE. *400 Parnassus Ave., near 3rd Ave., tel. 415/476–3700.*

EAST BAY

➤ **BERKELEY** • **Berkeley Comprehensive Family Planning Clinic.** Cost: sliding. Services: GYN, STD; free, anonymous HIV testing. *830 University Ave., at 6th St., tel. 510/644–8571.*

Berkeley Free Clinic. Cost: free. Services: DEN, GM, GYN, STD. *2339 Durant Ave., at Dana St., tel. 510/548–2570.*

Berkeley Women's Health Center. Cost: sliding. Services: GM, GYN, OB, STD. *2908 Ellsworth St., 1 block from Ashby Ave., tel. 510/843–6194.*

West Berkeley Health Center. Cost: sliding. Services: DEN, EYE, GM, GYN, PED, STD. *2031 6th St., at University Ave., tel. 510/644–6939.*

➤ **OAKLAND • Asian Health Services.** Cost: sliding. Services: GM, GYN, PED, STD; HIV services. *310 8th St., Room 200, at Harrison St., tel. 510/763–4411.*

Central Health Center. Cost: sliding. Services: GM, GYN, PED, STD. *470 27th St., near Telegraph Ave., tel. 510/271–4263.*

East Oakland Health Center. Cost: sliding. Services: DEN, EYE, GM, GYN, PED, STD. *7450 E. 14th St., at 74th Ave., tel. 510/430–9401.*

La Clinica de la Raza. Cost: free with $25-per-year family membership. Services: DEN, EYE, GM, GYN, OB, PED, STD; there's a special "teen clinic," too. *1515 Fruitvale Ave., at E. 14th St., tel. 510/534–0078.*

Native American Health Center. Cost: sliding. Services: GM, GYN, PED, STD; HIV services. *3124 E. 14th St., near Fruitvale Ave., tel. 510/261–1962.*

West Oakland Health Center. Cost: sliding. Services: DEN, EYE, GM, GYN, OB, PED, STD. *700 Adeline St., btw 7th and 8th Sts., tel. 510/835–9610.*

Women's Choice Clinic. Cost: sliding. Services: GYN, OB, STD. The clinic also offers Chinese medicine and acupuncture. *2930 McClure Ave., btw 29th and 30th Sts., tel. 510/444–5676.*

MARIN COUNTY **Marin Community Clinic.** Cost: sliding. Services: GM, GYN, PED. *250 Bon Air Rd., on the grounds of Marin General Hospital in Greenbrae, tel. 415/461–7400.*

Marin County STD Clinic. Cost: $20 for adults, free for those under 18. Services: STD. *920 Grand Ave., San Rafael, tel. 415/499–6944.*

SOUTH BAY **Drew Health Foundation Community Medical Clinic.** Cost: sliding. Services: DEN, EYE, GM, GYN, PED, STD. *2111 University Ave., East Palo Alto, tel. 415/328–5060.*

Seton Medical Center Family Health Care Program. Cost: free. Services: GM, GYN, PED, STD. *1900 Sullivan Ave., Daly City, tel. 415/992–4000.*

PHONES AND MAIL

The area code for Oakland, Berkeley, and the East Bay is **510;** for San Francisco, Marin, and Palo Alto, it's **415;** and for San Jose and Santa Cruz, it's **408. Postal Answer Line** (tel. 415/695–8760) is a 24-hour automated service that provides info on post office hours, postal

Who to Call When Nobody Else Is Home

No need to spend money on a 900 line just because you're sitting by the phone feeling bored. The Bay Area offers plenty of 24-hour information lines to amuse you at any hour of the day or night. For starters, try the Public Library's Dial-a-Story (tel. 415/626–6516), where the tale changes once a week. Then move on to the U.C. Berkeley Seismographic Station (tel. 510/642–2160) for the latest on any recent earthquakes. Call the Audubon Society's Rare Bird Summary (tel. 510/524–5592) for a rhapsodic account of local sightings of unusual birds. The Morrison Planetarium Information Line (tel. 415/750–7141) tells you all you need to know about sky watching; and the Hearing Society Dial-a-Test (tel. 415/834–1620) lets you know if the old eardrums are still in working order. If you've still got nothing better to do, there's always that old standby, the Grateful Dead Hotline (tel. 415/457–6388).

rates, and more. A good all-purpose source of information is the front matter of the San Francisco or Oakland *Yellow Pages,* which lists community organizations, public transit information, maps, descriptions of tourist attractions and community parks, seating plans for Bay Area theaters, and much more.

Working Assets Long Distance Company (701 Montgomery St., 4th Floor, San Francisco 94111, tel. 800/788–8588) is a long-distance telephone company that gives you more than tearjerker TV ads with moms and daughters spending quality time on the phone. They actually donate 1% of your long-distance phone bill to nonprofit groups such as Amnesty International, the National Gay and Lesbian Task Force, the National Minority Aids Council, and Planned Parenthood. Subscribers get to vote by mail to decide how much should go to each group, as well as make free calls to selected politicians and business leaders on Mondays. It's easy as pie to join—just call them and they'll set you up.

MEDIA

DAILY PAPERS The Bay Area's two big dailies, the **San Francisco Chronicle** and the **San Francisco Examiner,** are equally unremarkable. The "Chron" does have some great columns, and it has strangely endeared itself to local readers, despite its lightweight coverage. The combined *Chronicle-Examiner* Sunday paper comes with the "Pink Pages," useful for its extensive movie reviews and listings of all sorts of upcoming events.

The **Oakland Tribune,** formerly one of the country's premier African-American–owned dailies, was recently bought by a large newspaper chain. The paper is stronger on community happenings than politics. Many Berkeleyites read the student-produced **Daily Californian,** which has recently come out only two–three times a week due to financial problems. There's been some talk about their return to daily publication, but at press time they had no firm plans. The **Marin Independent Journal** focuses mostly on Marin County, but also tackles some more general issues. The big surprise in Bay Area dailies is the **San Jose Mercury News,** a paper that's well read throughout the area and highly respected in the journalism community. It's stronger on national and international news than most Bay Area papers.

WEEKLY PAPERS San Francisco sustains two excellent free alternative weeklies, the **SF Weekly** and the **Bay Guardian.** The *Guardian* has full listings of San Francisco's cultural events, but is especially strong on local and national politics. Around election time, the *Guardian* offers extensive analyses of local, state, and national candidates along with their recommended slate. Their column "Cost of Living" tells you how to manage life in the city on a budget, with tips on dealing with landlords, the phone company, etc. Best of all, the paper carries the entertaining and educational sex question-and-answer column "Ask Isadora." Look for the *Guardian*'s "Best of the Bay Area" special every August. The *Weekly* is strong on cultural events in the Bay Area, but skimpy on news and commentary.

The SF Weekly sex-advice column "Savage Love" is fun and informative (if you need advice on having your nipples tattooed, that is), but "Ask Isadora" Alman has described her competitor's column as "monumentally offensive."

The **East Bay Express** comes in two parts: the front section includes articles, and "Billboard" has the best events listings in the East Bay as well as a huge classified section. While folks sometimes make fun of the idiosyncratic *Express* for its marathon front-page articles, it's one of the few papers willing to publish thorough pieces in an age of sound bites and MTV.

Other weeklies in the Bay Area are the Marin County **Pacific Sun,** which has an events calendar but dubious politics and a cheesy tone, and the much better Santa Clara **Metro,** which covers the whole South Bay with high-quality feature articles and event listings.

MONTHLY PUBLICATIONS San Francisco Focus is published by KQED, and members receive it free. Not surprisingly, it has an arts focus, with theater and opera listings and profiles of local artists, and it's geared toward a rich-white-liberal audience. (Witness the personal ads, which cost $5 a word and often run to 50-plus-word descriptions of lonely doctors and lawyers who "love fine wine, ocean breezes, and gourmet cooking" and seek "professionally established, classy partner with great warmth and panache, who understands investments.") But this monthly magazine sometimes surprises its readers with high-quality articles on controversial local and national issues. If you're not a KQED member, a subscription costs $19 a year; call 415/553–2800 to sign up. You can also find *Focus* at some newsstands for $1.95. In the East Bay, *The Monthly,* heavy on local ads and light on journalism, presents *Focus* with little competition, but at least it's free.

GAY PUBLICATIONS The *Bay Times* comes out every two weeks and has a left-of-center bent. This was the paper responsible for the downfall of police chief Richard Hongisto; he was buried in negative publicity when he tried to pull a controversial *Bay Times* issue from the shelves. It serves as an information network for the gay, lesbian, and bisexual communities, listing clubs, political organizations, AIDS organizations, information hotlines, and much more.

San Francisco's other major gay paper, the free *Bay Area Reporter,* appears every Thursday and offers excellent political and social commentary, personals, an arts and style section, and several great contributing writers, including Rachel Pepper. The *Reporter* is also stronger on lesbian issues than the other gay papers. For a more conservative gay perspective, pick up *The Sentinel,* which emphasizes national gay news and has an interesting column called "This Week in Leather." The section "168 Hours" is an excellent listing of arts, films, literary events, and social goings-on. In the South Bay, the biweekly *Out Now!* is a San Jose–based forum for local gay and lesbian news and community happenings.

On Our Backs and *Deneuve* are two popular lesbian pseudo-porn mags, both based in San Francisco. Pick them up at A Different Light (489 Castro St., tel. 415/431–0891), the Bay Area's best gay bookstore, along with some other gay magazines you won't find at your corner newsstand. Among the store's wide selection of queerzines, published by special-interest groups that sometimes consist of as few as one member, are *Bear,* the magazine for big, hairy, husky men, and the men who love them; *Girljock,* the tongue-in-cheek magazine for girls who like sports; *Girlfriend,* aimed at men who do drag; and *Raw Vulva,* for the bike-riding dyke.

RADIO STATIONS The Bay Area radio scene isn't as bleak as you might think after hearing all those Top-40, classic rock, and soft-rock megastations as you twirl the dial. Browse the left end of the FM range to find some less conventional programming. Berkeley's **KALX** (90.7 FM), a typically cool, alternative college station run by an all-volunteer staff 24 hours a day, can be

Desperately Seeking . . .

If you read enough Bay Area papers you'll soon realize that all classified sections are not created equal. The free weeklies are short on nuts-and-bolts info, but make up for this in entertainment value. Take a gander at the Bay Guardian's relationships department, where ads promise everything from fairytale romances to "oral worship." The SF Weekly's personals are even more experimental (requests for hermaphrodites are not uncommon). The East Bay Express is less dominated by personal ads; look here for massage therapy, counseling, and housing in Oakland and Berkeley. Daily papers like the Chronicle and the Examiner are much stronger on employment and housing opportunities than any of the free weeklies. The Oakland Tribune lists tons of rentals all over Alameda County, and the San Jose Mercury News is full of job listings and cars for sale. The gay and lesian Bay Times has an extensive resource guide, pointing you to hundreds of organizations that deal with issues like addiction and recovery, parenting, and AIDS. The classified section of the Bay Area Reporter is dedicated solely to personals, and is chock-full of pictures of mostly nude males with captions like "Ex football player rubs you the right way."

counted on for the eclectic, the avant-garde, and the noisy. They have some excellent regular programs: "Women Hold Up Half the Sky" (Sat. 11–noon) features interviews with fierce and fabulous women from around the country, and "Straightjackets" (Tues. 9–9:30 PM) deals with issues of gender and (homo)sexuality. Unfortunately, you can rarely pick up KALX's signal from San Francisco. **KUSF** (90.3 FM) comes out of the University of San Francisco, playing new music, ethnic music, and specialty shows.

Much-loved, listener-sponsored **KPFA** (94.1 FM) broadcasts all over central and Northern California. You can listen to classical, reggae, rap, soul, blues, and national news all in one place. Also look for interviews with artists and members of special-interest groups you didn't even know existed. Although some programs are a bit off-the-wall, there's no better place on the dial for music and news programs of every variety. **KFJC** (89.7 FM) operates from Foothill College in the Los Altos Hills. They play every kind of music you can think of, but are best known for their outstanding specialty shows, including the award-winning "Norman Bates Memorial Soundtrack Hour," playing your favorite TV and movie themes Saturday 9–noon; "Phil's Garage," featuring grungy garage-band music Saturday 7–10 PM; and the news show "One Step Beyond" on Sunday 7–11 PM. Again, listeners in San Francisco are subject to the whims of atmospheric conditions when tuning in.

News junkies have a few different options. On the AM dial, **KCBS** (740 AM) has rapid-fire news bites around the clock. They may not have the most in-depth coverage, but they certainly have the quickest. For higher-quality reportage, try **KQED** (88.5 FM), which broadcasts a lot of National Public Radio programming ("All Things Considered" starts at 2 PM and the BBC starts at 1 AM). **KALW** (91.7 FM) also plays NPR and BBC throughout the day.

RESOURCES FOR GAYS AND LESBIANS

Even if you're not looking for them, resources for the gay community will jump out at you. Publications focusing on gay issues can be found in most San Francisco cafés and in gay-oriented bookstores and cafés in other parts of the Bay Area. San Francisco has the *Bay Times,* the *Bay Area Reporter,* and *The Sentinel;* and the South Bay has *Out Now!* (for more information, *see* Gay Publications, *above*). The San Francisco gay community, particularly in the Castro area, is extremely supportive and close-knit. If you're trying to find your niche (be it a support group or a political organization), some friendly asking around at one of the Castro cafés or diners should get you helpful advice, if not a pal. **Café Flore** (*see* Chapter 5), despite all the winking and wagging of butts going on, is actually a great spot to start getting down to business with those in the know. If you don't find the resources you're looking for in the gay papers or by poking around the Castro, get a copy of the 200+ page *Gaybook* ($9.95), published by Rainbow Ventures Publishing (584 Castro St., Suite 632, tel. 415/928–1859). Each biannual edition contains a resource guide listing organizations that cater to gays and lesbians as well as a classified advertising section. If you're traveling, pick up Bob Damron's Address Book ($13.95 plus $5 shipping), which lists services and entertainment options for gay men, or The Women's Traveler ($10.95 plus $5 shipping), with resources for lesbians and women in general. Both are available through the Damron Company (tel. 415/255–0404).

In Berkeley, several blocks from campus, the **Pacific Center for Human Growth** (2712 Telegraph Ave., at Derby St., tel. 510/548–8283) is a well-known gay and lesbian gathering place. The organization offers counseling, social gatherings, rap sessions, and support groups (covering stuff like coming out, jealousy in relationships, parents, etc.). Also check out their bulletin boards, littered with tidbits that run the gamut from apartments for rent to invitations to socials. You can drop in weekdays 10–10 or Saturday 10–4 to see what's going on and to use any services. The Pacific Center's **Gay, Lesbian, and Bisexual Switchboard** (tel. 510/841–6224) doles out information and referrals.

In San Francisco, the **Lavender Youth Recreation and Information Center** (127 Collingwood St., at 18th St., tel. 415/703–6150, hotline 415/863–3636 or 800/246–7743) is a social and support organization for gays, lesbians, and transgenders 23 years old and younger. If you call the hotline Monday–Wednesday 4–9 PM or Thursday–Sunday 6:30–9 PM, you can talk to other young gays and lesbians, or a counselor (at off hours, you get recorded info). **Communi-**

ties **United Against Violence** (973 Market St., Suite 500, tel. 415/777–5500, 24-hour emergency hotline 415/333–4357) provides crisis counseling and referrals for gays and lesbians who are victims of anti-gay violence.

In Palo Alto, the **Stanford Lesbian/Gay/Bisexual Community Center** (Fire Truck House, Stanford Campus, tel. 415/725–4222 or 415/723–1488 for event information) knows all about gay and lesbian happenings around campus. They'll refer you to a vast number of support groups and resources. During the school year, the center is generally open weekdays noon–4; during summer, its hours are weekdays noon–1. The place is staffed by volunteers (who have other lives), so it's best to call ahead to see if anyone will be there.

One of the few positive things to emerge from the AIDS epidemic is the gay community's creation of a tremendous flood of support groups, political organizations, and other AIDS-related services. If you or a loved one has AIDS, or you just want to learn more about it, San Francisco is the place to be. For starters, head to the **San Francisco AIDS Foundation** (25 Van Ness Ave., tel. 415/864–5855), an umbrella organization that can direct people to whichever AIDS-related group best suits them. **Shanti Project** (525 Howard St., tel. 415/864–2273) is a big organization that offers assistance to people with AIDS. They provide emotional support and have housing and activities programs. For late-night counseling or information, call the **AIDS/HIV Nightline** (tel. 415/668–AIDS, 800/273–AIDS in Northern California) 5 PM–5 AM seven nights a week. If you're pissed about the AIDS crisis and want to do something about it, call **ACT-UP SF** (tel. 415/677–7988). Making headlines for its confrontational tactics, ACT-UP rallies for increased AIDS research and an end to discrimination against those living with AIDS. You can attend a meeting every Thursday at 7:30 PM in the Women's Building (3543 18th St.). **ACT-UP East Bay** (tel. 510/547–7538) meets monthly at different locations; call for specifics.

Generally, lesbian resources are much harder to ferret out. The Castro is definitely slanted toward gay men, and women should branch out geographically to find what suits them. A good move is to check out Valencia Street in San Francisco's Mission district, home to several women's bookstores and organizations. **Old Wives' Tales** (1009 Valencia St., at 21st St., tel. 415/821–4675) sells feminist and lesbian books of every stripe and sponsors readings and lectures. Berkeley is another good spot for lesbian resources and hangouts. In particular, the bookstore and coffeehouse **Mama Bears** (6536 Telegraph Ave., Berkeley, tel. 510/428–9684) offers readings and social events in a warm, supportive environment. The lesbian-owned and -operated **Tea Spot Café** (2072 San Pablo Ave., Berkeley, tel. 510/848–7376) is another happening spot—look in the papers for readings and other evening activities.

RESOURCES FOR PEOPLE OF COLOR

Northern California has a rich mix of ethnicities, but the melting pot is often more like a tossed salad, with everyone maintaining strong individual cultural identities. A wealth of resources support, educate, celebrate, and bring together people of color in the Bay Area. In addition to community organizations, look into student services and groups at the universities.

AFRICAN-AMERICAN RESOURCES The **Black Women's Resource Center** (518 17th St., Suite 202, Oakland, tel. 510/763–9501) works to establish, improve, and maintain support systems that empower African-American women, especially those with low incomes. They offer information and referrals and publish a newsletter for women in the community. The **Northern California Center for African-American History and Life** (5606 San Pablo Ave., Oakland, tel. 510/658–3158) is an extensive museum, archive, and research center. The preeminent local African-American bookstore is **Marcus Books** (3900 Martin Luther King Jr. Way, Oakland, tel. 510/652–2344).

The **Center for African and African-American Art and Culture** (762 Fulton St., San Francisco, tel. 415/928–8546) sponsors poetry readings, a variety of speakers, and storytelling in the African tradition and has research materials that people can borrow. The **Oakland History Room** (tel. 510/238–3222) in the main branch of the Oakland Public Library (125 14th St., btw Oak and Madison Sts.) has an extensive archive of past African-American life in Oakland. Bill Sturm, who runs the room, is reputed to know everything.

ASIAN-PACIFIC RESOURCES Asian Immigrant Women Advocates (310 8th St., Suite 301, Oakland, tel. 510/268–0192) works to empower immigrant Asian women through leadership development and education. The **East Bay Vietnamese Association** (1909 E. 14th St., Suite 201, Oakland, tel. 510/533–4219) provides employment services and other assistance for the Vietnamese community. In San Jose, **Korean American Community Services** (2750 Westfield Ave., San Jose, tel. 408/248–5227) helps recently arrived Koreans with English skills and other issues. **Filipinos for Affirmative Action** (310 8th St., Suite 308, Oakland, tel. 510/465–9876), a nonprofit social agency, works with the community on employment issues, AIDS and substance abuse education, and activism. The **Japan Pacific Resource Network** (310 8th St., Suite 305B, Oakland, tel. 510/891–9045) can point you to all sorts of resources for the Japanese community in the Bay Area. The **Chinese Cultural Center** (750 Kearny St., 3rd Floor, San Francisco, tel. 415/986–1822) is dedicated to the preservation of Chinese culture and community. Stop by and talk to the helpful staff for information on Chinese community events in the area.

CHICANO/LATINO RESOURCES San Francisco's entire Mission district is a resource for Chicanos and Latinos, with its theater groups, cultural centers, and zillions of Latino-owned restaurants and bookstores. One important meeting place is the **Mission Cultural Center** (2868 Mission St., btw 24th and 25th Sts., San Francisco, tel. 415/821–1155), site of an art gallery and dance, music, and theater classes. **La Peña Cultural Center** (3105 Shattuck Ave., Berkeley, tel. 510/849–2568) has concerts and dances, workshops, a store with Latino books and music, a café, and a cooking school/caterer, Dos Burros (tel. 510/204–9733). In the South Bay, the **Centro Cultural Latino** (tel. 415/343–7476) has after-school and summer programs for Latino youth and sponsors cultural activities.

NATIVE AMERICAN RESOURCES The **International Indian Treaty Council** (123 Townsend St., Suite 575, San Francisco, tel. 415/512–1501) is an information center that works with indigenous people both locally and around the world, promoting sovereignty, human rights, and indigenous prisoners' rights. They work as a consultant to the United Nations. The **American Indian Center of Santa Clara Valley, Inc.** (919 Alameda, San Jose, tel. 408/971–9622) has a spectrum of support services and a reference library (tel. 415/971–0772). The **Native American Health Center,** a free clinic open to anyone, has two locations in the Bay Area (56 Julian Ave., San Francisco, tel. 415/621–8051; and 3124 E. 14th St., Oakland, tel. 510/261–1962).

RESOURCES FOR WOMEN

The most comprehensive resource center in the Bay Area is the **Women's Building** (3543 18th St., San Francisco, tel. 415/431–1180), which provides a wealth of information for women. The building houses nine women's organizations, including the **National Organization for Women (NOW), San Francisco Women Against Rape (SF WAR),** and **Mujeres Unidas y Activas.** They can also help you find housing, health care, employment, or just about anything else. Regular meetings at the Women's Building include NOW (the third Tuesday of the month at 7 PM) and **Women Embracing Life** (Mondays at 6:45), a support group for women with HIV.

In the East Bay, one of the best resources is the **Women's Resource Center** (250 Golden Bear Center, U.C. Berkeley, tel. 510/642–4786). Come here to get referrals for other organizations. Only U.C. students and staff can check out materials from the book and audiovisual collections, but anyone can dig through the community resources files, with info on support groups, internships, grant opportunities, and more.

An important women's health resource is **Planned Parenthood** (815 Eddy St. Suite 200, San Francisco, tel. 415/441–5454; 482 West MacArthur Blvd., Oakland, tel. 510/ 601–4700), a pro-choice family-planning clinic (see Low-Cost Medical Aid, above). The **Women's Needs Center** (1825 Haight St., San Francisco, tel. 415/487–5607) offers pro-choice gynecological services for low-income women, and anonymous HIV testing for men and women. San Francisco Women Against Rape (see above) runs a 24-hour crisis hotline (tel. 415/647–7273 or 510/845–RAPE). Female victims of domestic violence can call **A Safe Place** (tel. 510/536–7233), a shelter for battered women, 24 hours a day. The **Women's Action Coalition (WAC)** (1360 Mission St., btw 9th and 10th Sts., tel. 510/869–2584) is an open alliance of

15

women committed to direct-action support of women's rights. Biweekly meetings are held in the Mission Street office; free child care is provided.

The free **Bay Area Businesswomen's Directory** (5337 College Ave., Suite 501, Oakland, tel. 510/654–7557), published biannually, is a resource guide for women in the workforce. Its purpose is to assist women on their way to economic independence. Their monthly *Bay Area Businesswomen's Calendar* has articles on issues of interest to women, as well as a schedule of upcoming events. **Mama Bears** (Telegraph Ave., Oakland, tel. 510/428–9684) stocks female-oriented literature, sponsors readings, and can refer you to other bookstores around California if they don't have what you want. The **Women of Color Resource Center** (2288 Fulton St., Suite 103, Berkeley, tel. 510/843–9272) publishes the excellent book *Women of Color, Organizations and Projects: A National Directory* ($8.95 plus shipping), which points you to hundreds of organizations dedicated to women of almost every ethnicity. The **Young Women's Christian Association** (620 Sutter St., San Francisco, tel. 415/775–6502) offers social-service programs and lodging referrals for women. The San Francisco office can refer you to the six other YWCAs in Marin and the East Bay.

RESOURCES FOR THE DISABLED

The Bay Area is an important center for disabled resources, thanks mostly to Berkeley's **Center for Independent Living,** started in the early '70s by a group of disabled people who fought for their right to be accepted at the University of California at Berkeley. There are now over 300 independent living centers around the nation, working for rights for the disabled, helping disabled people understand their own potential, and giving referrals. You'll find several in the Bay Area: in Berkeley (2539 Telegraph Ave., tel. 510/841–4776); in Hayward (439 A St., tel. 510/881–5743); in San Rafael (710 4th St., tel. 415/459–6245); in Santa Clara (1601 Civic Center, Suite 100, tel. 408/985–1243); and in San Francisco (70 10th St., tel. 415/863–0581). The San Francisco office is especially helpful. Ask for Tricia Leetz, who knows Bay Area resources like the back of her hand.

Transit organizations in the Bay Area have joined ranks to create an ID card that gives disabled people discounts on travel throughout nine Bay Area counties; each transit company decides what kind of a discount to give. You can get the pass at any transit office by filling out a form and getting proof from your doctor. The **BART Customer Service Office** (800 Madison St., at the Lake Merritt BART station, tel. 510/464–7136) can tell you where you buy a $16 ticket for a mere $1.60. All BART stations have elevators. San Francisco MUNI's **Elderly and Handicapped Discount ID Office** (tel. 415/923–6070) gives the same information about MUNI passes. You'll pay 35¢ instead of $1 to ride MUNI; monthly passes for the disabled are $8. **AC Transit** (tel. 510/891–4777) issues a disabled ID card allowing the bearer to pay 55¢ instead of $1.10 to ride the bus. To find out which bus routes are wheelchair accessible, contact their bus information line (tel. 510/839–2882). On **Golden Gate Transit** (tel. 415/332–6600), you get 50% off the price of bus fare. Call them to find out which buses are wheelchair accessible. If you call the day before you plan on traveling, they'll make sure to put the right bus on the route.

Some major car-rental companies are able to supply hand-controlled vehicles with a minimum of 24 hours advance notice. **Avis** (tel. 800/331–1212) will install hand-control mechanisms at no extra charge if given a day's notice. **Hertz** (tel. 800/654–3131, TDD 800/654–2280) asks for 48 hours notice (except at San Francisco International Airport, where a day will suffice). Rental companies often can't install hand controls on their least expensive cars.

Grand Mar (1311 63rd St., at Doyle St., Emeryville, tel. 510/428–0441) rents and repairs wheelchairs. Manual wheelchairs rent for $10 the first day, $5 each subsequent day, or $55 a month; power wheelchairs are $20 a day, $348 a month. **Abbey Home and Healthcare** (390 9th St., San Francisco, tel. 415/864–6999) rents manual wheelchairs for $56 a month.

American Foundation for the Blind (111 Pine St., San Francisco, tel. 415/392–4845) has brochures and catalogues to help people access resources. **Lighthouse for the Blind and Visually Disabled** (20 10th St., San Francisco, tel. 415/431–1481) has assistant devices (canes, talking watches) and can direct people to support groups. **Lion's Blind Center** in Oakland (tel. 510/450–1580) or San Jose (tel. 408/295–4016) also has resources for the blind. **Peninsula Center for the Blind** (4151 Middlefield Rd., Suite 101, Palo Alto, tel. 415/858–0202) has orientation and mobility specialists, social workers, and short-term counseling. For the hearing impaired, **Hearing Society for the Bay Area** (870 Market St., Suite 330, tel. 415/693–5870, TDD 415/834–1005) provides social services, interpreting, vocational rehab, and referrals.

ACCESS/ABILITIES (P.O. Box 458, Mill Valley 94982, tel. 415/388–3250) is a small travel center that provides travel opportunities for the disabled. They've got info on accessible tours and they customize itineraries for both the Bay Area and other places in the country. The non-profit organization **Environmental Traveling Companions** (Fort Mason Center, Landmark Building C, tel. 415/474–7662) organizes cross-country skiing, kayaking, and rafting trips for the physically disabled and other people with special needs—cancer survivors, the developmentally disabled, etc.—as well as the population at large. Their prices are very reasonable (one-day trips start at about $58 per person), and they're willing to negotiate if you're truly unable to pay. In the East Bay, **Bay Area Outreach and Recreation Program** (tel. 510/849–4663) organizes sports events and outdoor activities for the disabled, with programs for youth, adults, and seniors.

SPECTATOR SPORTS

The Bay Area is fertile ground for spectator sports, with two pro baseball teams, a championship football team, an NBA franchise, enthusiastic college sports rivalries, and thousands of loyal fans. The city's major sports venue is the unfortunately located **Candlestick Park** (south of S.F. in Daly City), where the San Francisco Giants play baseball and the San Francisco '49ers play football. The park's management has recently sunk $5 million into renovation, adding 130,000 square feet of Kentucky Blue Grass and 1,600 new seats, but that doesn't alter the fact that the 'Stick is butt cold most days and almost every night. To get to Candlestick Park, take U.S. 101 south to the Candlestick exit, or catch the Muni 9X "Ballpark Express" at the Sutter Street exit of the Montgomery BART station. Round-trip costs $5, $2 for those with a MUNI pass, and buses leave every 10 minutes, starting 90 minutes before the game on weekdays or three hours before on weekends. SamTrans also has buses from the Palo Alto Transit Center for $3 round-trip. Call 800/660–4BUS for departure times, which vary according to game time.

It's easy for Giants fans to show their loyalty: Just sitting through a game at the freezing 'Stick is enough to test the most ardent fan's dedication.

If you can't bring yourself to watch baseball with your mittens on, go see the Oakland Athletics play at the **Oakland Coliseum** (tel. 510/639–7700); the Golden State Warriors play basketball in the Coliseum's indoor stadium next door. The Coliseum emphasizes propriety, safety, and a family atmosphere (there's a kiddie play area under the stadium). You can reach it by taking I–880 to the Hegenberger Road exit, or, if you want to avoid parking fees and traffic, taking Fremont BART to the Coliseum Station.

BASEBALL The baseball rivalry between San Francisco and the East Bay came to a dramatic head in the 1989 "Bay Series," when the American League's **Oakland A's** and the National League's **San Francisco Giants** duked it out for the championship, and God intervened to sever the bridge between east and west with a major earthquake. But usually the competition between the two teams is less heated, and many fans are perfectly happy to alternate between cheering the A's on at the Oakland Coliseum (*see above*) and rooting for the Giants at Candlestick Park (*see above*).

Unfortunately, the A's haven't been playing up to par in recent years, and even the Giants struggled in '94, until the baseball strike forced the season to an early close. Still, as long as games are being played, the low, low price makes this the most accessible professional sport in the Bay Area. You can enjoy a bleacher seat for just $5 at the Stick or $4.50 at the Coliseum. Especially at Candlestick, the bleachers are a great deal: They command a better view than many of the $7 seats, and they're a good place to get a good look at Barry Bonds. At the Coliseum, those who don't want to slum it with the bleacher bums can get half-price tickets to the plaza level ($11) or upper reserved ($7) seats with a student ID. For a printed pocket schedule of games and information about A's tickets, call 510/638–0500 Monday–Saturday 9–5. For Giants information and schedules, call 415/467–8000 weekdays 8:30–5:30. To charge tickets for either team, call BASS (tel. 415/776–1999 or 510/762–BASS), but expect to pay an extra $3–$4 per ticket plus $2.65 per order in service charges. Unless you think the game will be a sellout, get your tickets at the stadium box office.

FOOTBALL Along with the Pittsburgh Steelers and the Dallas Cowboys, the **San Francisco '49ers** hold the NFL record for most Super Bowls won. Because of their consistent success, the '49ers have built up a huge fan base from all over Northern California, and tickets for home games at Candlestick Park (the season runs Sept.–Jan.) are nearly impossible to get. Season-ticket holders have a lock on most seats, and when the rest go on sale in July, they usually sell out within the hour, despite the $40 price tag. Call the ticket office (tel. 415/468–2249) to find out what day tickets go on sale (usually mid-July). Then all you can do is call BASS (tel. 415/776–1999 or 510/762–BASS) at 9 AM that day and hope you get through before someone else snatches the last ticket.

BASKETBALL Many people feel that the **Golden State Warriors** are on the brink of an NBA championship. Number-one draft pick and NBA Rookie of the Year Chris Webber gave the team a huge boost last season, as did Latrell Sprewell, one of the only second-year players in the NBA to make the All-Star team. If Tim Hardaway returns as expected, after being out all last season with knee injuries, they might just go all the way. Tickets, which go on sale in late September or early October, sell out fast. They're available through BASS (tel. 415/776–1999 or 510/762–BASS) for $17.50–$28. To reach the Warriors' business office (weekdays 8:30–5), call 510/638–6300.

HOCKEY Hardly an article was written about the San Jose Sharks last season that didn't contain the words "storybook season" and "Cinderella team." After the previous season's 11-71-2 effort, the Sharks managed to go seven games against the Toronto Maple Leafs in the Western Conference semifinals before finally giving up their Stanley Cup dreams. At press time, the NHL lockout was still in effect, and game schedules were still undecided. When available, tickets to games in the new San Jose Arena ($15–$71) are expected to sell quickly; call 408/287–4275 for information. The season runs from October to April. From San Francisco, you can take CalTrain (see Getting In, Out, and Around by Train, above) to the San Jose Arena, and they even run a late train back to S.F. after the game. There's a shuttle to and from parking lots in downtown San Jose.

COLLEGE SPORTS Most college sports in the Bay Area take place at either U.C. Berkeley (called "Cal" by sports fans) or Stanford University in Palo Alto. Both schools are supported by a huge alumni base who love to recapture their youth by getting sloshed and cheering like banshees at school events. The **Cal Bears** football team, which plays in Memorial Stadium on the east side of campus, has improved a bit in recent years. But whether or not it's a winning season, even the most blasé Berkeley bohemian may work up an ashamed sweat over the "Big Game" between Cal and Stanford.

When hoops star Jason Kidd announced his decision to enter the NBA draft in 1994, coach Todd Bozeman cried at the press conference; and you can be sure thousands of **Cal basketball** fans were doing the same. Top recruit Jelani Gardner, a member of the 1994 U.S. Olympic Festival's West Team, has his work cut out for him if he's going to fill Kidd's high-tops. But losing Kidd and Lamond Murray hasn't done too much to dampen fans' enthusiasm: Tickets for the '94–'95 season, played on campus at Harmon Gym, were sold out and had a 1,500-person waiting list by the summer of '94. Luckily, it's much easier to get tickets to the few games each season (six in '94–'95) that are played at the Oakland Coliseum.

To buy tickets for Cal sports, call 800/GO–BEARS. Football tickets cost $12 for general admission, $20 for reserved seating. Basketball tickets for games at the Coliseum cost about $16. Baseball, played at Evan's Diamond on the corner of Bancroft Way and Oxford Street, costs $5 for adults, $3 for Cal students and minors.

Stanford's spectator sports revolve mainly around the university's football team, **The Cardinal** (named for the color, not the bird), which plays at Stanford Stadium. Tennis, baseball, and many championship women's teams also draw a crowd. Palo Alto may seem a little out of the way to some people, but Stanford fans are gung-ho. The school is notorious for its goofy band. For information on tickets for all Stanford sports, call 800/BEAT–CAL, weekdays 9–4. Football tickets cost $9 general admission, $20 reserved. Tickets to basketball games, played at Maples Pavilion, go on sale in September.

At both Cal and Stanford, women's sports are strong and getting stronger, thanks to the recent enforcement of federal funding statute Title IX. Cal women's soccer, softball, and basketball are acclaimed teams, and Stanford's women's basketball team is a consistent NCAA championship contender.

FESTIVALS

JANUARY In addition to the ballet and chamber orchestra seasons, January is a big month in the California whale-watching season, which runs through April. Patient watchers bundle up and pull out their binoculars at Point Reyes (*see* Chapter 8). The rangers at the Bear Valley Visitor Center (tel. 415/663–1092) can tell you how many beasties have swum past in the past few days.

Tet Festival. This one-day street fair is held on the Saturday nearest the Vietnamese New Year (the first new moon after January 20). The streets around the Civic Center come alive with performances by Vietnamese, Cambodian, and Laotian singers and dancers, booths selling Southeast Asian delicacies, and community services distributing information. The festival is not just a celebration of the New Year, but also of the diverse neighborhood in which it takes place. *Tel. 415/885–2743.*

FEBRUARY **Chinese New Year and Golden Dragon Parade.** Celebrate the dawn of the Year of the Boar (year 4693 on the lunar calendar) with the largest Chinese community in North America. The Chinatown Chamber of Commerce (730 Sacramento St., tel. 415/982–3000) has the lowdown on cultural events, which take place January 31–February 11. The justly famous Golden Dragon Parade explodes with fireworks and a riot of colorful costumes at 6 PM on February 11. *Tel. 415/982–3000.*

MARCH During **Tulipmania** (Mar. 4–18), over 35,000 tulips bloom around Pier 39. You can walk around on your own, or show up at the Entrace Plaza any morning at 10 for a free guided tour.

St. Patrick's Day Parade. Boasting shamrocks, Guinness stout, and enough green to make even Mother Nature envious, this parade is a party set in motion. The United Irish Cultural Center sponsors the parade, which winds through San Francisco to City Hall on March 12, 1995, at 12:30. Despite the recent politicization of the parade, with "Gaylic Pride" and "IRA All the Way" banners popping up, the emphasis is still firmly on green beer and Irish folk tunes. *Tel. 415/661–2700.*

In 1994, the Irish Lesbian and Gay Organization marched in the St. Patrick's Day Parade for the first time, voicing their support of gays in Boston, where the parade was cancelled to disallow gay participation.

APRIL **Cherry Blossom Festival.** On April 15, 16, 22, and 23, 1995, this cultural festival in Japantown features such traditions as ancient tea ceremonies and martial arts and cooking demonstrations. Nearly 400 Japanese performers come to dance, and there are numerous exhibits of Japanese art. Perhaps the most popular attraction is the taiko drum performance on Saturday night. For a schedule of events, send a self-addressed, stamped envelope to Cherry Blossom Festival, Box 15147, San Francisco 94115. The festivities conclude with a 2½-hour parade. Most events are free. *Tel. 415/563–2313.*

San Francisco International Film Festival. From April 6 to April 20, 1995, the oldest film festival in the United States features two straight weeks of movies and seminars and many opportunities to mingle with the creative minds behind them. Films range from the almost mainstream (Almódovar) to the truly obscure. Screenings take place at the Pacific Film Archive in Berkeley, the Kabuki 8 and the Castro Theatre in San Francisco, and Landmark's Palo Alto Square. *Tel. 415/567–4641. Admission: $7 per event.*

Whole Life Expo. If your energy needs to be rechanneled, come to this New Age fest, held at the Fashion Design Center (8th and Brannan Sts., next to Concourse Exhibition Center). On April 28–30, over 250 booths display their energy pyramids, massage tools, and sprout-growing paraphernalia. The biannual festival also happens the third week in October, when the emphasis is on food and health. *Tel. 415/721–2484. Admission: $7 Fri., $12 Sat. or Sun.*

MAY **Bay to Breakers.** Listed in the *Guinness Book of World Records* as the world's largest foot race, this zany 7½-mile race pits world-class runners against costumed human centipedes and huge safe-sex condom caravans. The half-comical, half-serious event attracts more than 100,000 people who get a charge out of running (or walking, or drinking) from the Financial District across San Francisco, through Golden Gate Park, and out to Ocean Beach. The race takes place the third Sunday of every May. Entry forms start appearing in the *San Francisco Examiner* (*see* Media, *above*) March 1. If you like crowds and silly fun, this is the event for you, but be warned that you could spend 45 minutes just jostling your way across the starting line. *Tel. 415/777–7770.*

Carnaval. On Memorial Day Weekend, long after Carnaval celebrations in New Orleans and Rio are over, the Mission district revives the party. Dozens of South American musical groups and the Aztec group Xiuhcoatc Danza Azteka are just a few of the people likely to participate. The parade along Mission and 24th streets generally starts at 11 AM on Sunday, though it was noon before anyone caught a glimpse of marchers last year. The fair on Harrison Street (btw 16th and 22nd Sts.) features food, craft booths, and stages. Escola Nova de Samba and Caribbean All-Stars are popular performers here. *Tel. 415/826–1401.*

Cinco de Mayo. Vibrant mariachi bands and colorful Mexican folklorico dancers congregate in the Mission district the weekend nearest May 5. On Sunday, floats, bands, and salsa dancers wearing little besides feathers parade through the Mission, starting at 24th and Bryant streets and ending at 8th and Market streets. The festival has been marred by post-celebration violence in recent years, but the '94 celebration went off virtually without a hitch. *Tel. 415/647–8622.*

Festival of Greece. On May 19–21 the emphasis is on food—moussaka, dolmas, baklava—and wine, but music and Greek crafts also make an appearance. Costume-clad dancers perform for the crowds, but when the bands pull out their bouzoukis, everyone gets in on the action. Each year a few celebrities make an appearance; in past years, Jeff Smith (the Frugal Gourmet) gave a demonstration, and George Stephanopolos showed up to cook some dolmas. The festival takes place at the Greek Orthodox Cathedral of the Ascension (4700 Lincoln Ave., Oakland), from approximately 11 to 11 Friday and Saturday and noon to 9 on Sunday. *Tel. 510/531–3400. Admission: about $5.*

JUNE Summer brings out all the neighborhood celebrations, including the **Haight Street Fair** (tel. 415/661–8025), the **Polk Street Fair** (415/346–4561), the **North Beach Fair** (tel. 415/403–0666), and the **Union Street Spring Festival** (tel. 415/346–4561), all of which feature craft booths, music, and food.

Festival at the Lake. Because police and young festival-goers clashed after Lake Merritt's 1994 Festival at the Lake, many talked about moving or canceling the East Bay's largest urban fair in '95. Those who feel the police overreacted hope that the fair, which features crafts, international food, storytelling, and world music, will return to the lake the first weekend in June. Call for the latest. *Tel. 510/286–1061. Admission: about $7.*

Free Folk Festival. It's surprising that more Bay Area residents haven't been turned on to the free, feel-good festival that takes place for two days every June at the John Adams Campus City College (1860 Hayes St., at Masonic Ave.). Bring your guitar, harmonica, or whatever you can carry a tune on to the workshops and impromptu jam sessions that spring up between concerts of folk, blues, and international music. It's a very loosely organized event, and participants change yearly, but if you call the college (tel. 415/561–1908) they should be able to tell you what's up.

Juneteenth. The day Lincoln's Emancipation Proclamation was read in Texas is celebrated in nearly every city in the Bay Area, mostly by a scattered series of community events; keep your eye on local papers for information as June 19th approaches. For info on San Francisco festivities, call the Western Addition Cultural Center (tel. 415/776–0363). One of the larger events is the **Oakland Juneteenth Celebration,** held at Lakeside Park at Lake Merritt. Organizers emphasize cultural enrichment and the history of the African-American community. The family-oriented festival is expanding to two days in 1995; show up at the park June 17 and 18 noon–6 for big-name blues and R&B acts, ethnic food booths, arts and crafts, and lots of activities for the kids (face painting, clowns, and an interactive play area). *Tel. 510/238–2193.*

Lesbian and Gay Freedom Day Parade and Celebration. This is San Francisco at its queer best. The parade traditionally attracts huge names in the gay community; writer Armistead Maupin was one of the grand marshals in 1994. The 1995 parade and street festival will take place on June 18th, but at press time the location was up for debate—the celebration has grown so large that it's hard to find a place with adequate space. *Tel. 415/864–3733.*

JULY–AUGUST In late July and early August, look for the **Jewish Film Festival** (tel. 510/548–0556), the largest of its kind in the world, in Berkeley and San Francisco.

Fourth of July Waterfront Festival. The biggest Independence Day celebration in the Bay Area takes place along the waterfront between Aquatic Park and Pier 39. Fireworks explode from several locations; stake out a place on the grass early to ensure a good view. Festivities start in the afternoon, when Bay Area musicians play at stages along the waterfront. At press time, they hadn't firmed up plans for 1995; call as the holiday nears for more details. *Tel. 415/777–8498.*

Intertribal Powwow. The Oakland Zoo has teamed up with the Intertribal Friendship House to put on this one-day event, where Native American dancers and drummers get a chance to shake their feathers, while vendors sell Native American crafts. The event generally takes place in late July in the Zoo Meadow, but call the number below for the latest information. *Tel. 510/632–9525.*

Jazz and All That Art on Fillmore. In the 1940s, '50s, and '60s, the Fillmore area was locally famous for its happening jazz and blues clubs. The clubs disappeared with gentrification in the '70s, but performers revive the tradition the first weekend of every July on Fillmore Street between Post and Jackson. Musicians like 72-year-old S.F. native Charles Brown play every day from 10 to 6, while crowds wander among booths laden with arts and crafts. And, of course, there's the requisite number of outdoor cafés serving everything from barbecue ribs to knishes. Admission to all shows is free. *Tel. 415/346–4446.*

KQED International Beer and Food Festival. If you have $35 to spare, join 5,000 San Franciscans at the Concourse Exhibition Center on Saturday, July 8, from 1 to 4 PM and sample 250 different beers. It's the largest international beer festival in the nation, featuring beers from around the world, as well as domestic microbrews. There's live music on two stages, and food booths sell everything from Thai cuisine to pizza. Free cable-car shuttles run from the Civic Center BART station. KQED suggests that you get tickets in advance by calling the number below; members get a 15% discount on advance tickets. *Tel. 415/553–2200.*

SEPTEMBER **Festival de las Americas.** This Mission district festival, celebrating the independence of Mexico and seven other Latin American countries, attracts over 80,000 people to 24th Street between Mission and Hampshire streets. The socially responsible, alcohol-free, family-oriented event promotes pride in the Latino community. Latino musicians, ethnic food, and booths selling original crafts crowd the streets Sunday, September 18, from 11 to 6. *Tel. 415/826–1401.*

Opera in the Park. To kick off the opera season, the San Francisco Opera presents a free concert in Golden Gate Park's Sharon Meadow the Sunday after the first performance of the season, usually the week after Labor Day. The program isn't announced until the day of the show, but it usually features a few high-powered singers appearing as guest performers with the opera. *Tel. 415/861–4008.*

San Francisco Blues Festival. You get big-name performers for big bucks at the oldest blues festival in the country. The venue is Fort Mason's scenic Great Meadow, at the corner of Marina Boulevard and Laguna Street. The lineup for the 1995 festival, September 23 and 24, had yet to be set at press time, but past performers have included B.B. King and the Robert Cray Band. One-day tickets are $16.50 in advance, $20 at the door; two-day tickets are $28, advance purchase only. Performances take place 11–5:30 each day, and all seating is on the lawn. A free kick-off concert happens at the Justin Herman Plaza on September 22. *Tel. 415/826–6837.*

San Francisco Shakespeare Festival. Free performances of a selected Shakespeare play begin Labor Day weekend in San Francisco's Golden Gate Park. In 1995, the play will also be staged at San Jose's St. James' Park, Oakland's Duck Pond Meadow, and, for the first time, at a location in Walnut Creek. At press time, the prevailing theory was that *As You Like It,* directed by Albert Takazauckas, would be the '95 play. Call for exact performance dates. *Tel. 415/666–2221.*

OCTOBER **Castro Street Fair** and **Halloween.** October is the best month to be in the Castro. On the first Sunday of the month, the Castro Street Fair brings out crafts vendors; booths run by community, health, and social organizations; and musical entertainment. The month winds up with the wild and wacky Castro Street Halloween extravaganza, where the good, the bad, the bizarre, and the ugly emerge, as beauties in drag parade around. *Tel. 415/467–3354.*

Great Halloween Pumpkin Festival. Though it takes place in the city, this free festival features all the country traditions—hayrides, pie-eating contests, a pumpkin weigh-off, and a costume parade. Bring the kids for trick-or-treating or pumpkin carving. The two-day event traditionally takes place on San Francisco's Polk Street (btw Broadway and Filbert St.) one or two weekends before Halloween, but call for the latest. *Tel. 415/346–4446.*

NOVEMBER Right after Thanksgiving, there's a **Christmas Tree Lighting Ceremony** at Pier 39 on Fisherman's Wharf (tel. 415/981–8030). Also look for the traditional Mexican celebration of **Día de los Muertos,** the Day of the Dead, on November 2 in San Francisco (tel. 415/826–8009). Derived from Aztec rituals and the Catholic All Souls' Day, the holiday is commemorated in the Mission with art exhibitions and a parade (usually starting from the Mission Cultural Center).

Run to the Far Side with Gary Larson. Over 13,000 people dressed like their favorite Gary Larson characters compete in a 5-kilometer walk and a 10-kilometer run through Golden Gate Park the Sunday after Thanksgiving. The cost is about $18 if you preregister, $22 on the day of the race; the event benefits the California Academy of Sciences' environmental education programs. *Tel. 415/221–5100.*

Show up late on the last day of the San Francisco Book Festival to get the best discount deals on all sorts of new books.

San Francisco Book Festival. Bibliophiles eagerly await this big festival at the Concourse Exhibition Center. Over 300 booths representing big publishers and small alternative presses show off their books, often selling them at a discount. About 250 authors are here to read and sign their books; Isabel Allende, Tony Hillerman, and June Jordan are just a few who have appeared in recent years. The 1995 festival will take place November 4 and 5. Though it has traditionally been free, a $2 admission charge was imposed in 1994; apparently the "Keep the Festival Free" donation boxes at the entrance didn't have the desired effect. *Tel. 415/861–BOOK.*

DECEMBER In celebration of the season, the American Conservatory Theater (345 Mason St., San Francisco, tel. 415/749–2228) presents *A Christmas Carol* every year.

CLIMATE

The Bay Area is home to something called "micro-climates." In lay terms, this means that while you're burning furniture to stay warm in San Francisco's Sunset district, your friend is talking to you cordless and poolside in 80° Palo Alto, a mere 45 miles away. And when you call the **National Weather Service** (tel. 415/364–7974) to try to figure out what to wear, they tell you something helpful about "highs from the upper 50s to the low 90s." At least if you call between 10 AM and 6 PM you can talk to a real live meteorologist, who might be able to narrow things down a bit. For ski conditions in Northern California, Tahoe, or the Sierras, call the **California State Automobile Association's Ski Report** (tel. 415/864–6440).

SAN FRANCISCO A local writer in the *East Bay Express* put it best: When it comes to San Francisco weather, "summer is winter, winter is spring, and fall is summer." In sum, it never snows here, but it's cold and windy a lot of the time—except in September and October, the Indian summer months. Late fall gets real cold, it rains pretty often in winter, and June is notoriously blustery and foggy. The average high temperature is 69°, the average low 46°.

EAST BAY The East Bay tends to be a few degrees warmer than San Francisco. Summer is mild, fall hot, winter unpredictable, and spring mild again. Overall, the climate here is pretty fabulous, especially if you enjoy mellow, overcast days or cool but sunny afternoons. It's smart to layer your clothing, because there's nothing to guarantee that the morning's foggy turtleneck weather won't betray you and become an afternoon heat wave. Highs average 72°, lows 43°.

MARIN COUNTY In a region of micro-climates, Marin goes one better: Even within the county, the weather differs from town to town. The coast is usually fogged in, the bayside towns of Tiburon and Sausalito get a cool breeze, and San Rafael checks in at a solid few degrees warmer than most of the Bay Area (with an average summer high of 82°).

SOUTH BAY Don't move to the South Bay if you thrive on unpredictability. Spring and fall are sunny and warm, and summer is sunny and hot (the average summer high in San Jose is 81°). In the winter, things cool down to a medium rare, with lows dipping to 40°.

VISITOR INFORMATION

SAN FRANCISCO Write or call the **San Francisco Convention and Visitors Bureau** to receive free info about hotels, restaurants, festivals, and shopping. *201 3rd St., Suite 900, 94103, tel. 415/974–6900. 3 blocks from Montgomery BART. Open weekdays 8:30–5.*

Walk This Way

Have a laugh at all the bus-riding, pastel-clad, camera-toting tourists that infiltrate Fisherman's Wharf if you like, but don't let them turn you off tours entirely. Walking tours are a booming business in San Francisco, and even longtime residents can learn something from the enthusiastic guides, who know the city's neighborhoods inside out. Wok Wiz Chinatown Tours and Cooking Company (tel. 415/981–5588) leads the popular "I Can't Believe I Ate My Way Through Chinatown" tour ($50). Though the name is pure fromage, this is a great way to single out the neighborhood's best restaurants and learn a lot about Chinese cuisine from cookbook author Shirley Fong-Torres. Tours usually start on Saturday mornings at 10 and end, according to Shirley, "when the first person explodes." Wok Wiz's other tours cost only about $25–$35, and some include stops for dim sum along the way. Trevor Hailey (375 Lexington St., tel. 415/550–8110), a prominent member of the San Francisco lesbian community, leads a highly recommended tour of the city's famous gay neighborhood called Cruisin' the Castro ($30). The 3½-hour tour, which includes brunch, leaves about four times a week; call for reservations. Finally, to see San Francisco for free, call City Guides (tel. 415/557–4266), whose frequent guided walks are sponsored by the San Francisco Public Library. Tours, which cover almost every corner of town, include Roof Gardens and Open Spaces, the Telegraph Hill Hike, Art-Deco Marina, and the Mission Murals. Quality of these tours varies according to the skills of the library volunteer, but it's hard to beat being shown around the city for free by an enthusiastic local.

Visitors can stop in for maps and brochures at the city's **Visitor Information Center** in the lower level of Hallidie Plaza, next to the Powell Street BART station at Powell and Market streets. Their phone number also connects you to an events hotline, with the latest info on goings-on in the city. *Tel. 415/391–2000. Open weekdays 9–5:30, Sat. 9–3, Sun. 10–2.*

EAST BAY The **East Bay Regional Parks District** has maps and information about the 46 parks and 13 regional trails in the Oakland hills. *2950 Peralta Oaks Ct., at 106th St., tel. 510/635–0135. Open weekdays 8:30–5.*

The **Oakland Convention and Visitors Bureau** (1000 Broadway, Suite 200, tel. 510/839–9000), open weekdays 8:30–5, is geared toward convention-goers, but the staff is happy to answer all inquiries. Pick up a copy of their small pamphlet, "The Official Visitors Guide," which lists dozens of museums, historical attractions, and community events. To reach the office, take BART to 12th Street Station and walk down Broadway to 11th Street. For recorded info on the arts, theater, sports, and all sorts of entertainment, call Oakland's **Cultural Arts Division** (tel. 510/835–2787).

MARIN COUNTY The **Marin County Chamber of Commerce** distributes the free *Weekender Magazine,* which lists live music and cultural events in the area. *30 N. San Pedro Rd., Suite 150, San Rafael, tel. 415/472–7470. Open weekdays 9–5.*

Point Reyes National Seashore's **Bear Valley Visitors Center** has exhibits on park wildlife, topographical and hiking maps, and loads of information on exploring the peninsula. Look for a sign marking the turnoff for the center half a mile past Olema on Route 1. *Tel. 415/663–1092. Open weekdays 9–5, weekends 8–5.*

Muir Woods Visitor Center. *Tel. 415/388–2596, or 415/388–2595 for recorded information. Take U.S. 101 north to the Rte. 1/Stinson Beach exit and follow the signs to Muir Woods. Open daily 9–5:30.*

The **West Marin Chamber of Commerce** has a free newsletter, "The Coastal Traveler," with great information on out-of-the-way beaches, bike rides, and backpacking trips. *Box 1045, Rte. 1, Point Reyes Station, tel. 415/663–9232. 2 mi north of Olema on Rte. 1. Open Mon., Thurs., and Fri. 10–5, weekends and holidays 11–5.*

SOUTH BAY The **Santa Clara Convention and Visitors Bureau** (2200 Laurelwood Rd., Santa Clara, tel. 408/296–7111) is open weekdays 8–5. Visit the **San Mateo County Convention and Visitors Bureau** (111 Anza Blvd., Burlingame, tel. 415/348–7600) weekdays 8:30–5.

The **Pacifica Chamber of Commerce** has info on Pacifica and Montara, as well as limited materials about Half Moon Bay and points south. *450 Dondee St., Pacifica, near Rockaway Beach, tel. 415/355–4122. Open weekdays 9–noon, 1–5, weekends 10–4:30.*

The friendly staff at the **Half Moon Bay Chamber of Commerce** will give you more info than you ever wanted on Half Moon Bay and the immediately surrounding area, as well as a smattering of maps and brochures for the entire San Mateo County Coast. *520 Kelly Ave., Half Moon Bay, tel. 415/726–8380. Open weekdays 10–4.*

At the **Half Moon Bay State Parks District Office** you'll find limited information on state parks and beaches from Montara to Año Nuevo. *95 Kelly Ave., Half Moon Bay, tel. 415/726–8800. Open weekdays 8–5.*

EXPLORING THE BAY AREA

2

By Lisa Roth and Timothy McIntyre

You'll never run out of opportunities for adventure in the Bay Area, no matter how much time you have to explore. San Francisco alone offers a dozen distinct neighborhoods made for walking. A cosmopolitan, almost European, feeling pervades the city, and an endless string of shops, parks, and cafés invites you to stop and soak up the atmosphere. On days when you feel more rugged, head for Marin County's stunning cliffs, forests, and beaches, an impressive backdrop to the multimillion-dollar homes that dot the landscape. The East Bay offers acres of hilly parks with incredible views of the city and the ocean beyond. Also in this direction lie Berkeley, known for its university, its radical politics, and its wacky street people; and Oakland, a sprawling, unpretentious city with a strong African-American identity. Then there's the South Bay, 70 or so miles of that banal suburban flavor the rest of the region lacks.

San Francisco

No matter how well you think you know San Francisco, the dense, eclectic city will surprise you every time you take a walk. There's always something you're not prepared for—a poignant exchange with a stranger, a view entirely altered by fog or sunlight, a piece of fruit getting ready to drop from the tree in the middle of a busy urban neighborhood. And damn, it all changes so quickly. One minute you're marveling at the frenetic pace of Financial District workers and the next you're walking through Chinese herb shops and produce markets. You leave that noisy Italian café where you downed a cappuccino and biscotti, and 10 minutes later you're gazing at the Golden Gate Bridge from the water's edge. Bored? You should be ashamed of yourself.

You can spend endless days—and no money at all—just kicking around the hilly streets. Pontificate about the latest artistic trend as you gallery-hop South of Market; get your exercise climbing through other people's backyards on hidden stairway streets; gawk at the mansions that dominate the peaks of Pacific Heights and the Presidio; or get lost for a day or two in Golden Gate Park. When your dogs get tired, as they inevitably will on the dizzying hills in some parts of the city, hop a bus for a higher-speed version of the San Francisco scene. You can get a MUNI transportation map at most liquor and grocery stores for $2; carry it with you, and when you're all worn out you should be able to find a line to take you someplace interesting.

San Francisco

Golden Gate Bridge

Golden Gate
National
Recreation
Area

PACIFIC OCEAN

The Presidio

Baker
Beach

Phelan
Beach

W. Pacific Ave.

Land's
End

Lincoln
Park

Lake St.

SEACLIFF

Clement St.

Point
Lobos

8th Ave.

Arguello Blvd.

Presidio Ave.

Masonic Ave.

Cliff
House

Geary Blvd.

43rd

34th

25th

19th

Balboa St.

Turk

Ave.

Ave.

Ave.

Ave.

RICHMOND

Fulton St.

Golden Gate Park

HAIG
ASHB

Kennedy Dr.

Middle Dr.

Jr.

Martin

Luther

King

Dr.

Stanyan St.

Clayton St.

Lincoln Way

Judah St.

28th Ave.

Funston Ave.

7th Ave.

Clarendon Ave.

Lawton St.

Ocean Beach

Great

Highway

Noriega St.

Ortega St.

SUNSET

19th Ave.

Dewey Blvd.

Tw
Pe

41st Ave.

Sunset Blvd.

Quintara St.

McCoppin
Square

Taraval St.

Larsen
Park

14th Ave.

Mt.
Davidson

Vicente St.

Dr.

Yerba Buena Ave.

Stern Grove

Portola

Monterey

Blvd.

Miramar
Ave.

Monte

San Francisco
Zoo

Sloat Blvd

STONESTOWN

Juniper Serra Blvd

Ocean Ave.

Harding
Park

Skyline Blvd.

Lake Merced

San Francisco
State Univ.

Font Blvd.

Lake Merced Blvd.

Holloway Ave.

Garfield St.

Plymouth Ave.

280

Brotherhood
Way

N

0   1 mile

0   1 km

San Francisco Bay

Marina
Green

Fort
Mason

Pier
39

Fisherman's
Wharf

MARINA

Bay St.

NORTH
BEACH

Coit
Tower

San Francisco-Oakland
Bay Bridge

101

Lombard St.

Hyde St.

Columbus

RUSSIAN
HILL

TELEGRAPH
HILL

(tunnel)

PACIFIC
HEIGHTS

Broadway

101

CHINATOWN

FINANCIAL
DISTRICT

Washington St.

Sacramento St.

California St.

Grant Ave.

Powell St.

NOB HILL

80

UNION
SQUARE

China
Basin

Pine St.

Gough St.

Van Ness Ave.

Post St.

Geary St.

1st St.

2nd St.

Mission St.

Bush St.

Laguna St.

3rd St.

Divisadero St.

Steiner

JAPAN-
TOWN

Turk St.

4th St.

St.

5th St.

Geary

Franklin St.

Market St.

6th St.

SOMA

Townsend St.

Blvd.

Golden

Gate

Ave.

Alamo
Square

Fulton St.

9th St.

Felsom

Harrison

Bryant

Central Basin

Fell St.

WESTERN

10th St.

Brannan St.

7th St.

HT-
URY

Haight St.

ADDITION

Central
Skyway

7th St.

280

Buena
Vista
Park

Castro St.

Duboce Ave.

101

3rd St.

17th St.

Potrero Ave.

Mariposa St.

Market St.

Mission
Dolores
Park

MISSION

Harrison St.

POTRERO

Pennsylvania Ave.

Indiana St.

CASTRO

20th St.

South Van Ness Ave.

Mission St.

Valencia St.

San Francisco
General
Hospital

3rd St.

Dolores St.

Guerrero St.

Army St.

Islais Cr. Channel

India
Basin

NOE
VALLEY

25th St.

Diamond St.

280

Oakdale Ave.

Hunters
Point

Bosworth
St.

Quesada Ave.

rey Blvd.

Fwy.

Silver Ave.

outhern

Ave.

GLEN
PARK

Felton Ave.

lboa
Park

Alemany Blvd.

Excelsior Ave.

101

n Jose

Mission St.

Persia St.

Moscow St.

Ave.

John
McLaren
Park

Mansell St.

Gilman Ave.

3rd St.

Geneva

France Ave.

Ave.

Jamestown

Candlestick
Park

South
Basin

TO COW
PALACE

Major Sights

With the exception of Fisherman's Wharf, which bludgeons visitors with its banality, San Francisco's major sights are major for a reason. Even the most jaded residents can't help but inhale a reverent breath at the sight of the Golden Gate Bridge looming overhead. The Alcatraz tour, for all its hype, explores such a fascinating place, on such a genuinely stark, scary island, that it doesn't come off as idiotic. That is the city's true appeal: Despite the best efforts of merchants selling tourist schlock, the spirit of San Francisco refuses to yield, and the real city pulses through the neon. Except at Fisherman's Wharf.

GOLDEN GATE BRIDGE

Nearly 2 miles long, the bridge to end all bridges has come to symbolize San Francisco more than any other monument. This masterpiece of design and engineering, which links San Francisco to its wealthy neighbor, Marin County, has withstood winds, fogs, suicides, and the weight of several hundred thousand people who showed up to celebrate its 50th birthday back in 1987. The bridge is painted International Orange for visibility in fog (so the seagulls don't crash into it). The cables that support it are over 3 feet in diameter and the combined lengths of the individual strands would wrap around the earth three times.

In order to catch a glimpse of the bridge, you'll have to scale a hill or two in the city or head to the waterfront near Fisherman's Wharf. And of course, you'll want to cross it. Bus 28 will drop you at the toll plaza, from which point you can hoof it or hitch. The walk takes about an hour and the wind can be freezing. There's also something satisfying about crossing the bridge by bike; and there's even a gorgeous way to get there, via Lincoln Boulevard in the Presidio. (To reach Lincoln, take a gentle ride west down Lombard Street, or go for the screaming downhill adventure by approaching from the south on Presidio Boulevard.)

ALCATRAZ ISLAND

Known as the Rock, Alcatraz Island served for 60 years as the nation's most notorious federal penitentiary, holding high-risk prisoners in its isolated maw. Al Capone, Robert "The Birdman"

Four Great Views of Golden Gate Bridge

- *Up close, from the pier in front of the Maritime Museum, just west of Fisherman's Wharf. Walk all the way out until you feel almost surrounded by water and you'll see the bridge, picture perfect, in one direction and the city looking like a toy in the other.*

- *From Fort Point, a brick and granite fortification that defended the bridge from 1861 to 1943, when the army transferred it to the National Park Service. Brave the rough winds and climb up to the roof for superlative views of the Golden Gate directly above you. A trail connects the fort to the bridge's toll plaza. Fort Point is open daily 10–5, and admission is free.*

- *From Baker Beach. The bridge looms above to your right, the ocean extends forever to your left, and the hilly, green Marin Headlands lie right in front of you. It's one of the most beautiful views in the city.*

- *From Grizzly Peak Boulevard in the Berkeley Hills as the sun sets behind it, way in the distance.*

Stroud, and Machine Gun Kelly were among the more famous bad guys who got "Rock fever" gazing out day after day at the bittersweet sight of San Francisco.

Of course, ever since the prison closed in 1963, people have been trying to get onto Alcatraz Island rather than off it. In 1969, a group of Native Americans occupied the land in an attempt to reclaim it, saying that a federal treaty of 1868 allowed Native Americans to use all federal territory that wasn't actively being used by the government. After almost two years, the U.S. government forced them off. The bloody incident is recounted in the island's small museum, and graffiti still reminds visitors that "This is Native American Land."

Today the island is part of the national park system, and tourists visit the grounds in hordes— though even heavy weekend crowds don't affect the lonely, somber, abandoned feel of the place. Rangers on Alcatraz offer a variety of free talks, including one that explores the island's history as a 19th-century military fort, one about the Native American occupation, and one on Alcatraz's unique properties as part of an island chain in San Francisco Bay. Check for schedules at the ranger station at the ferry landing when you arrive or call the dock office at 415/705-1042.

The **Red and White Fleet** (tel. 415/546-2896 for info or 415/546-2700 for tickets) ferries you to the island from San Francisco's Pier 41. The price ($8.75) includes the ferry ride and an audiocassette tour of the prison itself (tapes are available in several languages, and the average tour takes about 2½ hours). You can skip the cassette tour and pay only $5.75, but the tape, which features former inmates and guards talking about their experiences on Alcatraz, is one of the best parts of the experience. Ferries leave San Francisco 9:30 AM–2:15 PM year-round and until 4:15 PM June–August. You'll need a Visa, AmEx, or MasterCard to reserve tickets by phone. If you're buying tickets in person, especially during summer, show up *several days* in advance at the ferry ticket office (open 8–5) at Pier 41. If you're going to risk same-day purchase, arrive before 10 AM. To get here, take Bus 32 from the Ferry Building downtown.

FISHERMAN'S WHARF

This is San Francisco's prize tourist trap, specially designed to make you spend money. The astounding thing about the Wharf is that it seems to be a tourist attraction that draws visitors solely on the basis of being a tourist attraction. As Gertrude Stein said, "There's no there there." You'll enjoy the semblance of an authentic experience only if you arrive in the misty early morning hours (around 5 AM) to watch the fishing boats unload. Otherwise, it's schlock city. Take your friends from out of town—they'll insist on going anyway—but don't let this be their main memory of San Francisco.

Once the domain of Italian fishermen, Jefferson Street, the wharf's main drag, is now packed with tourists, expensive seafood restaurants, tacky souvenir shops, and expensive "museums" like the **Wax Museum, Ripley's Believe It or Not!,** the **Guinness Museum of World Records,** and the **Medieval Dungeon** (featuring graphic re-creations of torture devices from the Middle Ages). Each can be yours for the low admission price of $6–$8.75. Dream on, bloodsuckers. The only thing that remains fairly authentic (albeit rather pricey) is the array of seafood stands. Buy clam chowder ($3–$4) or a half-pound of shrimp ($6) from one of the sidewalk vendors and a loaf of sourdough bread ($2.50–$3) from the **Boudin Bakery** (156 Jefferson St., tel. 415/928-1849), and eat on one of the piers, dangling your legs over the side and watching cruise ships and fishing boats glide in and out. Then hightail it out of there to catch a ferry to Alcatraz or Angel Island (*see* Tiburon and Angel Island, in Marin County, *below*) or walk over to Fort Mason to see the museums.

If you must stick around the wharf, check out the **Maritime Museum** (Beach St., at foot of Polk St., tel. 415/929-0202), housed in an art-deco building that features all sorts of artifacts from the maritime history of San Francisco. The museum is free, but if you have $3 to spare ($2 for students), you might have more fun climbing around on one of the old ships at Hyde

Just in case you're gathering tidbits of San Francisco lore, Jonathan Winters was once briefly institutionalized after he climbed the mast of the Balclutha and hung from it, shouting "I am the man in the moon!"

29

Street Pier, just down the street. Among the ships docked there are the *Balclutha*, a 100-year-old square-rigged ship, and the *Eureka*, an old ferry that now holds a classic car collection.

Three shopping complexes girdle the wharf: **Pier 39**, the **Cannery**, and **Ghirardelli Square**. Owned by the billionaire Bass brothers of Texas, Pier 39 is a bland imitation of a turn-of-the-century seaport village that more resembles the shopping mall that might surface in your worst nightmares. Its one redeeming quality is the swarm of sea lions that took over several of the marina docks next to the development a few years ago and have refused to leave. To shake off the lingering "I'm-being-ripped-off" feeling you get if you spend any time at Pier 39, eat at the Eagle Café (*see* Chapter 4), and take a moment to read the yellowed news clippings describing how the establishment was lifted whole from its former location in 1978 and plunked down on the upper level of the pier.

A former Del Monte peach-canning facility, the **Cannery** (Jefferson, Leavenworth, Beach, and Hyde Sts., tel. 415/771–3112) is now a gallery of chic boutiques. Chocolate is no longer made on-site at **Ghirardelli Square** (900 North Point St., tel. 415/775–5500), but you can buy it here in bars or topping a huge, tasty ice-cream sundae ($5.50). If the word "crafts" makes you think of dolls with crocheted dresses fitted over toilet paper rolls, take a look at the impressive, cutting-edge contemporary crafts at the small **California Crafts Museum** (Rose Ct., Ghirardelli Sq., tel. 415/771–1919; donation requested). The easiest way to reach Fisherman's Wharf from downtown is via Bus 32 from the Ferry Building (at the end of Market Street). Or fulfill your other tourist obligation by taking a cable car from Powell Street (*see* Getting In, Out, and Around, in Chapter 1) to the end of the line (a nice metaphor for Fisherman's Wharf).

COIT TOWER

Though built to memorialize San Francisco's volunteer firefighters, the 210-foot, concrete observation tower on Telegraph Hill is perhaps more reminiscent of the woman who left the funds to build it, Lillie Hitchcock Coit (1843–1929). An eccentric San Francisco legend in her own time, heiress Coit was a cross-dresser (in men's clothes she could gain access to the most interesting realms of San Francisco) who literally chased fire engines around town. Most people agree the building looks like a fire nozzle, though, supposedly, that was not intentional.

Sunset is the best time to visit Coit Tower—the crowds are thinner, parking is a bit easier, and the bay looks downright spectacular.

The walls inside the lobby are covered with Depression-era murals in the style of Diego Rivera, painted by local artists as a Public Works of Art project. **City Guides** (tel. 415/557–4266) offers free descriptive tours of the murals every Saturday at 11 AM, which include the second-floor works normally closed to the public. For $3, the elevator inside the tower will take you to the top for a drop-dead, golly-it's-pretty, 360° view of Golden Gate Bridge, the Bay Bridge, and Alcatraz Island. One warning: If you have a car, you will probably get a headache trying to park near Coit Tower on summer weekends. *1 Telegraph Blvd., tel. 415/362–0808. Take Bus 30 or 45 from Market and 3rd Sts. downtown; get off at Washington Sq., walk 2 blocks east on Union St., turn left on Kearny St. Or take Bus 39 from Fisherman's Wharf to top of Telegraph Hill. Hours depend on weather; usually open summer, daily 9:30–7; winter, daily 10–6.*

GOLDEN GATE PARK

The western keyhole to San Francisco is Golden Gate Park, a massive, splendid strip of nature that covers over a thousand acres (it's less than a mile wide but 4 miles long). The park is packed with zillions of varieties of plant life, wooded areas, wide swaths of grass, and tiny gardens, as well as more urban attractions like museums, sporting activities, and open-air performances. And, as an added bonus, if you make it all the way to the western end of the park you'll hit Ocean Beach and the Pacific. Bordered on its east side by the Haight-Ashbury district, the park has always been a natural hangout for the countercultural folks that crowd that neighborhood: Hippie historians should note that Ken Kesey and friends celebrated the first **Human Be-In** here on January 14, 1966.

Golden Gate Park

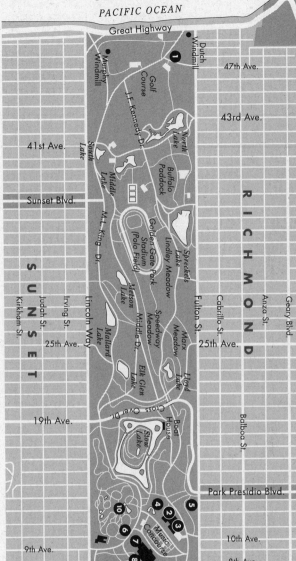

PACIFIC OCEAN

Great Highway

Dutch
Windmill

47th Ave.

Murphy
Windmill

43rd Ave.

Golf
Course

North
Lake

J.F. Kennedy Dr.

41st Ave.

South
Lake

Buffalo
Paddock

Sunset Blvd.

Middle
Lake

M.L. King Dr.

Golden Gate Park
Stadium
(Polo Field)

Lindley Meadow

Spreckels
Lake

R I C H M O N D

Geary Blvd.

Anza St.

Cabrillo St.

Fulton St.

Metson
Lake

Marx
Meadow

Speedway
Meadow

Middle Dr.

Lloyd
Lake

25th Ave.

25th Ave.

S U N S E T

Judah St.

Irving St.

Lincoln Way

Mallard
Lake

Elk Glen
Lake

Kirkham St.

Cross Over Dr.

Boat
House

19th Ave.

Stow
Lake

Balboa St.

Park Presidio Blvd.

10

4
2
3

5

10th Ave.

6

Music
Concourse

8th Ave.

9th Ave.

7
8
9

6th Ave.

7th Ave.

11

J.F. Kennedy Dr.

3rd Ave.

12

Tennis
Courts

Children's
Playground

McLaren
Lodge
(Park HQ)

Arguello Blvd.

Kezar
Stadium

Kezar
Pavilion

Stanyan St.

N

0
0

500 meters

1/2 mile

Once a collection of sand dunes, Golden Gate Park was designed in 1868 by a 24-year-old civil engineer with no prior experience (his bid was the lowest) and landscaped by John MacLaren. The park is the largest of its kind and much prettier than New York's Central Park, despite the claim of that park's designer, Frederick Law Olmsted (who also designed the Stanford University campus), that "beautiful trees could not be made to grow in San Francisco." Today, blue gum eucalyptus, Monterey pine, and Monterey cypress trees, not to mention one of the world's foremost horticultural displays, are peppered throughout in the park.

Strybing Arboretum and Botanical Gardens (tel. 415/661–1316), near the museum complex, has 70 dazzling acres of plants, featuring some 5,000 specimens arranged by country of origin, genus, and fragrance. With its koi fish ponds, 18th-century Buddha, and meditative paths, the **Japanese Tea Garden** (tel. 415/752–4227) is one of the park's star attractions—well worth the $2 admission (tea is extra). The Hagiwara family took beautiful care of the garden until they, along with other Japanese-Americans, were sent to internment camps during World War II. In 1994, on the garden's 100th-year anniversary, a new cherry blossom tree was planted in memory of the internees. The park's first building was the delicate Victorian **Conservatory** (off Kennedy Dr., near east entrance, tel. 415/752–8080), a knock-off of London's Kew Gardens that features a tropical garden and exotic orchids.

The park's many free gardens include the **Shakespeare Garden,** which features all the types of plants that are mentioned in Shakespeare's works—don't eat the nightshade. With its benches and quotations engraved in bronze, it's perfect for a contemplative moment, whereas the **Rose Garden**, especially in early June, is too rambunctious to be at all contemplative. There's also **Rhododendron Dell, Fuchsia Garden,** and the **Queen Wilhelmina Tulip Garden,** with its two nearby Dutch windmills. A herd of bison even inhabits the park near its northwest end, although it usually takes some effort to discover where they are in the large paddock.

The park's fixtures also include three world-class museums: The **Asian Art Museum,** the **M. H. de Young Memorial Museum**, notable for its collection of American art, and the **California Academy of Sciences**, a complex of natural science facilities (*see* Museums and Galleries, *below*). Stoner types will undoubtedly make the pilgrimage at least once to the **Laserium** (tel. 415/750–7138), where *Dark Side of the Moon, Lollapalaser,* and other high-tech music and light shows are projected on the planetarium's dome. Shows are held nightly Thursday–Sunday, and admission is $7.

On Sundays, John F. Kennedy Drive, the park's main thoroughfare, is closed to car traffic between Stanyan Street and 19th Avenue, and flocks of bikers, in-line skaters, and skateboarders take over. Hang out by the Conservatory and watch some expert bladers do their thing.

Golden Gate Park is bordered by Stanyan Street, the Great Highway, Lincoln Way, and Fulton Street. Several places near the park rent bikes and in-line skates. **Park Cyclery** (1749 Waller St., at Stanyan St., tel. 415/751–8383) rents mountain bikes for $5 an hour or $30 a day. **Skate Pro Sports** (27th Ave. at Irving St.; tel. 415/752–8776), near a less traveled part of the park, offers a good deal on blades: $20 a day including pads and helmet. To reach the park from downtown or Civic Center, take Bus 5, 71, or 73.

Neighborhoods

The best way to experience San Francisco's neighborhoods is to plunk yourself down in one and walk until you drop, preferably into a chair on some café patio. You can look at a map and plan your walks, or skip the map, start off in an interesting spot, and just go for what looks good. Certain parts of the city lend themselves especially well to the second type of exploration, where you surrender to the whims of the streets. One such area is the Mission–Noe Valley–Castro region. Get off BART at 16th and Mission streets, and head west on 16th or south on Mission or Valencia, or a little bit of both. Either direction gets you a tableau of neighborhood life, funky shops, galleries, and cafés and restaurants aplenty.

DOWNTOWN

For better or worse, Downtown is grand old San Francisco, the San Francisco of tea dances and cocktail hours and piano bars and fedoras and big overcoats in winter. All you have to do is look up at all the beautiful architectural details and you could forget what decade it is. There's the modern face of downtown—big consumerism, big cafeterias, and waitresses with big hair. But look a little lower and you'll descry dozens of low-rent electronics stores and hundreds of homeless people. It's typical cosmopolitan walking territory, with all of the fascinating and horrifying elements of urban American life.

UNION SQUARE Union Square might be considered the center of the city if it weren't so soulless. The square, bordered by Powell, Post, Stockton, and Geary streets, was named in honor of rallies held prior to the Civil War in support of the Union. Some San Franciscans will tell you the name more appropriately refers to the huge demonstrations held here in the 1930s by labor organizations, which at one point effectively shut down the city for a week.

Today, Union Square consists of a park (graced with a few palm trees to remind you that you're still in California) encircled by a ring—make that a solid gold band—of the most elegant stores and boutiques in the city, including I. Magnin, Neiman-Marcus, Saks, Chanel, Tiffany, Cartier, Hermès, and Gump's. The park can be a relaxing place to rest your weary feet after a hard day's window-shopping, if you don't mind pigeons and homeless folks as your companions. By nightfall it starts to get a little seedy, and it may be time to hop a MUNI out of here.

Heading south on Powell Street from Union Square, you'll come to the intersection of Market and Powell. Everyone passes through here: proselytizers, street musicians, artists, punks, young professionals, flower vendors, protesters, dogs, pigeons, and tourists in matching jogging suits. Especially tourists in matching jogging suits. All converge around the cable-car turnaround, the Powell BART station, Woolworth's with its astonishingly inflated prices, and the **San Francisco Visitor Information Center** (900 Market St., tel. 415/391–2000), tucked below the street in the submerged Hallidie Plaza.

The stretch of **Market Street** near Union Square is home to a string of cheap fast-food joints, the Emporium department store, and, adjoining it, San Francisco's latest monument to the shopping gods, the **San Francisco Shopping Centre** (865 Market St., at 5th St., tel.

Two Mind-Blowing San Francisco Tours

- *When city-style craziness has just about done you in, surrender yourself to the calming influence of Golden Gate Park (see Major Sights, above). Romp among the rhododendrons and spend a meditative moment among delicious-smelling eucalyptus trees. To induce a rapture that will last for days, head west to Ocean Beach and the Pacific, and then north to Lands End, a quiet, green, almost wild chunk of land where the ocean and bay meet. The views of the water, the Golden Gate Bridge, and the Marin Headlands are not of this world, which is entirely the point.*

- *The 22 Fillmore bus transports you from the picturesque marina on the north side of the peninsula—within spitting distance of its obnoxiously yuppie bars—across town through the Mission, by the Valencia Gardens Housing Project, past South of Market's warehouses and railroad tracks, all the way to the city's industrial east shore. Jump off at 3rd and 18th streets, and find the Mission Rock Resort (817 China Basin St., tel. 415/621–5538), facing a little marina and complete with a shoreside bar and grill. On sunny summer Sundays, blues bands often play.*

Chestnut St.

Lombard St.

①

②

Octavia St.

Gough St.

Franklin St.

Van Ness Ave.

Polk St.

Larkin St.

Hyde St.

Leavenworth St.

Greenw

Filbert S

Union S

RUSSIAN HILL

Green St.

Vallejo St.

Broadway

Broadway Tunnel

PACIFIC HEIGHTS

Pacific St.

Jackson St.

Taylor St.

Alta Plaza

Washington St.

Lafayette Park

Clay St.

Leavenworth St.

Jones St.

N(
H

Sacramento St.

California St.

Pierce St.

Steiner St.

Fillmore St.

⑪

Pine St.

Bush St.

Webster St.

Buchanan St.

Laguna St.

Gough St.

Franklin St.

Van Ness Ave.

POLK GULCH

Larkin St.

Hyde St.

Sutter St.

Post St.

JAPANTOWN

Polk St.

Geary St.

③
④
⑤ ⑥

O'Farrell St.

Ellis St.

⑳

Eddy St.

Turk St.

Golden Gate Ave.

McAllister St.

㉑
㉒
㉔
㉖

Fulton St.

Market St.

Alamo Square

CIVIC CENTER

㉓
㉕

Grove St.

Hayes St.

㉗ Civic Center
ba BART Station

8th St.

7th St.

Ansel Adams Center, **33**

Bank of America World HQ, **39**

Cable Car Museum, **10**

Cartoon Art Museum, **35**

Center for the Arts, **31**

Chinatown Gate, **38**

Chinese Historical Society of America, **18**

Chinese Telephone Exchange, **14**

Circle Gallery, **36**

City Hall, **24**

City Lights Bookstore, **9**

Coit Tower, **7**

Crocker Plaza, **37**

Embarcadero Center, **40**

Ferry Building, **42**

Glide Memorial Methodist Church, **20**

Golden Gate Fortune Cookie Factory, **12**

Grace Cathedral, **11**

Hallidie Building, **40**

Herbst Theatre, **22**

Jackson Square, **16**

Japan Center, **6**

Jewish Community Museum, **44**

Justin Herman Plaza, **41**

Kabuki Hot Springs, **4**

Kabuki 8 Theatres, **3**

Lombard Street, **2**

Louise M. Davies Symphony Hall, **25**

Main Library, **26**

Old Mint, **28**

Pacific Stock Exchange, **41**

Palace of Fine Arts, **1**

Peace Plaza, **5**

Downtown San Francisco

0   1/2 mile

0   500 meters

KEY
----- Cable Car

San Francisco Bay

N

Chestnut St.
Lombard St.
NORTH BEACH
Columbus Ave.
Grant Ave.
Mason St.
Powell St.
TELEGRAPH HILL
7
8
9
10

The Embarcadero
Front St.
Davis St.

Stockton St.
Montgomery St.
Sansome St.
Battery St.
12
13 14 15
16
17
Waverly Pl.
CHINATOWN
Kearny St.
18
19 Halleck St.
Drumm St.
Davis St.
Front St.
FINANCIAL DISTRICT
40
41
42

38
39
Embarcadero BART Station
41
40
37
UNION SQUARE
Union Square
36 Maiden Ln.
Montgomery St. BART Station
42
Fremont St.
Beale St.
Main St.
Spear St.
Steuart St.
43 44

Market St.
SOMA
New Montgomery St.
2nd St.
3rd St.
31 32
35
34
30
29
28
Powell St. BART Station
Mission St.
4th St.
5th St.
6th St.
Howard St.
Moscone Center
33
Folsom St.
Harrison St.
Bryant St.
Townsend St.
Brannan St.
Hawthorne St.
1st St.
80
The Embarcadero
45

Portsmouth Square, **15**
Rincon Center, **43**
San Francisco Centre, **29**
San Francisco Museum of Modern Art, **32**
South Park, **45**
Tin Hou Temple, **13**
Transamerica Pyramid, **17**
Transbay Terminal, **42**

United Nations Plaza, **27**
Veterans Building, **21**
Visitor Information Center, **30**
War Memorial Opera House, **23**
Washington Square, **8**
Wells Fargo History Museum, **19**
Yerba Buena Gardens, **34**

35

415/495–5656). Come if only to ride the vertiginous spiral of escalators that surrounds the open interior of the building, seven stories high and leading up to Nordstrom's. A few blocks south, the **Old Mint** (88 5th St., at Mission St., tel. 415/744–6830), built in 1874, houses a free museum where you can strike your own mint medallion on an old press.

➤ **MAIDEN LANE** • This short alley off the east side of Union Square was once the lair of the "cribs" or brothels that formed the center of a world-renowned and extremely violent red-light district. Now it's a shopping arcade for the thick-walleted, and the site of San Francisco's only Frank Lloyd Wright building, the **Circle Gallery** (140 Maiden Ln., tel. 415/989–2100), which served as the prototype for the Guggenheim Museum in New York. Wright also designed the gallery's gorgeous teak cabinets. (An interesting bit of trivia: The gallery's bubble ceiling costs $4,000 to clean.) The gallery sells paintings by artists as incongruous as Donna Summer, Yaacov Agam, and fashion illustrator René Gruau.

FINANCIAL DISTRICT San Francisco is the financial capital of the West Coast, and the center of San Francisco's Financial District is **Montgomery Street,** the "Wall Street of the West," where the towers of wealth block all sun at street level. This part of town once bordered the water, and the district is built on the remains of hundreds of abandoned ships and docks. Nowadays, traffic lights stop vehicles in all four directions to allow busy office workers to cross diagonally and bicycle messengers to cheat death.

Since you're in the Financial District, you may as well see what those monstrously large California banks are doing with your savings. You'll find the glowering **Bank of America World Headquarters** at the corner of Kearny and Pine streets. Its north plaza is graced with a black granite shard of public art officially called _Transcendence,_ but popularly known as "The Banker's Heart." Up on the 52nd story in the elegant **Carnelian Room** (tel. 415/433–7500), you can nurse a $6.50 cocktail and gaze in wonder at the city below. Bank of America's rival, Wells Fargo Bank, offers you the free **Wells Fargo History Museum** (420 Montgomery St., tel. 415/396–2619), detailing the history of California's oldest bank and interminably celebrating the short-lived but picturesque Pony Express. Nearby, two giant sculptures, _Earth's Fruitfulness_ and _Man's Inventive Genius,_ attempt to inject some life and soul into probably one of the least fruitful, least inventive places in the city: the **Pacific Stock Exchange,** on the south side of Pine Street at Sansome. It's closed to the public.

➤ **TRANSAMERICA PYRAMID** • A high concentration of San Francisco's architectural landmarks are here, including the Transamerica Pyramid (600 Montgomery St.), _the_ distinguishing feature of the San Francisco skyline, whose perky peak locals studiously ignore. You

Welcome All Ye Sinners

Ever been to church and come away humming, tapping your toes, and with the phone number of the stranger you sat next to, without having seen a single religious icon? At Glide Memorial United Methodist Church, the Sunday morning "celebration" is presided over by a beaming Reverend Cecil Williams in his colorful robe. Instead of organ music, a band and choir belt out popular songs. People in the audience stand up and groove with the music when the spirit moves them. It gets crowded and hot in here, so try to arrive a few minutes early. Celebrations at Glide attract all ethnicities, classes, and sexual orientations. Bobby McFerrin often comes to Glide, and Bill Clinton and Maya Angelou stopped in when they were in town. Among the many community programs offered at Glide are a daily free meal program, an HIV/AIDS project, a families in crisis center, recovery programs for men and women, and women's health services. Celebrations occur every Sunday morning at 9 and 11. 330 Ellis St., at Taylor St., tel. 415/771–6300. From Powell St. BART/MUNI, walk 1 block on Powell St., turn left on Ellis St.

can ride the elevator to the 27th-floor observation area for a bird's eye view of Coit Tower and down Columbus Avenue, but the building itself seems much less impressive once you're in it, which takes away half the fun. A block north, **Jackson Square**, lined with expensive antiques shops and upholstery stores, has some of the only buildings that survive from the days when this area was overrun with brothels and saloons. The old-time atmosphere of gentility and calm (see what happens when you renovate) contrasts markedly with the greed-and-skyscrapers feel of the rest of the Financial District.

➤ **CROCKER PLAZA** • When you can't stand the crowded Downtown streets anymore, head for soothing Crocker Plaza, where you can sit at a table, read the *Wall Street Journal*, and nurse a double-cappuccino. For a good overview of downtown, head to the top of the **Crocker Galleria** (50 Post St., near Montgomery St.). This three-level mall, almost certain to be beyond your price range, has a completely free rooftop garden where you can chill, eat lunch, and look down at the bewildered tourists and bustling corporate tools. Two blocks northeast, the 1917 **Hallidie Building** (130 Sutter St.), dedicated to the inventor of the cable car, has the dubious distinction of being the first glass curtain office structure.

EMBARCADERO The Embarcadero, Spanish for "wharf," looks more like a string of office buildings than anything vaguely maritime. In the center of it all, at the end of Market Street, stands the **Ferry Building.** The 230-foot clock tower and terminus for transbay ferries before the Bay Bridge was built is now merely a convenient and attractive landmark. You may have gathered here with a thousand or so of your fellow San Franciscans last time you marched in a pro-choice, antiwar, or gay pride rally. This is also where you can catch the ferry for Sausalito or Larkspur (*see* Getting In, Out, and Around, in Chapter 1).

➤ **EMBARCADERO CENTER** • Dominating the Embarcadero is the concrete Embarcadero Center, on Sacramento Street between Battery and Drumm streets. The center is a conglomeration of four nearly identical office towers connected to each other by bridges, with shops and restaurants below that cater to a corporate crowd. From a distance they look like rectangular pancakes planted in an unnaturally tidy row; they get prettified in December when they're festively lit. The five-screen **Embarcadero Center Cinema** was scheduled to open in December 1994; more likely, it won't be finished until April 1995. Call 800/733–6318 for the latest details. The fifth tower you'll see is the **Hyatt Regency Hotel,** which offers occasional tea dances (finally, a place to wear your Easter hat and little white gloves!) and an elevated, revolving bar with an incredible view of the city and the bay. Unless you're going through Benetton withdrawal, save your shopping expeditions for other areas of town.

If you've sold out to the corporate interests but still have a politically correct bone or two left in your body, leave your office at 5:30 PM the last Friday of every month and head to Justin Herman Plaza for Critical Mass, a group of hundreds of environment-friendly downtowners, bike messengers, and cycle-rights activists who protest by biking home from work.

➤ **JUSTIN HERMAN PLAZA** • Between the Embarcadero Center and the Ferry Building stretches Justin Herman Plaza, a favorite haunt of the office bag-lunch crowd and young skateboarders who favor long expanses of brick and concrete. Here, Jean Dubuffet's mammoth stainless-steel sculpture *La Chiffonière* poses like a Napoleonic Pillsbury doughboy. Armand Vallaincourt's huge building-block fountain looks just a little too much like prehistoric plumbing, but you can gambol among its girders even when the water is streaming through. The plaza hosts sporadic free concerts and shows, usually Wednesdays or Fridays at noon when the weather is nice. During a free, unannounced concert by the band U2 in the plaza in 1988, Bono spray-painted the fountain, earning the ire of city officials, who were waging a war against graffiti at the time. (Bono later apologized.) The "anarchistic" gesture is recorded for posterity in the movie *Rattle and Hum*.

➤ **RINCON CENTER** • Another water adventure awaits nearby at the stately, restored Rincon Center, formerly a post office. The outside of the building is unassuming—you'll recognize it by the raised blue dolphins on its sides—but inside there's a newly restored 1940s lobby and a stately atrium into which a tall, shimmering column of rain descends. The social realist murals in the lobby depict the history of California, including the oppression of Native Americans and the exploitation of workers by capitalist overlords. *101 Spear St., at Mission St., tel. 415/543–8600.*

CIVIC CENTER

The Civic Center is the locus of the city government and home of many of the city's cultural events, including dance, opera, and theater. It's also where a good percentage of San Francisco's homeless have camped out since the 1940s. To reach the area, take BART to the Civic Center stop, or catch any of a thousand buses down Market Street.

CITY HALL City Hall, built in classic Beaux Arts style, dominates the scene with its bronze rotunda. In the early '60s, protesters were washed down City Hall's central stairway with giant fire hoses, while the hearings of the Un-American Activities Committee went on inside, all of which is depicted in the amusing government propaganda effort (now a cult film) *Operation Abolition.* Joe DiMaggio and Marilyn Monroe got married here on January 15, 1954. On February 14, 1991, scores of gay couples lined up to get "married" in celebration of the passage of San Francisco's Domestic Partners Act the previous November. Has this building seen some crazy times or what? *Between Van Ness Ave. and Grove, McAllister, and Polk Sts.*

At City Hall in 1978, conservative ex-city supervisor Dan White shot and killed Mayor George Moscone and Supervisor Harvey Milk, the first openly gay person elected to public office in the United States.

Surrounding City Hall are many of the city's cultural mainstays. On Van Ness Avenue the **Louise M. Davies Symphony Hall** and the **War Memorial Opera House** offer San Franciscans their fill of high culture (*see* Symphony and Opera, in Chapter 6). You can catch a variety of cultural events, including concerts, readings, and lectures at the **Herbst Theatre.** Volunteers conduct 75-minute tours of these three buildings every Monday on the hour and half hour from 10 to 2, leaving from the Grove Street entrance of Davies Symphony Hall. Call 415/552–8338 for more info. The **San Francisco Main Library** (Larkin St., at McAllister St., tel. 415/557–4400), which will move around the corner in the spring of 1996, has a fine collection of books, records, CDs, and San Francisco memorabilia. If you're walking around the area, head to **Hayes Street** between Franklin and Webster streets; it's loaded with specialty shops, art galleries, cafés, and restaurants.

Across from City Hall on the south side is the large plaza where those protest marches that started at the Ferry Building usually end up, culminating in a big rally (including a couple of 200,000-plus ones during the Persian Gulf War) and an occasional riot. Leading away from City Hall toward Market Street is the **United Nations Plaza**, presided over by a dramatic statue of Simón Bolívar commemorating the founding of the United Nations in San Francisco in 1945. A major thoroughfare and the widest street in the city, **Van Ness Avenue** leads north from Market Street to the Golden Gate Bridge. It's flanked by a themeless hodgepodge of businesses grouped in uncanny multiples: steak houses, electronics stores, bakeries, movie theaters, car dealerships. The street is notably drab from the Civic Center all the way to Lombard Street.

Brown Bag Opera

The San Francisco Opera Center takes opera to the streets, presenting lunchtime concerts in their Brown Bag Opera series. Young singers belt out arias over downtown traffic, often with piano accompaniment—quite a sight. Performances are held in spring, summer, and during the Christmas season. You can also count on several concerts on Fridays at 12:15 PM at 1 Bush Street, in the sunken courtyard at the corner of Sansome Street. Call 415/565–6343 for current schedules.

POLK GULCH Once the gay heart of San Francisco, Polk Gulch is now the second-most prominent gay area after the Castro district. Polk Gulch is part yuppie neighborhood, part urban blight. It's a good place to buy roasted coffee at the two **Royal Ground** locations (2216 Polk St., near Vallejo St., tel. 415/474–5957; 1605 Polk St., at Sacramento St., tel. 415/749–1731) as well as leather and Spandex for cousin Bob back east. Two of its big industries, drug sales and prostitution, don't exactly attract the tourist buses. Rumor has it that the call boys get more expensive by the block—the most expensive block is the stretch from Bush to Pine streets. The bargain basement is around Geary Street.

Once you get past the sleaze, Polk Street makes a nice walk to the Aquatic Park and Fisherman's Wharf. The street is lined with small businesses and cafés, including **Les Croissants** (1406 Polk St., btw Pine and California Sts., tel. 415/922–3286), a popular place to drink coffee, eat sandwiches, and loiter. Satisfy your carnivorous cravings at **Hot 'n' Hunky** (*see* Chapter 4) with a burger and a Ménage à Trois (fried mozzarella, mushrooms, and zucchini) on the side. Bus 19 from Civic Center BART runs up Polk Street.

CHINATOWN

The best way to experience San Francisco's Chinatown—possibly the most famous immigrant community in the world and certainly one of the most distinctive—is to go in hungry and energetic, with open eyes and ears. The shops are nice and all, but the real appeal of Chinatown is its street life. On **Grant Avenue,** flocks of visitors shuffle wide-eyed, clutching bamboo back scratchers they just bought for $1.50. Stray from here and you're more likely to see residents shopping for groceries and carrying grandchildren down the street on their backs. In fact, no matter how tourist-oriented some of the shops are, no matter how many times the neighborhood makes its obligatory appearance in travel guides, Chinatown remains steadfastly a residential area, where the largest Chinese community outside Asia has made

Gay and Lesbian San Francisco

San Francisco promotes the fact that it is a gay city, the gayest in the world, even. Gays and lesbians are the city's most prominent special-interest group. Depending on the neighborhood you visit, the population can be as much as 95% gay, and it really is feasible for lesbian women and gay men to go about their lives in San Francisco dealing exclusively with other gays and lesbians, both in business and in pleasure. And while gay people are still the victims of violence, at least here many such cases are fully documented and prosecuted.

San Francisco's most concentrated gay neighborhood is the Castro district, followed closely by Polk Gulch. Although there isn't a lesbian neighborhood per se, many young lesbians gravitate to the Mission district. Bernal Heights seems to attract slightly older lesbians, and the more upwardly mobile lesbian set heads to Noe Valley. Valencia Street in the Mission is home to the greatest concentration of women-oriented shops and is the street most likely to see lesbians walking hand in hand.

The city has a vital gay club scene, but if you're not into clubs you'll still find plenty of activities to thrill you. There's a thriving café culture, the flagship of which is probably Café Flore (see Chapter 5). San Francisco also features a good number of gay theater productions, poetry readings, and comedy shows, all of which are listed in gay-oriented publications like the "Bay Times" and "The Sentinel."

its home for about 130 years and established businesses and cultural organizations. Today, though, many Chinese and other Asians are moving away from the cramped conditions in Chinatown in favor of more residential neighborhoods like the Richmond and Sunset districts. For an historical look at Chinese immigration to San Francisco and the development of Chinatown, visit the **Chinese Historical Society of America** (*see* Museums and Galleries, *below*).

Don't miss the huge, week-long, colorful Chinese New Year's festival held during the first new moon in February. Come early to get a spot for the final parade, a riot of firecrackers, dancers, and painted dragons.

To reach Chinatown, take Bus 45 from Market and Third streets. You'll know you've made it to the 16-block neighborhood when you see street signs in Chinese. The best way to enter is through the dragon-crowned **Chinatown Gate** on Grant Avenue at Bush Street, where the sense of being in a different world is suddenly quite palpable. Or enter through **Portsmouth Square** on Washington Street (at Kearny Street), where dozens of old Chinese men gather in groups, gambling or shooting the breeze.

GRANT AVENUE Grant Avenue is the main tourist thoroughfare in Chinatown, crowded with souvenir shops, Chinese restaurants, and intricate red, green, and gold lampposts. The old **Chinese Telephone Exchange** building, now the Bank of Canton, stands at 743 Washington Street, at Grant Avenue. It's both architecturally and historically interesting; operators here had to memorize the names of all their customers, and speak English and five Chinese dialects. Chinatown's residents spend their time on **Stockton Street,** packed with grocery stores, bakeries, and trade and service shops. Between these two main drags, narrow alleys hide the secrets of the real, untouristed Chinatown, a community that has existed as long as San Francisco.

WAVERLY PLACE One of the most interesting streets is Waverly Place, off California and Clay streets, between Grant and Stockton streets. You may remember the name from Amy Tan's *The Joy Luck Club*; it's also known as the "street of painted balconies." There are Chinese temples along Waverly Place, including the purportedly oldest in the city, the **Tin Hou Temple** (125 Waverly Pl., top floor). Also don't miss nearby **Ross Alley,** between Grant and Stockton and Jackson and Washington streets, the home of the **Golden Gate Fortune Cookie Factory** (56 Ross Alley), where you can watch old women fold cookies and also pick up risqué fortunes to slip to whomever you'd like to see blush. At the end of Ross Alley is **Jackson Street,** where you'll find several Chinese herbal medicine shops, the walls of which are lined with a multitude of drawers containing the magic plants.

NORTH BEACH

Walk north on Columbus Avenue from the Columbus and Broadway intersection (long the site of one of San Francisco's best-known red-light districts) and you'll find yourself in the heart of

Park yourself in a café in North Beach and spend the afternoon watching the twentysomething crowd try to capture the spirit of their famous Beat predecessors, whom James Baldwin called "uptight, middle-class white people, imitating poverty, trying to get down, to get with it . . . doing their despairing best to be funky."

the legendary Italian district where the Beat movement was born. Nowadays North Beach offers an incredible selection of restaurants, delis, and cafés, not to mention a lingering aura of the alternative culture that thrived here during the 1950s. Poets and writers like Jack Kerouac, Lawrence Ferlinghetti, and Allen Ginsberg came to North Beach from New York around 1953 to write, play music, and generally promote a lifestyle that emphasized Eastern religion, free love, drugs, and crazy new means of artistic expression. From this movement sprang Ferlinghetti's **City Lights Bookstore** (261 Columbus Ave., tel. 415/362–8193), which to this day continues to publish and sell works by little-known, alternative authors, as well as stuff by the Beats, even though they've been anthologized to high heaven and hardly qualify as alternative any more. The recently renamed **Jack Kerouac Lane** is right next to the store. In 1994, Ferlinghetti received the same honor: An alley off Union Street near Stockton Street was renamed **Via**

Ferlinghetti. The short, dead-end street is barely longer than its new name —and as purists are quick to point out—it should be "vicolo," which means alley, not "via," a thoroughfare.

Those looking to immerse themselves in Beat history can poke around **Vesuvio** (255 Columbus Ave., tel. 415/362–3370), a bar just across the alley from City Lights, where the boys undoubtedly consumed more than one glass of red, and **Caffè Trieste** (601 Vallejo St., at Grant Ave., tel. 415/392–6739), which fueled the Beats with their favorite legal amphetamine (and whose clientele, some 35 years later, still looks pretty beat).

Lay a poem or a stick of incense in front of **29 Russell Street,** between Larkin and Hyde streets and Union and Green streets, where Kerouac crashed with Neal and Carolyn Cassady for a time in the early '50s. (His relationship with Neal is immortalized in his popular tome *On the Road,* though *The Subterraneans* will give you a better feel for Kerouac's North Beach days.) Then pay homage to the **Wentley Apartments,** where Ginsberg composed *Howl.* The **North Beach Museum,** on the mezzanine level of Eureka Federal Savings (1435 Stockton St., at Columbus Ave., tel. 415/391–6210), contains a handwritten manuscript of Ferlinghetti's "The Old Italians Dying" about the old men of North Beach.

Although the Beats reached their peak back in the late 1950s, and the number of Italian-Americans living in North Beach is diminishing, the neighborhood remains one of the most interesting to explore, with some shops and watering holes that have been catering to the same clientele for the last 40 years. In addition to having some of the city's best restaurants, the area has plenty of specialty shops for all you grazers. Among the most authentic old-time businesses are **Figoni Hardware** (1351 Grant Ave., tel. 415/392–4765), a musty, dark repository for tools and other useful knickknacks, and the **Shlock Shop** (1418 Grant Ave., tel. 415/781–5335), an even darker, mustier place that specializes in, well, schlock. Look here first for that used porkpie hat or Las Vegas snow globe you've been dying for.

Some people choose to live in North Beach—and subject themselves to dealing with tourists on a daily basis—just for the food the neighborhood offers. Stop in at **Liguria Bakery** (1700 Stockton St., at Filbert St., tel. 415/421–3786) for focaccia right out of the oven. **Molinari Delicatessen** (373 Columbus Ave., at Vallejo St., tel. 415/421–2337) has an insane selection of salami, olive oils, cheeses, pastas, wines, chocolate, and bread to sate your need for a coma-inducing picnic at **Washington Square Park** (*see* Parks, *below*). To get here, take Bus 30 or 45 from Market and 3rd streets.

NOB HILL AND RUSSIAN HILL

The most classically elitist of San Francisco's many elitist districts is **Nob Hill**, the locus for all sorts of establishments that cater to San Francisco high society, and all sorts of great views that even the downtrodden will enjoy, assuming they can drag themselves up here. North of Nob Hill lies **Russian Hill**, originally the burial ground for Russian seal hunters and traders, which today houses a combination of old Victorian homes, new high-rises, and some of the city's most elite addresses.

A steep walk (or an expensive cable-car ride) north from Union Square brings you to the hilltop estates of four of the city's biggest entrepreneurs, now the site of the city's poshest hotels. Ignore the looks of suspicious doormen as you nose around the lobbies of the **Fairmont Hotel,** at California and Mason streets; the **Mark Hopkins,** across California Street from the Fairmont; and the **Stanford Court Hotel,** at California and Powell streets. See how many times you can ride up and down the glass elevator at the Fairmont before the management ever-so-politely suggests that you scram.

If you're anywhere near the Fairmont Hotel, you're a big goob if you don't have a drink in its South Pacific-themed Tonga Room, with cocktails in coconuts, a $2 happy-hour buffet (weekdays 5–7), and lashing rains every hour on the hour.

CABLE CAR MUSEUM On your way from Nob Hill to Russian Hill, check out the (somewhat less thrilling) Cable Car Museum, which exhibits photographs, scale models, and other memorabilia from the cable car's 121-year history. From the adjacent overlook you can gander at the brawny cables that haul the cars up and down the city's hills. *1201 Mason St., at Washington St., tel. 415/474–1887. Admission free. Open daily 10–5.*

GRACE CATHEDRAL Come to Grace Cathedral and repent for all the trouble you've caused the employees at Nob Hill's fancy hotels. The cathedral is a nouveau Gothic structure that took 53 years to build; it's essentially a poured-concrete replica of an old European-style cathedral. The gilded bronze doors at the east entrance were taken from casts of Ghiberti's *Gates of Paradise* on the baptistery in Florence. For a truly sublime experience, come for the singing of **vespers** every Thursday at 5:15 PM; an all-male choir will lift you out of the muck of your petty little world and leave you feeling almost sanctified. Guided tours of the cathedral are free, but donations are accepted. To get here, take Bus 1 from Embarcadero BART and MUNI Station to Sacramento and Jones streets. *1051 Taylor St., at California St., tel. 415/776–6611. Admission free.*

You might have to buy a postcard to capture a picture-perfect image of Lombard Street as it is scheduled to undergo unsightly street repairs for four months starting in February 1995.

LOMBARD STREET AND AROUND Since you've made it all the way up here, don't miss the chance to do some strenuous walking around Russian Hill's well-maintained streets. The most famous is undoubtedly **Lombard Street,** the block-long "crookedest street in America." It descends the east side of Russian Hill in eight switchbacks between Hyde and Leavenworth streets. If you're a lowly pedestrian negotiating this trafficky route, look out for crazy drivers from the Midwest who would just love to crush you as they lose control of the rental car.

The insanely steep Russian Hill has a number of funky little stairway streets that wind through the trees or lead up to miniature parks. Try the steps at Lombard and Larkin streets; you'll eventually reach a small rest spot with benches, plants, and an incredible view of the Golden Gate. The stairs at Taylor and Vallejo streets lead up small alleys to two beautiful old houses, **Russian Hill Place** and **Florence Place.** Vallejo Street at Mason turns into a set of steps that will transport you to **Ina Coolbrith Park,** a hilly spot with outrageous views of the bay and Alcatraz; on Taylor Street between Green and Union, a wooden staircase leads up to **Macondray Lane,** a tiny, cobblestone alley lined with houses on one side and foliage on the other. Also look for the dark, wood-shingled houses designed by Willis Polk that date from before the 1906 earthquake. One lies on the **1000 block of Green Street,** which also contains one of the city's two remaining eight-sided houses, built in the 1850s, as well as a firehouse dating from 1907.

THE PRESIDIO AND MARINA

You'll certainly feel like you've traveled someplace else when you hit the Marina district, but it may not be a place you wanted to go. Stretching over a gorgeous strip of waterfront between Fort Mason and the Presidio, the Marina provides a home—actually a series of pricey, Mediterranean-style homes—for San Francisco's yuppies. Apparently it's a good example of an entire Art Deco neighborhood, or at least that was the idea. Business suits and athletic wear (depending on whether one is in "work" or "leisure" mode) are the uniforms of choice, and the mostly characterless specialty shops, cafés, and restaurants in the neighborhood reflect the lifestyle of its inhabitants. Aspiring yuppie types come to the Marina's main drag, **Chestnut Street,** from all over the city to chow down and drink up at innumerable restaurants and bars, and to hunt for an acceptable mate.

Even if it's not your scene, you'll probably find yourself wandering Chestnut Street at some point. It's the most convenient place to come for a bite to eat or a drink after visiting Fort Mason; and to boot, the insanely well-stocked **Safeway** (15 Marina Blvd., btw Laguna and Buchanan Sts.) right across the street from Fort Mason provides cheap, good food for those staying in the **San Francisco International Youth Hostel** (*see* Hostels, in Chapter 7) or those walking around Fisherman's Wharf with a pained, hungry look on their face.

PALACE OF FINE ARTS At the far western edge of the Marina sits the Palace of Fine Arts, which looks just like a classic Roman temple, complete with columns and a pond in front (a bunch of these were built for the 1915 Pacific Expo, but only this one remains). It's a great place to get photos of you or a loved one lounging languidly, half-naked. Inside, you'll find the **Exploratorium** (*see* Museums and Galleries, *below*), a hands-on museum devoted to making science interesting for common folk. If you're visiting on Sunday, Bus 76 from Montgomery BART and MUNI Station takes you within a few blocks of Fort Mason, skirts the southern edge of the Marina, passes the Palace of Fine Arts, and goes all the way to Golden Gate Bridge. Otherwise, pick up Bus 30 from Montgomery BART and MUNI Station, which follows a similar route, but stops short of the Presidio. *Baker and Beach Sts., tel. 415/567–6642.*

FORT MASON Fort Mason, a series of warehouses built on piers, forms the Marina's eastern border. Once an army command post, Fort Mason is now a nexus of artistic, cultural, and environmental organizations, as well as small specialty museums (*see* Museums and Galleries, *below*). Although it's fairly quiet most days (except for a trickle of people taking advantage of classes, lectures, and museums), Fort Mason is well worth a trip or two. While you're here, read through their newsletter, which details what's going on this month (you can pick one up at the museums).

But let's face it: You're probably coming here not to fill your mind with all this great culture but to fill your belly at the renowned vegetarian restaurant **Greens** (*see* Chapter 4), also tucked into one of the warehouses. If you're too immobilized after the meal to even think about a museum tour, relax at the **Book Bay Bookstore** (Building C, Fort Mason Center, tel. 415/771–1076), run by the Friends of the San Francisco Public Library, where you can still get a book for a quarter. From Fisherman's Wharf it's about a ten-minute walk west; go past the Maritime Museum and the Municipal Pier, climb the forested hill where the hostel is, and as you descend on the other side you'll see it spread out on the waterfront. *Fort Mason general info: tel. 415/441–5706. MUNI Buses 22, 28, 30, 42, 43, 47, and 49.*

THE PRESIDIO The Presidio, a huge chunk of prime waterfront land stretching from the western end of the Marina all the way over to Golden Gate Bridge, is one of the oldest military installations in the country. The land was officially turned over to the National Park Service on October 1, 1994, but the army will remain here for a while in a reduced capacity. Since it's some of the most desirable real estate in the city, profit-hungry developers are fighting like cats and dogs over its future, with open-space conservationists putting their two cents in, too.

Detractors of Park Presidio point out that although its transformation was supposed to serve as a model for sustainable development, big businesses like PG&E, rather than community-based alternatives, threaten to take control of the park's facilities. The park service's plan for transforming existing buildings will take years to complete; it is yet to be determined how much of the park will remain and how much will become developed. But there are a few things you can count on: rolling hills crossed by plenty of trails and paths through cypress and eucalyptus forests; military buildings; and war-era houses. Check out the **Officer's Club** (Moraga Ave.) which contains one adobe wall reputed to date from 1776, the year the base was founded. Find out more about the Presidio's history at the **Presidio Army Museum** (Funston Ave., at Lincoln Blvd., tel. 415/921–8193).

The views from the Presidio out over the bay are terrific. The easiest way to get here is to drive toward the water on Van Ness Avenue, turn left on Lombard Street, and then follow the signs. Otherwise, take Bus 38 from the Montgomery BART and MUNI Station downtown to Geary Boulevard and Presidio Avenue, and switch to Bus 43, which will take you into the Presidio.

PACIFIC HEIGHTS

Rising above the Marina—in more ways than one—Pacific Heights is the posh neighborhood of Victorian mansions that stretches up from Van Ness and over to the Presidio, between California and Union streets. The mostly residential area is broken by **Fillmore Street**, separating the eastern and western halves with its upscale boutiques and trendy restaurants. If you like that sort of thing, the stretch of Fillmore from Bush Street to Jackson Street, known as **Upper Fillmore**, is a "cute" area in which to stroll, browse, and have a cup of espresso. Pacific Heights's defining characteristics, however, are the Victorian mansions, spared from the 1906 fire that ravaged the city east of Van Ness Avenue (houses along Van Ness were dynamited in order to create a firebreak).

HAAS-LILIENTHAL HOUSE A good place to start your tour of Victorian Pacific Heights is at the Haas-Lilienthal House, the only one that's open to the public. Modest in comparison to the mansions that once stood along Van Ness, the 1886 Queen Anne-style house is now the property of **The Foundation for San Francisco's Architectural Heritage**, headquartered here. The trick is, in order to step inside and see the original furnishings, you must join an hour-long, docent-led tour. These leave Wednesday noon–3:15 and Sunday 11–4 whenever a small group is gathered. Meet here at 12:30 PM on Sundays for a free walking tour covering the surrounding blocks of Victorians and Edwardians—and learn once and for all that these terms refer to periods (1837–1901 and 1901–1911, respectively), not styles. *2007 Franklin St., near Washington St., tel. 415/441–3000. Admission: $5.*

LAFAYETTE PARK From the Haas-Lilienthal House, walk one block south to the corner of California Street to the **Coleman House** (1701 Franklin St.), closed to the non-lawyer needing public (it's filled with law offices). The tower, prominently displayed on the corner, is what makes this a Queen Anne tower house. Turn right on California Street and right again on Octavia Street to reach Lafayette Park. Visited by dog walkers, picnickers, and sun bathers, the park's expansive lawns slope to a wooded crest, just as a well-behaved, English-style garden should. On the north side of the park, behold the **Spreckels Mansion** (2080 Washington St.), an imposing 1913 French Baroque structure now owned by Danielle Steele and her husband. You can see the effects of San Francisco's moist and salty air on the ill-chosen Utah Limestone, which has noticeably eroded. Blame architect George Applegarth (who also designed the California Palace of the Legion of Honor).

UNION STREET AND COW HOLLOW

Conventional tourist wisdom has it that Union Street between Gough and Steiner, with its rows of sparkling, refurbished Victorian houses and clean streets, evokes the feeling of classic San Francisco; and it does indeed clobber you on the cranium with quaintness. Dozens of restaurants, cafés, hair and nail places, boutiques, and galleries (all housed in "cute" Victorians) vie for your attention and your dollars. If you've come to San Francisco to shop and lounge about without such nasty distractions as homeless people or street life, perhaps Union Street is for you. It *is* beautifully located just a few blocks from the Marina and the waterfront, and the pace here *does* seem remarkably relaxed, albeit at the cost of diversity and soul.

If you do elect to come for some window shopping or a latte, try to stop in at **Carol Doda's Champagne and Lace Lingerie Boutique** (1850 Union St. No. 1, tel. 415/776–6900), owned by the woman who led the vanguard to legalize topless dancing in the 1960s, when she became the first woman to bare her breasts as part of a respectable nightclub show (she never waitressed again). If you get lucky, Carol herself will be on hand to advise you on all of your intimate apparel needs.

Other neighborhood landmarks include the **Wedding Houses** (1980 Union St., near Buchanan St.), two identical houses built side by side by a man for his two daughters, who happened to be getting married at the same time. He stationed the houses next to each other so he could keep an eye on his daughters. These days, all he'd see are two stunning Victorians filled with upscale shops. The Vedanta Society of Northern California's **Old Temple** (2963 Webster St., at Filbert St., tel. 415/922–2323), a Hindu Temple built in 1905 (closed to tourists), combines all the best elements of Victorian architecture and the Taj Mahal. No joke. Bus 41 from Embarcadero BART and MUNI Station runs down Union Street.

JAPANTOWN

The modern Japantown, which spans the area north of Geary Street between Fillmore and Laguna streets, consists mostly of the massive, somewhat depressing, shopping complex called Nihonmachi, better known as the **Japan Center**. The community was once much larger, until it was dispersed during World War II when California made a practice of dumping Japanese-Americans in concentration camps.

The **Peace Plaza** and five-story **Pagoda** in the Japan Center still remain, however, designed by architect Yoshiro Taniguchi as a gesture of goodwill from the people of Japan. The plaza is landscaped with traditional Japanese-style gardens and reflecting pools, and is the site of many traditional festivals throughout the year. The **Nihonmachi Street Fair** (tel. 415/431–6197), held in early August, is a two-day festival celebrating the contributions of Asian Americans to the United States. There are several shops selling Japanese wares, as well as a number of good restaurants, in the area.

To relax after a tough day, try a Japanese steam bath at the **Kabuki Hot Springs** (1750 Geary Blvd., tel. 415/922–6000 or 415/922–6002 for appointments), where you can use the steam room, sauna, and hot and cold baths (all sex-segregated) for $10, or get a 25-minute shiatsu massage and unlimited bath use for $35. The bath is reserved for women on Sunday, Wednesday, and Friday; men get to use it the rest of the week. Also in the Japan Center, the **Kabuki 8 Theaters** (1881 Post St., tel. 415/931–9800) shows first-run films in a high-tech complex. If you're coming for a movie, take advantage of the Kabuki's validated parking in the Japan Center; your parking choices outside are pretty seedy. On public transportation, Buses 2, 3, 4, and 38 will deposit you in Japantown from the Montgomery BART and MUNI Station.

RICHMOND DISTRICT

In the eyes of many San Franciscans, the Richmond district, a sprawling, unassuming area north of Golden Gate Park, might as well be the suburbs. In a lot of ways, the quiet streets and rows of bland townhouses feel like suburbia prime, and that's exactly what has attracted lots of families here. A big Southeast Asian and Chinese population has settled in the Richmond, and the main shopping blocks on **Clement Street** between Arguello Boulevard and 8th Avenue contain a dizzying array of produce markets, Chinese herb shops, and Asian restaurants, as well as a smattering of Irish pubs and a couple of good used bookstores. Bus 2 from Montgomery BART and MUNI Station downtown will get you here.

Clement Street can be a comforting place to hang out—sometimes it's good to spend time in a family-oriented neighborhood, even if you came to San Francisco to get away from one. Show up here after a day in Golden Gate Park or at the beach for a stroll and some tasty, cheap food. **Haig's Delicacies** (642 Clement St., tel. 415/752–6283), a one-of-a-kind market and delicatessen, imports interesting food items from the Middle East, India, and Europe and is a great place to stock up on picnic goods. **New May Wah Supermarket** (547 Clement St., no phone) offers a huge number of special ingredients (sauces, tea, noodles, and much, much more) for Chinese, Vietnamese, Thai, or Japanese food. Also don't miss **Green Apple Books** (506 Clement St., tel. 415/387–2272) for a huge selection of new and used books—you could lose yourself in this store for days.

HAIGHT-ASHBURY DISTRICT

East of Golden Gate Park sits the Haight-Ashbury district, the name of which still strikes fear in the hearts of suburban parents everywhere. The Haight began its career as a center for the counterculture in the late 1950s and early '60s when some of the Beat writers, several more or less illustrious fathers of the drug culture, and bands like the Grateful Dead and Jefferson Airplane moved in. There went the neighborhood. Attracted by the experimental, liberal atmosphere, several hundred thousand blissed-out teenagers soon converged on the Haight to drop their body weight in acid, play music, sing renditions of "Uncle John's Band" for days at a time, and generally do things for which they would feel incredibly silly 20 years later. But like the '60s themselves, the Haight's atmosphere of excitement and idealism was pretty much washed up by 1970 or so.

HOME SWEET HOME:

- *Janis Joplin: 112 Lyon St. between Page and Oak Sts.*
- *The Grateful Dead: 710 Ashbury St. at Waller St.*
- *The Manson family: 636 Cole St. at Haight St.*
- *Jefferson Airplane: 2400 Fulton St. at Willard St.*
- *Sid Vicious: 26 Delmar St. at Frederick St.*

UPPER HAIGHT Since the 1970s, the stretch of Haight Street between Divisadero and Stanyan streets has gone through various stages of increasing and decreasing seediness and gentrification. Its countercultural spirit survives largely in terms of the goods you can buy—like bongs, leather harnesses, and rave wear. The youthful slackers who come to live here still try

Chilling by the Ocean

Step off the bus at Ocean Beach in your bikini top and flip-flops, all sunscreened and ready to catch some rays, and you may be in for a big shock. San Francisco's beaches, though numerous and lovely, rarely greet you with the kind of radiant heat and sun that'll make you crave a swim in the ocean. Residents quickly learn to use the beaches listed below for things other than swimming, like meditating, kite flying, exercising their dogs, and walking (try the 7-mile trek from Fort Funston to Ocean Beach).

- *Fort Funston. San Francisco's most remote beach and nice to visit before or after the zoo. People also hang glide here. Take Bus 88 from the Balboa Park BART station.*

- *Ocean Beach. The surfers' beach, the tourists' beach, the family beach, the walkers' beach. It's all-purpose. Besides the sand and water, attractions include the Cliff House, a restaurant and historic San Francisco landmark perched on the cliffs, and the National Park Service office, where you can pick up information on the Golden Gate National Recreation Area. Right across the plaza from the park service office is the excellent, off-beat Musée Mécanique (see Museums and Galleries, below). Just west of the Cliff House lie the ruins of the formerly grand Sutro Baths, a huge complex of fresh and saltwater pools modeled after ancient Roman baths (they were torn down in 1966). People still climb around on the foundation of the baths, trying to get a look at some sea lions or crustaceans. Remember the scene from "Harold and Maude" that was shot here? To reach Ocean Beach take the N Judah streetcar from any downtown underground MUNI station.*

- *Lands End. A nude beach that's no longer exclusively gay. It's rocky and unsafe for swimming, but you'll find some sand as well as a respite from the wind in the small walled-off areas that people have built. To get here from downtown, go west on Geary Street and turn right on El Camino del Mar. From the parking lot at the end, take the steps down by the flag and head east on the trail. When it branches, head down to the beach.*

- *China Beach. Stroll through the Seacliff neighborhood (million-dollar homes tucked between Lands End and the Presidio) to reach this small beach with views of the Golden Gate, or take Bus 1 from Clay and Drumm streets near the Embarcadero.*

- *Baker Beach. Beautiful views of the Marin Headlands, the Golden Gate Bridge, and the bay. One end sees families, tourists, anglers, and wealthy homeowners taking their dogs for a walk; the other end is a nude beach. Take Bus 1 from Clay and Drumm streets near the Embarcadero, and transfer to Bus 29 heading into the Presidio.*

to maintain some aura of rebelliousness, wearing black, riding motorcycles, piercing body parts, and listening to dissonant music at bars like **The Thirsty Swede** or to live jazz and swing at **Club Deluxe** (*see* Bars, in Chapter 6), though they are less attracted to the neighborhood's historical legacy than they are to the cheap apartments and upper Haight's bars and cafés. Not to mention restaurants like **Crescent City Cafe** and the **Pork Store Café** (*see* Chapter 4). You can still buy drugs at the intersection of Haight Street and Golden Gate Park; in fact, it's pretty rare to walk through the Haight *without* being offered shrooms, green kind buds, or doses. Neo-hippies still play guitar on the street corner, but somehow it seems like it's all been done before, and the revolution is nowhere in sight.

The upper Haight doesn't have any major sights or attractions. It's more a place where people come to hang out or to shop. In addition to the used-clothing standbys **Wasteland** and **Buffalo Exchange** (*see* Secondhand and Outlet Clothing, in Chapter 3), you'll find T-shirts on the Haight that you just can't get anywhere else. The Grateful Dead, Speed Racer, Alfred E. Newman, Bob Marley and more of the Grateful Dead cover the walls of **Haight-Ashbury T-Shirts** (1500 Haight St., at Ashbury St., tel. 415/863–4639). Down the street, the **Haight-Ashbury Free Medical Clinic** (558 Clayton St., at Haight St., tel. 415/431–1714) has been offering free medical care ever since drug-related illnesses became a big problem on the Haight in the '60s. Just east of Masonic Street, strategically located **Pipe Dreams** (1376 Haight St., tel. 415/431–3553) is a well-endowed head shop adjacent to a tattoo parlor. When the weather is warm, head down the street to **Buena Vista Park** (*see* Parks, *below*), which has become a hangout/meeting spot/home for skaters. At the other end of Haight Street, smoke a peach-flavored hookah at **Kan Zaman** (1793 Haight St., btw Shrader and Cole Sts., tel. 415/751–9656), a Middle Eastern restaurant where you can lounge comfortably on pillows and glare out the window at rich kids on the sidewalk trying too hard to look down-and-out in their Docs.

LOWER HAIGHT Despite everything you've heard, the hip, alternative Haight-Ashbury of the '60s isn't dead, it's just relocated. The Lower Haight picks up where the '60s and '70s left off at around Haight and Fillmore, with an authentic collection of disaffected youth and bedraggled Victorian houses. On a stroll down the street you're bound to see an American flag hanging upside down from an iron window grate and a variety of stolen goods for sale. Not to mention ornery drunks, trash, and more than a few drug dealers. Don't be scared away, simply exercise your street sense, especially late at night. In the depths of Lower Haight, **Café International** (508 Haight St., near Fillmore St., tel. 415/552–7390) plays those old Donovan songs you thought you'd finally rid yourself of. Join the neo-beatniks and punks for brunch at **Spaghetti Western** (*see* Chapter 4), or head to **Naked Eye News and Video** (533 Haight St., tel. 415/864–2985) for underground magazines and avant-garde videos. If you're ready for that beer in a laid-back bar, try the **Toronado** or, across the street, **Mad Dog in the Fog**, with more of an English-pub-meets-lower Haight atmosphere (*see* Bars, in Chapter 6). Buses 6, 7, 66, 71, and 73 will get you to the Haight from downtown Market Street—hardly the Magic Bus, but you'll have to make do.

COLE VALLEY If you duck off the Upper Haight, you'll find that the neighborhoods abound with lavishly detailed Victorians. Follow Cole Street south a few blocks to an area known as **Cole Valley,** a quiet neighborhood with the requisite number of corner markets, flower stands, cafés, and restaurants. By the time you hit Carl Street, you'll understand why this mellow, upscale neighborhood is so popular (and why housing is so hard to find here).

CASTRO DISTRICT

When the concentration of rainbow flags adorning businesses and homefronts becomes increasingly dense, and pink triangle bumper stickers are more the rule than the exception, you know you're nearing the Castro, the city's gay center. Since the early 1970's, the area around Castro Street has been attracting gay men and women from around the world. Before the AIDS epidemic, it was known as a spot for open revelry, disco music pumping 24 hours a day. The community is definitely less celebratory since the first days of open gay pride, but especially on weekends, it still bustles with people on the streets, in the bars, at the gyms, socializing and checking one another out.

The heart of the district is **Castro Street,** between Market and 19th streets. At the southwest corner of Market and Castro, where the K, L, and M MUNI lines stop, is **Harvey Milk Plaza,** named in honor of California's first openly gay elected official. On November 27, 1978, Milk and then-Mayor George Moscone were assassinated by Dan White, a disgruntled former supervisor. That night, 40,000 San Franciscans gathered at the plaza and proceeded to City Hall in a candlelight march, a procession that is repeated each year.

One block away, 18th and Castro streets meet at the gayest four corners in the world. On weekends, people here hand out advertisements and discounts for clubs and upcoming queer events and canvas for political causes. The 24-hour Walgreens at 18th and Castro is one of the biggest distributors of AZT, the drug prescribed to treat HIV—something to think about as you're buying your bubble gum or saline solution. The photo shop on the northeast corner displays pictures of happy couples from the latest gay festival or event.

All the shops, bars, and cafés in the neighborhood cater to the gay community. Travel agencies bill themselves as gay and lesbian vacation experts and card shops have names such as **Does Your Mother Know** (4079 18th St., tel. 415/864–3160). The **Castro Theater** (*see* Movie Houses, in Chapter 6) is an impressive repertory house that hosts the San Francisco Lesbian and Gay Film Festival each summer. This is also a good area to pick up information on gay and, to a lesser extent, lesbian resources—try **A Different Light Bookstore** (*see* Books, in Chapter 3), with an extensive collection of lesbian and gay literature. Look for special interest listings, free publications, and advertisements for clubs or events in neighborhood shop windows.

Don't leave the Castro without catching a film at the art deco Castro Theater, complete with a live organist and trippy ceiling decorations.

The Castro is filled with unique gift shops and boutiques, especially those selling men's clothing. At **Man Line** (516 Castro, tel. 415/863–7811), you can buy Keith Haring earrings and a rainbow-striped robe for yourself, and for your home, a decorative wine bottle holder and an American flag in red, white, and Roy G. Biv. **Under One Roof** (2362 Market St., tel. 415/252–9430), adjacent to the NAMES Project Foundation (*see below*), gives 100% of its profits to AIDS organizations. The shop carries license plate holders bearing pink triangles, red ribbon pins, and a good selection of soaps, lotions, books, cards, and wind chimes. Don't step into **Jaguar** (4057 18th St., tel. 415/863–4777) unless you're prepared to be confronted with a foot-long silicon fist and other "objects of art" and books on how to use them. Visit **Gauntlet** (2377 Market St., at Castro St., tel. 415/431–3131), the friendly neighborhood piercing studio, to see photos of piercing possibilities and to chat with the knowledgeable staff.

The social hub of the neighborhood is east of Harvey Milk Plaza at **Café Flore** (*see* Chapter 5), where the eyes turn and the gossip mills churn. Closer to Castro Street, **The Café** (*see* Bars, in Chapter 6), is the only bar in the area where women represent a majority of the clientele. At the intersection of Castro and Market streets, **Twin Peaks** (401 Castro St., tel. 415/864–9470) has the distinction of being the first gay bar in the city with transparent windows. Note that Castro area bars get going in the afternoon. Why waste any time?

If you're in the city around the end of June or on Halloween, come to the Castro to witness two of San Francisco's craziest parties—the **Lesbian and Gay Freedom Day Parade** (usually held on the last Sunday in June) and the Castro Street **Halloween** party (*see* Festivals, in Chapter 1), in which thousands of gorgeous men in drag perform cabaret shows for onlookers roaming Castro Street. Both events attract tens of thousands of participants.

NAMES PROJECT FOUNDATION For a sobering reminder of the greatest crisis facing the gay community, drop by the NAMES Project Foundation's **Visitor Center and Panelmaking Workshop,** where panels from the now famous NAMES Quilt—a tribute to those who have died of AIDS—are displayed. The project started in 1987 when gay rights activist Cleve Jones organized a meeting with several others who had lost friends or lovers to AIDS, in hopes that they could create a memorial. They decided on a quilt that was to feature panels dedicated to individuals who have succumbed to the disease, each panel to be created by loved ones of the deceased. The idea caught on big and people from all over the country sent in quilt panels. To date, the entire quilt has been displayed in front of the White House four times (it now contains more than 26,000 panels). There are always some on display in the San Francisco office, as well as in other offices all over the world. For those who are interested in creating a panel, sewing machines, fabric, company, and support are available here. *2362 Market St., tel. 415/863–1966. Open Mon.–Wed. and Fri. noon–7, weekends noon–5.*

TWIN PEAKS Looming high above the Castro, Twin Peaks is one of the few places in the city where you can see both the bay and the ocean, and everything in between. Naturally, it's one of the prime make-out spots in San Francisco. If you surface long enough to look at the view, you'll have to admit it's truly spectacular—definitely worth the hassle of getting here on public transportation. Bring a picnic, and budget at least 30 minutes to walk up and around this twin-peaked mountain. When the Spanish came to this area in the 18th century, they named the peaks *Los Pechos de la Choca* (the Breasts of the Indian Maiden). Just another example of missionaries hard at work converting the heathens. To reach Twin Peaks, take MUNI Bus 37 from Castro and Market streets.

NOE VALLEY

Lying one major hill away from the hectic Mission and Castro districts, Noe Valley seems like their sedate older sister—you know the type, the one who traded the glitz and glamour and hard edges of city life for a more domestic arrangement. Home to large numbers of babies and dogs and those who love them, Noe Valley provides a sunny, neighborly venue for the eco-conscious set to convene and exchange childcare advice.

The main drag, **24th Street** beginning at Church Street and heading several blocks west, has plenty of solid, old-timey restaurants, pubs, and clothing stores, as well as a few trendy upstarts. **Global Exchange** (3900 24th St., near Sanchez St., tel. 415/648–8068) satisfies the neighborhood's social conscience: It's an international organization that promotes exchange between the United States and developing countries. In their Noe Valley store they sell crafts their representatives have bought from all over the world and distribute information on exchange programs and dire situations worldwide. Gift shops that smell nice and invariably

Great San Francisco Views

- **Treasure Island.** A slightly different angle reinvigorates the familiar San Francisco skyline. The Bay Bridge, dramatically draped in lights, frames the panorama. By car, take the Treasure Island exit from the Bay Bridge and park at the water's edge.

- **The 49-Mile Drive.** Start at the Civic Center and head north on Van Ness, following the blue-and-white signs with seagulls on them. This is the full San Francisco tour, with all the well-known scenic and historic draws. The route is marked on a free map you can get from the Visitor Information Center.

- **Upper Market Street.** Where Portola Street ends and Market Street begins, near Twin Peaks, you'll find a gorgeous view of the city and the East Bay.

- **Tank Hill.** Take Stanyan Street south and go left on Belgrave Avenue until it dead-ends. Follow the footpath to the high, craggy outlook and gaze to your heart's content. This is one of the finest views of San Francisco.

- **Top of the Mark.** The lookout point at the top of the Mark Hopkins Hotel, on Nob Hill at the corner of California and Mason streets, is accessible only to those in proper attire who are willing to pay dearly for a drink with a great view.

Univ of
San Francisco

Fulton St.

Masonic Ave.

Central Ave.

Lyon St.

Grove St.

Alam
Squa

Shrader St.

Cole St.

Clayton St.

Ashbury St.

Hayes St.

Divisadero St.

Fell St.

Stanyan St.

Oak St.

Page St.

Golden Gate Park Panhandle

Haight St.

**HAIGHT
ASHBURY**

Waller St.

Alpine Ter.

*Golden
Gate
Park*

Clayton St.

Downey St.

Ashbury St.

Delmar St.

Waller St.

West

*Buena
Vista
Park*

Buena Vista Ave.

Buena Ter.

Buena Vista

14th

Henr

Beulah St.

**Kezar
Stadium**

Frederick St.

Buena

Buena Vista
Way

East

Willard St.

Carl St.

**COLE
VALLEY**

*Corona
Heights
Park*

15t

Be

Parnassus Ave.

States St.

Woodland

Grattan St.

Belvedere St.

Roosevelt

Saturn

St.

**Castro St.
MUNI Station**

1

Edgewood Ave.

Alma St.

Rivoli St.

Ord St.

Harvey
Milk
Plaza

3

**Univ of
Calif
San Francisco**

17th St.

Corbett

Ave.

Castro St.

Carmel St.

Caselli Ave.

Collingwood St.

▲ *Mt. Sutro*

Belgrave Ave.

Ave.

Graystone

Yukon St.

Corwin St.

CASTRO

Clarendon

Mtn Spring Ave.

Twin

Ter.

St Germain Ave.

Palo Alto Ave.

Peaks

Ave.

Dellbrook

**TWIN
PEAKS**

Blvd.

Clarendon Ave.

Graystone Dr.

Ave.

Corbett

Ave.

Burnett

Douglass St.

Eureka St.

Diamond St.

Panorama

Dr.

▲▲

Market St.

Hoffman Ave.

*Midtown
Terrace
Rec Ctr*

Glenview Dr.

Panorama

Skyview Way

Knollview Way

Peaks

Twin
Peaks
▲

parkridge

Crestline Dr.

Dr.

Grand View Ave.

Fountain St.

Homestead St.

Dellbrook Ave.

N
↗

Twin
Peaks
Blvd.

Clipper St.

Way

0 ——— 440 yards

0 ——— 400 meters

Portola Dr.

Amethyst

Way

Café Flore, 2
Castro Theatre, 3
Gold Fire Hydrant, 5
Mission Cultural Center, 9
Mission Dolores, 4
NAMES Project, 1
New College of California, 8
Precita Eyes Mural Arts Center, 6
Women's Building, 7

WESTERN ADDITION

Van Ness MUNI Station

10th St.

11th St.

Mission St.

South Van Ness Ave.

Howard St.

12th St.

Fillmore St.

Webster St.

Brady St.

Gough St.

Otis St.

Hermann St.

Duboce Ave.

oce Park

101

Market St.

Clinton Park

Brosnan St.

14th St.

Church St. MUNI Station

Dolores St.

Ramana Ave.

Guerrero St.

Valencia St.

Caledonia St.

Minna St.

Mission St.

Natoma St.

Shotwell St.

Landers St.

15th St.

Albion St.

Sharon St.

Prosper St.

Pond St.

16th St/Mission BART Station

16th St.

2

17th St.

Chula Ln.

4

Sycamore St.

17th St.

Noe St.

18th St.

Oakwood St.

Linda St.

Lapidge St.

7

Lexington St.

San Carlos St.

18th St.

Mission Dolores Park

19th St.

19th St.

20th St.

rty St.

I. St.

20th St.

5

MISSION

21st St.

Guerrero St.

Fair Oaks St.

Valencia St.

Bartlett St.

Mission St.

Capp St.

South Van Ness Ave.

Church St.

Chattanooga St.

Dolores St.

22nd St.

varado St.

Vicksburg St.

Sanchez St.

23rd St.

lizabeth St.

24th St/Mission BART Station

24th St.

9

E VALLEY

Jersey St.

25th St.

Osage Al.

Lilac St.

Clipper St.

26th St.

Army St.

27th St.

Mission St.

6

Duncan St.

51

carry some combination of ethnic crafts, wind chimes, crystals, stationery, candles, lotions, oils, and fancy cookie cutters pop up at least once a block in this neighborhood. Doesn't sound tempting? Grab a cup of espresso at **Spinelli** (3966 24th St., near Noe St., tel. 415/550–7416), kick it on one of the benches outside, and contemplate which brie you're going to bring home from the **24th St. Cheese Co.** (3893 24th St., tel. 415/821–6658). For the melodically inclined, the **Noe Valley Ministry Presbyterian Church USA** (1021 Sanchez St., tel. 415/282–2317) features an eclectic assortment of performances, including traditional Scottish and Celtic music, modern jazz, and Indian music.

Noe Valley was once an enclave of Irish and German immigrants. These days, you can still find grandmotherly types gabbing in German on Sunday morning ambles. Pick up a bottle of bitters, some Bavarian music, and a packet of gummy bears at **Lehr's German Specialties** (1581 Church St., tel. 415/282–6803). Top it off with a sit-in-your-gut wurst and yummy goulash soup at **Speckmann's** (1550 Church St., tel. 415/282–6850), which also has a deli stocked with your favorite German specialties (nothin' like bloodwurst for breakfast).

Murals with a Mission

For a little over 20 years now, artists in San Francisco have actively explored the tradition of mural painting by creating huge, vibrant works on walls all over the city. You'll find the largest concentration of these in the Mission district, many done in the tradition of Mexican muralists like Diego Rivera. Within an area of about eight blocks in the southeast part of the Mission, you can see about 60 murals. The Precita Eyes Mural Arts Center (348 Precita Ave., near Folsom St., tel. 415/285–2287) offers an excellent two-hour tour of said murals, led by one of its muralists-in-residence, along with an introductory slide show. Tours cost $3 and leave from the center every Saturday at 1:30 PM. Otherwise, you can stop by any weekday between 1 and 4 and pick up a copy of their handy "Mission Mural Walk" map for a $1 donation. To get here take Bus 27 from 5th and Market downtown, and get off at 27th and Harrison; the center is right across the park.

A do-it-yourself tour could start at the Arts Center and go down Harrison Street (drug activity makes it best to do this stretch in the daytime). Make sure to duck into Balmy Alley (btw Harrison St. and Treat Ave., and 24th and 25th Sts.), an entire alley of garage and fence murals begun in 1971, mostly depicting scenes of and issues surrounding Central America. The stretch of 24th Street from Mission to Potrero teems with murals in every corner. A little farther north (btw 22nd and 23rd streets and Folsom and Shotwell), the trilingual César Chávez School is bedecked with an incredible array of murals by children and adults. The small panels along the top depict each letter of the alphabet in English, Spanish, and American Sign Language. Another heavy concentration of murals lies along Mission between 20th and 26th, including one right by the 24th and Mission BART station that seems to depict BART being built on the backs of the people. "Inspire to Aspire," a huge tribute to local idol Carlos Santana, decorates three buildings at South Van Ness and 22nd streets. Begun in 1993, the Clarion Alley Mural Project (between 16th, 17th, Mission, and Valencia streets) is a site for emerging artists; look for it right near the Elbo Room.

MISSION DISTRICT

Unplagued by fog, the sunny Mission district—named after the Spanish Mission Dolores (*see below*) and stretching from the South of Market area to Army Street—was once San Francisco's prime real estate, first for Ohlone Native Americans and then for Spanish missionaries. Over the years, various populations, primarily European, have given way to immigrants from Central and South America, and the Mission isn't as prized a territory as it used to be. The community today is low-income and primarily Latino, though it also includes a significant contingent of artists and radicals of all ethnicities. The neighborhood is colorful and friendly, a great place to hang out, but it can also be dangerous. Women won't feel comfortable walking alone here at night, and while you can actually find a parking space, you might think twice about leaving your car.

The Mission provides a bounty of cheap food, especially in the form of huge Mexican burritos and succulent tacos made up fresh in the numerous storefront taquerias. The area also abounds with specialty bookstores, relatively inexpensive alternative theater companies, and an increasing variety of bars, some of which offer live music, poetry readings, and dance spaces. Two BART stations (one at Mission and 16th, the other at Mission and 24th) put you right in the heart of things.

Much of the artsy scene, with its bookstores, cafés, and theaters, is concentrated in the northern half of the Mission, while the southern half is predominantly Latino-oriented businesses. The scene is most densely Mexican and Latin American on **24th Street,** between Mission and Potrero. A lively, sometimes hectic area, the strip is filled with people shopping at the many cheap produce stands, markets, and *panaderías* (bakeries). Just in case you need to chase down your taqueria burrito with something sweet, head down to 24th and York streets, where you can have homemade ice cream at the **St. Francis Soda Fountain and Candy Store** (2801 24th St., tel. 415/826–4200), or grab a pair of tongs and pick out a pastry or three at **La Mexicana Bakery** (2804 24th St., tel. 415/648–2633)—it'll still cost less than a scone from your favorite café.

VALENCIA STREET A good place to discover the offbeat side of the neighborhood is on Valencia Street (a block west of Mission St.) between 16th and 24th streets. This low-key strip is lined with cafés, secondhand furniture and clothing stores, galleries, garages, **Epicenter** (*see* Records, Tapes, and CDs, in Chapter 3), and a variety of bars. The **New College of California** (50 Fell St., off Van Ness Ave., tel. 415/241–1300), a center for alternative education, offers a renowned degree in poetics, innovative programs like Art and Activism, and an excellent women's resource center. Around the corner is the **Women's Building** (3543 18th St., tel. 415/431–1180), a meeting place for progressive and radical political groups. The building received a beautiful face-lift with the recent completion of the mural *Women's Wisdom Through Time.* Look for Audre Lorde, Georgia O'Keefe, and Rigoberta Menchú, among many other women's names woven into the fabric of the mural.

Back on Valencia Street, **Yahoo Herb'an Ecology** (968 Valencia St., tel. 415/282–WORM) specializes in worm boxes for composting. They also sell herbal teas, organic seeds, and products made of hemp fiber. At **Botanica Yoruba** (998 Valencia St., at 21st St., tel. 415/826–4967), you can pick up incense, candles, herbs, oils, and make an appointment for a spiritual consultation. The street is also the site of several good used and new bookstores, including the leftist **Modern Times** (888 Valencia St., tel. 415/282–9246) and the feminist **Old Wives' Tales** (1009 Valencia St., tel. 415/821–4675). Also check out **Good Vibrations** (*see* Specialty Items, in Chapter 3), a user-friendly vibrator and sex-toy store that's so respectful of the sacred act you could almost bring your mom here.

16TH STREET A busier and denser off-shoot of Valencia Street, 16th Street, between Mission and Guerrero, has its own share of hip cafés, bars, cheap restaurants, unusual shops, plus an independent movie theater, **The Roxie Cinema** (*see* Movie Houses, in Chapter 6). Two blocks north of Valencia, the **Pink Paraffin** (3234 16th St., tel. 415/621–7116) is noteworthy for its collection of second-hand religious items, cement gargoyles, reproductions of early-American gravestones, and brand-new Virgin Mary night lights. Just north of here, **Red Dora's Bearded Lady** (*see* Chapter 5), a lesbian-owned café, is the only full-time dyke space around.

DOLORES STREET AND MISSION DOLORES West of the busy, sometimes dangerous, thoroughfares of Mission and Valencia streets, the scene becomes green, hilly, and residential. Dolores Street, divided by a row of palm trees, marks the edge of the district. While the Castro, just west of here, is where many gay men call home, Dolores Street and the surrounding residential area is quietly though not exclusively lesbian. San Franciscans converge upon the expansive **Mission Dolores Park** (*see* Parks, *below*) to stretch their limbs and absorb some vitamin D, and tour buses make the pilgrimage stop at the old mission, two blocks away.

Though it's made of humble adobe, **Mission Dolores,** the oldest building in San Francisco, has survived some powerful earthquakes and fires. It was commissioned by Junípero Serra to honor San Francisco de Asís (St. Francis of Assisi) and completed in 1791. The Spanish nicknamed it Dolores after a nearby stream, *Arroyo de Nuestra Señora de los Dolores* (Stream of Our Lady of the Sorrows), and the name stuck (though the river is gone). Mission Dolores is both the simplest architecturally and the least restored of all the California missions, with a bright ceiling in a traditional Native American design painted by local Costanoan Indians. The mission bells still ring on holy days, and the cemetery next door is the permanent home of a few California celebrities, including San Francisco's first mayor, Don Francisco de Haro. For the $1 admission you get an informative pamphlet on the history of the mission, access to a small museum with old artifacts, plus as much time as you like in the fascinating old cemetery and the mission itself. *16th and Dolores Sts., tel. 415/621–8203. Admission: $1. Open weekdays 8–3:30, weekends 9–4.*

The gold fire hydrant on the corner of 20th and Church streets kept pumping water when the others went dry during the firestorm that followed the 1906 earthquake.

SOUTH OF MARKET

Lots is going on in SoMa (so named for its supposed resemblance to New York's SoHo) these days. The vast neighborhood, consisting mostly of warehouses and their occupants (industrial workshops, nightclubs, artists' studios, and racks and racks of clothes), is becoming the new center of San Francisco's cultural offerings. For the moment, however, parts of SoMa still look like an industrial wasteland, a thriving home to factory outlets and design firms. During the day, shoppers are out in force for leather, beauty products, work clothes, and office supplies needs, or anything else you can think of (*see* Chapter 3). At 660 3rd Street you'll find the ultimate bargain basement, **660 Center** (btw Brannan and Townsend Sts., tel. 415/227–0464), a conglomeration of 22 outlet stores under one roof.

Artists and musicians who work out of their studios are a major part of the SoMa landscape. A number of the city's best museums and galleries are also here, including **New Langton Arts** and the **Ansel Adams Center** (*see* Museums and Galleries, *below*). And then there's the **Cartoon Art Museum** (814 Mission St., at 4th St., tel. 415/546–3922), which will teach you all you ever wanted to know about the history of the cartoon. The museum recently moved and should be opening to the public in March of 1995. Admission is $3 ($2 students). Past exhibits have included the making of *Snow White* and a retrospective of illustrator Edward Gorey's work.

Cheap warehouse space and a lack of neighbors to disturb have also brought SoMa a happening nightlife (*see* Chapter 6). Such perennially fashionable discos as **Club Townsend** and **1015 Club** are here for the duration, and the stretch of Folsom Street between 7th and 11th streets has sprouted numerous bars, live-music venues, restaurants, and cafés. Toward the water, the downtown business scene has spread south of Market, but you'll still find several semi-hip, semi-yuppie cafés and restaurants around the surprisingly green **South Park** (*see* Parks, *below*).

YERBA BUENA GARDENS The city has undertaken big construction projects along 3rd Street, including Yerba Buena Gardens, part of a long-range redevelopment plan that has been in slow progress for the past 30 years. After long and drawn out rehousing plans and a good dose of bureaucratic disputes over a formerly run-down, 12-block area near downtown which used to have many low-rent hotels, October 1993 finally saw the opening of the 8.3-acre arts and performance space. On the east side of the garden complex, the **Center for the Arts** houses galleries (*see* Museums and Galleries, *below*) and a theater (*see* Theater and Dance, in Chapter 6) meant to expose and celebrate the multicultural nature of the Bay Area. Critics point out that the multicultural emphasis may be at the exclusion of mainstream arts. Others smirk at the money spent building the center: $41 million. *701 Mission St., tel. 415/978–2787.*

Aside from the performing and visual arts, Yerba Buena Gardens offers a welcome respite from the frenzy of downtown; it's just a couple blocks southeast of the Powell Street BART station. Take a walk along the paths of the grassy, spacious esplanade to the Martin Luther King, Jr. Memorial: twelve glass panels engraved with quotes of Dr. King in English and in the languages of each of San Francisco's sister cities all behind a shimmering waterfall. A retail and entertainment center is busily being constructed on the west side and 1995 will see the opening of the **San Francisco Museum of Modern Art** (*see* Museums and Galleries, *below*), across the street from the Center of the Arts and the newly relocated **California Historical Society** (678 Mission St., at 3rd St., tel. 415/567–1848). The latter will be opening in spring of 1995. A Children's Center should open in 1996, and the Mexican Museum will make its new home here around 1998.

Parks

Along with Golden Gate Park (*see* Major Sights, *above*), the grandaddy of them all, the city has an abundance of smaller strips of greenery where you can cavort like a hyperactive kid when your energy overflows, or rest when your feet have become a little too accustomed to the feel of pavement. In several of these, the sheer horticultural magnificence and diversity will amaze you as you laze beneath cypress or gaze at palms and say: "I *am* in California! So why is it so damn cold?"

ALAMO SQUARE This brief flash of green near the lower Haight lies across the street from the **Painted Ladies,** probably the most famous row of houses in the city (featured on hundreds of postcards and the opening credits of several TV shows set in San Francisco). The Ladies comprise six beautifully restored, brightly colored Victorians sitting side by side on a steep street with the downtown skyline looming majestically behind. To get here, take Bus 6, 7, 66 or 71 to Haight and Steiner streets, and walk north on Steiner up to Hayes Street.

AQUATIC PARK The only chlorophyll to be found here is a small splotch of grass in front of the Cannery, but the real reason to come to this "park" just west of Fisherman's Wharf (*see* Major Sights, *above*) is to stroll on its pier, which extends like a big apostrophe into the bay. From the pier's west side you can gaze at choppy seas, the Golden Gate, and the great ocean beyond. This is the ideal place to eat that cup of chowder or chocolate bar you just bought over in Tourist Hell.

BUENA VISTA It ain't called Buena Vista ("good view") for nothing. Set on a steep hill covered with cypress and eucalyptus and tumbling down toward Haight Street at about 100 miles per hour, Buena Vista offers potheads, dog walkers, and lovers some serious inspiration to do their thing. The park has a reputation for being dangerous at night, but in the daytime it's a largely undiscovered escape from the Haight's asphalt chaos. From the summit, the views of the Golden Gate, the ocean, the Bay Bridge, and downtown create a mystical backdrop for whatever activity you choose to indulge in. Here's a great place to check out the hilly, water-locked stretch of land the city is built on, to imagine the time when it was just a big sand dune, and to contemplate what an 8.0 earthquake would look like from up here. The park fronts Haight Street at the intersection of Haight and Lyon; from downtown, take Bus 6, 7, 66, or 71 up Market Street and get off at Lyon Street.

DUBOCE PARK Dogs and 20-year-olds with assorted tattoos, drug habits, and musical instruments seem especially drawn to this tiny park, which is crammed in between the lower Haight and the Castro and offers no view beyond that of MUNI streetcars trundling by (it's on the N Judah line, which runs from downtown Market Street out to the Sunset). Despite its utter averageness compared to such jewels as nearby Buena Vista or Alamo Square, it's a grassy enough place to enjoy the cup of coffee or piece of pizza you just bought on lower Haight Street; and unlike the other two, it requires barely any energy to reach. Slacker heaven.

GLEN CANYON Hidden in a part of the city that isn't crawling with visitors, Glen Canyon Park might just give you back all the resources city life so quickly depletes. Eucalyptus trees loom above you and scent the air, zillions of birds sing to you and only you, and grass-covered slopes lead down to a shady path, equal parts poison oak and soothing stream. There are even rocks to climb on. Take BART to Glen Park, walk uphill on Bosworth Street to the end, and go hiking. Don't tell anybody.

MISSION DOLORES PARK In a sunny residential area between the Mission and Castro districts, beautiful Dolores Park tends to attract picnickers, families with children, dogs and their owners, and men in Speedos if the weather is right. Set on a gently sloping hill, the park contains tennis courts, a basketball court, a playground, palm trees, and wide expanses of grass where you can catch some of the city's hard-to-find rays. Head toward the west and southwest edges of the park (where the serious sun-worshippers hang out), for spectacular views of the city and the Bay Bridge. While the open areas feel quite friendly and safe, the thoroughfare down the middle of the park seems to be where dealers and sketchy-looking types hang out. Avoid this area at night. *Btw Dolores, Church, 18th and 20th Sts. From Downtown take J Church MUNI to 18th or 19th Sts.*

For all you radical leftists out there, the San Francisco Mime Troupe (tel. 415/285–1717) performs free in Mission Dolores Park on July 4 and Labor Day. On weekends in between, look for them in venues throughout the Bay Area.

SOUTH PARK Set in the middle of the warehouse-laden, hip, and utterly ungreen South of Market district is a welcome surprise: South Park, a tree-filled square which looks like it just dropped in from Paris to say hi, has a playground, several cafés and restaurants, inviting benches, and a bit of quiet. It's a perfect old-fashioned antidote for those postmodern moments when you feel like you've spent the whole day on the set of *Mad Max*. Weekdays, graphic artists, writers, architects, and attorneys pass through here sipping their lattes. Sundays, when the surrounding cafés, offices, and galleries are closed, are quietest. *South Park Ave., off 2nd and 3rd Sts., btw Bryant and Brannan Sts.*

SUTRO FOREST Sometimes you'll be walking around the city and off in the distance you'll see a big patch of trees. You know it's not Golden Gate Park, but it looks awfully tempting anyway. This wild, densely forested place is Sutro Forest, off Stanyan Street, right behind the UCSF Medical Center. Just when you think it might be possible to get lost along one of its deserted, overgrown trails, among the ferns and ivy-covered eucalyptus trees, you stumble upon UCSF residence halls. The least strenuous way to get here is to take the N Judah MUNI to Willard Street, head south on Willard, right on Belmont Avenue, and left on Edgewood Avenue until it dead ends. There's your hiking trail.

WASHINGTON SQUARE Old men chewing on long-dead cigars and a Romanesque church whose bells ring on the hour give this park between Filbert, Union, Powell, and Stockton streets a distinctly European feel. An Italian-style picnic grabbed from any of North Beach's numerous delicatessens, a bottle of Chianti hidden discreetly in a brown paper bag, and someone you feel like relaxing with will only heighten the good vibes. Make the hike to **Coit Tower** (*see* Major Sights, *above*), a few steep blocks east of the park, to work off those Italian calories. From Market Street downtown, take Bus 15 or 30 to get here.

Museums and Galleries

On a rainy day, you should take a look at some of the most diverse museums on the West Coast. The big ones, especially the Asian Art Museum, are comparable to those found anywhere else in the country, but it's worth checking out the little, free, funky ones, for tastes eclectic and perverse. Note that one of San Francisco's major museums, the Legion of Honor, is closed through 1995.

If you're looking for big names and relatively mainstream art, head Downtown; a stone's throw from Montgomery BART and Union Square lie no fewer than 30 galleries. The thickest concentrations are along the first three blocks of Grant Street, the 100 block of Geary, the 100 and 200 blocks of Post, and the 200 block of Sutter. You'll find more eclectic galleries scattered South of Market and along Hayes and Grove streets between Van Ness and Laguna, near the Civic Center. Keep an eye out for two monthly publications that contain gallery listings and notices for events in the arts community: the *San Francisco Gallery Guide,* a brochure published by the **William Sawyer Gallery** (3045 Clay St., tel. 415/921–1600), and the newspaper *San Francisco Arts Monthly.* Both are available at galleries throughout the city.

South of Market galleries to check out include **New Langton Arts** (1246 Folsom St., btw 8th and 9th Sts., tel. 415/626–5416), a well-established, non-profit exhibit and performance space with a variety of multimedia events, and **Capp Street Project** (515 2nd St., btw Bryant and Brannan Sts., tel. 415/495–7101), which presents site-related installations in its new SoMa location. Two worthwhile photography galleries are **Vision Gallery** (1155 Mission St., btw 7th and 8th Sts., tel. 415/621–2107) and **SF Camerawork** (70 12th St., tel. 415/621–1001).

AFRICAN AMERICAN HISTORICAL AND CULTURAL SOCIETY Aimed at exploring and disseminating African-American culture, this place offers a contemporary art gallery featuring works by African and African-American artists, exhibits like "The African Legacy in Mexico," an intriguing gift shop that sells jewelry and artifacts, and a historical archive and research library. In addition, the museum has performing-arts classes and lecture series. *Building C, Room 165, Fort Mason Center, tel. 415/441–0640 or 415/979–6794 (events hotline). Donation requested. Open Wed.–Sun. noon–5.*

ANSEL ADAMS CENTER If you're even remotely interested in serious photography, come here. The largest repository of art photography on the West Coast, the Ansel Adams Center has five rotating exhibits, one of which is devoted to Adams's work. Born of the Friends of Photography, a national group founded by Adams, the center serves photographers with publications, awards, an educational series taught by famous shutterbugs, and an incredible bookstore. The center's 1993 Annie Leibovitz retrospective put it on the pop-culture map. *250 4th St., btw Howard and Folsom Sts., tel. 415/495–7000. Admission: $4, $3 students; free first Tues. of month. Open Tues.–Sun. 11–5, first Thurs. of month 11–8.*

ASIAN ART MUSEUM Housed in the same building as the M. H. de Young (*see below*), this is the West's largest Asian museum. The first floor is devoted to Chinese and Korean art; the second floor holds treasures from Southeast Asia, India and the Himalayas, Japan, and Persia. The museum hosts about three exhibitions a year, either showcasing a visiting exhibition or drawing on pieces from its own collection that aren't already on permanent display. Past exhibits have included two world-class shows on the sacred art of Tibet and the sculpture of Indonesia. *John F. Kennedy and Tea Garden Drs., Golden Gate Park, tel. 415/668–8921. Admission: $5; free first Wed. of month, first Sat. of month until noon. Open Wed.–Sun. 10–5, until 8:45 first Wed. of month.*

CALIFORNIA ACADEMY OF SCIENCES This huge natural-history complex actually houses several separate museums, the **Steinhart Aquarium,** and **Morrison Planetarium** (*see* Golden Gate Park, in Major Sights, *above*). Its biggest draw is the aquarium's **Fish Roundabout,** which places you in an underwater world of 14,500 different creatures. The living coral reef, with its fish, giant clams, and tropical sharks, is super cool. Go mid-morning so you can watch the penguins and dolphins at feeding time. If earthquakes are inextricably linked with San Francisco in your imagination, try the trembling earthquake floor in the Space and Earth Hall of the **Natural History Museum.** The Life through Time Hall, which chronicles evolution from the dinosaurs through early mammals, the Birds of a Feather Exhibit, which explores the learning of birds, their languages, songs, and physical features, and the photo exhibit on North American endangered species, are also worth checking out. *Btw John F. Kennedy and Martin Luther King, Jr. Drs., Golden Gate Park, tel. 415/750–7000; laser shows at planetarium, tel. 415/ 750–7138. Admission to museum and aquarium: $7, $4 students; free first Wed. of month. Admission to planetarium $2.50, to laser shows $7. Open daily 10–5.*

CENTER FOR THE ARTS The Center for the Arts at Yerba Buena Gardens, a two-story glass, metal, and stone structure, houses three spacious galleries exhibiting contemporary works, usually of emerging local and regional artists; a media screening room showing videos and films; and a multi-use forum. The idea of this visual arts center is to reflect San Francisco's multicultural community and its range of human issues in a space that is welcoming, unpretentious, and appealing to as large a community as possible—how very San Francisco. Opening season saw artwork by prison inmates, people from the Tenderloin's Hospitality House, artists who use Renaissance painting techniques to express contemporary social issues, and panels from the NAMES Project Memorial Quilt. The Center's high-tech theater (*see* Theater and Dance, in Chapter 6) next door promotes local, multicultural talent. *701 Mission St., at 3rd St., tel. 415/978–2700 or 415/978–2787. Admission: $3; free first Thurs. of month. Open Tues.–Sun. 11—6.*

CHINESE HISTORICAL SOCIETY OF AMERICA This nonprofit organization houses a modest museum in its basement headquarters. Historical photos and graphics accompanied by interesting and often moving explanations trace the experiences of Chinese Americans from the 1850s. Among other artifacts, the small museum contains opium pipes, a *queu* (long braid men used to wear as a symbol of allegiance to the Manchu emperor of China before the 1911 Revolution), an altar built in the 1880s, and a parade-dragon head from 1909, one of the first to use lights. *650 Commercial St., btw Kearny and Montgomery Sts., tel. 415/391–1188. Admission free, donations accepted. Open Tues.–Sat. noon–4. Closed major holidays.*

EXPLORATORIUM Come here for the ultimate fourth-grade field trip you never took—it's a great place for children and grown-ups to learn about science and technology in a big, drafty warehouse. In the more than 650 exhibits, many of them computer-assisted, a strong emphasis is placed on interaction with the senses, making it especially popular with people on hallucinogenic drugs. Advance reservations are required for the excellent crawl-through **Tactile Dome**, where you slither through several small rooms in complete darkness. *3601 Lyon St., btw Marina Blvd. and Lombard St., tel. 415/561–0360. Admission: $8, $6 students, $4 disabled; free first Wed. of month. Open Tues.–Sun. 10–5 (Wed. until 9:30); Memorial Day and Labor Day 10–5.*

GALERIA DE LA RAZA Founded in 1970 by artists of the Chicano Arts movement, this was the first Mexican museum in the United States, and it remains an influential cultural resource. Eight major exhibits are presented each year along with numerous community-arts programs. *2857 24th St., at Bryant St., tel. 415/826–8009. Admission free. Open Tues.–Sat. noon–6.*

JEWISH COMMUNITY MUSEUM This handsome, small museum features revolving exhibits that trace important moments in Jewish history and the works of Jewish artists—contemporaries as well as old masters. Past exhibits that drew a lot of attention included one on Chagall and one entitled "Bridges and Boundaries," exploring the relationship between African Americans and Jews. *121 Steuart St., btw Mission and Howard Sts., tel. 415/543–2090 or 415/543–8880 (recorded message). Embarcadero BART. Admission: $3, $1.50 students. Open Sun.–Wed. 11–5, Thurs. 11–7. Closed Jewish holidays.*

KEANE EYES GALLERY This entire gallery is devoted to that cornerstone of American kitsch, the Keane painting. Back in the 1960s a husband and wife started painting poor little waifs with enormous vacuous eyes—you know the ones. America loved them, America hated them. Rush over and check it out. *651 Market St., tel. 415/495–3263. Admission free. Open weekdays 10–6, Sat. 10–4.*

MEXICAN MUSEUM A unique center for Mexican and Chicano culture in the United States, the museum has an impressive 9,000-object permanent collection. Despite its relatively small space, it's scored impressive exhibits of Diego Rivera and Frida Kahlo. Less mainstream shows with themes like Chicano graffiti art are also showcased. *Building D, Fort Mason Center, tel. 415/441–0404. Admission: $3, $2 students; free first Wed. of month, noon–8. Open Wed.–Sun. noon–5.*

M. H. DE YOUNG MEMORIAL MUSEUM This is San Francisco's big, mainstream museum—the one that puts up those international traveling exhibits that draw art lovers out of the suburbs. Past shows have included the King Tut exhibit, Andrew Wyeth's Helga paintings, the Dutch Masters, and the Dead Sea Scrolls. The museum is best known for its substantial survey collection of American art, from paintings and sculpture to decorative arts, textiles, and furniture. Some pieces survive from as far back as 1670, and the artists represented include

Sargent, Whistler, Church, and Wood. Don't miss the great gift shop and garden café. Docent-led tours are offered on the hour. Call the recorded message to find out about special lectures and events. If you're a student, you can get a $35 membership that gets you free admission for an entire year. *Btw John F. Kennedy Dr. and 8th Ave., Golden Gate Park, tel. 415/750-3600 or 415/863-3330. Admission: $5; free first Wed. of month, other Wed. half-price after 5; free first Sat. of month until noon. Open Wed. 10-8:45; Thurs.-Sun. 10-5.*

MISSION CULTURAL CENTER This Mission district landmark has not only gallery space but classrooms, dance spaces, painting studios, and a theater, all devoted to promoting the arts in the Latino community. Call or stop by for a complete rundown of events, including exhibits, performances, lectures and classes. *2868 Mission St., btw 24th and 25 Sts., tel. 415/821-1155. Admission and hours vary.*

MUSEE MECANIQUE This quirky museum lurks near the Cliff House at the end of Geary Boulevard. As museums go, the Mécanique is tops, stuffed with antique carnival attractions like player pianos, marionette shows, and fortune tellers. Admission is free, but bring a pock-etful of change (mostly quarters) to play with all the gadgets. Don't miss the miniature amuse-ment park—complete with a Ferris wheel—built out of toothpicks by inmates at San Quentin. *1090 Point Lobos Ave., tel. 415/386-1170. Admission free. Open weekdays 11-7, weekends 10-8.*

MUSEO ITALOAMERICANO Exhibits celebrate Italian and Italian-American cultural contri-butions in a large gallery space. There's often a special exhibit on display, in addition to the permanent collection. Sometime in 1995, look for the show on the last 85 years of the Alpha Romeo and for the exhibition on Tina Modotti's photographs. They have shows on architecture as well. *Building C, Room 100, Fort Mason Center, tel. 415/673-2200. Admission: $2, $1 students. Open Wed.-Sun. noon-5.*

ROBERT KOCH GALLERY Although most everything here is for sale, you'll probably come simply to see the latest photography exhibit, whether it's documenting Ginsberg and the Beat generation or a 1930s Russian hydroelectric project. Call for the latest exhibit info and ask about occasional readings and lectures. *49 Geary St., 5th floor, btw Kearny and Grant Sts., tel. 415/421-0122. Admission free. Open Tues.-Sun. 11-5:30 (first Thurs. until 9).*

SAN FRANCISCO MUSEUM OF MODERN ART The first time you see the new SFMOMA, you'll do a double take. Designed by Swiss architect Mario Botta, the brick and stone building is dominated by a huge, cylindrical skylight trimmed with black and white stripes of stone. Due to open in January 1995, the space doubles that of the museum's prior home at the War Memorial Veterans Building, where it opened in 1935 as the West Coast's first museum devoted to 20th-century art. The permanent collection contains paintings and sculpture that represent the major modernist and postmodernist movements. It was one of the first museums to showcase art photography, and its collection of contemporary photos is vast. Newer pursuits include architecture and design and video installations. Inaugural exhibitions include a study

Monthly Free Days at San Francisco Museums

Ansel Adams Center: first Tuesday 11-5. Asian Art Museum: first Wednesday 10-8:45 and first Saturday 10-noon. Center for the Arts: first Thursday 11-6. Exploratorium: first Wednesday 10-9:30. Mexican Museum: first Wednesday, noon-8. M. H. de Young Museum: first Wednesday 10-8:45 and first Saturday 10-noon, half-price admission Wednesdays 5-8:45. San Francisco Museum of Modern Art: first Tuesday 10-6, half-price admission Thursdays 5-9. California Academy of Sciences: first Wednesday 10-5.

of the influence of photographic images on contemporary art, an architecture and design exhibition on the museum itself, and a show on William Klein's New York. *151 3rd St., tel. 415/357–4000. Admission: $7, $3.50 students; free first Tues. of month, half-price Thurs. 5–9. Open Tues.–Sun. 11–6 (Thurs. until 9). Closed major holidays.*

Cheap Thrills

Proud of its healthy contingent of bohemians and starving artists, the city seems to cater, in some ways, to those perpetually low on cash. In addition to the thrills listed below, consider some of the cheap forms of entertainment discussed in other sections, such as author readings, open mike nights at bars and cafés, museum free days, Sunday morning celebrations at Glide Church (*see box above*), and the many annual festivals and street fairs (*see* Festivals, in Chapter 1).

Golden Gate Ferries (*see* Getting In, Out, and Around, in Chapter 1), the commuter ferry between San Francisco and Sausalito and San Francisco and Larkspur, offers the cheapest way to experience the bay in a boat ($3–$5). They have all the features you've come to associate with fine ferry travel: outdoor decks, food for sale, a complete wet bar, and no irritating commentary.

The **Anchor Brewing Company** (1705 Mariposa St., at De Haro St., tel. 415/863–8350), on Potrero Hill east of the Mission district, offers free brewery tours, including a history of the brewery, a step-by-step explanation of the brewing process, and, yep, free samples at the end. Tours run twice a day June–August, and once a day the rest of the year. You *must* make reservations three to four weeks in advance.

Drink beer, listen to live blues, and watch big boats pull in and out of the bay every Sunday afternoon at 2 at **Mission Rock Resort** in China Basin. To get here, take Bus 22 to the intersection of 18th and 3rd streets, walk down 3rd one block to Mariposa Street, and head toward the marina.

An especially discombobulating and/or morbidly fascinating diversion awaits you in the Richmond district at the **Neptune Society Columbarium**, a four-story Beaux Arts structure displaying urns that contain the cremated remains of San Francisco's dearly departed. The domed structure alone can make you kind of dizzy: a perfect circle with niches carved throughout and doors leading to rooms with elaborate display cases and 19th-century stained glass. Get the greens keeper going and he'll tell you all sorts of interesting stories. *1 Lorraine Ct., tel. 415/221–1838. Off Anza St. btw Stanyan and Arguello Sts. Admission free. Open daily 10–1.*

Wise Fool Puppet Intervention is a theater-arts project that brings giant puppets and stilt characters to the city's streets and public parks. The puppets and masks are handmade with recycled materials. The processions and performances are moving, magical, and just might inspire you to sign up for a volunteer program in your own community. They also hold open workshops, where you can help build a puppet or make a mask and then join one of the processions (you pay only for materials). For more info call 415/905–5958.

East Bay

So you've had a burrito at every taqueria in the Mission. You've worn a groove in your seat at your favorite San Francisco café, and you know where each book at City Lights is shelved. You've had more than your share of great times in the city by the bay, but at the moment you're asking yourself somewhat anxiously: What next?

Luckily, the funk and soul of San Francisco extend beyond the city limits. Only a bridge away lie Berkeley and Oakland, each with its own character and some attractions the city can't match—from the hip-hop Oaktown beat to the hippie parade in Berkeley. Whether you're looking for a New Age healing session or a grungy blues band, odds are good that you'll find it somewhere in the East Bay.

Berkeley

Berkeley and the **University of California** may not be synonymous, but they're so interdependent, it's difficult to tell where one stops and the other begins. You won't find many knapsack-toting students in the upscale neighborhoods that buffer the north and east sides of campus, but for the most part Berkeley is a student town, dominated by the massive U.C. campus and its 33,000 enrollees. Because of its offbeat, radical reputation, the university attracts every sort of person imaginable—from artists, anarchists, and hypergenius intellectuals to super-jocks, sorority girls, and fashion slaves, not to mention the stubbornly apathetic and the piously ideological, and of course the food snobs, intellectual snobs, and people whose only professed prejudice is against snobbishness itself. The city's liberal bent has led detractors to describe it as Berzerkeley and the People's Republic of Berkeley, but residents sometimes see this as a compliment. Berkeley thrives on being different and cutting-edge, which has helped keep it culturally diverse and politically adventurous—a breeding ground for social trends and all things alternative.

You know the university is of prime importance when people name parts of the city in reference to the campus. Southside, or the area south of campus, is dominated by chaotic **Telegraph Avenue,** while Northside, the area (surprise) north of campus, is more refined, consisting of peaceful residential areas, English-style gardens, and Berkeley's **Gourmet Ghetto,** home of the famed Chez Panisse and other upscale restaurants. The Berkeley Hills, rising north and east of campus, offer the huge **Tilden Regional Park** and several lovely smaller gardens. The campus itself is surprisingly beautiful, crisscrossed by numerous walking paths and a creek, and overgrown with eucalyptus groves. Unfortunately, much of west Berkeley is grimy and run-down, though the marina does have sparkling views of San Francisco and the Golden Gate Bridge.

To visitors, it may seem as if Berkeley citizens exude a bit of moral superiority—nowhere else does the cashier at the store make the question "Paper or plastic?" sound like a political interrogation.

No matter what part of town you're in, you're never far from movie houses and bookstores geared toward the young and ideological, used-clothing stores, and cafés and restaurants that cater to student budgets. Except for the occasional droves who come to Berkeley for demonstrations, with hopes of getting tear-gassed, arrested, or just stoned out of their minds, San Franciscans don't get over here much. But don't be afraid to make the easy journey from the city to load up on espresso, organic produce, and alternative literature. Whatever your pleasure, be careful: People who hang out in Berkeley too long look up from their granola 20 years later only to realize they forgot to pursue the American Dream.

MAJOR SIGHTS

TELEGRAPH AVENUE When most people think of Berkeley, they think of Telegraph Avenue, which begins at the campus and runs south into Oakland. Whether you love it or hate it, this congested and colorful avenue is the spiritual heart of Berkeley—a five-block-long jumble of cafés, bookstores, art shops, students, long-haired hippies, homeless buskers, metaphysical warriors, and wide-eyed tourists. Every day—rain or shine—troops of street vendors line the avenue, selling everything from handmade jewelry and imported crafts to crystals, incense, and tie-dyed T-shirts. New Age prophets offer tarot and numerology readings to passersby while baggy-jeaned hip-hop fans skateboard down the sidewalks. Telegraph today is a unique fusion of '60s and '90s counterculture, and the two elements blend nicely. Get your karma healed at the **Berkeley Psychic Institute** (2436 Haste St., tel. 510/548–8020), popular with all sorts of New Agers and alternative enthusiasts. They offer a free weekly healing clinic Monday evening; psychic readings, by appointment only, are $20.

Shops along Telegraph (*see* Chapter 3) come and go, but neighborhood landmarks include **Rasputin's Records** and **Leopold Records**, both at Durant Avenue, and both featuring that rare medium: vinyl. Book lovers should check out **Cody's Books** (at Haste St.) and **Moe's** (btw Haste St. and Dwight Way). Cody's hosts regular readings and has probably the largest selection of

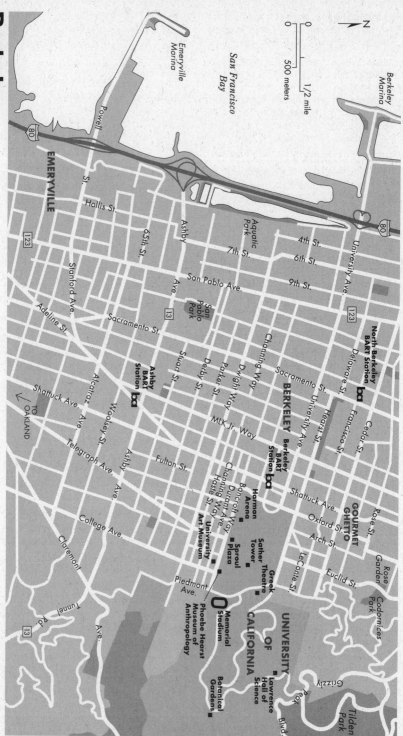

Berkeley

N

0
1/2 mile

0
500 meters

San Francisco Bay

Berkeley Marina

Emeryville Marina

Powell St.

80

EMERYVILLE

Hollis St.

123

Stanford Ave.

Adeline St.

65th St.

Ashby Ave.

San Pablo Ave.

San Pablo Park

Aquatic Park

7th St.

4th St.

6th St.

9th St.

University Ave.

13

Sacramento St.

Stuart St.

Derby St.

Parker St.

Dwight Way

MLK Jr. Way

Channing Way

Sacramento St.

University Ave.

Delaware St.

Francisco St.

Cedar St.

North Berkeley BART Station

BERKELEY

GOURMET GHETTO

Rose St.

Hearst St.

Shattuck Ave. TO OAKLAND

Alcatraz Ave.

Woolsey St.

Telegraph Ave.

Ashby Ave.

Fulton St.

College Ave.

Claremont Ave.

Tunnel Rd.

13

Piedmont Ave.

Ashby BART Station

Berkeley BART Station

Harmon Arena

Bancroft Way

Durant Ave.

Haste St.

Channing Way

University Art Museum

Phoebe Hearst Museum of Anthropology

Sather Tower

Sproul Plaza

Greek Theatre

Memorial Stadium

UNIVERSITY OF CALIFORNIA

Shattuck Ave.

Oxford St.

Arch St.

LeConte St.

Euclid St.

Rose Garden

Codornices Park

Lawrence Hall of Science

Botanical Gardens

Grizzly Peak Blvd.

Tilden Park

123

80

new books in the area, while Moe's specializes in used and rare books. For candles, incense, black-light posters and, er, any other recreational needs, stop by Berkeley's only remaining head shop, **Annapurna** (2416 Telegraph Ave., at Channing Way, tel. 510/841–6187).

Berkeley is a haven for street musicians. In particular, look for the **Spirit of '29,** a local Dixieland blues and jazz ensemble distinguished by what so many of the other players lack—harmony. They're not very punctual, but about once a week they set up on the corner of Telegraph and Bancroft and let it loose (try calling 510/655–3024 for more info on where to find them). As always, a small donation is encouraged.

If you're lucky, you may cross paths with the Bubble Lady (poet and bubble maker), Rare (lunatic and sports-trivia fiend), the Hate Man (high heels, lipstick, and a professed hatred for everything and everybody), or any of the other wacked-out denizens who give Berkeley its odd appeal.

UNIVERSITY OF CALIFORNIA CAMPUS Established in 1868 as the first branch of the statewide University of California system, U.C. Berkeley has the privilege of calling itself "Cal." The campus retains some of the beauty and gentility of its early years (especially in the old brick and stone buildings scattered about campus), some of the fire of the revolutionary 1960s (check out Sproul Plaza at noon), and some of the apathy and complacency of the 1980s (also visible on Sproul Plaza at noon). On a walk through campus you'll find peaceful glades, imposing academic buildings in the style known as brutalism, and battalions of musicians, random dogs, zealots, and students "on their way to class" (i.e., napping in the sun). For a map, stop by the **Student Union Building** on the west side of Sproul Plaza (*see below*). Inside the lobby there's a small visitor center staffed by students. For a free student-led tour of campus, held on Monday, Wednesday, and Friday at 10 AM and 1 PM, meet at a second visitor center (101 University Hall, tel. 510/642–5215), at the corner of University Avenue and Oxford Street on the west side of campus.

➤ **SPROUL PLAZA** • Just north of the Telegraph and Bancroft intersection, Sproul Plaza is widely known as the spot where the Free Speech Movement began in 1964. Look inside **Sproul Hall** (the nearby white, imposing administration building) for a display of photographs from this first demonstration, in which 3,000 students surrounded a police car that was holding a man arrested for "disturbing the peace" and distributing political flyers. Both the man and car were released after 32 hours, but Berkeley's activists had found a worthy cause. Today, Sproul Plaza is a source of endless entertainment for locals and tourists alike, where some of Berkeley's most famous loonies get a chance to match wits. Here's your chance to see a man in a bra and high heels heckle an evangelist who's preaching damnation and hellfire to fornicators and sodomites, or engage in a debate on foreign policy or the existence of God with street philosophers of all stripes, or listen to an endless stream of bad show tunes sung by the intensely annoying Rick Starr, who apparently believes his unplugged Mr. Microphone reaches a national audience. **Lower Sproul Plaza,** just a staircase west of Sproul Plaza, is the site of sporadic free noon concerts (usually held on Fridays during the school year) as well as weekend jam sessions by a ragtag group of bongo drummers (the very same drummers who give editors at the Berkeley Guides intense headaches while we *try* to edit but can't *hear* ourselves *think* because of all the damn *drumming* going on *right* outside our office). Bring your own pot and kettle and join in, or just hang and listen. Nearby **Zellerbach Hall** (*see* Theater and Dance, in Chapter 6) brings more professional productions to campus; check the box office for upcoming events.

➤ **SATHER GATE AND DOE LIBRARY** • North of Sproul Plaza, pass through Sather Gate, the main entrance to campus until expansion in the 1960s. The second building on your right, Doe Library, is worth a look for its cavernous and beautiful reference room and the cozy **Morrison Reading Room** (open weekdays 10:30–5). Stop in the latter if you want to curl up somewhere and recuperate from the incessant flow of people outside. The subdued brass lamps, oak paneling, and ornate tapestries inspire calm, and anyone is welcome to peruse the international newspapers and magazines, listen to their compact discs and records with headphones, or just plant themselves in a cushy, leather easy chair.

Adjacent to Doe on the east side is the **Bancroft Library,** which houses an amazing collection of historical documents, rare books, and old photographs. On permanent display in the administrative office is a gold nugget purported to have started the California Gold Rush when it was discovered on January 24, 1848. The area roughly between Doe and Moffitt Library is currently closed off for construction, making a walk across campus even more convoluted than it used to be. **North Addition,** a mostly underground building which connects the two libraries, opened in 1994 to alleviate traffic problems.

➢ **CAMPANILE AND SURROUNDINGS** • Directly east of Bancroft Library is **Sather Tower,** more commonly known as the Campanile, a 307-foot clock tower modeled after the one in Venice's Piazza San Marco. The carillon is played daily, weekdays at 7:50 AM, noon, and 6 PM, Saturday at noon and 6; and Sunday at 2 for an extended 45 minutes. You can watch the noon performances from the approximately 200-foot observation deck, open Monday–Saturday 10–3:30, Sunday 10–1:45. You reach the deck via an elevator (50¢); if you ask nicely, the elevator operator may stop briefly on the way up and show you the room filled with thousands of bones from all sorts of long-dead animals (those crazy paleontologists). Even if you miss the carillon show, the views from the observation deck are stunning.

Southeast of the Campanile, **South Hall** is the only one of the original university buildings still standing. Walk east toward the hills and you'll pass the **Hearst Mining Building,** a masterpiece of Beaux Arts architecture designed by John Galen Howard. If you continue up this road, you'll eventually run into Piedmont Avenue and the **Hearst Greek Theatre.** This is a good place to catch concerts. Designed by Julia Morgan, it's a replica of the theater in Epidaurus, Greece.

If you're feeling studious (or want to remember what it's like to feel studious), slip into one of the larger lecture halls on campus, like Wheeler Auditorium, Rooms 155 and 145 of Dwinelle Hall, or the Physical Sciences Lecture Hall, and imbibe some wisdom.

Continuing south on Piedmont, you'll pass the **California Memorial Stadium,** home of the Golden Bears football team. At the intersection with Bancroft Way is the **International House,** a dormitory that provides rooms for international students and hosts cultural events. The café in the "I House," as it's called, is a good place to grab a Greek lunch of dolmas, pita, and hummus ($4.25) or an Italian soda ($1). A block away, at Bancroft Way and College Avenue, a small plaza con-

People's Park

It was over this university-owned plot of land just east of Telegraph Avenue, between Haste Street and Dwight Way, that students erupted into protest in 1969, after the university tried to replace the park with a dormitory. Within a few days, thousands of students and locals converged here and refused to leave, preferring instead to celebrate people's power with music and generous doses of LSD. The university reacted by erecting a chain-link fence around the park, and the ensuing protests ended in nasty battles with the police, the death of one man, the dropping of tear gas on Sproul Plaza, and the 17-day occupation of Berkeley by the National Guard. Over the years, the land has become a hangout for the city's growing homeless population, and the university has attempted to regain control of the land several times. In 1991, officials tried to beautify the park and build a few volleyball courts, but many residents saw the effort as a thinly disguised scheme to dislocate the homeless and hippies who call the park home. After several riots, the Berkeley police stood 24-hour guard at the park, mostly to protect a handful of volleyball-loving students from hecklers. The park continues to sport sandy volleyball courts and basketball courts, but many residents would like to see it become a historical landmark.

tains the **Boalt School of Law.** Nearby are **Wurster Hall** (a brutalist monstrosity that houses the architecture and environmental-design schools, a fact many find highly ironic) and **Kroeber Hall,** which contains the Museum of Anthropology (*see* Museums, *below*).

NEIGHBORHOODS

UNIVERSITY AVENUE University Avenue stretches all the way from I–80 and the bay to the U.C. campus, providing easy access to (or a quick escape from) downtown Berkeley and the university. It's not as walker-friendly or trendy as some of Berkeley's other neighborhoods, and you won't find as many people wandering around, but it teems with budget ethnic restaurants, cafés, and foreign clothing stores, as well as car-part places, futon shops, and gas stations. In case you missed the first run of *Brazil* or this year's Festival of Animation, the **U.C. Theater** (*see* Movie Houses, in Chapter 6) shows a diverse range of classics, along with weekly midnight performances of *The Rocky Horror Picture Show.*

Near I–80 at the far end of University, **Takara Sake** (708 Addison St., 1 block south of University Ave., tel. 510/ 540–8250)—one of only three makers of *sake* (Japanese rice wine) in the United States—offers daily tastings and a slide show for free. They're open daily noon–6.

Warm windy days were meant to be spent at the **Berkeley Marina,** on the water a half-mile west of I–80. The views of San Francisco and the Golden Gate Bridge are stunning, and you can even take a free spin around the bay with the **Cal Sailing Club** (west end of University Ave., tel. 510/287–5905). Otherwise, flop down on the grass and watch local kids flying their dragon kites. To reach the marina, take Bus 51 west from Berkeley BART.

NORTH BERKELEY Grad students, professors, and over-30 locals frequent Northside, lending it a calmer and more upscale atmosphere than you'll find on the frenzied Southside. The neighborhoods here are architecturally diverse, with many homes dating from the 1920s, and the streets are worth exploring on foot. Cafés and restaurants line a block-long section of **Euclid Street,** where it dead-ends at the campus. A less student-filled area is the **Gourmet Ghetto,** around Shattuck and Vine streets. Here you'll find specialty stores, bookshops, and hordes of restaurants. Look for that obscure treatise on Nietzsche at **Black Oak Books** (*see* Chapter 3) or just grab a cuppa joe at **Peet's Coffee & Tea** (2124 Vine St., one block east of Shattuck Ave., tel. 510/841–0564) and kick back with the locals who hang out at this colorful corner. You'll find more stores on **Solano Avenue** (go north on Shattuck Avenue, which turns into Solano) including the always-packed and ever-delicious **Zachary's Pizza** (1853 Solano Ave., one block west of The Alameda, tel. 510/525–5950) with their Chicago-style pies running about $13. **The Bone Room** offers live tarantulas, dinosaur bones, and any other living or fossilized paleontological necessities (1569 Solano Ave., at Peralta Ave., tel. 510/526–5252).

For a thrill guaranteed to last a lifetime, get a tattoo; there are several reputable artists in the Berkeley area. The Tattoo Archive (2804 San Pablo Ave., Grayson St., tel. 510/548–5895) abounds with design ideas, while Blue Buddha Tattoo (1959 Ashby Ave., across from Ashby BART, tel. 510/549–9860) offers a more Zen-like tattooing experience.

BERKELEY HILLS The hills east of campus contain some of the area's nicest homes and parks, including the massive Tilden Park (*see* Parks and Gardens, *below*), and offer incredible views of San Francisco and the bay. **Grizzly Peak Boulevard,** a curvy two-lane road leading far up into the hills, is a great place to get an overview of the city and campus. Around sunset, motorcyclists hang out and drink beer in the turnoffs. To reach Grizzly Peak Boulevard, take Centennial Drive, which leads away from California Memorial Stadium (directly east of campus). Along the way on Centennial, you'll pass the woodsy **Berkeley Hills Fire Trail,** popular among joggers and hikers, as well as the U.C. Botanical Garden (*see* Parks and Gardens, *below*) and the Lawrence Hall of Science (*see* Museums, *below*). If you choose to enter the hills by following Euclid Street north from campus instead, you'll pass the Berkeley Rose Garden (*see* Parks and Gardens, *below*).

PARKS AND GARDENS

`TILDEN REGIONAL PARK` The only regional nature area accessible by public transportation, Tilden Park offers more than 2,000 acres of forests and grasslands. Some days, simply driving through the park's winding roads is escape enough from the urban congestion of the lowlands. Follow the signs to **Inspiration Point** for an uncluttered view of two reservoirs and rolling hills where lazy cows graze. If you feel inclined to stay awhile, Tilden offers picnic spots (call 510/636–1684 to reserve a group picnic area) and miles of hiking and biking trails (*see* Chapter 8).

Tilden Nature Area Environmental Education Center (EEC) (tel. 510/525–2233; open Tues.–Sun. 10–5), at the north end of the park, is just completing renovations and now has a new watershed exhibit. EEC sponsors a number of naturalist-led programs; pick up a copy of the *Regional Parks* monthly at the center for more info. If you want to take a nature walk on your own, you can borrow or buy a self-guided trail booklet at the center. For a nice, easy walk (about a mile), take the **Jewel Lake Trail** loop from the EEC office and look out for the salamanders. To make friends with furry or feathered animals, bring green, leafy vegetables to the nearby **Little Farm.**

Rumor has it that Lake Anza is a popular spot for skinny-dipping under a full moon.

Want to escape the heat of the dry hillside? If you don't mind sharing a small lakeside beach with a bunch of toddlers in Mickey Mouse swimsuits, Tilden's **Lake Anza** (tel. 510/848–3028) makes a good swimming hole. The water is clean and the beaches sandy, but you may have to compete with a Girl Scout troop or two for precious towel space on hot summer days. A changing facility is open when the lifeguards are on duty, May 12–October 28, daily 11–6. While the lifeguards are around, you pay $2. At all other times you swim for free and at your own risk.

Other park activities include pony rides ($1.50), a merry-go-round (60¢), a botanical garden of California plants (free), the 18-hole **Tilden Golf Course** (call 510/848–7373 for reservations), and a miniature steam train ($1.25) that takes passengers on a 12-minute ride around the south end of the park. Rides operate on weekends and holidays when school is in session and daily during spring and summer vacations.

To reach the park, take Bus 67 from Berkeley BART to the end of the line. If you're driving, take University Avenue east from I–80 to Oxford Street, go left on Oxford, right on Rose, and left on Spruce to the top of the hill, cross Grizzly Peak Boulevard, make an immediate left on Canon Drive, and follow the signs. The park is closed 10 PM–5 AM.

`BERKELEY ROSE GARDEN/CODORNICES PARK` North of campus on Euclid Avenue, between Bayview Place and Eunice Street, you'll find the multilevel rose garden, an amphitheater with roses, benches aplenty, more roses, and a good view of the bay. Built during the Depression, it's an attractive spot for a picnic or a moment of solitude. If you prefer parks where you can hear children's voices, head across the street to Codornices Park. Here you'll find all the park favorites, including basketball courts, a baseball diamond, swings, grass and sand, and picnic areas, but the star attraction is the long concrete slide. If you're brave, line up behind the kids and swoosh down on a piece of cardboard. At the back of the park, hiking paths lead up the mountain along Codornices Creek. To reach the rose garden and the park, walk north from campus on Euclid Street for 15 minutes, or take Bus 65 from Berkeley BART.

`INDIAN ROCK PARK` If you head north on Shattuck Avenue, the street dead-ends at Indian Rock Road, where you'll see enormous volcanic rock thrusting from the hillside. There was no way for developers to sandblast the monstrosity, so they left it alone; the city eventually transformed the area into a park. The view of Solano Avenue far below, Albany Mill in the distance, and the Marin Headlands is humbling. Rock climbers can practice their sport on the north side of the boulder, though steps are available for the elevationally challenged. The park is open dawn to dusk.

`UNIVERSITY OF CALIFORNIA BOTANICAL GARDEN` The Botanical Garden, used by the university for research and education purposes, is notable for the diversity of its collection—10,000 species of plants from around the world, all neatly labeled for your enlightenment. Its location in sloping Strawberry Canyon, with a variety of exposures, provides habitats diverse enough to grow plants from Southern African deserts and Himalayan forests. The garden is divided into theme areas, and features three indoor exhibits and a slew of paths to explore. If you need a quick breather, sit on a rock along Strawberry Creek in the cool and shady **Asian Garden**, choose a bench near the sunny cactus garden, or lie out on the grass. If you make it to the top of the garden, you'll be rewarded with a view of the bay framed by green. The garden is especially colorful in spring, when the extensive rhododendron collection is in full bloom. Check the Visitor Center for bulletins on various plant seminars or upcoming educational enrichment programs offered to the public, and take home some outdoor plants, for sale at bargain prices. The garden is quiet, and sees primarily older tourists, but that doesn't mean you should miss it. *Centennial Dr., tel. 510/642–3343. Take Bus 65 from Berkeley BART, or take Hill Service Shuttle at Hearst Mining Circle on campus, or walk 15 min uphill from Memorial Stadium. Admission free. Open daily 9–4:30. Tours weekends at 1:30.*

MUSEUMS

PHOEBE HEARST MUSEUM OF ANTHROPOLOGY This is one of Berkeley's best museums, with rotating exhibits that cover everything from ancient America to Neolithic China. Also on display are artifacts used by Ishi, the lone survivor of California's Yahi tribe, who was brought to live at the museum in 1911 after gold miners slaughtered the rest of his tribe. Keep your eyes open for the student art displays lining the halls to the museum entrance—you'll see modern sculpture and painting. *Kroeber Hall, U.C. Berkeley campus, tel. 510/642–3681. Admission: $2, free for students. Open weekdays 10–4:30 (Thurs. until 9), weekends noon–4:30.*

LAWRENCE HALL OF SCIENCE Perched on a cliff overlooking the East Bay, this science museum and research center was founded as a memorial to Ernest O. Lawrence, the university's first Nobel laureate, who created the cyclotron and helped design the atom bomb. Somewhat contradictorily, the exhibits here lean toward the life sciences; most of them are hands-on and geared toward children. On weekends, and daily during summer, you can catch films, lectures, laboratory demonstrations, and planetarium shows. LHS sponsors after-school and summer classes (mostly for the young'uns) and science programs for both children and adults. Recent exhibits have included life-sized mazes, laser shows, and presentations about the brain. Call ahead to find out what's currently showing. On the hillside outside the museum's rear patio, look for the long, slender pipes sticking out of the ground. The 36 harmonized aluminum pipes are part of a wind organ. If you walk among them when the wind is blowing, you'll hear their music; play with the tones by turning one of the six movable pipes. *Centennial Dr., near Grizzly Peak Blvd., tel. 510/642–5132. Drive east (toward the hills) on Hearst St. and follow the signs, or take Bus 18 from Berkeley BART to end (ask driver for a transfer, redeemable at museum for $1 off admission), or take Hill Service Shuttle from Hearst Mining Circle on campus. Admission: $5, $4 students and seniors; planetarium shows $1.50 extra. Open daily 10–5.*

Don't leave Berkeley without seeing a movie at the Pacific Film Archive (see Movie Houses, in Chapter 6), a university-run cinema with an excellent platter of alternative, international, and generally obscure flicks.

UNIVERSITY ART MUSEUM A low-key cement building with balcony galleries, the UAM houses the largest university-owned collection in the country, mostly contemporary European and American works. It features a permanent exhibit of Hans Hoffman paintings donated by the artist. You can wander through the peaceful outdoor sculpture garden for free, and there's a café with slightly pricy but good food. The UAM is also the home of the Pacific Film Archive, on the ground floor. *2626 Bancroft Way, tel. 510/642–0808. Admission: $6, $4 students and seniors, free Thurs. 11–noon and 5–9. U.C. employees and students admitted free. Open Wed.–Sun. 11–5, Thurs. 11–9.*

Oakland

If you expect Oakland to dazzle you like San Francisco, save the $2 BART fare for a cup of coffee. Oakland isn't glitzy or chic; it's a predominantly working-class community where people go about their business and have a hell of a good time on Saturday night. It's the home of the West Coast Blues and, more recently, the Oaktown school of rap and funk, whose practitioners include local artists MC Hammer, Digital Underground, Too Short, Tony Toni Tone, Oaktown 3-5-7, and Tupac Shakur. The city is full of seedy clubs—the sort of places where pool sharks named Shorty and Duke hang out—and folks getting down. Okay, so it's a bit dirty, ugly, and slummy, but in an odd way, that's the root of Oakland's appeal.

Oakland is one of the main shipping ports in the United States and a major West Coast rail terminus. On the down side, the city has had economic hardships, and for years has been notorious for its high crime rate. You'll see a depressing number of drunks and crack addicts on the streets. Though the downtown area has benefited immensely from a slew of urban renewal projects, the streets are still dangerous at night.

In October 1991, a brush fire in the Oakland-Berkeley Hills went out of control, fanned by high winds and years of drought. Hundreds of homes were burned to the ground, several people were killed, and several U.C. professors lost major portions of their life work. The rebuilding continues, under restrictions on the materials people can use and the flora they can plant.

But there's a lot to discover in Oakland. Stroll around **Lake Merritt**, or wander wide-eyed through the untouristy **Chinatown** (downtown between 7th, 10th, Harrison, and Franklin streets). The recently restored **Old Oakland** and the barrios and food stands in **Fruitvale** (near Fruitvale BART) are worth exploring. Afterwards, grab a coffee in the trendier areas around Grand Avenue, College Avenue, or Piedmont Avenue. If the city is fraying your nerves, head for the hills to the east. While many of the multimillion-dollar homes here were destroyed in the October 1991 fire, the area manages to retain the look and feel of the 1930s, when Oakland was mostly a cluster of ranches, farms, and lavish summer estates. The parks here are rugged and undeveloped, and give an idea of what the topography was like when the Ohlone Native Americans first lived here 2,000 years ago. You'll need a car to explore the hills, but most everything else is within reach of a BART station.

Free walking tours are available May 1 to October 31 from the **City of Oakland Walking Tours** (tel. 510/238–3234) promptly at 10 AM; call for current itineraries. For those interested in a historical and architectural perspective, **Oakland Heritage Alliance** (tel. 510/763–9218) offers $6 tours on weekends in July and August. The **Port of Oakland** (tel. 510/272–1200) offers free, 90-minute boat jaunts on Oakland Harbor every month; call ahead to make reservations.

MAJOR SIGHTS

LAKE MERRITT AND LAKESIDE PARK Lake Merritt, a 155-acre oasis in the middle of urban Oakland, is filled with shady trees, meandering paths, and old men feeding the ducks. The lake was created in 1860 when a tidal saltwater lake was dammed. Artificial though it may be, Lake Merritt has the distinction of being the first national wildlife refuge in the United States. **Lakeside Park** (tel. 510/238–3091), on the north shore, has picnic facilities, Japanese and herb gardens, frequent music events, and boat rentals at the **Sailboat House** (tel. 510/444–3807). For $6–$8 an hour (plus a $10 deposit) you can paddle or canoe on the lake; sailboats are $6–$12 an hour (plus $20 deposit). Otherwise, take a tour of the lake aboard the *Merritt Queen,* a replica of a Mississippi River steamboat ($1.50). If you prefer to remain on shore, a 3-mile walking path encircles the lake.

Each June, Lake Merritt is the site of Oakland's **Festival at the Lake** and the **Juneteenth Festival** (*see* Festivals, in Chapter 1). Year-round, it's a nice place for an afternoon nap or stroll and easily reached from downtown. Walk a quarter-mile southwest from the 12th Street or 19th Street BART station, or go directly to the Lake Merritt BART station. Nearby, you can tour the **Camron-Stanford House** (1418 Lakeside Dr., tel. 510/836–1976), the only remaining Victo-

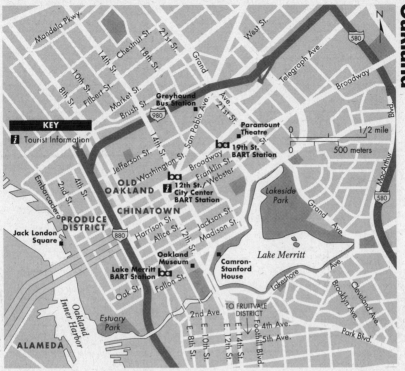

rian building in this formerly bourgeois neighborhood. Tours ($2; free first Sunday of month) are offered Wednesday 11–4 and Sunday 1–5.

JACK LONDON SQUARE Although born in San Francisco, Jack London spent his early years in Oakland before shipping out on the adventures that inspired *The Call of the Wild*, *The Sea Wolf*, and *The Cruise of the Snark*. In an effort to make a buck and draw a Fisherman's Wharf-type crowd, Oakland created Jack London Square, a collection of waterfront boutiques and restaurants on the Oakland Embarcadero, at the end of Broadway west of downtown. In particular, look for **Heinhold's First and Last Chance Saloon** (56 Jack London Sq., tel. 510/

Marching to a Different Beat

Like San Francisco and Berkeley, Oakland has a reputation for being a center of alternative culture and revolutionary politics. The militant and still widely debated Black Panther Party began here. In the 1970s, the city was also headquarters for the Symbionese Liberation Army, who kidnapped Patty Hearst and demanded as part of her ransom that food be distributed to Oakland's poor. Even the city's most famous literary figure, Jack London, was steeped in controversy—an ardent socialist and debauched trouble maker, he wanted California to form its own country (although that's hard to detect in those two novels about dogs).

839–6761), one of Jack's debauched hangouts. Next door is a reassembled Klondike cabin that Jack once spent a winter in—when it was in Alaska. The square is designed to make you spend money, so patronize the specialty shops and upscale eateries in the **Jack London Village** with care. If you're interested in Jack the writer, check out the collection of letters, manuscripts, and photographs in the public library's **Oakland History Room** (125 14th St., tel. 510/238–3222).

OLD OAKLAND As a busy transportation hub and the last stop for the Transcontinental Railway, Old Oakland boomed in the late 1800s. Those years saw the construction of some of the finest Victorian homes in the West. All the houses have been restored and decorated with period furniture, and they're open to the public at seemingly random hours. The neighborhood also contains several interesting art galleries. The member-supported **Pro Arts Gallery** (461 9th St., tel. 510/763–4361), in addition to displaying local artists' works, sponsors **East Bay Open Studios,** in which artists' workspaces are opened to the public for two weekends in June. Old Oakland is between 7th Street, 10th Street, Broadway, and Jefferson Street, about three blocks south of 12th Street BART.

MORMON TEMPLE The Mormons have received a lot of flak for believing the Garden of Eden may be in Mississippi, for building their temples near major freeways to attract distraught souls, for barring women from many church services, and for spending millions of dollars on elaborate, marble-covered temples. Well, come see for yourself. Free tours of the outside only are given daily 9–9. Pick up a souvenir in the visitor center, or watch their 15-minute video about Joseph Smith and the gang. *4770 Lincoln Ave., tel. 510/531–1475. Take Lincoln Ave. exit off Warren Freeway (a.k.a. Hwy. 13), or Bus 46 from Oakland Coliseum BART.*

PARAMOUNT THEATRE First-time visitors to Oakland are generally surprised by the Art Deco architecture around the 19th Street BART station. Some buildings have fallen into disrepair, but the Paramount Theatre, an architectural masterpiece, still hosts dance, music, and film events. If you can't attend a show, you'll still be able to afford the two-hour tour ($1), offered the first and third Saturday of each month. Meet at the box office on 21st Street near Broadway at 10 AM. For concert info, thumb through the free weekly *East Bay Express* or call the box office. *2025 Broadway, tel. 510/465–6400. 1½ blocks north of 19th St. BART.*

MUSEUMS

Oakland has a number of excellent museums. In particular, stop by the **Ebony Museum of Art** (30 Alice St., tel. 510/763–0745), which features work by African and African-American artists. It's open Tuesday–Saturday 11–6, Sunday noon–6, and admission is free. Also free is the **Creative Growth Art Center** (355 24th St., tel. 510/836–2340), which displays arts and crafts by disabled artists. It's open weekdays 10–4, but closes one week out of every five, so call ahead.

CENTER FOR AFRICAN AMERICAN HISTORY AND LIFE The center's Northern California branch focuses on the history of Africans in North America, with a special emphasis on Oakland and the Bay Area. Check out the library and the displays of personal mementos from Bay Area residents. *5606 San Pablo Ave., tel. 510/658–3158. Open Tues.–Fri. 10–5:30. Take Bus 72 north on Broadway from downtown.*

OAKLAND MUSEUM The three permanent collections at the Oakland Museum present the Golden State from the perspectives of art, history, and ecology. For those with California culture shock, the historical hall puts today's multicultural population into context. Its extensive mixed-media exhibits document the rise and fall of the Ohlone people (the region's first inhabitants), and tackle the issues of urban violence and Oakland's subsequent deterioration. Other exhibits include Spanish-era artifacts, a fire truck that battled San Francisco's 1906 fire, and some hokey relics from the 1967 "Summer of Love." The hall of natural sciences offers a simulated walk through the state's eight biotic zones and a view of the plants and animals of each. The changing shows in the art hall feature work by California artists. Be sure to visit the museum's terraced gardens and the nearby Estuary Park, a 22-acre sculpture garden. *1000 Oak St., tel. 510/238–3401. 1 block east of Lake Merritt BART. Admission: $4, $2 students. Open Wed.–Sat. 10–5, Sun. noon–7. Wheelchair access.*

CHEAP THRILLS

When sitting under a shady tree sounds like nirvana, head to the **Mountain View Cemetery,** a peaceful place to get your emotional and metaphysical bearings. Interspersed among the acres of tombstones are dozens of gaudy chapels and morbid funerary pyramids—the final garish homes of people like Ghirardelli and Crocker (of Crocker Bank). Bus 59 from downtown will drop you a block away. When you're ready to rejoin the living, head down Piedmont Avenue (which intersects the south boundary of the cemetery) for a nice lunch, a new dress, or a stiff drink. *5000 Piedmont Ave., tel. 510/658–2588. Gates open weekdays 8–4:30, weekends 10–4.*

Locals get a kick out of wandering around at 3 AM in the **Produce District** (between Broadway, Webster, 2nd, and 3rd streets, a block up from Jack London Square) to watch the vendors setting up shop. It's reassuring to see all this excitement in the wee hours of the morning, when most of Oakland looks like a ghost town. After you've had your fill, walk down to the 24-hour **Jack London Café** (on Embarcadero and Broadway) for some pancakes.

If you're in a playfully immature kinda mood and have the requisite child companion, visit **Children's Fairyland,** where you can climb around on cool scenes from children's stories and nursery rhymes. It's located on the north shore of Lake Merritt (*see above*). After you're finished horsing around, rent a miniature toy paddle boat for a few bucks and ride around on the lake; boat houses are on the north and west sides of Lake Merritt.

Marin County

Just across the Golden Gate Bridge, Marin is the state's richest county, an upscale playground for children old enough to remember Woodstock. Everywhere you turn you'll see an odd combination of hippie ideals and yuppie wealth. Expensive estates are buffered by ragged log cabins, and Porsches and BMWs park next to aging Volvo station wagons and VW vans.

The reason so many '60s-refugees-turned-'80s-success-stories want to live here—and the reason you'll want to visit despite the price tag—is Marin's incredible natural beauty. The county encompasses stunning ocean views, thick redwood forests, and rural back roads tempered by sheep ranches and country farms. You could spend a lifetime hiking in Muir Woods and the Point Reyes National Seashore, and it's hard to act blasé about the view from **Route 1,** no matter how many times you've driven the road.

Grateful Dead member Jerry Garcia, filmmaker George Lucas, and out-there musician Todd Rundgren are a few of the cultural heroes who live in Marin County.

Marin's upscale, touristed bayside towns, like Tiburon and Sausalito, are tougher for the young, budget-conscious visitor to love. You'll have to pick your way through an ostentatious show of wealth to find a cheap organic grocery store where you can stock up on supplies for your hike, an isolated, sunny field hospitable to hackysack players, and an unpretentious restaurant that serves reasonably priced seafood. But these things do exist. Many of Marin's best sights are well off the beaten path, but even the most rural corners are little more than two hours from San Francisco (except during rush hour, when it can take nearly an hour just to cross the bridge).

Marin Headlands

For a quick taste of what Marin County has to offer nature freaks, cross the Golden Gate Bridge, exit at Alexander Avenue, and drive up Conzelman Road to the Marin Headlands. Perched on a small bluff overlooking San Francisco Bay and the Pacific Ocean, the undeveloped, 1,000-acre headlands are a great place to snap a few photos or while away an afternoon. Thick fog often whips across the headlands, obscuring everything but the tips of the Golden Gate Bridge; but on a sunny day, the views of downtown San Francisco, the East Bay, and Point Reyes to the north are stunning. Hundreds of hiking and biking trails meander along the wind-beaten hills and cliffs (*see Hiking, in Chapter 8*).

The headlands were used as a military camp in the late 19th century, and during World War II emplacements were dug for huge 16-inch naval guns to protect the approaches to the bay. The guns were never installed, but you can still see the bunkers. Fortunately, the army handed the land over to the Golden Gate National Recreation Area, and not to eager developers. Most weekends—especially in summer—the area crawls with locals, but the farther north you hike, the fewer people you'll encounter. The unmarked coastal cliff trail is one of the most scenic and least traveled; drive all the way through the headlands to the **Marin Headlands Visitor Center** (tel. 415/331–1540) at Field and Bunker roads, walk as far out to the ocean as possible, and then turn north and look for a small dirt path. It ends 1½ miles farther on.

Sausalito

Only a few miles north of San Francisco, Sausalito flourished during the 1880s and '90s as a small whaling town, infamous for its saloons, gambling dens, and bordellos. It had a tough reputation, as the sort of place where sailors and riffraff could get drunk and cause trouble on the docks. Even after it became suburbanized in the 1940s, the town continued to attract an offbeat and raffish element, becoming a well-known artists' colony. Over the years, however, Sausalito's wharf rats have been replaced by lawyers and investment bankers, and this is now a bland, wealthy resort town, popular with yachters and San Francisco's upwardly mobile crowd. If you have unlimited time to explore the Bay Area, Sausalito is definitely worth a gander, but don't go out of your way. Parking is next to impossible, shops and restaurants are shockingly expensive, and you have to dodge camera-toting tourists who fill the sidewalks and streets.

Bridgeway is Sausalito's main thoroughfare, bordered on one side by waterfront restaurants and the bay, on the other by shops hawking pricey antiques or pastel-colored T-shirts and pelican paperweights. At the south end of Bridgeway, a 10-minute walk from the center of town, lies the Sausalito Ferry Terminal, where the commuter boat from San Francisco docks (*see* Getting In, Out, and Around by Ferry, in Chapter 1). Farther south—near the end of Bridgeway at Richardson Street—is Sausalito's oldest restaurant, originally known as **Valhalla.** Built in 1893, it was used as a backdrop in the classic 1940s film *The Lady from Shanghai.* Today it's just a Chart House restaurant with fantastic views and expensive (about $25) meals.

During the Great Depression, a local grocer graciously honored his customers' credit, preventing countless Sausalito residents from going hungry. Today, Yee Tock Chee Park stands as a monument to him, where Bridgeway meets the Bay.

At the four-story **Village Fair** (777 Bridgeway), a warehouse has been converted into one of the most attractive shopping malls around, complete with a little waterfall and more potted plants than you've ever seen in your life. You won't find too many bargains in the 30 or so stores here, which mostly sell gourmet cookware, expensive clothing, and useless collectibles. You can eat at the cheap **Village Delites** snack bar on the third floor, sitting in the flowery atrium, or head up to the top floor to **Café Sausalito** (tel. 415/332-6579), where you'll find semi-affordable fare (coffee $1.50, sandwiches about $5) and a phenomenal view of San Francisco and Angel Island.

About a mile north on Bridgeway, look for the **Bay Model,** an enormous working model of San Francisco Bay and the Sacramento–San Joaquin Delta. Don't expect a cute little replica of Coit Tower—this is strictly a scientific tool, used by the U.S. Army Corps of Engineers to study the tides and other forces affecting the bay. The detail of the model is amazing, right down to ebbing tides, actual South Bay mud flats, and rivers that flow at one-tenth of their actual velocity. *2100 Bridgeway, tel. 415/332-3871. Admission free. Open Tues.–Sat. 9–4.*

Tiburon and Angel Island

Some young urbanites come to Tiburon with picnic baskets in hand, and set out their spread on the harborfront lawns at the tip of the peninsula. Others dock their boats at the harbor and head to one of the many waterside cafés and restaurants. Do both these things and you'll have just about exhausted the possibilities for an afternoon in Tiburon. The atmosphere is relaxed and the views of Angel Island and San Francisco are great, but the small cluster of gift shops and pricey boutiques housed in wooden shingle buildings along the waterfront will seem cutesy and cloying before long. To rise above the strip of tourist shops on Main Street (both literally and figuratively), head up the hill to **Old St. Hilary's Historic Preserve,** which stands in a field of wildflowers on a lonely perch above town. The white, wooden Victorian church is run by the Landmarks Society as a historical and botanical museum. *Esperanza and Alemany Sts., tel. 415/435–1853. Admission free. Open Wed. and Sun. 1–4.*

If Tiburon is about to quaint you to death, hop a ferry to **Angel Island,** about a 15-minute ride. Here you can explore sandy beaches, eucalyptus groves, and old military installations (across Raccoon Straits), all crammed into a tiny state park within spitting distance of the Golden Gate Bridge. **Ayala Cove,** the area around the ferry landing, is congested with picnickers taking advantage of tables and barbecue grills; and the 5-mile perimeter road that rings the island, offering access to plenty of scenic and historic sites, is heavily traveled (for more info, *see* Hiking, in Chapter 8). But it's easy to escape the crowds. For the ultimate isolated picnic, schlep your stuff about a mile from Ayala Cove to **Camp Reynolds,** which functioned as an army camp from the Civil War to World War II. Plenty of people linger at the Commanding Officer's House along the road, but about a quarter mile down past the old army barracks at the water's edge you'll find some isolated picnic tables and an outstanding close-up view of the Golden Gate Bridge.

On the other side of the island is **Immigration Station,** where immigrants (mostly Asian) were detained when trying to enter the United States between 1910 and 1940. A few poems written by despairing immigrants are still etched into the walls. A **visitor information center** at Ayala Cove (tel. 415/435–1915) distributes leaflets about the island for about a quarter each.

Ferries (415/435–2131) leave for Angel Island from Tiburon's Main Street Pier at 10, 11, 1, and 3 on summer weekdays, and every hour from 10 to 5 on summer weekends. Boats depart from Angel Island 20 minutes after each boat docks. Round-trip fares are $5, plus $1 for bicycles (no cars). Schedules are subject to change, so call ahead for the latest. Ferries also leave from Fisherman's Wharf in summer. Those with their own aquatic transportation can dock at the island's boat slips for $5 a day, $9 overnight. For more information on hiking Angel Island, *see* Chapter 8.

Mill Valley

If you're headed to Route 1 and the coast, you'll pass through Mill Valley as soon as you get off U.S. 101 (at the Stinson Beach/Rte. 1 exit). This is a community of mansions and millionaires set amid the California redwoods—a sleepy town where people have paid dearly for their solitude and want to keep it that way. There aren't any official tourist sights, but a drive through the hills and forested canyons will explain why this is some of the Bay Area's most coveted real estate. If you want a break from driving, turn off on **Tennessee Valley Road** (*see* Hiking, in Chapter 8)—look for the road sign just before you get into town from the freeway. The road ends in a parking lot, from which you can hike or bike the dirt path that gently descends to the beach where, in 1853, the steamship *Tennessee* wrecked in dangerous surf.

In Mill Valley itself, stop by the **Depot Bookstore and Café** (*see* Chapter 5) for an espresso, and browse through the adjoining bookstore. If you're anxious to get an early start on the day, **Mama's Royal Café** (*see* Chapter 4) can fuel you up with a fine breakfast. After sunset, locals mosey over to the **Sweetwater** (*see* Chapter 6), where on any given night bluesman Roy Rogers or Huey Lewis might show up to jam. For a different side of the music scene, check out **Village Music** (9 E. Blithedale Ave., at Throckmorton Ave., tel. 415/388–7400). John Goddard has run the record shop, which specializes almost exclusively in vinyl, for over 25 years. The store has become a landmark on the international music map, attracting many big-name customers. A local waiter boasts of having run into Mick Jagger outside Village Music one day. No guarantees of similar brushes with greatness, but the store's well worth a visit if only to look at the memorabilia papering the walls.

San Rafael

Unassuming San Rafael, set between the foot of Mt. Tamalpais and San Rafael Hill, is ignored by most Bay Area residents. Maybe it would attract more day-trippers from foggy San Francisco if people realized it's almost always a few degrees warmer here than elsewhere in the Bay Area. In fact, that's exactly why the town was founded in the first place. In 1817, when Native Americans at San Francisco's Mission Dolores started dying at an alarming rate, missionaries built a hospital here so they could receive care in a more hospitable climate. The original buildings of the Mission San Rafael Archangel were torn down in the 1870s, but a replica of the **chapel** (5th and A Sts.), built of stuccoed concrete instead of the original adobe, now sits next to a gift shop selling histories of the mission and Catholic kitsch. If you drive up San Rafael Hill from the chapel, you'll see some of Marin County's ubiquitous million-dollar homes. A block away from the chapel, **4th Street** is the town's main drag, lined with cafés, some interesting used bookstores, and a large contingent of department stores. Far from thrilling, it's nonetheless a good place for an afternoon stroll and brunch with the Sunday paper.

Fourth Street is so quintessentially American that George Lucas used it as a backdrop for some scenes in his film "American Graffiti." Just off 4th Street is Lucas Road, where the director's studio Industrial Light and Magic lies.

North of downtown—take North San Pedro Road exit off U.S. 101—the enormous pink and blue **Marin Civic Center** (3501 Civic Center Dr., tel. 415/499–7407) has guided tours of its impressive complex, designed by architect Frank Lloyd Wright. Concerned with preserving the natural contours of the site, Wright integrated the buildings into the surrounding landscape, setting them around, in, and under three principal hillocks. The complex looks a lot like a bloated whale from the outside, but the inside has been heralded as one of the most functional and offbeat office spaces ever conceived. Tours are available by reservation, and there's a well-stocked information kiosk in the lobby (open weekdays 8–6) for walk-in visitors. For information on dance and drama performances in the adjoining theater, call 415/472–3500.

If you're tired of suburbia, drive 4 miles east on San Pedro Road to **China Camp State Park,** a beautiful 1,600-acre wilderness area on the fringe of civilization. Most people are surprised to find such a pristine slice of nature so close to a big city, and somehow it has remained undeveloped and unpublicized. Remnants of an old Chinese fishing village are still visible, and the oak knolls and saltwater marshes are great for hiking and camping (*see* Chapter 7). You pay about $3 in day-use fees to park your car most places in the camp. A parking lot at China Camp Point accesses a 5-mile hike along the well-marked **Shoreline Trail.** The **Bay View Trail,** a steeper schlep but wonderfully uncrowded, is a favorite of park rangers. Pick up a map marked with all the trails from the ranger station about halfway between the campground entrance and China Camp Point.

Muir Woods and Mt. Tamalpais

MUIR WOODS NATIONAL MONUMENT Judging from the crowded parking lot and tacky gift shop, the Muir Woods National Monument looks like just another overtouristed attraction to be avoided. This 550-acre park, however, contains one of the most impressive groves of redwoods in the world, some more than 250 feet tall and over 800 years old. It's crowded, to be sure, and a favorite destination of the older set, but you can find rugged, unpopulated trails that meander along cool, fern-filled ridges high above the clogged canyon. The **Panoramic Trail,** which is rarely crowded and begins just beyond the gift shop, leads 1½ miles to **Fern Creek Trail,** and returns to the gift shop after an easy mile-long descent. Along the way, you'll pass the **Bohemian** and **Cathedral groves,** two of the park's most impressive stands of redwoods (for more trail recommendations, *see* Hiking, in Chapter 8). To really avoid the camera-toting throngs, try to visit on a weekday morning, or even a rainy day.

Neither picnicking nor camping is allowed in the park, but snacks are available at the gift shop, along with every type of redwood souvenir imaginable. The **visitor center** (tel. 415/388–2595) organizes free nature walks through the woods; call for current schedules. The weather here is usually cool and often damp, so dress warmly. The woods lie off U.S. 101, 17 miles north of San Francisco. Take the Stinson Beach/Route 1 exit and follow signs. The monument is open daily 8 AM–sunset, and parking is free.

MUIR BEACH If you stick to Route 1 instead of following the turnoff to Muir Woods, you come to **Muir Beach,** a quiet strip of sand cluttered with oddly shaped pieces of driftwood and hundreds of tidal pools. Muir Beach was the site of the first coastal settlement north of San Francisco. The strikingly scenic beach attracts folks looking to get away and relax—not the Budweiser and volleyball crowd you'll find at Stinson Beach, 6 miles farther on.

If you really want to get a feel for Marin's landscape, park your car at Muir Beach and hike the **Coastal Trail** (see Hiking, in Chapter 8), which leads up a steep hill overlooking the ocean and crawls around a series of deserted coves and valleys. Return the same way and reward yourself with a pint of Guinness in front of the fire at the **Pelican Inn** (Rte. 1 at Muir Beach, tel. 415/383–6000 or 415/383–6005). The restaurant serves everything from fish-and-chips ($8) to prime rib ($17) and Yorkshire pudding ($2), along with a healthy sampling of British ales and bitters. There's a stone fireplace in the wood-paneled dining room and a dart board in the adjoining pub. Upstairs are six Tudor-style rooms ($155 a night) filled with antiques and canopied beds—about as atmospheric and rustic as they come. Ask the innkeeper about renting horses from the nearby stables: You can arrange moonlight gallops along the beach.

Not to belittle the beauty of Muir Woods, but it's a place you could take your grandma (and many people do). When you want to see Marin at its most powerful, go to the source—Mt. Tamalpais.

MT. TAMALPAIS STATE PARK Muir Woods is actually connected to the breathtaking Mt. Tamalpais near sea level on the eastern slope, but to reach the mountain you must follow separate signs from Route 1. The best months to visit are February through May, when wildflowers are in bloom (the California poppy blooms in March and the Marin iris in April). A good starting point for your exploration is the **Pantoll Ranger Station** (tel. 415/388–2070), where you can buy a 50¢ topographic map of Mt. Tam with all the trails and roads clearly shown. Mountain biking is big here (see Chapter 8), and the map distinguishes the fire trails (where biking is allowed) from the walking trails (where biking nets you a fat $100-plus fine). One beautiful and popular hike, the 2-mile **Steep Ravine Trail** (see Hiking, in Chapter 8), starts from the Pantoll station. Parking is $5 in the Pantoll parking lot, but you can park for free anywhere along the road—just make sure you're completely outside the white sideline. The place is packed on weekends, so you'll have trouble parking if you're not there before noon. You can camp at one of Pantoll's 15 walk-in sites ($14) or one hike-and-bike site ($3 per person), or head for the more primitive **Steep Ravine** campground and cabins off Route 1 (see Chapter 7).

The **summit** of Mt. Tam can be reached by car (look for the turnoff opposite Pantoll station) and the gates are open dawn to dusk. Unfortunately, the military owned the summit until recently

The Towering Legacy of John Muir

One hundred fifty million years ago, redwood trees grew throughout the United States. Today, the sequoia sempervirens can be found only in a narrow coastal belt that stretches from Monterey to Oregon. Muir Woods has been preserved by the federal government since 1908, primarily as a result of John Muir's campaign to save old-growth forests from destruction. His response: "This is the best tree-lover's monument that could be found in all of the forests of the world. Saving these woods from the axe and saw is in many ways the most notable service to God and man I have heard of since my forest wandering began."

and left the kind of squat buildings and strange towers only the military seems to use. According to one park aide, there are several full-size bowling alleys in one of the buildings. Try not to let the structures taint your view (and no, you can't have a game). Also near the summit is the **Mountain Theater,** where every summer for six consecutive Sundays a play or musical is produced. It's a landmark of the local scene and worth a look if you're around. Ask at the Pantoll station for performance and ticket information, or call 415/383–1100.

Stinson Beach

Six treacherous miles north of Muir Beach on Route 1 lies Stinson Beach, one of the most popular coastal towns in Northern California. It's loaded with rickety wooden houses and friendly general stores, and its beach—the longest in Marin County—has a beach-bum and barbecue appeal that's hard to find north of Santa Cruz. Despite Stinson's isolated location, the chilly water temperatures, and the threat of sharks lurking offshore, hordes of surfers and sun worshipers descend every weekend upon this town of 1,200. Even if you're not planning to surf or swim, the 20-minute (10-mile) drive from Muir Woods to Stinson, past towering cliffs and jagged granite peaks, is incredible. Traffic can be a problem on summer weekends, but there are plenty of scenic overlooks along the way to cushion the blow of bumper-to-bumper traffic.

The **Livewater Stinson Beach Surfshop** (3450 Rte. 1, tel. 415/868–0333) rents body boards ($8 a day), wet suits ($10 a day), and surfboards ($25 a day) year-round; just look for the building with a surfboard on the roof. If you're hungry, stop off at the **Parkside Café** (43 Arenal St., tel. 415/868–1272), with good burgers at the cheapest prices in town ($5–$6). Turn left at the stop sign on Route 1 and you'll run right into it. You can enjoy your meal at the park next door. You might also stop in to browse through the eclectic offerings at **Stinson Beach Books** (3455 Rte. 1, tel. 415/868–0700).

Along Bolinas Lagoon, just north of Stinson on Route 1, you'll find the **Audubon Canyon Ranch** (tel. 415/868–9244). On weekends between mid-March and mid-July, this 1,000-acre bird sanctuary and ranch (and its 10 or so hiking trails) are open to the public from 10 to 4, offering bird lovers the chance to watch blue herons and egrets up close. There's a small museum ("donation" required) with geological and natural-history displays, a bookstore, gift shop, and a picnic area.

For a different slice of nature, walk down to **Red Rocks Beach** (look for the pullout a few miles south of Stinson), where, during extremely low tides, caves containing hot springs are revealed. Be prepared—the locals are likely to be protective of their turf and entirely naked. Even when the caves are concealed by water, the beach is peopled by nudists. Leave your inhibitions in the car.

Bolinas

A few miles north of the Audubon Canyon Ranch (*see above*), at the end of an unmarked road running west from Route 1 (the first left you can make after circling the estuary), lies Bolinas, a town dedicated to discouraging tourism. Locals may not actually dislike the day and weekend trippers who cruise up and down Route 1 looking for quaint burgs to visit, but they loathe the idea of tacky Sausalito-style development. If you breeze into town to wander Main Street and do some shopping, you'll feel tolerated at best—rarely, if ever, welcome. You might brave the cold stares to witness the town's **Fourth of July** festivities, which have included outrageous parades and a tug-of-war with Stinson Beach (the loser ended up in the muddy mouth of the estuary between the two towns). One local described Bolinas as the "Zen-purity, earth-magnet, long-hair, free-to-do-what-you-want place to be, man," but a walk past the town's million-dollar homes makes you wonder how much residents really champion the ideals of the '60s.

Despite the elitism, you'll still find a few VW buses and bearded hippies strumming their guitars on street corners. The **Bolinas People's Store** (14 Wharf Rd., at Brighton Ave., tel. 415/868–1433) is famous for its fresh, high-quality local produce, grown by the same sweaty hippies who once gave Bolinas so much of its character. The only nightlife in town is **Smiley's**

Schooner Saloon (41 Wharf Rd., at Brighton Ave., tel. 415/868–1311). Huddled around the pool table and jukebox you'll find an odd combination of the suit-and-tie professional and the tie-dyed alternative fringe. For a bite to eat, go to the **Bolinas Bay Bakery and Café** (20 Wharf Rd., at Brighton Ave., tel. 415/868–0211), which offers fresh baked goods, pasta salads, and pizzas. Many items feature locally grown organic ingredients.

If the smell of patchouli is fraying your nerves, take Mesa Road 4½ miles north to the **Point Reyes Bird Observatory** (tel. 415/868–0655), a sanctuary that harbors 225 species of birds. It's open year-round, and admission is free. On your way, make the mile-long detour to **Duxberry Reef**, a peaceful breaker that's dotted with hundreds of tidal pools. To get there, go left on Overlook Drive and left again on Elm Avenue. For hikes in this area, *see* Hiking, in Chapter 8.

Point Reyes National Seashore

Exploring the Point Reyes National Seashore—a 70,000-acre jumble of marshes, ferocious cliffs, and undisturbed beaches—you'll feel a lot farther than 30 miles away from San Francisco. With its lush grazing land and rambling farms, Point Reyes could easily pass for the Scottish Highlands or western Ireland—minus the pubs. Even though it's isolated, Point Reyes is a manageable day trip from San Francisco, a drive of about 1½ hours each way. There are hundreds of hiking trails on the peninsula (*see* Hiking, in Chapter 8) and, if you want to spend the night, four backpackers-only campgrounds and an excellent hostel (*see* Chapter 7).

Twelve miles north of Bolinas on Route 1, you'll pass the block-long town of Olema; look for a sign marking the turnoff for Point Reyes at the end of the block of stores, and head for the **Point Reyes Visitor Information Center** (tel. 415/663–1092). This is the best place to begin your exploration; you can sign up for ranger-led interpretive hikes or get trail maps and camping permits. A short walk away, look for the reconstructed **Miwok Indian Village**, built on the ruins of a 400-year-old Miwok farming settlement. Also nearby is the **Bear Valley Trail**, a lightly traveled 4-mile hike that wanders through the woods and down to a secluded beach. If you can't make it to Point Reyes Lighthouse (*see below*), the Bear Valley Trail offers a good overview of the peninsula.

Two miles farther on, you'll pass through the quiet town of **Inverness**, an offbeat place with Czech restaurants and architecture. Coming across one of its oddly colored, intricately carved wooden houses can be somewhat disorienting after miles of trees and uncluttered coast, but its East European flavor is definitely real. In 1935, after a freighter ran aground in San Francisco Bay, a number of its Czech deckhands jumped ship and ended up here. Since then, dozens of Czech families have settled in Inverness, bringing both their culture and their cuisine. For some of the best dumplings this side of Prague, head to **Vladimir's** (12785 Sir Francis Drake Blvd., Inverness, tel. 415/669–1021), one of the town's pricey but excellent Czech restaurants. A meal costs around $15, and the restaurant's open Tuesday–Sunday.

West of Inverness, at the end of Sir Francis Drake Boulevard, lies a massive stretch of white sand known as **Drake's Beach**. It's often windy here and too rough for swimming (oh yeah— sharks swim offshore, too), but the beach is great for a relaxing day in the sun. Supposedly, Sir Francis himself landed here on his world tour; hence the name. Check with the visitor center for current regulations; if they give the okay, there's plenty of driftwood on the beach for an early evening campfire.

A quarter mile north of Drake's Beach, a sign directs you to the **Point Reyes Lighthouse** (tel. 415/669–1534) 6 miles to the west. It's open Thursday–Monday 10–4:30, and admission is free. Go even if you hate lighthouses; the best part of the trip is the drive itself, which winds through some downright incredible scenery. From the small parking lot, a steep trail leads down to the lighthouse, and a dozen or so trails are etched into the surrounding cliffs. If it's really clear you should be able to see San Francisco, but usually the thick fog provides little visibility. The hike to **Chimney Rock**, three-quarters of a mile away, is one of the most scenic; look for the trailhead in the parking lot.

To reach Point Reyes from San Francisco, take U.S. 101 north and cross the Golden Gate Bridge. If speed is more important than scenery, exit at Sir Francis Drake Boulevard and follow it west for 21 miles to the coast. Eventually, you'll end up 2 miles north of Olema on Route 1. Otherwise, take the Stinson Beach/Route 1 exit and enjoy the curvy, 29-mile scenic drive along the coast. On weekends, Golden Gate Transit can take you here by bus, but it's a long, complicated journey (*see* Getting In, Out, and Around, in Chapter 1).

There aren't too many places to eat in Point Reyes, so stock up in San Francisco or at the **Bovine Bakery** (11315 Rte. 1, 2 mi north of Olema, tel. 415/663–9420). They have excellent, reasonably priced sandwiches, pastries, and breads—the perfect makings for a picnic. The most popular stop, however, is Inverness's **Perry's Delicatessen** (12301 Sir Francis Drake Blvd., near Vallejo Ave., tel. 415/663–1491). For under $6, you can brown bag one of their shrimp or crab sandwiches and a freshly made garden salad. Also in Inverness is the **Gray Whale Inn** (12781 Sir Francis Drake Blvd., tel. 415/669–1244), a good pit stop for home-style pizzas, pastries, sandwiches, coffee, and beer. It's more expensive than Perry's, but the sunny patio is a good place to watch day fade into night.

The South Bay

A wannabe philosopher once said that middle America begins but a few miles away from San Francisco. Indeed, just south of the San Francisco International Airport, you'll notice a subtle change in scenery and ambience. It doesn't exactly hit you over the head, but as you travel south you'll see a rapid proliferation of shopping malls, industrial parks, tract homes, and brightly lit clusters of fast-food restaurants. Before you know it, the winding streets and frenetic energy of San Francisco seem miles away—you've entered suburbia. But life does not end here, all evidence to the contrary notwithstanding. The region has quite a few interesting, amusing, or just plain weird attractions that San Francisco snobs thoroughly underrate (or don't know about). A number of cities, including Palo Alto—home to the acclaimed Stanford University—make for easy day trips from San Francisco.

Best of all, there's **Route 1** and the secluded San Mateo County Coast—over 75 miles of winding shoreline and gently undulating hills that seem a world away from the overdeveloped inland communities. Along the highway are long, sandy beaches, frequently devoid of any life aside from the local sea lions and pigeons; small towns just beginning to awaken to their potential as tourist destinations; and redwood groves filled with great hiking trails. The only drawback to this part of the Bay Area is the weather. Though hilly inland areas like La Honda and Pescadero are nearly always warm in spring and fall, and hot (but not oppressively so) in summer, the beaches more often than not are windswept and chilly—better suited for a brisk walk than an afternoon of sunbathing. The quickest way to reach the northern end of the San Mateo County Coast from San Francisco is to follow I–280 south to Route 1; it'll only take 10–15 minutes to reach Pacifica from downtown.

Palo Alto

Palo Alto, about 30 miles south of San Francisco, is mostly known as the town where Stanford University was built, and it's certainly worth the drive just to check out the beautiful, 8,200-acre campus. However, contrary to popular Bay Area opinion, the town of Palo Alto itself has some cultural attractions worth a look, as well as a cute, if overpriced, downtown area. **University Avenue** is Palo Alto's main drag; if you take it all the way west past El Camino Real it'll metamorphose into **Palm Drive**, Stanford's entrance and main thoroughfare. University Avenue and its side streets are loaded with restaurants, music shops, galleries, boutiques, and bookstores. All are disappointingly upscale for a student shopping district, but at least the streets are punctuated by pleasant little plazas with benches and plants.

The huge, sprawling campus itself is best explored by bike, and the biking is even better in the foothills west of the university. For rentals, try **Bike Connection,** which can get you rolling on a mountain bike for $20 or a three-speed for $15. You must leave a deposit equal to the cost of the bike, either in cash (yeah, right), by check, or by credit card. *2086 El Camino Real, about 1 mi south of University Ave., tel. 415/424–8034. Open daily 10–8.*

STANFORD UNIVERSITY If you're curious to see what a $20,000-a-year education looks like, swing through the Stanford campus and check out the sights. Nicknamed "The Farm" because the land was once a stud farm (that's certainly not the case anymore), Stanford consists of look-alike, mustard-colored buildings that combine Romanesque squatness with the ranchy feel of a Spanish mission, giving the campus an austere and refined flavor.

From downtown, enter campus along the aptly named Palm Drive, which will take you to the **quad,** the heart of campus and a popular hangout with students. You can pick up free maps or take a guided walking tour from the **information office** here. The plaza is dominated by the spritely, Romanesque **Memorial Church,** finally open again after years of repairs following the 1989 earthquake. At the entrance to the quad, the grassy **Memorial Court** has a couple of Auguste Rodin statues—dedicated to Stanford men who died for their country—that depict some 14th-century English martyrs "at the moment of painful departure from their families and other citizens." Thrusting mightily into the sky just to the south is the 280-foot **Hoover Tower,** home of the ultra-conservative Hoover Institution for the Study of War, Revolution, and Peace. To get the classic view of campus and parts of Palo Alto, climb up to the tower's observation deck, which offers an excellent 360° vista.

Like many colleges these days, Stanford prides itself on tolerance and diversity, but last year a group of students destroyed a campus gay-pride statue, drawing the ire of leftists and the Bay Area's sizable gay community.

For now, the **Rodin Sculpture Garden** is as close as you'll get to **Stanford's Museum of Art,** seriously damaged in the 1989 earthquake and closed until at least June 1995. The 20 or so works by French sculptor Auguste Rodin (1840–1917) are clustered in a small area next to the museum. Most pieces depict nudes in various stages of pensiveness, ecstasy, or anguish. Check out the particularly intense Gates of Hell; the giant iron doors are the scene of lots of wild action. Descriptive tours are given at 2 PM Wednesday and on weekends; call for details. *Museum Way and Lomita Dr., tel. 415/723-3469. Look for signs about halfway up Palm Dr.*

STANFORD LINEAR ACCELERATOR Even if you're only vaguely interested in science, make the trek up Sand Hill Road (west from campus toward I–280) to see this masterpiece of modern ingenuity. The 2-mile-long atom smasher is amazing—thousands of house-size machines, dials, diodes, and scientists who get excited when you mention n-orbits and electrons. Reserve space in advance for the free two-hour tour, which includes a slide show and lecture (days and times vary); it's geared toward lay people and is extremely interesting. *2575 Sand Hill Rd., at Wickham Pl., Menlo Park, tel. 415/926-2204. From I–280 south take the Sand Hill Rd. exit toward Stanford.*

BARBIE HALL OF FAME "Barbie mimics society; whatever we've done, she's done," says Evelyn Burkhalter, founder of the Barbie Hall of Fame. She's put together the largest collection of Barbie dolls on public display in the world, with 16,000 of the plastic bombshells in resi-

When People Die, They Move to the Suburbs

If you're driving on I–280 down to Palo Alto, you'll pass by the small city of Colma, a modern-day necropolis filled with cemeteries and macabre graveyard art. In 1914, San Francisco's mayor ordered that all cemeteries relocate their occupants to Colma, since the city needed its land for its more active residents. Since then, nobody's been buried within San Francisco's city limits. The Colma Town Hall (1198 El Camino Real, at Serramonte Blvd., tel. 415/997-8300) offers a self-guided tour of the city's cemeteries ($2.50), from the prestigious Cypress Lawn to the eerie Pet's Rest, littered with flea collars and dog toys. Look for the graves of Dodge City's Wyatt Earp and former Phillie outfielder Lefty O'Doul.

dence. Evelyn says that Barbie has changed constantly and considerably over the years, and indeed, just about every fashion and lifestyle trend of the past few decades can be seen in these halls. Don't miss the infamous "talking-math Barbie," which says "math is *so hard*"— Mattel took a lot of heat from feminists for that one. *433 Waverly St., just off University Ave. in Palo Alto, tel. 415/326–5841. Admission: $4. Open Tues.–Fri. 1:30–4:30, Sat. 10 AM–noon and 1:30–4:30.*

NEAR PALO ALTO

NASA AMES RESEARCH CENTER At Moffett Field in Mountain View (about 5 miles southeast of Palo Alto), this 140-acre research center, devoted to the design of all types of flying machines, is a true technological trip. You can visit the **NASA Visitor's Center Museum** (open weekdays 8–4:30), which showcases aviation and space-flight paraphernalia, but the research facility itself is normally closed to the general public. The real score is to call ahead and sign up for one of the two or three escorted tours of the main plant they offer each week (days and times vary). Depending on what's available that day for snooping, the two-hour free tour may take you around flight simulators, design centers, retired research crafts, or construction hangars. *Tel. 415/604–6274. From U.S. 101, take Moffett Field exit, follow the arrow, turn left at intersection, and head toward the space shuttle.*

GREAT AMERICA If you've got the urge to spin around until you feel nauseated, eat gooey food, and buy monstrous pairs of sunglasses, head to this crayola-colored amusement park, loaded with excellent roller coasters and hokey gift shops. It's owned by the Paramount megacorporation, so you get movie-theme attractions like the **Days of Thunder** racing simulator and the amazing **Top Gun Jet Coaster.** The stand-up **Vortex** coaster was built a few years ago for $5 million, and **The Edge,** which all too vividly simulates a high-speed free-fall drop from the top of a cliff, is also popular.

To shave a few bucks off the price, call the number listed below and ask an operator about any current discount schemes (usually by bringing a Coke can or a token from some fast-food restaurant). Another tip: They don't let people bring food in (so you'll be forced to buy their pricey, greasy slop), but you can get around the rule by bringing your own chow, leaving it in a locker near the front gate, and eating in the picnic area outside. *Great America Pkwy., Santa Clara, tel. 408/988–1800. Take the Great American Pkwy. exit off U.S. 101, 35 mi south of San Francisco. Admission: $26. Open weekends 10–8, closed mid-Oct.–Mar.*

Pacifica and Montara

Pacifica and Montara—about 15 and 20 minutes south of San Francisco, respectively—mark the northern end of the spectacular, underpopulated San Mateo County Coast. Two particularly sleepy seaside towns on a coastline known for its lack of energy, Pacifica and Montara are great places for a quick escape from urban chaos. The "historic" section of Pacifica, located on the northernmost outposts of town, is full of unpretentious, bungalow-style homes that once served as weekend retreats for wealthy San Franciscans but today house a majority of the town's locals. Pacifica's small commercial district, to the south, is an eclectic combination of old mom-and-pop stores and upscale specialty shops, the latter suggesting that the town is growing a little weary of its backwater authenticity and wants to start attracting some of San Francisco's yuppie business. Bridging past and present are the old, paved boardwalk and fishing pier, which serve the same purpose today that they have all along. Come here to smell the salt water, feed the pigeons, and watch the local fishermen ply their trade; the pier also affords brilliant views of San Francisco and Marin County.

Pacifica's beaches lie south of town, and they're the attractions that lure most San Franciscans down this way. About 2 miles south of old Pacifica is **Rockaway Beach.** Two large dollops of sand on either end of this gorgeous cove are just large enough for half a dozen sunbathers, and your only other company will be a handful of surfers and fishermen. Immediately south of Rockaway you'll come to the more popular **Pacifica State Beach,** a long, sandy beach favored by surfers and a fair number of local sun worshipers. Pacifica is also home to some fine hikes; for more info, *see* Hiking, in Chapter 8.

Just a few miles farther removed from San Francisco, Montara is an even more inviting destination than Pacifica for those looking to explore the San Mateo County Coast's natural environment. The town is pretty much all beach, its commercial district nearly nonexistent. **Montara State Beach,** on the north end of town, is a wide, picturesque stretch of sand, less crowded than Pacifica. It's a good place to catch some rays, play frisbee, have a picnic, or take long walks. Half a mile farther north, **Gray Whale Cove State Beach** (tel. 415/728–5336) is an American anomaly: a government-supported clothing-optional beach. Entrance to the spectacular, secluded cove is $5 (or you can pay $175 for an annual pass, if you want to do a whole lot of nude bathing). Keep your voyeuristic tendencies in check—cameras are strictly forbidden. Immediately south of the Montara city limits, the **James V. Fitzgerald Marine Reserve** has some of the coast's richest tide pools. Go at low tide to check out abalone, barnacles, kelp, shells, and maybe an octopus or two; but remember, this is a reserve, so look, but don't touch. To reach the reserve from the Point Montara Lighthouse Hostel (*see* Chapter 7), where you can obtain a tidal timetable, take Route 1 south to California Avenue and turn right.

For a meal in Pacifica, head straight to Francisco Boulevard, just west of Route 1. Here you'll find **Pacifica Thai Cuisine** (1966 Francisco Blvd., tel. 415/355–1678), which features traditional specialties like chicken curry in coconut milk ($5.50), and the oddly named **Pacifica Harry** (1780 Francisco Blvd., tel. 415/738–8300), an upscale Chinese restaurant with enticing entrées like cashew-nut shrimp ($8). Both restaurants offer vegetarian options. **A Coastal Affair** (Rte. 1 at 8th St., tel. 415/728–5229), a third of a mile north of the Point Montara Lighthouse Hostel (*see* Chapter 7), is a combination craft gallery and café with excellent espresso ($1.75–$2.75) and some of the best granola ($2) you'll ever crunch. Half a mile south of the hostel, **El Gran Amigo** (2448 Rte. 1, tel. 415/728–3815) serves up a wide variety of authentic Mexican specialties like enchiladas ($5) and nachos ($2.50).

Half Moon Bay

Famous for growing Halloween pumpkins and Christmas trees, Half Moon Bay is an easygoing seaside town 28 miles south of San Francisco on Route 1 (known here as the Cabrillo Highway). With its small-town rural feel, natural beauty, and wealth of activities (well, compared to the other dinky villages around here), it's the most inviting of the coastal communities. The small downtown area, centered around **Main Street,** is cluttered with craft stores, produce markets, gardens, cafés, and unpretentious burger joints. If lolling on the beach is more your speed, follow Kelly Avenue west to the popular **Half Moon Bay State Beach,** actually a series of beaches covering over 2 miles. To avoid the $5 parking fee, walk from downtown. It will probably get unpleasantly cold near the water before too long, a perfect excuse to trek 2 miles inland along Route 92 and sample—free of charge—the local wines at **Obester Winery** (12341 San Mateo Rd., tel. 415/726–9463), open daily 10–5.

Half Moon Bay hosts literally dozens of annual festivals, any one of which you could plan a visit around. The largest and most popular one is the **Art and Pumpkin Festival,** held the weekend after Columbus Day. The high-spirited fall celebration includes live music, local foods, crafts, vendors, a children's parade, and outrageous pie-eating and pumpkin-carving contests. Also popular is the self-explanatory **Coastal Flower Market,** which takes place on the third Saturday of each month May through September. Other yearly events include the riotous **Human Race** every May, in which entrants use every wacky scheme they can devise to carry other contestants along the course; the **Brew Ha-Ha** beer-tasting festival each June; and a daring **Fly-In and Air Show** that takes place at Half Moon Bay's tiny airport in the fall. For more information on any of these festivals, contact the **Half Moon Bay Chamber of Commerce** (520 Kelly Ave., tel. 415/726–8380).

For a meal, Half Moon Bay offers everything from reasonably priced health-food counters to expensive seafood restaurants. The best of the former is the **Healing Moon Natural Foods Market and Café** (523 Main St., tel. 415/726–7881), serving homemade soups ($2) and garden burgers ($3.50). Open Monday–Saturday 10–6 and Sunday 11–5, the café has an excellent outdoor garden patio. Despite its chain-restaurant exterior, **3 Amigos** (200 N. Cabrillo Hwy., on Rte. 1 at Kelly Ave., tel. 415/726–6080) offers tasty, cheap Mexican food (veggie burritos $3) and every Mexican beer under the sun ($2.25) each day until midnight. You'll find reasonably priced seafood (a rarity in this area) at the **Flying Fish Grill** (99 San Mateo Rd., cnr Rte. 92 and Main St., tel. 415/712–1125), open daily 11:30–6. Chow down on clam chowder ($2) and a variety of deep-fried and grilled fresh fish ($6–$9).

San Gregorio to Año Nuevo State Reserve

The desolate stretch of coastline south of Half Moon Bay is nearly deserted year-round, and for good reason. The beaches here are cold; the choice of affordable food and lodging is limited; and the number of worthwhile "sights," depending on your criteria, can be almost negligible. But the very fact that the area is so empty makes up for all this. With the exception of Año Nuevo State Reserve during elephant-seal mating season, there's almost nothing you can do here that will require advance planning. The rich tide pools at Pescadero State Beach, the cliff-hugging Pigeon Point Lighthouse Hostel, and the sky-high trees lining Route 84 through La Honda all make this chunk of coast extremely worthwhile for people taking the slow road up or down the California shore.

SAN GREGORIO Although not much of a destination in itself, San Gregorio is a worthwhile stop if you're traveling up or down the coast between Santa Cruz and Half Moon Bay. The drive to this hitching post of a town, at the junction of Routes 1 and 84 (the latter is also known as La Honda Road), is half the fun, even if you don't come by the spectacular coast road. **Route 84,** the east–west road running to San Gregorio from I-280, is for the strong of stomach only; but if you can take it, you'll get a roller-coaster ride on a highway so thick with redwoods it barely sees the light of day. And best of all, the road spits you out at the isolated **San Gregorio State Beach,** where you can lie back and soak up some rays, or, more likely, throw on a fisherman's sweater and battle the wind as you watch the fog come rolling in. If you get too cold, the bluff north of the parking lot is a good place for a brisk, blood-warming walk.

If you're in the area, don't miss the **San Gregorio General Store** (tel. 415/726–0565; open daily 9–7), 1 mile east of Route 1 on Route 84. This eclectic, funky store, which has served the ranching and farming community since 1889, sells everything from used books and stuffed animals to cast-iron pots and antiques, and it doubles as the town saloon and community center. You might even catch some Bulgarian bluegrass or Irish R&B if you show up on the right weekend night.

LA HONDA If you're getting tired of relentlessly magnificent coastal scenery, the densely forested inland community of La Honda, 11 miles east of Route 1, is the perfect antidote. About the size of a postage stamp, La Honda seems almost lost in the shadow of countless giant redwoods on Route 84 (*see* San Gregorio, *above*). The town consists of a small market, a reasonably priced restaurant, a post office, and **Apple Jack's Tavern** (La Honda Rd., tel. 415/747–0331). The last is a scruffy bar you shouldn't miss, no matter what time of day you're passing through town. Apple Jack's is today's version of an Old West saloon: The men drink their whiskey straight up, the women are loud and boisterous, and a brawl seems ready to erupt any minute. You'll feel equally comfortable pulling up on a Harley Davidson or on a horse.

Apple Jack's in-your-face attitude is perhaps best characterized by a sticker behind the bar that reads "The meek shall inherit shit."

Even more than Apple Jack's, though, it's the old-growth redwoods surrounding La Honda that will make your visit here a mind-blowing one. If you don't have time to head north to California's logging country, La Honda is a surprisingly good substitute. Four—that's right, four—state and county parks ring this tiny town, and their forested hills provide excellent terrain for hiking, biking, and generally being inspired by the wonders of nature (for details on hiking, *see* Chapter 8).

Take Route 84 about a mile west of La Honda, make a left on Alpine Road, and 4½ miles later you'll come to the parking lot of **Pescadero Creek County Park** (for info call Memorial County Park, tel. 415/879–0238), a secluded expanse of fir- and pine-covered hills crisscrossed by a series of gentle streams. From the parking lot, follow the **Tarwater Trail Loop** in either direction for a moderate hike of about 2 miles, which will take you from a ridge with ocean views down through the scrub and into the redwoods. Don't blame PG&E for the crude oil bubbling in Tarwater Creek—it's natural. If you haven't had your fill of towering redwoods, Douglas fir, and pine trees, drive a bit farther along Alpine Road and you'll reach the turnoff for **Portola State Park** (Portola State Park Rd., tel. 415/948–9098), 2,400 acres of even more remote and scenic forest where the only drawback is the $5 parking fee. Just past the entrance to the park, the visitor center sells wood ($3) and trail maps ($1). For info on hikes here, *see* Hiking, in Chapter 8.

Two more woodsy parks lie on Pescadero Road, which meets up with Alpine Road a mile south of Route 84. The first is **Sam McDonald County Park,** a small, almost deserted redwood forest good for taking short hikes in complete solitude. Thankfully, there's no charge for day use of the park. A bit farther along Pescadero Road, you'll come to **Memorial County Park** (tel. 415/879–0238), the most developed of the four parks, whose attributes include a fresh-water swimming hole, picnic areas, and a number of short and medium-length hiking trails through the redwoods. The best (legal) mountain-biking trails in the area, actually located within the borders of Pescadero Creek County Park, are also accessible from Memorial. From Memorial's visitor center, take Pescadero Road back toward La Honda, turn right on Wurr Road, cross the bridge, and you'll come to the **Old Haul Road,** where you can ride to your heart's content. To avoid the $5 parking fee at Memorial, park on the side of the road just outside the entrance.

PESCADERO Over a hundred years ago, all the wooden buildings in the small fishing village of Pescadero were painted white, with paint that washed up on shore when the clipper ship *Carrier Pigeon* crashed into the rocks off Pigeon Point, a few miles south of town. Today, the country bakery, general store, local post office, and other shops that populate Pescadero still retain their whitewashed uniformity, giving this town, in the flatlands a mile inland from the coast on Pescadero Road, a calming, subdued ambience.

After you've rambled around the three blocks that make up Pescadero's commercial district, head straight to **Duarte's Tavern** (202 Stage Rd., at Pescadero Rd., tel. 415/879–0464), open 7 AM to 9 PM daily, a combination bar and restaurant that's been run by four generations of Duartes since the late 19th century. The homey restaurant serves everything from peanut butter and jelly sandwiches ($2.50) to lamb chops ($14), but it's most famous for its cream of artichoke soup ($4), fresh seafood plates ($6–$20), and homemade pies ($3).

On the coast just west of town, you'll find **Pescadero State Beach,** a long, sandy expanse with vibrant tidal pools, perfect for checking out the Pacific's aquatic community. Immediately

The Merry Pranksters

In the early 1960s La Honda was home to one of the hippie era's most renowned groups of psychedelic crazies, the Merry Pranksters. Led by the multitalented bohemian Ken Kesey, author of such acclaimed novels as One Flew Over the Cuckoo's Nest, the Merry Pranksters spent several years on a La Honda farm exploring the "states of non-ordinary reality" they achieved by dropping acid, eating mushrooms, and smoking dope. When La Honda became too limiting they outfitted an old school bus with psychedelic, day-glo paintings and filming and recording equipment, and set off to travel across the country, a journey made famous by Tom Wolfe in his popular chronicle "The Electric Kool-Aid Acid Test."

north of the beach is the **Pescadero Marsh Reserve,** a protected area favored by ornithologists. Guided walks leave from the parking lot Saturdays at 10:30 AM and Sundays at 1 PM year-round. If you prefer a hike or bike ride in the hills, **Butano State Park** (tel. 415/879–0173), 5 miles south of Pescadero on Cloverdale Road, has 20 miles of trails on 2,700 acres (for hiking info, *see* Chapter 8). You can reach the park from Gazos Creek Road, off Route 1 near Año Nuevo State Reserve (*see below*), or take Pescadero Road a couple miles east from town and head south on Cloverdale; there's a $5 parking fee. Although mountain bikes are forbidden on the park's trails, you can ride on any of the fire roads. Your best bet is to park at the entrance gate near the corner of Cloverdale and Canyon roads, about a mile north of the main park entrance, and ride the **Butano Fire Road.** If you're in good shape you can take it all the way to the **Olmo Fire Road,** which leads back to the park's main drag, and pedal back to your car.

ANO NUEVO STATE RESERVE Named by explorer Sebastian Viscaino on New Year's Day 1603, the Punta del Año Nuevo is one of the few places in the world where you can safely view live elephant seals close up. Not only that, if you're here between December and March, you get to see them do the wild thing. During mating season, you'll need to make reservations up to eight weeks in advance through MISTIX (tel. 800/444–PARK), and you can only visit the reserve on one of their 2½-hour guided walks ($2, plus a $4 parking fee). If you're lucky, you may also catch sight of migrating gray whales during the mating season.

Since drag queen Divine kicked the bucket some years ago, this may be your only chance to watch overfed, under-exercised, 200-pound-plus honking balls of blubber perform their mating rituals. Don't miss it.

At other times of the year, you can check out the elephant seals resting on the rocks (or sometimes butting heads) by obtaining a free visitor's permit when you show up (parking is still $4). The path to the beach from the parking lot is 1½ miles long; and if you come in spring, you'll be treated to the sight of thousands of colorful wildflowers as you make your way toward the elephant seals. If seals bore you, Año Nuevo is also a great surfing beach—a local secret. The surfers can be territorial about their beach and hostile toward visitors, so try to act like you know what you're doing. The reserve, 22 miles north of Santa Cruz, is on Route 1 and can be reached on San Mateo Bus 96C.

Just south of Año Nuevo, you can pick ollalieberries in summer, pumpkins in October, and kiwifruit in November and December at **Coastways Ranch** (640 Rte. 1, tel. 415/879–0414). You generally pay for your pickings by the pound, and prices are reasonable. This is also the place to pick up a Christmas tree when the season rolls around.

Big Basin Redwoods State Park

One of the flagships of the California state-park system, Big Basin, 23 miles northeast of Santa Cruz, overwhelms you with thousands of acres of gigantic old-growth redwoods, lofty Douglas firs, rushing streams, and flowing waterfalls. All sorts of wildlife call Big Basin home, including black-tailed deer and an occasional fox, bobcat, coyote, or mountain lion. Worthy of at least a day's visit ($5 per car), and more if you groove on the outdoors, this is one park where you must get away from the main roads to fully appreciate nature's splendor. So put on your hiking boots, get out of your car, and go commune with some trees who've been here about 1,500 years longer than you have.

Just past the main entrance you'll come to park headquarters (21600 Big Basin Way, tel. 408/338–6132), where helpful rangers can give you advice on which trails will best suit your desires and energy level, or simply sell you a map (75¢) and let you go to town. For a relatively easy hike through redwoods, firs, and tan oaks, and past **Sempervirens Falls,** pick up the Sequoia Trail from the south end of the parking lot and follow it to the Skyline-to-Sea Trail, which will take you back to the visitors' center. The 4½-mile walk takes two to three hours. If you've got a bit more ambition, take the Skyline-to-Sea Trail from the parking lot west to Berry Creek Falls Trail, and work your way back to the visitor's center on the Sunset Trail. The 10½-mile loop, which affords views of the incredible 75-foot **Berry Creek Falls** and the Pacific, takes five to six hours. About half a mile up the trail, you'll find **Silver Falls** and **Golden Falls,** good options if you want to lose the crowds at Berry Creek. You can wade in pools, run through the falls themselves, or skip across the creek on the redwood logs.

The truly fit should take the 12½-mile **Skyline-to-Sea Trail**—arguably the most scenic hike in the park—all the way to the coast. This is the park's most popular trek, and those who've done it rave about how satisfying it is to reach the water after gazing at it earlier in the trail. If you want to tackle it, you'll need to leave a second car at the trail's endpoint at Waddell Beach. Also, the convergence of several trailheads a few miles into the walk necessitates either scrupulous attention to a map or a willingness to get lost. Mountain biking is allowed only on the fire roads in the park. Unfortunately, there aren't any good loops. Your best bet is to follow North Escape Road a short distance from park headquarters to **Gazos Creek Road,** a 14-mile fire trail that stretches to the coast.

Big Basin is an excellent place to camp. All of the 144 drive-in sites have picnic tables, fire pits, food lockers, and access to toilets and showers; most of them are spread out under the redwoods with lots of room for you to breathe; and many are near gentle streams. The sites, which fetch $14 in summer, go quickly on weekends; make reservations through MISTIX (tel. 800/444–PARK) up to eight weeks in advance. Even more lovely are the primitive sites ($7) at Big Basin's trail camps. Though fires in the trail camps are strictly forbidden, you'll be compensated by the seclusion and privacy of these sites, most less than 2 miles from a trailhead. Call the visitor center to reserve. To reach Big Basin from the north, take I–280 to Route 85 south (in Cupertino) to Route 9 south, and pick up Route 236 into the park.

SHOPPING

3

By Carmen Aguirre

Spending money is easy in the Bay Area. As if the vacuum effect that rent and food have on your wallet weren't enough, the city's stores will coax you into spending your last penny on some treasure, be it a Fred Flintstone lamp from the Haight, a low-rider bicycle from the Mission, or an extinct vinyl recording from one of SoMa's record shops. If you want to look even half as cool as most young people here, you've got your work cut out for you; but with a little effort and patience, you'll come across some real finds at decent prices.

Despite the expensive boutiques lining Union Street and the overpriced, sophisticated empo-ria of downtown's Union Square, San Francisco has a lot to offer the budget shopper. Infamous Haight Street is home to the *très* hip in fashion, but there are better thrift shops in the Mis-sion. Here you can find warehouses with everything from furniture to underwear, and you won't pay extra for atmosphere and attitude. Chinatown has tons of electronic goods and silk items; Fisherman's Wharf takes the prize for kitschy souvenirs; North Beach has unique (often expen-sive) specialty stores and boutiques; and SoMa has bargain warehouses that stock slightly flawed brand-name threads at damaged prices. Pick up *The Factory Outlet Shopping Guide,* or Sally Socolich's *Bargain Hunting in the Bay Area*, for an overview of the area's discount shop-ping; both are available at most local bookstores.

In the East Bay, you'll probably have better luck in Berkeley than Oakland. With the exception of a few small areas like **Piedmont Avenue** and **Rockridge** (College Ave., btw Alcatraz Ave. and Broadway), you won't find much to shop for here unless you're into discount emporiums. Addi-tionally, most Oakland stores are open 9–5, while the rest of the Bay Area seems to operate on a more worker-friendly 11-to-7 schedule. Instead, follow your nose to Berkeley's incense- and patchouli-scented Telegraph Avenue, which is all student, all the time. Stands selling tie-dyes, cheap silver earrings, and beaded necklaces line the avenue. Sweatshirt and T-shirt shops shove the Cal logo down your throat, and sandwiched in between are some fierce bookstores, music shops, and clothing stores.

If you (inexplicably) pine for overpriced, touristy boutiques, cross the Golden Gate Bridge to points north. Marin County is filled with small, expensive shops: Sausalito's are pretentious, and Tiburon's are just plain tacky. San Rafael may be less upscale, but it's no more exciting. Marin locals do their shopping in the city, as do residents of the South Bay. You'll frequently hear South Bay suburbanites complaining that it's bleak down here, but if malls are your gig, you've found your linoleum-lined paradise. Head down U.S. 101 to **Hillsdale Mall** in San Mateo or the **Stanford Shopping Center** in Palo Alto, and you'll realize all your white-bread dreams.

New Clothes

SAN FRANCISCO

You'll find everything from Armani suits to Afghani rugs in the city. Besides huge department stores like the **San Francisco Centre** (865 Market St., tel. 415/495–5656), which may make you tired of shopping before you've even found the right floor, San Francisco has zillions of boutiques—some snooty, some exotic, some painfully hip—and other cheaper, less pretentious stores that are still genuinely innovative.

Mega-department stores like Macy's, Nordstrom, Emporium-Capwell, and Nieman Marcus are perfect for the shopper with the patience of Buddha and the bank account of Trump.

Ambiance. Specializing in all things romantic, this boutique carries a large selection of pretty, flowing garments for women (dress prices average $50–$100). You can also pick up dainty necklaces, lacy picture frames, and elaborate jewelry boxes. *1458 Haight St., btw Masonic Ave. and Ashbury St., tel. 415/552–5095.*

Behind the Post Office. Stocked with the latest and greatest hip-hop gear, including smart-ass T-shirts, striped dresses, and baggy pants for when you're feeling phat, this tiny shop specializes in small and local labels. On Saturday local DJs spin tunes. This is also a great place to pick up 'zines and info on the city's underground graffiti and hip-hop scenes. *1504 Haight St., at Ashbury St., tel. 415/861–2507.*

Betsey Johnson. Postmodern designer-goddess Betsey Johnson brings you her outrageous women's fashions in a campy art-deco and neon-lights environment. The often silly clothes aren't cheap, but their limited appeal leads to regular half-off sales. *2031 Fillmore St., btw Pine and California Sts., tel. 415/567–2726. Other location: 160 Geary St., btw Stockton and Grant Sts., tel. 415/398–2516.*

Daljeets. *The* place to come if you're looking for arch-breaking heels, Daljeets carries flashy, rockin' women's evening wear. You'll also find a selection of equipment to help you punish that naughty significant other. *541 Valencia St., near 16th St., tel. 415/626–9000. Other location: 1744 Haight St., near Cole St., tel. 415/752–5610.*

Joshua Simon. This Noe Valley store stocks an eclectic selection of women's garments—from flowing pants and romantic-looking dresses to unusually woven vests and painted clothing. Some items are imported from Indonesia; others are fashioned by local designers. Either way, there are plenty of natural-fabric items. *3915 24th St., btw Sanchez and Noe Sts., tel. 415/821–1068.*

Na Na. Part of a national chain that has stores in New York and Los Angeles, Na Na sells trendy shoes and clothes, as well as a wide selection of "alternative" accessories, at fair prices. They have a number of small and local labels; and even the big-name lines aren't carried in bulk, so you won't look like everyone and their mother at the next party. *2276 Market St., near Noe St., tel. 415/861–NANA.*

Rolo. All three branches of this boutique, especially popular among gay and lesbian club-goers, carry some really groovy threads. The store on Market is heavy on conservative wear for men; the Howard Street store features a flashier women's selection; and the Mill Valley branch emphasizes casual clothes for women. *1301 Howard St., at 9th St., tel. 415/861–1999. Other locations: 2351 Market St., near Castro St., tel. 415/431–4545; 438 Miller Ave., near Camino Alto, Mill Valley, tel. 415/383–4000.*

Shoe Biz. Outfit yourself for a stroll down Haight Street with a pair of happening stompers from Shoe Biz. The friendly, well-pierced staff will set you up with a pair of sneakers, D.M.'s, or anything else your feet desire. *1446 Haight St., at Masonic Ave., tel. 415/864–0990.*

Used Rubber USA. No, you won't find recycled-condom wear here; the name refers to the store's propensity for making garments out of old inner tubes. They also use brass, cotton, and canvas made from hemp. The displays are striking, the clothing unique, but hopefully used rubber does not represent the future of urban fashion. The Haight Street store has recently been made an outlet, with large discounts on damaged items and last year's styles. *597 Haight St., at Steiner St., tel. 415/626–7855. Other location: 1423 Grant Ave., btw Green and Union Sts, 415/421–2721.*

EAST BAY

Although you can find almost anything in San Francisco, the East Bay, with its masses of students, fills its own niche. Come here to find street vendors, excessive quantities of "alternative" wear, and lower prices than those across the bay.

Deep Threads. Hip-hop fans rejoice: Deep Threads has all the baggy jeans, baseball caps, beanies, and hooded T-shirts you could possibly want. They also carry decks, trucks, and wheels, if you're in the market for a new rig. This is a good source for info on the Oakland hip-hop scene. *5243 College Ave., Oakland, at Broadway, tel. 510/653–4790.*

If your feet are sore and you're tired of being hassled for spare change, cruise into X-Large, grab a seat on the couch, and browse through one of the mags stacked on the table.

Futura. Berkeley's primary Haight Street–style boutique outfits both sexes in trendy new and used clothes. Many items here appear in stores across the bay for much more. *2360 Telegraph Ave., Berkeley, near Durant St., tel. 510/843–3037.*

Urban Outfitters. This place—sort of a left-of-center Gap—is actually part of a chain, though it feels one-of-a-kind with its unusual assortment of casual urban wear, as well as jewelry, shoes, and stuff for your apartment. This is the place to come if you like your new duds to look used and alternative. In a perfect marketing ploy for the twentysomething generation, a portion of the profits go to various good causes. Accessories are cheap, but a T-shirt could run you $30. *2590 Bancroft Way, Berkeley, btw Bowditch St. and Telegraph Ave., tel. 510/486–1300.*

X-Large. New to Berkeley, X-Large has brought cool clothes, fat hip-hop beats, and a comfortable couch to Telegraph Avenue. It's part of the chain fronted by Beastie Boy Mike D, and Sonic Youth bassist Kim Gordon has taken the time to design some of the threads for all you hip-hop bettys—so you *know* they're cool. The Berkeley store has DJs spinning every Saturday, and the San Francisco location hosts once-a-month parties complete with DJs, kegs, and small discounts if you can present one of their mailers (sign up for the mailing list next time you're in the store). *2422 Telegraph Ave., Berkeley, near Channing St., tel. 510/849–9242. Other location: 1415 Haight St., San Francisco, near Masonic Ave., tel. 415/626–9573.*

Secondhand and Outlet Clothing

SAN FRANCISCO

Naturally, the Mission and the Haight abound with vintage clothing, secondhand duds, and thrift shops. Stray from the big names—Wasteland and Buffalo Exchange among them—to the smaller shops for more interesting hunting and more substantial savings. Walk Mission and Valencia streets between 15th and 18th streets and you'll find all kinds of places. If you want to browse Haight Street, start at Fillmore Street and go all the way up to Stanyan Street. If your time is limited, the upper Haight (from Masonic to Stanyan) has a much wider variety of stores than the lower Haight. Those who take their thrifting seriously will want to head off the trendy path to Divisadero Street between Pine and Bush streets, or to Fillmore Street between Bush and Sacramento streets. Both areas have cheap thrift stores and slightly nicer vintage-clothing stores.

AAardvark's Odd Ark. AAardvark's keeps the thrifty crowd coming back with a wide selection of used clothing. It's a good source for basics, like men's cotton dress shirts and vintage Levi's. *1501 Haight St., at Ashbury St., tel. 415/621–3141.*

American Rag Compagnie. This store mixes old and new, and while none of it is cheap, the dreck has been filtered out, the clothes are in good shape, and everything is sanitized for your protection. They've got possibly the best selection of black vintage dresses in San Francisco, plus racks of stylish suits and hip, retro-looking jackets. *1305 Van Ness Ave., btw Sutter and Bush Sts., tel. 415/474–5214.*

Buffalo Exchange. This thrift store doesn't try to be hip (or at least it's not too successful), but the selection is large and pretty cheap. They also offer competitive prices on any clothes you want to sell. *1555 Haight St., btw Ashbury and Clayton Sts., tel. 415/431–7733. Other locations: 1800 Polk St., btw Washington and Jackson Sts., tel. 415/346–5726; 2512 Telegraph Ave., at Dwight Way, Berkeley, tel. 510/644–9202; 3333 Lake Shore Ave., Oakland, tel. 510/452–4464.*

Clothes Contact. This is a real thrift shop, where shirts are between $3 and $4, dresses cost $5, and Levi's run $10. It's an especially good place to come if you have a weakness for funky old dresses, or you're a man in dire need of a suit and a Hawaiian print tie. *473 Valencia St., near 16th St., tel. 415/621–3212.*

Community Thrift. This huge emporium in the Mission sells extremely cheap clothes, furniture, records, books, shoes, jewelry, the whole nine yards. Come here if you really want to save money. *623 Valencia St., btw 17th and 18th Sts., tel. 415/861–4910.*

Construction Zone. Do as the signs urge and DRESS UP YOUR MAN in an occupational uniform or otherwise enticing costume. You and your construction worker, military man, or cowboy will be all set to hang out with the boys at the YMCA. *2352 Market St., near Castro St., tel. 415/255–8585.*

Crossroads Trading Co. This secondhand clothing store has three locations in the Bay Area, all with a small, carefully selected, and relatively cheap stock. They'll also buy your old clothes at great prices. *2231 Market St., btw Sanchez and Noe Sts., tel. 415/626–8989. Other locations: 1901 Fillmore St., at Bush St., tel. 415/775–8885; 5636 College Ave., near Keith St., Berkeley, tel. 510/420–1952.*

Departures from the Past. This immaculate vintage shop has formal attire and costumes for both sexes, as well as casual wear from eras past. The stock is heavy on accessories and hats. They'll rent any item in the store for half the price on the tag, including penguin suits, which rent for about $30–$55 per night. *2028 Fillmore St., btw California and Pine Sts., tel. 415/885–3377.*

Esprit Factory Outlet. You, too, can look like a fresh-scrubbed and slightly artsy young American, and now at substantial savings! *499 Illinois St., at 16th St., tel. 415/957–2550. 1 block east of 3rd St. in Potrero Hill district.*

Gabardines. This shop has a good selection of '40s-style clothing and overalls, all very reasonably priced. *342 Divisadero St., btw Page and Oak Sts., tel. 415/864–7034.*

Goodwill. The biggest chain of thrift stores in the Bay Area is sure to have a location near you. The constantly rotating inventories are typically more tacky than trendy, but if you search hard you're bound to find a worthwhile bargain. For those who've just moved to the Bay Area, Goodwill is also the place for $30 couches, $5 chairs, and 20¢ coffee mugs. *820 Clement St., btw 9th and 10th Aves., tel. 415/668–3635. Other locations: 1700 Fillmore St., at Post St., tel. 415/441–2159; 1700 Haight St., at Cole St., tel. 415/387–1192.*

New Government. This is the place to go if you're nostalgic for '70s pop culture. Sean Cassidy T-shirts and Three's Company posters ($18–$20) litter the collection of bell-bottoms and go-go boots. Famous regulars here include rock legend David Bowie and Dee-Lite diva Lady Miss Kier. *1427 Haight St., near Masonic Ave., tel. 415/431–1830.*

Scarlett's Vintage Clothing. This cluttered shop is a surrogate grandmother's closet, complete with hats and hat boxes, dresses, shoes, cashmere sweaters, and costume jewelry—though Grandma probably wouldn't make you pay $75 for her old coat. *2121 Fillmore St., btw Jackson and California Sts., tel. 415/346–3770.*

Thrift Town. A large, traditional thrift store and sometime repository of decades-old designer clothing and accessories, Thrift Town offers a fine selection of bric-a-brac. It's a good source for anything from spectator pumps to acrylic sweaters to used cribs. *2101 Mission St., at 17th St., tel. 415/861–1132.*

Wasteland. One of the most popular secondhand stores in San Francisco, Wasteland brings you the trendy and outrageous at reasonable prices, including a groovy selection of bell-bottoms and other fashion items you hoped to never see again. It's also a good source for vintage costume jewelry. *1660 Haight St., btw Belvedere and Clayton Sts., tel. 415/863–3150.*

Worn Out West. San Francisco can be counted on to supply what you can't find back east, and this Castro district store does its part by providing secondhand western wear and leather goods to budget-conscious cowboys manqué. *582 Castro St., btw 18th and 19th Sts., tel. 415/431–6020.*

EAST BAY

The East Bay has a great variety of thrift stores, especially along Telegraph Avenue near the U.C. campus in Berkeley; on College Avenue in Rockridge; and along lower Solano Avenue near Albany. The farther you stray from the hip stores (i.e., the ones with velvet in the windows), the more likely you are to find a real steal, like a $5 pair of Levi's that some collector would pay $100 for. Unfortunately, this kind of thrifting requires a keen eye and a car, since you'll eventually end up in small, out-of-the-way thrift stores in suburban sprawlvilles like Hayward, ruthlessly shoving innocent shoppers aside as you search for the jeans with the golden rivets.

Bizarre Bazaar. This upscale store is stocking less and less used clothing (it's hard to find good vintage clothing these days, the owners complain) and is leaning more toward accessories and small antiques. If you're looking for a pair of cufflinks or a dainty watch, you're in luck. Though the clothing selection is minimal, girls who like to play dress-up may find that perfect (and expensive) evening dress and matching tiara. *5634 College Ave., Oakland, tel. 510/655–2909. At Keith St., near Rockridge BART.*

Children's Home Society Thrift Shop. Here's a junky thrift store where ugly household goods are complimented by even uglier clothes. Still, it's a good place to find coffee mugs and ashtrays that walk the line between tacky and beautiful. *2440 Telegraph Ave., Oakland, at 25th St., tel. 510/451–0266. Open Mon.–Fri. 11–3.*

Madame Butterfly. This small shop stocks dainty little dresses, hats, gloves, and rhinestone jewelry from eras past. *5474 College Ave., Oakland, tel. 510/653–1525. At Taft St., 2 blocks south of Rockridge BART.*

Mars Mercantile. Formerly a branch of the Wasteland (*see above*), this vintage clothing store has the flashiest window displays in Berkeley. Although not cheap, the merchandise is selectively chosen and well organized. There's a sizable quantity of funky secondhand shoes. *2398 Telegraph Ave., at Channing Way, Berkeley, tel. 510/843–6711.*

Rockridge Rags. Browse through the orderly racks of secondhand clothing and you'll find lots of stuff to wear when you're doing temp work—you'll find the occasional Bill Blass skirt or Anne Klein suit. Lucky bargain hunters may nab an elegant but cheap garment for a dressy night out. *5711 College Ave., Oakland, tel. 510/655–2289. Next to Rockridge BART.*

Sharks. Come here for jeans, fatigues, and other military wear, mixed in with some homely Hawaiian shirts and pearl-studded sweaters. *2505 Telegraph Ave., Berkeley, at Dwight Way, tel. 510/841–8736.*

Slash. With its huge stock of cheap Levi's ($15), overalls ($20), and other pants for rugged living, Slash feels like somebody's messy closet. Yet rifling through the mixed piles of clothing on the floor is part of the fun. *2840 College Ave., Oakland, tel. 510/841–7803. At Russell St., 1 block north of Ashby Ave.*

Books

SAN FRANCISCO

Looking for some reading material to divert your attention, increase your attention span, or act as a prop when you're lounging in a café? You have over 200 bookstores to choose from, new and used, small and huge, general and specialized, for every interest, language, and purse size. Don't ignore the smaller used bookstores peppered throughout the city (there are zillions in the Mission and the Haight): It's more exciting to poke through cluttered stacks, possibly stumbling upon a rare treasure, than to search a computer roster at an enormous chain store for the title you want. If you don't find what you're looking for at the bookstores below, try **Books Inc.** (3515 California St., btw Laurel and Spruce Sts., tel. 415/221–3666; 140 Powell St., tel. 415/397–1555) or **Stacey's Bookstore** (581 Market St., tel. 415/421–4687; 219 University Ave., Palo Alto, tel. 415/326–0681).

Bound Together Book Collective. Here you'll find anarchist literature from all over the world, as well as nifty stickers declaring you vehemently anti-establishment. *1369 Haight St., btw Masonic and Central Sts., tel. 415/431–8355.*

City Lights, the legendary home of the Beat Generation, was once busted on obscenity charges for selling Allen Ginsberg's poem "Howl."

City Lights. For some, a trip to San Francisco is not complete without an evening spent browsing the stacks at City Lights, surely the city's most famous bookstore. Owned by poet Lawrence Ferlinghetti, City Lights is *the* source for Beat literature, much of it published under the store's own imprint. It also stocks a wide selection of poetry and art books, plus some very obscure, very expensive titles. *261 Columbus Ave., at Broadway, tel. 415/362–8193.*

A Clean Well-Lighted Place for Books. The name says it all at this pleasant bookstore, with lots of new, quality fiction and a wide selection of general-interest books. They're famous for hosting readings by well-known authors. *601 Van Ness Ave., in Opera Plaza, tel. 415/441–6670.*

Columbus Books. Before you drop a bundle on that shiny new book at City Lights, sneak over to this huge used bookstore and see if you can find it cheaper. *540 Broadway, btw Columbus and Kearny Sts., tel. 415/986–3872.*

A Different Light. You'll find a large selection of new lesbian- and gay-oriented literature here. They also carry queerzines (*see* Gay Publications, in Chapter 1), T-shirts, and stickers. Readings are held on a regular basis. *489 Castro St., near 18th St., tel. 415/431–0891.*

European Book Company. Come here for European magazines and newspapers. It's also a good source for foreign-language dictionaries and travel guides. *925 Larkin St., btw Geary and Post Sts., tel. 415/474–0626. Open weekdays 9:30–8:30, Sat. 9:30–5.*

Green Apple Books. Not for the anal, this big, ramshackle store in the Richmond district jumbles together the new, the used, and the rare; a walk through feels like an exceedingly satisfying foray into Grandma's attic. It's one of the city's best bookstores, and the staff is knowledgeable and friendly. **Ninth Avenue Books** in the Sunset district is a smaller branch of Green Apple. *Green Apple: 506 Clement St., btw 6th and 7th Aves., tel. 415/387–2272. Ninth Avenue: 1348 9th Ave., btw Judah and Irving Sts., tel. 415/665–2938.*

Kinokuniya Bookstores. More than 60,000 titles in Japanese and English cover all aspects of Japanese politics, economics, and culture. You can find Japanese grammar and language books, magazines, and music. Look for the store on the upper level of the Kinokuniya Building in the Japan Center. *1581 Webster St., btw Post and Geary Sts., tel. 415/567–7625.*

Marcus. Here you'll find titles on all aspects of African and African-American culture, including history, religion, fiction, and art. They also carry some music and posters, and there's a great selection of children's and young-adult literature. *1712 Fillmore St., btw Post and Sutter Sts., tel. 415/346–4222.*

Modern Times. Leftists can choose from lots of titles with a progressive political bent; popular topics include theory, current affairs, poetry, women's issues, and art. There's an extensive Spanish-language section. The store hosts regular readings and forums, often with a political focus. *888 Valencia St., btw 19th and 20th Sts., tel. 415/282–9246.*

Old Wives' Tales. And young career women's tales, and middle-aged divorced mothers' tales, and some pimply, troubled adolescent girls' tales, too. Specializing in women's issues and women authors, this is a good resource for feminists of all ages. *1009 Valencia St., btw 21st and 22nd Sts., tel. 415/821–4675.*

San Francisco Mystery Bookstore. This Noe Valley shop stocks everything imaginable for the armchair gumshoe in your life. New and used books, both in and out of print, abound; they even stock a few gay and lesbian mysteries. *746 Diamond St., at 24th St., tel. 415/282–7444. Open Wed.–Sun. 11:30 AM–5:30 PM.*

Sierra Club Bookstore. Along with a wide range of titles on all aspects of environmentalism, including political tomes, nature poetry, and practical guides for hiking and camping, they stock topo maps and kids' books. The staff knows reams about all things outdoorsy. *730 Polk St., btw Eddy and Ellis Sts., tel. 415/923–5600.*

Small Press Traffic. Struggling writers should stop by this Mission-district bookstore to find out about the local literary scene. It's got a great collection of small-press and self-published titles and hosts a variety of literary events and workshops. *3599 24th St., at Guerrero St., tel. 415/285–8394. Open Tues.–Sat. noon–6 PM.*

Would-be writers take note: Small Press Traffic is the ultimate place to peruse, ponder, and peddle obscure poetry.

William Stout Architectural Books. This store in Jackson Square stocks a comprehensive collection of architecture books and magazines from both Europe and the United States. *804 Montgomery St., btw Jackson and Pacific Sts., tel. 415/391–6757.*

EAST BAY

The East Bay intelligentsia doesn't have to look far for quality new and used books. With a huge university in its midst and more pretentious intellectuals per square mile than anywhere outside the Academie Française, you'll find enough bookstores to keep you occupied for a year. For the densest concentration of books, check out Telegraph Avenue and its offshoots, directly south of the university. Some excellent book shops lie a bit farther from campus, for those who get hives when they get too close to institutions of higher learning.

Black Oak Books. Grad students and professors frequent this huge, well-stocked new and used bookstore in North Berkeley, which hosts numerous readings. The store sells a beautiful collection of broadsides (profound quotations from literary works, artfully arranged on heavy decorative paper)—an excellent gift for the serious bookworm. *1491 Shattuck Ave., at Vine St., Berkeley, tel. 510/486–0698.*

Cody's. Here's a Berkeley institution if there ever was one. Take a break from Telegraph Avenue and ponder the stacks and stacks of shiny new volumes, covering every imaginable genre—from poetry and philosophy to travel, toy trains, and happy books for kids. They also have an extensive periodicals section and host regular readings by potentially famous authors. *2454 Telegraph Ave., at Haste St., Berkeley, tel. 510/845–7852.*

Don't read alone: On Fridays and Saturdays, Cody's is something of a pickup joint for earnest intellectuals.

Gaia Books. A great East Bay resource for books on alternative spirituality, ecology, holistic health, and sexuality, Gaia occupies a bright, airy space that's perfect for its regular readings and lectures, which usually cost a few dollars. *1400 Shattuck Ave., at Rose St., Berkeley, tel. 510/548–4172.*

Half-Price Books. They sell all sorts of titles you'd actually want to read (especially quality fiction) for less than you'd spend on a cappuccino. You can browse at the Berkeley location while waiting for a table at the Blue Nile (*see* Chapter 4, Food); they'll call your name in the store.

2525 Telegraph Ave., btw Parker St. and Dwight Way, Berkeley, tel. 510/843–6412. Other location: 1849 Solano Ave., near the Alameda, Albany, tel. 510/526–6080.

Mama Bears. This store specializes in all kinds of women's literature. It hosts live readings and workshops. *6536 Telegraph Ave., at 66th St., Oakland, tel. 510/428–9684.*

Moe's. Moe's has become one of Berkeley's most successful bookstores, thanks to the efforts of the gruff, cigar-chomping owner, Moe Moskowitz. Browse his five floors of new, used, and antique books, with a strong emphasis on the used and antique part. Humanities and social-science grad students save big bucks by buying their course texts here. *2476 Telegraph Ave., btw Haste St. and Dwight Way, Berkeley, tel. 510/849–2087.*

Shambhala. This is one of the area's best sources of literature on Eastern religions (and Western slants on Eastern religions). Shambhala also specializes in magic and other non-Christian types of spirituality. *2482 Telegraph Ave., btw Haste St. and Dwight Way, Berkeley, tel. 510/848–8443.*

University Press Books. Titles from over 100 university presses represent the absolute latest in intellectual thought on a variety of topics. Buy a hot treatise on cultural theory and read it at the Musical Offering café next door—make sure everyone can see the title as you read. *2430 Bancroft Way, btw Telegraph Ave. and Dana St., Berkeley, tel. 510/548–0585.*

Walden Pond. This large store offers the best selection of new books in downtown Oakland and hosts regular readings by relatively big names. *3316 Grand Ave., near Grand Lake Theater, Oakland, tel. 510/832–4438. Take I–580 to Grand Ave. exit (not West Grand Ave.) and go left on Grand Ave.*

MARIN COUNTY

Copperfield's Books (tel. 707/578–8938), a local chain, has seven stores around Marin County and the Wine Country. **A Clean Well-Lighted Place for Books** (*see above*), a San Francisco stalwart, has a branch in Marin (2417 Larkspur Landing Circle, tel. 415/461–0171) and another in the South Bay (21269 Stevens Creek Blvd., Cupertino, tel. 408/255–7600).

The Bearded Giraffe. If your karma's out of kilter, this shop sells "Books for Lighting the Inner Lamp." Once you've inhaled their incense, bought a small Buddha, and picked up a new or used copy of the *I Ching*, you'll be one step closer to nirvana. Bargain books out front go for as little as 50¢. *1115 Bridgeway, Sausalito, tel. 415/332–4503.*

Book Passage. This Corte Madera store has the best selection of travel books in the Bay Area, and regularly holds author signings and workshops on travel writing. Book Passage also has a wide selection of general-interest books and recently added an extensive mystery and used-book annex. A café with outdoor seating serves pastries and fancy coffees. *51 Tamal Vista Blvd., Corte Madera, tel. 415/927–0960.*

SOUTH BAY

Peninsula residents were thrilled when **Barnes and Noble** (1940 S. El Camino Real, tel. 415/312–9066), a large bookstore with an unparalleled magazine section, made its way into San Mateo. **Crown Books,** a chain that sells discount books, has stores throughout the South Bay. If you prefer used books, get hold of the *Northern California Book Finder* ($6), a little directory of used book shops that's sold at The Book Nest (*see below*).

The Book Nest. This rust-colored, Cape-Cod-style house has mostly hardbacks, including some old editions that date back to 1830. Ed, the owner, probably won't mind if you curl up in a fluffy Victorian chair with Dickens and an old teddy bear (a pile waits in the children's room). Don't miss the box of free books by the front door. If you want to make Ed happy, ask to see a rare or autographed Steinbeck edition, his specialty. *366 2nd St., Los Altos, tel. 415/948–4724. Take I–280 to El Monte Ave. east, turn left on Foothill Expressway, right on San Antonio Rd., left on Lyell St., and right on 2nd St.*

Kepler's. This upscale Menlo Park bookstore has over 125,000 titles for you to peruse. Pick up a book to keep you busy while you sip coffee and munch on a sandwich ($4–$6) at Café Borrone (tel. 415/327–0830) next door. *1010 El Camino Real, Menlo Park, tel. 415/324–4321. Take Marsh Rd. west from U.S. 101, turn left on Middlefield Rd. and right on Ravenswood Ave. to El Camino Real.*

Megabooks. The classical music emanating from the radio should ease your claustrophobia as you walk through the narrow, maze-like aisles of tall bookshelves. While this store sells mostly used books, it also offers discounted new books, including some paperback bestsellers at 25% off. *444 University Ave., Palo Alto, tel. 415/326–4730. Open Mon.–Sat. 10–6.*

Printer's Inc. This café/bookstore features special-interest titles in addition to standard material. They host readings three to four times a week; call or stop by for a schedule. Find a 'zine that interests you from their extensive selection (about 900 titles), and head to the café (tel. 415/323–3347) for a cuppa joe and a sandwich ($6) or salad ($6–$7). *310 California Ave., at Birch St., Palo Alto, tel. 415/327–6500. Take Oregon St. exit from U.S. 101, turn right on El Camino Real to California Ave. Other location: 301 Castro St., at Dana St., Mountainview, tel. 415/961–8500.*

Records, Tapes, and CDs

The Bay Area music scene ranges from hip hop to punk rock, from grunge to gangsta rap, and record shops cater to most every taste (or lack thereof). Haight Street in San Francisco is loaded with new- and used-music stores whose inventories include as much Grateful Dead as hard-to-find, alternative imports. Berkeley's Telegraph Avenue is also a good bet, with more than a few excellent used-music shops. Throughout the Bay Area, jazz and classical abound, whether you're in a massive **Tower Records** or a mom-and-pop shop in Marin County.

SAN FRANCISCO

Gaia Mantra. This elaborately decorated hole-in-the-wall has a vinyl listening room where you can check out the ambient/techno/acid/trance record collection. There's also a decent CD and tape selection. If you can't make it in, no worries—you can access their catalogue and make purchases via e-mail (mantra@£:netcom.com). *511 Valencia St., at 16th St., tel. 415/487–9728.*

Groove Merchant. Come here for soul, funk, and rare groove—vinyl only. There are plenty of great finds for the collector, DJ, and serious amateur. *776 Haight St., btw Pierce and Scott Sts., tel. 415/252–5766.*

Old Wives' Tales. This women's bookstore in the Mission has a wide variety of female vocalists, lesbian artists, and music with a feminist message. It's all on cassette only. *1009 Valencia St., btw 21st and 22nd Sts., tel. 415/821–4675.*

Prince Neville's Reggae Run-Ins. Jah, mon, this is a reggae wonderland, with records, tapes, videos, T-shirts, jewelry, and other paraphernalia in red, gold, black, and green. *505 Divisadero St., btw Fell and Hayes Sts., tel. 415/922–9037.*

Reckless Records. A good source for used cassettes and CDs, Reckless also carries new stuff. They specialize in independent and corporate rock, hip hop, and soul. *1401 Haight St., at Masonic St., tel. 415/431–3434.*

Recycled Records. This smallish store in the Haight buys and sells used CDs and vinyl. They usually have a lot of indie, jazz, and blues in stock. *1377 Haight St., at Masonic St., tel. 415/626–4075.*

Rough Trade. They've got new and used tapes, LPs, and CDs; and they're especially strong in imports, independent music, and reggae. In their listening area you can check out new releases that you probably won't find at Tower. *1529 Haight St., btw Ashbury and Clayton Sts., tel. 415/621–4395.*

Samiramis Imports. This import store has a big selection of Middle Eastern music on record and tape. *2990 Mission St., at 26th St., tel. 415/824-6555.*

Streetlight Records. Because they buy and sell for great prices here, they pull in the collections of eclectic music enthusiasts, which means their selection of records, tapes, and CDs is usually off-beat and always fresh. Streetlight was voted favorite music store by readers of the *SF Weekly. 3979 24th St., btw Noe and Sanchez Sts., tel. 415/282-3550. Other location: 2350 Market St., near Castro St., tel. 415/282-8000.*

No need to come all the way into the city to pick up salsa, banda, and mariachi music. Discoteca La Fiesta (2607 Middlefield Rd., Redwood City, btw MacArthur and Douglas Aves., tel. 415/366-0502) caters to the South Bay's Latino community with all of the above plus Spanish-language videos.

Tower Records. The branch on Columbus Avenue and Bay Street, near Fisherman's Wharf, has an excellent selection of international music, specially designed to calm pangs of overseas homesickness. Otherwise, this chain record emporium offers a wide spectrum of new rock and pop, as well as some jazz, hip hop, classical, and show tunes. *Columbus Ave. and Bay St., tel. 415/885-0500. Other locations: 3205 20th Ave., in Stonestown Galleria, tel. 415/681-2001; 2280 Market St., at Noe St., tel. 415/621-0588; 2727 S. El Camino Real, San Mateo, tel. 415/570-4600; also see East Bay, below.*

EAST BAY

Ready to spend a few hundred dollars on music? You can't do much better than to head over to Berkeley. Within five blocks of the U.C. campus sit no fewer than four enormous record stores, each with a dizzying selection of new and used titles. Even the most insanely picky or eccentric collector should find the jazz, grunge, indie, hip-hop, rap, or New Age 7" she's been searching for.

Amoeba. Among the stores that serve the Berkeley campus, Amoeba has the best selection of new and used 7" records. You'll find a well-rounded selection of jazz, international music, and rock, spiced up with plenty of indies, imports, and used videos. If you're selling old records, Amoeba generally pays a fair price. *2455 Telegraph Ave., at Haste St., Berkeley, tel. 510/549-1125.*

Leopold's. The Bay Area source for new hip hop, soul, and funk—on record, tape, and CD— Leopold's also carries a lot of jazz and world music. They even have large Celtic and movie-soundtrack sections. *2518 Durant Ave., near Telegraph Ave., Berkeley, tel. 510/848-2015.*

Rasputin's. Berkeley's largest selection of new and used CDs, records, and tapes is housed in a massive, three-story glass coliseum. On weekends you can check out an act by a local band between DJ spinnings. If you're a vinyl hound, check out **Rasputin's Records** (2332 Telegraph Ave., no phone) a few doors up, but plan ahead—it's only open weekends. *2350 Telegraph Ave., at Durant Ave., Berkeley, tel. 510/848-9005.*

Music for Rebels

In San Francisco you can buy records and foment revolution at the same time. Epicenter (475 Valencia St., at 16th St., tel. 415/431-2725), an anarchist-oriented community center, has a huge selection of new and used punk-rock albums, as well as pool tables, bulletin boards, and a library with tons of independent 'zines. It's an awesome resource for the new radical in town. Come by weekdays 3-8, Saturday noon-8, or Sunday noon-7.

Tower Records. While Amoeba and Rasputin's are the places for alternative and used music, Tower sells only new and mostly mainstream records, tapes, and CDs. Still, because they're a huge corporation, they sometimes have better deals on blank tapes and Top 40 bestsellers. If you love classical, check out **Tower Classical** (2585 Telegraph Ave., tel. 510/849-2500), a few blocks from the main branch. *2510 Durant Ave., at Telegraph Ave., Berkeley, tel. 510/841-0101.*

Household Furnishings

The Bay Area has three main peddlers of things cheap and used: the **Salvation Army, Goodwill,** and **St. Vincent de Paul,** each with numerous outlets on both sides of the bay. The Salvation Army is best for $5 lamps and $10 office desks, Goodwill for 20¢ ashtrays and $1 mugs proclaiming "I Luv U Grandma," St. Vincent de Paul for $15–$50 sofas, chairs, desks, and ancient televisions and stereos.

Noe Valley, particularly Church Street between 19th and 27th streets, is garage-sale paradise. So, too, are Dolores and Guerrero streets between 16th and 24th.

SAN FRANCISCO

There is so much free or extremely cheap furniture in this city, it's ridiculous. Garage sales, sidewalk sales, and yard sales abound; look at the classified ads in the *Bay Guardian,* the *S.F. Weekly,* or the *San Francisco Chronicle* for the organized ones, and on telephone poles for signs advertising the more impromptu sales. Valencia and Mission streets, from 14th to 20th streets, have a number of used-furniture shops and thrift stores where you can find all kinds of cheap stuff. Try **Community Thrift** or **Thrift Town** (*see* Secondhand and Outlet Clothing, *above*) for the largest selections at the best prices.

Cookin': Recycled Gourmet Appurtenances. Here are used fondue makers, espresso pots, cookie cutters, Jell-O molds, pots, pans, and everything else your kitchen is begging for that you can't afford new. *339 Divisadero St., btw Oak and Page Sts., tel. 415/861-1854.*

Hocus Pocus. Junk and treasures are jumbled together in this groovy shop in the Mission, where you can pick up everything from cheap knickknacks to overpriced antiques. *900 Valencia St., at 20th St., tel. 415/824-2901.*

One Person's Garbage . . .

The cheapest furniture of all comes from the street on certain very special days. Scavenging is best on the last and first days of every month, when people are moving in and out of their apartments and throwing their sofas to the winds of fate. Even better, however, is the mythic Neighborhood Cleanup, a day when residents of a particular neighborhood are allowed to leave furniture, appliances, and any other large pieces of so-called junk on the street; in the morning, the city hauls it away for free. Most residents will put their stuff out around 8 or 9 at night, and it behooves you to get at it early (like 10 or 11), because secondhand-furniture salespeople love to sweep everything into their big trucks. The quality of your haul will vary from neighborhood to neighborhood, but Russian Hill, Pacific Heights, and the Marina generally have the most tony goods. For specific Neighborhood Cleanup dates in San Francisco, call Sunset Scavenger (tel. 415/330-1355). In Berkeley, where Neighborhood Cleanup happens only once a year in each neighborhood, call Berkeley Refuse (tel. 510/644-8856).

Jim's Used Furniture. Looking like it's been here for decades, Jim's attracts cheap-furniture hunters willing to venture off the well-shopped part of Valencia Street. Seek and ye may find a neat chair for $10 or a worn coffee table for $5. *1499 Valencia St., at 26th St., tel. 415/285–2049.*

EAST BAY

Crate and Barrel Outlet. This is the only outlet store in the state for Crate and Barrel's popular wooden furniture, kitchenware, and decorative items (rugs, placemats, candelabras, and the like). Most of the stock is made up of irregular or discontinued items; but everything is quite functional, and items are priced about 30%–50% lower than at their regular stores. *1785 4th St., btw Virginia and Hearst Sts., Berkeley, tel. 510/528–5500.*

Urban Ore. Need a new door, or a new doorknob, or a new chandelier, or a new toilet bowl, or some other piece of junk you didn't even know you wanted until just now? Head on over to this outdoor treasure trove (or junkyard, depending on how you look at it) and leave raving about your incredible find. *7th St., at Gilman St., Berkeley, tel. 510/559–4450.*

Warm Things. This factory outlet specializes in goose-down comforters, pillows, and featherbeds. You can get a comforter for $100 or a feather bed for $75. *6011 College Ave., at Claremont Ave., Oakland, tel. 510/428–9329.*

Whole Earth Access. Though the prices aren't super-cheap, this unique outlet store is good for one-stop home decorating, especially if your home's a little yuppie-ish. They've got stereos, TVs, computers, kitchen appliances (including neat juicers and espresso makers), some furniture (imported tapestries, wicker and bamboo items), books, clothes, and shoes. *2990 7th St., at Ashby Ave., Berkeley, tel. 510/845–3000.*

SOUTH BAY

Goodwill. Palo Alto's Goodwill doesn't have the variety of merchandise that Thrift Mart (*see below*) has, but on the whole the stuff is nicer, thanks to donations of clothes, books, dishes, and the like by wealthy residents. *4085 El Camino Way, Palo Alto, off El Camino Real south of Stanford, tel. 415/494–1416.*

Thrift Mart. You name it, this thrift store has got it. Boasting "the lowest prices in California," Thrift Mart features everything from skis to bras to stuffed animals. Come on a Sunday or Wednesday and receive a 30% reduction on all purchases. *92 W. El Camino Real, Mountain View, near Grant Rd., tel. 415/961–2616. Take I–280 to Rte. 85 north to El Camino north, or take U.S. 101 to Rte. 237 southwest to El Camino north.*

Specialty Items

SAN FRANCISCO

San Francisco attracts weird specialty goods the way a black hole attracts—well, you get the idea. Maybe it's because the city harbors special-interest groups and bizarre individuals in such abundance; maybe it's because people come here to create a lifestyle for themselves and need the proper accessories. The Castro, naturally, abounds with places to create almost any kind of queer lifestyle; the Haight offers lots of head shops and tie-dye boutiques; and those who want to flirt with the occult can visit the Mission or the Haight. If you have no lifestyle, try **Macy's** downtown.

ART AND PHOTOGRAPHY **Adolph Gasser.** Your best source for photography and video equipment, Gasser has the largest inventory of such items in northern California. *181 2nd St., btw Howard and Mission Sts., tel. 415/495–3852. Other location: 5733 Geary Blvd., at 22nd Ave., tel. 415/751–0145.*

Art Rock Gallery. Put Nirvana or Siouxsie and the Banshees on your wall for $10 and up. Handmade silk-screened posters run $15–$20. *1153 Mission St., btw 7th and 8th Sts., tel. 415/255–7390.*

Womancrafts West. This unique gallery and art store displays and sells textiles, jewelry, quilts, sculpture, paintings, and other items by women from different traditions. Come check out exhibits like felt rugs woven by the Sisters of the Moon Felt Collective. You might take home some jewelry, candleholders, or art postcards, but the big items will likely be out of your price range. *1007½ Valencia St., at 21st St., tel. 415/648–2020. Closed Mon.*

ASSORTED GIFTS **Planet Weavers Treasure Store.** Politically correct products, especially those related to environmental concerns, abound in this Unicef-run store. They've got a colorful selection of drums, maps, toys, textiles, hammocks, and eco-conscious games for kids. A portion of the proceeds goes to the children's fund. *1573 Haight St., btw Ashbury and Clayton Sts., tel. 415/864–4415.*

Under One Roof. They share a roof with the NAMES project and sell goods gathered from 62 AIDS organizations. The profits generated go back to the organization that supplied the product. You'll find all kinds of gifts, including T-shirts with radical queer slogans, household goods, and cards. *2362B Market St., btw Noe and Castro Sts., tel. 415/252–9430.*

BODY PRODUCTS **The Body Shop.** This international corporation brought natural health and beauty aids—and a modicum of environmental and political consciousness—to the shopping malls. They sell reasonably priced soaps, lotions, essential oils, and other fun stuff and provide informational pamphlets on their business practices (buying certain ingredients from tribes in the Amazon rain forest, for example). *865 Market St., in San Francisco Centre, tel. 415/281–3760. Other locations: 16 California St., at Drumm St., tel. 415/397–7455; 2106 Chestnut St., at Steiner St., tel. 415/202–0112.*

New York Cosmetics & Fragrances. Come here for name-brand cosmetics and perfumes at a discount. *318 Brannan St., btw 2nd and 3rd Sts., tel. 415/543–3880.*

Skin Zone. All sorts of lotions, facial masks, shampoos, and other personal-care items will help you start your new life soft and shiny. *575 Castro St., btw 18th and 19th Sts., tel. 415/626–7933.*

GAMES AND TOYS **Basic Brown Bear Factory and Store.** Tour one of the few remaining teddy bear factories in the United States on Saturdays at 11 and 2. You can purchase an ursine companion on your way out. *444 DeHaro St., at Mariposa St., tel. 415/626–0781.*

FAO Schwarz Fifth Avenue. Remember in the movie *Big* when Tom Hanks performs "Chopsticks" by jumping around on an enormous piano keyboard? He was in FAO Schwarz, home to some of the most lavish, elaborate toys you'll ever find. To feel especially starry-eyed and amazed (or nauseated, depending on your tastes), come near holiday time, when Mummy and Daddy are buying Junior a mini-Mercedes and kids are begging and drooling in every corner. *48 Stockton St., at O'Farrell St., tel. 415/394–8700.*

Gamescape. They've got sci-fi and war board games, playing cards, gambling paraphernalia (for recreational use only, of course), tarot cards, and lots more for those long, boring winter nights. *333 Divisadero St., btw Page and Oak Sts., tel. 415/621–4263.*

HATS AND JEWELRY **African Outlet.** Reasonably priced African textiles, shell jewelry, hats, and other African accessories line the walls of this shop. *524 Octavia St., btw Hayes and Grove Sts., tel. 415/864–3576.*

Nancy's Originals. Here you'll find hats for the urban dweller: porkpie, Bogart-type, and a bunch of hats reminiscent of the Jackson Five. *1429 Haight St., btw Masonic Ave. and Ashbury St., tel. 415/861–3910.*

LEATHER GOODS **Coyote Leather.** Come here for gorgeous custom and handmade Western boots in colorful, exotic leathers—"the Rolex of boots," they like to call them. Pair them with one of their beaded garments, and you're ready to enter that barrel-racing contest. *509 Columbus Ave., btw Union and Green Sts., tel. 415/433–5487.*

North Beach Leather. Ignore the snippy staff and browse to your heart's content through the intricately designed, richly colored, and expensive leather and suede garments. *190 Geary St., at Stockton St., tel. 415/362–8300. Other location: 1365 Columbus Ave., at Beach St., tel. 415/441–3208.*

MAGIC AND WITCHCRAFT **Lady Luck.** The proprietor of this tiny shop is so convincing that even the most bitter cynic will feel compelled to buy a hope candle. The devotional candles, oils promising love, and wide selection of incense will thrill your favorite mystic. *311 Valencia St., btw 14th and 15th Sts., tel. 415/621–0358.*

Skin & Bones & Sticks & Stones. You must make an appointment to see the proprietor's collection of human skulls, but lesser bones are on display, as are ingredients for magic potions, incenses, special rocks, and quirky pieces of jewelry. You can also talk to their live doves. *210 Fillmore St., near Haight St., tel. 415/864–2426.*

PAPER, CARDS, AND STATIONERY **Does Your Mother Know . . .** This queer card shop features coming-out cards, same-sex love cards, and funny gay-humor cards. They also have some gift items of the jewelry and T-shirt variety. *4079 18th St., near Castro St., tel. 415/864–3160.*

Kozo Handmade Paper. Beautiful Japanese stationery, blank books, wall hangings, and other frivolities cost a pretty penny here. *531 Castro St., btw 18th and 19th Sts., tel. 415/621–0869.*

SEX ACCESSORIES **Good Vibrations.** This cooperatively owned, feminist sex shop in the Mission stocks a dazzling selection of vibrators (in fact, there's even an antique vibrator museum). They've also got other sex toys, videos, and literature on all topics sexual. The store is specially designed to make women feel comfortable (though men are equally welcome). If you think all sex shops are sleazy, you obviously haven't been here. *1210 Valencia St., at 23rd St., tel. 415/974–8980.*

Image Leather. They'll accommodate all of your intimate leather needs with a wide variety of nipple rings, harnesses, whips, collars, and boots. *2199 Market St., btw Noe and Church Sts., tel. 415/621–7551.*

SKATEBOARDS AND MOTORCYCLES **Dudley Perkins Harley-Davidson.** This is the oldest Harley-Davidson dealership in the world. Check out the vintage Harleys for sale and on exhibit. *66 Page St., btw Franklin and Gough Sts., tel. 415/703–9494.*

Deluxe. This San Francisco skate shop provides a relatively upscale environment where you can kick back with the regular posse of skaters and watch a couple videos of the sport. Street wear (T-shirts $10) and decks ($40–$45) abound, and the store features works (including display mannequins) by local skater/artist Kevin Ancell. *1831 Market St., btw Guerrero and Octavia Sts., tel. 415/626–5588.*

Magri Motorcycles. The motorcycle enthusiast and historian will appreciate this store's emphasis on hard-to-find British and American bikes, including Vincent, Indian, Norton, and BSA. *1220 Pennsylvania Ave., btw 25th and Army Sts., tel. 415/285–6735. Closed Sun. and Mon.*

MISCELLANEOUS **Bob Mandell's Costume Shop, Inc.** Ball gowns, fake hands, clown ruffles, vampire teeth, capes, and other miscellany await you, for the holidays or every day. *1135 Mission St., btw 7th and 8th Sts., tel. 415/863–7755.*

Gauntlet. The well-trained staff at Gauntlet will gladly pierce your nose, eyebrow, tongue, belly button, and/or ears. The setting is clean and relaxed, and they won't let you out of the shop without fully explaining how to care for your new flesh accessory. If you're already pierced, Gauntlet has a small selection of silver and gold studs and rings. *2377 Market St., at Castro St., tel. 415/431–3133. Open daily noon–7 (until 9 Thurs. and Fri.).*

Guitar Solo. You probably can't afford a 1968 Ramirez or one of the upper-end steel-string guitars sold here, but it's still fun to dream. And if you're looking for that obscure piece of music, you're in luck. If it's still in print, they'll order it . . . if it isn't already in stock. You'll find an extensive (and frighteningly expensive) selection of concert classical guitars, as well as some less upscale models. Read the flyers around the counter or ask the knowledgeable staff about local guitar teachers and upcoming concerts. *1411 Clement St., btw 15th and 16th Aves., tel. 415/386–0395.*

Naked Eye Video. This is definitely not Blockbuster. Come here for offbeat and hard-to-find titles (to rent or buy), and peruse the rack of tattoo and alternative-lifestyle magazines. *533 Haight St., btw Fillmore and Steiner Sts., tel. 415/864–2985.*

Workingman's Headquarters. This has to be the coolest, most ancient and ramshackle, packed-to-the-gills hardware store around. Stuff hangs from the ceiling, the walls, the counters, the employees . . . everywhere. It's great. *2871 Mission St., near 25th St., tel. 415/282–2403.*

Yahoo Herb'an Ecology. No bloodshot eyes here—the name refers to the shop's promotion of urban ecology through the sale of compost materials (such as worm boxes and organic seeds). They also sponsor fundraising benefits that include hip-hop shows and poetry readings. Call before stopping by; the staff takes regular siestas. *968 Valencia St., btw 20th and 21st Sts., tel. 415/282–9676. Closed Sun.–Mon.*

EAST BAY

Body Time. The oldest body shop in the Bay Area makes a huge variety of natural skin- and hair-care goods. They also carry loofahs and sponges. The woman-owned and -run business manufactures its products locally. *2911 College Ave., at Ashby St., Berkeley, tel. 510/845–2101. Other locations: 1942 Shattuck Ave., at Berkeley Way, Berkeley, tel. 510/841–5818; 2509 Telegraph Ave., at Dwight Way, Berkeley, tel. 510/548–3686; 5521 College Ave., btw Ocean View and Lawton, Oakland, tel. 547–4116.*

Games of Berkeley. This large toy store is for the kid in all of us, whether your inner child requires board games, puzzles, cards, or small plastic things that dangle from the end of a pencil. *2010 Shattuck Ave., near University Ave., Berkeley, tel. 510/540–7822.*

Lhasa Karnak. An excellent source of herbs and herbal knowledge, Lhasa Karnak has some extremely helpful and friendly employees. Take advantage quick—before the FDA outlaws it. *1938 Shattuck Ave., at Berkeley Way, Berkeley, tel. 510/548–0372. Other location: 2513 Telegraph Ave., at Dwight Way, Berkeley, tel. 510/548–0380.*

Movie Image. This is the place for film noir in Berkeley. Most titles are for rent only, but a few new and used videos are sold. If you're looking for a hard-to-find classic, the friendly staff will order it. *64 Shattuck Sq., Suite A, near University Ave., Berkeley, tel. 510/649–0296.*

Oak Barrel. This Berkeley home-brew shop stocks everything you need to make a 5-gallon jug of ale. Besides beer-making equipment, you'll also find plenty of recipe and how-to books. *1443 San Pablo Ave., at Page St., Berkeley, tel. 510/849–0400.*

Subway Guitars. This hole-in-the-wall is where Billy Bragg buys and repairs his guitars when he's in town; it's also a great place to browse and drool over classic models. Rumor has it that Joe Satriani used to give lessons out of Subway when he lived in the Bay Area. *1800 Cedar St., at Grant St., Berkeley, tel. 510/841–4105.*

MARIN COUNTY

Marin City Flea Market. If you can wade through the absolute mountains of stuff here, you might find a real bargain, but don't hold your breath. It's strictly for true flea-market hounds, who show up in the hope of unearthing obscure treasures. You'll have to drag your butt out of bed early for this one, because it's open Saturday 6 AM–5 PM, Sunday 5 AM–4 PM. *147 Donahue Rd., at Drake Rd., tel. 415/332–1441. Off U.S. 101 at the Sausalito exit.*

Sausalito Vintage Guitars. Jamey Bellizzi and Charles Peterson have crammed a small but interesting collection of electric, acoustic, and (a few) classical guitars into this tiny store on the second floor of the Bridgeway shopping strip. They aren't exactly giving them away, but you might be able to bargain (a little). *719 Bridgeway, Sausalito, tel. 415/332–1399.*

SOUTH BAY

Bucket of Suds. What looks like another auto-body shop on Old County Road is really a new vendor of beer-brewing and wine-making supplies. A starter kit for beginners ($50) contains a fermentation tank, a bottle capper, and a New Brewers' Handbook, among other necessities. Ben, the owner, will help you get started, and he plans to offer classes in the evenings. He brews much more than he can drink, so ask him for a sample. *317 Old County Rd., Belmont, tel. 415/637–9844. Take U.S. 101 to Ralston Ave. west and turn right on Old County Rd.*

House of Humor. "Will work for sex" and "I'd rather be a smart ass than a dumb shit" are among the pithy proverbs that grace the T-shirts sold in this costume/magic/gag shop. Don't miss the Elvis clock, which gyrates with every swing of his pendulum legs. Mountain View also has a House of Humor (131B E. El Camino Real, at Grant Rd., tel. 415/965–4116). *747 El Camino Real, btw Broadway and Brewster Aves., Redwood City, tel. 415/368–5524.*

Leather Masters. Handcuffs, black-leather jockstraps and garter belts, and harnesses dripping with chains are just a few of the items displayed in this store geared toward the S&M community. You have your pick of massage oils, how-to sex books, and literature by and for the gay community. Plus you can get any part of your body pierced—$10 for above the neck, $15 for below (jewelry costs extra). *969 Park Ave., San Jose, tel. 408/293–7660. Take I–280 to Bird Ave. exit, and turn left on Park Ave. from Bird Ave.*

FOOD

4

By AnneLise Sorensen and Kelly Green

The Bay Area has more than 4,000 restaurants to satisfy everyone from lobster lovers to tofu fanatics. In particular, waves of Asian and Mexican immigrants have made San Francisco a hotbed of cheap taquerias, divey-looking but excellent Chinese restaurants, gracious Thai and Vietnamese establishments, reasonably priced sushi houses, and Korean and Mongolian barbecue joints. Also look for a slew of superb new Greek and Mediterranean restaurants, most serving up heaping, inexpensive platters of food with unique spices that make for a refreshing change from traditional American fare.

These restaurants come equipped with a seemingly endless selection of restaurant reviews, dutifully pasted up in almost every window. Don't assume this little strip of paper means the place is any good, however. Always check the date of the review, since writers frequently update their impressions, and restaurants regularly change hands and chefs. One of the more reliable reviewers is Jim Wood, who writes for the *Examiner.* San Francisco's two biggest free weeklies, *SF Weekly* and the *Bay Guardian,* both have extensive dining reviews and are good sources for new budget restaurants. Dan Leone of the *Guardian* can be counted on for reliable (and witty) advice.

San Franciscans like to repeat this bit of trivia: If every one of the city's residents were to go out to dinner at the same time, there would be enough seats for all of them.

The Bay Area is renowned as the birthplace of California cuisine, which is based on the idea that fresh, home-cultivated ingredients (no matter how expensive) are vital to the success of a dish, and that portions are to be savored, not shoveled in. If it weren't for Berkeley chef Alice Waters, who in 1971 opened the now legendary **Chez Panisse** (1517 Shattuck Ave., Berkeley, tel. 510/548–5525), you might—horror of horrors—never have heard of sun-dried tomatoes, free-range chicken, goat cheese, or arugula. But if you don't have $65 to drop for one of Chez Panisse's five- to six-course meals, the Bay Area still has plenty to offer. Probably the cheapest sit-down meals you'll find are at the hordes of taquerias in San Francisco's Mission district, where a huge, messy burrito can be yours for under $5.

San Francisco

Any one of San Francisco's neighborhoods is likely to boast more good restaurants than exist in most American cities. The diverse population here provides an opportunity to experience authentic dishes from around the world at reasonable prices. Head to North Beach for Italian food, the Mission for Mexican food, and Chinatown for—you guessed it—Chinese fare. If you're

103

after more exotic flavors, some excellent Burmese, Indonesian, Cambodian, and Afghan restaurants have recently taken the city by storm.

CASTRO DISTRICT

The Castro district teems with cute, slightly pricey restaurants, many with outdoor patios for optimum people watching. Brunch seems to be the Castro's favorite meal. Join the masses some weekend by rolling out of bed around 11, donning your shades, and setting out for a long afternoon of Bloody Marys. There's no better way to start (or rather, spend) the day. The Castro's two hottest brunch spots are **Café Flore** (*see* Chapter 5) and the **Patio Café** (*see below*). Mimosas and espressos flow freely on weekend mornings, and the crowd is always jovial and loud. Ranking a close third is **Pasqua** (tel. 415/626–6263), at the corner of Castro and 18th streets. Packed with toned, tanned Castro locals who come for the excellent scones and coffee and stay for the GQ-style social scene, Pasqua is great on a sunny day, when everyone spills onto the outside benches. The Castro's after-hours eating scene is just as lively—you'll find a bunch of 24-hour diners and late-night pizza joints in the area.

➢ **UNDER $5** • **Hot 'n' Hunky.** This pink, perky little restaurant with a preponderance of Marilyn Monroe posters on the walls is a Castro institution for thick, juicy burgers, served until midnight on weekdays and 1 AM on weekends. Ordering burgers with names like the "macho man" (three patties; $4.25), "I wanna hold your ham" (burger with ham and swiss; $4), and "Ms. Piggy" (burger with cheddar and bacon; $4) is half the fun. *4039 18th St., near Castro St., tel. 415/621–6365. Other location: 1946 Market St., at Duboce St., tel. 415/621–3622. No credit cards.*

Marcello's. These guys conjure up some of the best pizza in San Francisco right across the street from the Castro Theatre (*see* Movie Houses, in Chapter 6)—very convenient when it's almost show time. They sell by the slice ($1.75–$2.50) or the pie ($7.50–$18.50), and you can always find unusual ready-made combo slices like spinach, black olives, and feta; or ham and pineapple. They're open real late on weekends, in case you've got the munchies. *420 Castro St., near Market St., tel. 415/863–3900. Open Sun.–Thurs. 11 AM–1 AM, Fri.–Sat. 11 AM–2 AM. No credit cards.*

➢ **UNDER $10** • **Amazing Grace.** This cafeteria-style, no-nonsense vegetarian restaurant offers an inventive and tasty array of dishes that change daily. An order of Moroccan vegetables with couscous, or tofu loaf with a cashew and mushroom sauce, will run you $4.25. You can also feast on delicious soups and curry dishes. *216 Church St., at Market St., tel. 415/626–6411. Open Mon.–Sat. 11–10. No credit cards.*

Bagdad Café. Hogging an entire street corner to itself (no small feat in the packed Castro), this 24-hour restaurant is as famous for its expansive, street-level windows—in an area where people watching is a high art—as its home-style breakfasts. Two eggs with home fries cost $4.25; sandwiches run $5–$6. *2295 Market St., at 16th St., tel. 415/621–4434. Wheelchair access. Open daily 24 hrs. No credit cards.*

Josie's Cabaret and Juice Joint. By night it's a well-known performance venue; by day it's an easygoing neighborhood hangout offering a 100% vegetarian menu of fresh organic juices, salads, sandwiches, and breakfast items. Vegetarian entrées of any kind won't cost much over $5, and you can get a small salad, soup, or a fruit smoothie for less than $3. Come on a sunny day and eat outside on the pretty back patio. *3583 16th St., at Market St., tel. 415/861–7933. Open daily 9–8. No credit cards.*

La Méditerranée. This small, personable restaurant on the edge of the Castro district serves great Middle Eastern and Greek food, including dolmas, salads, hummus, baba ghanoush, and levant sandwiches (appetizers cost $4–$6; entrées go for $6–$10). If everything sounds good, get the Middle Eastern combination plate—two meaty phyllo pastries, a levant sandwich, luleh kabob, and salad ($7). Dessert lovers shouldn't miss the *datil* ($3.50), a dense roll of dates, phyllo dough, nuts, and cream that is surely one of the most decadent things on the planet. *288 Noe St., at Market St., tel. 415/431–7210. Open Sun. and Tues.–Thurs. 11–10, Fri.–Sat.*

11–11. Other locations: 2210 Fillmore St., at Sacramento St., tel. 415/921–2956; 2936 College Ave., Berkeley, near Ashby Ave., tel. 510/540–7773.

No-Name (Nippon) Sushi. Everybody calls it No-Name Sushi, even though the proprietors did eventually put up a tiny cardboard sign in the window officially dubbing it "Nippon." This tiny, wood-paneled restaurant in the Castro district almost always has a line out the door, because it serves huge, delicious sushi combos at staggeringly low prices—try $6–$10 on for size. No alcohol is served. *314 Church St., at 15th St., no phone. Open Mon.–Sat. noon–10 PM. No credit cards.*

Orphan Andy's. If you're looking for inexpensive American grub late at night, head to this small, atmospheric Castro hangout adorned with red vinyl booths, a lunch counter, and a jukebox. Bring a date and pretend you're Joanie and Chachi (or, more likely, Richie and Fonzie) in a secluded back booth at 3 AM. Burgers cost $5, and omelets run between $4 and $6. *3991 17th St., at Market and Castro Sts., tel. 415/864–9795. Open daily 24 hrs. No credit cards.*

Patio Café. The Castro's premiere brunch spot operates out of an enormous converted greenhouse complete with fake parrots perched among the foliage. Enough Bloody Marys ($3) are consumed here to conk out a small army. Eggs with home fries go for $4–$5, and decadent cheese blintzes with cherry sauce are $7. You can also chow on sandwiches, burgers, and pastas (all $7). *531 Castro St., btw 18th and 19th Sts., tel. 415/621–4640. Open daily 8–4 and 4:30–10.*

Sparky's. This 24-hour diner has a menu with shades of Denny's, but—for what it's worth—a *much* trendier clientele. To fill your hip quotient, arrive at 3 AM in your Doc Martens and join the throngs of hungry clubbers who come for burgers ($6), pizzas ($10–$14 for a small), and breakfast (bulging omelets $6–$7). *242 Church St., near Market St., tel. 415/621–6001. Open daily 24 hrs.*

Thailand Restaurant. Climb the stairs to this second-story Thai restaurant and feast on some of the best food the Castro (hell, San Francisco) has to offer. Directly across the street from the Castro Theatre (*see* Movie Houses, in Chapter 6), this dainty spot serves up a mean plate of pad Thai ($6) and an excellent *pad kao pod* (sautéed chicken with garlic and baby corn; $6). Even if you're not an appetizer person, the *goong gra bawg* (shrimp in a crispy batter; $6) is a must. *488A Castro St., btw Market and 18th Sts., tel. 415/863–6868. Open Mon.–Thurs. 11–10, Fri.–Sat. 11–10:30.*

➤ **UNDER $15 • Anchor Oyster Bar.** Small, bright, and clean, the Anchor draws a crowd that likes to chow down on reasonably priced oysters ($7 for six), not to mention innovative pasta and seafood dishes ($10–$15) and awesome clam chowder ($3). *579 Castro St., btw 18th and 19th Sts., tel. 415/431–3990. Open weekdays 11:30–10, Sat. noon–10, Sun. 4:30 PM–9:30 PM.*

CHINATOWN

Finding something to eat in Chinatown will probably be one of your easiest and most pleasurable projects. Steer clear of the glaringly tourist-oriented places (where you have to ask for chopsticks and the patrons are all carrying shopping bags of souvenirs), and instead wander through the heart of Chinatown—Washington, Clay, and Sacramento streets between Mason and Kearny—until you find a restaurant that has the four elements that spell success: small, divey, cheap, and packed with locals.

➤ **UNDER $5 • Kowloon.** One of the few all-vegetarian restaurants in Chinatown, Kowloon packs in the tree huggers and true Buddhists with its excellent selection of vegetarian dim sum. A pot sticker or a dense mushroom cake sells for only about 60¢. If you get impatient eating your meal one item at a time, choose from a huge number of rice dishes (brown rice optional) for $3–$5, topped with such exotica as vegetarian duck gizzards and vegetarian pork tripe. *909 Grant Ave., near Washington St., tel. 415/362–9888. Open daily 9–9. No credit cards.*

Lucky Creation. This small restaurant in the heart of Chinatown serves fantastic meatless fare. From the green sign to the green tables and menus, this place is loud and clear about its aims to please the vegetarian palate—and it's cheap. Mixed veggies over rice go for $3.75, and braised eggplant in a clay pot will run you $4. *854 Washington St., near Stockton St., tel. 415/989–0818. Open Thurs.–Tues. 11–9:30. No credit cards.*

➢ **UNDER $10 • Chef Jia's.** Next door to the ever-popular tourist magnet House of Nanking (*see below*), Chef Jia's manages to survive, indeed thrive, thanks to its top-notch Hunan and Mandarin cuisine. It's noisy and crowded, and the decor leaves a lot to be desired, but the onion cakes ($1.50) and the spicy yams in garlic sauce ($4) are both to-die-for. Best of all, you'll be halfway through your mouthwatering chicken breast with yams ($5) before the Nanking diehards even reach the front door. *925 Kearny St., btw Jackson and Columbus Sts., tel. 415/398–1626. Open daily 11–10. No credit cards.*

House of Nanking. This Chinatown hole-in-the-wall offers excellent Shanghai home cooking at low prices. The tiny space is constantly packed (a line stretches out the door), the decor is nonexistent, and the no-nonsense waiters keep you on your toes. Ask for the delicious shrimp cakes in peanut sauce ($4.50)—they're not on the menu—or try the chicken Nanking ($5), a version of General Tso's chicken. *919 Kearny St., btw Jackson and Columbus Sts., tel. 415/421–1429. Open weekdays 11–10, Sat. noon–10, Sun. 4 PM–10 PM. No credit cards.*

Lotus Garden. Chinatown locals and out-of-towners pile into this second-story vegetarian Chinese restaurant. Skilled chefs work wonders with wheat gluten, coming up with such treats as sautéed puffballs in curry sauce ($4.75). The sweet-and-sour vegetarian pork ($5.25) and hot-and-sour soup ($3.75) are also big hits. The pleasant smell of incense wafting through the restaurant comes from the Taoist temple directly above. *532 Grant Ave., at California St., tel. 415/397–0707. Open daily 11:30–9.*

R&G Lounge. You couldn't call it lively (in fact, it's a bit sterile and depressing), but the R&G Lounge serves super-fresh seafood dishes. Worth trying are the oyster clay pot ($7) and the mushrooms with bok choy ($6.25), the latter featuring delicate greens. Go for lunch ($4–$5) and watch the staff prepare egg rolls ($4) in the dining room. *631B Kearny St., btw Sacramento and Clay Sts., tel. 415/982–7877. Open daily 11–9:30.*

Royal Hawaii Seafood Restaurant. This is the original source for dim sum in San Francisco, and one of the least expensive (dishes run $2–$3.50). It's a large, bustling Chinatown hangout, especially at lunch on the weekend. The evening yields decent dinner fare, like the flavorful garlic chicken over rice ($6.50). *835 Pacific Ave., at Stockton St., tel. 415/391–6365. Open daily 7:30–3 and 5–10.*

CIVIC CENTER

For a bite on your way to the art museum or a cuppa joe after the opera, walk along **Hayes** and **Grove streets** between Franklin and Laguna—the area is a prime example of gentrification in progress, with trendy cafés and restaurants sprouting up right beside depressed, dingy storefronts. **Spuntino** (524 Van Ness Ave., at McAllister St., tel. 415/861–7772) is perfect if you're headed to the movie theaters on Van Ness Avenue. Salads are about $5 and *panini* (Italian sandwiches) go for $7.

➢ **UNDER $5 • Tommy's Joynt.** This lively cafeteria-style hofbrau and bar is a longtime San Francisco fixture. Specialties include buffalo stew ($6) and bean-and-beer soup ($2.50). They also serve inexpensive carved-meat sandwiches ($3.50) and dinner platters, as well as a vast selection of obscure beers from around the world ($2.50–$3). *1101 Geary St., at Van Ness Ave., tel. 415/775–4216. Wheelchair access. Open daily 10 AM–1:30 AM. No credit cards.*

➢ **UNDER $10 • Ananda Fuara.** Escape from grimy Market Street into this soothing vegetarian restaurant with sky-blue walls. Servers sway by the tables in flowing saris, bringing sandwiches ($5) and entrées like curry with rice and chutney ($7). The massive Brahma burrito ($5) will fill you for the rest of the day. *1298 Market St., at 9th St., tel. 415/621–1994. Open Mon.–Tues. and Thurs.–Sat. 8–8, Wed. 8–3. No credit cards.*

Grubstake. Housed in a converted railroad car in Polk Gulch, this late-night eatery serves decent breakfasts ($5) and thick, messy burgers ($5–$6). Ask for the delicious homemade quince jelly (made from apples) to spread atop your toast. *1525 Pine St., btw Polk St. and Van Ness Ave., tel. 415/673–8268. Open weekdays 5 PM–4 AM, weekends 10 AM–4 AM. No credit cards.*

Moishe's Pippic. This Chicago-style Jewish deli near the Civic Center will satisfy the corned-beef pangs of relocated, alienated East Coasters. They've got it all: kosher salami, hot dogs, corned beef, chopped liver, pastrami, tongue, bagels and lox, matzo ball soup, Polish sausage, knishes. . . . It'll almost make living in California bearable. Hot dogs start at $2.50, sandwiches at $5. *425A Hayes St., at Gough St., tel. 415/431–2440. Open weekdays 8–4, Sat. 9:30–4. No credit cards.*

Racha Café. In a city filled to the brim with Thai restaurants, this is an exceptional choice, for both the food and the service. Try the spicy mint chicken (around $6) or the vegetables with peanut sauce ($6). *771 Ellis St., at Polk St., tel. 415/885–0725. Wheelchair access. Open daily 11–9.*

Vicolo. Popular with the symphony crowd, this pizzeria serves up gourmet slices and pies in a hard-to-find Civic Center alleyway. Choose from basic varieties (cheese, pepperoni, sausage, veggie, and lowfat) or several more exciting seasonal selections. Prices are high, but the corn-

Food Snob for a Day

There's a tier of restaurants in San Francisco that are hopelessly out of reach for most of us except on that one glorious day of the month: payday. In the euphoric 24 hours before the rent and credit-card demons start toying with your conscience, you are the richest, hippest, swankiest person in the city—and that's when you call a friend, put on your finest duds, and splurge like hell at one of San Francisco's toniest restaurants, where diners regularly pay $40 and up per person. Critics and locals argue endlessly about which is the best restaurant in San Francisco, "the best" being gauged by criteria like attentive service, chic ambience, and artistic presentation. Among those vying for the top title are:

- Stars. Inventive California cuisine. Nearby, at 500 Van Ness, Stars Café isn't as good as the mother restaurant, but it's not as expensive either. 150 Redwood Alley, off Van Ness Ave., tel. 415/861–7827.

- Postrio. California cuisine with Asian and Mediterranean influences. 545 Post St., btw Taylor and Mason Sts., tel. 415/776–7825.

- Bix. A '90s version of a '40s supper club, featuring classic American fare. 56 Gold St., at Montgomery St., tel. 415/433–6300.

- Square One. International cuisine, but look for a Mediterranean emphasis. 190 Pacific St., at Front St., tel. 415/788–1110.

- Aqua. Seafood with a French accent. 252 California St., btw Battery and Front Sts., tel. 415/956–9662.

- Restaurant Lulu. Rustic cuisine from the French and Italian rivieras, served family style. 816 Folsom St., btw 4th and 5th Sts., tel. 415/495–5775.

meal crust makes a slice more filling than it appears. A piece of, say, wild mushroom pizza ($3.50), plus a Caesar salad ($5) shared with a friend, may well suffice. *201 Ivy St., btw Franklin and Gough Sts. and Hayes and Grove Sts., tel. 415/863–2382. Open Mon.–Thurs. 11:30–11, Fri.–Sat. 11:30–11:30, Sun. 2 PM–10 PM. Other location: 473 University Ave., Palo Alto, near Cowper St., tel. 415/324–4877. From U.S. 101, take University Ave. exit west (toward Stanford). Wheelchair access. Open Sun.–Thurs. 11:30–10, Fri.–Sat. 11:30–11.*

> **UNDER $15** • **Golden Turtle.** Here you can consume some of San Francisco's best Vietnamese food in high style (among some carved wood pieces that look like they belong in an Asian art collection). The barbecued quail is excellent ($6), and a number of vegetarian dishes, such as spicy lemongrass vegetable curry ($9), round out the menu. *2211 Van Ness Ave., btw Broadway and Vallejo St., tel. 415/441–4419. Open Tues.–Sun. 5 PM–11 PM.*

Phnom Penh. With its lace curtains and dainty table settings, this little place in the Civic Center looks ready for an elaborate tea party. Despite the rawness of the neighborhood, expect friendly service and excellent Cambodian food, including coconut-milk curries ($7–$8) that you can order with chicken, prawns, or halibut; and lots of spicy grilled-meat dishes ($8.50). You can get lunch for about $6. *631 Larkin St., near Eddy St., tel. 415/775–5979. Open weekdays 11–3 and 5–9, Sat. 5–9, Sun. 5–8:30.*

Swan Oyster Depot. The genial staff welcomes you with open arms and will promptly set you up with a bowl of clam chowder, thick sourdough bread, and an Anchor Steam beer for a fiver. Don't be surprised if you find yourself ordering a half-dozen oysters or cracked Dungeness crab. Such gluttony will set you back $20, but you just won't care. *1517 Polk St., btw California and Sacramento Sts., tel. 415/673–1101. Open Mon.–Sat. 8–5:30. No credit cards.*

Politicians can open their mouths wider than the tiny Swan Oyster Depot, which consists of nothing more than a lunch counter, a few stools, and the best damn seafood in town.

> **UNDER $20** • **California Culinary Academy.** How'd you like to eat someone's homework assignment? You can at the Culinary Academy, where fledgling chefs prepare food under the watchful eyes of their instructors. The results vary, but it's worth a shot. The academy offers two restaurants. At Careme, the more formal one (lunch $10–$15, dinner $13–$19), you can watch student chefs at work. The Grill offers basic grill food for lunch ($4–$9) and buffet dinners ($10–$12) nightly. *625 Polk St., at Turk St., tel. 415/771–3500. Open weekdays noon–1:30 PM and 6 PM–8:30 PM.*

Miss Pearl's Jam House. Miss Pearl's live reggae and calypso music (Thurs.–Sat. nights) and "soul-food Sunday" gospel performances attract a young, lively crowd. You'll have to traipse through a scuzzy neighborhood to get here, but once you arrive you can eat poolside (weekends only; the pool belongs to the attached Phoenix Hotel) or in the Jamaican-style dining room. In addition to the regular selection of Caribbean entrées ($12–$18), the restaurant serves inventive appetizers, like corn and manchego cheese *arepas* (corn fritters) with smoked tomato salad ($5). The Jamaican-style jerk chicken ($11) is famous in these parts. *601 Eddy St., at Larkin*

Reach Out and Taste Something

No longer do you have to rely on the old standbys—Chinese and pizza—for delivered food. If you're willing to pay a $6-per-restaurant delivery fee, two delivery services, Waiters on Wheels (tel. 415/252–1470) and Dine-One-One (tel. 415/771–DINE), will bring you hot meals from a slew of San Francisco restaurants. You can order anything from burgers to Italian to Greek and Mediterranean. To start your browsing, pick up their free delivery guides at street boxes—usually near newspaper stands—in the Financial District and other parts of the city. You can also call and have them mail you a guide.

St., tel. 415/775–5267. Open Tues.–Thurs. 6 PM–10 PM, Fri.–Sat. 6 PM–11 PM, Sun. 11–2:30 and 5:30–10.

Zuni Café. Watch yuppies and artist kids with trust funds sneer at each other over oysters ($1.50 each) at this crowded, sleek café on Market Street. Zuni provides friendly service and really decadent food for those times when you're in a what-the-hell frame of mind. It's most fun to come for appetizers and drinks. Try the famous Caesar salad ($8)—regulars swear it's the best they've ever had. Another popular item is roasted chicken for two ($28) with Tuscan bread and salad. *1658 Market St., btw Haight and Page Sts., tel. 415/552–2522. Open Tues.–Sat. 7:30 AM–midnight, Sun. 7:30 AM–11 PM.*

DOWNTOWN

Downtown abounds with old, classic restaurants that evoke San Francisco's golden years, and lunch counters that still feature blue plate specials and chocolate malts. **Lori's Diner** (336 Mason St., at Geary St., tel. 415/392–8646), earnestly nostalgic for the '50s, is open 24 hours, as is **Pine Crest** (401 Geary St., at Mason St., tel. 415/885–6407), a slightly less ersatz version on the same theme. In recent years, haunts catering to a high-rolling Financial District clientele have flourished, and you'll also run into the occasional health food joint trying to keep all those executives from succumbing to heart disease at a young age. The **International Food Fair** (24 Ellis St., at Market St.) probably contains the highest concentration of cheap food in all of downtown: Persian, Greek, Burmese, Korean, Mexican, Japanese, Chinese, and American fast-food stands rub shoulders, offering $3–$5 lunch specials. The **Bush and Kearny Food Center** (cnr Bush and Kearny Sts.) is a good place to look for Chinese, Mexican, and Thai dishes for less than $5.

➤ **UNDER $5 • Specialty's.** This trio of tiny take-out stands bakes six kinds of bread, including potato-cheese and carrot-curry, on which they will make any of 40—count 'em, 40—fresh sandwiches (most around $3–$4). They also sell soup ($2–$3) and insanely rich sweets. If you don't feel like eating on the sidewalk, take your lunch over to the rooftop garden at Crocker Galleria (cnr Kearny and Post Sts.) and have a feast. *312 Kearny St., btw Bush and Pine Sts.; 22 Battery St., at Bush and Market Sts.; 150 Spear St., btw Mission and Howard Sts. Tel. 415/788–BAKE for daily specials, 415/512–9550 for phone orders. Open weekdays 6–6. No credit cards.*

How to Eat for Free, Get Sloshed, and Network at the Same Time

Happy Hour, that ritual of working stiffs that offers free hors d'oeuvres to anyone who buys a drink, is of course commemorated in San Francisco. You can nosh on some pretty wonderful food in these places, including pizza, chicken wings, nachos, egg rolls, and fried calamari. Some of the happiest hours in town include the Starlight Roof in the Sir Francis Drake Hotel (450 Powell St., at Sutter St., tel. 415/392–7755; Mon.–Sat. 4:30–7), the Achilles Heel (1601 Haight St., at Clayton St., tel. 415/626–1800; Wed.–Fri. 5–7), the Cadillac Bar (1 Holland Ct., off Howard St. btw 4th and 5th Sts., tel. 415/543–8226; weekdays 4–6:30), the London Wine Bar (415 Sansome St., btw Sacramento Ave. and Clay St.; weekdays 5–7), ¡WA-HA-KA! (1489 Folsom St., at 11th St., tel. 415/861–1410; weekdays 5–8), and Bull's Texas Café (25 Van Ness Ave., at Market St., tel. 415/864–4288; weekdays 4:30–6:30). There's enough free food to keep you sated for weeks. Drinks range anywhere from $2 to $6—and if you have too many, your name may end up in some Rolodexes you'll later regret.

➤ **UNDER $10** • **101 Restaurant.** In the downtrodden Tenderloin, this highly respected restaurant serves up tasty *chao tom* (shrimp and sugarcane; $8), *ga xao lang* (coconut chicken and lemongrass; $5.25), and other Vietnamese favorites. At lunch they have a great $4.75 special that includes soup, an imperial roll, and your choice of barbecued beef, chicken, or pork. *101 Eddy St., at Mason St., tel. 415/928–4490. Open Mon.–Sat. 11–9.*

Clown Alley. This splashy burger joint is popular with the Financial District's lunchtime crowd and late-night North Beach revelers in need of a red-meat fix. Tasty, messy burgers ($4–$5) are the name of the game, and big fries and shakes round out the menu. *42 Columbus Ave., at Jackson St., tel. 415/421–2540. Open Mon.–Thurs. 7 AM–12:30 AM, Fri.–Sat. 7 AM–3 AM, Sun. 9 AM–10:30 PM. No credit cards. Other location: 2499 Lombard St., at Divisadero St., tel. 415/931–5890.*

The Fruit Gallery. Come here for healthy food in a bright, clean space that features changing art exhibitions. The quality of the art varies, but the food remains steadfastly wholesome and reasonably priced. Breakfasts ($2–$6) include egg dishes and various members of the granola family. For lunch try a veggie burger with a side salad ($6.25), grilled chicken (about $6), or healthful soups and salads. *301 Kearny St., at Bush St., tel. 415/362–2216. Open Mon.–Thurs. 7 AM–3 PM and 5 PM–9 PM, Fri. 7 AM–3 PM.*

Tu Lan. This place welcomes street-smart diners with terrific Vietnamese food in a really seedy downtown location. The expansive menu (entrées $3.75–$6.25) includes plenty of choices for vegetarians. Sit at the packed counter and watch the kitchen staff prepare your food, including addictive imperial rolls ($4) and chicken with five herbs ($5). *8 6th St., at Market St., tel. 415/626–0927. Open Mon.–Sat. 11–9. No credit cards.*

➤ **UNDER $15** • **Café Bastille.** Stop by for neat little French appetizers, like onion soup, pâté, or baked goat cheese on eggplant ($3–$5), in a happening, Frenchy atmosphere. For a more substantial meal, they've got sandwiches ($5–$7), crepe dinners ($6.50), or real meat-and-potatoes fare ($7–$10). Filled with quasi-hip Financial District workers and bohemians with a few bucks to blow, the café gets pretty fun and friendly, especially on Thursdays, Fridays, and Saturdays, when the live jazz is going. *22 Belden Pl., btw Pine and Bush Sts. and Kearny and Montgomery Sts., tel. 415/986–5673. Open Mon.–Wed. 11:30–10, Thurs.–Sat. 11:30–10:30.*

The food at Café Claude is so good, the atmosphere so nearly authentic, that you may burst out with some bad French, which your waiter will enjoy ridiculing.

Café Claude. Live jazz accompanies your meal most nights at this youthful but bourgeois French bistro in the Financial District. With a more relaxed atmosphere than Café Bastille (*see above*), this is a great place to while away a lazy afternoon. The menu includes two types of salad ($2.50–$7), soup ($4), and hot and cold sandwiches and entrées ($8–$10). *7 Claude La., off Bush St. btw Grant and Kearny Sts., tel. 415/392–3505. Open Mon.–Wed. 8 AM–9 PM, Thurs. 8 AM–10 PM, Fri. 8 AM–11 PM, Sat. 8 AM–12:30 AM.*

Il Fornaio. This posh but sterile restaurant serves authentic Italian cuisine at surprisingly reasonable prices. The pizzas ($8–$11) are baked the old-fashioned way—in a brick, wood-burning oven—and the pastas are usually terrific, especially the angel-hair pasta with fresh tomatoes and basil ($10). A spin-off, the Il Fornaio Bakery (2298 Union St., tel. 415/563–0746), serves pizza by the slice ($3.75) and mouthwatering loaves of Italian bread ($3–$4). *1265 Battery St., at Greenwich St., tel. 415/986–0100. Open Sun.–Thurs. 8 AM–11 PM, Fri.–Sat. 8 AM–midnight. Other location: 520 Cowper St., Palo Alto, near University Ave., tel. 415/853–3888. Open Mon.–Thurs. 7 AM–11 PM, Fri.–Sat. 7 AM–midnight, Sun. 8 AM–11 PM.*

Sol y Luna. Smack in the heart of downtown, this upscale Spanish restaurant serves excellent *tapas* (appetizers), including *gambas al ajillo* (prawns sauteed with garlic and olive oil; $5.50) and *berenjena* (grilled eggplant in roasted tomato sauce; $3.75). Make a meal of them, or splurge on the *paella marinera* (Spanish rice topped with prawns, scallops, clams, mussels, cod, and vegetables; $13). Wednesday through Saturday nights you can dance away your dinner to live Latin music. *475 Sacramento St., btw Battery and Sansome Sts., tel. 415/296–8696. Open weekdays 11:30–2:30 and 5:30–10, Sat. 5:30–10.*

Yank Sing. With a location in the Financial District and one South of Market, Yank Sing is a great place to feast on dim sum (small dumplings that you choose from passing carts and pay for by the plate) in a tasteful, modern setting. A meal should cost about $10–$15 per person, but watch out: Let your appetite run away with you and next thing you know your pants are unbuttoned, your head is nodding, stacks of plates are sliding off the table, and the waiter's handing you a bill the size of Beijing. *427 Battery St., at Clay St., tel. 415/362–1640. Open weekdays 11–3, weekends 10–4. Other location: 49 Stevenson Pl., btw 1st and 2nd Sts., tel. 415/495–4510. Open weekdays 11–3.*

FISHERMAN'S WHARF

Steer clear of the mediocre, high-priced seafood restaurants that compete for tourist bucks all along the wharf. The best dining experience you could have here would involve a loaf of sour-dough, some shrimp or perhaps a crab, a bottle of wine, a perch on the pier, and a tantalizing dining partner. The corner of **Jefferson** and **Taylor streets** is jam-packed with street stands that hawk all sorts of seafood goodies, including shrimp, prawn, or crab cups ($2.50) and thick clam chowder in a bread bowl ($3.50).

➢ **UNDER $10** • **Buena Vista Café.** This brass-and-wood bar just down the road from Fisherman's Wharf at the Hyde Street cable-car turnaround serves burgers and sandwiches ($4–$7.50), as well as Irish coffee, which they strenuously claim to have introduced to America. While the tourists are sometimes packed in elbow to elbow, it manages to retain its dignity. *2765 Hyde St., tel. 415/474–5044. Open weekdays 9 AM–2 AM, weekends 8 AM–2 AM. No credit cards.*

Eagle Café. Lifted whole from its former location two blocks away and dropped onto the upper story of Pier 39, this bar/restaurant is authentically rustic, unlike the rest of this area. Windows and patio tables offer a view of the waterfront and Alcatraz. It's a good place to eat a bowl of clam chowder ($4) or a burger ($5) and plan how you're going to escape Fisherman's Wharf. After lunch, the Eagle becomes a bar only. *Upper level, Pier 39, tel. 415/433–3689. Wheelchair access. Kitchen open Mon.–Sat. 7:30 AM–2:30 PM, Sun. 7:30 AM–3 PM. No credit cards.*

HAIGHT-ASHBURY DISTRICT

The Haight abounds with good breakfast places, including the Pork Store Café, the Crescent City Café, and Kate's Kitchen (*see below*). These places are full to the brim with the youth of today—in case you can't tell, they're the ones who are smoking, wearing black, looking like hell, and sucking on coffee like it's the primal life force. For dinner the Haight offers a few trendy hot spots and a preponderance of pizza joints, which provide the necessary carbohydrates to propel you to the next bar.

➢ **UNDER $10** • **All You Knead.** This classically Californian establishment has lots of items on the menu with sprouts and/or avocado. The decor is spartan, but the upper-Haight slackers who flow in and out of here are looking to nibble indifferently on a big salad with herbal vinaigrette dressing ($4), not to gaze at the insipid art exhibits on the walls. A jumbo quesadilla with veggies and a salad will set you back $5; a hot dish of eggplant parmesan sells for $6. *1466 Haight St., at Ashbury St., tel. 415/552–4550. Open Mon.–Thurs. 8 AM–10:45 PM, Fri.–Sat. 8 AM–midnight.*

Crescent City Cafe. Every so often, we at the *Berkeley Guides* find a restaurant that we like so much, we don't want to review it. The situation is especially grave in the case of this New Orleans–style café, which has just six small tables and maybe a dozen counter seats. Whatever you do, please do not come for brunch on weekends, when you'll find Berkeley editors gorging themselves on Andouille hash ($5.75) and hefty plates of pork chops and eggs ($6). Another bad time to come is Thursday night for the barbecued-rib special ($8). Do us a favor and order your po-boy catfish sandwich ($6) to go. *1418 Haight St., at Masonic St., tel. 415/863–1374. Open daily 8–4 and 5–10.*

Kan Zaman. Patrons pack into this trendy Mediterranean restaurant to sit on big floor pillows, listen to hypnotic Middle Eastern music, and indulge in hummus ($2.75), baba ghanoush ($2.75), and spinach pies ($3). If you need that final push to reach a dreamlike state, fork over $7 for a huge hookah (a traditional water pipe) with your choice of flavored tobacco—the apple is especially good. On Friday, Saturday, and Sunday nights the Fat Chance Belly Dancers do their seductive thing. *1793 Haight St., at Shrader St., tel. 415/751–9656. Open Mon. 6 PM–midnight, Tues.–Fri. noon–midnight, weekends noon–2 AM. No credit cards.*

Kate's Kitchen. Kate's is the biggest thing to hit Haight Street since LSD. The crowd may be grungy, but the food is positively wholesome. Chummy servers bring you specials like lemon-cornmeal pancakes with fresh fruit ($5 short, $7 tall) or an omelet with cilantro pesto, tomatoes, feta, and roasted chilis ($7). Split the hush puppies with honey butter ($1.75 for six) among your table as an appetizer. On weekends you'll line up outside with people who look cool (or at least try to) even with a hangover. *471 Haight St., btw Fillmore and Webster Sts., tel. 415/626–3984. Open Tues.–Fri. 8 AM–2:45 PM, weekends 9–3:45.*

Massawa. If you've never had Ethiopian food before and you (1) like to eat with your hands, (2) relish unusual spices, or (3) are one of those ignoramuses who is guilty of making dumb jokes about Ethiopian cuisine, you must come here. You get a dinner platter filled with tender lamb or beef ($6–$8), usually with side portions of lentils, greens, or yellow split-pea paste (they have all-vegetarian dishes as well). All plates come with *injera*, a flat, spongy bread used instead of silverware to scoop up food. *1538 Haight St., btw Ashbury and Clayton Sts., tel. 415/621–4129. Open Tues.–Sun. noon–9:30.*

Pork Store Café. This Haight Street breakfast joint is a great place to eat away your hangover. Mounds of grits ($1.50), big fluffy omelets ($4.25–$5.50), and plate-size pancakes (a chocolate short stack is $4) are all slapped together on the same griddle. While you're waiting in line (with a cup of complimentary coffee), check out the collection of posters from Haight-Ashbury street fairs past—they're almost as entertaining as the stream of locals strutting by. *1451 Haight St., btw Ashbury St. and Masonic Ave., tel. 415/864–6981. Open Mon.–Sat. 7 AM–3 PM, Sun. 8 AM–4 PM. Other location: 372 5th St., at Harrison St., tel. 415/495–3669.*

Spaghetti Western. The pierced and tattooed set eats breakfast and then hangs around all day at this chaotic lower-Haight spot. Gorge yourself on the spuds o'rama ($4), a huge, quivering mound of home-fried potatoes topped with cheese and sour cream, or the thick sourdough French toast ($4.50). *576 Haight St., near Steiner St., tel. 415/864–8461. Open weekdays 7 AM–3:30 PM, weekends 8 AM–4 PM.*

Squat and Gobble Café. This big, sprawling café-turned-breakfast spot serves up home-style breakfasts to lower-Haight types who come armed with the Sunday paper, a pack of Marlboro reds, and nothing to do all day. Try the massive lower-Haight omelet, with fresh veggies, pesto, and cheese ($4.75), or any number of inventive crepes, including the Zorba the Greek, with feta, olives, artichokes, spinach, and cheddar ($6). If you're the type who needs a pot of coffee before you can focus, be aware that refills are not free. *237 Fillmore St., btw Haight and Waller Sts., tel. 415/487–0551. Open daily 8 AM–9 PM. No credit cards.*

➣ **UNDER $15** • **Cha Cha Cha.** You'll enjoy the skillfully prepared tapas and the pseudo-Catholic icons on the walls, but you'll wait all night for a table. The heyday of this Caribbean joint has lasted a little too long, as evidenced by the wanna-be-hip crowd it now draws. Entrées range from $10 to $15, but it's de rigueur to stick to tapas like fried plantains with black beans and sour cream ($4.50) or shrimp sautéed in Cajun spices ($5.50). Wash it all down with plenty of sangria (which can also help your potential two-hour wait fly by in a veritable blur). To avoid the crowds, come for a late lunch during the week (they close from 3 to 5, though). *1801 Haight St., at Shrader St., tel. 415/386–5758. Open Mon.–Thurs. 11:30–3 and 5–11, Fri. 11:30–3 and 5–11:30, Sat. 10–4 and 5–11:30, Sun. 10–4 and 5–11. No credit cards.*

Ganges. Those who think vegetarian food is dull and tasteless should come to this small Indian restaurant. The delicious, extra-spicy Surti cuisine, which contains no meat, no fish, and only homemade cheeses, can fill you up for about $10; but if you order the "number one" package (raita, papadum, chapati, chutney, appetizer, rice, vegetable, curry, and dessert), you'll have a feast for under $15. À la carte curry dishes like *chana masala* (a garbanzo-bean delicacy) and stuffed zucchini cost $5.50. Friday and Saturday nights musicians play the sitar and tabla. *775 Frederick St., btw Stanyan and Arguello Sts., tel. 415/661-7290. Open Tues.–Sat. 5 PM–10 PM.*

If you don't feel like sitting at one of the Ganges's tables, you can remove your shoes and park yourself on cushions in the back room, though after a couple of Taj Mahal beers, standing up may pose something of a challenge.

Thep Phanom. This small, daintily decorated lower-Haight Thai establishment finally seems to be nearing the end of its trendy period, when hour-plus waits were common. If you come at the right time, it can be a relaxing place to grab a savory bowl of *tom kha gai* (coconut chicken soup; $7). Critics also rave about the duck dishes and curries, but expect to pay a bit more than you normally do for Thai entrées ($8–$10 instead of the standard $6–$7)—the price of inventiveness and fame. *400 Waller St., at Fillmore St., tel. 415/431-2526. Open daily 5:30 PM–10:30 PM.*

JAPANTOWN

In the **Japan Center,** the veritable heart of Japantown, a bunch of decent restaurants—spanning a wide range of price categories—display their edibles via shiny photos or shellacked plastic miniatures. If nothing piques your interest, explore the surrounding streets for older, more divey places that occasionally turn out to be gems. The cheapest option of all is to visit the Japanese market **Maruwa,** on the corner of Post and Webster streets. Along with fruits and vegetables and all manner of Japanese products, a delicatessen offers sushi, rice and noodle dishes, and individual cuts of meat. When you're done eating, go blow the rest of your money on a cheesy action movie at the multi-screen Kabuki Cinema (*see* Movie Houses, in Chapter 6), in the same complex.

➤ **UNDER $10 • Isobune.** Patrons at this touristy but fun sushi restaurant pack in around a large table, elbow to elbow, and fish their sushi off little boats that bob about in the water in front of them. Kimono-clad chefs deftly mold the sushi and replenish the boats' cargo as fast as they are emptied. Prices range from $1.20 for two pieces of octopus or fried bean cake to $2.50 for two pieces of salmon roe or red clam. *Japan Center, 1737 Post St., tel. 415/563-1030. Open daily 11:30–10.*

Mifune. A steady stream of Asian and American patrons slurp up cheap, tasty *udon* and *soba* noodles and *donburi* (rice) dishes in the simple dining room of Mifune. The noodles, which come with various meats and vegetables, cost anywhere from $3.50 for a plain broth to $8.50 for one with jumbo shrimp. *Japan Center, btw Geary and Fillmore Sts., tel. 415/922-0337. Open daily 11–9:30.*

➤ **UNDER $15 • Sanppo.** Japanese restaurants, like Japan, have a reputation for costliness. But Sanppo, a longtime Japantown fixture, offers familiar specialties at prices that won't break the bank, including vegetable tempura for $8, grilled salmon for $9, and three six-piece avocado sushi rolls for $6.25. *1702 Post St., at Buchanan St., tel. 415/346-3486. Open Tues.–Sat. 11:30–10, Sun. 3–10.*

MARINA DISTRICT

A few blocks inland from the wharf, lots of upscale restaurants, from grills to sushi spots to California-cuisine eateries, line **Chestnut** and **Union streets**. It's a nice area to take your honey to dinner when she passes the bar exam.

➤ **UNDER $10 • Angkor Palace.** Excellent Cambodian food—a must if you like fish—is served in a fantasy-blue dining room by waiters dressed in traditional Cambodian clothing. The stir-fried mushrooms ($5) and steamed baby eggplant ($5) are especially tasty. Wimps *can* be seated on chairs, but this is one of those places where you really should take off your shoes and sit on the floor. *1769 Lombard St., at Octavia St., tel. 415/931-2830. Wheelchair access. Open daily 5 PM–10:30 PM.*

Hahn's Hibachi. This tiny restaurant, little more than a take-out counter, dishes up healthy portions of delicious Korean-barbecued chicken, beef, or pork with rice and kimchi for about $5–$6. Vegetarians will pay even less ($4) for a bowl of vegetable *udon* (noodle soup). So many people order take-out that there's rarely a wait for the five or so tables. *3318 Steiner St., btw Chestnut and Lombard Sts., tel. 415/931–6284. Open Mon.–Sat. 11:30–10. Other location: 1710 Polk St., at Clay St., tel. 415/776–1095. No credit cards.*

➤ **UNDER $15 • Doidge's Kitchen.** If anyone asks you to "do breakfast," this is likely to be the spot they pick. Curtains shelter the upscale Doidge's from the street life outside. Expensive and delicious California-cuisine breakfasts run the gamut from a chutney omelet with sour cream ($7.50) to French toast with strawberries and bananas ($8.50). Reserve in advance. *2217 Union St., at Fillmore St., tel. 415/921–2149. Open weekdays 8 AM–1:45 PM, weekends 8 AM–2:45 PM. No credit cards.*

➤ **UNDER $25 • Greens.** On your birthday, or if you want a treat after a long day of museums and cultural enrichment, head here. This place will make you entirely reevaluate your notion of vegetarian dining. No Kraft macaroni and cheese or carrot sticks here—Greens serves state-of-the-art vegetarian food in a beautifully spacious, gallery-like setting with a romantic view. Soups, salads, and bread by the Tassajara Bakery are all highly recommended, but be prepared for small portions and haughty waiters. Sunday brunch is probably the best deal here; full dinners cost around $20. *Bldg. A, Fort Mason, tel. 415/771–6222. Open Tues.–Fri. 11:30–1:45 and 5:30–9:30, weekends 11:30–2:15 and 6–9:15.*

MISSION DISTRICT

Here you can wander from taqueria to café to bookstore to taqueria again in a salsa-induced state of bliss. To add to the zillions of Mexican and Central American spots that already crowd the neighborhood, a rash of trendy new restaurants has sprouted up on **16th Street** between Valencia and Guerrero. What other two-block area do you know that offers eight different types of cuisine for no more than $10 per person? The Mission's restaurants are accessible from either the 16th and Mission BART station or the 24th and Mission BART station.

➤ **UNDER $5 • Cancun Taqueria.** In the midst of Mission Street's mayhem sits this *típico* taqueria, which serves one of the best veggie burritos ($3) around, chock full of beans, rice, and thick avocado slices. The tasty enchilada platter ($5) is also a big hit. *2288 Mission St., btw 18th and 19th Sts., tel. 415/252–9560. Open weekdays 10 AM–12:30 AM, weekends 10 AM–1:30 AM. No credit cards.*

Casa Sanchez. With a colorful outdoor patio that's great for sunny days and warm nights, Casa Sanchez is just about everyone's favorite taqueria. Fiercely loyal patrons come back again and again for the homemade tortillas, chips, and salsa. Hefty combo platters ($4–$5) will fill you to the bursting point. *2778 24th St., tel. 415/282–2400. Open weekdays 8 AM–7 PM, Sat. 8–6. No credit cards.*

El Farolito. Nowhere else can you stagger in for a burrito ($2.50–$3.50) as late as 3 AM (4 AM on Sat.). The grimy, cafeteria-style atmosphere is depressing, but after a couple of drinks in the wee hours of the morning, you probably won't even notice. *2777 Mission St., at 24th St., tel. 415/826–4870. No credit cards.*

El Toro. This lively corner taqueria is the land of choice: black beans or pinto, refried or whole, and no less than ten kinds of meat for your burrito ($3–$5), including *lengua* (tongue) and *cabeza* (head). You'll have plenty of time to study the menu, since the line often snakes out the door. It's a good place for gringos: The burritos are a little on the bland side. *598 Valencia St., at 17th St., tel. 415/431–3351. Open daily 11–10. No credit cards.*

El Trébol. What El Trébol lacks in decor, it quickly makes up for with incredibly cheap Central American fare and an animated, Spanish-speaking clientele. Specialties include *salpicón* (chopped beef), *chancho con yuca* (fried pork with cassava), and *pollo encebollado* (chicken with onions). Most entrées come with beans, rice, and tortillas, and all cost under $4. *3324 24th St., at Mission St., tel. 415/285–6298. Across from 24th St. BART. Wheelchair access. Open weekdays noon–9, Sat. noon–8.*

La Cumbre. Large, colorful Mexican paintings line the walls, and the requisite Virgin Mary statue guards the front door of this bustling taqueria. The burritos with *carne asada* (marinated beef; $2.50–$5) are so good they can bring a vegetarian back to the herd, so to speak. Dinner platters ($7) with meat, beans, and rice will fuel you through the night and most of the next day. *515 Valencia St., at 16th St., tel. 415/863–8205. Open Mon.–Sat. 11–10, Sun. noon–9. No credit cards.*

New Dawn. This slacker hangout dishes out hangover breakfasts loaded with cholesterol, fat, starch, and everything else you need to ensure you remain immobilized for the rest of the day. Try the huge portion of veggie home fries, an assortment of vegetables topped with a load of potatoes ($5.50), or go the familiar route with a basic two-egg breakfast ($3.50). *3174 16th St., btw Valencia and Guerrero Sts., tel. 415/553–8888. Open weekdays 8 AM–2 PM, weekends 8–3. No credit cards.*

New Dawn is decorated with the most bizarre collection of kitsch you've ever seen, including a life-size Jesus wearing sunglasses.

Pancho Villa. This always-packed taqueria is a step above the myriad others, with a full range of dinner plates, including garlic prawns ($6) in addition to your basic burrito ($3.25). The eclectic, ever-changing artwork is always fun to peruse, and Pancho Villa has the distinction of being the only taqueria with a doorman. *3071 16th St., btw Mission and Valencia Sts., tel. 415/864–8840. Open daily 10–midnight. No credit cards.*

➤ **UNDER $10** • **Café Sanchez.** At this small café in Noe Valley, owned and sometimes gruffly run by two women, you'll find young families politely vying with local hipsters for outdoor tables. Gourmet ($5–$7) omelets are served with fresh-baked muffins and enough home fries to let you skip lunch. Large, rich espresso drinks ($2), which come in bowls instead of mugs, should help you fight off the inevitable food coma. Later in the day, pick up hefty sandwiches like roasted eggplant and fontina ($6.25) on warm focaccia. *3998 Army St., at Sanchez St., tel. 415/641–5683. Wheelchair access. Open Tues.–Fri. 7:30 AM–9:30 PM, Sat. 8 AM–9:30 PM, Sun. 8–8.*

Country Station Sushi Café. Wedged between the taquerias and seedy liquor stores on Mission Street, Country Station is a small, friendly sushi bar in an unlikely location. You'll have to tolerate Holly Hobby decor (fake cherry tree, straw hats, and country music), but the fresh sushi rolls ($1–$4)—including some unusual combinations like Robin's Roll, with avocado, cucumber, lettuce, mango, and sesame seeds ($3.50)—are among the cheapest around. The 54-piece mixed sushi platter, available for take-out only (order 2 hrs in advance), is an incredible deal at a scant $12. Those who don't like sushi can choose from the dinner menu ($7.50–$9.50), which features a variety of chicken, beef, and pork dishes (cooked, of course). *2140 Mission St., btw 17th and 18th Sts., tel. 415/861–0972. Open Mon.–Sat. 5:30 PM–10 PM. Wheelchair access. No credit cards.*

Esperpento. Tapas and sangria have lately become very popular for a reasonably priced and festive dinner. When this tapas joint opened in the Mission in 1992, it skyrocketed to instant popularity, as lines out the door on weekends will attest. Brightly lit and decorated with all sorts of surreal, Daliesque touches, it serves delicacies like garlic shrimp ($6), red pepper salad ($4), and *tortilla de patatas* (potato and onion pancake; $4.75), as well as huge paella dinners ($26 for two). Come here with a bunch of friends to celebrate something, like the end of the day. *3295 22nd St., btw Valencia and Mission Sts., tel. 415/282–8867. Open daily 5 PM–10 PM. No credit cards.*

Mission Grounds. This unassuming spot on 16th Street in the Mission serves up delicious, cheap crepes, and a few egg dishes on the side. You can choose from 18 different fillings, including spinach, ham, cheese, mushrooms, and other savory pickings. For dessert, the chocolate or apple crepes and the blintzes are delicious. With coffee, your French comfort food will cost $4–$7. *3170 16th St., btw Valencia and Guerrero Sts., tel. 415/621–1539. Open daily 7 AM–10 PM. No credit cards.*

Nicaragua. The fried plantain and cheese dinners ($4–$6) are, in the words of one Nicaraguan, an "explosion of flavors." The restaurant is a classic dive, with plastic tablecloths, cheesy pictures of Nicaragua on the walls, and a jukebox that plays Mexican and Central American music.

The area is seedy, though, so be careful around here at night. *3015 Mission St., near Army St., tel. 415/826–3672. Open Thurs.–Tues. 11–9:45. No credit cards.*

Panchita's. You could walk down 16th Street a hundred times without noticing this basic but excellent Salvadoran restaurant. If your idea of charming includes mismatched silverware, a jukebox loaded with mariachi bands, and home-cooked food, plan on eating many meals here. For breakfast there's *huevos rancheros* (eggs with tortillas, salsa, and guacamole; $4.75), for dinner *camarones al ajillo* (garlic shrimp; $9) and *plantanos con crema* (fried bananas with refried beans and cream; $4.75). The best deal is the king-size super burrito ($4). *3091 16th St., at Valencia St., tel. 415/431–4232. Open Sun.–Thurs. 9 AM–11 PM, Fri.–Sat. 9 AM–2 AM.*

Ti Couz. A youngish crowd lines up outside the door, waiting to get a crack at the succulent, piping-hot crepes whipped up at this Mission joint, styled after Breton creperies in western France. You'll want one of the light pancakes for dinner *and* dessert, no doubt: The main course, with savory fillings like spinach, mushrooms, and ricotta, will run you $3–$5, while a sweet crepe will set you back $2–$5. The atmosphere is warm and friendly, perfect for dinner on a long summer evening or lunch on a rainy afternoon. *3108 16th St., at Valencia St., tel. 415/252–7373. Open weekdays 11–11, Sat. 10 AM–11 PM, Sun. 10–10.*

➤ **UNDER $15 • La Rondalla.** A strolling mariachi band passes by iron-haired waitresses serving up decent, reasonably priced Mexican dinners in a room decorated with Christmas ornaments year-round. If that isn't enough of a draw, it's open until 3:30 AM—plenty of time for you to drink margaritas ($10.50 a pitcher) and shout yourself hoarse over the music. The enchilada, taco, and chili relleno combination goes for $8.50. *901 Valencia St., at 20th St., tel. 415/647–7474.*

Rita's Bar/Timo's. Rita does the alcohol and Timo the food, and the result is a success. The menu at this dimly lit, cozy restaurant features a huge selection of Spanish- and Mediterranean-style tapas, including delicate salads ($4–$6), roasted potatoes with garlic mayonnaise ($4), grilled prawns ($7.50), calamari ($5.50), and salt-cod potato cake with mint salsa ($7.25). Come with friends and order a slew of different tapas, along with some Sangre de Toro wine. *842 Valencia St., at 19th St., tel. 415/695–7887. Dinner Sun.–Wed. until 10:30, Thurs.–Sat. until 11:30.*

Scenic India. This small restaurant serves up excellent *saag paneer* (spinach with homemade cheese; $7), shrimp *tandoori* (baked in a clay oven; $13), and other traditional Indian specialties. Delicious breads ($2 each) help keep the curries and other spicy sauces from going to waste in the bottom of your bowl. Think of the slow service as a bonus, not a drawback—you get that much more time to knock back your fill of Taj Mahal beers. If the portions were a little bigger and the prices a couple dollars lower, Scenic India would be perfect. *532 Valencia St., btw 16th and 17th Sts., tel. 415/621–7226. Open Mon. 5 PM–10 PM, Tues.–Sun. 11–3 and 5–10.*

NORTH BEACH

This old-time Italian neighborhood wows the hungry visitor with strong coffee, fresh pasta, spicy sausages, and the highest concentration of restaurants in the city. **Columbus Avenue** and **Grant Avenue** north of Columbus are lined with reliable, reasonably priced Italian restaurants from which you can pick and choose. If you overindulge, go to the nearby Church of Saints Peter and Paul to atone for your gastronomic sins.

Nose rings and tattoos are de rigueur at the Art Institute Café, and a sign at the counter promises PSEUDO-BOHEMIANS WELCOME.

➤ **UNDER $5 • San Francisco Art Institute Café.** Usually the only way you can eat with a view like this is by dressing up, subjecting yourself to a rude waitstaff, and dishing out large amounts of cash in a top-floor restaurant of a downtown skyscraper. Not here! A couple of steep blocks up Russian Hill from North Beach, this café inside an art school provides all of the view and none of the pretentiousness of those *other* places. On top of that, you get great food cheap: A superlative garden burger costs only $4, as does a regular burger. Sandwiches run about $4. *800 Chest-*

nut St., 1½ blocks uphill (west) from Columbus Ave., tel. 415/749–4567. Open weekdays 9–9, Sat. 9–4. No credit cards.

➤ **UNDER $10** • **Bocce Café.** Most dishes are $6–$8 at this high-ceilinged restaurant hidden away from the craziness of North Beach. For your money you'll get a fresh Caesar or chicken salad, or a large individual pizza, or a choice of four types of pasta with about 15 sauces (including mussels, feta, olive and tomato, and risotto with wild mushrooms), or an oven dish like lasagna. When it's warm, you can eat in the garden, sometimes to the strains of live jazz. 478 Green St., at Grant Ave., tel. 415/981–2044. Open daily 11–11.

Caffe Europa. You'll feel like you've just stepped into Mom's kitchen when you enter this tiny, unassuming restaurant in the middle of Columbus Avenue, and you may marvel at how many times you strolled right by and didn't even see it. Ravioli, lasagna, pasta, polenta, and cannelloni dinners with salad and bread are $4.50–$6, while a bowl of minestrone with bread goes for just $2.50. The owners make you feel like you've been coming here forever. 362 Columbus Ave., at Vallejo St., tel. 415/986–8177. Open weekdays 7:30 AM–midnight, weekends until 1 AM. No credit cards.

Hunan. This old North Beach favorite put the "hot" in hot-and-sour chicken ($7). Come for painfully spicy but delicious MSG-free Chinese food. The space resembles a big warehouse, perfect for when you and 20 of your closest friends want to get obnoxious. 924 Sansome St., near Broadway, tel. 415/956–7727. Open daily 11:30–9:30. Other locations: 674 Sacramento St., near Kearny St., tel. 415/788–2234; 1016 Bryant St., btw 8th and 9th Sts., tel. 415/861–5808.

Il Pollaio. This small Italian kitchen overlooking Columbus Avenue serves grilled chicken, and lots of it, in a homey, casual atmosphere. You can get a terrific half chicken with salad, bread, and wine for less than $10; without the wine it's around $7. 555 Columbus Ave., near Washington Sq., tel. 415/362–7727. Open Mon.–Sat. 11:30–9.

L'Osteria del Forno. In this small North Beach restaurant and café, the ambience is Italian, right down to the crockery. Salads, antipasti, and sandwiches ($3–$5) feature Mediterranean touches like red peppers, imported cheese, and Greek olives. The pizza has won a few kudos, too. You can get it by the slice ($2–$4) or by the pie (small $10–$12). 519 Columbus Ave., at Green St., tel. 415/982–1124. Open Mon., Wed.–Thurs. 11:30–10, Fri.–Sat. 11:30–10:30, Sun. 1 PM–10 PM. No credit cards.

Mario's Bohemian Cigar Store and Café. With about 10 tables and a big wood bar, this old-time Italian establishment has been packing 'em in and feeding 'em strong espresso, a glass of Chianti, or a beer for the last 50 years. You can also get a fine sandwich (meatball, roasted eggplant, Italian sausage, chicken, etc.) on homemade focaccia bread ($5–$6). The windows overlook Washington Square Park and the Church of Saints Peter and Paul, in case you didn't already feel like you were in Italy. 566 Columbus Ave., at Union St., tel. 415/362–0536. Open Mon.–Sat. 10 AM–midnight, Sun. 10 AM–11 PM. No credit cards.

North Beach Pizza. Everyone swears this spot serves the best pizza in North Beach, and after one cheesy, decadent bite, you'll agree. From a bustling kitchen come messy, heaping pizzas like Verdi's special, with spinach, pesto, onions, and feta cheese (medium $15). The only drag is that they don't sell by the slice. 1499 Grant St., at Union St., tel. 415/433–2444. Open Mon.–Thurs. 5 PM–11 PM, Fri.–Sat. 11 AM–1 AM, Sun. 11–11. Wheelchair access. No credit cards. Other locations: 1310 Union St., at Vallejo St., tel. 415/433–2444; 800 Stanyan St., at Beulah St., tel. 415/751–2300; 4789 Mission St., btw Persia and Russia Sts., tel. 415/586–1400.

➤ **UNDER $15** • **Capp's Corner.** Capp's doesn't have the best food in North Beach, but it's always a party. Come to this crowded but comfortable Italian restaurant for lunch during the week, when former boxing manager Joe Capp himself, wearing fedora and trench coat, seats the customers. A complete five-course dinner ($10.50–$13.50), served family style, includes minestrone soup, salad, pasta, and an entrée, plus the mandatory dish of spumoni ice cream. After the meal, you can catch Beach Blanket Babylon (see Theater and Dance, in Chapter 6) right next door. *1600 Powell St., at Green St., tel. 415/989–2589. Open weekdays 11:30–2:30 and 4:30–midnight, Sat. 4:30–midnight, Sun. 4–midnight.*

The Gold Spike. It first opened as a candy store back in 1927 (conveniently manufacturing bathtub gin on the side), but for over 50 years now this cluttered, unpretentious restaurant has served up reasonably priced Italian fare to loyal regulars and gawking tourists. Once you get over the baffling array of trinkets on display, you can sit back and enjoy entrées like eggplant or chicken parmigiano, sautéed calamari (around $10), and basic pasta dishes ($7–$9). *527 Columbus Ave., btw Union and Green Sts., tel. 415/986–9747. Open Mon.–Tues., Thurs.–Fri. 5 PM–10 PM, weekends 5–10:30.*

Helmand. This North Beach favorite serves Afghan food—an unusual specialty, even for San Francisco—and presents a perfect opportunity for budget eaters to experience a new cuisine in an elegant setting. Lamb, chicken, and vegetarian entrées run $8–$14, and once you see how lovely and well-presented everything is, you'll agree it's one of the best deals in San Francisco. *430 Broadway, btw Kearny and Montgomery Sts., tel. 415/362–0641. Open Sun.–Thurs. 6 PM–10 PM, Fri.–Sat. 6–11.*

➢ **UNDER $20** • **Buca Giovanni.** This rustic, bricked-in cave at the bottom of a short stairway features solid northern Italian food in an area sadly lacking it. Dishes like rabbit with prosciutto, mushrooms, and Italian liqueur ($16) seem to come straight out of a rural Italian farmhouse. The *salsa rossa,* a sun-dried tomato, anchovy, and caper spread that comes with your bread, is incredible. *800 Greenwich St., at Mason St., tel. 415/776–7766. Open Tues.–Sat. 5:30–10:30.*

RICHMOND AND SUNSET DISTRICTS

From the way that San Franciscans talk, you'd think that the Richmond and Sunset districts were in another county. The fact is that these districts (flanking Golden Gate Park) are only a few minutes away from the Haight and Japantown by car, or three to four more stops on the MUNI. For a little extra effort you get good, cheap food and the opportunity to brag about "exploring the city" to your friends. In the Richmond district, Vietnamese, Chinese, Thai, and Japanese places line **Clement Street** between Arguello Boulevard and 9th Avenue and between 20th and 25th Avenues. You'll find produce markets along this stretch that brim with items unfamiliar to the Western eye. On the other side of the park in the Sunset district, **Irving Street** between 5th and 25th avenues yields numerous Chinese and Thai restaurants. You'll also find excellent Mediterranean delis, where you can purchase take-out tubs of hummus, falafel, and tabouleh.

➢ **UNDER $10** • **Empress Garden.** Although the Sunset district teems with Chinese restaurants, this tastefully decorated establishment has muscled its way to the top. Every night of the week Asian locals pack in around the party-size tables. Chicken dishes are about $5, but the house specialty, minced or deep-fried squab ($8–$10) is worth the splurge. An inlaid fish tank filled with live, kicking crabs attests to the food's freshness. *1386 9th Ave., btw Irving and Judah Sts., tel. 415/731–2388. Open daily 11:30–9:30.*

Shangri-La. This all-vegetarian Chinese restaurant in the Sunset district offers a delicious array of dishes, including bean-curd balls with garlic sauce ($4.75), vegetarian chicken with black-bean sauce ($5.25), and golden-brown gluten with sweet-and-sour sauce ($4.75). Although the faux wood walls and inadequate lighting may be a turnoff, the food definitely makes up for the blah decor. *2026 Irving St., btw 21st and 22nd Aves., tel. 415/731–2548. Open daily 11:30–9:30.*

➢ **UNDER $15** • **Angkor Wat.** Though this Cambodian restaurant has won its fair share of awards, it's not immediately apparent why this place stands out. But if you put aside your high expectations you'll find decent food and elegant surroundings, not to mention a Cambodian dance performance on Friday and Saturday nights. Appetizers like papaya salad and chicken satay cost about $3; entrées, including a great barbecued pork, run $8–$11. *4217 Geary Blvd., at 6th Ave., tel. 415/221–7887. Open Sun.–Thurs. 5 PM–10 PM, Fri.–Sat. 5–10:30.*

Khan Toke Thai House. This attractive, dimly lit Richmond district restaurant serves Thai cuisine that always seems to be winning some prize in a "Best of the Bay Area" contest. As an added bonus, they make you take off your shoes and sit on the floor to eat. Most dishes cost $5–$10. *5937 Geary Blvd., at 24th Ave., tel. 415/668–6654. Open daily 5–11.*

If you're feeling erudite, choose from a special section of Khan Toke's menu called "Thai Curries Mentioned in Thai Literature."

SOUTH OF MARKET

The SoMa warehouse wasteland yields surprisingly good restaurants on the unlikeliest, grimiest corners. Wander along **Folsom Street** between 7th and 12th streets, or on **11th** and **9th streets** between Howard and Harrison, and you'll have the SoMa eating scene in the palm of your hand. Oddly, there are very few late-night eating spots to satiate clubbers' cravings. Besides Hamburger Mary's (*see below*), you can try **20 Tank Brewery** (316 11th St., at Folsom St., tel. 415/255–9455; *see* Chapter 6), which serves sandwiches ($3–$5), nachos ($3.75–$5.75), and other munchies until 1 AM, and beer until 1:30. **Pizza Love** (1245 Folsom St., btw 8th and 9th Sts., tel. 415/225–LOVE) has cheap pizza slices ($1.75, toppings 25¢ each) until midnight Sunday–Wednesday, 2 AM Thursday, and 4 AM Friday and Saturday. The place brings new meaning to ugly decor, but at 4 AM who cares?

➤ **UNDER $10** • **Hamburger Mary's.** The messy hamburgers ($5–$8) and the cluttered decor go together wonderfully. Come by at 1 in the morning to hang out with SoMa clubbers in various states of drunkenness and undress. Vegetarians can feast on the tofu burger ($6) or the Meatless Meaty, a hot sandwich of mushrooms, cream cheese, and olives ($7). *1582 Folsom St., at 12th St., tel. 415/626–5767. Open Tues.–Fri. 11:30 AM–1 AM, weekends 10 AM–2 AM.*

Manora's Thai Cuisine. The location on Folsom is trendier than most Thai restaurants in the city, and big crowds wait at the bar before being seated. The Mission branch is smaller and quieter. At both, the fresh, attractive dishes are worth the wait. Garlic quail is $7.50, and spicy Japanese eggplant with prawns goes for $7. *3226 Mission St., at 29th St., tel. 415/550–0856. Open Tues.–Sat. 5 PM–10 PM. Other location: 1600 Folsom St., at 12th St., tel. 415/861–6224.*

¡WA-HA-KA! Popular with large, jovial groups, this Mexican eatery specializes in California-style burritos. Grab a ¡WA-HA-KA! burrito or an order of Baja rolls (Mexican sushi) before you head off to the nearby clubs; either one runs $4.50 à la carte, or $6 with rice, beans, and salad. The margarita cantina opens at 5; a WA-HA-Karita can be yours for $2.50. *1489 Folsom St., at 11th St., tel. 415/861–1410. Open Mon.–Wed. 11:30–10, Thurs. 11:30–11, Fri.–Sat. 11:30 AM–1 AM, Sun. 5 PM–10 PM. No credit cards. Other location: 2141 Polk St., btw Broadway and Vallejo St., tel. 415/775–1055.*

➤ **UNDER $15** • **Ace Cafe.** Ingest some nouvelle Tex-Mex cuisine in a dark, roadhouse-style café with postmodern wood furnishings. The food is inventive and reasonably priced: A tender prawn quesadilla with salsa fresca and cilantro pesto will deplete your funds by $7; for clams and mussels in a saffron broth, you'll fork over $9. *1539 Folsom St., btw 11th and 12th Sts., tel. 415/621–4752. Open weekdays 5:30 PM–11 PM, weekends 6 PM–1 AM.*

Acorn. Come on a warm day and station yourself on the back patio of this flowery, romantic café—a surprising find in industrial SoMa. The inventive, changing menu will do you right for lunch or weekend brunch (dinner, at $20 and up, is a little steep). Lunch entrées might include a potato-cheddar frittata with ratatouille ($7) or garlic-roasted artichoke with marinated clams and mussels ($10.50). For the nutritionally correct, they use organic produce whenever possible. *1256 Folsom St., btw 8th and 9th Sts., tel. 415/863–2469. Open for lunch Tues.–Fri. 11–5, for dinner Wed.–Sat. 6–10, for brunch Sat.–Sun. 10:30–3.*

South Park Café. Only minutes away from the seedy streets and empty warehouses South of Market lies South Park, which could easily double as a refined European town square. Pretend you're Hemingway, Gertrude Stein, or Henry Miller in glorious Parisian exile while you gnaw on *boudin noir* (blood sausage; $10) and *frites* (french fries; $1.75), and watch the world go by. This French bistro opens at 8 AM for fresh croissants and coffee and stays open for country-cooked lunches and dinners. Lunch costs between $5 and $10 and dinner between $6 and $15. *108 South Park Ave., btw 2nd and 3rd and Bryant and Brannan Sts., tel. 415/495–7275. Open for coffee weekdays 8 AM–10 PM, for meals weekdays 11:30–2:30 and 6–10, Sat. 6 PM–10 PM.*

East Bay

With all of San Francisco's diverse dining choices, why leave the city when you want a meal? Well, believe it or not, the East Bay actually outdoes San Francisco in some types of cuisine. This is the best place to find an Ethiopian meal, or to pick up a barbecued-rib dinner. Oakland's Chinatown rivals San Francisco's in authenticity, and Berkeley offers a more upscale breakfast scene than the Haight for about the same price.

BERKELEY

Berkeleyites take their food very seriously. California cuisine, designer fuel for the yuppie generation, got its start here. The area around Shattuck Avenue and Cedar Street has become known as the Gourmet Ghetto—it's home to a number of high-quality restaurants, including the famed Chez Panisse (*see* chapter introduction, *above*). On Telegraph Avenue between Dwight Way and the U.C. campus, you'll find the city's cheap restaurants, serving fast food with a Berkeley twist (heaping green salads and gourmet sandwiches are far more common than burgers). West of campus, along University Avenue, there's a string of mostly Asian and Indian restaurants. In Albany, just north of Berkeley, Solano Avenue is lined with cafés, sandwich shops, and upscale restaurants that cater to the neighborhood's students, professors, and granola-fied yuppies.

➤ **UNDER $5** • Telegraph Avenue near the Berkeley campus is full of places that cater to students and their thin pocketbooks. Several food carts park along Bancroft Avenue where

Great Licks

Slurp it, lick it, let it melt all over your face and hands. Along with Ghirardelli (see Fisherman's Wharf, in Chapter 2), the spots listed below should take care of all your ice cream needs.

- *Ben & Jerry's. This super-rich, politically correct ice cream is available right on the corner of Haight and Ashbury streets and at a stand at Fisherman's Wharf on Pier 39. Cherry Garcia and Wavy Gravy are the flavors of choice on Haight Street, naturally. 1480 Haight St., tel. 415/249–4685.*

- *St. Francis Soda Fountain and Candy Store. They make their own ice cream, syrups, and candy at this old-fashioned soda shop in the Mission district. Venture into the pink interior, order a phosphate, an egg cream, or a chocolate malt, and wax nostalgic. 2801 24th St., at York St., tel. 415/826–4200.*

- *Swensen's. Climb to the top of Russian Hill and you'll find the original Swensen's ice cream parlor. You'll probably need a respirator and a chocolate double dip to get you going again. Cnr of Union and Hyde Sts., tel. 415/775–6818.*

- *Toy Boat. Come here for a scoop and marvel for hours at the hundreds of old and new toys lining the walls. 401 Clement St., at 5th St., tel. 415/751–7505.*

Telegraph ends, selling everything from bagels and smoothies to Japanese food, burritos, and stuffed potatoes. For pizza with an "eat-it-or-screw-you" attitude, stop by the infamous **Blondie's** (2340 Telegraph Ave., near Durant Ave., tel. 510/548–1129), popular with street freaks and bleary-eyed students in need of a midnight pepperoni fix. The stand-up counter is loud and always packed, the deranged, rude employees provide constant entertainment, and your filling, greasy slice costs $2. For a $2 hot dog or Polish sausage, make the short walk to **Top Dog** (2534 Durant Ave., at Bowditch St., no phone), just east of Telegraph. Across the street in the Durant Food Court, 10 small places, including American, Chinese, Japanese, and Mexican, vie to serve you a big meal for about $3.50. A few blocks south of campus at Dwight Way, **Ann's Soup Kitchen and Restaurant** (2498 Telegraph Ave., tel. 510/548–8885) dishes out exceptionally cheap breakfasts, homemade soups, salads, and sandwiches ($1.75–$3).

Café Intermezzo. This Berkeley institution, with a harried, occasionally rude staff, indisputably serves the biggest and best salads around. The veggie delight ($4.50) is a family-size mound of greens topped with kidney and garbanzo beans, hard-boiled egg, sprouts, and croutons, plenty to share with a friend. Salads are served with homemade dressing and include a slab of fresh-from-the-oven honey wheat bread. Or try one of the humongous sandwiches on inch-thick slices of the same delicious bread ($4.50). *2442 Telegraph Ave., at Haste St., tel. 510/849–4592. Wheelchair access. Open daily 8:30 AM–10 PM.*

Cheese Board Pizza Collective. If you can get to this makeshift pizza café during their ridiculously short open hours, you will experience one of Berkeley's true delights. An offshoot of the Cheese Board Collective down the street (*see* Specialty Markets and Delicatessens, *below*), this tiny kitchen offers just one kind of pizza each day, always vegetarian and made with such toppings as eggplant, red peppers, pesto, feta or goat cheese, and cilantro. Seating space is limited to a few tables inside and on the sidewalk, but regulars overflow onto nearby walls and benches. If you're lucky, you might even catch some live jazz piano while you eat. A whole pie is $12, a slice $1.50. *1512 Shattuck Ave., btw Cedar and Vine Sts., tel. 510/549–3055. 8 blocks north of Berkeley BART. Wheelchair access. Open Tues.–Thurs. 11:30–2, Mon. and Fri. 4:30–around 6:30, Sat. noon–2.*

➤ **UNDER $10** • **Berkeley Thai House.** The interior of this restaurant near the Berkeley campus is about as boring as it gets, but the peaceful patio, set off from the street by tall bushes and lined with flowers, is a wonderful place to escape the Telegraph Avenue crowds. Locals and students in the know come to wolf down pad Thai ($4.25) and other reasonably

Would You Like a Little Buddha With That?

Looking for something a little more exciting than eggs and toast this weekend? On Sundays between 10 and 3, families set up food stands, tables, and folding chairs in the sunny courtyard behind the Thai Buddhist Temple and Cultural Center in Berkeley and serve up homemade Thai specialties. Exchange your money for tokens and choose from a heaping plate of pad Thai; a spicy soup of noodles, meatballs, and beef; or various seafood curries ($3 each). The freshly sliced mango over sticky rice with coconut cream ($3) is particularly refreshing. Side dishes, including neat packages of glutinous rice filled with taro root, banana, or coconut and wrapped in banana leaves, are $1. Be brave and taste one of the artistic-but-hard-to-identify desserts ($1.50) stacked next to Thai iced tea and iced coffee (50¢ each). This brunch is popular among Thai families and anthropologist types; proceeds benefit the temple. On your way out, check the information board, with listings of Thai language and yoga classes. 1911 Russell St., Berkeley, btw Martin Luther King Jr. Way and Otis St., tel. 510/540–9734. 1 block north of Ashby BART.

priced lunch specials ($4.50–$5.50). For dinner, try the *mus-s-mun* (beef with red curry, peanuts, potatoes, carrots, and coconut milk; $6), and wash your meal down with a Thai beer ($2.50). *2511 Channing Way, at Telegraph Ave., tel. 510/843–7352. Open Mon.–Thurs. 11–9:30, Fri.–Sat. 11–10, Sun. 2–9:30.*

Bette's Oceanview Diner. In the midst of the home-decoration stores on 4th Street (near I–80), this bright, crowded '50s-style diner offers yummy breakfasts and lunches from the grill ($5–$8). Bette's takes a more upscale approach than the usual diner: Instead of bottled Thousand Island, you'll find homemade dressings ($3.75). Grilled American cheese and white bread? Try Jack and cheddar on sourdough ($4.75). If you're not up for a half-hour wait on weekend mornings, Bette's To Go next door offers take-out salads ($2–$4 for ½ pint) and sandwiches ($3.50–$4.50). *1807A 4th St., off University Ave., tel. 510/644–3230. Wheelchair access. Open Mon.–Thurs. 6:30 AM–2:30 PM, Fri.–Sun. 6:30 AM–4 PM.*

Blue Nile. This is one of Berkeley's best Ethiopian eateries, serving everything from thick split-pea stew and pepper-cooked beef to *tej* (honey wine) and freshly blended fruit shakes. The food is served family style, and you use *injera* (spongy unleavened bread) instead of silverware to scoop it up. As with most restaurants along Telegraph Avenue, the Blue Nile attracts lots of U.C. students and faculty. Plates are about $6–$8 for dinner, $5 for lunch. *2525 Telegraph Ave., btw Dwight Way and Parker St., tel. 510/540–6777. Wheelchair access. Open Mon.–Sat. 11:30–10, Sun. 4 PM–10 PM.*

Brick Hut Cafe. This mom-and-mom café, owned and operated by women, is one of the best breakfast spots around. The creative dishes include Wendy's waffle ($5), baked with cheddar cheese and bacon inside, and eggs with homemade pesto ($5.50). For lunch, they serve salads, burgers, and sandwiches. The Brick Hut is busy on Sundays, but you probably won't have to wait more than 15 minutes, and if you're in a rush, you can share a large communal table. *3222 Adeline St., near Fairview St., tel. 510/658–5555. About 3 blocks north of Ashby BART. Wheelchair access. Open weekdays 7:30 AM–2 PM, weekends 8:30–3.*

Cafe Panini. It's hard to believe that the peaceful, umbrella-shaded tables of this gourmet sandwich spot lie so close to noisy Shattuck Avenue. A popular lunch destination for local office workers, the open-air café, hidden away in sunny Trumpetvine Court, serves sandwiches with a Mediterranean flair. The menu, consisting of a half-dozen inventive selections, changes daily; a typical choice is smoked Black Forest ham with Cambozola cheese, green apple, lettuce, and raspberry vinaigrette ($5.50); or vegetarian eggplant Romanesco with white cheddar, tomatoes, greens, and red onions ($5.50). *2115 Allston Way, tel. 510/849–0405. Enter from Shattuck Ave., at Trumpetvine Court, btw Center St. and Allston Way (across from Berkeley BART). Open weekdays 7:30 AM–4 PM, Sat. 10–4.*

Cha Am. This airy restaurant feels removed from Shattuck Avenue, even though its greenhouse-like window seats overlook the street. In a city that abounds with Thai food, Cha Am is among the best. In particular, try the magical *dom-ka gai* (chicken and coconut soup; $6) or the mixed seafood plate with chili, garlic, and vegetables ($8.75). *1543 Shattuck Ave., at Cedar St., tel. 510/848–9664. 7 blocks north of Berkeley BART. Open Mon.–Thurs. 11:30–4 and 5–9:30, Fri. 11:30–4 and 5–10, Sat. noon–4 and 5–10, Sun. 5–9:30.*

Chester's Cafe. Looking out over the bay from Chester's sunny upstairs deck is one of the best ways to start a lazy weekend morning. The friendly staff will do you up with mug after mug of hot coffee and a brunch with all the fixings. Weekend specials include eggs Juneau (poached eggs and smoked salmon on an English muffin topped with Hollandaise sauce; $7.50). If you wake up on the lunch side of brunch, the warm chicken salad with sautéed red, yellow, and green bell peppers ($7) is a savory choice. *1508B Walnut Ave., at Vine St., tel. 510/849–9995. Open Mon.–Sat. 8 AM–9 PM, Sun. 8–5.*

Homemade Cafe. You'll have a hard time deciding what to order from the extensive menu, and you'll probably have to wait for a table (at least on weekends), so grab a cup of coffee and a menu, park yourself on the sidewalk, and start deliberating. The whole-wheat buttermilk waffle made with cinnamon and nutmeg ($3) sounds like one of the less indulgent items, until you start adding pecans (75¢) and homemade blueberry sauce ($1.50). Also popular are the ethnically inspired *matzoh brei* (matzo with scrambled eggs and cheese; $5) and the famous home-fry heaven (home fries with cheese, salsa, sour cream, and guacamole or pesto; $4.50). *2454 Sacramento St., at Dwight Way, tel. 510/845–1940. Open weekdays 7 AM–2 PM, weekends 8–3.*

Juan's Place. This traditional Mexican restaurant has the feel of an old cantina, complete with piñatas, mirrored beer ads, and cheesy portraits of matadors. Juan's dishes out large portions of standard fare, including tacos, burritos, and tamales. The crab enchilada with red sauce and cheese ($7 for two) overflows with tender crabmeat. Try a wine margarita ($2.50 a glass, $10 a pitcher) from the adjoining bar. Juan's is stuck on the fringes of Berkeley, surrounded by steel factories and warehouses. *941 Carleton St., at 9th St., tel. 510/845–6904. 2 blocks west of San Pablo Ave. Open weekdays 11:30–10, weekends 2–10.*

Rick and Ann's. Join East Bay yuppies in bicycle shorts (with babies and dogs in tow) as you wait for the best breakfast in town—and in Berkeley, that's really saying something. Try the "down south" ($7), a combo of two cornmeal pancakes, two spicy turkey sausages, and two fluffy scrambled eggs with cheese. The special omelets and scrambles are also delicious, as is the French toast, made with challah (egg bread). *2922 Domingo St., near Ashby St., tel. 510/649–8538. Across from Claremont Hotel. Open Tues.–Sun. 8–2:30 and 5:30–9:30.*

Saul's. This is the closest thing to a New York deli in the East Bay. Shelves of Manischewitz products line the entry, and a glass deli counter displays bowls of chopped liver, sauerkraut, and whole smoked fish. Sandwiches ($5–$7) are stuffed with pastrami, corned beef, brisket, or tongue. Jewish specialties include knishes ($3), potato latkes with sour cream and applesauce ($6 for three), and matzo-ball soup ($3.50). Saul's gets noisy and crowded during peak hours; if you come at lunch, expect a wait for a table or get your food to go. *1475 Shattuck Ave., at Rose St., tel. 510/848–3354. 8 blocks north of Berkeley BART. Open daily 8:30 AM–9:30 PM.*

Shilpa. Come here for tasty northern and southern Indian cuisine at very reasonable prices. Spicy dishes and flavorful curries are yours for the taking at the excellent all-you-can-eat lunch buffet ($7), served daily 11:30–2:30. Grad students from nearby labs recommend the *aloo gobi masala* (cauliflower and potato curry; $6) and the spicy red lentil curry ($5.50). Dinner ($8–$10) is accompanied by live music on Friday and Saturday nights. *2175 Allston Way, at Oxford St., tel. 510/849–5451. Wheelchair access. Open daily 11–10.*

Zachary's Chicago Pizza Inc. People rave about the spinach and mushroom special ($16.50 for a medium), but whatever toppings you choose to fill your pizza, they'll come surrounded by a wall of bready crust and topped with a layer of mozzarella and stewed tomatoes. Zachary's may have lines going out the door, but it's definitely worth the wait. Though they don't take reservations, you can place your order so the pizza will be ready when your table is. At lunch, grab a thin slice for $1.75–$3. *5801 College Ave., near Rockridge BART, tel. 510/655–6385. Other location: 1853 Solano Ave., Berkeley, btw Colusa and Fresno Aves., tel. 510/525–5950. Both wheelchair accessible. Both open Sun.–Thurs. 11–9:30, Fri.–Sat. 11–10:30.*

➢ **UNDER $15** • **Pasand Madras Cuisine.** If you feel like going for the gusto at this southern Indian restaurant, get a complete *thali* dinner, including lentil curry, lentil vegetable soup, spicy tamarind soup, yogurt with vegetables, a selection of Indian flat breads, rice pilaf, sweet mango chutney, and a dessert surprise. The boneless ginger chicken masala curry ($8 à la carte, $10.50 thali) is a winner, as are the vegetable curries ($5.50–$9.50), though even the ones labeled spicy are pretty tame. A raised seating area offers views of cross-legged sitar and tabla players who perform during dinner; and an adjoining lounge features live jazz nightly. *2286 Shattuck Ave., at Bancroft Way, tel. 510/549–2559. 1 block south of Berkeley BART. Wheelchair access. Open Sun.–Thurs. 11–10:30, Fri. and Sat. 11–11.*

➢ **UNDER $20** • **Sushi Ko.** The decor at this Berkeley restaurant is simple, and the food is exceptional. Check out the special rolls, listed on a board by the sushi bar. The spider roll, filled with soft-shell crab, fish eggs, cucumber, and lettuce ($7), is a good bet, as is the spicy tuna handroll ($3.50). In addition to delicate and flavorful sushi, Sushi Ko has unusual cooked dishes like grilled calamari with ginger sauce ($5.50). *64 Shattuck Sq., near University Ave.,* *tel. 510/845–6601. 1 block north of Berkeley BART. Open Mon.–Thurs. 11:30–2 and 5:30–9:30, Fri. 11:30–2 and 5:30–10, Sat. 5:30–10, Sun. 5:30–9:30.*

Venezia. This restaurant goes to great lengths to evoke the atmosphere of a Venetian piazza. The walls are painted to look like Italian shops and houses, with protruding wrought-iron balconies and flower boxes, and a clothesline is strung overhead, complete with drying boxers. Luckily, the food measures up to the decor. Start with the *insalata di pollo* (salad with smoked chicken, pistachios, grapefruit, and scallions; $5.50) and check the board for daily pasta and fresh fish specials, like grilled salmon with olive-fennel relish ($13). *1799 University Ave., at Grant St., tel. 510/849–4681. Wheelchair access. Open Mon.–Thurs. 11:30–2:30 and 5:30–10, Fri. 11:30–2:30 and 5–10, Sat. 5–10, Sun. 5–9:30.*

➢ **UNDER $30 • Chez Panisse Café.** The world-famous Chez Panisse restaurant may be out of reach, but the café upstairs serves many of the same dishes for half the price, and there's less silverware to contend with. You can make same-day lunch reservations, but for dinner you just have to suffer—go early and expect to wait an hour or more for a table. Among the starters, Heidi's garden salad with goat cheese ($7) is exquisite. The café is noted for its pizzas ($13.50–$15); the prosciutto, garlic, and goat cheese calzone makes a great appetizer to share or a main dish for one. The café feels like an upscale living room, and patrons sport everything from jeans to suits and evening wear. *1517 Shattuck Ave., at Cedar St., tel. 510/548–5049. 7 blocks north of Berkeley BART. Open Mon.–Sat. 11:30–3:30 and 5–11:30.*

OAKLAND

From southern-style barbecue shacks to Salvadoran holes-in-the-wall, Oakland is loaded with cheap and colorful eateries. Because the population is so diverse, you can find just about every type of cuisine imaginable, so explore this area with eager taste buds and an open mind. The center for Asian food is **Chinatown,** a less touristy version of its counterpart across the bay. Downtown between 7th, 10th, Harrison, and Franklin streets, Chinatown offers increasing numbers of Southeast Asian restaurants and markets, as well as the older and more established Chinese ones. The **Fruitvale** district, encompassing the neighborhoods around the Fruitvale BART station, has dozens of cheap Mexican and Central American restaurants. It's safest to restrict your visits here to the daylight hours. If you don't feel like having an adventure along with your meal, two long avenues in Oakland offer a wide selection of familiar delis, burger joints, and gringo burrito shops. From downtown, Bus 59 or 59A will take you north on Broadway to **Piedmont Avenue;** for **College Avenue,** take BART or Bus 51 or 51A to Rockridge.

➢ **UNDER $5 • Taqueria Morelia.** Come to this Oakland joint for one of the best quesadillas ($2) around, a fried flour or corn tortilla oozing cheese and sprinkled with chopped tomatoes and cilantro. Locals of all ages flow between the restaurant and adjacent dive bar, **Talk of the Town,** carrying plastic baskets of tacos and burritos ($2.50–$4 each) and cheap beer. The specialty here is *cabeza* (beef head), but true carnivores should head down the street to **El Taco Zamorano,** a silver truck parked at the corner of East 14th and High streets, where the delicious burritos ($2), tacos ($1), and tortas are filled with beef head, beef tongue, and pork skins. *Morelia: 4481 E. 14th St., near High St., tel. 510/535–6030. About 7 blocks southeast of Fruitvale BART. Open daily 10–10.*

➢ **UNDER $10 • Asmara Restaurant.** Colorful baskets and rugs suspended from the ceiling cheer up the drab interior of this East African restaurant in North Oakland. Sample three of the excellent entrées in the combination platter, either meat ($5.50 lunch, $8 dinner) or vegetarian ($5 lunch, $7.50 dinner). The red lentil stew is the most flavorful of the vegetarian dishes. Those who like lamb should try *ye-beg alicha,* made with curry and spices ($4.75 lunch, $7.50 dinner). In keeping with Ethiopian tradition, food is served family style with injera bread and a notable lack of utensils—this is not a good place for a first date. *5020 Telegraph Ave., near 51st St., tel. 510/547–5100. Wheelchair access. Open Mon., Wed., Thurs. 11:30 AM–10 PM, Fri.–Sat. 11:30 AM–11 PM, Sun. noon–10 PM.*

Barney's Gourmet Hamburger. This Solano Avenue joint specializes in gourmet burgers, like the Parisian, served on a baguette with bleu cheese ($5). The prices are reasonable and the portions enormous. They even cater to those trying to avoid red meat—you can order your burger with grilled chicken instead. Round off your meal with an order of fries and a chocolate malt. *5819 College Ave., near Chabot Ave., tel. 510/601–0444. Open Mon.–Thurs. 11–10, Fri.–Sat. 11–10:30, Sun. 11–9:30. Other locations: 4162 Piedmont Ave., at Linda Ave., Oakland, tel. 510/655–7180; 1591 Solano Ave., at Ord Way, Albany, tel. 510/526–8185; 4138 24th St., at Castro St., San Francisco, tel. 415/282–7770.*

Flint's. Regarded by some as the best barbecue shack in the world, Flint's caters to large appetites during the wee hours. Choose from ribs, beef, or chicken (around $7) piled high on a paper plate, crowned with a couple slices of all-American white bread (to soak up the grease) and potato salad. Sandwiches are around $5. You'll be getting your food to go, as there are no seats here. *6609 Shattuck Ave., at 66th St., tel. 510/653–0593. 2 blocks south of Ashby BART. Open weekdays 11 AM–2 AM, weekends until 4 AM.*

Gaucho's Café. Enormous burritos, tostadas, and delicious tacos—all with a strong California influence—are served up at this unassuming bright-yellow café. The vegetarian burrito ($4.25) with mixed squash and carrots is an herbivore's south-of-the-border fantasy. Meatier choices include barbecued chicken, prawns, and Mandarin duck. Order to go or eat at one of the few outdoor tables. *5295A College Ave., near Broadway, tel. 510/652–3402. Open daily 11–9:30.*

Lois the Pie Queen. Despite the name, most people come to this Oakland eatery for breakfast, not dessert. A family-run diner (vinyl swivel chairs and root-beer floats) that's gone California chic (pink walls and espresso drinks), Lois's offers all the breakfast favorites as well as excellent burgers and fries. Two eggs with homemade biscuits and grits are $4, and the tuna melt is $3.50. Don't forget the pies that made Lois monarch; a slice of sweet potato or lemon icebox goes for $2.50–$3. *851 60th St., 1 block west of Martin Luther King Jr. Way, tel. 510/658–5616. Open weekdays 7 AM–2 PM, Sat. 7–3, Sun. 7–5.*

Los Cocos. Fruitvale's best (and only) Salvadoran restaurant is famous for its fried bananas ($4.50) and *pupusas* (stuffed tortillas; $3 for two). It may not look like much from the outside (or the inside, for that matter), but the food is excellent and cheap. The friendly family of cooks chatting in the small open kitchen brings life to the sparse yellow room. *1449 Fruitvale Ave., at 14th St., tel. 510/536–3079. Wheelchair access. Open Tues.–Sun. 11–10.*

Mama's Royal Cafe. Although you can get lunch here after 11:30 AM, the restaurant's real raison d'être is breakfast (served until closing). Huge omelets ($5.50–$9), which come with home-style potatoes, fruit, and a muffin, are available in no fewer than 31 flavors. The fresh-fruit crepes ($5.75) and the popular eggs Benedict ($8.25) could send you into a cholesterol-induced coma. You can eat in a room covered with old-fashioned aprons or one that displays vintage radios. *4012 Broadway, at 40th St., tel. 510/547–7600. Open weekdays 7 AM–3 PM, weekends 8–3. No credit cards.*

Nin Yang. Although it's in Oakland's Chinatown, Nin Yang serves authentic Burmese cuisine. The atmosphere is less than intimate, but the service is fast and cordial. Concentrate on the Burmese specialties rather than the supplementary Chinese dishes. Especially tasty are the curry chicken noodle soup ($5.50), the ginger salad ($5.50), and the curry fish ($9). They also serve vegetarian entrées. *301 8th St., at Harrison St., tel. 510/465–6924. Wheelchair access. Open Tues.–Thurs. 11–9, Fri.–Sat. 11–9:30, Sun. noon–9. Other location: 6048 College Ave., at Claremont Ave., tel. 510/655–3298.*

Phó' Lâm Viên. This Vietnamese restaurant in Oakland's Chinatown is worth a trip for those with a sense of culinary adventure. Ignore the piped-in Muzak and focus on pork with fish sauce, spicy lemongrass gluten, and all sorts of other dishes you never even knew you wanted ($5–$7). The beverages are no less exotic—you can quench your thirst with a concoction made from seaweed, barley, dried longan, lotus seed, and apples ($1.50) or a tall glass of pennywort juice ($1). *930 Webster St., btw 10th and 11th Sts., tel. 510/763–1484. Open Sun.–Mon., Wed.–Thurs. 11–11, Fri.–Sat. 11 AM–midnight.*

Starlite Restaurant II. Smack in the middle of Chinatown, the Starlite boasts a daunting 17-page menu. Most of the Vietnamese and Chinese entrées, including *phó-bo* (a vat of soup with rice noodles, veggies, and your choice of meat), run $4–$6, and all are amply sized. Top off your meal with *café sũa hay nóng* ($1.75), a brew-it-yourself dark French coffee mixed with condensed milk and poured over ice. *820 Franklin St., near 9th St., tel. 510/444–1142. Open weekdays 9–9, weekends 9 AM–10 PM.*

Tin's Teahouse. On the edge of Oakland's Chinatown, Tin's serves great dim sum for about $5 per person. Feast on shark's-fin dumplings, chicken buns, stuffed bell peppers, and taro triangles. One house specialty is steamed rice-noodle crepes with shrimp, beef, or pork. *701 Webster St., at 7th St., tel. 510/832–7661. Open Mon., Wed.–Fri. 9–3, weekends 8:30–8:30.*

➤ **UNDER $15** • **Anna's.** Anna chooses her recipes from all over the world: On any given night, she might offer Kenyan coconut chicken with plantain ($10), Marrakesh lamb stew ($10), or Cuban black-bean soup with corn bread ($4.50). You'll catch some kind of live music, often folk or mellow jazz, on the weekend. *6420 Shattuck Ave., near Alcatraz Ave., tel. 510/655–5900. Open Tues.–Sun. 5:30 PM–9:30 PM.*

Anna's international cooking has a reassuring down-home flavor, and when she's done in the kitchen, she may even sing you a song.

The Cantina. On a yuppified stretch of Park Boulevard east of Lake Merritt in Oakland, this upscale, Americanized Mexican restaurant attracts a lively crowd. Chicken Caesar salad ($8) and the Cantina club burrito with chicken and bacon ($8.50) are popular choices. Vegetarian renditions of classic meat dishes feature mushrooms, spinach, onions, zucchini, and red peppers. Happy-hour specials (3–7 PM) such as 25¢ tacos change daily and are best when accompanied by a margarita. *4239 Park Blvd., near Wellington St., tel. 510/482–3663. Wheelchair access. Open Sun.–Thurs. 11:30–10, Fri.–Sat. 11:30–10:30.*

Le Cheval. After you've made it past the scary laughing buddhas at the door of this Vietnamese restaurant, you get to warm up with the popular firepot soup (medium $14), which mixes prawns, calamari, clams, fish balls, and fresh vegetables. Vegetarians will feel at home with dishes like sautéed eggplant and tofu ($6.50). Follow it all up with a cup of *café phin* ($2), a sweet but strong coffee prepared iced or hot with condensed milk. *1007 Clay St., at 10th St., tel. 510/763–8495. Open weekdays 10–10, Sat. 11:30–10, Sun. 4:30–10. Wheelchair access. Other location: 344 20th St., in Kaiser Center, tel. 510/763–3610.*

➤ **UNDER $30** • **Bay Wolf.** Walking into this elegant restaurant, you might think you're entering someone's beautiful home. Inside you're treated to friendly service and excellent food that mixes Provençal, northern Italian, and California influences. The menu, featuring entrées in the $13–$17 range, changes every two weeks and includes such tasty creations as smoked trout salad with arugula, pickled beets, and dill crème fraîche; and grilled duck with ginger-peach chutney. When it's warm enough, you can dine on the outdoor patio. *3853 Piedmont Ave., btw 40th St. and MacArthur Blvd., tel. 510/655–6004. Open weekdays 11:30–2 and 6–10, weekends 5:30–10.*

Kincaid's Bayhouse. On the waterfront at Oakland's Jack London Square, this spiffy restaurant spit-roasts, sear-grills, and hardwood-broils steaks and seafood. Savor the renowned crab cakes ($17, $8 as an appetizer) or the coconut-beer prawns ($14.50, $7 as an appetizer). Even if you can't afford a meal here, you can hang out at the bar during happy hour (weekdays 4:30–6:30) and watch sailboats breeze into the harbor. *1 Franklin St., in Jack London Sq., tel. 510/835–8600. Wheelchair access. Open Mon.–Thurs. 11:15–9:30, Fri. 11:15–10, Sat. 11:30–10, Sun. 10:30–9.*

Marin County

In this land of the rich and established, it's hardly surprising that most restaurants cater to older folks with cash to blow. You'll have to look hard for budget eats, and don't expect anything too exciting—Marin is no hotbed of ethnic diversity. Your best bet is to pack a picnic and dine in the open, far away from the din of well-heeled civilization. For restaurants on the Marin County Coast, including Stinson Beach, Bolinas, and Point Reyes, *see* Marin County, in Chapter 2.

SAUSALITO

Restaurants and cafés line **Bridgeway,** Sausalito's main street, but they're generally overpriced and touristy. Expect to pay at least $15–$20 for seafood and waterfront vistas. If you head one block inland from Bridgeway to **Caledonia Street,** you'll find much better bargains without the tourist brouhaha. Even better, picnic at one of the grassy areas between Bridgeway and the bay.

➤ **UNDER $10 • Hamburgers.** If you're lucky enough to see a few locals in Sausalito, it'll be in the line for this hole-in-the-wall. All they do are a few variations on the hamburger ($4–$5) and fries ($1.50) theme. Most people take their food to one of the benches in the park outside rather than eat in the steamy restaurant. If neither option appeals to you, head to Paterson's Bar next door, where they'll serve you the same burger for about a buck extra. *737 Bridgeway, tel. 415/332–9471. Open daily 11–5.*

Lighthouse Coffee Shop. Open at the crack of dawn seven days a week, Sausalito's Lighthouse has surprisingly cheap breakfasts and lunches, generally priced under $6. They specialize in hearty Danish food: Try Danish meatballs with potato salad ($6), or the Copenhagen burger ($7), with horseradish, pickles, capers, onion, and egg yolk. This is a no-frills sort of place, popular with just about everybody. *1311 Bridgeway, tel. 415/331–3034. Open weekdays 6:30 AM–3 PM, weekends 7–3.*

Stuffed Croissant. This is *the* stop for picnickers attempting to avoid Sausalito's overpriced restaurants. The tiny mom-and-pop deli offers sandwiches ($4–$5.50), soups, decadent desserts, and simple breakfast fare ($1–$5). Look for day-old pastries that sell for a song. You can eat at the counter, or get it to go like everyone else. *43 Caledonia St., 1 block inland from Bridgeway, tel. 415/332–7103. Wheelchair access. Open Mon. 6:30 AM–9 PM, Tues.–Sat. 6:30 AM–10 PM, Sun. 7:30 AM–9 PM.*

➤ **UNDER $15 • Arawan.** This unpretentious restaurant isn't much to look at, but once you eat here you'll see why loyal Thai-food devotees patronize the place regularly. The lunch specials are standard (pad Thai is $5.25), but they pull out all the stops at dinner, when a chef with poetic leanings serves up savory entrées ($6–$9) like "spicy angel of the sea" (fried calamari with chili garlic sauce) and "shrimp lost in the woods" (shrimp with snow peas, bamboo shoots, and black mushrooms in oyster sauce). *47 Caledonia St., 1 block inland from Bridgeway, tel. 415/332–0882. Open Mon.–Sat. 11:30–3 and 4:30–10, Sun. 4:30–10.*

TIBURON

In general, Tiburon's restaurants are more notable for their views than for their food. Restaurants and cafés line **Main Street.** Most offer decks hanging out over the bay, but you'll pay for the privilege of gazing at the San Francisco skyline or Angel Island. If you're really short of money, pack a picnic, take a ferry over from San Francisco (*see* Chapter 1), and eat on the grass at the tip of the peninsula. You'll find a Safeway and some delis a few blocks from the waterfront on Tiburon Boulevard, if you left your baguettes and Brie behind.

➤ **UNDER $10 • Conditori Sweden House Café.** This Tiburon café serves up fresh and unusual breakfasts (all with limpa bread, a type of Swedish rye) on a peaceful wooden deck jutting out into the water. Regulars order the Swedish pancakes with lingonberries and sour cream ($6). Also check out the granola with yogurt ($5.50) or fresh seasonal fruit ($6.75). *35 Main St., tel. 415/435–9767. Open Mon.–Thurs. 8–6, Fri.–Sat. 8–10, Sun. 8–7.*

➤ **UNDER $15 • Sam's Anchor Cafe.** One of Tiburon's least expensive waterfront restaurants, Sam's attracts a lot of Marin County locals, who cram onto the deck sipping Famous Ramos gin fizzes ($4.50) and Bloody Marys. Even on wet and windy days, diehards eat big brunches (served on weekends until 2:30) or dinner on the deck. Hearty breakfast dishes are $6.50–$9; if you're feeling adventurous, try the Hangtown Fry omelet ($7.50) with oysters, bacon, scallions, and cheese. Fresh fish dishes are $8–$15, burgers $7–$9, sandwiches $5.50 and up. *27 Main St., tel. 415/435–4527. Wheelchair access. Open Mon.–Thurs. 11–10:30, Fri. 11–11, Sat. 10 AM–11 PM, Sun. 9:30 AM–10:30 PM.*

➤ **UNDER $20** • **Guaymas.** It's not cheap, but this restaurant next to the Tiburon ferry landing serves some of the best, most authentic Mexican food in the Bay Area. If you're on a tight budget, fill up on the fresh corn tortillas and three salsas brought to your table before you order, and stick to the appetizers ($4–$9). As well as the usual quesadillas, look for *chalupas* (tortilla pockets with chicken breast, cheese, and jalapeños; $4.75), *cazuelitas* (potato and corn tortillas with baked zucchini and cheese; $4), and cute baby tamales. If you want to go all out, tack on a main course ($9–$18)—there are heaps of seafood options. The outside deck is heated, but for once the colorfully decorated interior is as attractive as the view. *5 Main St., tel. 415/435–6300. Wheelchair access. Open Sun.–Thurs. 11–10, Fri.–Sat. 11–11.*

Order a Guaymas margarita to find out what the drink is supposed to taste like.

MILL VALLEY

You'll pass through Mill Valley if you're headed to the attractions along coastal Route 1—Muir Woods, Mt. Tamalpais, Stinson Beach, and Point Reyes. If you're eager to push on through to the coast, grab a quick slice of thin pizza ($2–$3), served by a guy who actually speaks Italian, at **Stefano's Pizza** (8 East Blithedale Ave., at Throckmorton Ave., tel. 415/383–9666). Locals also recommend the Chinese food at **Jennie Low's** (38 Miller Ave., at Sunnyside Ave., tel. 415/388–8868), where spicy eggplant is $6.50 and Hunan prawns go for $9.

➤ **UNDER $10** • **Mama's Royal Café.** If you're anxious to get an early start on the day, this funky café serves unbeatable huevos rancheros ($6) and *huevos con nopales* (eggs with cactus; $6). It's full of thrift-store artifacts and psychedelic murals, and has plenty of outdoor seating. At lunch, Mama features the "Hippie-crit" ($6)—one nature-burger patty, one free-range beef patty—for the wanna-be vegetarian who's not quite there yet. Live acoustic music ranging from folk to blues to rock plays Tuesday–Saturday nights, and there's no cover charge. *393 Miller Ave., at Locust Ave., tel. 415/388–3261. Open weekdays 7:30 AM–2:30 PM, weekends 8:30–3.*

SAN RAFAEL

Compared to most of Marin County, San Rafael has a down-to-earth restaurant scene, with lots of cafés, Mexican joints, and other ethnic eateries lining **4th Street** downtown.

➤ **UNDER $10** • **Royal Thai.** You'd hardly expect to find great Thai food in a leafy court-yard called the French Quarter in San Rafael, but people all over the Bay Area rave about this great restaurant, started by a couple who defected from the kitchen at San Francisco's popular Khan Toke Thai House (*see above*). The friendly staff serves up no-frills seafood and curry dishes for less than $8 in a restored Victorian house. *610 3rd St., at Irving St., tel. 415/485–1074. Open weekdays 11–2:30 and 5–10, weekends 5–10. Other location: 951 Clement St., San Francisco, at 11th Ave., tel. 415/386–1795.*

San Rafael Station Café. This breakfast and lunch spot has a real neighborhood feel—pictures of people's pooches line the mirror behind the counter. Locals hang out here on weekends reading the paper and ingesting phenomenal amounts of cholesterol. Omelets of every persuasion run $4–$8, and sandwiches are $3.50–$7.50. *1013 B St., btw 4th and 5th Sts., tel. 415/456–0191. Wheelchair access. Open weekdays 6:30 AM–3 PM, weekends 8–3.*

➤ **UNDER $15** • **Mayflower Inne.** Few people would mistake the British pub grub here for haute cuisine. Still, their fish and chips ($7.50) and hearty sandwiches ($6) are some of the best lunch deals in town. And if you're sick of delicate California cuisine, you'll appreciate dinners like the huge ploughman's platter ($10) or bangers 'n' mash ($11). The less hungry can wash down snacks like chicken wings ($5) with one of nine rotating tap beers. An adjacent specialty store is piled high with British food items. *1533 4th St., tel. 415/456–1011. From U.S. 101 north, take Central San Rafael exit to 4th St. and turn left. Wheelchair access. Kitchen open weekdays 11:30–10, weekends 5–10.*

South Bay

Most restaurants on the suburbanized peninsula south of San Francisco are predictably bland. You'll find a cluster of semi-intriguing restaurants around Palo Alto and the Stanford campus, but they're not as cheap as the eats in most student areas. You might do better to head out to the coast—the food's certainly no more exciting, but it's bound to taste better when you're gazing out at the roaring Pacific. For coastal restaurants, *see* The South Bay, in Chapter 2.

PALO ALTO

University Avenue, which runs into Stanford's campus, is one long food court, with cutesy, yuppified restaurants everywhere you look. You'll pay just enough more than usual for your burrito, your burger, or your beer to make it annoying.

> **UNDER $10 • The Dutch Goose.** It doesn't get any more all-American than this grungy sports bar near Stanford—just ask the beer-bellied regulars who congregate at the front tables seven nights a week. Cheeseburgers are $3.50, and you'll pay $7 for a dozen steamed clams. Bring a sharp object and carve your name in the table. *3567 Alameda de las Pulgas, Menlo Park, tel. 415/854-3245. Exit I-280 at Sand Hill Rd. toward Stanford, and turn left on Junipero Serra Blvd., which becomes Alameda de las Pulgas. Open Mon.–Sat. 11 AM–2 AM, Sun. 11 AM–1 AM.*

Jing Jing. This popular Chinese restaurant near the Stanford campus is the place to come for spicy food. You're sure to run into students and professors, as the large tables are the locus of many a departmental lunch. Most dishes are in the $5–$10 range, though lunch specials run only $4–$5. Expect a wait. *443 Emerson St., off University Ave., tel. 415/328-6885. Open Mon.–Sat. 11:30–2 and 4:30–9:30, Sun. 4:30–9:30.*

Mango Café. Overlook the tacky bamboo sticks and fish nets, and enjoy authentic Jamaican dishes like hot curried goat with vegetables ($9) or jerked joints, a spicy chicken dish ($5.50). Fruit-juice smoothies ($3), served in glasses the size of fishbowls, come in a wide range of exotic flavors. *483 University Ave., at Cowper St., tel. 415/325-3229. From U.S. 101, take University Ave. exit west (toward Stanford). Wheelchair access. Open Mon.–Sat. 11–3 and 6–10. No credit cards.*

Miyake Sushi. If you don't mind eating over the din of saké-drinking college students and waiters yelling orders across the restaurant, you'll get surprisingly good sushi at a truly reasonable price—about $1–$2 per piece. For just a bit more, you can order specialties like the Tarzana roll (yellowtail, wild carrots, sprouts, and flying fish roe; $4). They also have a small menu of teriyaki and tempura dinners ($7–$12). There's almost always a wait. *261 University Ave., btw Bryant and Ramona Sts., tel. 415/323-9449. Wheelchair access. Open daily 11:30–10.*

Oasis Beer Garden. This grubby but immensely popular hangout near the Stanford campus serves tasty burgers and sandwiches ($4–$7). You can play pinball, watch sports on TV, read what's carved into your table, or soak up sun at one of the outdoor tables. *241 El Camino Real, tel. 415/326-8896. Just north of Stanford campus, at Cambridge St. Open daily 11 AM–1:30 AM, bar open until 2 AM.*

> **UNDER $15 • Sushi Ya.** The regular clientele, a mix of students and office workers, will more than vouch for the sushi and sashimi here. This inconspicuous restaurant near Stanford's campus does a good business in all the staples, from yellowtail and tuna rolls ($3.30 each) to *kaiso* (seaweed) salad ($6). The fried soft-shell crab ($9.50) is especially good. There are a few tables, but most patrons prefer to sit at the bar and chat with the owner while he skillfully prepares the food. *380 University Ave., btw Waverly and Florence Sts., tel. 415/322-0330. From U.S. 101, take University Ave. exit west. Wheelchair access. Open weekdays 11:30–2 and 5:30–9:30, Sat. 5–9:30.*

Specialty Markets and Delicatessens

SAN FRANCISCO

Grocery shopping in San Francisco need not be a mundane chore. Not only is there a store for every imaginable cuisine, ethnicity, and dietary restriction, but the act of buying groceries can also serve as valuable cruising and scamming time for busy San Franciscans. In two easy steps you can check out a potential love interest *and* make sure they're not committing any food faux pas. Stores whose windows can be counted on to steam up on occasion include the **Safeway** in the Marina district, where yuppies size up each other's sportswear and fret about the onset of love handles; the Safeway on Market and Church streets, for all types of gay men; the Harvest Ranch Market (*see below*), for the young, health- and fashion-conscious gay and lesbian set; and the Mission's Rainbow Grocery (*see below*), for lesbians and politically radical types of all persuasions. You may leave the house with a list reading "lettuce, toilet paper, marshmallow cream" and come home with a whole lot more.

If all you want is cheap and unusual food items, don't restrict yourself to the big stores: Head instead to San Francisco's rich, colorful neighborhood markets. In the Mission, you'll find markets stocking piñatas, fresh tortillas, and several varieties of chili powder. The Asian markets on Clement Street in the Richmond district will cheaply accommodate your every produce need, the delis in North Beach will load you down with extra-virgin olive oil and fresh mozzarella, and the Mediterranean and Middle Eastern delis on Irving Street in the Sunset district pack up pints of hummus and tabouleh. Once you see what the city has to offer, you'll never go back to Safeway again—unless you're lonely.

Holey Bagel. Several locations dole about 15 varieties of fresh, chewy bagels, and the cream cheese comes plain ($1.25) or whipped up with things like chives, lox, and sun-dried tomatoes ($1.75). The 24th Street branch is a popular hangout on weekend mornings. *3218 Fillmore St., at Lombard St., tel. 415/922–1955. Other locations: 1206 Masonic Ave., at Haight St., tel. 415/626–9111; 3872 24th St., at Sanchez St., tel. 415/647–3334.*

Just Desserts. Since 1974, this excellent bakery has captured the hearts and stomachs of the Bay Area with its decadent desserts—and they've got a mile-long list of awards to prove it. Following the motto "No mixes, no preservatives, no freezing, no compromise," Just Desserts produces sweet treats to die for: lemon tarts; carrot, chocolate fudge, and sour cream cakes; cheesecakes; and buttermilk raisin scones ($1.25–$3.50 a piece). Since hooking up with Tassajara Bakery (*see below*), they also offer mouthwatering breads and baguettes. Look for branches throughout the Bay Area; the main location on Church Street in San Francisco has a beautiful outdoor courtyard. *248 Church St., at Market St., tel. 415/626–5774. Open Mon.–Thurs. 7–11, Fri. 7–midnight, Sat. 8–midnight, Sun. 8–11.*

Harvest Ranch Market. Come to this always-busy market in the heart of the Castro for all your nutritious-food needs. The aisles are packed with organic produce, organic bulk foods (including 10 varieties of cereal), and tons of canned goods—most *sans* fat and preservatives. They also offer an organic salad bar and the ever-popular Tassajara bread. The outside benches are popular munching (and flirting) spots on the weekends—sit awhile and you may just meet that dark, organic stranger. *2285 Market St., near Noe St., tel. 415/626–0805.*

Molinari Delicatessen and **Lucca Delicatessen.** Although these two establishments lie miles apart from each other (Molinari is in the heart of North Beach, Lucca in the Mission district), they have similar selections, prices, and jovial Italian service. At both you can get reasonably priced homemade pastas, cheeses, vino, and bread, and anything else decadent and Italian you can think of (except Pia Zadora). Enormous sandwiches, dripping with fresh mozzarella and a trillion slices of salami, make both places popular lunchtime spots. *Molinari: 373 Columbus Ave., at Vallejo St., tel. 415/421–2337. Lucca: 1100 Valencia St., at 22nd St., tel. 415/647–5581; 2120 Chestnut St., at Steiner St., tel. 415/921–7873.*

Rainbow Grocery. This cooperatively owned and run grocery store on the edge of the Mission district stocks organic produce, oils, honey, syrup, grains, pastas, herbs, spices, and other stuff in bulk. They've got just about every food item a vegetarian could dream of. The attached general store is your source for vitamins, herbal supplements, health books, and natural soaps. They also provide a bulletin board and a card file, if you're looking for a room or a ride or a futon or a dog or a cause. *1899 Mission St., at 15th St., tel. 415/863–0620.*

Real Foods. This delicatessen on the upscale stretch of Polk Street sells all sorts of prepared food items (salads, casseroles, noodle dishes, desserts) to folks who have sauntered down from Russian Hill to see what the peasants are up to. If you've got a little extra cash to blow on a gourmet picnic you're in the right place; and if not, you can always enjoy a coffee and a cookie while those around you spend big bucks. Real Foods also has a grocery store and deli in Cole Valley, near the Haight. *2164 Polk St., at Vallejo St., tel. 415/775–2805. Other location: 1023 Stanyan St., at Carl St., tel. 415/564–1117.*

Tassajara Bakery. The bakery that began in a kitchen at the Tassajara Zen Center in Marin County never advertised itself as the purveyor of nirvana in every bite; that's something you have to discover on your own. In addition to many unusual varieties of freshly baked bread, Tassajara sells healthy, hearty soups, excellent vegetarian sandwiches, focaccia bread drizzled with herbs and garlic, and other food items in a tranquil location a few blocks from the upper Haight. They've recently merged with the outstanding local chain Just Desserts (*see above*), so you don't have to worry about coming away too healthy. *1000 Cole St., at Parnassus St., tel. 415/664–8947.*

Your Black Muslim Bakery. Specializing in "good-for-you" baked goods, this bakery, with two outlets in San Francisco and six in the East Bay, is a haven for vegans and the health-conscious. Most items contain no sugar, salt, milk, or eggs. The natural sweet rolls ($3), honey and carrot pies ($10), and honey chocolate chip cookies ($3 for 5) are excellent. They also sell vegetarian sandwiches and tofu burgers ($4–$5), as well as all-natural beverages ($2–$3). Every outlet also carries books on black history and displays posters and brochures about events in the African-American community. *609 Cole St., at Haight St., tel. 415/387–6384. Open Mon.–Sat. 10–8. Other S.F. location: 160 Eddy St., btw Mason and Taylor Sts., tel. 415/929–7082. Main bakery in Oakland: 5832 San Pablo Ave., btw Stanford Ave. and 59th St., tel. 510/658–7080.*

EAST BAY

Berkeley is enamored of European-style specialty markets, but even these come with a Berkeley twist (i.e., heavy on organic and pesticide-free produce, light on butcher shops). On Shattuck Avenue north of University Avenue, the Gourmet Ghetto is filled with grocery stores, bakeries, and specialty stores. **The Cheese Board** (1504 Shattuck Ave., btw Cedar and Vine Sts., tel. 510/549–3183) is one of the few successful collectives remaining in Berkeley and features an incredible selection of cheeses and freshly baked breads. Stop by in the morning for a scone or a sourdough cheese roll ($1). The staff likes nothing better than to explain the subtle variations in cheeses to you, and they'll give you free samples as they help you choose.

Near the south end of Shattuck, **Berkeley Bowl Marketplace** (2777 Shattuck Ave., at Stuart St., tel. 510/843–6929) represents alternative grocery shopping at its best. The organic produce selection is endless, the bulk grains come cheap, the seafood department features the freshest fish in Berkeley at a reasonable price, and the "environmentally friendly" selection is stunning. In Emeryville, a branch of the chain **Trader Joe's** (5796 Christie Ave., at Powell St., tel. 510/658–8091) sells inexpensive wine and beer, and lots of very affordable gourmet food. A decent bottle of wine will only set you back about four bucks. **Seabreeze Market** (598 University Ave., tel. 510/486–8119), near the Berkeley marina, offers fresh shellfish, fruits, and vegetables. They also serve sandwiches and daily specials that you can eat at picnic tables overlooking the bay.

For bagels, try the very popular **Noah's Bagels** (3170 College Ave., tel. 510/654–0944; 2344 Telegraph Ave., tel. 510/849–9951; 1883 Solano Ave., tel. 510/525–4447), a New York–style shop famous for its flavored cream-cheese schmears. A bagel with lox schmear is $2.25. Noah's also has a branch in San Francisco's Sunset district (742 Irving St., at 9th St., tel. 415/566–2761) and one in the Marina district (2075 Chestnut St., btw Steiner and Fillmore Sts., tel. 415/775–2910).

Berkeley is full of specialty bread outlets offering fresh-baked loaves, like seeded baguettes or potato rosemary bread, still warm from the oven. If you can't make it down to their retail outlets, both **Semifreddi's** (372 Colusa Ave., Kensington, tel. 510/596–9935) and **Acme bread** (1601 San Pablo Ave., Berkeley, tel. 510/524–1327; 2730 9th St., Berkeley, tel. 510/843–2978) supply many Bay Area markets with fresh bread daily. Or visit **Il Fornaio** (2059 Mountain Blvd., Oakland, tel. 510/339–3108), a slick European café chain with branches in Oakland, San Francisco, and Marin. If you can deal with the atmosphere, you'll be rewarded with interesting (but expensive) breads.

In downtown Oakland, you'll find a huge variety of ethnic markets. Chinatown is full of Chinese and Southeast Asian groceries. Nearby, on 7th Street between Broadway and Washington, **Mi Rancho** (464 7th St., at Broadway, tel. 510/451–2393) offers ready-made tacos (95¢) and burritos ($2.50–$4) and sells the fixings for making your own. **Housewives Marketplace** (8th and Jefferson Sts., tel. 510/444–4396) is a warehouse full of specialty stands with a southern flair. You'll find a small grocery store, a deli, a butcher, a fish and seafood counter, a sausage shop, and dried goods like beans, roasted peanuts, and mix for Cajun jambalaya. Locals come here for fresh produce and smoked meats like ham hocks. A few stands offer fast-food items like Louisiana burgers with jalapeño cheese ($3.50). **G. B. Ratto & Company** (821 Washington St., btw 8th and 9th Sts., tel. 510/832–6503) is your source for delicacies like buffalo-milk mozzarella and many varieties of olive oil. They also prepare sandwiches and have everything you need for a gourmet picnic.

MARIN AND THE SOUTH BAY

The draw at the airy **Windsor Vineyards** wine shop in Marin County is that you can taste the wines, all made at their winery in the Russian River Valley, before you buy. They have about 20

Farmers' Markets

One of the best ways to get organic produce cheaply is to go to local farmers' markets, which usually take place once or twice a week. The farmers' market at the Civic Center's United Nations Plaza happens Wednesday and Sunday 8 AM–5 PM, and is chock full of fruits, vegetables, breads, honey, jellies, and salsas. Another market bustles at the Ferry Building, at the end of Market Street downtown, on Saturday from 9 AM to 1 PM. And at Alemany Boulevard and Crescent Avenue in Bernal Heights, just south of the Mission district, residents do some serious produce shopping Saturday 6–6.

Every Friday from 8 to 2, you can meet the East Bay's farmers and bakers at the Old Oakland Certified Farmers' Market (Broadway and 9th St., tel. 510/452–FARM). Oakland's other farmers' market takes place at the Jack London Waterfront (Broadway and Embarcadero, tel. 510/798–7061) Sundays 10–2. You can also stock up on farm-fresh products at one of Berkeley's farmers' markets, sponsored by the Ecology Center (tel. 510/548–2220). They happen every Saturday 10–2 on Center Street at Martin Luther King Jr. Way, Sunday 11–3 on Haste Street at Telegraph Avenue, and Tuesday from 2 until dusk on Derby Street at Martin Luther King Jr. Way.

In Marin, the Downtown San Rafael Farmers' Market (tel. 415/457–2266), which takes place every summer Thursday from 6 to 9 PM on 4th Street, is more like a weekly block party than a simple produce sale. Locals come to buy handicrafts, listen to live music, and let the kids take pony rides.

bottles for sampling, but they suggest you only try six (which is none too stingy). You won't find any Grand Crus here, but there are plenty of wines you can afford—some go for as little as $6 a bottle. *72 Main St., Tiburon, tel. 415/435–3113. Open Sun.–Thurs. 10–6, Fri.–Sat. 10–7.*

The South Bay's **Whole Foods Market,** part of a Bay Area chain, has an amazing bakery and deli section, featuring everything from gourmet vegetarian and vegan dishes to huge sandwiches loaded up with turkey, ham, or roast beef. Try the Hunan chicken, at a steep but almost justifiable $8 per pound. The organic produce is the freshest in town, but the prices throughout the market are a bit on the expensive side. The deli section has tables, just in case you can't wait until you get home to start scarfing that turkey sandwich ($4.50). *774 Emerson St., Palo Alto, at Homer St., tel. 415/326–8676. Wheelchair access. Open daily 9 AM–10 PM. Other locations: 3000 Telegraph Ave., Berkeley, at Ashby St., tel. 510/649–1333; 414 Miller Ave., Mill Valley, at Evergreen Ave., tel. 415/381–1200.*

Reference Listings

BY TYPE OF CUISINE

AMERICAN

UNDER $5
Café Intermezzo (Berkeley)
Hot 'n' Hunky (Castro)
New Dawn (Mission)
San Francisco Art Institute Café (North Beach)
Specialty's (Downtown)
Tommy's Joynt (Civic Center)

UNDER $10
All You Knead (Haight-Ashbury)
Bagdad Café (Castro)
Barney's Gourmet Hamburger (Berkeley)
Bette's Oceanview Diner (Berkeley)
Brick Hut Cafe (Berkeley)
Buena Vista Café (Fisherman's Wharf)
Café Sanchez (Mission)
Chester's Cafe (Berkeley)
Clown Alley (Downtown)
Crescent City Cafe (Haight-Ashbury)
The Dutch Goose (Palo Alto)
Eagle Café (Fisherman's Wharf)
Flint's (Oakland)
The Fruit Gallery (Downtown)
Grubstake (Civic Center)
Hamburger Mary's (South of Market)
Hamburgers (Sausalito)
Homemade Cafe (Berkeley)
Kate's Kitchen (Haight-Ashbury)
Lois the Pie Queen (Oakland)

Mama's Royal Café (Mill Valley)
Mama's Royal Café (Oakland)
Moishe's Pippic (Civic Center)
Oasis Beer Garden (Palo Alto)
Orphan Andy's (Castro)
Patio Café (Castro)
Pork Store Café (Haight-Ashbury)
Rick and Ann's (Berkeley)
San Rafael Station Café (San Rafael)
Saul's (Berkeley)
Spaghetti Western (Haight-Ashbury)
Sparky's (Castro)
Squat and Gobble Café (Haight-Ashbury)
Stuffed Croissant (Sausalito)

UNDER $15
Ace Cafe (South of Market)
Acorn (South of Market)
Doidge's Kitchen (Marina)
Sam's Anchor Café (Tiburon)

UNDER $20
California Culinary Academy (Civic Center)
Zuni Café (Civic Center)

UNDER $25
Greens (Marina)

UNDER $30
Bay Wolf (Oakland)
Chez Panisse Café (Berkeley)
Kincaid's Bayhouse (Oakland)

BURGERS

UNDER $5
Hot 'n' Hunky (Castro)

UNDER $10
Barney's Gourmet Hamburger (Berkeley)
Buena Vista Café (Fisherman's Wharf)
Clown Alley (Downtown)
The Dutch Goose (Palo Alto)
Grubstake (Civic Center)
Hamburger Mary's (South of Market)
Hamburgers (Sausalito)
Oasis Beer Garden (Palo Alto)
Orphan Andy's (Castro)
Sparky's (Castro)

CHINESE

UNDER $5
Kowloon (Chinatown)
Lucky Creation (Chinatown)

UNDER $10
Chef Jia's (Chinatown)
Empress Garden (Richmond/Sunset)
Jennie Low's (Mill Valley)
Jing Jing (Palo Alto)
House of Nanking (Chinatown)
Hunan (North Beach)
Lotus Garden (Chinatown)
R&G Lounge (Chinatown)
Royal Hawaii Seafood Restaurant (Chinatown)

Shangri-La (Richmond/Sunset)
Tin's Teahouse (Oakland)

UNDER $15
Yank Sing (Downtown)

ETHIOPIAN

UNDER $10
Asmara (Oakland)
Blue Nile (Berkeley)
Massawa (Haight-Ashbury)

FRENCH

UNDER $10
Mission Grounds (Mission)
Ti Couz (Mission)

UNDER $15
Café Bastille (Downtown)
Café Claude (Downtown)
South Park Café (South of Market)

UNDER $30
Bay Wolf (Oakland)

INDIAN

UNDER $10
Ananda Fuara (Civic Center)
Shilpa (Berkeley)

UNDER $15
Ganges (Haight-Ashbury)
Pasand Madras Cuisine (Berkeley)
Scenic India (Mission)

ITALIAN

UNDER $5
Marcello's (Castro)

UNDER $10
Bocce Café (North Beach)
Caffe Europa (North Beach)
Cafe Panini (Berkeley)
Il Pollaio (North Beach)
L'Osteria del Forno (North Beach)
Mario's Bohemian Cigar Store and Café (North Beach)

North Beach Pizza (North Beach)
Vicolo (Civic Center)

UNDER $15
Capp's Corner (North Beach)
The Gold Spike (North Beach)
Il Fornaio (Downtown)

UNDER $20
Buca Giovanni (North Beach)
Venezia (Berkeley)

JAPANESE

UNDER $10
Country Station Sushi Café (Mission)
Isobune (Japantown)
Mifune (Japantown)
Miyake Sushi (Palo Alto)
No-Name (Nippon) Sushi (Castro)

UNDER $15
Sanppo (Japantown)
Sushi Ya (Palo Alto)

UNDER $20
Sushi Ko (Berkeley)

MEDITERRANEAN AND MIDDLE EASTERN

UNDER $10
Kan Zaman (Haight-Ashbury)
La Méditerranée (Castro)

MEXICAN AND CENTRAL AMERICAN

UNDER $5
Cancun Taqueria (Mission)
Casa Sanchez (Mission)
El Farolito (Mission)
El Toro (Mission)
El Trébol (Mission)
La Cumbre (Mission)
Pancho Villa (Mission)
Taqueria Morelia (Oakland)

UNDER $10
Gaucho's Café (Oakland)
Juan's Place (Berkeley)

Los Cocos (Oakland)
Nicaragua (Mission)
Panchita's (Mission)
WA-HA-KA! (South of Market)

UNDER $15
The Cantina (Oakland)
La Rondalla (Mission)

UNDER $20
Guaymas (Tiburon)

PIZZA

UNDER $5
Blondie's (Berkeley)
Cheese Board Pizza Collective (Berkeley)
Marcello's (Castro)
Stefano's Pizza (Mill Valley)

UNDER $10
North Beach Pizza (North Beach)
Vicolo (Civic Center)
Zachary's Chicago Pizza Inc. (Berkeley)

SEAFOOD

UNDER $15
Anchor Oyster Bar (Castro)
Sam's Anchor Café (Tiburon)
Swan Oyster Depot (Civic Center)

UNDER $30
Kincaid's Bayhouse (Oakland)

SPANISH AND CARIBBEAN

UNDER $10
Esperpento (Mission)
Mango Café (Palo Alto)

UNDER $15
Cha Cha Cha (Haight-Ashbury)
Rita's Bar/Timo's (Mission)
Sol y Luna (Downtown)

UNDER $20
Miss Pearl's Jam House (Civic Center)

THAI

UNDER $5
Thai Buddhist Temple
(Berkeley)

UNDER $10
Berkeley Thai House
(Berkeley)
Cha Am (Berkeley)
Manora's Thai Cuisine
(South of Market)
Racha Café (Civic Center)
Royal Thai (San Rafael)
Thailand Restaurant (Castro)

UNDER $15
Arawan (Sausalito)
Khan Toke Thai House
(Richmond/Sunset)

Thep Phanom (Haight-
Ashbury)

VIETNAMESE AND CAMBODIAN

UNDER $10
101 Restaurant (Downtown)
Angkor Palace (Marina)
Phó' Lâm Viên (Oakland)
Starlite Restaurant (Oakland)
Tu Lan (Downtown)

UNDER $15
Angkor Wat (Richmond/
Sunset)
Golden Turtle (Civic Center)
Le Cheval (Oakland)
Phnom Penh (Civic Center)

OTHER

UNDER $10
Conditori Sweden House
(Swedish; Tiburon)
Hahn's Hibachi (Korean;
Marina)
Lighthouse Coffee Shop
(Danish; Sausalito)
Nin Yang (Burmese;
Oakland)

UNDER $15
Anna's (International;
Oakland)
Helmand (Afghan; North
Beach)
Mayflower Inne (British;
San Rafael)

SPECIAL FEATURES

BREAKFAST/BRUNCH

UNDER $5
Ann's Soup Kitchen and
Restaurant (Berkeley)
New Dawn (Mission)
Thai Buddhist Temple
(Berkeley)

UNDER $10
All You Knead (Haight-
Ashbury)
Bette's Oceanview Diner
(Berkeley)
Brick Hut Cafe (Berkeley)
Café Sanchez (Mission)
Chester's Cafe (Berkeley)
Conditori Sweden House
(Tiburon)
Crescent City Cafe (Haight-
Ashbury)
The Fruit Gallery (Downtown)
Homemade Cafe (Berkeley)
Kate's Kitchen (Haight-
Ashbury)
Lighthouse Coffee Shop
(Sausalito)
Lois the Pie Queen (Oakland)
Mama's Royal Café (Mill
Valley)
Mama's Royal Cafe (Oakland)
Mission Grounds (Mission)
Pasqua (Castro)
Patio Café (Castro)
Pork Store Café (Haight-
Ashbury)

Rick and Ann's (Berkeley)
San Rafael Station Café
(San Rafael)
Spaghetti Western (Haight-
Ashbury)
Squat and Gobble Café
(Haight-Ashbury)
Tin's Teahouse (Oakland)

UNDER $15
Acorn (South of Market)
Doidge's Kitchen (Marina)
Sam's Anchor Café (Tiburon)

DINNER AND ENTERTAINMENT

UNDER $10
Bocce Café (North Beach)
Kan Zaman (Haight-
Ashbury)
Shilpa (Berkeley)

UNDER $15
Angkor Wat (Richmond/
Sunset)
Anna's (Oakland)
Café Bastille (Downtown)
Café Claude (Downtown)
Ganges (Haight-Ashbury)
La Rondalla (Mission)
Pasand Madras Cuisine
(Berkeley)
Sol y Luna (Downtown)

UNDER $20
Miss Pearl's Jam House
(Civic Center)

LATE-NIGHT EATS

UNDER $5
Cancun Taqueria (Mission)
El Farolito (Mission)
Marcello's (Castro)
Pizza Love (South of
Market)

UNDER $10
20 Tank Brewery (South of
Market)
Bagdad Café (Castro)
Buena Vista Café (Fisher-
man's Wharf)
Clown Alley (Downtown)
The Dutch Goose (Palo
Alto)
Flint's (Oakland)
Grubstake (Civic Center)
Hamburger Mary's (South of
Market)
Lori's Diner (Downtown)
Oasis Beer Garden (Palo
Alto)
Orphan Andy's (Castro)
Pine Crest (Downtown)
Sparky's (Castro)

UNDER $15
La Rondalla (Mission)

OUTDOOR EATING

UNDER $5
Casa Sanchez (Mission)

UNDER $10
Berkeley Thai House
(Berkeley)
Bocce Café (North Beach)
Cafe Panini (Berkeley)
Café Sanchez (Mission)
Chester's Cafe (Berkeley)
Conditori Sweden House
Café (Tiburon)
Gaucho's Café (Oakland)
Josie's Cabaret and Juice
Joint (Castro)
Oasis Beer Garden (Palo Alto)
Patio Café (Castro)

UNDER $15
Acorn (South of Market)
Café Bastille (Downtown)
Café Claude (Downtown)
Sam's Anchor Cafe (Tiburon)

UNDER $20
Guaymas (Tiburon)
Miss Pearl's Jam House
(Civic Center)

UNDER $30
Bay Wolf (Oakland)

VEGETARIAN

UNDER $5
Cheese Board Pizza Collective (Berkeley)

Kowloon (Chinatown)
Lucky Creation (Chinatown)

UNDER $10
Ananda Fuara (Civic Center)
Lotus Garden (Chinatown)
Shangri-La (Richmond/
Sunset)

UNDER $15
Ganges (Haight-Ashbury)

UNDER $25
Greens (Marina)

CAFÉ CULTURE   5

By AnneLise Sorensen and Kelly Green

These days, you can find espresso in the strangest of places—Iowa, movie the-
aters, even 24-hour convenience stores—but a few cafés in Berkeley and San Francisco can
boast of having had the same java-obsessed customers for more than 30 years. The rest of the
world is finally realizing what participants of Bay Area coffee culture have known all along: that
four shots of espresso is the best legal high around. San Francisco's cafés can be as crowded
on Friday nights as the local bar; and meeting for coffee isn't just something to do when you're
bored, it's a cherished way of life.

Bay Area cafés come in every style and price level and play every type of background music imaginable. You can drink your morning espresso in a small establishment with sofas and classical
music, your noon latte in a postmodern warehouse space with a bunch of people in Armani suits,
and your evening cappuccino in a place where English is rarely spoken and the jukebox plays
opera. If you like to hang out with students and New Age prophets, head to Berkeley. If you prefer a more stylish, older crowd, check out San Francisco's North Beach. If you're into black
leather, long hair, and tattoos, your next stop should be a Haight Street café. In an effort to be
true to the "culture" part of café culture, many Bay Area cafés do a lot more than crank out coffee. Local artists are invited to display their works on café walls, and on weekend evenings, cafés
feature readings and open-mike nights (*see box* An Open Mike in San Francisco, *below*).

SAN FRANCISCO

San Francisco is a city of people who believe strongly in the connection between coffee and the
arts. Early converts to the café-as-muse philosophy included renegades Kerouac and Ginsberg,
who held all manner of performances at the still-pumping Caffe Trieste in North Beach. With
its European-style park and tiny streets, North Beach is still a popular place to grab a demi-
tasse on a rainy day, especially if you have someone to hold hands with under the table. Modern hipsters, however, have headed south to SoMa, the Haight, and especially the Mission. The
new hotbed of experimental art in San Francisco, the Mission has sprouted java-spewing
refuges for bohemians new and old, who write poems, novels, letters, and laundry lists as they
soak up the atmosphere.

DOWNTOWN **Café de la Presse.** This French-owned, international newsstand and café can
be a vital source of rejuvenation when the Financial District gets you down. After a day of dodging suits, the inordinate number of tourists here will almost seem refreshing. Preferred reading
material: *Le Monde. 342 Grant Ave., btw Sutter and Bush Sts., tel. 415/398–2680. Open
Mon.–Sat. 7 AM–11 PM, Sun. 7 AM–10 PM.*

Paninoteca Palio d'Asti. This very modern Italian café attracts suits, Italophiles, and espresso junkies with its powerful coffee ($1.70 for a single espresso) and damn good lunch items. You'll find an extensive array of *panini* (Italian sandwiches on focaccia bread); try the San Pietro (prosciutto and pungent Italian cheese; $5.50) or the San Secondo (fresh mozzarella, roasted peppers, and Gorgonzola; $5.25). On sunny days, they set up tables on nearby Commercial Alley. Preferred reading material: conservative Italian newspapers (in Italian, of course), *The Washington Post. 505 Montgomery St., near Sacramento St., tel. 415/362–6900. Open weekdays 7–4.*

CIVIC CENTER AND POLK GULCH **Mad Magda's Russian Tea Room and Café.** The deep-blue ceiling is dotted with yellow stars, the walls sprout onion domes, the peaceful garden is scattered with statues, and a tarot and tea-leaf reader waits to tell you all—what a way to relax after swallowing too much culture at the Museum of Modern Art. Some have complained about the service and cleanliness level, though. Sandwiches ($3–$5) come with provocative names like the Khrushchev (ham, Swiss, and herb mayo) and the Fabergé eggplant (eggplant, mozzarella, and basil). Preferred reading material: *Alice in Wonderland. 579 Hayes St., near Octavia St., tel. 415/864–7654. Open Tues.–Fri. 9–9, Mon. and Sat. 9–7, Sun. 10–7.*

Main Squeeze. If you find yourself dazed in the Civic Center, duck over to this space-age café and juice joint on Polk Street, innovatively designed with industrial materials molded into postmodern pieces of fruit. They specialize in juices ($2.50–$3.50) and have a decent breakfast

Choosing Your Poison

If the only two choices you know for coffee are "black" or "with creamer," you're going to be overwhelmed by Bay Area coffee houses. Practically every café here offers drinks whose names span four different languages. Here's a handy little cheat sheet to help you keep your cool and order like a sophisticate.

- *ESPRESSO comes in very tiny cups and is made by pumping steam instead of water through finely ground coffee. After two espressos, you may feel happy and giddy. After four, you will definitely need to be peeled off the ceiling.*

- *CAPPUCCINO is espresso topped with thick milk foam, with a sprinkling of chocolate on top.*

- *CAFFE LATTE is espresso with a lot of steamed milk and a little foam.*

- *Order CAFE AU LAIT and you'll get French roast coffee with steamed milk.*

- *KAFFE MIT SCHLAG is espresso with whipped cream, also known as espresso con panna.*

- *ESPRESSO MACCHIATO is an espresso with a tiny bit of milk foam.*

- *In a bold departure from the java tradition, CAFFE MOCHA is hot chocolate fortified with espresso.*

- *A DEPTH CHARGE is regular coffee with a shot of espresso in it.*

- *A WHY BOTHER is a double-decaf latte with nonfat milk, and a CUPPA JOE is simple diner coffee.*

and lunch menu that's 100% vegetarian, with some vegan items. Focaccia sandwiches ($4–$5) and soups ($2.50) cater to the healthy crowd. Preferred reading material: *Vogue, Yoga Journal*. 1515 Polk St., at California St., tel. 415/567–1515. Open Mon.–Sat. 8 AM–10 PM, Sun. 9 AM–10 PM.

NORTH BEACH Café Puccini. This small, cozy North Beach café offers the perfect refuge on a rainy day. The jukebox plays opera and a little Sinatra; and the sandwiches, including prosciutto on focaccia ($5) and the vegetarian special (mozzarella, tomatoes, and bell peppers; $6), make great meals. Preferred reading material: *Learn to Knit in 10 Easy Steps*. 411 Columbus Ave., at Vallejo St., tel. 415/989–7033. Open daily 6 AM–11:30 PM.

Caffè Greco. An international crowd fills this attractive café, whose windows overlook Columbus Avenue. You'll find a colorful selection of desserts—the decadent tiramusù ($4) is worshipped by regulars. The staff pumps out rich Italian espresso ($1.50 a cup), the stereo plays bad Italian pop music, and the place bustles day and night. Preferred reading material: Sunday *New York Times*. 423 Columbus Ave., btw Vallejo and Stockton Sts., tel. 415/397–6261. Open Mon.–Fri. 7 AM–midnight, Sat.–Sun. until 1 AM.

Greco uses Illy Caffè, reputed to be the best espresso in existence.

Caffe Trieste. This is the legendary home of the Beat generation; it was here that Kerouac and his gang oozed cool from every pore. The café doesn't seem to have changed a bit: It's as smoky as ever, with '50s decor and an opera-spouting jukebox. All drinks are $3.50 and the coffee is delicious, though they have a poor selection of pastries. Saturday afternoons at 1:30 PM, the owner's family serenades guests with anything from old Italian tunes to opera. Preferred reading material: *The Beat Reader*. 601 Vallejo St., at Grant St., tel. 415/392–6739. Open Sun.–Thurs. 6:30 AM–11:30 PM, Fri.–Sat. 6:30 AM–12:30 AM.

HAIGHT-ASHBURY DISTRICT The Crepery Café. This fetching café serves an extensive menu of crêpes with such fillings as strawberries and cream or hot brandied bananas (both are $4). You can also get dinner crêpes (chicken and vegetables, beef stroganoff) with salad for $7. Cole Valley locals, UCSF medical students, and Haight Street hipsters make up the crowd listening to Kate Bush and Sinead O'Connor. Preferred reading material: *Gray's Anatomy*. 86 Carl St., at Cole St., tel. 415/566–4433. Open Mon.–Sat. 9 AM–10 PM, Sun. 9–9.

Ground Zero. This stark place is the official café of the Apocalypse. The walls are faux granite, the floor unfinished wood and concrete, and the patrons founding members of the despairing

Plug In, Tune In, Drink Up

If you're curious about the so-called "Information Super Highway," or if face-to-face interaction just isn't your thing, try out San Francisco Net, a computer network that connects several cafés in the Bay Area. As you sit drinking your latte, you can delve into cyberspace and exchange messages with people at other cafés hooked up to the system. Here's how it works: You put in your quarter (yes, it costs money), log on with any name you want, and chat away, feeding the computer more money every so often. Who knows—maybe you'll find your future mate. But then again, you may just meet a bunch of technoids who have nothing better to do. S.F. Net can be found in 13 San Francisco cafés, including Brainwash (1122 Folsom St., at Langton St., tel. 415/861–3663), the two Jammin' Java locations (701 Cole St. and 398 Judah St., tel. 415/668–JAVA), and Muddy Waters (521 Valencia St., at 16th St., tel. 415/863–8006). You can also log on with your computer at home if you have a modem. Drop by a participating café for the number to dial.

generation. In addition to traditional café fare, you can get steamed eggs ($3.50) and draught beer. Preferred reading material: anything by Ray Bradbury. *783 Haight St., btw Pierce and Scott Sts., tel. 415/861–1985. Open weekdays 7 AM–11 PM, weekends 8 AM–11 PM.*

The Horseshoe. Here you'll find more disaffected youths with tattoos, piercings, and time on their hands than perhaps anywhere else in the city. Come for a strong cuppa joe (some think the strongest in town), peruse the millions of flyers on the walls seeking band members and housemates or advertising upcoming artistic events, and leave toying with the idea of just a small tattoo. Preferred reading material: *Modern Primitives, Guitar* magazine. *566 Haight St., near Steiner St., tel. 415/626–8852. Open daily 7:30 AM–1 AM.*

Jammin' Java. This sunny café, which serves great, strong coffee ($1.25–$2), light food (quiche $3.50), and lackluster desserts, is a welcome respite from the frenzy of nearby Haight Street. The indoor and outdoor tables are populated day and night, and an interesting variety of music plays overhead. Preferred reading material: *Harper's. 701 Cole St., at Waller St., tel. 415/668–5282. Open daily 7 AM–11 PM. Other location: 398 Judah St., at 9th Ave., tel. 415/566–JAVA. Open daily 6:30 AM–midnight.*

Tassajara Bakery. Although it's known throughout the Bay Area for its healthful breads (*see* Specialty Markets in Chapter 4), Tassajara also doubles as a tranquil café where older Cole Valley residents spend hours chatting and reading. And you'd be hard-pressed to find better café eats anywhere else: Snack on the excellent cookies (50¢–$1) or try the focaccia topped with tomato and basil ($2.50). Preferred reading material: *The Three Pillars of Zen. 1000 Cole St., at Parnassus St., tel. 415/664–8947. Open Mon.–Sat. 7 AM–11 PM, Sun. 8 AM–11 PM.*

CASTRO DISTRICT **Café Flore.** The Castro's premier gay hangout, Flore is a hotbed of activity day and night, drawing pseudo-artists, political activists, and trendy boys from all over. If you can't find a place at one of the outside tables, strike a pose and loiter until someone makes room for you—sharing tables is de rigueur. Expect noise, commotion and, in the midst of it all, an incredibly attractive someone sipping chamomile tea and looking furtively your way. Preferred reading material: Jean Genet (just pretend to read). *2298 Market St., at Noe St., tel. 415/621–8579. Open Sun.–Thurs. 7:30 AM–11:30 PM, Fri.–Sat. until midnight.*

Café Flore is also known as Café Bore, Café Floorshow, Café Hairdo, Café Hairdon't, Café Hairspray, and Café le Pretense.

Cup a Joe. This funky place with lavender walls has all the ingredients of a successful café: a mean cuppa joe at the lowest price in town (80¢ for an espresso), tasty pastries ($1.50–$2.50), and a clientele of art students. The café hosts spoken-word performances Tuesday nights at 8 PM and sponsors events like an evening of readings by disabled poets. Preferred reading material: the *Bay Times*, Armistead Maupin. *3801 17th St., at Sanchez St., tel. 415/252–0536. Open weekdays 7 AM–10 PM, weekends 8 AM–10 PM.*

Jumpin' Java. Sit down with a good read, a powerful cup of coffee (medium $1), and a spinach-and-cheddar quiche ($3.25) and make a night of it. Hell, come here every night. Rarely does one find such a centrally located café (steps away from Market Street in the Castro) with zero pretension, no grating music, and no squealing groups of work buddies. Students, gays, and young couples (dressed in black or college sweatshirts) make up the crowd. Preferred reading material: anything by Rita Mae Brown. *139 Noe St., btw Henry and 14th Sts., tel. 415/431–5282. Open daily 7 AM–10 PM.*

MISSION DISTRICT **Café Istanbul.** Owned by a man from Syria, Istanbul serves authentic and delicious Middle Eastern food (entrées $1–$4) and beverages ($1–$3) in a dark, tapestried setting. Score a place on the pillowed platform, take off your shoes, and hunker down with a pot of tea and some delicately flavored *dolmas* (grape leaves), or baklava and a pot of Turkish coffee. A wide variety of Middle Eastern music plays in the background; and there's live music Thursday and Friday evenings and belly dancing Wednesday nights. The latter is free, but reservations are required. Preferred reading material: anything by Rumi. *525 Valencia St., btw 16th and 17th Sts., tel. 415/863–8854. Open daily 11–11.*

Café Macondo. Jazz or Latin American music plays on the stereo at this serious, politically left café in the Mission. The patrons are here for serious study or conversation; and the oak tables and vintage lamps make it wonderfully easy to bury your nose in a book and write off the afternoon. Culinary offerings include fresh salads ($3–$5) and *empanadas,* a Chilean pastry filled with potatoes and vegetables ($4). Preferred reading material: Noam Chomsky. *3159 16th St., near Guerrero St., tel. 415/863–6517. Open daily 9 AM–11 PM.*

La Bohème. Right across the street from the BART station, this Mission-district institution has supplied locals with hearty breakfasts (fruit and granola, poached eggs, bagels, and the like) for years and years. Day and night, a steady stream of jazz or Stevie Wonder flows from the stereo while a multiracial, all-ages crowd gathers at the big, antique-looking tables. Preferred reading material: anything by Pablo Neruda, in Spanish. *3318 24th St., at Mission St., tel. 415/285–4122. Open daily 6 AM–11 PM.*

Red Dora's Bearded Lady. A self-proclaimed "dyke café (everybody welcome)," this small coffee house is a visible expression of San Francisco's young, energetic queer culture. It's decorated with votive candles and mismatched furniture and blasts a variety of contemporary music. There's a lovely garden in back. Dora's serves the usual café eats, plus a tasty breakfast burrito with black beans and the works ($4) and a tofu burger ($4.50). Spoken-word and musical performances take place most Fridays and Saturdays at 8 PM after the café has closed, but call ahead to confirm. Preferred reading material: *On Our Backs. 485 14th St., at Guerrero St., tel. 415/626–2805. Open weekdays 7–7, weekends 9–7.*

OTHER NEIGHBORHOODS So you've ventured beyond the parts of the city where cafés run two to a block. Shame on you. Luckily, there are places to get your caffeine fix in almost every neighborhood, for those times when you're visiting your aunt, expanding your horizons, getting a part for your car, or going to the dentist.

Blue Danube. A homey Richmond-district café with ceiling fans and changing art exhibits, the Danube is a great place to dig into the books you just bought down the street at Green Apple (*see* Chapter 3, Shopping). The café serves breakfast (Denver omelet with hash browns; $4), sandwiches ($4), beer, and wine, so you could conceivably spend all day here. Monday through Friday 5–8 PM is happy hour, with popcorn for all. The place is full of college students, resident youth with time on their hands, and thirtysomethings who never forgot how to laze away the weekend in a café. Preferred reading material: *Sassy* magazine, *S.F. Weekly. 306 Clement St., btw 4th and 5th Aves., tel. 415/221–9041. Open Mon.–Thurs. 7 AM–11:30 PM, Fri.–Sat. 7 AM–12:30 AM, Sun. 7 AM–11 PM.*

An Open Mike in San Francisco

Like their Beat predecessors, bohemians today enjoy airing their ghastly, turbid secrets to strangers at coffee houses. That's what open-mike poetry is all about—occasionally fabulous, more often incomprehensible, sometimes offensive, sometimes silly, always San Francisco. If you can wow these audiences with your poetry, you've got it made.

Cafés usually have scheduled readers before opening the mike to the public. Jammin' Java (see above) offers poetry with some music and performance art at 8 PM on Wednesdays. Red Dora's Bearded Lady (see above) features poetry, comedy, and music at 8 PM Fridays and Saturdays. The Blue Monkey (see below) has mostly poetry, with some music and storytelling, at 7:30 PM on Tuesdays. Café International (508 Haight St., at Fillmore St., tel. 415/552–7390) offers readings—often with an ethnic bent—at 8:30 PM on Fridays. Brainwash (1122 Folsom St., at Langton St., tel. 415/861–3663) features poetry and other readings at 8 PM on Saturdays.

The Blue Monkey. A quiet, small café with a gorgeous mural on the wall and open-mike nights (*see* box *above*), the Blue Monkey lies just a block off Fillmore Street, right where the neighborhood is transformed from the Fillmore of expensive boutiques and restaurants to the Fillmore of liquor stores and housing projects. Preferred reading material: anything by Amiri Baraka. *1777 Steiner St., btw Sutter and Post Sts., tel. 415/929–7117. Open Mon.–Fri. 7–6 (Tues. until 10:30 PM), Sat. 7:30–4, Sun. 8–3.*

Tart to Tart. The only problem with this large, lively café in the Sunset district (near UCSF Medical School) is the military-style seating at long tables that are in no way conducive to intimate conversation. Otherwise, this place whips up a mean cup of coffee and plenty of excellent desserts ($1.50–$3.25), salads ($4), and entrées. Preferred reading material: *Parenting* magazine. *641 Irving St., btw 7th and 8th Aves., tel. 415/753–0643. Open weekdays 7:30 AM–11 PM, Sat. 8:30 AM–midnight, Sun. 8:30 AM–11 PM.*

BERKELEY

Without its cafés, the People's Republic of Berkeley would collapse. Students would have nowhere to be seen while "studying"; skate punks would have nowhere to hang while cutting class; artists and poets would have no place to share their angst. Luckily, within a square mile of the U.C. campus no less than 50 cafés peacefully coexist. Smokers, however, should take note: In 1994, Berkeley banned smoking in all indoor and outdoor cafés.

Café Fanny. Owned by Chez Panisse maven Alice Waters, Café Fanny draws young mothers and tofu yuppies to its shady patio. The food's not exactly cheap, and the portions are small: If you're on a tight budget, get the bowl-sized latte ($2) and the homemade granola ($4), or try the buckwheat crêpes ($4.75), available with a variety of fillings. On your way home, stop next door at Acme Bread for a fresh-baked baguette. Preferred reading material: Marcel Pagnol, *Fanny. 1603 San Pablo Ave., at Cedar St., tel. 510/524–5447. Open weekdays 7–3, Sat. 8–4, Sun. 9–3.*

Caffè Med is where Allen Ginsberg wrote much of his famous poem "Howl." Even so, this landmark Berkeley café almost shut its doors for good in July 1994. Thanks to the uproar raised by loyal patrons, the Med is now remaining open.

Caffè Mediterraneum. The Med, featured in the film *The Graduate*, has nurtured countless bursts of inspiration and the occasional failed revolution. Because it's located away from campus at the south end of Telegraph Avenue, it's less frequented by students and more popular with hardened, lifelong Berkeleyites. Besides espresso drinks and desserts, the Med's small kitchen (open daily 8–3) serves omelets, sandwiches, burgers, and pasta at reasonable prices. The café—but not the second-floor rest room—is wheelchair accessible. Preferred reading material: Jack Kerouac, *On the Road. 2475 Telegraph Ave., btw Haste St. and Dwight Way, tel. 510/549–1128. Open daily 7 AM–11 PM.*

Caffè Strada. There's very little indoor seating, but the sprawling outdoor patio attracts a good mix of architecture students, frat and sorority types, and visiting foreigners. It's a social café, so don't expect to get much work done. Instead, bring a newspaper, relax in the sun, and eavesdrop while you sip your latte ($1.50) and munch on your pastry ($1–$2). Preferred reading material: *San Francisco Chronicle. 2300 College Ave., at Bancroft Way, tel. 510/843–5282. Open Mon.–Sat. 7 AM–11:30 PM, Sun. 8 AM–11:30 PM.*

Carreras Café and Gallery. Emeryville, the small collection of converted warehouses and artists' lofts between Berkeley and Oakland, is experiencing a cultural renaissance of sorts, as is evident in its burgeoning café scene. Carreras, the best of the lot, is housed in a one-story brick warehouse whose tall ceilings provide ample space for the paintings by local artists that adorn the walls. The café caters to young artsy types more than to students, but this is a good place for anyone to have an Anchor Steam beer ($2.50) after a long day. The food's not cheap (a sandwich costs $6–$7), but the desserts are worth the price. The selection changes daily and features such specialties as the raspberry linzer torte ($3.50). Preferred reading material: *The Spirit of Community and the Reinvention of American Society. 1290 Powell St., at Hollis St.,* *tel. 510/547–6763. From I–80, take Powell St. off-ramp and head north. Wheelchair access. Open Mon. 7 AM–11 PM, Tues.–Fri. 7 AM–midnight, Sat. 9 AM–midnight.*

The Musical Offering. With its airy interior and constant stream of classical music, this café caters to a tweedy and mature crowd. Coffees, sandwiches, vegetarian fare, and soups are sold in front, classical CDs and cassettes in back. The smoked trout salad will set you back $6; a latte is $1.50. Shopper's hint: Buy a CD or tape on the composer's birthday and receive a 20% discount. Preferred reading material: the *Brandenberg Concertos. 2430 Bancroft Way, near Telegraph Ave., tel. 510/849–0211. Open daily 8–8, music store open daily 10–9.*

Nefeli Caffè. Owned by a couple of charming Greek gentlemen, this quality coffee house on the north side of the U.C. campus is popular with students and professors for its innovative, reasonably priced menu. The impressive selection of Italian-style panini includes a great one with eggplant, roasted peppers, feta, and Kalamata olive spread ($4.25). Nefeli also has a variety of wine and beer, as well as sangria ($2.75). Sample the caffè freddo (espresso, sugar, and Sambuca; $1.75), a house specialty. Poetry readings take place Monday nights, followed by open-mike performances. Preferred reading material: anything by Nikos Kazantzakis. *1854 Euclid Ave., at Hearst St., tel. 510/841–6374. Open Mon.–Thurs. 7 AM–10 PM, Fri. 7 AM–midnight, Sat. 8 AM–midnight, Sun. 8 AM–10 PM.*

The Tea Spot. This enormous, easygoing women's café in West Berkeley has all kinds of things going on, including readings, gay and lesbian comedy nights, lectures, and art exhibitions. The

Folger's? Hah!

Someday, when the novelty of the café scene wears off, you'll be faced with making your own cup of coffee. And that means you have to buy a can of tasteless beans at the market, right? Nah. Just visit one of the Bay Area's numerous purveyors of by-the-pound gourmet coffees. Be prepared to face a million choices when you walk in: Sumatra or house blend? Ground or whole? It'll make your head spin.

Peet's Coffee and Tea is the undisputed java champion. Each store has pamphlets describing 33 kinds of coffee, and order forms in case you want to send a pound to your aunt in Chicago. The chain also sells "coffee hardware" (mugs, coffee makers, and so on) and a wide variety of teas. The original Peet's is in Berkeley (2124 Vine St., at Walnut St., tel. 510/841–0564); the newest location is in San Francisco (2257 Market St., at Noe St., tel. 415/626–6416).

Starbuck's was founded in Seattle at the start of the recent coffee craze, but aggressive expansion has carried it all the way down the West Coast. The San Francisco location (3995 24th St., at Noe St., tel. 415/826–1118) will give you a free cup of coffee when you buy a pound of beans. The quality is consistent, though the stores have as much ambience as a Carl's Jr. Also vying to sell beans to the wired consumer are San Francisco's Spinelli stores. A popular location is in the Haight-Ashbury (919 Cole St., at Carl St., tel. 415/753–2287.)

If big business gives you hives, try the independent java shop Uncommon Grounds in Berkeley (2813 7th St., btw Hines and Greyson Sts., tel. 510/644–4451), which sells beans retail and wholesale. Or head for Royal Ground Coffee in San Rafael (see below), whose sign boasts THE BEST BUZZ IN THE BAY AREA.

tea selection ($1.25 a cup) includes such soothing flavors as mango, vanilla, sassafras, and burgundy cherry. The Tea Spot also serves innovative breakfasts like blueberry rice pancakes ($5.25) and delicious lunches ($5–$7). Preferred reading material: anything by Sara Schulman. *2072 San Pablo Ave., btw University and Addison Sts., tel. 510/848–7376. Open Tues.–Fri. 7:30 AM–2 PM, Sat.–Sun. 8 AM–2 PM.*

MARIN COUNTY

For such a Sunday-stroll sort of place, Marin doesn't have as many cafés as you might expect, and what coffee houses there are make you pay for atmosphere and a view. You're best off in San Rafael, where the cafés offer above-average food and drinks and often have live music to boot. In Tiburon, **Conditori Sweden House** (*see* Chapter 4) is the best choice, especially if you like decadent desserts.

Depot Bookstore & Café. In downtown Mill Valley, this friendly café is a favorite with mountain bikers after a run down Mt. Tamalpais. On weekends, local families and tourists overflow from the café's patio into the town square, where serious chess-playing goes on. If you get there early, grab a Parisian ham and cheese on baguette ($1.75); they often run out by midday. Pick up a latte ($2) before you head into the bookstore section across the café's counter. Preferred reading material: anything by Barbara Kingsolver. *87 Throckmorton Ave., at Miller St., Mill Valley, tel. 415/383–2665. Open Mon.–Sat. 7 AM–10 PM, Sun. 8 AM–10 PM.*

Jazzed. Modeled after bohemian cafés of the '60s, this smoke- and alcohol-free club has photos of jazz legends on the wall and a small leave-a-book, take-a-book library. Lattes are the specialty (a double is $2.50), and the menu offers a light repast. Have a bowl of seafood gumbo ($6) and sit out on the patio under the stars; it's a great way to pass an evening. There are free live jazz performances every night; don't forget to tip the musicians. Preferred reading material: Nat Shapiro, *The Jazz Makers. 816 4th St., at Lincoln Ave., tel. 415/455–8077. From U.S. 101, take Central San Rafael exit and turn left. Wheelchair access. Open Tues.–Thurs. 9 AM–10 PM, Fri.–Sat. 9 AM–11 PM, Sun. 9–6.*

Royal Ground Coffee. Casual, sunny, littered with newspapers and a hip crowd, Royal Ground will make you feel right at home—if you love places where the employees are given free rein to be obnoxious and play loud music. The coffee, brewed at ROCKET-FUEL STRENGTH, as the sign on the wall proclaims, is also sold by the pound. A latte costs $1.75, and for 50¢ extra they'll make it with soy milk. They also have board games for your entertainment. Preferred reading material: *Come As You Are: The Story of Nirvana. 1146 4th St., at B St., San Rafael, tel. 415/455–0107. From U.S. 101, take Central San Rafael exit to 4th St. and turn left. Wheelchair access. Open Mon.–Thurs. 6:30 AM–11 PM, Fri.–Sat. 6:30 AM–midnight, Sun. 7 AM–11 PM.*

PALO ALTO

Palo Alto's cafés reflect the affluence of residents (rumored to have the highest average income in the Bay Area) and the diversity (or lack thereof) of the student population at nearby Stanford University. Most are located a few blocks off the main drag, University Avenue. These clean, upscale establishments serve good coffee, but they're not what you might call "homey."

Café Borrone. Nowhere are caffeine and literature more happily fused than at Café Borrone, next to the excellent bookstore Kepler's (*see* Chapter 3). A yuppie crowd of Kepler's customers ensures that the café's brick patio is almost always full; and the menu offers such interesting concoctions as the café Borrone—espresso, chocolate, steamed milk, cinnamon, nutmeg, whipped cream, and almonds ($3). The owner often books Dixieland jazz bands on weekend nights. Afterwards, head to the B.B.C. Pub or the King's Arms Pub (both next door) for a pint. Preferred reading material: *New York Times Book Review. 1010 El Camino Real, btw Ravenswood and Santa Cruz Aves., Menlo Park, tel. 415/327–0830. Wheelchair access. Open Mon.–Thurs. 7 AM–11 PM, Fri.–Sat. 8 AM–midnight, Sun. 8 AM–11 PM.*

Caffè Verona. Locals roll into this airy, high-ceilinged café after 5 PM to eat dinner or share a bottle of Chianti. The espresso-swigging college students arrive around 7 or 8 PM; some even manage to study amid the conversation and clanking dishes. The menu is pricey (a single latte costs $2.25 and tortellini with tomato cream sauce is $7.25), but you'd be hard-pressed to find anything cheaper in this upscale neighborhood. Preferred reading material: Ernest Hemingway, *The Sun Also Rises. 236 Hamilton Ave., btw Emerson and Ramona Sts., tel. 415/ 326–9942. Wheelchair access. Open Mon.–Thurs. 7 AM–11 PM, Fri. 7 AM–midnight, Sat. 8 AM– midnight, Sun. 8–5.*

Red Rock Coffee Company. This small café, housed in an old bank building, sells coffee makers, ceramic mugs, and pounds and pounds of coffee from South America, Africa, and the Far East. Red Rock makes a great café orgeat (almond-flavored latte; $2.50), but the main attraction here is the live music at 7 or 8 PM, usually folk during the week and blues on the weekends. Preferred reading material: *San Jose Mercury News. 201 Castro St., at Villa St., Mountain View, tel. 415/967–4473. Take U.S. 101 to Moffett Blvd. west, which becomes Castro St. Wheelchair access. Open weekdays 7:30 AM–10 PM, Sat. 8 AM–10 PM, Sun. 10–4.*

Rodger's. To hang with a down-to-earth crowd, visit this friendly café popular with students. The menu offers sandwiches and salads ($5–$6) and all kinds of coffee—the adventurous can try the mocha monkey (coffee with banana syrup and chocolate; $2.75); for the rest of us, there's always the good old latte ($2.25). Sit on the sidewalk patio and watch the throngs of people rush past on University Avenue. Preferred reading material: *The History and Geography of the Human Gene. 250 University Ave., in Plaza Ramona, tel. 415/324–4228. Wheelchair access. Open Mon.–Thurs. 7 AM–10 PM, Fri. 7 AM–11:30 PM, Sat. 8 AM–11:30 PM, Sun. 8 AM–10 PM.*

AFTER DARK 6

By Carmen Aguirre

The sun has edged its way into the ocean, leaving you to face that all-consuming question: What am I going to do tonight? Well, the Bay Area's got a lot of answers. If you don't find your scene in one of the area's 10,000 bars, you can go see an old movie in a funky theater, check out a live performance at a local club, head to a performance space to watch some unbridled genius, or shake your booty all night long at an underground party.

Local bars range from the seedy to the snooty, and it's not hard to find booze and fine entertainment under the same roof. Check the *SF Weekly,* the *Bay Guardian,* or flyers posted in the hipper parts of town—the Mission, the Haight, and SoMa—for details. The weeklies are prime resources for info on dance clubs that travel from spot to spot, but you should also drop by clothing and record stores, which often have the lowdown on music and clubs. The *Bay Times* is a good place to look for gay and lesbian listings.

If you are interested in disco dancing, tattooed rockers, or the gay scene and all of its sub-scenes, you're best off in the city. Otherwise, the East Bay has plenty of bars and a handful of good places to hear live music. Come to Oakland to sample world-class blues and jazz, or to Berkeley if you just can't get enough of watching drunken frat boys harass sorority girls. Flip through the free weekly *East Bay Express* for a complete events calendar, including films, lectures, readings, and music.

Marin County and the South Bay offer notoriously little in the way of nightlife. Bay Area residents flock to Marin by day to stroll by the water and eat picnic lunches, but when the sun sets the area becomes very, very quiet. You can thumb through the free entertainment guide *Weekender Magazine, Marin Edition,* but all it'll tell you is that most Marinites head for Oakland or San Francisco to shake their booties. Still, if you missed the last bus for the city, you should be able to ferret out a local bar and maybe some live music in Marin; and even the South Bay offers a few diversions near the Stanford campus.

Bars

SAN FRANCISCO

In San Francisco, choosing a place to drink is no easy matter. Maybe you're looking for Dr. Martens and grunge rock, maybe black leather and chaps. Or maybe you're more comfortable around football posters and college sweatshirts, or perhaps even cowboy hats and pickup trucks. In any case, San Francisco caters to tastes subtle and flamboyant, and you shouldn't have any trouble finding a new favorite bar. One very serious piece of advice: Take the bus or call a cab, but do not drink and drive in this city of hills, fog, and one-way streets.

DOWNTOWN/CIVIC CENTER The downtown area isn't the greatest place to be after sundown, unless you enjoy getting heckled by streetwalkers in microminis or witnessing shady business transactions. Nevertheless, there are a few bars worth braving if you have door-to-door transportation.

Edinburgh Castle. This diamond in the rough was established before the Tenderloin earned its reputation for squalor. A British pub with a beautiful bar, it's a great place to play darts, eat greasy fish-'n'-chips, sip pints of Guinness or Bass, and make friends with thick-accented U.K. types. *950 Geary St., btw Larkin and Polk Sts., tel. 415/885–4074.*

E'space. The vibes are hip and European at this sleek, low-key, French-owned wine bar and gallery space. Stop in for a glass of wine after work and stay for the evening; on Friday nights you'll be treated to live jazz or spoken-word performances. *520 Hayes St., btw Octavia and Laguna Sts., tel. 415/861–4657.*

Hollywood Billiards. The 37 tables here make Hollywood a must for those who are serious about shooting stick, but amateurs should have no fear of being relegated to the well-lit corners. You'll get plenty of chances to play, and when you need a break (so to speak), this 24-hour establishment also boasts the city's longest bar. *61 Golden Gate Ave., btw Jones and Taylor Sts., tel. 415/252–9643.*

QT. At the "Quick Trick" you can cozy up to hustlers, drag queens, or "appreciative older gentlemen" in an unassuming atmosphere (read: lots of mirrors). There's live music Thursday, Friday, and Saturday nights, and strip shows most Sundays and Tuesdays. Legend has it that the owner gave Anita Baker her start. *1312 Polk St., btw Bush and Pine Sts., tel. 415/885–1114.*

NORTH BEACH North Beach is famous for its Italian restaurants, cafes, and tiny cobblestone alleys. While it lacks the loud nightlife of some other San Francisco neighborhoods, you'll find a surprising number of low-key hangouts for the educated, less trendy bar hopper.

Savoy-Tivoli. The front doors open when the weather's nice, making the Savoy prime territory to drink wine, watch the world go by, and generally feel like you're in Italy. This North Beach institution caters to those recuperating from a hard day in the Financial District. *1434 Grant Ave., btw Union and Green Sts., tel. 415/362–7023.*

Specs'. This is a classic North Beach hangout for the perennially half-sloshed—a jovial, divey, no-attitude sort of place where, if the conversation sucks, you can gaze all night at the quirky memorabilia on the walls. *12 Saroyan Pl., tel. 415/421–4112. In the alley across the street from City Lights Books.*

Tosca. This lovely, cavernous establishment in North Beach is renowned for its liqueur-laced coffee drinks, its beautiful old espresso machine, its opera-only jukebox, and its celebrity patrons (Francis Ford Coppola and Mikhail Baryshnikov are what you might call regulars). *242 Columbus Ave., at Broadway, tel. 415/391–1244.*

Vesuvio. A bohemian hangout during the Beat era, Vesuvio has somehow managed to avoid having the life stamped out of it by tourist boots. Have a glass of red and peruse the copy of *Howl* you just bought a few doors up at City Lights, or listen for words of wisdom from the wizened crowd of regulars. *255 Columbus Ave., at Broadway, tel. 415/362–3370.*

NOB HILL AND RUSSIAN HILL This area caters to an upscale, often touristy crowd. There are a few bars that the city's more conservative youth swear by, but Nob and Russian hills are dominated by four- and five-star hotels, and don't offer much to the barfly.

Johnny Love's. Fledgling yuppies let their hair down and dance on the tables at this Russian Hill lounge, much touted by the press as *the* singles bar for post-college types who have managed to find a steady job. In other words, it's the most upscale meat market in town. *1500 Broadway, at Polk St., tel. 415/931–8021.*

The Tonga Room. This Tiki kitsch-o-rama bar is custom-made for tourists who think it's still 1955, but you'll secretly love the bamboo-and-palm-leaf decor as much as they do. The waiters wear mumus; a simulated rainstorm occurs regularly in the simulated lagoon; and, best of all, your potent drink ($6–$10) comes with fruit, umbrellas, and all sorts of paraphernalia. *Fairmont Hotel, California and Mason Sts., tel. 415/772-5278.*

Every 30 minutes or so, a small hurricane blows through the Tonga Room, and at 8 PM most nights a soft-rock band performs from a thatched hut in the middle of a lagoon.

Top of the Mark. San Francisco's classic, old-time cocktail lounge matches expensive drinks and a snooty clientele with breathtaking views of the city. All kinds of locals consider this *the* place to be seen in heels and pearls or a suit. *1 Nob Hill, at the top of the Mark Hopkins Hotel, tel. 415/392-3434. Cnr of California and Mason Sts.*

MARINA DISTRICT You'll feel most at home in the Marina if you're the type who wears pearls or agonizes over which tie to wear with the blue pinstripe. The bars here often seem sleazy in a Ken-does-Barbie sort of way.

Pierce Street Annex Drinking Establishment. The Annex is typical of the many bars in the "Triangle," a walkable section of the Marina/Pacific Heights known for its look-alike taverns and expensive sidewalk eateries. It's packed with aspiring yuppies and those who claim allegiance to a fraternity or sorority. There's a dance floor and occasional karaoke nights, and Thursday is "Asian Theme Night." *3138 Fillmore St., at Greenwich St., tel. 415/567-1400.*

HAIGHT-ASHBURY DISTRICT Ah, Haight-Ashbury—over 25 years of hipness. This neighborhood may overdo it at times, but the crowd is always on the heels of the latest trend, and there are plenty of spots where you can toss down a few.

Casa Loma. The crowd here is sort of a punk-rock/hip-hop fusion, but the jukebox is current and loud, the pool is cheap (50¢), and the drinks are stiff. The hotel upstairs offers a ready haven if you happen to find the hipster of your dreams. *610 Fillmore St., at Fell St., tel. 415/552-7100.*

The Deluxe. Come on the weekend to this snazzy, slick bar, order a martini, and take a look around: You'll get the uncanny feeling that the year is 1945. Patrons enjoy donning their finest '40s duds (hairdos and shoes included) and acting very cool. There will usually be a crooner, with backup swing band, or at least a DJ doing an all-Sinatra marathon. On weekends expect a $3–$5 cover. *1511 Haight St., btw Ashbury and Clayton Sts., tel. 415/552-6949.*

The Gold Cane. With very little in the way of atmosphere or trendiness, and the cheapest drinks on the street, this is a good place to pound a few cold ones before heading out to hear some music. *1569 Haight St., btw Ashbury and Clayton Sts., tel. 415/626-1112.*

Mad Dog in the Fog. This British-style pub in the heart of the lower Haight is frequented by people who don't mind communicating in screams over loud grunge music and cold, frothy beer. You can also play darts here; and during the day you might get lucky and enjoy a moment

Anchors Aweigh

So you want a drink, but that buck you thought you had has mysteriously disappeared with your roommate. Don't despair—there may be hope yet. Call the Anchor Brewing Company, feign deep interest in touring their brewery, and make an appointment. If you can stand 20 minutes of learning about Anchor Steam Beer, you'll receive all the free samples you can consume (within reason) at the end. 1705 Mariposa St., at DeHaro St., tel. 415/863-8350. Call weekdays 9–5.

of peace on the back patio. In the mornings, they serve up greasy English-style breakfasts. *530 Haight St., btw Fillmore and Steiner Sts., tel. 415/626–7279.*

Midtown. Watch lower Haight Street have a beer. The clientele is young, tattooed, perpetually smoking, and good at pool. Arrive early to get a table on weekends, as the crowd can be fierce in the standing room. *582 Haight St., btw Fillmore and Steiner Sts., tel. 415/558–8019.*

Murio's Trophy Room. Murio's is often overcrowded with bikers and Haight Street slackers, but it can be fun and low-key on weekdays. If the conversation bores you, there's a pool table, jukebox, and TV. *1811 Haight St., btw Shrader and Stanyan Sts., tel. 415/752–2971.*

The Noc Noc. Step inside this lower-Haight institution and you'll find yourself in a postmodern cave complete with chunky Flintstones-style furniture. Expect a healthy variety of beers, a couple kinds of wine and sake, and all manner of tunes passing through the speakers. It's a favorite of visiting Europeans. *557 Haight St., btw Fillmore and Steiner Sts., tel. 415/861–5811.*

The Toronado. A narrow, dark dive in the Haight with lots of folks in leather and lots of beer on tap, the Toronado makes a good casual hangout—boisterous and loud compared to the generally cool climate of the Haight. It's got one of the widest selections of microbrewed beer in the city, and the jukebox features a refreshing mix of kitschy country-and-western in addition to the standard grunge anthems. *547 Haight St., btw Fillmore and Steiner Sts., tel. 415/863–2276.*

CASTRO DISTRICT This safe, very gay quarter of San Francisco plays host to some of the wildest festivals in the city. Though you're far more likely to kindle a romance here if you're enamored of the same sex, you'll always encounter flamboyance, cleanliness, and folks eager to celebrate.

The Café. This large, plush bar with mirrored walls and neon lights caters mainly to lesbians, although gay men also frequent the place. Play pool or hang out on the patio and watch the Castro go by. *2367 Market St., near Castro St., tel. 415/861–3846.*

The Detour. Minimally decorated with a chain-link fence and pool table, this bar caters to a youngish leather-queen-wanna-be crowd with goatees. Even without a dance floor, the urgent techno-house music causes the level of sexual frustration in the room to skyrocket. Beers are $1 on Friday and Saturday nights. If you forget the address, listen for the music, since the black-on-black sign is impossible to see at night. *2348 Market St., btw Castro and Noe Sts., tel. 415/861–6053.*

Midnight Sun. Three video screens help alleviate the need for conversation in this crowded vanilla bar, showing a mix of weird TV and current music videos. *4067 18th St., near Castro St., tel. 415/861–4186.*

The Orbit Room. Besides having a groovy name, the Orbit has a smart-looking, high-ceilinged drinking area where you can enjoy a cocktail or espresso with a mostly straight crowd that doesn't mind the artsy, slightly uncomfortable bar stools. The subdued lighting, stucco walls, and innovative interior-design scheme make you feel like you're on display at some swank art gallery. *1900 Market St., at Laguna St., tel. 415/252–9525.*

Twin Peaks. David Lynch has nothing to do with this casual, lounge-like gay bar; in fact, the Peaks has been around for more than 15 years, and proudly claims to have been the first gay bar in the city with clear floor-to-ceiling windows. On weekends expect big crowds and an older, established clientele. *401 Castro St., at Market St., tel. 415/864–9470.*

MISSION DISTRICT Lately, the Mission has been sprouting hip bars, cafés, restaurants, and clubs faster than a Chia pet. This neighborhood, however, has long had a shady reputation. The poorly lit side streets are the most dangerous, but even on more heavily trafficked streets like Valencia and Mission, bar hoppers shouldn't scoot from bar to bar alone.

The Albion. Come here for a young crowd, a fine pool table, and loud grunge rock; it's all served up in the glow of pink neon lights. *3139 16th St., btw Valencia and Guerrero Sts., tel. 415/552–8558.*

The Elbo Room. Although it may initially strike you as just another Mission watering hole, as the night progresses, the Elbo Room offers none (elbow room, that is). Live jazz and hip-hop acts, as well as occasional DJs, attract the crowds, and the drinks are cheap enough ($2–$3) to keep you around all night. *647 Valencia St., near 17th St., tel. 415/552-7788.*

The 500 Club. Here's a little slice of Americana, complete with a huge neon sign and two pool tables packed much too close to the walls. Everyone here has checked their pretentiousness at the door and succumbed to the lure of cheap American beer. *500 Guerrero St., at 17th St., tel. 415/861-2500.*

The city's best margaritas come from Puerto Allegre (546 Valencia St., btw 16th and 17th Sts., tel. 415/626–2922), across the street from the Elbo Room. Order a strawberry and munch on some tortilla chips to get you fueled up for the evening ahead.

The Lone Palm. There's something about this place that's reminiscent of a David Lynch film. The neon palm out front? The surreal comments your waitress makes? The funny facial tics of the guy at the counter? Hard to say, but they combine to make this quiet bar a dark, retro, generally weird place to have a cocktail. *3394 22nd St., btw Guerrero and Dolores Sts., tel. 415/648-0109.*

The Rite Spot. This outer-Mission bar, a casual local hangout, offers the ubiquitous pool table and a young, bohemian crowd shootin' the shit. *2099 Folsom St., at 17th St., tel. 415/552-6066.*

The Uptown. Sit at the long oak bar and get rowdy with friendly barflies, grab a game of pool with neighborhood hipsters, or stand on the corner watching hookers and drug dealers do their thing. The groovy jukebox is outgunned occasionally by live bands playing jazz and blues; Sunday evenings are a good bet for music. *200 Capp St., at 19th St., tel. 415/861-8231.*

Zeitgeist. This is the original no-frills biker bar, for every kind of biker. In the afternoons, it fills with bike messengers relating the day's near encounters with the Big Grille in the Sky; by night the BMW motorbike crowd clogs the outdoor deck, waiting their turn at the lone pool table. The Geist is trendier and friendlier than your average biker hangout. *199 Valencia St., at Duboce Ave., tel. 415/255-7505.*

SOUTH OF MARKET South of Market, a.k.a. SoMa, has few bars but lots of dance clubs waiting to happen. Come early and sip a few before the sweaty crowds invade.

Julie's Supper Club. Past music greats (captured in black-and-white photos) gaze down at professionals and pre-professionals nibbling interesting appetizers and sipping cocktails. The art-deco interior and innovative menu make it worth a visit after work or before hitting the clubs. Appetizers, including calamari and trout with a delicate sauce, run $3–$6. *1123 Folsom St., near 7th St., tel. 415/861-0707.*

Moe's Tavern

Now that The Simpsons has moved to Sunday nights, you may not feel so lame when you stay home to watch. But you'll have a lot more fun getting your Homer fix at the Rat and Raven (4054 24th St., near Church St., tel. 415/550–9145), where every Sunday you can enjoy a loud and clear episode of "The Simpsons," plenty of beer (though no Flaming Moes), and a crowd of folks who know what you mean when you say, "It's funny, because it's true." Arrive at 7 PM to get a seat. If you can't make it all the way to Noe Valley, watch Marge and Homer at the Zeitgeist (199 Valencia St., at Duboce Ave., tel. 415/255–7505), which has recently begun screening Beverly Hills 90210 and Melrose Place, too.

20 Tank Brewery. Catch a few pints (brewed on the premises) before heading across the street to DNA or Slim's, or skip the clubs and just catch the pints. Located in a beautiful old warehouse, the 20 Tank resists that common brewery pitfall of resembling a big frat party by attracting a reasonably diverse mix of patrons. They also serve appetizers and sandwiches. *316 11th St., near Folsom St., tel. 415/255–9455.*

The Up and Down Club. Sleek deco digs and live background jazz make this the lounge of choice for those who like to pretend San Francisco is New York City. Upstairs you'll find a DJ laying down tracks. *1151 Folsom St., btw 7th and 8th Sts., tel. 415/626–2388.*

EAST BAY

BERKELEY Berkeley doesn't offer high-concept bars, but you'll find plenty of casual places to have a beer. Needless to say, don't come to Berkeley if you don't like to drink with college students.

The Albatross. This no-nonsense, no-attitude pub attracts both students and working folk. The cheap beer (starting at $1.25) tastes even better with free popcorn, and there's a dart board and cozy fireplace. *1822 San Pablo Ave., btw Hearst Ave. and Delaware St., tel. 510/849–4714.*

Bison Brewing Company. Berkeley's most colorful crowd, all fully pierced and tattooed, call Bison home when they want to drink, but any beer enthusiast will want to try the homemade stout, ale, and cider. Live bands, ranging from blues to Irish folk, entertain Thursday through Saturday ($1–$2 cover charge). Happy hour (weekdays 4–6) features $1.75 pints and attracts huge crowds. *2598 Telegraph Ave., at Parker St., tel. 510/841–7734. 5 blocks south of U.C. campus. Wheelchair access.*

Brennan's. The bar is woefully nondescript, but the specialty drinks make it worth the trip. Try the Irish coffee ($2.75) or a white Russian ($3.25), guaranteed to put a spark in your step. Popular with bar scum and heavy drinkers, this is as far from student Berkeley as you can get. *720 University Ave., near the Marina, tel. 510/841–0960. Take Bus 51 from Berkeley BART to University Ave. and 4th St.*

Café Bistro. The low lighting and smoky European feel make this place popular with the beret-and-spectacles set. Nightly background jazz accompanies your Gitane and glass of brandy. *2271 Shattuck Ave., tel. 510/848–3081. 4 blocks south of Berkeley BART at Durant Ave.*

The Ivy Room. The pool table costs only two quarters, Patsy Cline rules the jukebox, and Bud is $2 a bottle. Come on down and join the bar rats. *860 San Pablo Ave., near Solano Ave., tel. 510/524–9220. Take Bus 43 from Berkeley BART and get off on cnr of San Pablo and Solano Aves.*

Jupiter. This large, open wine-and-beer bar near the Berkeley BART station is popular with less schmoozy, more down-to-earth Berkeley residents. Huge round tables and an eccentric collection of beers ($3.25–$3.75) make this a great place to relax with a group of friends. *2181 Shattuck Ave., near Center St., tel. 510/843–8277.*

Le Bateau Ivre. Neither the elegant bar nor the adjoining upscale restaurant is cheap, but both are beautifully decorated in a French château style. There's a fireplace in the back room and a candle on every table—perfect for a romantic bottle of wine with your significant other. Cheese and fruit plates are $7, and a decadent slice of cheesecake goes for $3.50. Le Bateau Ivre also serves one of the creamiest pints of Guinness west of Dublin. Dress ranges from formal to blue jeans and sweaters. *2629 Telegraph Ave., near Parker St., tel. 510/849–1100. 6 blocks south of U.C. campus.*

Leona's. Although it sits about seven steps away from the Berkeley campus, this little lounge just upstairs from the famous blues club Larry Blake's manages not to feel too obnoxiously collegiate. Come after school or work for a plate of free hors d'oeuvres and a stiff, cheap drink ($2.50–$3). *2367 Telegraph Ave., btw Durant Ave. and Channing St., tel. 510/848–0886.*

The Pub. This unpretentious hole-in-the-wall is great for cheap pints and thick coffee—the sort of place where the barflies blend into the woodwork and don't bother you. Its overstuffed sofas, oak tables, and pipe-tobacco aroma go nicely with that novel you're reading or writing. If you forget your book, borrow one of theirs. It teems with students on weekend nights, but during the week things are generally quiet. *1492 Solano Ave., tel. 510/525–1900. Take Bus 43 north from Berkeley BART to Solano and Santa Fe Aves.*

Spats'. The inventive drink selection rivals anyone's anywhere: Choose from concoctions like the Nutty Buddy (Frangelico, cream, and crème de cacao; $4.25) or the Scorpion (rums, fruit juices, brandy, almond flavor, and two straws; $8.75). Then settle into a cushy old Victorian sofa in the parlor-like bar, and let yourself slip into romantic reminiscences. *1974 Shattuck Ave., tel. 510/841–7225. 2 blocks north of Berkeley BART at University Ave.*

Triple Rock Brewery. At this popular microbrewery, the 1950s reign supreme, with goofy posters and nostalgic knickknacks lining the walls. On weekend nights, look for grad students talking shop, frat and sorority types pounding homemade ale (it comes in light, red, or dark), and office workers unwinding after a stressful day. The crowd is loud and raucous in a collegiate sort of way, but folks are friendly. During the day, munch on excellent pub food (nachos, grilled sandwiches, and the like) on the outdoor patio. *1920 Shattuck Ave., at Hearst Ave., tel. 510/843–2739. 3 blocks north of Berkeley BART. Wheelchair access.*

OAKLAND Did your last evening in San Francisco end in a conversation about Wim Wenders? The merits of Treasury bills versus mutual funds? Heidegger and the Who of Dasein? Don't get discouraged—the bars in Oakland are much cheaper, more sincere, and generally rougher around the edges.

The Alley. This is the only bar in Oakland where you can sit at a piano and sing along with your drunken compadres. It's been in business since the late 1940s and has the clientele to prove it. It's dark, musty, and unassuming—a great place to hang out with low-key locals. Live piano music usually begins at 9; drinks are $3–$5. *3325 Grand Ave., tel. 510/444–8505. East of Lake Merritt, 2 blocks south of Piedmont Ave.*

At the Alley, sit next to the piano, and don't be shy about singing your favorite Barry Manilow or Sinatra song. It's like karaoke, but without the subtitles and cheesy video.

Chalkers Billiard Club. Looking for a game of snooker or pool? Chalkers is one of the nicest pool halls in town, decorated in a Miami Vice color scheme and loaded with dozens of well-maintained tables. It's a yuppie hangout (their motto is "for civilized fun"), but the full bar and reasonably priced snack counter help make up for the crowd. *5900 Hollis St., at 59th St., Emeryville, tel. 510/658–5821. 1 block north of Powell St. off I–80. 21 and over.*

George and Walt's. G&W's is a stylish place filled with pool tables and comfortable booths, though on weekend nights you should probably steer clear unless you like hanging with crowds of U.C. Berkeley students. *5445 College Ave., tel. 510/653–7441. 1 block north of McNally's (see below).*

The Kingfish. No-nonsense drinking and camaraderie are the norm at this dark, lively sports bar. Order yourself an ice-cold beer and bide your time: It's only a matter of minutes before someone starts talking about the A's. Drinks start at $2. *5227 Claremont Ave., tel. 510/655–7373. Take Bus 40 north on Telegraph Ave. from MacArthur BART; get off at Claremont.*

The Lobby. With its soft couches, low lights, and live jazz Friday through Sunday, this is a good place for a beginner to seduce somebody. Drinks are $3–$4. *5612 College Ave., tel. 510/547–9152. 1 block south of Rockridge BART.*

McNally's Irish Pub. This place has the smell and feel of a real Dublin pub. Grab a pint of Guinness, Bass, or Harp and warm yourself by the stone fireplace. There's a decent jukebox and a bumper-pool table in back. *5352 College Ave., tel. 510/654–9463. 4 blocks south of Rockridge BART.*

Pacific Coast Brewing Company. In Old Oakland, this brew pub serves three kinds of homebrew and 16 other beers on tap. It's popular with the thirtysomething crowd and a bit yuppie, but the beers are top rate. They serve lunch from 11:30 to 4 and dinner Monday–Saturday until

10:30 (9 on Sunday); the burgers, grilled specials, and salads range from $3.50 to $10. Drinks run $3–$3.50. *906 Washington St., at 10th St., tel. 510/836–2739. Walk 3 blocks southwest on Broadway from 12th St. BART, then 1 block west to Washington St.*

Oliveto. Although it's more restaurant than bar, Oliveto is a good choice for solid pints and fine California-Italian appetizers. The soothing interior, done in salmon-colored pseudo adobe with wrought-iron furnishings, will make you forget your hectic day. The clientele includes yuppie commuters fresh off the BART and kids on furlough from the nearby art school. *5655 College Ave., tel. 510/547–5356. Across from Rockridge BART.*

MARIN COUNTY

Tiburon's only happening nightlife is at **Sam's Anchor Café** (*see* Chapter 4), where yuppies sit on the deck downing Bloody Marys while young hipsters hang out at the bar watching sports on TV. Other Marin cities have a bit more going for them. Though you won't find any places to groove to dance tunes, there are a few good bars where you can drink beers with middle-age locals and listen to blues.

Flatiron Sports Bar and Late Night Grill. If you're a buff guy in an A's cap, or would like to meet one, this is the place for you. The decor is strictly cheesy sports bar—beach towels with team logos hang from the ceiling, and five different TV screens go at once. The large menu offers myriad variations on the hot dog, hamburger, and nachos theme (about $5–$7). If you can identify everyone the dishes are named for—including Chris Speier and Jerry Goff—you've been watching too much ESPN. *724 B St., San Rafael, tel. 415/453–4318. From U.S. 101, take Central San Rafael exit to 2nd St., turn left, and go about a mile to B St.*

4th Street Tavern. This place tries hard to be a dive, but it's just a little too upscale. The patrons are a very dressed-down, late-thirties crowd, and the proprietors live up to their promise: "No Cover, No Minimum, No Attitude." Live music starts at 9:30; you'll hear the blues band before you see the small sign and the Harleys parked outside. *711 4th St., San Rafael, tel. 415/454–4044. From U.S. 101, take Central San Rafael exit to 4th St. and turn left.*

 No Name Bar. This place hops almost every night of the week, with a rowdy post-thirties clientele and lots of live music, usually blues, jazz, or Dixieland. The shady garden out back, where the staff sometimes cooks up oysters on the half shell ($1.50 each), is a little more sedate, but not much. *757 Bridgeway, Sausalito, tel. 415/332–1392.*

 Paterson's Bar. Like its neighbor the No Name Bar (*see above*), Paterson's has lots of live music, but the jazz is usually cool rather than hot and the locals brood over their beer instead of dance in the aisles. Paterson's has no kitchen of its own, but during the day it serves burgers ($5.50–$6) from the restaurant next door. *739 Bridgeway, Sausalito, tel. 415/332–1264.*

Smiley's Schooner Saloon. This laid-back and mostly local place is the oldest continually operated saloon in California. Blues play on Friday and Saturday nights; cover is usually free on Fridays, $6–$7 on Saturday night, when the biggest names play. Pool sharks can compete for $100 in the weekly Tuesday night tournament. *41 Wharf Rd., Bolinas, tel. 415/868–1311.*

Tiburon Tommie's. The decor is strictly Polynesian, right down to the gaudy flowered shirts on the two friendly old bartenders. Tiburon Tommie's serves lots of fruity drinks, some in bowls with long straws. The "outrigger" ($3), with lemon, lime, grenadine, pineapple, and rum, is especially popular. A few of the bar seats face the water, but there's no outdoor deck. *41 Main St., Tiburon, tel. 415/435–1229. Closed Mon.–Tues.*

PALO ALTO

Palo Alto's bar scene caters to the law- and business-school crowd. If a night of trading war stories from the investment banking front doesn't sound like a good time, there are a couple of grungy burgers-and-beer joints near campus where you can while the night away watching sports on TV, playing pinball, or carving your name into the table. Try the **Oasis Beer Garden** or the **Dutch Goose** (*see* Chapter 4) for a down-and-dirty evening.

Blue Chalk Café. At night this Southern-style restaurant turns into a bar frequented by T-shirted college students and business-suited yuppies. Patrons can shoot pool at one of four small tables ($10 an hour before 7 PM, $12 after) in a well-lit, smoke-free environment. The music and the drinks sport a New Orleans style—try the Hurricane ($7), a 22-ounce punchlike concoction of light rum, dark rum, mashed fruit, and a secret syrup shipped in from The Big Easy. *630 Ramona St., btw Hamilton and Forest Aves., tel. 415/326–1020. Take U.S. 101 to University Ave., turn left on Ramona St.*

Gordon Biersch Brewery Restaurant. The homebrewed beer is well worth trying, but unless you're a massive corporate tool, you'll be embarrassed to be around so many suits and heels. If you brave the yuppie crowd, the rewards are free bread sticks and some fine beers: The lagers include an *export* (similar to a pilsner), a *märzen* (like the beer served in Munich during Oktoberfest), and a *dunkles* (a Bavarian-style, unfiltered dark beer). Ask for a sample set to taste a shot of each. Half a liter costs $3, while a 10-ouncer is $2. *640 Emerson St., tel. 415/323–7723. Take U.S. 101 to University Ave., exit west, and turn left on Emerson St. Wheelchair access.*

Clubs

Bay Area residents, like many city dwellers, take their nightlife very seriously. As a result, it's often hard for the uninitiated to break the ice with the club-going crowd and learn about the underground scene. Your best bet is to check smaller retail and record shops for flyers. Dance clubs that appear weekly at Bay Area bars are usually listed in the *SF Weekly* or *Bay Guardian*; *Klub* magazine is also a good resource. Always call ahead—the hot spots change as quickly as fashion fades.

SAN FRANCISCO

Those who want to dance in San Francisco definitely have options: Spaces large and small play music for every age, style, and level of rhythmic ability. There's a huge variety of quite casual and even reasonably priced dance venues. Many local bars will just stick a DJ in the corner and clear some tables away, creating a cheap instant disco. Dance purists can even find spaces that allow no alcohol or smoking. On the other end of the spectrum are the raves (*see box, below*)—still going strong in warehouses and fields—where substance abuse is by no means limited to alcohol and smoking.

STRAIGHT **Bahia Tropical.** An international crowd of all ages comes here for a samba fix. Wednesdays are reggae; other nights feature Afro-Brazilian music and shows by local dance troupes like Xinga Brasil. *41 Franklin St., at Market St., tel. 415/626–3306.*

Barefoot Boogie. Neither a drop of alcohol nor a puff of smoke enters the doors of this dance studio in the Mission district, but the moves people execute in various states of undress quite belie your expectation of a nice little straight dance party. The event takes place twice a week (Sundays and Wednesdays 7:30–10:30), and the music ranges from classical to deep house to samba to hip hop. People often bring their own drums and other rhythm keepers. The cover is $6. *Third Wave Dance Studio, 3316 24th St., at Mission St., tel. 415/282–4020.*

Café Bastille. This tiny European restaurant (*see* Chapter 4) in a cobblestone alley downtown hosts dancing and occasional jazz shows. The good-looking, well-dressed crowd doesn't lose an ounce of sophistication on the dance floor. Come on Bastille Day (July 14) for a great outdoor party. *22 Belden Pl., off Bush St. btw Kearny and Montgomery Sts., tel. 415/986–5673.*

Cat's Grill and Alley Club. Spend all night on the dance floor of this mostly after-hours club—if you get hungry, they serve food until 5 AM at the cheesy restaurant downstairs. *1190 Folsom St., near 8th St., tel. 431-3332.*

Cesar's Latin Palace. Cesar's Latin All-Stars play salsa most nights, with occasional guest artists. On weekends the club stays open until 6 AM. *3140 Mission St., near Army St., tel. 415/648–6611.*

Crash Palace. Formerly the Kennel Club, Crash Palace now serves up a spicier platter of events than the old hardcore standby did. It's decorated with couches and pool tables, so you'll find something to do if the entertainment—from comedy to live jazz to dance parties—doesn't thrill. Tuesday is "Speak Easy," a free evening of spoken word. *628 Divisadero St., at Grove St., tel. 415/931–1914.*

DNA Lounge. It's the dependable choice for late-night dancing (until 4 AM nightly) and eclectic live acts, from music to tattoo/piercing shows. Whether you come today or in five years, you can be sure of finding somebody interesting to talk to or dance with. *375 11th St., at Harrison St., tel. 415/626–1409.*

Nickie's BBQ. Red vinyl booths and Christmas lights decorate this racially mixed, mostly straight hole-in-the-wall that's admirably cheap (cover $3–$5) and entirely lacking in pretension. Excellent dance music—everything from '70s funk to soul to hip hop, not to mention some reggae, Latin, and world beat—booms through the speakers four to five nights a week. *460 Haight St., btw Webster and Fillmore Sts., tel. 415/621–6508.*

Wanna-be ravers who weren't cool enough to be invited can check out the list of raves posted at the store House Wares (1322 Haight St., tel. 415/252–1440).

The Upper Room. This tiny 18-and-over club, right next to the Civic Center BART station, has recently earned itself a name in the hip-hop/jazz/funk scene. Dance clubs, rap acts, and acid jazz groups pass through here regularly, and the club is sometimes used as a performance art space. Patrons manage to have a really good time, despite the no-alcohol, no-smoking policy. *7 Grove St., at Market St., tel. 415/861–0594. Above Burger King.*

Upstairs at the Elbo Room. Local hip-hop and jazz bands play here regularly to a jovial young crowd that likes to bust a move on the tiny dance floor. Weekends are usually reserved for DJs spinning funky tunes, but if you ain't got no beat, don't trip—there's a pool table and pinball machines in back. *647 Valencia St., near 17th St., tel. 415/552–7788.*

MIXED **1015 Club.** This place hosts various clubs on a nightly basis, including the Saturday-only "Spread" (tel. 415/431–2617), a huge queer dance party ($10 cover). On Friday, "Dakota" (tel. 415/431–1200) captures the history of disco in three rooms: deep funk and tribal beats in the basement, '70s disco in the Gold Room, and high house in the main dance pit. Dress up for this one. On Sunday mornings, the "Boogie Buffet" caters to hipsters who thrive on Bloody Marys

Rave Culture

It's been mainstream for a while now, and by the time you read this it may be dead. Then again, it may be driven back underground, and perhaps you won't be cool enough to find it. Either way, take this opportunity to sample the San Francisco rave scene—the enormous, ecstatic techno-shamanic trend that has permeated nightlife and fashion all over the city. The rave basically consists of a few thousand boys, girls, genderfucks, and offbeat others in wool ski caps and baggy clothes, who dance blissfully—and often nonstop—to thumping techno-house music. The drug of choice is MDMA (a.k.a. Ecstasy), which creates a state of general blissed-out-ness and a sense of being at peace with the world—all for the low, low price of about $20 and a vicious hangover the next day. These days, the most reliable information on good raves is Urb magazine, which thoroughly covers the Bay Area club scene. Otherwise, start talking to people, or look for flyers in the rave-wear shop House Wares (1322 Haight St., tel. 415/252–1440)— you're sure to find a tribe in short order. The average rave cover charge, minus drinks and illegal substances, is $10–$20.

and house. Dance in the dimly lit Gold Room, or lounge around under the giant skylight. Breakfast is served from 8 to 11. *1015 Folsom St., btw 6th and 7th Sts., tel. 415/431–0700.*

The Box. Come here for hard-core hip hop, funk, and house, with less attitude than most places because everybody's sweating on the dance floor. Go-go boxes mounted on the wall showcase dancers with breathtaking bodies at full throttle. This is technically a gay club, run by lesbians, but the multicultural crowd includes straights, too. (Simply put, it's a very popular club and everybody wants to go.) The most accomplished DJs and club dance troupes in the city appear here, including Page Hodel, S.F.'s most famous queer DJ. The Box happens Thursdays only. *715 Harrison St., btw 3rd and 4th Sts., tel. 415/972–8087.*

DV8. DV8 is the hippest of the hip. From private parties to roaming dance clubs, you can almost never go wrong stopping by this SoMa warehouse. Come on Saturdays for "Star 69," a new, predominantly gay dance party, and move it all night to deep house tunes. *510 Harrison St., near 1st St., tel. 415/957–1730.*

El Río. The atmosphere is casual at this neighborhood hangout for multiethnic nubos (new bohemians), lesbians, gay men, pool players, and regular folks who don't expect their dance club to come with valet parking. Tuesdays and Fridays feature "Club Enzinga," with international dance music, Wednesdays $1 drafts of Pabst's Blue Ribbon; Sundays are salsa time. The neighborhood isn't the best; avoid walking alone at night on Mission Street. *3158 Mission St., near Army St., tel. 415/282–3325.*

The Sound Factory. The latest, largest disco to roll into town is designed after clubs in Los Angeles and New York. Different rooms host a variety of acts and sounds, but deep house is the music of choice among the rave crowd. Call the information line for upcoming clubs and events. *525 Harrison St., at 1st St., tel. 415/543–1300.*

Trocadero Transfer. Wednesday nights only, Trocadero hosts "Bondage A Go-Go," where S&M dilettantes and beginners get together to get their feet wet. Start the evening off by handcuffing yourself to the bar for free drinks. Then proceed to another room where you can engage in a little light bondage or get whipped by an awfully professional-looking dominatrix. It's a sort of light intro to real underground S&M culture. The cover for this 18-and-over event is $5. *520 4th St., btw Bryant and Brannan Sts., tel. 415/995–4600.*

GAY AND LESBIAN For current listings of gay and lesbian discos, flip through *Odyssey Magazine,* a free monthly that covers the comings and goings (and gossip) of gay disco life. Look for it in cafés and bookstores around the Castro.

Club Townsend. This dance mecca hosts "Pleasuredome," San Francisco's most popular gay and lesbian club, on Sunday nights. The crowd is mostly male, but "Club Universe" on Saturdays and "Club King" on Wednesdays are less gender specific. All three clubs are flashy and groovy; don't bother showing up if you can't take the loud, deep sounds of house music. *177 Townsend St., btw 2nd and 3rd Sts., tel. 415/974–6020.*

The End Up. This club was recently elevated to legendary status, when *Details* magazine hailed it as *the* after-hours dance spot in San Francisco and *SF Weekly* readers voted it the best gay and lesbian club in the city. Venues change as fickle hipsters try to keep up with trends, but the End Up always has a sweaty crowd gettin' down. The bar features a pool table, a patio with an elevated deck, and a waterfall surrealistically situated almost underneath U.S. 101. Club covers range from $5 to $10; call the information line for details. *401 6th St., at Harrison St., tel. 415/543–7700.*

Esta Noche. Tucked away in the Mission, Esta Noche plays a good mix of Latin, house music, and '70s disco. The crowd consists mostly of young Latinos and the men who love them. European-American patrons are respectfully requested to refrain from doing the cha-cha. *3079 16th St., btw Mission and Valencia Sts., tel. 415/861–5757.*

Motherlode. This Tenderloin landmark is the city's most popular transvestite haven, although there's no dress code posted at the door. The area is often dangerous and the crowd sometimes seedy, but the flamboyant patrons provide an energetic, entertaining night of thrills. *1002 Post St., at Larkin St., tel. 415/928–6006.*

The Phoenix. This is a good place for shy types to pick up on a sexy new loverboy. Admission is free, and it's the only gay bar on Castro Street with a dance floor. *482 Castro St., btw 17th and 18th Sts., tel. 415/552–6827.*

Rawhide. Although this club specializes in country and western for gay men, all are welcome, and free swing dance lessons are given on some weeknights. Owner Ray Chalker, who also publishes the *San Francisco Sentinel,* roused the ire of gay political activists when he rented the club as a set for the film *Basic Instinct. 280 7th St., btw Howard and Folsom Sts., tel. 415/621–1197.*

The Stud. It's a San Francisco legend and a good watering hole any night of the week. Dress up or come as you are, and have some fun flirting with innocent out-of-towners. The Stud hosts "Junk," a thrash dance club for lesbians ($3) on Thursdays; Wednesdays feature "Oldies" and a beer bust ($2); and "80something," a new-wave dance party, takes place Sundays. *399 9th St., at Harrison St., tel. 415/863–6623.*

EAST BAY

The dance scene is much sparser here than in San Francisco. Check the *East Bay Express* under "Dance Clubs" for a thorough listing of clubs and a calendar of events. In a pinch, stop a fashion victim on the street and ask about the floating clubs that sometimes surface in East Oakland warehouses.

Blake's. This few-nights-a-week scene, basically just a DJ in the basement playing for Cal students and Oakland natives, is as hip as it gets in Berkeley. For around $3 you'll be jammed into a very sweaty basement that's ruled by funk, soul, hip hop, and rare groove sounds. Blake's may not be the pinnacle of cool, but it should serve your dance needs just fine. *2367 Telegraph Ave., Berkeley, near Durant Ave., tel. 510/848–0886.*

The Caribee Dance Center. Occasional live music and daily dance classes are supplemented five nights a week (Wednesday–Sunday) with dancing to reggae, salsa, and African music. Drinks cost $2–$5; the cover is $5–$10. *1408 Webster St., Oakland, tel. 510/835–4006. Take BART to 12th St., and go 2 blocks east from Broadway on 14th St.*

White Horse Inn. Get down under a gleaming disco ball at this very unpretentious place on the Oakland–Berkeley border. Most patrons are gay or lesbian, but other fun seekers are welcome as long as they behave themselves. A DJ is in the house Thursday–Saturday after 9 PM, and the bar's open daily 3 PM–2 AM. *6551 Telegraph Ave., Oakland, at 66th St., tel. 510/652–3820. Take Bus 40 north on Broadway from downtown Oakland to 66th St.*

PALO ALTO

Alberto's World Dance Music. If you've always admired salsa dancing from afar but never had the guts to try it, this 21-and-over club is a good place to start. On Tuesday and Thursday nights, $8–$10 buys you admission and lessons (7 PM). When the band starts playing around 9, you can put your new moves into practice. Other Latin dance classes are offered during the week, and reggae bands play Wednesdays. Pick up a monthly schedule outside the club. *736 W. Dana St., Mountain View, off Castro St., tel. 415/968–3007. Take U.S. 101 to Moffett Blvd. west, which becomes Castro St., and go left on W. Dana St. Wheelchair access.*

The Edge. The only sign of life on this quiet Palo Alto avenue is the Edge, an alternative 18-and-over club. Thursdays are free, but Tuesdays are more popular. Special "youth nights" are reserved for the 14-to-17 crowd; call for dates. Covers run $7–$8. If you dance until you starve, you can wolf down pizza in the adjacent Palermo Pizza restaurant, open as long as the club is. *260 California Ave., Palo Alto, tel. 415/324–3343. Take U.S. 101 to Oregon Expressway west, turn right on El Camino Real, and right on California Ave. Wheelchair access. No torn clothes allowed.*

Live Music

SAN FRANCISCO

Because of its propensity to draw artists and others willing to be outlandish for art's sake, San Francisco has an eclectic and extensive music scene. Sometimes you can see hugely talented bands for free in parks, bookstores, bars, cultural centers, and the occasional alley. In such venues, your money will go a long way (after all, Bud in a brown paper bag is cheap). As befits a world-class metropolitan center, there's also plenty of world-class talent, priced accordingly. Your best bets for up-to-the-minute music listings are the free *SF Weekly* and *Bay Guardian*, available at cafés and newsstands all over the city.

The **Great American Music Hall** (859 O'Farrell St., btw Polk and Larkin Sts., tel. 415/885–0750), a gorgeous old theater that serves as a mid-size concert venue, books an innovative blend of rock and world music. Tickets cost $8–$15. Bands on the verge of MTV stardom often play at the **Warfield** (982 Market St., btw 5th and 6th Sts., tel. 415/775–7722), or the historic, recently reopened **Fillmore** (1805 Geary Blvd.., at Fillmore St., tel. 415/346–6000), where tickets run $15–$20.

ROCK **Bottom of the Hill.** This neighborhood space at the bottom of Potrero Hill showcases a huge variety of local bands. Come here for a few nights and you'll acquire a comprehensive sense of the local music scene. On Sunday afternoons the all-you-can-eat barbecue ($3) draws mammoth crowds. *1233 17th St., at Texas St., tel. 415/626–4455.*

Brave New World. Brave new rock, jazz, and alternative local acts make this a great place to tap into the San Francisco underground scene. Don't forget to wear your nose ring. The cover is usually $5. *1751 Fulton St., at Masonic St., tel. 415/441–1751.*

Club Chameleon. Catch truly alternative up-and-coming local acts at this small space in the Mission. It's cheap, grungy and almost unpretentious. Friday's happy hour (4–7:30) features $2.25 pints. *853 Valencia St., btw 19th and 20th Sts., tel. 415/821–1891.*

Miss Pearl's Jam House. Most people come to Miss Pearl's to eat dinner (*see* Chapter 4) and drink margaritas, but don't overlook the live reggae music (Thurs.–Sat.), which is low-key and very danceable. *601 Eddy St., btw Polk and Larkin Sts., tel. 415/775–5267.*

Paradise Lounge. The quality of music varies widely (to put it kindly) at this hip cocktail lounge/cabaret; so, too, does the quality of the regular poetry readings upstairs. *1501 Folsom St., at 11th St., tel. 415/861–6906.*

The Thirsty Swede. Park your Harley and head inside this trendoid club for cheap beer and straight-ahead, Gothic rock and roll, both live and recorded. The Swede features free shows Sundays at 5 PM. *1821 Haight St., btw Shrader and Stanyan Sts., tel. 415/221–9008.*

JAZZ Don't fret if you missed the Summer of Love, because San Francisco is once again spearheading something new and wonderful: A rash of local bands have taken it upon themselves to explore and stretch the boundaries between funk, hip hop, and jazz. Venues like the Elbo Room (*see* Bars, above), Café du Nord, and Club 181 devote much of their booking time to these new acts. Names to look for are the Broun Fellinis (freestyle jazz with a funky bass line), Alphabet Soup (upbeat, reggae-influenced jazz with *two* rappers), Midnight Voices (leaning toward straight hip hop), and the Charlie Hunter Trio (more straight-ahead jazz).

You may recognize one of the band members of Midnight Voices from MTV's Real World.

Café du Nord. The specialty at this often overcrowded club is jazz you can afford. The $3–$5 cover charge gets you some fine local bands, pool tables, and the chance to stare at young San Franciscans sporting their finest duds, shaking their heads and snapping their fingers. *2170 Market St., btw Church and Sanchez Sts., tel. 415/861–5016.*

Club 181. A gorgeous, ancient jazz club that was closed in the '80s, the 181 recently reopened its doors to a whole new crowd. With a sizable clientele of jet-setting Euro types and rich kids, the 181 has become the chic place for those in their 20s to see, be seen, and eat a candlelight dinner. Club 181 attracts some great jazz and hip-hop shows; and if you don't sit down for dinner, you could even have an affordable evening. The cover runs $5–$10. Dress up. *181 Eddy St., near Taylor St., tel. 415/673–8181.*

El Río. It's mostly a dance club (*see* Clubs, *above*), but you can also catch live Latin jazz and samba here, in a casual and entirely unpretentious setting. *3158 Mission St., near Army St., tel. 415/282– 3325.*

Noe Valley Ministry Presbyterian Church USA. An adventurous booking policy draws some serious talent—from experimental jazz and blues artists to world music acts—into this no-smoke/occasional-drink church that moonlights as a theater. Cover charges range from $8 to $15. *1021 Sanchez St., near 24th St., tel. 415/282–2317.*

Pearl's. At this yup-scale jazz joint in North Beach, the surroundings are so comfy, the lights so low, that you could fall asleep. Luckily, the music is usually eye-opening, at least if mainstream jazz is your thing. Expect a middle-aged, well-heeled crowd. *256 Columbus Ave., at Broadway, tel. 415/291–8255.*

Spike's Café. A variety of acts comes through this small restaurant and performance space South of Market—everything from acoustic rock to avant-garde jazz and blues. It's a good place for a date or casual dinner. There are also occasional pool tournaments. *139 8th St., btw Mission and Howard Sts., tel. 415/626–7668.*

BLUES **Grant and Green Blues Club.** This dark, smoky bar hosts some out-of-hand blues shows, a welcome change in North Beach, where most residents sit in coffeehouses discussing their literary merits over a glass of wine. *1731 Grant Ave., at Green St., tel. 415/693–9565.*

Jack's. *The* place to hear blues on this side of the bay, Jack's serves up a wide variety of beers and some smoking jams seven nights a week in a relaxed, down-home atmosphere. John Lee Hooker has been known to stop by on occasion. *1601 Fillmore St., at Geary St., tel. 415/567–3227.*

Slim's. This club, owned by Boz Scaggs, features all types of American roots music. A wide variety of blues and jazz acts play here, not to mention the punkers, funkers, and gospel singers who also make occasional appearances. It's personable and fun for all ages (that is, all ages over 21). *333 11th St., btw Folsom and Harrison Sts., tel. 415/621–3330.*

The Spoken Word

The spoken-word scene, with its historic Beat connection, is enjoying a renaissance in cafés and bars throughout the Bay Area. In case you didn't know, the genre encompasses poetry, anti-poetry, monologues, howls, grunts, screams, and even readings of cereal boxes. Two places to experience all this first hand are The Chameleon (853 Valencia St., tel. 415/821–1891), which has spoken-word performances every Monday after 8:30 PM, and Café Babar (994 Guerrero St., tel. 415/282–6789), with spoken word every Thursday at 8 PM. For a more sedate evening, attend a free reading in Berkeley at Cody's (2454 Telegraph Ave., tel. 510/845–7852) or Black Oak Books (1491 Shattuck Ave., tel. 510/486–0698), where some big-name authors and poets meet to compare stanzas and the sizes of their grants.

EAST BAY

The East Bay music scene is fickle. Berkeley is better known for its student bars and cafés than for its music venues, and the only real exceptions are Blake's (for blues and jazz) and 924 Gilman Street (for straight-edge punk rock). Folk, jazz, and world music are well represented in the East Bay, but it's the soulful blues that lure people into the depths of Oakland, the self-styled Home of West Coast Blues.

ROCK **The Berkeley Square.** This was once the hippest venue in Berkeley for alternative music, both local and big-name, and it still attracts some national bands occasionally. However, its golden years have passed; nowadays, the Square caters to the young and fashionable (i.e., East Bay high-school kids). Call for current schedules. *1333 University Ave., tel. 510/841–6555. Take Bus 51 west from Berkeley BART to San Pablo and University Aves. 18 and over.*

Merchant's Lunch. Lace up your Doc Martens on Friday and Saturday nights and head to this downtown Oakland club for loud alternative rock. Covers hover around $3–$5. *401 2nd St., in Jack London Sq., tel. 510/465–8032.*

924 Gilman Street. This all-ages, alcohol-free cooperative features local hard-core garage bands and occasional big-name acts. The music is generally loud and aggressive, the crowd young, sweaty, tattooed, and not afraid to throw themselves around. Most shows cost $5, and you have to buy a $2 membership (valid for one year) to get in the first time. *924 Gilman St., at 8th St., Berkeley, tel. 510/525–9926.*

Stork Club. The country-and-western flavor and Christmas lights decorating this downtown Oakland dive make it a great watering hole. Recently, they've booked some decent local alternative bands and have started to attract a hip crowd. *380 12th St., near Webster St., tel. 510/444–6174.*

JAZZ Jazz greats come through Oakland on a regular basis, making appearances at established venues and putting on special shows. **Koncepts Cultural Gallery** (tel. 510/763–0682) hosts a fall series that includes a jazz duet festival, a jazz fest for families, and "Jazz in Tongues," a spoken-word event.

Kimball's East. In Emeryville, a small community tucked between Berkeley and Oakland, look for this excellent jazz and supper club, which books big-name jazz musicians Wednesday to Sunday. Covers range from $12 to $25. The downstairs venue, **Kimball's Carnival,** draws big names in Latin jazz and Caribbean music. Covers here are $10 and up, and you can expect to share the club with a sizable contingent of older professional types. *5800 Shellmound St., tel. 510/658–2555. From MacArthur BART take Bus 6 or 57 west on 40th St. to Pacific Park Plaza.*

Yoshi's. Yoshi's is a historic club and restaurant that serves up sushi and jazz in sophisticated syle. The clientele knows its music; past acts have included Cecil Taylor, Anthony Braxton, and Ornette Coleman. Visit while you can—Yoshi's is scheduled to close down in April 1995, and may or may not relocate to Jack London Square. Covers vary from $5 to $30. *6030 Claremont Ave., Oakland, tel. 510/652-9200. From Rockridge BART, walk about 3 blocks north on College Ave. and turn left on Claremont Ave.*

BLUES In the years following World War II, Oakland gave birth to the gritty, hurts-so-bad-I'm-gonna-die music known as the West Coast blues. Even after 50 years, it still flourishes in clubs and bars all over town. Dedicated to the preservation of blues, jazz, and gospel, the **Bay Area Blues Society** (tel. 510/836-2227) sponsors shows and festivals year-round, and is a wellspring of information about West Coast blues.

Oakland's blues scene is rough around the edges, but that only adds to its smoky, sweaty, raspy charm.

Blake's. This restaurant and jazz joint was opened in the late 1940s, and since then it's become a Berkeley legend. The upstairs dining room serves decent food to a yuppie crowd, but the cramped basement downstairs—a no-frills bar with a sawdust-covered floor—occasionally hosts some of the best blues acts in the area, plus the occasional alternative rock band. Covers are $5 and up; thumb through the *East Bay Express* or call for current listings. *2367 Telegraph Ave., Berkeley, near Durant Ave., tel. 510/848–0886.*

Eli's Mile High Club. The reputed birthplace of West Coast blues remains a consistently good bet. It's a small, basic club with a pool table, soul food, and music Wednesday to Sunday. The kitchen opens around 6:30 and music starts by 9; covers run $3–$8. *3629 Martin Luther King Jr. Way, Oakland, tel. 510/655–6661. From Berkeley take Bus 15 to 15th St. and Martin Luther King Jr. Way.*

The Fifth Amendment. Quality blues and jazz acts play to a largely African-American crowd of professionals, students, and neighborhood old-timers. Expect a cover charge of $5–$10 and some absolutely searing music. Dress up a bit. *3255 Lakeshore Ave., Oakland, at Lake Park Way, tel. 510/832–3242. From MacArthur BART, take Bus 57 to Lakeshore Ave.*

FOLK The Freight and Salvage. At this low-key coffeehouse you'll find Berkeley's thriving (and aging) folk-music community enjoying a wide variety of standards—everything from world-class accordionists to spoken word to political protest songs. Tickets cost $7–$13. *1111 Addison St., Berkeley, near San Pablo Ave., tel. 510/548–1761. Wheelchair access.*

The Starry Plough. This popular Irish-style pub near the Berkeley-Oakland border offers an eclectic mix of folk music (especially Irish) and not-too-extreme rock bands, usually for about $5. You can join the older, politically left crowd for a pint or two of Guinness, Bass, or Anchor Steam and a game of darts. Visit on Mondays at 7 PM for free Irish dance lessons. *3101 Shattuck Ave., Berkeley, at Prince St., tel. 510/841–2082. Take Bus 40 south from Berkeley BART to Ashby. Wheelchair access.*

WORLD MUSIC Ashkenaz. They call it "world music and dance"; essentially, it means there's a different live beat every night, from African and Cajun to Bulgarian folk. You can take dance lessons or just go at it. You won't find any brain-dead ravers here, only a devoted group of older locals and students out to broaden their cultural horizons. Vegetarian lunches are served Tuesday–Sunday. *1317 San Pablo Ave., Berkeley, tel. 510/525–5054. Take Bus 51 west on University from Berkeley BART; at San Pablo Ave., transfer to Bus 72 northbound and get off at Gilman St.*

La Peña. This Latin American cultural center offers a wide selection of live music, political lectures, performance pieces, and films on Central and South American issues. Many shows are benefits, so covers often masquerade as "donations" ranging from $5 to $10. *3105 Shattuck Ave., Berkeley, tel. 510/849–2568. Exit Ashby BART at Woolsey St. and walk 2 blocks east to Shattuck Ave.*

MARIN AND PALO ALTO

ROCK New George's. The frequent live music at this Marin County venue ranges from thrash to reggae to big-name rock bands. New George's can really cook when a hot band takes the stage, but often the less-than-hip, older crowd is pretty staid. Catch stand-up comedy on Tuesdays ($5), free live music on Wednesday, local bands on Thursdays ($1, students free), and bigger bands on weekends ($5–$15). Mixed drinks run about $3, and standard bar food (about $5) is served 11 AM–1 AM. During the day it's popular with slackers and Nam vets. *842 4th St., San Rafael, tel. 415/457–1515. From U.S. 101, take Central San Rafael exit to 4th St. and turn left. Closed Mon.*

Pioneer Saloon. A house of ill repute in the late 1800s, this dimly lit establishment near Palo Alto now sports live music every night—country and western on Tuesdays and rock the rest of the week, with an occasional R&B night. Bands start playing around 9:30, and admission is free before 8 (cover is $3–$5 otherwise). *2925 Woodside Rd., Woodside, at Whiskey Hill Rd., tel. 415/851–8487. Take I–280 to Woodside Rd. (Hwy. 84) west. Wheelchair access.*

Sweetwater. Once the sun sets in Mill Valley, locals mosey over to the Sweetwater. On any given night, bluesman Roy Rogers or Huey Lewis might show up to jam. The club is a Bay Area institution and, even though it's tiny, attracts some of the finest blues and R&B talents in the country. Cover ranges from $4 to $25. *153 Throckmorton Ave., at Miller Ave., tel. 415/388–2820.*

Movie Houses

If you're sick of mega-budget Hollywood productions, you can catch classic and obscure foreign flicks in San Francisco at the **Goethe Institut** (530 Bush St., at Grant St., tel. 415/391–0370), the **Alliance Française** (1345 Bush St., btw Polk and Larkin Sts., tel. 415/775–7755), and the **Instituto Italiano di Cultura** (425 Bush St., btw Grant and Kearny Sts., tel. 415/788–7142). They screen German, French, and Italian films, respectively, and host cultural activities. Call ahead to see if a film will be subtitled; if not, you may have to enlist a fascinating stranger to enrich your translation.

If you know the name of the blockbuster movie you'd like to see, call 415/777–FILM or 510/777–FILM, and the service will tell you where and when it's playing.

SAN FRANCISCO

San Francisco has a lot of cinema going on, much of it in funky repertory houses scattered throughout the city. For new releases, everyone goes to the **Kabuki 8** (1881 Post St., at Fillmore St., tel. 415/931–9800), even though some of the octoplex's screens are pretty small (ask which screen your movie's showing on, if you care). Tickets run about $7, but you get a $2 discount with student ID. Take advantage of their validated parking in the Japan Center, since some of the streets here aren't too safe for your car. The *Bay Guardian* and the *SF Weekly* have complete listings and reviews for both first-run theaters and rep houses.

During spring and summer three film festivals roll through town. In April look for the **San Francisco Film Festival** (tel. 415/931–3456), with features from all over the world. For the last two weeks in June, the much-loved **International Lesbian and Gay Film Festival** (tel. 415/431–1227), the largest such event in the world, coincides with Gay Pride Day. Then, just as you've caught your breath, and maybe even gotten a couple of bucks in your wallet, the **Jewish Film Festival** (tel. 510/548–0556) breezes into town for the last two weeks in July (one week at the Castro Theatre in San Francisco and one week at the U.C. Theater in Berkeley).

If all this action inspires you to try making your own movies, a great resource is **Artists' Television Access** (992 Valencia St., at 21st St., tel. 415/824–3890), a nonprofit media-arts center in the Mission founded eight years ago to perpetuate knowledge about television, video, and film. Show your very own homemade video to other artists and get feedback. They also have editing facilities for rent at reasonable rates and offer workshops on production and editing. Their screenings of unusual and offbeat films provide a night of cheap entertainment at $3–$5.

Castro Theatre. The most beautiful place to see a film in San Francisco is the Castro, which shows a wide selection of rare, foreign, and offbeat films that play anywhere from a night to a week. The Castro specializes in Audrey Hepburn and Bette Davis flicks and other classics of gay culture, as well as new releases of interest to lesbian and gay viewers. The little man who rises out of the floor playing the Wurlitzer organ is guaranteed to make you giggle for the sheer kitschiness of it all. *429 Castro St., btw Market and 18th Sts., tel. 415/621–6120.*

The Red Vic. This is the only theater in town with couches. How cool. Films range from the artsy to the cultish to the rare, and you can order herbal tea or coffee to accompany your popcorn with yeast. *1727 Haight St., btw Cole and Shrader Sts., tel. 415/668–3994.*

The Roxie. Movie snobs unite! This theater in the Mission district shows political, cult, and otherwise bent films. The audience can get raucous, probably because they're blowing off steam after carrying the weight of the world on their shoulders all day long. *3117 16th St., at Valencia St., tel. 415/863–1087.*

EAST BAY

Along with several big cinema complexes that show first-run releases, Berkeley has two theaters that specialize in the rare, the old, and the avant-garde. The **U.C. Theater** (2036 University Ave., tel. 510/843–6267), which has been in operation since 1917, shows foreign films and classics that change nightly; double features are juxtaposed with great care and creativity. The theater is cavernous, the seats lumpy, and the popcorn refreshingly cheap. In case you've never seen a real performance of *The Rocky Horror Picture Show,* it plays here at midnight on Fridays and Saturdays.

The **Pacific Film Archive,** in the U.C. Art Museum, caters to hard-core film enthusiasts with an impressive collection of rare titles. Films change nightly and often center around a certain theme (past offerings have included film portrayals of people with disabilities and an evening of Clint Eastwood films). Filmmakers often show up to discuss their work. Admission usually costs about $7, $5 for PFA members. No popcorn or drinks are allowed. *Entrance at 2621 Durant Ave., Berkeley, near College Ave., tel. 510/642–1124.*

PALO ALTO

You won't find the kind of offbeat theaters you get in Berkeley or San Francisco, but plenty of first-run movie houses pervade the Palo Alto area. If you've got the urge to do the Time Warp again, head to the **Varsity Theater** (456 University Ave., tel. 415/323–6411), which shows *The Rocky Horror Picture Show* every Saturday at midnight. Tickets are $6.75 each, $3.75 if you dress—or undress—yourself appropriately.

Stanford Theater. If seeing old movies on TV doesn't satisfy you, come watch them on the big screen in this restored theater, which rarely shows a movie made after 1960. It presents a series of film festivals throughout the year, usually centered around an actor or director such as Groucho Marx or Alfred Hitchcock. An organist entertains the crowd nightly before and after the 7:30 show and provides accompaniment for silent films. *221 University Ave., Palo Alto, off El Camino Real, tel. 415/324–3700. Take University Ave. exit west from U.S. 101. Admission: $6 for a double feature. Wheelchair access.*

Theater

While it doesn't carry the national reputation of New York, Los Angeles, or Chicago, the Bay Area has a diverse and affordable theater scene. The region is especially noted for its experimental theater, with a particular emphasis on multimedia productions and solo performers. The *SF Weekly,* the *Bay Guardian,* and the "Pink Pages" of the Sunday *Examiner-Chronicle* carry listings for special events.

SAN FRANCISCO

Most mainstream, Broadway-type musicals and dramas in town play at the **Curran Theater** (445 Geary St., tel. 415/474–3800). The city's principal repertory theaters are **ACT** (345 Mason St., tel. 415/749–2228), **Eureka Theater** (2730 16th St., tel. 415/558–9898), and **Magic Theater** (Fort Mason, tel. 415/441–8822). ACT is well-established and features mostly tried-and-true favorites; the latter two host well-mounted productions that lean toward the moderately experimental. **Theater Artaud** (450 Florida St., at 17th St., tel. 415/621–7797) regularly programs avant-garde dance, drama, and multimedia work. **Life on the Water** (3435 Army St., Suite 110, at Valencia St., tel. 415/824–9394) and **Climate Theater** (252 9th St., btw Folsom and Howard Sts., tel. 415/626–9196) are smaller venues, handling local and touring works of an experimental and multicultural nature, including monologues, political satires, and performance art. **Theater Rhinoceros** (2926 16th St., near Mission St., tel. 415/861–5079) is dedicated to all kinds of gay theater.

Above Brainwash. Local theater companies and performers present one- and two-act plays in this SoMa theater located above everyone's favorite café/laundromat. *1122 Folsom St., btw 7th and 8th Sts., tel. 415/362–7703.*

Asian American Theater Center. Local and traveling productions focus on different aspects of the Asian-American experience. It's a good place to see comedy. *403 Arguello Blvd., at Clement St., tel. 415/751–2600.*

Beach Blanket Babylon. This wacky talent show is the longest-lived musical revue in history, and for good reason. It features high production values, impeccable timing, well-practiced musicians, polished performers, extra-large headgear, and a zesty, zany script that changes often to incorporate topical references and characters. Twenty-plus bucks is a high price to pay, but BBB is notable for spending significant amounts of its profits on local charities. If you're under 21, you can only attend Sunday matinees. Be sure to reserve tickets well in advance. *Fugazi Hall, 678 Green St., tel. 415/421–4222. Shows Wed.–Sun.*

George Coates Performance Works. Avant-garde productions are put on by technological theater wizard George Coates and his company. *110 McAllister St., at Leavenworth St., tel. 415/863–8520.*

Intersection for the Arts. San Francisco's oldest alternative arts center continues to give exposure to new artists, playwrights, poets, writers, and actors. This is a good place to catch artists just before their big break: They often feature local talent of very high caliber. Depending on when you come, you might get to see a play, a visual art installation, and/or a series of readings. *446 Valencia St., btw 15th and 16th Sts., tel. 415/626–2787.*

Josie's Cabaret and Juice Joint. This medium-size cabaret in the Castro district features lesbian and gay performers who do everything from stand-up comedy to caustic monologues. Tickets cost $8 and up; it's a great place to take a date. *3583 16th St., near Market St., tel. 415/861–7933.*

Komotion International. This artists' collective, run by volunteer labor, acts as a recording studio for over 40 musicians, as well as a performance space/art gallery. They regularly host music, poetry readings, dance and theater performances, multimedia events, and benefits for various good causes. *2779 16th St., btw Folsom and Harrison Sts., tel. 415/861–6423.*

Lorraine Hansberry Theater. An alternative theater, Lorraine Hansberry specializes in productions by African-Americans. *500 Sutter St., at Powell St., tel. 415/288–0320.*

The Marsh. This small, experimental venue in the Mission offers performers and playwrights a shot at public exposure, and offers you the chance to say you saw them here first (for $5), before they got big and commercial. If you happen to be a blossoming performer, stop in for a schmooze. The Marsh sometimes hosts big productions on tour from New York City and beyond. *1062 Valencia St., btw 21st and 22nd Sts., tel. 415/641–0235.*

Téatro Misión. Inside the Mission Cultural Center, Téatro Misión features adventurous, politically topical works, including a variety of Spanish-language pieces aimed at the Mission's Mexican, Central American, and Chicano communities. *2868 Mission St., btw 24th and 25th Sts., tel. 415/695–6970.*

Theater on the Square. This downtown theater specializes in musicals and dance performances. *450 Post St., btw Powell and Mason Sts., tel. 415/433–9500.*

Lofty Ambitions

The latest trend among broke, innovative San Franciscans with an eye for art has been to turn loft-style apartments, cafés, and galleries into showcases for all kinds of talent. Kiki (43 14th St., at Guerrero St., tel. 415/863–5454) has art showings; Epicenter Zone (415 Valencia St., at 16th St., tel. 415/863–3321) offers performances, classes, and shows; and Luna Sea (2940 16th St., Suite 216C, btw Capp and South Van Ness Sts., tel. 415/863–2989) hosts a variety of feminist events from readings to workshops. The underground nature of the scene and the sometimes sketchy locations mean a low cover price, and the low-key atmosphere attracts an abundance of raw talent.

Surprisingly, Berkeley doesn't have a strong theatrical tradition. There are a number of good companies in town, but not enough to sustain innovative drama on a regular basis. This said, the **Berkeley Repertory Theater** (2025 Addison St., tel. 510/845–4700) is an extremely popular ensemble, performing everything from Beckett to Corneille to Mamet. After noon on the day of a show you can get half-price tickets for the otherwise expensive ($21–$27) performances. Other Berkeley-area companies include the **Black Repertory Group** (3201 Adeline St., tel. 510/652–2120), whose performances address all aspects of the African-American experience, and the **Blake Street Garage** (2029 Blake St., tel. 510/548–3360), whose offbeat and casual shows gave birth to Whoopi Goldberg's career. **La Val's Subterranean** (1834 Euclid Ave., tel. 510/843–5617) offers small productions and works-in-progress by local artists in an unlikely location underneath a pizza joint. At **Zellerbach Playhouse** (tel. 510/642–9988), on the U.C. campus, you can catch productions that feature actors, playwrights, and directors from Cal's dramatic arts department.

Call 510/835–ARTS, Oakland's 24-hour arts and entertainment hotline, for weekly listings of theater, music, and dance events.

Dance

Besides the world-class San Francisco Ballet (*see below*), the city has a variety of local companies that reflect the diversity and eclecticism of the Bay Area. When large troupes or festivals come into town, they often end up at the **Palace of Fine Arts Theater** (3301 Lyon St., at Bay St., tel. 415/563–6504) in the Marina district. More experimental mid-size companies often perform in the Mission at **Theater Artaud** (450 Florida St., at 17th St., tel. 415/621–7797). For funky local companies and the extremely cutting edge, try **Footwork Dance Studio** (3221 22nd St., btw Mission and Valencia Sts., tel. 415/824–5044). **Third Wave Dance House** (3316 24th St., at Mission St., tel. 415/282–4020) is a good place to see shows by local choreographers and ethnic dance. Check the entertainment sections of the *SF Weekly* and the *Bay Guardian* for all the latest info.

TIX Bay Area (251 Stockton St., btw Post and Geary Sts., tel. 415/433–7827) offers half-price, same-day tickets for theater, dance, opera, and music events (cash only). The kiosk is open afternoons and evenings Tuesday–Saturday.

Performances of the **San Francisco Ballet** (tel. 415/703–9400) are held at the Opera House (*see* Opera, *below*), the **Center for the Arts at Yerba Buena Gardens** (700 Howard St., at 3rd St., tel. 415/978–2787), and various other theaters around the bay. The 1995 season will include the "United We Dance" festival, with performances from around the globe in honor of the 50th anniversary of the signing of the United Nations International Charter. Students can try for same-day rush tickets to the ballet (with discounts of 50% and up); go to the box office the afternoon of your performance and hope for the best. You could probably get away with using an old student ID, but don't say you heard it here.

On the U.C. Berkeley campus, Zellerbach Hall provides a venue for nationally and internationally famous dance companies, symphony orchestras, and musicians. For information on this season's lineup, call **Cal Performances** (tel. 510/642–9988).

Symphony

The **San Francisco Symphony**, the big cheese of Bay Area orchestras, plays from September to May. The symphony has become a major musical force in recent years under the musical direction of Herbert Blomstedt and has been able to attract stellar guest musicians like soprano Jessye Norman and pianist Van Cliburn. Blomstedt will be turning over his baton to Michael Tilson Thomas at the end of the 1994-95 season, so hurry if you want a chance to see him conduct. The latter half of the 1994–95 season will include a performance of Britten's *War Requiem*, child prodigy violinist Sarah Chang, and Beethoven's *Missa Solemnis*. Tickets for box seats can be as high as $65, but terrace seats behind the stage are sold for $9–$12 starting two hours before each performance. If terrace seats sell out, sometimes they sell remaining second-tier balcony seats for $15. Second-tier balcony seats sold in advance are about $23. *Davies Symphony Hall, cnr Van Ness Ave. and Grove St., tel. 415/431–5400.*

In the East Bay, try to catch the **Berkeley Symphony Orchestra** (tel. 510/841–2800), which performs periodically at Zellerbach Hall on the U.C. campus. Under the innovative direction of Kent Nagano, the symphony has delved into some very unorthodox but intriguing areas, including a Frank Zappa piece complete with life-size puppets. Beyond that, Zellerbach Hall offers a wide range of classical performances; call **Cal Performances** (tel. 510/642–9988) for information. For chamber music (as well as jazz and world music) in a peaceful, intimate setting, try the **Maybeck Recital Hall** (1537 Euclid Ave., tel. 510/848–3228), designed by revered Berkeley architect Bernard Maybeck, or **St. John's Presbyterian Church** (2727 College Ave., tel. 510/845–6830).

The **Stanford University Symphony** (tel. 415/723–3811) plays four concerts a year on campus. Buy tickets ($8 adults, $5 students) at Tressider ticket office in the student union. On the cheap end of the spectrum, you can see the **California Youth Symphony** (tel. 415/325–6666), which performs at the San Mateo Performing Arts Center and the Flint Center at De Anza College. Tickets cost $6, $3 for students.

If you're not sure you like this classical music stuff enough to pay money for it, catch a free classical concert every Tuesday at 12:30 PM at Old Saint Mary's Cathedral (cnr Grant and California Sts.) in San Francisco, courtesy of the **Noontime Concerts Series** (tel. 415/288–3840). An even better option in summer is the **Stern Grove Midsummer Music Festival** (*see* Cheap Thrills, San Francisco, in Chapter 2). Otherwise, the **U.C. Music Department** (tel. 510/642–4864) hosts free noontime concerts during the school year at Hertz Hall or Morrison Hall on the Berkeley campus, generally on Wednesdays. Most of the performers are students, but then again, most of the students are incredibly talented.

Opera

The **San Francisco Opera,** one of the best companies in the country, has a regular season that generally runs from early September to mid-December, plus a short summer season. The opera is known for taking some risks; in 1995, Bobby McFerrin is scheduled to debut his own opera (with Ishmael Reed as his librettist). Ticket prices range from $15 to about half your monthly paycheck; the cheapest seats sell out first, so plan in advance. One of the best deals going for those with a student ID is same-day rush tickets, which allow you to buy remaining seats (including real expensive ones) to some performances for only $25. Rush tickets aren't available, however, for performances which are nearly sold out. Standing-room tickets, though, are available for every show. If you line up at 10:30 the morning of the show and pay $8, you earn the right to stand through your favorite opera. Performances take place in the War Memorial Opera House, near the Civic Center. *301 Van Ness Ave., at Grove St., tel. 415/864–3330.*

The **Berkeley Opera** (715 Arlington St., tel. 510/841–1903) presents quality productions on a smaller scale (they usually manage three operas a year).

A Requiem for the Masses

You've sung yourself stupid in the shower, but now it's time to try something a little more advanced. Most Mondays in summer, directors of Bay Area choral groups lead classical sing-alongs at the Mountain View Center for the Performing Arts (tel. 415/903–6000). Just bring $10–$12 and your voice, and you'll learn to sing masses and requiems by Bach, Beethoven, and Brahms, among other famous composers. The center is located at the corner of Castro and Mercy streets, in Mountain View's Civic Center complex. Take U.S. 101 to Moffett Boulevard west, which becomes Castro Street.

WHERE TO SLEEP   7

By Timothy McIntyre

Unless you have a specific reason to stay in the 'burbs, your best choice for almost any kind of lodging in the Bay Area is San Francisco. You'll find some truly unusual bed-and-breakfasts here, and even the cheap hotels have a little character. But if your goal is to escape the city for the night or the weekend, head straight for Marin County's hostels and campgrounds. In places like Point Reyes (*see* Chapter 2) and the Marin Headlands, you'll find more gorgeous open space than you'd believe could exist so close to the city, and a night at a woodsy hostel or beach campsite will run you less than $10. Otherwise, you're stuck with grimy motels in the East Bay, astronomically priced bed-and-breakfasts in Marin County, or chain hotels filled with business travelers in the South Bay.

San Francisco

For an expensive city, San Francisco has a surprisingly large assortment of reasonably priced accommodations. For a great no-frills deal, stay in one of nine hostels, where a bed will only set you back about $12, or in one of the residential hotels that populate downtown, SoMa, and North Beach. For a bit more ($30–$50 a night), many small downtown hotels offer charming "European-style" rooms (i.e., the toilet's down the hall). Then there's a genre that might be called the specialty hotel, some of which may cause you to shake your head and sigh, "Only in San Francisco." You've got your leather-and-Levi's gay B&B, your art B&B complete with easels and lots of good light, and the inn whose nightly accommodations include the "Summer of Love Room" and the "Japanese Tea Garden Room."

If you don't reserve one to two weeks in advance in summer, you may be exiled to the strip of generic motels along **Lombard Street** in the Marina district, about a 20-minute bus ride from downtown (on Bus 76), but quite close to Fisherman's Wharf. On Lombard, you'll pay an annoying $50–$70 for a double—stay here only as a last resort. The places listed below will put you up for a night, a week, or (in some cases) a month; and if you just can't leave, we've included some tips on how to find a long-term home.

HOTELS AND MOTELS

Directions below are given from the downtown BART/MUNI stations along Market Street. To reach the stations from the San Francisco International Airport, take SamTrans Bus 7F or 7B. Either one will drop you off on Mission Street, which runs parallel to Market a block to the south; just ask the driver for the stop nearest your station.

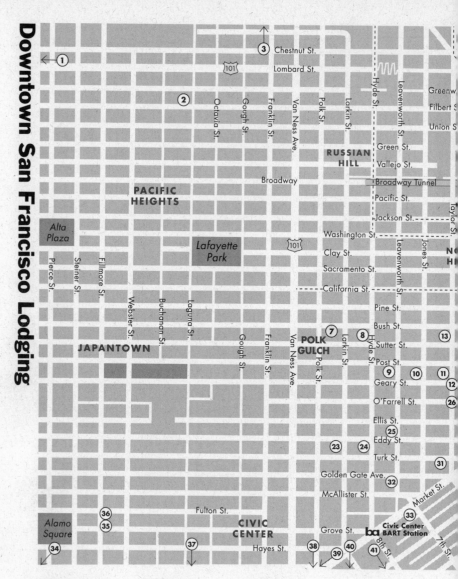

Chestnut St.

Lombard St.

Octavia St.

Gough St.

Franklin St.

Van Ness Ave.

Polk St.

Larkin St.

Hyde St.

Leavenworth St.

Greenw

Filbert

Union S

RUSSIAN HILL

Green St.

Vallejo St.

Broadway Tunnel

Pacific St.

Jackson St.

Taylor St

PACIFIC HEIGHTS

Broadway

Alta Plaza

Lafayette Park

Pierce St.

Steiner St.

Fillmore St.

Webster St.

Buchanan St.

Laguna St.

Gough St.

Franklin St.

Van Ness Ave.

Washington St.

Clay St.

Sacramento St.

California St.

Leavenworth St.

Jones St.

N
H

Pine St.

Bush St.

Sutter St.

Post St.

Geary St.

O'Farrell St.

Ellis St.

Eddy St.

Turk St.

Golden Gate Ave.

McAllister St.

POLK GULCH

Polk St.

Larkin St.

Hyde St.

JAPANTOWN

Fulton St.

CIVIC CENTER

Grove St.

Hayes St.

Alamo Square

Market St.

Civic Center BART Station

8th St.

7th St.

Adelaide Inn, **11**

Aida Hotel, **33**

Albergo Verno, **25**

Alexander Inn, **26**

Amsterdam, **13**

Art Center Bed and Breakfast, **2**

AYH Hostel at Union Square, **27**

Brady Acres, **10**

Cornell Hotel, **17**

David's Hotel, **12**

Europa, **5**

European Guest House, **40**

Fort Mason International Hostel, **3**

Globetrotter's Inn, **29**

Golden Gate Hotel, **14**

Grand Central Hostel, **38**

Grant Hotel, **16**

Grant Plaza Hotel, **20**

Green Tortoise Hostel, **6**

Grove Inn, **35**

Herbert Hotel, **28**

Hotel Astoria, **21**

Hotel One, **24**

Hyde Plaza Hotel, **8**

Interclub Globe Hostel, **41**

James Court, **7**

Marina Motel, **1**

Metro Hotel, **34**

Olympic Hotel, **30**

Pacific Tradewinds, **19**

Pensione International, **9**

Pensione San Francisco, **39**

Phoenix Hotel, **23**

San Francisco Residence Club, **18**

San Francisco RV Park, **42**

San Francisco Zen Center, **37**

San Remo Hotel, **4**

San Francisco
Bay

KEY
---- Cable Car

N

0   1/2 mile

0   500 meters

④ Chestnut St.

Lombard St.

NORTH BEACH

TELEGRAPH HILL

Columbus Ave.

Grant Ave.

Powell St.

Mason St.

Stockton St.

Montgomery St.

Sansome St.

Battery St.

The Embarcadero

Front St.

Davis St.

Drumm St.

⑤

⑥

FINANCIAL DISTRICT

Waverly Pl. — ⑲

CHINATOWN

Kearny St.

Halleck St.

Front St.

Davis St.

Embarcadero BART Station ba

⑱

⑯ ⑳ ㉒

⑮ ⑰ ㉑

⑭

UNION SQUARE

Union Square

Maiden Ln.

Montgomery St. BART Station ba

Market St.

SOMA

New Montgomery St.

1st St.

2nd St.

3rd St.

Hawthorne St.

Fremont St.

Beale St.

Main St.

Spear St.

Stewart St.

⑳ ⑦

㉘

㉚

Powell St. BART Station ba

Mission St.

4th St.

5th St.

3rd St.

Moscone Center

Folsom St.

Howard St.

Harrison St.

Bryant St.

Brannan St.

The Embarcadero

Townsend St.

80

㊷

Sappho's, **36**

Sheehan, **14**

Temple Hotel, **22**

YMCA Central Branch, **32**

Youth Hostel Centrale, **31**

DOWNTOWN Stay downtown if you want to be surrounded by fog, tall buildings, old architecture and restaurants (at least, old by California standards), and tourists. Sleeping downtown offers the added advantage of easy proximity to North Beach, Fisherman's Wharf, Chinatown, and Union Square. The neighborhood is packed with high-priced corporate hotels; you'll need to check side streets for more reasonable rates. It's deserted and not always safe here at night, so be alert.

Most of the small European-style hotels are downtown, adding to the feeling that you've stepped through a time warp into the '40s.

➤ **UNDER $40** • **Herbert Hotel.** The proprietor of this residential hotel, about a block from Union Square, rents out only a few rooms by the night ($30 for a double with private bath), but you can't beat his weekly rates: $85 for a double with shared bath, $110 for a double with private bath. The place is clean and the mid-size rooms aren't bad, although the decor won't win any prizes. The hotel usually doesn't take reservations from tourists, but if you call a couple days ahead and explain your plans, the manager may hold a room for you. *161 Powell St., btw Ellis and O'Farrell Sts., tel. 415/362–1600. From Powell St. BART/MUNI Station, walk north 1½ blocks on Powell St. 90 rooms, 45 with bath.*

Hyde Plaza Hotel. In limbo between Van Ness Avenue, the Tenderloin, and Nob Hill, this European-style hotel offers basic, comfortable furnishings in 50 rooms, most with shared bath. Nightly rates run anywhere from $30 per double to $45 for a room sleeping four; the weekly rate for a double is about $130. The beautiful old building has an adjoining restaurant. *835 Hyde St., near Sutter St., tel. 415/885–2987. From Montgomery BART/MUNI Station, walk northeast 1 block to Sutter St.; take Bus 2, 3, or 4 to Hyde St. Luggage storage.*

James Court. Near Nob Hill and Chinatown, the James Court offers airy, medium-size doubles with TV and phones for $35–$45; for a double with kitchenette you'll pay $50 (rates are subject to change because the hotel is changing ownership). Four people can get a room for $45 per night, which is as cheap as a youth hostel, and this is one of the safer parts of downtown. *1353 Bush St., btw Larkin and Polk Sts., tel. 415/771–2409. From Civic Center BART/MUNI Station, take Bus 19 to Sutter and Polk Sts., walk 1 block north on Polk St. and turn right. 37 rooms, most with shared bath. Luggage storage, laundry. Reservations recommended.*

Olympic Hotel. The Olympic is centrally located near Union Square and the Powell Street BART/MUNI Station. The clean, small rooms are basic and functional, though the building is slightly run-down. Lots of backpacker types, not all American, stay here. Reserve at least a week in advance in summer. A single or double with shared bath is $30, and rooms with private bath are $45. *140 Mason St., at Ellis St., tel. 415/982–5010. From Powell St. BART/MUNI Station, walk 1 block east on Eddy St. and ½ block north on Mason St. 120 rooms, about half with bath.*

Temple Hotel. Across the street from the Bank of America building, this small residential hotel is a throwback to earlier days in a neighborhood of high-rises and big bucks. Opinions on the decor are mixed: Some find it tasteful, others say "hideous," and remark that the carpets could use a good cleaning. Older travelers and some international backpackers make up the clientele. Doubles with private bath are $45, with shared bath $35. The hotel also offers weekly rates starting at $147, so you can take your time checking out nearby Chinatown and North Beach. *469 Pine St., btw Montgomery and Kearny Sts., tel. 415/781–2565. From Montgomery BART/MUNI Station, walk 3 blocks north to Pine St. and turn left. 88 rooms, 24 with bath. Reservations recommended in summer.*

➤ **UNDER $55** • **Adelaide Inn.** This place, just minutes from Union Square, is comfortable in a kitschy, Swiss way (you'd expect a cuckoo clock on the mantelpiece, if they had a mantelpiece). It's very popular with Europeans. Rates include a continental breakfast, and some kitchen facilities are available. Singles run $32–$38, doubles $42–$48, depending on room size and availability. *5 Isadora Duncan Ln., off Taylor St., tel. 415/441–2261. From Montgomery BART/MUNI Station, take Bus 38 to Geary and Taylor Sts., walk ¾ block north on Taylor St., and turn left. 18 rooms. Reserve in summer.*

Grant Hotel. The gaudy red decor won't appear in *Interior Design Monthly* any time soon, but this hotel's location on Nob Hill, two blocks from Union Square and Chinatown, is unbeatable.

The rooms have furniture that looks like it came from Grandma's basement, clean bedding, TVs, phones, and private baths—not bad for $49 per double. Try to reserve about a week in advance in summer, or show up the morning of the day you arrive, when there may be cancellations. *753 Bush St., btw Powell and Mason Sts., tel. 415/421–7540. From Powell St. BART/MUNI Station, walk 5½ blocks north on Powell St. and turn left. 60 rooms.*

Pensione International. About a 10-minute walk from Union Square, you'll find small, clean rooms with character at this hotel with a very helpful staff. Rates start at $50 for doubles with shared bath, $70 for those with private bath. Prices are $10 cheaper in the off-season, and complimentary breakfast is always included. *875 Post St., btw Hyde and Leavenworth Sts., tel. 415/775–3344. From Powell St. BART/MUNI Station, take Bus 27 to Leavenworth and Post Sts. 43 rooms, some with bath.*

➤ **UNDER $65** • **Brady Acres.** Come to this small, comfortable hotel near the Theater District if you're sick of being on the road and want a place that feels like home. Each room includes a kitchenette with microwave, toaster, and coffeemaker, and the bathrooms have real towels, just like Mom gives you. Your phone comes with an answering machine, and all rooms have TVs and radios with cassette players. The management goes out of its way to make guests feel at home. Those who can spare $50–$60 for a single, $60–$75 for a double, should look no further for a way to escape the travel blues. Ask for current weekly specials. *649 Jones St., btw Post and Geary Sts., tel. 415/929–8033 or 800/627–2396. From Montgomery BART/MUNI Station, take Bus 38 to Geary and Jones Sts. 25 rooms. Laundry. Reservations recommended in summer.*

Golden Gate Hotel. At this small hotel on top of Nob Hill, the spotless rooms are decorated country-style, with wicker, antiques, floral wallpaper, and fresh flowers. The management is a delight, too. Rooms with shared bath ($59 per double) are a better bargain than the slightly larger ones with private bath ($89 per double). The hotel offers a continental breakfast and afternoon tea in the front sitting room, where you'll meet travelers from all over. Reserve two to three weeks in advance in summer; you also need to make a deposit. *775 Bush St., btw Powell and Mason Sts., tel. 415/392–3702. Follow directions to Grant Hotel (see above). 23 rooms.*

Hotel One. A lot of French and German tourists stay at this clean hotel, which sits on one of the Tenderloin's less hectic blocks, not far from downtown and the Civic Center. Although the atmosphere and furnishings are drab, all rooms have TVs and private baths. You pay $45–$55 per single and $55–$65 per double (each additional guest $5). Take a bus or cab from Market Street at night, as this area is seedy. *587 Eddy St., btw Hyde and Larkin Sts., tel. 415/775–5934. From Civic Center BART/MUNI Station, walk 5 blocks north on Hyde St. and turn left. 65 rooms. Reservations with credit card.*

San Francisco Residence Club. In a spectacular location at the top of Nob Hill, this place serves as both a reasonably priced hotel and a genteel, old-time residence club. Families, couples, and single people from all over the world stay here, but the atmosphere is definitely yuppieish. A large double with shared bath costs $55 and up; singles start at $38. They also have weekly and monthly rates. All rates include a big breakfast and dinner in the warmly lit dining room. The Donahues, who operate the hotel, know how to make guests feel at home; prepare for some pampering. *851 California St., btw Stockton and Powell Sts., tel. 415/421–2220. From Embarcadero BART/MUNI Station, take California St. cable car to Powell St. Laundry. $100 deposit required.*

Sheehan. The building was formerly a YWCA, so guests have free use of a gym and swimming pool. Clean, dorm-like rooms with shared bath run $50 per single, $60 per double; for a room with a private bath, you pay $70–$99. Breakfast is included. *620 Sutter St., at Mason St., tel. 415/775–6500 or 800/848–1529. From Montgomery BART/MUNI Station, walk 1 block northeast to Sutter St., and take Bus 2, 3, or 4 to Mason St. 70 rooms, 54 with bath.*

➤ **UNDER $85** • **Alexander Inn.** Two blocks west of Union Square, the Alexander is an upscale version of a European-style hotel, with deferential employees, sunny rooms, real wood furniture, and an international clientele. Most rooms have private baths, color TVs, and coffeemakers. If you're willing to share a bath, you pay a super-low $35; otherwise, singles and doubles are $72 (triples $84). Reserve at least a week in advance. *415 O'Farrell St., at Taylor*

173

St., tel. 415/928–6800 or 800/843–8709. From Powell St. BART/MUNI Station, walk 2 blocks west on Eddy St., 2 blocks north on Taylor St. 76 rooms, most with bath.

Amsterdam. For a Victorian bed-and-breakfast two blocks from Nob Hill, this is a sweet bargain: $69 for two people, $60 for one (rates are lower off-season). The smallish rooms have cable TV and private baths, some of which could use a good scrubbing. When the temperature drops to a windy 50° at night and you just can't face going out, you'll be stoked about the reading room. *749 Taylor St., btw Sutter and Bush Sts., tel. 415/673–3277 or 800/637–3444. From Montgomery BART/MUNI Station, walk 1 block northeast to Sutter St., and take Bus 2, 3, or 4 to Taylor St. 34 rooms.*

Cornell. This small, French country-style hotel on Nob Hill offers beautifully decorated doubles (a bit heavy on flowers and lace) for $80–$90. The French owners operate a small restaurant in the cellar with a $14 prix-fixe menu, stained glass, and groovy medieval accoutrements on the walls. *715 Bush St., btw Powell and Mason Sts., tel. 415/421–3154. From Powell St. BART/MUNI Station, walk 5½ blocks north on Powell St. to Bush St. and turn left. 55 rooms, all nonsmoking.*

➢ **UNDER $100 • David's Hotel.** The rooms at this hotel on Theater Row are small but spotless. The best part of staying at David's, though, is the deal you get from the Jewish delicatessen downstairs. Breakfast is free, and you get a 25% discount on lunch and dinner, which makes the room rates seem extraordinarily cheap, since non-guests must fork over $13 just to get a Reuben sandwich. A single room is $69, a double $89. David's also provides free airport transportation and free parking for all guests, many of whom hail from the New York area. One floor of the hotel is reserved for nonsmokers. *480 Geary St., at Taylor St., tel. 415/771–1600 or 800/524–1888. From Powell St. BART/MUNI Station, walk 2½ blocks north on Powell St. and 2 blocks west on Geary St. 50 rooms. Wheelchair access.*

CIVIC CENTER The area around the Civic Center should be a great place to stay: Davies Symphony Hall, the Opera House, the Museum of Modern Art, and a host of theaters are all within easy walking distance, and many of the city's public transport lines converge here. Sadly, the Civic Center can also be quite intimidating, especially at night, because of the large homeless population.

➢ **UNDER $40 • Aida Hotel.** Tourists from all over the world crash at this centrally located hotel on Market Street, a block from Civic Center BART. For $37 you get a double with TV and phone (bath down the hall); for $8 more, your room will have a private bath. The rooms are typical of all motels, but at least they're new and clean. And since there are 165 of them, you can probably get something at the last minute, even during high season. *1087 Market St., at 7th*

The Phoenix Rises from the Ashes of the Tenderloin

In the squalid Tenderloin district, home of strip bars and streetwalkers, the Phoenix Hotel has built a strong reputation among young hipsters. Bands like the Red Hot Chili Peppers, NRBQ, Simple Minds, and Living Colour have stayed here; and original work by Bay Area artists spices up the tropical Southwest design scheme. A special legal exemption had to be obtained for the Phoenix's swirling black-tile pool bottom. In-room massage and body work is available, and the hotel is joined at the hip, as it were, to the lively Miss Pearl's Jam House (see Chapter 4). In high season, you'll pay $89 for a single or double, but rates go down as much as $20 in winter, depending on demand. 601 Larkin St., at Eddy St., tel. 415/776–1380. Take Bus 31 from Embarcadero, Montgomery, or Powell St. BART/MUNI Station, get off at Larkin St.

St., tel. 415/863–4141. From Civic Center BART/MUNI Station, walk 1 block northeast on Market St. Luggage storage.

YMCA Central Branch. The Golden Gate YMCA isn't quite the young men's paradise envisioned by the Village People, since women can stay, too. But it does offer functional, clean rooms in the seedy Tenderloin, with complimentary continental breakfast and use of the gym facilities. Singles are $28, doubles $38, and almost all the rooms share baths. Five less expensive beds (around $15) are reserved for students as a hostel-type thing, but these are often booked up. International Student Identification Card (ISIC) holders get a 10% discount on the regular rooms. *220 Golden Gate Ave., btw Hyde and Leavenworth Sts., tel. 415/885–0460. From Civic Center BART/MUNI Station, walk 3 blocks north on Hyde St., right on Golden Gate Ave. 104 rooms. TV room. Wheelchair access.*

➤ **UNDER $55 • Albergo Verona.** In a neighborhood that's central but sketchy, this beautifully renovated, turn-of-the-century hotel attracts German, French, and Italian tourists. Rooms, some with private bath, are a good deal at $40–$50 for a double. They also have 14 dorm spaces in two-, four-, and six-person rooms, which rent for $17 per person; all rates include morning coffee and doughnuts. *317 Leavenworth St., at Eddy St., tel. 415/771–4242. From Powell St. BART/MUNI Station, walk 4 blocks west and turn right. 67 rooms.*

Pensione San Francisco. This well-located establishment near the Civic Center has managed to retain some character without getting all bourgeois and expensive. Rooms feature little decorative touches like bedposts and framed pictures, as well as refrigerators. The shared bathroom facilities are clean. A complimentary continental breakfast is served in a sunny eating area that doubles as a TV room. Reserve at least two weeks in advance (with credit card or one night's deposit) during summer. Rates are $42–$45 for a single, $52–$55 for a double. *1668 Market St., btw Franklin and Gough Sts., tel. 415/864–1271. From Van Ness MUNI Station, walk 1 block southwest on Market St. 36 rooms.*

CHINATOWN Chinatown is noisy, often smelly, and right in the center of the action. This is tourist central, bounded on one side by North Beach and on the other by downtown and Union Square. Grant Street overflows with electronics stores and T-shirt stands, so if you're in search of authenticity, you'll need to branch out to the side streets.

➤ **UNDER $40 • Hotel Astoria.** This hotel near the Chinatown gates is a real bargain if you're prepared to share a bathroom: Pleasantly decorated singles with TVs cost $31, doubles $36 (two twin beds). If you want a private bath, expect to pay $61 for a double. Although the rooms are decent and clean, the best thing about Hotel Astoria is its location, in a relatively safe neighborhood blocks away from Union Square and North Beach, and inches from Chinatown. Europhiles will be glad to know that the Goethe Institute is next door and that a café and an international newsstand specializing in French publications sit right across the street—but you didn't come to Chinatown to sip espresso with Europeans, did you? *510 Bush St., at Grant*

Zen and the Art of Sleeping

If you have an honest interest in enlightenment and aren't just looking for a cheap place to crash, the San Francisco Zen Center, between the Civic Center and the lower Haight, has a few rooms for visitors. You get a spotless, nicely furnished room overlooking a courtyard ($30–$40 for a single, $40–$50 for a double with shared bath), plus a hearty breakfast. This working temple also offers a guest-student program ($10 a night) in which you adhere to the meditation, work, and meal schedule of the center for one to six weeks. You should reserve in advance, especially during summer. 300 Page St., at Laguna St., tel. 415/863–3136. From Market St. downtown, take Bus 7 or 71 to Page and Laguna Sts.

Ave., tel. 415/434–8889. From Montgomery BART/MUNI Station, walk 2 blocks west on Post St., 2 blocks north on Grant Ave. 80 rooms. Reservations with credit card.

➤ **UNDER $55** • **Grant Plaza.** Near the entrance to Chinatown, this large, characterless hotel offers a bargain for groups of four: two double beds for $62. That's comparable to hostel rates, and you get some luxuries that AYH doesn't provide, like private baths, color TVs, and phones. If you're not traveling in a posse, expect to pay $39–$42 for one person, $42–$52 for two. Families and older travelers occupy the small but immaculate rooms. 465 Grant Ave., btw Bush and Pine Sts., tel. 415/434–3883 or 800/472–6899. From Montgomery BART/MUNI Station, walk 2 blocks west on Post St., 2½ blocks north on Grant Ave. 72 rooms.

NORTH BEACH North Beach is a great place to stay: It's near downtown, Chinatown, and Fisherman's Wharf, and no part of the city feels more classically San Francisco. Unfortunately, this is also where most tourists congregate, and hotel rates are correspondingly high. You'll have to search hard for something affordable.

Come to North Beach if you want to be near many of the city's best restaurants, bars, and cafés; even the tacky strip joints are here.

➤ **UNDER $40** • **Europa Hotel.** Sandwiched between two establishments boasting "Live! All-nude Girls!" this place tries hard to be a lone bastion of morality. The sign at the counter prohibits visitors after 6 PM, illegal drugs, weapons, pets, alcohol, and loud noise. The security entrance (guests are buzzed in) makes it fairly safe, though it looks divey—and some strange characters were spied wandering the incense-scented halls. If you don't mind street noise, ask for a room with a view of Broadway and Columbus to alleviate the hotel's musty barrenness. Better yet, pay $30 for a double, shower in the ugly but functional shared bathroom, and spend your time and savings on good coffee at a chic Italian café down the street. 310 Columbus Ave., at Broadway, tel. 415/391–5779. From Montgomery BART/MUNI Station, walk one block southwest on Market St. to Kearny St.; take Bus 15 to Columbus Ave. and Broadway. 76 rooms, none with bath.

➤ **UNDER $65** • **San Remo Hotel.** A short walk from both Fisherman's Wharf and North Beach, the San Remo is an incredible bargain in a pricey area. The hotel boasts helpful management, beautiful redwood furnishings, stained-glass windows, and quiet, spotless rooms. And get this: $55–$65 for a double with shared bath. 2237 Mason St., btw Francisco and Chestnut Sts., tel. 415/776–8688. From Powell St. BART/MUNI Station, walk ½ block northeast on Market St. to 4th St., take Bus 30 to Mason St., and walk north 2 blocks on Mason St. 64 rooms. Laundry. Reservations recommended in summer.

THE MARINA The Marina is a residential neighborhood popular with young corporate types. It's a long walk from North Beach, Chinatown, and downtown, but the views of the bay and the Golden Gate Bridge from the waterfront are tremendous, and the area is both quiet and safe. Nearby Union and Fillmore streets offer a good selection of yuppiefied restaurants and singles bars. Unfortunately, most of the cheap lodging in this area lies along busy **Lombard Street,** a main artery leading to the Golden Gate Bridge that's lined with run-down motels, gas stations, and cheap restaurants.

➤ **UNDER $85** • **Marina Motel.** This Spanish-style stucco motel is a few bucks cheaper than other Lombard Street lodges. Doubles go for $70, slightly more in the peak season. About half the rooms have kitchens. 2576 Lombard St., btw Broderick and Divisadero Sts., tel. 415/921–9406. From Montgomery BART/MUNI Station, walk 1 block southwest on Market St. to 3rd St., take Bus 30 to Broderick and Chestnut Sts., walk 1 block south on Broderick St., and turn left. 38 rooms.

➤ **UNDER $100** • **Art Center Bed and Breakfast.** Staying here is like visiting your country uncle, if you have one that paints. The inn, near the Presidio and Union Street, is filled with paintings and art-related knickknacks. If you like to take brush to canvas yourself, the proprietors will be glad to set up an easel for you, and they've got a very inspirational garden in back. Two studios and a pair of two-room suites ($85–$95) all have double beds, TV and radio, microwave ovens, hot plates, and refrigerators. A three-room apartment with the same amenities runs $125 for two people. The owners like to call this place a country inn with a city built

Haight, Castro, and Mission Lodging

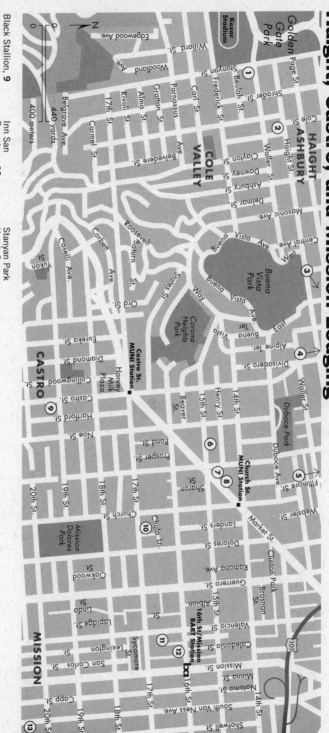

around it; when you see it you'll understand why. *1902 Filbert St., at Laguna St., tel. 415/567–1526. From Embarcadero BART/MUNI Station, take Bus 41 to Laguna St., walk 1 block north on Laguna St., and turn left. Reserve 1–2 weeks in advance in summer.*

HAIGHT-ASHBURY AND WESTERN ADDITION

All kinds of rock bands (the Dead, Jefferson Airplane), poets (Allen Ginsberg), psycho cult families (the Mansons), and runaway hippie children have settled in the Haight at various times, and it remains a fun, eclectic neighborhood. Staying here will give you a great introduction to how the post-college set lives in San Francisco, and it puts you close to other alternative neighborhoods like the Castro and the Mission.

> **UNDER $55 • Metro Hotel.** This hotel, whose neon sign lights up a major street near the Haight, is a good middle-range option. Sometimes, rock bands scheduled to play at nearby clubs stay here. The whole place was recently redone and the 23 rooms are large and comfortable. Try to get a room in the back, away from the street noise. Singles and doubles each cost $45 (add $10 for a third person). *319 Divisadero St., btw Oak and Page Sts., tel. 415/861–5364. From Market St. downtown, take Bus 7 or 71 to Divisadero and Haight Sts.; walk north on Divisadero St. 1½ blocks. Luggage storage. Reservations recommended in summer.*

The Haight has strict zoning codes limiting hotel construction. Only a few hotels have survived the bureaucratic red tape, and those that have are able to exploit you, since there's a high demand and short supply—remember Chapter One of your economics book?

> **UNDER $85 • The Grove Inn.** This reasonably priced B&B near Alamo Square, only blocks from the Opera House, provides a quiet refuge from the bustle of the city. Double rooms with private bath ($75) or shared bath ($65) are furnished with real and faux antiques; singles ($50) share a bath. Though the neighborhood isn't the safest, this is a great, personable alternative to bigger, uglier, and equally expensive chain motels in the area. *890 Grove St., at Fillmore St., tel. 415/929–0780. From Market St. downtown, take Bus 21 to Hayes and Fillmore Sts.; walk 1 block north on Fillmore St. Reservations recommended.*

Stanyan Park Hotel. So your bell-bottoms reek of stale incense, you've been humming Led Zeppelin songs for days, and your eyes will quit on you if you have to look at anything else tie-dyed.

Sappho Watches Over Her Sisters

Just arrived in San Francisco and haven't got a place to stay? In transition from temporary housing to something more permanent? Traveling through the city and need a safe, affordable room for the night in a single-sex environment? Then, if you're female, head immediately to Sappho's (859 Fulton St., near Fillmore St., tel. 415/775–3243). This women's residence, a seven-bedroom Victorian house in the Western Addition, serves a unique and important purpose: to provide a secure, welcoming space for single women who need a temporary home for the night or the week or the month (they have monthly rates October–April). Not only do you get a bed in a two- or three-person room for $15 a night, but they also provide resources to help you find employment and housing. Guests have use of a shared kitchen, outdoor barbecue pit, and meditation garden. If you get lucky, you may share quarters with an all-girl punk band or lesbian film directors in town for the film festival. They have some rules (no men upstairs, limited smoking areas, clean up after yourself), but they're all meant to enhance the feeling of comfort and cooperation: The ultimate aim is to bring together women of different ethnicities, economic backgrounds, and sexualities to learn from and support one another.

You need a healthy dose of Victorian furniture, brass fixtures, and intelligible conversation. This hotel on the eastern edge of Golden Gate Park can provide a respite from the Haight's craziness, but you'll pay $78 for a standard single or double. The rooms are immaculate and the service agreeable. *750 Stanyan St., btw Waller and Beulah Sts., tel. 415/751–1000. From Market St. downtown, take Bus 71 to Haight and Stanyan Sts., walk 2 blocks south on Stanyan St. 36 rooms. Wheelchair access. Reservations recommended.*

➤ **UNDER $100** • **The Red Victorian.** At this immensely popular Haight Street relic, each room is decorated according to a particular theme. Come here if you want to crash in the Japanese Tea Garden Room ($96), the Summer of Love Room (complete with a tie-dye canopy and authentic '60s posters; $86), or the Skylight Room (painted in deep jewel tones and featuring a skylighted ceiling; $86). Some rooms are more gimmicky than others, but it's clear from the moment you walk in that the proprietors take great care with every aspect of this place, from the quirky decorative touches to the warmth of the employees. *1665 Haight St., btw Belvedere and Cole Sts., tel. 415/864–1978. From Market St. downtown, take Bus 7 or 71 to Haight and Cole Sts. 17 rooms, most with shared bath. Reservations recommended in summer.*

CASTRO DISTRICT The most prominent gay neighborhood in the country naturally offers a wide variety of gay and lesbian accommodations. Although the ones right near Castro Street are pricey, a couple on upper Market shouldn't totally wipe you out. Reserve way, way, way in advance near the time of the Gay and Lesbian Freedom Day Parade (end of June) and near Halloween, when revelers from all over converge at Castro and Market streets to dance the night away.

➤ **UNDER $55** • **Twin Peaks.** If you don't mind heavy traffic outside and a distinct odor (curry powder? bad incense?) wafting through the halls, you can get a great deal here: Doubles are just $38 ($45 with private bath). The decor is nondescript (early Motel 6), but firm beds and clean bathrooms more than compensate. They also have weekly rates of $135–$170, depending on room size. You should be able to get a room any time, but they recommend calling first, and you may need to reserve in advance around Gay and Lesbian Freedom Day and Halloween. *2160 Market St., btw Church and Sanchez Sts., tel. 415/621–9467. From any BART/MUNI station downtown, take MUNI K, L, or M to Church St. Station, and walk 1 block southwest on Market St. 60 rooms.*

Perramont Hotel. At press time, this hotel was under renovation, but it's set to reopen in early 1995 with refurbished rooms for less than $50. It's situated right on Market Street, two blocks north of Harvey Milk Plaza. Call ahead for specific info. *2162 Market St., btw Church and Sanchez Sts., tel. 415/863–3222. From any BART/MUNI station downtown, take MUNI K, L, or M to Church St. Station, and walk one block southwest on Market St.*

➤ **UNDER $85** • **House O'Chicks.** This women-only guest house, two blocks from Harvey Milk Plaza, is an incredible find for a distinctive clientele. The people who run it also live here (the first thing they say when you arrive is "Welcome to our home"); and they prefer to talk to you over the phone to make sure you'll enjoy the atmosphere, which is artsy, homey, very sex-positive, and very gay-positive. Each of the three rooms (two are usually available for guests) has a custom-made mattress, a TV, and a stereo with CDs; they all share a bath. Rates are $50 per single, $75 per double; near Gay and Lesbian Freedom Day, though, you'll pay $100 for a double. *2162 15th St., btw Market and Noe Sts., tel. 415/861–9849. From any BART/MUNI station downtown, take MUNI K, L, or M to Church St. Station; walk 1 block southwest on Market St. to 15th St. and turn right. Call for reservations.*

Each room at the House O'Chicks has a TV and VCR, and you get access to their collection of films, including plenty of lesbian porn. The women-only hotel welcomes lesbian honeymooners.

➤ **UNDER $100** • **The Black Stallion.** The city's only leather-and-Levi's B&B provides gay men, as well as a few lesbians and adventurous straight couples, with an immaculate, comfortable home base from which to explore the Castro and San Francisco. The hotel, situated three blocks south of Harvey Milk Plaza, has nine rooms ($85–$110, depending on the season and room size), which

179

feature a variety of original artwork and sculptures, as well as gorgeous woodwork and one working fireplace. None has a private bathroom, though. Room rates include a hearty breakfast and unlimited use of the kitchen and sun deck. Reserve way in advance for summer and Halloween. *635 Castro St., at 19th St., tel. 415/863-0131. From any BART/MUNI station downtown, take MUNI K, L, or M to Castro St. Station, and walk south 2 blocks on Castro St.*

MISSION DISTRICT This lively, colorful neighborhood is home to the city's burgeoning Mexican and Central American communities, as well as a sizable population of lesbians and young, politically radical types. It's not the safest part of San Francisco, but right now it's a hotbed of experimental, bohemian life.

➣ **UNDER $40** • **Curtis Hotel.** The Mission has its share of shady characters, but the owner of this hotel works hard to keep the riffraff out. That means a lot of rules, such as "no loud disturbing noises after 9 PM," as well as a ban on alcohol and parties. Still, if you can hold your reveling tendencies in check, a sweet deal awaits: A clean single room with shared bath is just $85 a week (they have no doubles). Guests must pay in advance (checks are not accepted) and flash a picture ID. If you get too wild, the owner will throw you back out on the street. Yikes. *5595 Valencia St., near 16th St., tel 415/621-9337. From Mission/16th St. BART, walk one block west on 16th St., turn left on Valencia. 50 rooms. $2 key deposit.*

Eula Hotel. The drab purple carpets and musty rooms are a turnoff, and the management wins no hospitality points, but this hotel's location in the heart of the Mission makes it worth considering. Single rooms are $30, doubles just $35. *6031 16th St., btw Mission and Valencia Sts., tel. 415/621-6847. From Mission/16th St. BART, walk 1 block west on 16th St. 22 rooms, most with shared bath.*

➣ **UNDER $85** • **Dolores Park Inn.** If you want to do it up right without confining yourself to a stuffy part of town, come to this lovely B&B on a sedate street between the Mission and the Castro, one block north of Mission Dolores Park. A Victorian home built in 1874, it's quiet, restful, and almost entirely furnished with antiques. You can get a single room for $65; doubles run $75–$155, and all rooms give you access to the beautiful garden and parlor. The price includes a full breakfast. *3641 17th St., near Dolores St., tel. 415/621-0482. From any BART/MUNI station downtown, take MUNI J to 16th and Church Sts., walk 1 block south on Church St. to 17th St., and turn left. 5 rooms.*

The Inn San Francisco. Even though you'll probably only be able to afford a small room with shared bath, this sumptuous Victorian-style hotel in an unremarkable section of the Mission is flabbergastingly lovely—you'll be glad you came all the way out here to stay. The entire place is furnished with antiques, crystal, stained glass, and Oriental carpets, and each room is decorated differently. The smaller ones feature various color schemes with fancy touches, while the larger ones have such extras as a sun deck, a fireplace, a Jacuzzi, or a claw-foot bathtub. Other perks include a big breakfast in the morning, a peaceful garden with a gazebo and hot tub, and a parlor with complimentary sherry. Rooms with shared bath start at $75; those with private bath start at $95 (and go up to $195). *943 S. Van Ness Ave., near 21st St., tel. 415/641-0188. From the 24th and Mission BART Station, walk 1 block east to S. Van Ness Ave., then 3 blocks north.*

HOSTELS

You should definitely make reservations before you arrive in San Francisco. Hostels affiliated with American Youth Hostels (AYH), the American branch of Hostelling International (HI), offer a certain welcome predictability, but private hostels are often cheaper, and you'll meet a more eclectic crowd.

AYH Hostel at Union Square. A block from Union Square, this huge hostel sleeps more than 220 people in rooms with one to four beds ($15 a bed for members, $18 for nonmembers). The interior is bright and pleasant, and the hostel includes such amenities as a TV room and a kitchen (with microwaves, toasters, and refrigerators). Bulletin boards offer info on nightlife and other San Francisco attractions. About 20% of the rooms are set aside for reservations; you must reserve at least 48 hours in advance and you can stay a maximum of six days in high season, 14 days otherwise. *312 Mason St., btw O'Farrell and Geary Sts., tel. 415/788-5604.*

*From Powell St. BART/MUNI Station, walk 2 blocks north on Powell St., 1 block west on O'Far-
rell St., and turn right. No curfew, no lockout. Wheelchair access.*

European Guest House. A good choice for those who want to take advantage of the nightlife in
SoMa (South of Market), this mid-size hostel offers decent if unspectacular lodging in four-person dorms ($12 per person) or rooms sleeping two ($14 per person). It's got a sun roof, a common room, and a kitchen, and there's no curfew. *761 Minna St., near Mission St. btw 8th and
9th Sts., tel. 415/861–6634. From Civic Center BART/MUNI Station, walk 2 blocks down 8th
St. and turn right. Laundry.*

Ft. Mason International Hostel. This AYH hostel, perched high above the waterfront, will dazzle you with its views of the bay and the Golden Gate Bridge. The rules are tedious and complex, however, so pay close attention. It's almost impossible to stay here unless you reserve.
Reservations (by phone or in person) must be made at least 24 hours in advance with a credit
card, or by sending the cost of your first night's stay at least two weeks prior to your arrival, with
the names and genders of the people in your party and the dates you intend to stay. Get here
really early if you don't have a reservation. Beds are $14 a night for both members and non-
members. During summer you can stay a maximum of 14 nights. There's no curfew, but you've
got to perform a chore each day, and smoking is not allowed. Whew. *Bldg. 240, Box A, Ft.
Mason 94123, tel. 415/771–7277. From Transbay Terminal, take Bus 42 to Van Ness Ave.
150 beds. No curfew, lockout 11 AM–3 PM. Reception open daily 7 AM–2 PM and 3 PM–midnight. Laundry, free bike and luggage storage, kitchen, common room, free linen.*

Globetrotter's Inn. Its lack of restrictions (curfew, chores, etc.) and small size (it sleeps only 39
people) are among the strengths of this independent hostel on the edge of the down-and-out
Tenderloin district. It's not as new or sunny as some of the others, but the staff has done its
best, putting artwork on the walls and creating a comfortable common space with a TV, plants,
and a 24-hour kitchen. A space in a double or a four- or six-person dorm costs $12; singles are
$24. Lots of young people stay here while looking for a more permanent situation, and the bul-
letin board lists job openings on a regular basis. *225 Ellis St., btw Mason and Taylor Sts., tel.
415/346–5786. From Powell St. BART/MUNI Station, walk 1 block north on Powell St. and
1½ blocks west on Ellis St.*

Grand Central Hostel. The transformation of this flophouse-turned-hostel, in a central but
seedy location, has been snazzily accomplished. Dorms are $12 a night, or $65 a week in winter; singles run $20 a night, doubles $30. Other perks include an exercise room, unlimited free
coffee, all kinds of social events, free linen, a pool table, a jukebox, table tennis, and TV rooms.
Americans must have a passport or travel documents to stay here. *1412 Market St., at 10th
and Fell Sts., tel. 415/703–9988. From Van Ness MUNI Station, walk 1 block northeast on
Market St. 122 rooms. No curfew, no lockout. 21-day maximum stay.*

Green Tortoise Guest House. One of the best hostels in San Francisco, Green Tortoise is smack-
dab in the middle of hip North Beach, just blocks from the Financial District and Chinatown.
Cool Euro-backpackers inhabit most of the rooms, which are clean, spacious, and rarely vacant—call ahead. There's no curfew or lockout, and the managers are friendly and laid-back.
A single bunk is only $12, and a private double is $35. *494 Broadway, btw Columbus Ave. and
Kearny St., 5 blocks north of TransAmerica Pyramid, tel. 415/834–9060. 40 rooms. Laundry,
kitchen, common rooms, sauna.*

Interclub Globe Hostel. Intended for international travelers (you can be American, but you've
got to have a passport), this South-of-Market hostel has fewer rules and a warmer, more relaxed
atmosphere than some others. Not only that, they've got a pool table and a sun deck with a
great view of the city. The hostel is freshly painted in vibrant colors, with pages from slick German art magazines stuck on the walls. Guests sleep four to a room, and each room has a bathroom; there's one floor for nonsmokers. A bed is $15 in summer, $10 in winter, and $12
during spring and fall. Check out the SoMa map on the bulletin board, which shows you where
to find the good bars, cafés, and restaurants. An adjoining café serves cheap meals. *10 Hallam Pl., near Folsom St. btw 7th and 8th Sts., tel. 415/431–0540. From Civic Center
BART/MUNI Station, walk 3 blocks down 8th St. to Folsom St., turn left, and go ½ block to
Hallam Pl. No curfew, laundry.*

Pacific Tradewinds. The antithesis of an institutional hostel, this homey place in Chinatown has only four rooms (with a total of 28 beds), plus a warm common space and a kitchen. There's no official lockout (although they like people to be gone during the afternoon), and if you want to come in after midnight, the proprietors will give you a key. They'll also share all kinds of information with you about cheap restaurants and other attractions in the area. Beds are usually $14 a night, but the price fluctuates, so call ahead. The maximum stay is 14 days, though you may be able to negotiate a longer one. *680 Sacramento St., near Kearny St., tel. 415/433–7970. Luggage storage.*

Youth Hostel Centrale. If you look up the word "dive" in the dictionary, you'll find this hostel, whose bright new awning only amplifies the surrounding squalor. Weigh carefully the pros and cons of spending $14 for one person, $24 for two. The 18 rooms are private, but you share a bath. Wash your hands after you touch the doorknob. *166 Turk St., btw Taylor and Jones Sts., tel. 415/346–7835. From Powell St. BART/MUNI Station, walk 1 block southwest on Market St., 1½ blocks east on Turk St.*

CAMPGROUNDS

In the city, forget about pitching a tent. If you want to camp, head out of San Francisco, especially north or south on Route 1 along the coast. In a little over half an hour, you should find some spectacular pockets of nature (*see* Marin County and The South Bay in Chapter 2).

San Francisco RV Park. This is as close as you'll get to a campground inside city limits, though the South-of-Market location is more concrete jungle than natural paradise. You can't use a tent here, but you can hook up your recreational vehicle at one of the 200 sites. Rates are $34 a night, less in winter. *250 King St., tel. 415/986–8730. Store, laundromat, propane; city tours and car rental available.*

LONGER STAYS

So you think you want to stay a while? Monthly rents in San Francisco can range from $250 for a closet in an eight-bedroom house, to $350–$450 for an average room, to $500–$850 for studios and one-bedrooms. Still want to stay? If so, there are several ways to find a place to live in the city. If you need a whole apartment or house, investigate the classified ads in the *San Francisco Chronicle* and *San Francisco Examiner,* or visit a rental agency with private listings. **Community Rentals** (470 Castro St., tel. 415/552–8868; 1724 Sacramento St., tel. 415/474–2787), for example, provides about 1,400 listings of apartments, flats, and houses in San Francisco. You tell them what you're looking for (price range, neighborhood, type of housing) and they give you listings, each with about a quarter-page of info. Their fee is $75 for two months, $50 of which is refundable if you don't find a place through them. San Francisco's neighborhoods are each quite distinctive, and you can pick from an array of lifestyles—the sanitized hipness of North Beach, home of MTV's *Real World*; the grunge-hippie fusion thang over in the Haight; the gay culture of the Castro district; or the city's new bohemian hangout, the Mission district.

Industrious folks with a room for rent will often stick up a little flyer, with 10 to 15 adjectives strung together ("Bass-playing, cat-owning vegetarian household seeks gay, guitar-playing, nonsmoking, spiritual roommate for jam sessions and hearty soup . . . ") in order to find their soul (room)mate.

One of the cheapest ways to find an apartment is simply by walking. Many landlords with places to rent post FOR RENT signs in the windows, with details about the apartment and a phone number to call. The best strategy is to settle on a neighborhood that you like and walk the streets, jotting down the numbers and addresses of places for rent, and then calling to set up appointments to see them.

If all you're looking for is a sublet, or a room in someone else's apartment, you've got all kinds of options. Struggling artists and musicians and other poor folks often take their chances with the bulletin boards that appear in just about every café in the city. Another free way to find roommates is at **Rainbow Grocery** (*see* Specialty Markets and Delicatessens, in Chapter 4). A set of file boxes at the store contains listings, both sublet and long-term, for politically left types with their futons on their backs and their cats in a cage.

Those who can spend a little money to find a home often have good luck with one of the roommate referral agencies in town. For a fee of $25–$50, these agencies will give you access to computer listings of places with vacant rooms, tailored to your price range, personality, room requirements, food preferences, music tastes, neuroses, and whatever else you and your potential housemates want to declare about yourselves. Most agencies let you view the listings for as long as it takes to find a good living situation, and they provide as much as a page of information about each. Agencies include the **Original S.F. Roommate Referral Service** (610A Cole St., at Haight St., tel. 415/558–9191), which charges $34 for four months of service; **Great Roommates Etc.** (552 Castro St., Suite B, btw 18th and 19th Sts., tel. 415/626–1542), which charges $30 for three months; and **Roommate Network** (3129 Fillmore St., near Union St., tel. 415/441–2309), which charges $50 for indefinite use to "working professionals." Many people also find roommates through the classified ads under "Shared Housing" in the *Bay Guardian* and *S.F. Weekly.*

East Bay

BERKELEY

Lodging in Berkeley is either shabby or downright expensive—sometimes both. Most of the city's motels are on **University Avenue,** west of campus. Your life isn't necessarily in danger here, but don't expect much more than red velvet curtains, the reek of cheap perfume, and a prostitute to share a balcony conversation with. In general, it's best to stick to the part of University Avenue close to campus; the farther west you go, the shoddier the surroundings become. If you're not concerned about price or atmosphere, you can always settle for the generic blue-and-white **Travelodge** (1820 University Ave., tel. 510/843–4262), three blocks from campus, where basic, very clean doubles start at $76. To reach the motels on University Avenue from Berkeley BART, either walk two blocks north to University and head west, or let Bus 51 carry you to your destination.

In mid-May, when thousands of graduating Berkeley students don their caps and gowns, reservations for nearly all motels and hotels become *absolutely* essential. Most of the nicer places sell out four to five months in advance. All lodgings add 12% tax to the prices listed below.

Berkeley has no youth hostels, but the **YMCA** (2001 Allston Way, tel. 510/848–6800)—open to both men and women—is cheap and within easy reach of Berkeley's sights. Its 88 dorm-style singles go for $25 a night and are available on a first-come, first-served basis. You share a common bathroom, so leave your modesty at home. After 14 days of "residence," you're eligible to stay longer at around $100 a week.

➤ **UNDER $55** • **Berkeley Motel.** The dank rooms ($46 a night) have no phones, but you're within easy walking distance of Shattuck Avenue's stores and restaurants, and Berkeley BART is only three blocks away. If you can deal with grimy beds and foul-smelling bathrooms, go for it. Reservations are required. *2001 Bancroft Way, at Milvia St., tel. 510/843–4043. From Berkeley BART, walk 2 blocks south to Bancroft Way and 1 block west to Milvia St.*

Campus Motel. If you get your jollies from good hygiene, check out this motel, just a few blocks farther west on University Avenue than the Motel Flamingo (*see below*). Bedspreads and curtains look and feel freshly laundered, you could eat off the bathroom floor, and dust is tackled by the ultra-competent cleaning staff before it even has a chance to settle. Singles are $45, doubles $50. *1619 University Ave., btw McGee Ave. and California St., tel. 510/841–3844. 23 rooms.*

Capri Motel. The owner/manager of this motel tries hard to keep it cleaner and safer than its graffiti-covered neighbors on this section of University Avenue. Singles go for $36 and doubles for $45. Rooms are drab but neat, and you might actually enjoy taking a shower here—the bathroom scum is minimal. *1512 University Ave., at Sacramento St., tel. 510/845–7090. 26 rooms. Reservations recommended in summer.*

Golden Bear Motel. The nicest budget lodging in town is on the edge of Berkeley. All its rooms are clean, sunny, and show a modicum of taste. The surrounding neighborhood isn't very safe, so be wary walking around at night. Doubles with queen-size beds are $46, tax included. Bus 52 across the street will whisk you to the Berkeley campus. *1600 San Pablo Ave., tel. 510/525–6770. From Berkeley BART, take Bus 51 west on University Ave. to San Pablo Ave.; then transfer to Bus 72 going north on San Pablo Ave. or walk the 5 blocks. Luggage storage.*

Travel Inn. This pink motel is cheap, clean, and far enough from the street that you don't hear the noise. The spacious rooms are decorated with furniture probably purchased at a garage sale: putrid orange lamps with rusting bases and beds that seriously sag. But for 25¢, "Magic

Putting Up Mom and Dad

Going crazy trying to tidy up the apartment before the folks come into town? Forget the cleaning frenzy, keep the ashtrays in view, and book Mom and Pop into one of Berkeley's posh hotels. The popular Durant Hotel (2600 Durant Ave., tel. 510/845–8981), where doubles start at $97, is the closest to campus and the dorms. The lobby is quite elegant and the beds are big and comfy, though the dull earth-tone decor is a downer.

The frou-frou set will be delighted with Gramma's Rose Garden Inn (2740 Telegraph Ave., tel. 510/549–2145). As you open the little gates from grimy Telegraph Avenue, you enter a wonderland of chintz, flower beds, and cute stone paths. Doubles in the main house are $85; the surrounding cottages offer more spacious, higher-priced rooms ($125–$145). All rooms include a complimentary breakfast (champagne brunch on Sundays) and wine and cheese in the evenings.

The Berkeley City Club (2315 Durant Ave., tel. 510/848–7800), designed by Julia Morgan, wins the architecture award hands down. Its gorgeous high ceilings and Moorish/Gothic touches have made it a historical landmark. The rooms, sparsely furnished in neo-blah, are a let-down, but half of them boast bay views. The club offers a swimming pool and a fitness center. Doubles run $85, breakfast and parking included.

Doubles at the French Hotel (1538 Shattuck Ave., btw Cedar and Vine Sts., tel. 510/548–9930), North Berkeley's little Euro inn, go for $85 (they have one room for $68), and the location is prime. All rooms have a minuscule but sunny patio, and most come with a complimentary breakfast. Connected to the hotel is a hugely popular café, packed with yuppies slurping espresso. The surrounding neighborhood, nicknamed the "Gourmet Ghetto," overflows with bookstores and great restaurants.

If you really want luxury, check out the Claremont Resort, Spa, and Tennis Club (Ashby and Domingo Aves., tel. 510/843–3000), a striking all-white palace in the Oakland/Berkeley Hills. The prices will stun you as much as the building: Bay-view doubles go for $199 and hillside-view doubles for $179 (subtract $30 from rates if you're staying on Friday or the weekend). Ouch. As a guest, though, you can used the heated pools, saunas, whirlpools, and tennis courts.

Fingers" will do their thing to your bed. As the instructions explain, "It quickly carries you into the land of tingling relaxation and ease." How can you resist? Singles are $35, doubles $42. *1461 University Ave., btw Sacramento and Acton Sts., tel. 510/848–3840. 42 rooms.*

➤ **UNDER $65** • **Motel Flamingo.** Flanked by gray, run-down buildings on a gray, run-down street, this motel has bland rooms with a musty smell, faded bed covers, and orange-brown decor (imagine how it harmonizes with the Pepto Bismol–pink exterior). However, it's one of the closest motels to campus (five blocks west) and the manager Andy is helpful and enthusiastic. Singles are $55, doubles $60–$70 (prices go down $10 in the off-season). *1761 University Ave., at Grant St., tel. 510/841–4242. 29 rooms. Luggage storage.*

UNIVERSITY HOUSING University Guest Housing offers summer dorm accommodations on the Berkeley campus for $34–$44 per night. You'll most likely stay at **Stern Hall** (2700 Hearst Ave., at Highland Pl., tel. 510/642–9701), next to the Greek Theater on the northeast side of campus. It's a cut above the usual depressing Berkeley dorm: The rooms are standard (bed, desk, chair), but the upstairs has a comfy lounge with piano, and the downstairs features a rec room with a pool table, ping pong, and a vending machine. The dorm is pretty quiet, and you can buy breakfast in the dining hall. Reservations are required. If you call early enough (a month before you arrive) you can probably live in the dorms all summer (June–Aug.), as long as you're prepared to pay that much.

LONGER STAYS Every fall, thousands of Berkeley students scramble to find a place to live. Those that hit the jackpot with a cheap apartment or room close to campus are too wise to give it up come summer vacation. Their solution is to sublet the space (at about two-thirds the normal rent) to people like yourself. Look for sublets in the *Daily Cal,* the weekly *East Bay Express,* or the *East Bay Guardian,* all free publications available in most cafés around Bancroft and Telegraph avenues. A number of cafés, including **Café Milano** (near cnr Telegraph and Bancroft avenues), have large bulletin boards boasting a glorious mess of flyers and scraps of paper with apartment listings. **Sproul Plaza,** on the Berkeley campus, is another bulletin-board resource.

Berkeley students with ID can go to the **Housing and Dining Services** office for free (2401 Bowditch St., tel. 510/642–3106) and ask to see rental listings. If you get tired of bearing the burden on your own, try a rental agency like **The Berkeley Connection** (2840 College Ave., tel. 510/845–7821), which charges $25–$50, or **Homefinders** (2158 University Ave., tel. 510/ 549–6450), which charges $55 for 30 days (if you don't find a place in that time, you get a $30 refund). These companies will give you a long list of properties for rent in the area; for short-term housing, however, you're better off looking on your own.

Another option for longer stays are the student-owned and -operated co-ops. Inquire at the **University Students' Cooperative Association** (2424 Ridge Rd., tel. 510/848–1936) about what's available. The co-ops are open to students from any college, and for $700–$1,200 you can stay in them all summer (mid-May–mid-Aug.). Ask about the all-vegetarian **Lothlorien** (2405 and 2415 Prospect St., tel. 510/540–9200), southeast of campus, where you can frolic with hippies in the Jacuzzi, or the nearby women-only **Sherman Hall** (2250 Prospect St., tel. 510/540–9220), one of the cleanest and best-maintained co-ops. Also worth looking into are **Rochdale Village** (2424 Haste St., tel. 510/548–8608) and the **Northside Co-op** (2526 and 2540 Le Conte Ave., no phone), both co-ops/apartment villages. If you're not a student, you may be able to bend the rules a little by wandering into one of the larger co-ops, like grimy **Cloyne Court** (2600 Ridge Rd., tel. 510/549–6300). Feign desperation, share whatever you have on you, and you may be offered someone's floor space for a while.

If you can stand dirt, loud music, a plain room (just a bed and a desk), and frat guys, Berkeley's fraternities offer cheap summer lodging.

Berkeley's **fraternities** are also up for grabs in the summer. The price is, in their lingo, stylin': Generally you'll have to fork out only about $500 for the whole summer. The fraternities lie southeast of campus, on and around Piedmont and Channing avenues. You can try calling, but generally no one answers the house phone; you're better off just scouting the neighborhood on foot. Head east up Bancroft, turn right at Piedmont, and start your hunting (fraternities often advertise by hanging a big sign on their house). When something catches your eye, knock on the door and ask for the house manager. Scope out the bathrooms and kitchens—one glance should tell you if the place is livable. The list of frats that rent rooms changes every summer, so stop by **102 Sproul Hall** (Sproul Plaza, at Bancroft and Telegraph Aves., tel. 510/642–5171) for a complete list of addresses and phone numbers. **Sigma Chi** (2345 College Ave., tel. 510/540–9148) has recently been renovated and is nicer than most.

OAKLAND

Oakland's budget lodging scene isn't a pretty sight, price-wise or safety-wise. Hotels are either geared toward businesspeople on expense accounts, or they're smack in the middle of a grimy, scary neighborhood. If you're sniffing around for a budget bed, you should probably go back to Berkeley. Of course, if you're desperate, hundreds of faceless chain motels ($50–$75 a night) can give you a room in downtown Oakland and around the airport. Sad to say, Oakland has no youth hostels.

Along West MacArthur Boulevard, near the MacArthur BART Station in North Oakland, there's a string of motels used for illicit, after-hours business transactions. Women should not stay here alone. On West MacArthur east of Telegraph, you'll find a few reasonably priced motels in semi-safe surroundings. Check out the **Imperial Inn** (490 W. MacArthur Blvd., at Telegraph Ave., tel. 510/653–4225), where mediocre singles go for $30, doubles for $35.

➤ **UNDER $40** • **Avondale Residence Hotel.** In central Oakland, this place offers singles only, but the price is unbeatable: $20–$30 for a room with private bath. The manager is extremely gracious, but rooms can be noisy at night. You should watch out for yourself here, although the neighborhood is relatively safe compared to some other parts of Oakland. *540 28th St., tel. 510/832–9769. From Berkeley, take Telegraph Ave. into Oakland, turn right on 28th St. 57 rooms. Laundry, parking.*

Broadway Motel. It's a grimy dirtbag of a place, but at least it's in a reasonably safe neighborhood. Avoid the grungy upstairs rooms. Singles run $30, doubles $32. Across the street is Dave's Coffee Shop, a hopping 24-hour diner where your cup of coffee is refilled incessantly and the waitresses sport bouffant do's. *4140 Broadway, at 41st St., tel. 510/653–0458. From downtown Oakland, take Bus 51 north on Broadway and get off at 41st St.*

➤ **UNDER $55** • **Civic Center Lodge.** This lodge is a proud member of Oakland's exclusive "centrally-located-and-cheap" club, within easy reach of the waterfront, Lake Merritt, and the downtown bars and restaurants. It offers basic, no-frills doubles for $48; singles are $38. *50 6th St., tel. 510/444–4139. From Lake Merritt BART, walk down Oak St. to 6th St. and turn left. 32 rooms.*

➤ **UNDER $65** • **Travelodge.** Smack up against Chinatown, and within walking distance of Lake Merritt, downtown Oakland, and the waterfront, the Travelodge rents basic and dark but clean rooms with queen-size beds for $64. Your view is of rooftops, antennae, and the like. *423 7th St., tel. 510/451–6316. From 12th St. BART, walk south 6 blocks on Broadway. 130 rooms. Free parking. Wheelchair access.*

CAMPING You can camp at one of the 75 sites at **Anthony Chabot Regional Park** (tel. 510/562–CAMP), east of Oakland. Tent sites are $13 a night, hookups $18; you also have to fork over a $4 reservations charge. The place puts up traveling backpackers and hippies, but it's never too crowded. The sites are about a mile from Lake Chabot, and a 9-mile trail meanders around the lake (*see* Chapter 8). You need your own wheels to get here. From downtown Oakland, take I–580 east toward Castro Valley to the Redwood Road exit. Turn left as you get off the highway and follow Redwood Road for about 4½ miles to the park gate. Once you enter, it's another 2½ miles to the campground.

Marin County

Hotel accommodations definitely don't come cheap in Marin. The best way to keep enough money in your pocket for a cup of coffee is to spend the night in the great outdoors. If you've got cash to spare, though, the **Bed and Breakfast Exchange of Marin** (contact Suellen Lamorte, tel. 415/485–1971) offers a helpful service, booking either brief or extended stays in private homes and bed-and-breakfasts for $55–$150. She can also set you up in a houseboat.

ALONG U.S. 101

SAUSALITO While hundreds of tourists crowd Sausalito's streets during the day, all but the richest have to find somewhere else to spend the night. Unless you're prepared to pay astronomical prices for a view of the bay, head elsewhere—preferably to the hostel in nearby Ft. Barry (*see below*).

➢ **UNDER $85 • Alta Mira Continental Hotel.** This Spanish-style hotel in the Sausalito hills offers amazing views of the bay, but you'll pay dearly for them. Doubles without views start at $70; rooms with a view will set you back anywhere from $115 to $170. If you're relegated to one of the cheaper rooms, you can still enjoy a view of the bay by having a drink on the terrace. The stately rooms are tastefully decorated with antiques, and all rooms come with TV and telephones. *125 Bulkley Ave., tel. 415/332–1350. From U.S. 101, take the Sausalito exit and follow signs to Sausalito's Bridgeway Ave. Turn right at Princess Ave. (the 9th light) and go 3 blocks. 28 rooms. Reservations recommended.*

➢ **HOSTEL • Golden Gate AYH-Hostel.** Built in 1907, this hostel is only a five-minute drive from the Golden Gate Bridge in historic Ft. Barry. Set amid the beaches and forest of the headlands, the hostel has a communal kitchen, a laundry room, a tennis court, and a common room with a fireplace. Beds cost $9 a night and are often available at the last minute, but call at least one week in advance if you have your heart set on staying. Membership is not required. If you're coming from San Francisco on Golden Gate Transit, catch the Sausalito bus and ask to be let off at the bottom of the Alexander Avenue off-ramp; from there it's a 3-mile hike to the headlands. *Ft. Barry, Bldg. 941, tel. 415/331–2777. From U.S. 101, take Alexander Ave. exit, cross under freeway, and make first right after MARIN HEADLANDS sign. After 1 mi, turn right on McCullough Rd., left on Bunker Rd., and follow signs to hostel. 66 beds. No curfew.*

TIBURON AND ANGEL ISLAND Not surprisingly, expensive Tiburon offers no reasonably priced lodging. If you don't want to head down to the Golden Gate Hostel, a few miles south (*see* Sausalito, *above*), consider a ferry trip to Angel Island for a night of camping.

➢ **CAMPING • Angel Island State Park.** Get away from it all without losing sight of good old San Francisco. Nine showerless environmental campsites ($9 per night) lie at the end of a 2-mile hike on Angel Island. The views of San Francisco are amazing, and the campground is usually only about half full, so you won't feel claustrophobic. For directions to Angel Island, *see* Tiburon and Angel Island, in Chapter 2. *Tel. 415/435–1915 for info, 800/444–PARK for reservations. Barbecue grills, pit toilets, running water.*

MILL VALLEY AND CORTE MADERA Staying in Mill Valley gives you easy access to Muir Woods, Mt. Tamalpais, and coastal Route 1. But as long as you're this close, why not push on to Mt. Tam's more scenic Steep Ravine cabins and campsites (*see below*)?

➢ **UNDER $85 • HoJo Inn.** Corte Madera's branch of the Howard Johnson motel-and-coffee-shop chain provides clean, comfortable rooms and efficient service. A tiny rose garden, colorful flower pots, and small children (the owners' kids) playing in the parking lot lend the place a bit of character. During the week, rooms sleeping two are $59, and rooms with two double beds are $69, but be prepared for prices to change according to season, day of the week, position of the moon, whatever (add $10 on weekends). Rooms come with TV, telephone, a small refrigerator, and occasionally a microwave. *1595 Casa Buena Dr., Corte Madera, tel. 415/924–3570. Off U.S. 101 at the Paradise/Tamalpais exit. 18 rooms.*

Travelodge. Yes, you've seen them along the freeways, but this one's a little different—it's actually kind of attractive. The bleached-wood exterior gives it a beachy feel, despite the fact that a small marsh is the closest body of water. The interior is typical of the chain, and you'll fall asleep to the sound of cars rushing by. Singles cost $63, doubles $73. *707 Redwood Hwy., Mill Valley, tel. 415/383–0340. From U.S. 101 south, take Seminary Dr. exit and turn right.*

SAN RAFAEL San Rafael is Marin County's most down-to-earth town, and boasts the region's best nightlife, stores, and cafés. While the hotels here could hardly be called budget, they're at least more reasonable than the options in the surrounding area.

➤ **UNDER $55** • **National 9 Inn.** This lavender motel differs little from the neighboring San Rafael Inn (*see below*) except in its color, the slightly lower price, and the absence of a pool. The managers are apathetic, but the rooms are clean. Singles run $45 and doubles are $50. Views of the freeway abound. *855 E. Francisco Blvd., tel. 415/456–8620 or 800/524–9999. From U.S. 101 north, take Francisco Blvd. exit, left on Bellum Blvd., left on E. Francisco Blvd. 18 rooms.*

Panama Hotel. You'll feel a million miles away here, which is why it's not uncommon for locals to use this hotel as an escape from the real world. The very private rooms are individually decorated, some with canopy queen beds and some with claw-foot tubs. All rooms come with TV, and some of the higher-priced ones offer kitchenettes and patios. The hotel restaurant has a mouthwatering menu and a beautiful outdoor area draped with wisteria. The owner is terrific, the setting is perfect, the location is convenient, and—most amazing—the prices are reasonable. Rooms without bath start at $45; those with bath range from $70 to $125. *4 Bayview St., tel. 415/457–3993. From U.S. 101 north, take Central San Rafael exit, left on 3rd St., left on B St., and go 4 mi to where it becomes Bayview St. 15 rooms, 9 with bath. Reservations recommended.*

➤ **UNDER $65** • **San Rafael Inn.** It's your basic generic pink motel, but the owners are friendly, the rooms are clean, and a pool and Jacuzzi lie right across the parking lot from your room. Singles run $52, doubles $56–$75, and all rooms come with telephones and TV (some have a mini-fridge). Request a room toward the back to avoid freeway noise. *865 E. Francisco Blvd., tel. 415/454–9470. Follow directions to National 9 Inn (see above). 32 rooms. Wheelchair access.*

➤ **UNDER $85** • **425 Mission.** This wood-shingled cottage, an easy walk from old San Rafael, offers homey rooms furnished with antiques, rosewood and wicker furniture, and the occasional claw-foot tub. The downstairs living room is a comfortable place to watch the news, listen to music, or read a book. You can hang out on the deck when the weather is nice. Rooms range from $70 to $95, and include a gourmet breakfast and use of a hot tub in the backyard. If you stay a while, the innkeeper will do your laundry for free, just like Mom. *425 Mission Ave., tel. 415/453–1365. From U.S. 101 north, take Central San Rafael exit, go 5 blocks to Mission Ave., and turn right. 4 rooms, 2 with bath. Reservations recommended.*

➤ **CAMPING** • **Back Ranch Meadows Campground.** The trappings of civilization fade as you enter the 1,600-acre China Camp State Park, only 4 miles northeast of San Rafael. Here you can pitch your tent at one of 30 walk-in campsites near San Pablo Bay. The sites aren't far from the parking lot, or from each other, but they're well sheltered by oak trees. Sites are $14 per night ($12 off-season). Call MISTIX (tel. 800/444–PARK) to reserve. *Tel. 415/456–0766. Take N. San Pedro Rd. exit east from U.S. 101 in San Rafael, and follow signs. Parking: $3. Hot water, showers, flush toilets, fire pits.*

COASTAL ROUTE 1

MT. TAMALPAIS In addition to Steep Ravine, you can also camp at the **Pantoll** site on Mt. Tamalpais (*see* Chapter 2).

➤ **CAMPING** • **Steep Ravine Campground and Cabins.** Off Route 1 in Mt. Tamalpais State Park, Steep Ravine has six walk-in campsites for $9 per night, and cabins (up to five people) for $30 per night. If you can deal with a pit toilet, this place is absolutely unbeatable—just you and a few other guests sharing almost the entire dramatic coast as far as the eye can see. Unfortunately, Steep Ravine is not an unknown gem, and the cabins book up well in advance. *Tel. 800/444–PARK for reservations. From U.S. 101, take Stinson Beach/Rte. 1 exit and follow Rte. 1 until you see signs.*

STINSON BEACH Stinson Beach is full of nauseatingly quaint bed-and-breakfasts that cost upward of $90 a night. Instead, head to the **Stinson Beach Motel** (3416 Rte. 1, tel. 415/

868–1712), which has inviting doubles starting at $60, all with private bath and set around a shady garden.

POINT REYES In addition to its excellent hostel, Point Reyes National Seashore has four free campgrounds, open to backpackers only, in isolated wilderness areas. You may have to hike in as far as 6 miles to reach one, but that's part of the appeal.

➤ **HOSTEL • Point Reyes AYH-Hostel.** Eight miles west of the Point Reyes Visitor Center, this hostel is popular with both foreign travelers and local college kids. It makes a great base camp for excursions onto the peninsula, and there are hundreds of hiking trails nearby. The hostel's two common rooms have wood-burning stoves and loads of reading material. Dorm beds cost $9 per night for members, $12 for nonmembers. Reservations are advised, but they're not accepted over the phone; either write (enclose a check or money order) or show up in person as early as possible. *Box 247, Point Reyes Station 94956, tel. 415/663–8811. From Rte. 1 in Olema, left (west) on Bear Valley Rd. 1 block beyond the stop sign. 1½ mi farther, left at LIGHT-HOUSE/BEACHES/HOSTEL sign, go 6 mi, and turn left on Crossroads Rd. Reception open daily 7:30–9:30 AM and 4:30–9:30 PM. 44 beds. Communal kitchen, linen rental, on-site parking.*

➤ **CAMPING •** To reserve campgrounds in Point Reyes, call the **Point Reyes Visitor Information Center** (tel. 415/663–1092) up to one month in advance on weekdays between 9 AM and noon. Trails to the campgrounds leave from the visitor center, which is on the entrance road (turn left off Rte. 1 just past Olema). All the sites have picnic tables and pit toilets, but none has running water or allows fires, so bring plenty of supplies and warm clothing.

It's a 3-mile hike from the youth hostel parking lot (*see above*) or a 9-mile trek from the visitor center to **Coast Camp,** but you'll sleep within a stone's throw of the water at any of the 15 sites. People tend to avoid **Glenn Camp** because it's 5 miles from the nearest road, but it's great if you don't mind the hike. Surrounded by trees in a quiet valley, the 12 sites feel thoroughly apart from the reek of civilization. The 16 sites at **Sky Camp** are the most popular at Point Reyes. You'll have to take a steep 2½-mile trail from the visitor center to get here, but the ranger can direct you to a pullout up the road that's a gentler 1-mile hike from the camp. The campground is perched on a small mountain ridge with an outstanding view of the peninsula and seashore. For the true misanthrope, **Wildcat Camp,** a gnarly 6½ miles from the nearest road, has 12 sites scattered in a dense thicket. Privacy is never a problem.

Samuel P. Taylor State Park. Six miles east of Point Reyes on Sir Francis Drake Boulevard, this park has 60 sites that go for $14 per night (hike/bike $3 per person). They feature—blessing of all blessings—hot showers, at 25¢ for 5 minutes. Reservations can be made through MISTIX (tel. 800/444–PARK); during summer, even weekdays get booked up. If you do get in, you're in for a treat of the redwood variety. Think about taking the hike up to Barnaby Peak (4–5 hrs round-trip). It's a beautiful campground and redwood grove, not as overrun as Muir Woods. Golden Gate Transit Bus 65 stops at the park on weekends and holidays (*see* Coming and Going by Bus, in Chapter 1). *Tel. 415/488–9897. Take U.S. 101 to Sir Francis Drake Blvd. exit, and go west on Sir Francis Drake Blvd. about 15 mi.*

The South Bay

Along U.S. 101, the South Bay embodies much of what California has become deservedly infamous for: strip malls, fast food, and endless strings of chain motels. You'll find these motels at just about every freeway off-ramp, and even the budget ones run $50–$70 for a double. You're much better off staying on the coast, or in the region's two excellent hostels. For longer stays, consult *The Metro,* which lists summer sublets and long-term rentals. College bulletin boards are also promising places to look for apartments; try Stanford's, in **Tressider Union.**

PALO ALTO

While Palo Alto isn't exactly thrilling, it's probably the most happening place to stay in the South Bay. Stanford University students support a good number of restaurants, bars, and cafés, all a little on the pricey side.

➤ **UNDER $55** • **Coronet Motel.** Traffic on El Camino Real makes this place noisy, but the Coronet wins points for location and value. It's only a few blocks from the university, and Stanford Shopping Center is a short drive away. Doubles are $44, singles $40, and the rooms are quite comfortable, if not exactly modern. *2455 El Camino Real, btw California Ave. and Page Mill Rd., tel. 415/326–1081. From U.S. 101 south, take Embarcadero Rd. exit west, turn left on El Camino Real. 21 rooms, 14 with kitchenette.*

Stanford Arms Motel. This old-California-style motel is less generic than most others in its price range, and it's conveniently located near the Stanford campus and the Stanford Shopping Center. The rooms are clean, if a bit tired-looking; singles go for $35 and doubles for about $38 ($2 extra for rooms with kitchenette). *115 El Camino Real, at Harvard St., Menlo Park, tel. 415/325–1428. From U.S. 101 south, take Embarcadero Rd. exit west to El Camino Real and turn right. 14 rooms.*

➤ **UNDER $100** • **Cowper Inn.** This Victorian bed-and-breakfast is the perfect place for your parents to stay when they're in town. The spacious rooms are filled with antiques, yet they retain a fresh and airy feeling. Doubles start at $55 with shared bath, $97 with private bath. Breakfast is included, and all rooms have phones and cable TV. Mom and Dad can relax with a glass of sherry in the parlor before heading out to take you to an expensive dinner. *705 Cowper St., tel. 415/327–4475. From U.S. 101 south, take University Ave. exit west 2–3 mi, turn left on Cowper St., and go 2 blocks. 14 rooms, 12 with bath. Reservations recommended.*

HOSTELS **Hidden Villa Hostel.** In the Los Altos Hills between Palo Alto and San Jose, this is an actual working farm—complete with animals and organic gardens. Set in a 1,500-acre canyon, the hostel offers easy access to hiking trails and peaceful dirt roads. Large rustic cabins dot the canyon, each with communal bathroom facilities. Bring your own food. Unfortunately, public transportation doesn't come anywhere near here. HI members pay $9 a night, nonmembers $12. *26870 Moody Rd., Los Altos, tel. 415/949–8648. From San Francisco, take I–280 south past Palo Alto to the El Monte/Moody Rd. exit, turn right (southwest) on El Monte Ave. and left on Moody Rd. at stop sign, and go 1.7 mi. Reception open daily 7:30 AM–9:30 AM and 4:30 PM–9:30 PM. Closed June–Aug.*

Sanborn Park Hostel. This hostel is one of the most beautiful in California, perfectly situated for avid hikers and easily reached by public transportation. The main cottage, a wooden cabin that dates from 1908, is surrounded by the dense redwood forest of Sanborn Park, also home to a nearby nature museum. Hostelers stay in a large hall and have access to a rec room, a volleyball court, a grill, laundry facilities, and the standard HI kitchen, all for a mere $7.50 (members) and $9.50 (nonmembers). It's a busy place, but they try to find room for anyone who shows up. You need to bring your own food; as the only restaurants and grocery stores are in Saratoga, 4 miles away. *15808 Sanborn Rd., Saratoga, tel. 408/741–0166. Take I–280 south to Saratoga/Sunnyvale exit, turn right, go 5½ mi to Rte. 9. Turn right (toward Big Basin), go 2½ mi, turn left at SANBORN SKYLINE COUNTY PARK sign, go 1 mi, and turn right. Otherwise, take Bus 54 from Sunnyvale Caltrain station, get off at Saratoga post office, and call hostel for a ride. Reception open daily 5 PM–11 PM. Curfew 11 PM, lockout 9–5. Rental sheets 50¢. Wheelchair access.*

THE SAN MATEO COUNTY COAST

The undiscovered coast south of San Francisco yields isolated beaches and some of the area's most striking scenery. Surprisingly, Half Moon Bay, the largest and most centrally located town, is not the best choice for accommodations, since all its offerings are quite expensive. Instead, head for the coast's two gorgeous hostels, either of which could easily make a claim to be the best lodging deal in the Bay Area.

PACIFICA AND MONTARA If the spots listed below are full, try the all-too-familiar **Day's Inn** (200 Rockaway Beach, tel. 415/359–7700 or 800/522–3772) on Rockaway Beach, half a mile north of Pacifica State Beach, which offers clean, large doubles starting at $55 on weekdays and $65 on weekends, including free continental breakfast.

➤ **UNDER $55** • **Marine View Motel.** With roomy doubles ($42) that include enough carpeted floor space for at least six, this run-down but acceptably clean motel is the best bet in Pacifica. For dealing with the slightly annoying noise from Route 1, you'll be rewarded with an easy walk to the beach and the old town. *2040 Francisco Blvd., Pacifica, tel. 415/355–9042. 14 rooms, some with wheelchair access. If manager is out, inquire in Room 7.*

Sea View Motor Lodge. Another version of Motel-6-by-the-Sea, the Sea View runs a couple bucks more than the Marine View (*see above*), which it closely resembles. Doubles are $45 on weekdays, $50 on weekends. *2160 Francisco Blvd., Pacifica, tel. 415/359–9494.*

➤ **HOSTEL** • **Point Montara Lighthouse AYH-Hostel.** This functioning lighthouse and its adjoining hostel are perched on a cliff offering incredible views of the coast, half a mile south of Montara State Beach off Route 1. The attraction of Point Montara Lighthouse reaches well beyond the usual audience for hostels: Expect anyone from San Franciscans on a weekend break to German travelers on a cross-country trek, and look for a few 40- and 50-year-olds scattered among the twentysomethings. The comfortable living room has a fireplace; and there's a communal kitchen, a dining area, even an outdoor redwood hot tub ($5 per person for half an hour, two-person minimum). Beds go for $9 ($12 nonmembers), and everyone must do a small chore. If you're taking the coastal bus from San Mateo or Daly City, tell the driver you're going to the hostel and the bus will drop you off within 100 feet. Reservations can be made anywhere from six months to three days in advance and are recommended for summer weekends. *Rte. 1 and 16th St., Montara, tel. 415/728–7177. Take SamTrans Bus 1L southbound from Daly City BART; ask driver to let you off at 14th St. 45 beds. Curfew 11 PM. Reception open daily 7:50–9:30 AM and 4:30–9:30 PM. Laundry, deposit of first night's fees required.*

HALF MOON BAY Lodging is quite expensive here. If you can afford it, the **Old Thyme Inn** (779 Main St., tel. 415/726–1616), dating from 1899, is the nicest bed-and-breakfast in town. Each of its seven rooms is named and decorated after a different herb, each has an old-fashioned claw-foot bathtub, and some have a whirlpool or a fireplace. Rates range from $75 to $150 and include a hearty breakfast. If all else fails, a new, 20-room **Ramada Inn** (3020 Rte. 1, tel. 415/726–9700 or 800/2–RAMADA) on the north end of town has doubles starting at $65 weekdays, $85 weekends, including breakfast and private bath.

An overnight stay in Half Moon Bay can be relatively cheap if you camp. Otherwise, expect to pay through the nose. The tiny town has virtually no lodging under $50, though it offers four hotels for over $200 a night.

➤ **UNDER $65** • **Cameron's Inn.** This tiny place on the southern outskirts of town has three clean, simple doubles with a distinctly European feel. Big beds and fine art prints lend some style to the rooms, all of which share a common bath. You'll hear big-rigs downshifting on the freeway as you drift off, but at $50 on weekdays and $60 on weekends, it's about as cheap as you'll find anywhere in the area. *1410 S. Cabrillo Hwy. (Rte. 1), tel. 415/726–5705.*

➤ **CAMPING** • **Francis Beach at Half Moon Bay State Beach.** Its 55 characterless sites ($14 a night) at the base of a small sand dune feature picnic tables, food lockers, and fire pits. Because of its proximity to downtown, this place attracts teenage partiers and weekend-warrior types, especially during summer. Though you'll fall asleep to the sound of waves and arise to the smell of the sea, it's hardly the great outdoors. All sites are doled out on a first-come, first-served basis. *95 Kelly Ave., tel. 415/726–8820. Take Kelly Ave. west from Rte. 1 in Half Moon Bay. Cold showers, flush toilets. No open fires permitted.*

LA HONDA If you're considering spending a night or two in La Honda, you have four excellent choices: Three of the area's parks have campgrounds, and in one there's a backpacker's hostel. The **Hiker's Hut** in Sam McDonald State Park, a bargain at $4.50 a night per person, has sleeping space for 14 (bring your sleeping bag), pit toilets, and kitchen facilities in a Scandinavian A-frame cabin atop a ridge, a fairly steep 1½-mile hike from the parking lot. From the deck, you can see the ocean on a clear day. The only bummer is that reservations (which include a deposit) must be made by mail—and for Saturdays in summer, the hostel fills up two to three months in advance. Reserve through the Loma Prieta chapter of the Sierra Club (3921 E. Bayshore Rd., Palo Alto 94303, tel. 415/390–8411). For info on Sam McDonald State Park, including directions, *see* The South Bay, in Chapter 2.

➤ **CAMPING** • If you want to pitch a tent, the most developed sites are in **Portola State Park** and **Memorial County Park,** while **Pescadero Creek County Park** has more primitive, secluded hike-in campgrounds. Memorial offers 135 quiet sites scattered in a thick old-growth forest ($12), all with picnic tables, fire pits, and hot showers. Although popular with car campers on summer weekends, the campground is sparsely visited at other times. Sites are allotted on a first-come, first-served basis. In Portola State Park, the 53 "family" and seven hike-in campsites ($14) see little light in their cool berth beneath the redwoods. The family sites have running water, showers, fire pits, and picnic tables. Reserve through MISTIX (tel. 800/444–PARK). For a spot at one of Pescadero Creek's 15 hike-in sites ($7), buried in dense second-growth forest along the river, contact the rangers at Portola State Park (tel. 415/ 948–9098). For directions to these parks, and information on exploring them, *see* The South Bay, in Chapter 2.

PESCADERO If you want a bed, a shower, the beach, or all three in this pristine coastal town, the Pigeon Point Hostel is definitely the place to go.

➤ **HOSTEL** • **Pigeon Point Lighthouse Youth Hostel.** Perched on a small bluff 5 miles south of Pescadero State Beach, this place has four bungalow-style dorms overlooking miles of unblemished coast, an outdoor hot tub ($3 per person per half-hour), and free tours of the historic lighthouse on the grounds. The Pigeon Point Hostel tends to enchant its guests and destroy their will to leave—perhaps accounting for the three-night maximum stay. A night in any of the 54 comfortable beds costs $9, or $12 for nonmembers; and all the guests must do a chore during their stay. *Pigeon Point Rd. and Rte. 1, tel. 415/879–0633. Take SamTrans Bus 96C from Daly City BART. Curfew 11 PM. Check-in 7:30–9:30 AM and 4:30–9:30 PM. Wheelchair access. Reservations recommended.*

➤ **CAMPING** • In **Butano State Park,** 27 drive-in campsites ($14) and 18 hike-in sites ($7) lie peacefully among the redwoods waiting patiently for the few visitors who venture this way. The drive-in sites have fire rings, picnic tables, and food lockers. Reservations can be made through MISTIX (tel. 800/444–PARK) up to eight weeks in advance, but you'd have to be pretty anal to think you need them. None of the sites has showers, so be prepared to revel in your natural odors. For directions to Butano and more info on the park, *see* The South Bay, in Chapter 8.

OUTDOOR ACTIVITIES

8

By Lisa Roth

One young Berkeley resident gets up before dawn to windsurf for several hours before going to work. Another local, with a degree in economics, is content to keep his job as a bicycle mechanic because it allows him a daily mountain-biking jaunt through the forest. Then there's the 40-year-old attorney who leaves work in time to grab a longboard and catch some evening waves. It's no surprise—many people choose to live in the Bay Area precisely because it's so easy to drive 15 minutes from the city and enjoy some of the most spectacular natural attractions this country has to offer. The cool, moist woodlands of Marin County are prime territory for hikers, bikers, horseback riders, and bird watchers. The afternoon breezes make San Francisco Bay ideal for windsurfing. And when the summer winds die down, you can put away your sail and dust off the surfboard for the winter waves. With so many sporting options and such a moderate climate, it's hard for Bay Area residents to think of excuses to stay inside.

In fact, so many locals head for the mountains and coast that it's sometimes hard to distinguish those places from the city you just left behind. Outdoor enthusiasts are often outraged to find that their favorite recreation spot is more congested than the freeway at rush hour. Mountain bikers lock horns with hikers, and hikers with equestrians; novice surfers get in the way of expert surfers, and ultimate Frisbee players fight soccer players for field space. It's the price of convenience. If you're trying to escape humanity as well as exhaust fumes and urban neurosis, you'll need to drive a little farther than 15 minutes.

If you want to escape the weekend crowds, avoid Marin County and Point Reyes. The South Bay is undiscovered in comparison to its northern neighbors, and the farther you go from the city, the more likely you are to encounter true solitude among the redwoods. The parks in the East Bay hills don't get the harsh wind and dense fog of the coast, though they're not nearly as lush. If you just want to let off some steam after work, the concentration of young people in San Francisco and Berkeley makes it easy to find a pickup game of basketball, volleyball, soccer, or ultimate Frisbee at a nearby park or rec center.

A great place to start exploring the Bay Area's outdoor opportunities is **Outdoors Unlimited,** a co-op fueled by funds from U.C. San Francisco and the community. Volunteers here teach clinics on everything from sea kayaking to rock climbing to CPR. They organize backpacking and cycling outings and even moonlight kayak trips. While UCSF students have priority in signing up for some of the activities (which are unbelievably cheap, and sometimes even free), the general public is welcome. OU is also a great resource for information on specialized co-ops and networks, and they offer a variety of rentals. To receive their quarterly newsletter, send one stamped (52¢), self-addressed envelope to Outdoors Unlimited, Box

0234 A, University of California, San Francisco 94143. *Office: cnr. of 3rd and Parnassus Aves., beneath UCSF library, tel. 415/476–2078. Open Mon., Tues., Fri. 11:30–1:30 and 5–7, Wed.–Thurs. 11:30–1:30 and 4–6.*

Berkeley's **Cal Adventures** reserves the best deals for U.C. students, but it's also a great resource for the community, with a wide variety of affordable lessons and outings. When you complete classes in such sports as sailing, kayaking, and windsurfing, you're eligible to rent equipment at low prices. *Recreational Sports Facility, U.C. Berkeley, 2301 Bancroft Way, tel. 510/642–4000 or 510/643–8029. Open Mon.–Thurs. 11–6, Fri. 11–7.*

The best places to stock up on pamphlets, books, and maps are the **Sierra Club Bookstore**, in San Francisco (730 Polk St., tel. 415/923–5600) and Oakland (6014 College Ave., tel. 510/658–7470), and **REI** (1338 San Pablo Ave., tel. 510/527–4140) in Berkeley.

League Sports and Pickup Games

For city folk, pickup games and organized sports leagues are a great way to get the blood moving after a day in the office. You can join pickup games on just about every court and field in the Bay Area, though skill levels vary from place to place. Weekends draw the largest crowds, but warm weekdays and long evenings generally guarantee activity. Get in touch with your local community center, park department, or YMCA to get involved with activities in your neighborhood.

Coed volleyball and ultimate matches are not uncommon, but you'll be hard-pressed to find women out on the basketball courts and, to a lesser extent, on soccer fields during informal games. Luckily, female soccer and basketball leagues have popped up all over the Bay Area to pick up the slack.

The **Golden Gate Sport and Social Club** (tel. 415/921–1233), which sponsors a variety of sports in San Francisco, is made up primarily of young professionals from the Marina district. All their activities (except all-male basketball) are coed, and they're socially oriented: Players head to sponsor bars for a post-game beer and mourn the end of the season with a party. Indoor volleyball and basketball leagues operate year-round, and you can play ultimate Frisbee in winter and seven-a-side soccer in summer. The **Bay Area Outreach and Reacreation Program** (830 Bancroft Way, Berkeley, tel. 510/849–4663) sponsors athletics for people with physical disabilities, including motorized- and manual-chair basketball and soccer.

BASKETBALL Pickup games are almost universally male, and competition levels vary dramatically. In other words, peruse the courts in your neighborhood before you lace up those high-tops. To find out about men's leagues in the city, call Frank McKinney at the **Mission Recreation Center** (2450 Harrison St., tel. 415/695–5012) or Marty Arenas at the **Eureka Valley Recreation Center** (100 Collingwood St., 1 block from 18th St., tel. 415/554–9528). For information on women's leagues, contact Jim Jackson at the **San Francisco Recreation and Park Department** (tel. 415/753–7027).

➤ **WHERE TO PLAY** • The following courts usually get going weekday afternoons while it's still light out and weekend mornings between 8 and 11. **Grattan Playground** (Alma St., at Stanyan St.), near Golden Gate Park, sees a mixed group weekday afternoons around 3 or 3:30; weekends bring a bigger crowd and a higher level of play to the courts. In the Marina, the popular **Moscone Recreation Center** (Chestnut St., at Laguna St.) has courts with night-lighting and unforgiving double rims. Weekends tend to be a zoo. The skill level varies at the **Chinese Playground** (Broadway, at Larkin St.), but it's among the city's few lit courts, and people are almost always here in the evenings. Games at the **Potrero Hill Recreation Center** (Arkansas St., at 22nd St.) get pretty competitive, especially Monday and Thursday nights. Fights of the white-men-can't-jump variety are not uncommon on these well-lit courts. Four-on-four games get going early on the weekends at the small courts at **James Lick Middle School** (Clipper St., at Castro St.).

In North Berkeley, the short court at **Live Oak Park** (Shattuck Ave., at Berryman St.) hosts three-on-three games on weekends, but the wait can be unbearable. A more intimidating game goes on at **Ohlone Park** (Hearst St., near California St.).

SOCCER Those who thought there was no life after A.Y.S.O. will be happy to know that Bay Area soccer leagues were kicking long before the World Cup brought the sport to this country's attention. The **Golden Gate Women's Soccer League** has four divisions in the East Bay, Marin County, and San Francisco. To join for the fall or spring season, contact Janice Mullen (tel. 415/753–0946) or Ashley Young (tel. 510/658–8337). In the highly competitive men's **San Francisco Football Soccer League,** the players are a truly international crew. The season runs September–May, with six divisions playing all over the city on Sundays. Sunset Soccer Supply (*see below*) has a list of the coaches' phone numbers and game locations; try-outs are required. The high-caliber **Latin American Soccer League** (tel. 415/573–7444), with half as many divisions, fills in the summer gap for men's soccer. Several coed leagues keep you dribbling year-round: Contact the **San Francisco Co-Ed Recreational Soccer League** (tel. 415/330–8900) or Charles Jezycki of the **California Co-Ed Soccer Organization** (tel. 415/573–7444 or 415/697–4034, ext. 102) for more information.

Sunset Soccer Supply can hook you up with a new pair of cleats or help men interested in the San Francisco League find a team that has openings. The staff is up on the soccer scene and the shop carries the best supplies in the city. While you're here, pick up a free copy of the *Soccer America Yellow Pages* for a listing of leagues, clubs, and some tournaments. *3214 Irving St., btw 33rd and 34th Aves., San Francisco, tel. 415/753–2666. Open Mon., Wed.–Fri. 11–6, Sat. 10–6, Sun. 10–5.*

➤ **WHERE TO PLAY** • Sunday mornings year-round, a crowd gathers at the **Polo Field** in Golden Gate Park for an impromptu game of soccer. The almost exclusively male players represent a range of skill levels. League teams square off at **Beach Chalet,** at the western edge of the park. You'll find women's teams there on Saturdays and men's on Sundays. Wednesdays after work, post-college players kick around at the **Marina Green.** There are no lights here, so long summer days see more games than winter.

While San Francisco has it going on with league teams, Berkeley is the fat one when it comes to pickup games. The field at the top of Berkeley's **Clark Kerr Campus,** a.k.a. **Dwight/Derby** (btw Dwight Way and Derby St., east of Warring St.), has coed pickup games weekday evenings, women (usually) Tuesday or Thursday evenings, and mostly men on weekend mornings. It's a good place to come if you're looking for fun rather than competition. The scene quiets down some when school's not in session. Down the hill, **Willard Park** (Derby St., btw Hillegass Ave. and Regent St.) usually has Friday-afternoon pickup games from 2 or 3 until 6. Look for a friendly coed game (i.e., varied ages and skill levels) Tuesday, Thursday, and Friday noon to 1 at **San Pablo Field** (btw Mabel, Russell, Park, and Ward Sts). On the more serious side, astroturf pickup games take place weekdays at 5 and weekends at 4 at **Kleeberger Field** (Piedmont Ave., at Stadium Rim Way). It's mostly a male thang (ages 25–50), and testosterone levels are high.

ULTIMATE FRISBEE You'll find a huge Frisbee community in the Bay Area. Informal matches go on all the time, though sometimes it's hard to tell a pickup game from a picnic— post-game kegs are an unspoken tradition on nice days. Go to pickup games to get the scoop on leagues, club teams, and tournaments.

➤ **WHERE TO PLAY** • **Sharon Meadow**, off Kezar Drive in Golden Gate Park, sometimes sees coed pickup games of up to 40 people. Frisbee fanatics gather here every Tuesday and Thursday evening while it's still light out, and late mornings every weekend. **Julius Kahn Playground** (West Pacific Ave., btw Spruce and Locust Sts.), near the southeast corner of the Presidio, hosts pickup games Wednesday evenings and Saturday mornings.

In Berkeley, pickup ultimate follows soccer at 6 on Fridays in **Willard Park** (*see* Soccer, *above*). Discs have also been spotted flying at **North Field** (just north of Hearst Gym on the U.C. Berkeley campus) and up at **Clark Kerr** (*see* Soccer, *above*).

VOLLEYBALL The **Central YMCA** (220 Golden Gate Ave., tel. 415/885–0460) and the Richmond district's **S.F. Volleyball Association** (tel. 415/931–6385) have coed leagues nearly year-round; the former hosts open play between seasons for $3 a night. To join a women's vol-leyball league in San Francisco, contact Jim Jackson at the **San Francisco Recreation and Park Department** (tel. 415/753–7027), which sponsors several leagues for different skill levels. The season runs from October to mid-December. **Club One** (2 Embarcadero, tel. 415/788–1010) organizes the city's only sand-volleyball league. In summer, coed six-on-six beginner and inter-mediate games take place Tuesday–Thursday evenings at Embarcadero Beach, in Justin Her-man Plaza.

The **City of Berkeley Recreation Department** (tel. 510/644–6530) organizes a coed league with several seasons for advanced and recreational players. **City Beach Sports and Recreation Cen-ter** (4701 Doyle St., tel. 510/428–1221) in Emeryville offers some serious choices: five levels of play in men's, women's, and coed leagues, made up of teams of two, four, five, or six people. They have three hard courts and two sand, all indoors.

➤ **WHERE TO PLAY** • On weekends, people set up their own nets at the **Marina Green** and at the **Moscone Recreation Center** (Chestnut St., at Laguna St.). At both locations, you'll usually find high-skill two-on-two games. Also intimidating are the six-on-six weekend games at several spots along John F. Kennedy Drive in **Golden Gate Park.** You can rent nets for $11 for the weekend at **Outdoors Unlimited** (cnr. of 3rd and Parnassus Aves., beneath UCSF library, San Francisco, tel. 415/476–2078).

The S.F. Recreation and Park Department hosts Monday-night "skills and drills" from 6 to 7, followed by open play until 9:30, at **Kezar Pavillion,** between Stanyan and Beulah streets. In summer, the Pro-Am Basketball League has Monday games there, so the schedule switches to Tuesdays. These games generally attract a 20- to 30-year-old crowd. Admission is $2.

The only sand courts in the city are those that get hauled to Justin Herman Plaza each sum-mer, when the S.F. Recreation and Park Department and Club One (*see above*) sponsor **Embar-cadero Beach Sand Volleyball** (tel. 415/773–9803). Starting at the end of May, the smell of sunscreen permeates the Financial District, as corporate types loosen their ties and outside hitters drag themselves downtown for free open play weekdays and some weekends until the beginning of August.

In the East Bay, **People's Park** (*see* Chapter 2) has two outdoor sand courts, but you may have to fight for your right to play. Tuesday night, pickup games take place at the asphalt court in **Live Oak Park** (*see* Basketball, *above*). People also set up on the grass in **Ohlone Park** (Hearst Ave., btw. Sacramento Ave. and Milvia St.) and goof around Saturday morning. For $5, you can take part in open play at **City Beach** (*see above*) in Emeryville.

Hiking

You'll find an impressive array of hiking spots close to home where you can get away from car horns and concrete for the afternoon, work up a sweat, and marvel at giant trees, deep canyons, and the gloomy ocean. And if you hit the trail with **Golden Gate Hikers,** you may even score a date along the way. Sponsored by Hostelling International, this hiking club is filled with singles ages 25–50. You don't have to be an HI member to hike—just bring a buck for each event and a few dollars to cover transportation costs. Participants usually meet on Sundays at 9:30 AM at 2209 Van Ness Avenue (near Broadway) for day hikes; also look for a number of overnights throughout the season. For a free quarterly hiking schedule, write to 55 Vandewater St. #11, San Francisco 94133, or call the **Hikers' Hotline** (tel. 415/550–6321).

At **Outdoors Unlimited,** in true co-op spirit, all of the hiking trips are free—you only pay trans-portation costs. You don't need to be a member to participate; just sign up on the trip sheet posted at the OU office (*see* chapter introduction, *above*) up to 11 days prior to the trip. The **Sierra Club** also sponsors hikes all over the Bay Area. They're free, though a donation may be requested and carpoolers are expected to share gas, parking, and bridge tolls. Pick up a sched-ule at the Sierra Club Bookstore (*see* chapter introduction, *above*) or send a check for $4.50 (payable to the Sierra Club) to Chapter Schedule, 5237 College Ave., Oakland 94618.

SAN FRANCISCO Just because you can't tear yourself away from the city doesn't mean you can't escape the urban landscape (at least for a little while). If you don't have the wheels or the time to leave town, head out on the **Coastal Trail,** which follows San Francisco's shoreline from the cliffs near Golden Gate Bridge over dirt roads, onto residential sidewalks, around craggy headlands, and along the beach all the way down to Fort Funston. Some parts are better marked than others, but if you follow the shoreline, you should be okay. For a map of the route, pick up a free copy of the brochure "Golden Gate" at the **Golden Gate National Recreation Area Visitor Center** (Cliff House, Point Lobos Ave., tel. 415/556–8642).

The trail starts at the scenic overlook just east of the base of the bridge. It passes under the bridge anchorage and runs roughly parallel to Lincoln Boulevard. If you want to feel the sand between your toes, make a detour down to **Baker Beach** before heading down El Camino del Mar. Continue west along the paved road until the edge of Lincoln Park Golf Course, where you pick up the dirt trail again to your right. The most spectacular stretch begins here, leading through the craggy headland of **Land's End,** San Francisco's wildest little corner, full of rocky cliffs, grassy fields, insane views, and crashing surf. The cliffs here are unstable, so stay on trails, keep off the slippery rocks, and watch your footing. You'll pass the Cliff House and the **Sutro Baths.** Walk along San Francisco's longest stretch of beach for 4.7 miles, past Golden Gate Park and the San Francisco Zoo and on to Fort Funston. For info on the beaches and attractions along the way, *see box* Chilling by the Ocean, in Chapter 2.

On the other side of the bridge, the **Golden Gate Promenade** is a 3.5-mile, mostly asphalt path that traces the bay from Fort Point National Historic Site (*see* Chapter 2) to the **Hyde Street Pier.** The popular jogging route takes you by the windsurfers at Crissy Field, around the yacht harbor, past the Marina Green, and up and over the hill of Fort Mason to Aquatic Park by Fisherman's Wharf.

EAST BAY Those who can't resist a challenge perk up their ears at the mention of the 31-mile **Skyline Trail,** which runs through the East Bay's six major parks (*see below*). The trail, open to hikers and horseback riders, offers no camping opportunities except at its endpoint in Anthony Chabot Regional Park, so if you want to go the distance, you've got to do it in one day. The feat has been accomplished, but it requires an insane amount of energy and perseverance. If it makes you feel any better, Skyline isn't a particularly attractive trail (though you do get a nice view of the bay). For general information on the parks in the **East Bay Regional Park District,** call 510/562–PARK. The *East Bay Log* is a monthly newsletter filled with information on park activities. Call 510/635–0135, ext. 2200, to subscribe; a $15 donation is requested.

➤ **TILDEN REGIONAL PARK** • When Berkeleyites want to commune with nature, they head to Tilden Park in the Berkeley Hills. Here lie two of the highest points in the East Bay— **Volmer Peak** (1,913 feet) at the southern end of the park, and **Wildcat Peak** (1,250 feet) to the north. The hike to Wildcat Peak from **Inspiration Point** (for directions, *see Biking, below*) is just a moderate sweat-breaker. In fact, the trail, called **Nimitz Way,** is 4½ miles of wheelchair-accessible road. The hike should take a good two hours, during which you'll have plenty of time to absorb the view of the San Pablo and Briones reservoirs. Nimitz Way is a better bet than most of Tilden's poorly maintained dirt trails, on which poison oak and brambles run rampant.

You can disentangle yourself from the overgrown trails by heading to the more open and grassy north end of Tilden. Starting at Lake Anza, head northeast on the **Lake Anza Trail,** which encircles the lake. When you reach the far northeast corner of the lake, look for the **Wildcat Gorge Trail** on your left. The initial steep descent past a century-old springhouse is no indication of things to come: The trail tunnels through a wide, rocky gorge but eventually rises to 80 feet above the creek that carved it. Continue for a half-mile until the trail forks. To the right, the **Curran Trail** rises sharply to reach Inspiration Point in .7 miles. Otherwise, the Wildcat Gorge Trail, one of the nicest paths in Tilden, continues through groves of California bay laurels. About .3 miles up the trail on your right, you'll pass a hill with a practically vertical path upward (this isn't on the official Tilden map). At the top of the hill you'll have a 360° view of the park. Return to the Wildcat Gorge Trail and backtrack to Lake Anza for an easy to moderate 1½-hour hike.

For more hiking information or to arrange naturalist-guided tours, call Tilden's **Environmental Education Center** (tel. 510/525–2233). A moderate 3-mile, 800-foot climb through woods and fields to the top of Wildcat Peak begins at the center: Head east on **Laurel Canyon Trail,** cross the fire road, continue uphill, and turn left onto the **Wildcat Peak Trail.** A turnoff to your right leads all the way to the top, where you can look out over Oakland, San Francisco, and Marin. Head back down the way you came, turn right onto Wildcat Peak Trail, and go left on the **Sylvan Trail,** which leads back to the nature center.

To reach Tilden Park, take University Avenue east from I–80 to Oxford Street; go left on Oxford, right on Rose, and left on Spruce to the top of the hill. Cross Grizzly Peak Boulevard, make an immediate left on Canon Drive, and follow the signs.

➤ **WILDCAT CANYON REGIONAL PARK** • During summer and fall, Wildcat Canyon is the dried-up fire hazard adjoining Tilden Regional Park to the north. In winter, the 2,500-acre park is as green as a golf course, and in spring it erupts with wildflowers. You'll share the grassy hills and stunning views of San Pablo Bay with grazing cattle; don't forget to close the gates that block them from many of the canyon trails. The best trail loop is a moderate 4-mile hike: From the **Wildcat Creek Trail,** head up 1½ miles northeast through the tall grass on the **Mezue Trail** for an excellent view; then turn right and continue ¾ mile southeast along the paved **Nimitz Way.** The **Havey Canyon Trail** will return you to the Wildcat Creek Trail on a winding 1½-mile path (avoid this trail when it's wet, or you'll spend more time on your butt than your feet). Wildcat Canyon is easily accessed from Tilden Regional Park (*see above*) via either Wildcat Creek Trail (starting at the Environmental Education Center) or Nimitz Way (from Inspiration Point). The official entrance is at Alvarado Park, on the north end of the canyon, where parking is readily available. However, the major hiking trails are most easily accessed from Rifle Range Road, off Arlington Boulevard in the El Cerrito Hills. From I–80, exit east on Potrero Avenue, turn right onto Arlington Avenue, and go left on Rifle Range Road. The Wildcat Creek Trail picks up at a trailhead along Rifle Range Road. For more information call 510/236–1262.

➤ **REDWOOD REGIONAL PARK** • While the tourist hordes head to Muir Woods to see California redwoods, you can slip away to Redwood Regional Park in the East Bay. The park's original redwoods were mowed down at the start of the California gold rush, so the trees you'll see are youngsters—not even 100 years old. But unlike Muir Woods, where the trails sport guard rails, Redwood offers an environment rough enough to let you know you're outdoors and not at the mall.

Connecting the northern and southern entrances are two main trails that trace the perimeter of the park, the **East Ridge Trail** and the **West Ridge Trail.** The West Ridge Trail is the main thoroughfare through the park, and too much time on its broad path may get you flattened by a speed-crazed mountain biker. For two of the best hikes through this park, you'll only need to stick to this trail for a short while. From the Skyline Gate entrance, take the West Ridge Trail (the right-hand path) to the first trail that splinters off to the left, the **Stream Trail.** This mostly level 3-mile (one-way) hike heads down to the valley floor and follows the stream. If you'd

Thinking on Your Feet

If you can read a map while running at breakneck speed, dodging tree limbs, and leaping over fallen logs, you've got what it takes to go orienteering. You'll find people to join you in your crazy quests at the Bay Area Orienteering Club. Three or four times a month they plot a new route through the Bay Area (sometimes as far as Tahoe) and leave you to find your way along the marked path as fast as your feet can carry you, armed with a compass, a topographic map, and a suicidal drive. Events are $6–$10 for nonmembers; $12 will earn you membership and a spot on the mailing list. For more information call 408/255–8018.

rather explore the shady and secluded groves of redwoods, pass by the Stream Trail and take the **French Trail** in and out of ravines along the side of the canyon. To return to the Skyline Gate entrance, simply pick any trail heading up and to the right; you'll soon connect with the West Ridge Trail, which will lead you back to your car. *Tel. 510/ 635–0135, ext. 2578. From I–80, take Rte. 24 east to Sky- line Blvd. south; Skyline Gate entrance to park is on your left, after Huckleberry Botanical Preserve.*

➤ **ANTHONY CHABOT REGIONAL PARK** • This regional park east of Oakland and south of Redwood Regional Park takes up almost 5,000 acres, most of which are dry and unkempt. The park offers 31 miles of hiking trails through grassy valleys and along Lake Chabot. The **Lakeside Trail,** which traces most of the lake's 9-mile perimeter, is level, paved, and wheelchair accessible. The lake and its immediate surroundings are worth exploring (by foot or by rented boat), but beyond that, forget it. The ridge composing part of the **Skyline Trail** affords few scenic views and is dusty enough to choke a horse, not to mention the fact that the tranquility of your hike will be intermittently shattered by gunfire from the nearby rifle range. *Tel. 510/635–0135, ext. 2570, for camping and hiking info., or 510/582–2198 for lake info. From I–580 east, exit Fairmont Dr. east, which merges with Lake Chabot Rd.; then follow signs. Parking fee: $3.*

Hike the nature trail at Huckleberry Botanical Preserve in early spring and you might spy the first blossoms of the season; since the park is outside the fog belt, the plants bloom one to two months ahead of others in the vicinity. To reach Huckleberry, follow the directions for Redwood Regional Park.

MARIN COUNTY A short drive north from the city over the Golden Gate Bridge deposits you in Marin County, chock full of the kind of hiking most people will travel hours for—trails through virgin redwoods, over grassy mountain fields, and past dramatic surf. Many of Marin's best hiking spots, including Muir Woods, Mt. Tamalpais, and Point Reyes National Seashore, lie along Route 1, which winds up the coast.

➤ **MARIN HEADLANDS** • Just across the Golden Gate Bridge from San Francisco, the headlands are home to three parks. The **Tennessee, Gerbode,** and **Rodeo valleys** sprawl inland from the coast, sheltering diverse wildlife. To reach the headlands from San Francisco, take the first exit after the Golden Gate Bridge (Alexander Avenue); drive a short way up Conzelman Road, and follow signs for the park you want to visit.

For a leisurely stroll in the Rodeo Valley, take a spin around the perimeter of the **Rodeo Lagoon.** With all the opportunities to stop and look at the waterfowl, the 1½-mile tour may take longer than you think. For a better view and a more strenuous hike, charge north up the **Coastal Trail.** From the parking lot, head *up* the closed-off road (*not* the left stairway). Persevere for about 2 miles, turn right onto the **Wolf Ridge Trail,** and head up the grassy hill (alias Wolf Ridge) for 1.6 miles to the top. When you're ready to stop gazing at the Tennessee Valley, continue .7 miles down the verdant leeward side of the hill until it ends at the **Miwok Trail,** which you fol- low south. The trail wanders above the edge of the grassy Gerbode Valley, where you may spot a black-tailed deer or bobcat basking in the chaparral. In about 2 miles you'll be back at the Rodeo Visitor Center. *Ranger tel. 415/331–1540.*

The **Tennessee Valley Trail,** at the end of Tennessee Valley Road (from U.S. 101 north, take the Route 1 exit west and make the first left), is a broad path that meanders next to a small creek and through grassy fields for an easy 2 miles. In no time you'll be on the black, sandy **Ten- nessee Beach,** in the company of many families. Here you can see the namesake of the val- ley—the shipwreck of the SS *Tennessee.* If you're in the mood for something more strenuous, follow the Tennessee Valley Trail 1.3 miles from the parking lot and veer right onto the **Coastal Trail.** You may start to regret your decision when the going gets tough after ¾ mile; the trail wildly snakes above the secluded **Pirates Cove** for 2.2 miles, with stunning views of the jagged coast, and eventually leads you down to **Muir Beach** in the next .8 miles. Before you head back, relax a while at the **Pelican Inn** (*see* Muir Beach, in Chapter 2). On your return, see the less dramatic side of the Tennessee Valley by turning left off the Coastal Trail at **Coyote Ridge Trail** after .8 miles. Continue for 1½ miles and take the **Fox Trail** back to the Tennessee Valley Trail. You complete the 8-mile round trip with a short walk north, back to the parking lot.

➤ **ANGEL ISLAND** • Almost all 740 acres of this island in San Francisco Bay are covered with forest or sweeping grasses. **Perimeter Road,** which encircles the island, is wheelchair accessible but steep in some places. Hiking trails lead in from Perimeter Road. On the **Sunset Trail,** immediately southeast of the park headquarters, 2 miles of ascending switchbacks afford stunning views of San Francisco to the west. As you circle the 781-foot summit, **Mt. Caroline Livermore,** you'll reach a crossroads; take a left up the paved road to the top for a 360° view of the Bay Area. After you backtrack to the crossroads, return to your ferry via the **North Ridge Trail** to view the eastern side of the island. The entire loop, Angel Island's most difficult hike, takes 2½–3 hours. For information on how to reach the island, see Tiburon and Angel Island, in Chapter 2. For recorded information, call 415/435–1915; dial 415/435–5390 to speak to a ranger.

➤ **MUIR WOODS** • You'll share the awesome sight of ancient, towering redwoods (the oldest has been around over 1,200 years) with hordes of tourists who clog the paved paths on the valley floor. An estimated two million sightseers shuffle past the redwoods annually, but luckily, less than 10% venture on the network of hiking trails that start here. You can make a quick escape by following any of the trails that head up from the valley floor. The $1 brochure for sale at the park entrance and in the gift shop gives great explanations of flora and fauna and a complete trail map.

One way to avoid the crowds at Muir Woods is to come on a rainy day—yes, that's right, a rainy day. The forest's canopy is so dense that it keeps out much of the rain, and the dripping ferns and moss give the illusion that you've ventured into a rain forest.

For an easy 2-mile hike that will get you away from the crowds and give you a view of the redwoods, head to the fourth bridge from the park entrance and take the **Hillside Trail** to your left. For a more spectacular view and workout, head up the **Ben Johnson Trail,** starting from the same spot. You'll climb up through the forest for 2 miles (the last half-mile is quite steep) until you reach the top of a hill with a wonderful view of several canyons and the Pacific. You can either head east on the **Dipsea Trail** to complete a 4½-mile hike, or, if you're still full of energy, follow it 2 miles west down a steep gulch to **Stinson Beach.** The full hike is one of the best around, and it's over 9 miles, so you'll be damn pleased with yourself when you're done. If you're here on a weekend or holiday, you can cut down the hike back by hopping on Golden Gate Transit Bus 63 at the Stinson Beach park entrance. For $1.25 it'll transport you to Mountain Home Inn, where you can pick up the **Panoramic/Ocean View Trail,** which leads 2 miles downhill to the parking lot. Call 415/532–6600 for a schedule. Tel. 415/388–2596. From U.S. 101 north, take Stinson Beach/Route 1 exit and follow signs.

➤ **MT. TAMALPAIS** • On a clear day you can spot the Sierras from the top of Marin's highest mountain, Mt. Tamalpais ("Mt. Tam" to the natives). Of all Mt. Tam's well-worn trails, the trip to the top is the most popular. If you want to sweat a lot and hike over 3 miles on your journey to the summit, park at the Bootjack Campground and head north on the **Bootjack Trail.** At the Mountain Theater, turn right onto Ridgecrest Boulevard, following the well-marked paths to the summit. Or conserve your energy and drive up most of the way. If you park at the East Peak parking lot, you need only mosey an easy 7/10 mile on a paved road to the top for a spectacular view.

In the annual 7-mile Dipsea Race, usually held the second Sunday in June, runners take off from Mill Valley and sprint over Mt. Tamalpais before collapsing on Stinson Beach at the finish line. The race originated in 1905 and now attracts 1,500 manic runners.

The 2-mile **Steep Ravine Trail** follows a redwood-lined creek down to the ocean. The trail begins at the west end of the parking lot at **Pantoll Ranger Station** (tel. 415/388–2070); the trail map ($1) for sale here is an excellent investment. Along the trail, look for waterfalls, especially in springtime. It's all downhill to **Stinson Beach;** take the 1½-mile **Dipsea Trail,** or stick to the trail that leads to **Rocky Point** and the **Steep Ravine Environmental Camp,** where you can get a close look at teeming marine life. To get here from U.S. 101 in Marin County, take the Stinson Beach/Route 1 exit, and turn left at the first traffic light onto Route 1. Turn right onto Panoramic Highway and right again at the Pantoll Ranger Station on Ridgecrest Road.

➢ **BOLINAS** • Serious hikers should consider the **Palomarin Trail,** which stretches from Bolinas (*see* Marin County, in Chapter 2) to the edge of the Point Reyes National Seashore. The trailhead is at the end of Mesa Road, just past the bird observatory. For a healthy day hike, follow the trail to Bass Lake (5½ miles round-trip) or Pelican Lake (7 miles round-trip). Either way, you'll walk through eucalyptus groves and untamed wetlands, and along the edge of the cliffs that overlook the Pacific Ocean.

➢ **POINT REYES** • Even though it's not that far from the city, Point Reyes seems a world away. Gazing out at the rest of Marin County from here, you might get the feeling that you're on a separate island, which is almost true, except that the Tomales Valley joins the little archipelago to the mainland. The San Andreas fault runs right through the valley, putting Point Reyes on a different tectonic plate than the rest of the continent. Within the peninsula, the geography varies greatly; in just a few miles, you can see meadows, forests, peaks with panoramic vistas, craggy cliffs overlooking the ocean, and isolated coves. The area erupts with wildflowers from mid-February through July; and though winter sees a lot of rain, that's when the rivers and ponds teem with life and the whales migrate south. Point Reyes feels so far removed that you may not want to go home; fortunately, there are plenty of places to camp here (*see* Marin County, in Chapter 7).

The best place to gear up for hiking is the **Bear Valley Visitor Center** (tel. 415/663–1092), where you can get a trail map and talk to the rangers. To get here, take Bear Valley Road off Route 1 just west of the village of Olema. For a hike along a narrow peninsula, with the Pacific crashing on one side of you and Tomales Bay gently lapping the other side, head out to **Tomales Point,** the northernmost spot in the park. From the visitor center, take Bear Valley Road, go left at the stop sign on Sir Francis Drake Boulevard, and bear right at Pierce Point Road, which ends at the Historic Pierce Point Ranch. The **Tomales Point Trail** picks up here and heads right through the Tule Elk Range; keep your eyes peeled for the graceful animals. Three miles down the road, the official trail ends and the sandy footpaths to the cliffs (1½ miles) begin.

For a steep, strenuous hike, head to the highest point in the park, Mt. Wittenberg (1,407 feet). The **Mt. Wittenberg Trail** begins .2 miles from the Bear Valley Trailhead, at the south end of the parking lot by the visitor center. The trail rises 1,250 feet in elevation; the final push follows an unmaintained offshoot up to the peak, where you'll be rewarded with a panorama of land and sea. To get down, head back to the Mt. Wittenberg Trail, hang a right, then take the **Horse Trail** to the Bear Valley Trail, where another right completes your 6-mile loop.

SOUTH BAY The gently rolling hills that shelter the South Bay coast from the outside world provide excellent opportunities for hiking. Not only that, but you'll actually feel like you're heading into the country as you pass the small towns and farms south of San Francisco. Less popular than the hiking spots in Marin County, the South Bay's parks offer solitude—and you won't have to compete with mountain bikers for trail space. The inland town of **La Honda** on Route 84 (*see* San Mateo County Coast, in Chapter 2) is a good place to stop for picnic supplies before you head into one of the nearby state or county parks.

➢ **PACIFICA** • The hiking at **Sweeney Ridge** is mediocre, but its proximity to the city and its amazing view of the coastline make it a worthwhile getaway. The 1,047-acre park, which separates San Bruno from Pacifica, was added to the Golden Gate National Recreation Area in 1984. To reach the peak, hike 2 miles up a moderate grade through coastal scrub and grasslands that bloom with wildflowers in spring; the trailhead is at the end of Sneath Lane. A monument to the Spanish captain Gaspar de Portola, who supposedly discovered San Francisco Bay from this point in 1769, stands atop the peak. Most people are content to contemplate the view from here, but if you want to keep going you can hike the **Baquiano Trail** all the way down to Pacifica. Since the ridge is so close to the coast, you'll definitely encounter some wind, and you may have to combat zero visibility on foggy summer afternoons. To get here, take I-280 or Skyline Boulevard (Hwy. 35) to the Sneath Lane exit in San Bruno. Follow Sneath Lane west all the way to the Sweeney Ridge Gate. For information on ranger-led hikes call 415/556–8371.

San Pedro Valley County Park has several mellow hiking trails that take you through shady woods and meadows exploding with wildflowers. In winter and spring, the ½-mile **Brooks Falls Overlook Trail** offers great views of a three-tiered, 275-foot waterfall. The even shorter **Plaskon**

Nature Trail, which gives you the opportunity to get up close and personal with a variety of plant species and wildlife, is wheelchair accessible. For a longer hike, try the 4½-mile **Big Basin Canyon Trail** loop. The trail picks up about 1 mile into the San Pedro Valley and ascends gently for 2 miles to a series of 1,000-foot high overlooks. On a clear day, you can see the Farallon Islands. For more information and a detailed guide to the nature trail, stop by the **visitor center** (600 Oddstad Blvd., tel. 415/355–8289). To reach the park, take Route 1 into Pacifica and turn east on Linda Mar Boulevard. Follow that until it dead-ends, then make a right onto Oddstad Boulevard; the entrance is 50 yards up on the left.

➢ **LA HONDA** • Near tiny La Honda, 11 miles east of Route 1 along Route 84, lies scenic **Portola State Park.** Stop by the **visitor center** (tel. 415/948–9098) at the entrance for a trail map (75¢) and info on guided nature walks and other activities. For a moderately difficult 4½-mile hike through redwood groves, catch the steep **Coyote Ridge Trail** just north of the visitor center, follow it to Upper Escape Road, hang a left onto the **Slate Creek Trail,** shoot downhill on the steep **Summit Trail,** and follow the service road back to the visitor center. All told, the hike lasts two to three hours. To reach Portola, take I–280 to Route 84 west to Skyline Boulevard (Hwy. 35). Go south 7 miles, then turn west on Alpine Road. Parking is $5.

➢ **BUTANO STATE PARK** • This little-known state park in the Santa Cruz Mountains occupies a small canyon with diverse flora and fauna. Even when its campsites are full, you can still find solitude in Butano. Definitely invest in the 50¢ map available at the entrance station. In addition to marking the trails, it has information on the park's wildlife communities.

The beautiful **Little Butano Creek Trail,** about ½ mile from the entrance, takes you 3 miles along a creek and past old-growth redwoods. You can add about 2 more miles to the hike by following **Goat Hill Trail** from the fire road back to the main road. The **Jackson Flats Trail,** leading from the parking lot south of the entrance, begins a relaxing 1½-hour loop: Follow Jackson Flats to **Mill Ox Trail,** turn right down to the main road, make another right, and immediately go left onto the paved service road. Turn right down **Six Bridges Trail** and you'll eventually find yourself back at the parking lot. For a more strenuous hike and an incredible view on clear days, take the **Año Nuevo Trail** from the parking lot to the Año overlook, ½ mile away and about 800 feet up. Every Saturday and Sunday at 2, a ranger leads a 1½-hour nature walk, which leaves from the park's entrance.

To get to Butano, take Route 1 about 15 miles south of Half Moon Bay to Pescadero, turn left on Pescadero Road and right on Cloverdale Road, and go about 5 miles to the park entrance. It costs $5 to park within the grounds, but you can usually ditch your car for free at the turnoff just south of the Cloverdale Road entrance.

Biking

An incredible human-powered movement takes place in the Bay Area every month. Hundreds of recreational riders, cycling-rights activists, bike messengers, and businesspeople on their daily commute gather in downtown San Francisco and take off on a 1½-hour ride through the city. The group, called **Critical Mass,** is responding to the predominance of cars in the city by encouraging bicycles as an alternative means of transport. They meet around 5:30 on the last Friday of each month at Justin Herman Plaza to tie up traffic, piss off motorists, aggravate police officers, and generally have a good ol' time. The route is decided on the spot and varies each time, but usually ends at Dolores Park. The East Bay's Critical Mass gathers at the same time on the second to last Friday of the month at the downtown Berkeley BART. The East Bay group tends to be smaller and more politically active, as demonstrated by their pro-cycling chanting, anti-driving pamphlets, and occasional obstruction of the Bay Bridge. Police on bikes sometimes escort the San Francisco and East Bay groups in an effort to prevent problems and direct traffic.

If you want to rub spokes with other cyclists on a planned recreational ride, check out the calendar of events in the free monthly *Northern California Bicyclist*, available at bike shops. The **Sierra Club** (*see* Hiking, *above*) organizes group rides on various terrains from farmland to challenging hills. You need at least a 10-speed bike for all but the most level routes, and you must show up with a helmet. Pick up their activities schedule for a list of planned rides. The **Bicycling Group** co-op organizes rides about once a month, with an emphasis on social as well as physical activity; check out the bulletin board at Outdoors Unlimited (*see* chapter introduction, *above*) for specifics.

Northern Californians have the dubious distinction of having reinvented the wheel. Legend has it that mad scientists in Fairfax (some say Mill Valley) created the monster that became the mountain bike from the parts of racing ten-speeds and sturdy beach cruisers. But the mountain bike ultimately owes its existence to the invention of a reinforced tire rim that can withstand the punishment of riding over rocks and bumps. The notoriously hilly Bay Area provides some of the nation's best testing ground for your climbing machine. Unfortunately, there's

Roll, Roll, Roll Your Boat

Bay Area sea kayakers tackle waters both calm and rough. Beginners will get acquainted early on with Richardson Bay, between Tiburon and Sausalito in Marin County. With its calm waters, stunning scenery, and bird-watching opportunities, Richardson is a hot spot for novices, and it makes a good launching point for an intermediate-level trip to Angel Island or an advanced trip through the rough and dangerous currents under the Golden Gate Bridge. For even calmer waters, head farther north to Bolinas Lagoon, a protected estuary where you'll paddle past egret nesting sites and see more birds than you ever imagined. Drake's Estuary, another bird-infested spot, is a beautiful bay on the Point Reyes peninsula with calm waters for beginners. The placid waters of Tomales Bay, off the coast of Point Reyes National Seashore in Marin County, claim a resident flock of white pelicans as well as teems of jellyfish and starfish. Beginners and intermediates will feel comfortable in the western part of the bay, which offers stunning views of coves and beaches on shore.

To get in touch with the Bay Area kayak scene, contact Penny Wells of the Bay Area Sea Kayakers Co-op (tel. 415/457–6094). For $25 a year, you'll receive a newsletter and have access to frequent trips throughout the Bay Area. Also check the quarterly bulletin published by Outdoors Unlimited (see chapter introduction) for listings of free kayak and canoe workshops and volunteer-led trips. OU's day trips and moonlight paddles are the cheapest going—some are free, and for others you pay $50. Berkeley's Cal Adventures (see chapter introduction, above) also offers sea-kayaking day trips, instruction, and rentals.

Canoes and kayaks are all they do at California Canoe and Kayak (409 Water St., Jack London Sq., Oakland, tel. 510/893–7833 or 800/366–9804), and they're damn good at it. This retail store offers the widest range of classes and trips, including testosterone-free lessons and outings for women only. Sea Trek (Schoonmaker Point Marina, Sausalito, tel. 415/488–1000) also has classes and rentals, and they offer special kayak trips with naturalist guides. If you're looking to buy equipment, take a free spin on the water during Sea Trek's "Demo Days" before you lay down the cash. Like California Canoe and Kayak, they offer free testing of canoes and kayaks on a designated day each month from early spring through early fall.

intense competition for this prime real estate: Many hikers see bikers as a threat to their safety and to the land. The controversy has grown into a fight for control of state parkland, and bikers seem to be losing the battle. Bikes have been banned from most single-track trails in the Bay Area, leaving only fire roads for pedaling.

Mountain-bike technology is constantly being improved, and the innovations show in the price tag. Top-of-the-line bikes can easily sell for more than $500. Look for used bikes on bike-shop bulletin boards and in free magazines geared toward cyclists (pick them up in bike stores). Of course, the cheapest option is rental. **Karim's Cyclery** (2801 Telegraph Ave., Berkeley, tel. 510/841–2181) rents mountain bikes for $20 per day. Across the bay in Marin, **Wheel Escapes** (30 Liberty Ship Way, No. 210, Sausalito, tel. 415/332–0218) rents modest mountain bikes for $5 an hour or $21 a day. Higher-performance bikes cost $8 an hour or $35 a day. In San Francisco, **Park Cyclery** (1865 Haight St., at Stanyan St., tel. 415/751–RENT) rents mountain bikes for $5 an hour or $30 a day; **Magic Skates** (3038 Fulton St., at 6th Ave., tel. 415/668–1117) has them for $25 a day. Both are on the edge of Golden Gate Park.

WHERE TO BIKE

Most parks in the South Bay are completely closed to mountain bikers; for road rides in the area, *see* San Mateo County Coast, in Chapter 2.

SAN FRANCISCO San Francisco can be a tough city to ride in: You've got cars, jaywalking pedestrians, those damn streetcar tracks, one-way streets, and thigh-straining hills. But you also have an incredible variety of scenery within a relatively small area and less smog than in most big cities. If you plan on doing a lot of riding in the city, take a look at the *San Francisco Biking/Walking Guide*, a $3 map that shows street grades and bike-friendly routes. It's available at bike shops and outdoor-oriented bookstores.

The following 21-mile ride takes you through Golden Gate Park, into the Presidio, across the Golden Gate Bridge, and along the coast. Start at the west end of Golden Gate Park, where **Jonn F. Kennedy Drive** hits the Great Highway. Follow J.F.K. Drive to the east end of the park, turn left on **Conservatory Road,** and go left again on **Arguello Boulevard,** exiting the park. Hang a right on Moraga Avenue, then take another right onto **Presidio Boulevard.** Make a hard left onto **Lincoln Boulevard** almost immediately; it leads to the windy view area/toll plaza of the Golden Gate Bridge, where signs tell you how to cross according to the time and day of the week. When you return, follow Lincoln Boulevard in the direction you were heading; it turns into **El Camino del Mar Road.** At the Palace of Legion of Honor, the road veers right and becomes **Legion of Honor Drive** before dumping you back onto **Clement Street.** Turn right on Clement and follow it until it dead-ends, and take **Point Lobos Avenue** back to the Great Highway.

EAST BAY To escape the asphalt obstacle course of Berkeley's streets, take this 7-mile loop along the ridge of the Berkeley Hills and into Tilden. From the intersection of **Grizzly Peak Boulevard** and **Spruce Street** in North Berkeley, head south up the gradual incline of Grizzly Peak Boulevard. Not far beyond the two lookouts, make a left on **South Park Drive,** which takes you down through Tilden Park and past several picnic grounds. The street dead-ends at **Wildcat Canyon Road;** go left and ride over rolling hills past Lake Anza, back to the intersection with Grizzly Peak Boulevard. Taking this loop in the opposite direction involves potentially dangerous sharp curves and limited visibility. Spruce Street is the main access road to Grizzly Peak Boulevard north of town; **Tunnel Road,** which goes up into the hills past the Caldecott Tunnel, is the main access road to the south.

➤ **TILDEN/WILDCAT REGIONAL PARKS** • Named after Major Charles Lee Tilden, first president of the park-district board, Tilden Park contains 2,078 acres of eucalyptus trees and rolling hills, filled with hikers, picnickers, and families. Wildcat Regional Park, directly northwest of Tilden, is nowhere near as developed or crowded. Poison oak is common in both parks. As in most Bay Area parks, mountain bikes are limited to the fire trails.

A beautiful, moderately strenuous 13½-mile loop through both parks begins just west of Inspiration Point. Follow the rocky **Meadows Canyon Trail** to **Wildcat Creek Trail** and head right on the **Belgum Trail** for a steep and often muddy ascent of just under a mile. Make another right onto the **San Pablo Ridge Trail,** a steep grade that affords spectacular views of the bay. From here, you can pick up the paved **Nimitz Way Trail,** which leads back to Inspiration Point. For a shorter ride that avoids the most challenging stretch of the Belgum Trail, turn off Wildcat Creek Trail right onto **Conlon Trail.** To reach Inspiration Point by car, take the University Avenue exit from I–80, turn left onto Oxford Street when University ends, then turn right on Rose Street and left on Spruce Street. Follow Spruce over Grizzly Peak Road until it becomes Wildcat Canyon Road (about 20 minutes). Look for the Inspiration Point parking area on the left. To reach the Tilden Park rangers, call 510/562–7275.

➤ **REDWOOD REGIONAL PARK** • Over a hundred years ago, sailors entering San Francisco Bay used the giant redwood trees growing on the hills east of Oakland as a landmark. Unfortunately, most of those trees are now furniture. Only a few virgin redwoods remain in Redwood Regional Park, but the second-growth forest is still impressive. The 9-mile bike loop through the Redwood Forest is moderately difficult, with some strenuous areas. From Redwood Gate, follow the road past the picnic areas to the trailhead. **Canyon Trail** begins with a steep climb (which gets nice and muddy in the rainy season). After ½ mile, bear left on the **East Ridge Trail** for a gentle 3⅓-mile ascent up to the **West Ridge Trail.** The road levels out for a bit, but the downhill stretch has plenty of danger zones; so watch your speed. The West Ridge Trail eventually becomes the **Bridal Trail,** which runs into the Fern Dell Picnic Area. From here, turn right and take the road all the way back.

To get to Redwood Gate, take I–580 toward Hayward and exit at 35th Avenue/MacArthur Boulevard. Take 35th Avenue, which becomes Redwood Road, east past Skyline Boulevard. The park entrance is about 2 miles farther down the road. Parking inside costs $3 on weekends, but you can park along the road for free. To talk to a ranger, call 510/635–0135, ext. 2578.

➤ **ANTHONY CHABOT REGIONAL PARK** • Though the park's dusty trails sadly lack dramatic scenery and vistas, this is one of the few East Bay parks with a campground (*see* Chapter 7), and Chabot Lake's blue waters are a refreshing sight after a long haul. If you're looking for adventure, the 31-mile **Skyline Trail** (*see* East Bay, under Hiking, *above*) begins here and runs through six of the East Bay's major parks. You can ride it from Castro Valley all the way to Richmond, but you'll need to detour onto paved roads. To follow the Skyline Trail, look for signs with the red, white, and blue triangular insignia.

Bikers enjoy making the hilly 14-mile loop around Chabot Park. From the parking area at the marina, take the **West Shore Trail** to the **East Shore Trail.** Cross the bridge, turn right on **Live Oak Trail** for a steep ascent of just under a mile, and then turn right on **Towhee Trail** to the **Red Tail Trail.** Follow Red Tail Trail until you meet the **Grass Valley Trail.** From here, you can detour onto the Skyline Trail toward Redwood Regional Park, or follow the **Brandon Trail** to the **Goldenrod Trail,** ending up with a home stretch on the **Bass Cove Trail.** The entire loop is moderately strenuous.

To get to Anthony Chabot Regional Park, take Fairmont Drive east off I–580 to Lake Chabot Road. It costs $3 to park in the lot, but you can park along Lake Chabot Road for nothing. For biking and camping info, call 510/635–0135, ext. 2570; for lake info dial 510/582–2198.

MARIN COUNTY Ironically, the birthplace of the mountain bike is now a battleground where bikers are squaring off with hikers who want to keep the two-wheelers off the trails. Marin County has been particularly zealous about curtailing the use of mountain bikes. Trails that haven't been closed have a 15 mph speed limit (5 mph around turns), and rangers aren't shy about giving out hefty tickets ($180–$200) for violations. Some cyclists deliberately don't carry identification and give false names when rangers stop them. Other bikers have formed organizations to encourage better relations among everyone who wants to enjoy the wilderness. The **Bicycle Trails Council of Marin** (tel. 415/456–7512) maintains contact with park administrators and performs acts of community service, like leading bike trips for underprivileged urban kids and helping to maintain trails.

➤ **MARIN HEADLANDS** • The Marin Headlands, part of the **Golden Gate National Recreation Area,** are so close to San Francisco that most people leave the car at home and just bike to the park across the Golden Gate Bridge. The headlands are often foggy in summer and are always windy, so dress in layers. The trails, which start almost immediately on the north side of the bridge, are sure to be crowded on rare sunny weekends. If you're driving from the city, cross the Golden Gate Bridge and take the first exit (Alexander Avenue). Pass under the freeway, turn right before the entrance to U.S. 101 south, and follow the signs to the **visitor center** (tel. 415/331–1540). You can park there and pick up a map of legal trails between 9:30 and 4:30. Rangers sometimes lead mountain-biking tours; call for details.

A popular series of fire trails offers a great panorama of the Golden Gate and the Pacific. The 11½-mile loop described below is moderate, with some pretty steep sections. Take the **Miwok Trail** (from the parking area near the visitors' center) to the **Bobcat Trail,** and continue 3½ miles uphill to the **Marincello Trail.** This gravelly downhill run drops you on **Tennessee Valley Road,** which leads to the beach. To return, go back up Tennessee Valley Road and pick up **Old Springs Trail** (instead of Marincello) at the intersection by the Miwok Stable; you'll pass a set of perennial springs. Plan on getting muddy. At the Miwok Trail, hang a right and head back down to the trailhead.

➤ **MT. TAMALPAIS STATE PARK** • Mt. Tam's rangers take trail restrictions very seriously—some spend their whole day hunting for mountain bikers who are speeding or riding illegal trails. You should definitely get a map ($1) from the **ranger station** (tel. 415/388–2070) to see which trails are legal. To reach the station, follow U.S. 101 north from San Francisco and take the Route 1/Stinson Beach exit. Turn left onto Shoreline Highway and go 2½ miles to Panoramic Highway, which leads to the ranger station 5½ miles away. Parking at the station is $5, but you can park for free at the pull-out sites along the road.

The following bike ride takes you up to Mt. Tam's East Peak, for an exhilarating view from the top. Though you're climbing a mountain, the gradual gain in elevation makes this a relatively easy ride. If you continue past the East Peak, you're in for an all-day journey. From the ranger station, take the **Old Stage Road** uphill ½ mile to the West Point Inn, where you can grab a glass of lemonade. From the inn, go left on **Old Railroad Grade,** which runs for 2 miles almost to the top of Mt. Tam. It's one of the most popular rides on the mountain and gets quite crowded on weekends, so go carefully, especially on the way down.

From the top, you can either head back the way you came, or turn your ride into a 20-mile loop (total) that takes you back down Mt. Tam and halfway up again. If you've got the stamina, go down **East Ridgecrest Drive** and pick up the **Lagunitas–Rock Springs Trail,** which begins on the other side of the dirt parking lot. After a short climb, the trail descends to Lake Lagunitas, where you should turn right and go around the lake. Turn right again on **Lakeview,** and eventually you'll meet **Eldridge Grade,** where you start another ascent. Go left at **Indian** and enjoy a steep and bumpy downhill ride. Turn right on **Blithedale Ridge** (past the Hoo Koo E Koo Trail), and take either of two spurs that drop down to the right toward the **Old Railroad Grade.** When you hit West Point Inn—now are you ready for that lemonade?—go left on **Old Stage Road** and head back to the ranger station.

➤ **POINT REYES** • Most of the pristine trails in Point Reyes National Seashore are closed to bikers, but a few open paths and the park's paved roads make for scenic riding. A trail map from the **Bear Valley Visitor Center** (*see* Hiking, *above*), off Bear Valley Road from Route 1, should set you straight. For an easy, beautiful ride, take the **Bear Valley Trail** from the south end of the parking lot. About 3 miles into the ride, you'll reach a rack where you can lock your bike while you hike .8 miles out to the coast.

If you're up for something more serious, a strenuous 13-mile ride leaves from the Five Brooks parking area, off Route 1 about 3 miles south of Olema. Pick up the **Olema Valley Trail,** which leads to the **Randall Trail** (on the left); cross Route 1, ascend to Bolinas Ridge, and go right on the **Bolinas Ridge Trail.** About 1⅓ miles down the road, pick up the **McCurdy Trail,** cross Route 1 again, and take the Olema Valley Trail all the way back.

Surfing

If you want to take on the waves in the city, you're gonna earn your keep. The closest surf is brutal, paddling out can be exasperating, and the water is cold enough to make men remember that they have nipples, too. Surfers looking for forgiving conditions head south toward Santa Cruz. Anywhere you go in the Bay Area, though, swells are best during fall and winter, when storms far out at sea send ripples across the Pacific. Call **Wise Surfboards** (tel. 415/665–WISE) for a recorded message on conditions in the city.

Local surfers are territorial about their waves. They can be more hostile than the ocean when you violate surf etiquette, the unwritten law that the first person riding the wave has ownership. Novices should avoid practicing at popular, crowded spots like Rockaway Beach (*see below*), where there's competition for waves. In addition, the current around San Francisco claims lives every year. Beginners are best off heading north to Stinson Beach or south to Santa Cruz.

INSTRUCTION AND EQUIPMENT

If you can't find a friend to teach you, two world-class surfing instructors offer lessons near Santa Cruz. **Richard Schmidt** (tel. 408/423–0928) is a champion whose graceful style inspires his peers to sit back and take notes. The cheapest way to get any of the man's time is to take a surf class through the **Santa Cruz Parks and Recreation Department** (tel. 408/429–3663). A two-day group lesson, two hours daily, costs $63 for nonresidents of Santa Cruz, $55 for residents. Schmidt also offers private instruction, in which he guarantees to have first-time surfers riding their boards. A one-hour private lesson costs $50; equipment is included. **CLUB ED Surf and Windsurf School** (tel. 800/287–7873), run by Ed Guzman, also offers classes in Santa Cruz. Ed owns a concession stand on Cowell Beach, between the Dream Inn and the wharf. He's got boogie boards, windsurfers, kayaks, skim boards, surfboards, and an instructor for every skill level. His one-hour ($45) and two-hour ($75) group lessons start you off on an oversize board, perfect for beginners who don't yet have their balance. If you don't get the hang of it the first time, you can come back for another two-hour lesson for only $35.

In terms of equipment, think like a seal before you hit the water. All year round locals wear artificial blubber, in the form of boots, gloves, and full wet suits, 3–4/3 mm thick. The most common mistake newcomers to the area make is buying a board that's too small; a slightly longer, thicker board will help inexperienced surfers catch more waves. Check out the bulletin boards in surf shops to find something secondhand. **Wise Surfboards** (3149 Vicente St., San Francisco, tel. 415/665–7745) helps customers re-sell boards without taking a commission.

To rent a board in the city, go to **Outdoors Unlimited** (633 Parnassus Ave., near 4th Ave., tel. 415/476–2078); a weekend surfboard rental costs $8.50 and a 3-mm wet suit $12–$18. **Live Water** (3450 Rte. 1, Stinson Beach, tel. 415/868–0333) rents buoyant foam boards ($25 per day) for beginners. To the south, knowledgeable local surfers staff **Nor-Cal Surfshop** (5460 Cabrillo Hwy., Pacifica, tel. 415/738–9283), where you can rent a soft board for $10 a day.

The Smell of Blood

Shark trivia is a popular topic with surfers. Did you know that sharks never sleep, that they're not really fish (sharks' boneless bodies are composed of cartilage), or that the area stretching from Davenport (near Santa Cruz) to Stinson Beach is home to a large number of great whites? These indiscriminate eaters have been forced closer to shore as the seal population has decreased. Unfortunately, sharks have bad eyesight and mistake slick wet suits for shiny fur. Unlike the beast in Jaws, great whites don't usually bite off limbs in one gulp; they puncture their victims and circle until the prey bleeds to death. Surfers who have been bitten suggest hitting the shark on the nose to break its grip, then swimming like hell for shore. Sharks attack a few people annually, but that doesn't keep anyone out of the water. Surfers reason that if shark trivia scares you, you should try reading through car-crash fatality statistics sometime.

Sunlight Surfshop (575 Crespi Dr., Pacifica, tel. 415/359–0353) has similar boards, but the price depends on the board's size ($10–$15). If you call, you have to listen to a recording about current conditions before you can speak to a human.

WHERE TO SURF

Surf's up at **Ocean Beach,** west of Golden Gate Park, but you may wish it would go back down. Winter waves here get as big as anywhere in the world (20–25 feet), but only the insane tackle the biggest ones, because the shape of the wave is often poor. Even when the swells are manageable, the current is strong. You don't have to be an expert to surf Ocean Beach, but it's not a place to learn unless you're into self-abuse. Waves are cleaner at **Fort Point,** beneath the Golden Gate Bridge on the southeast side. This overlooked spot is quite convenient for city surfers, but the current and rocks may deter beginners.

If you're just starting out, drive north along Route 1 to **Stinson Beach.** The shallow beach break is not very demanding, and the waves are neither fast nor big. Stinson is a popular beach for sunbathing (or fog-bathing, as the case may be), but the water is rarely crowded. **Pacifica State Beach,** also known as **Linda Mar Beach,** is about 45 minutes south of San Francisco along Route 1. Pacifica breaks best at high tide, with smaller waves for beginners at the southern end of the beach. Just north of the rock promontory, **Rockway Beach** offers bigger waves, but it's more crowded and competitive. If you're adventurous, check out the underpopulated state beaches between Pacifica and Santa Cruz; for huge waves, head to **Mavericks Beach** in Half Moon Bay.

Windsurfing

The San Francisco Bay was ranked the third-best spot for windsurfing in the United States, after Oregon's Royal Gorge and Maui. Take advantage. Summer is the season to tack across the bay: From April to August, the wind blows west, providing optimal conditions for windsurfing almost anywhere in the Bay Area. Winds are sporadic during the rest of the year, blowing either north or south. During winter, the air can be as cold as the water, and you'll need a wet suit 3/2 or 4/3 mm thick. Some summer days are warm enough to go bottomless (in regard to wet suits, that is).

INSTRUCTION AND EQUIPMENT

Cal Adventures (*see* chapter introduction, *above*) offers cheap windsurfing lessons. Six hours of instruction on the bay, with an added hour of recreational windsurfing, costs $60 (less if you're a U.C. Berkeley student). After you've completed the course, you can buy a two-month pass for $100 that allows you to use windsurfing equipment during business hours (Mon. morning and all day Wed.–Sun.; closed Thurs. Nov.–Apr. 2).

The conditions on the bay are harsh for a beginning windsurfer, and you should consider learning on a lake. **Spinnaker Sailing** (3160 N. Shoreline Blvd., Mountain View, tel. 415/965–7474) offers beginning and advanced classes on an artificial lake. The two-day beginners' course costs $120. **Windsurf Del Valle** (Lake Del Valle, Livermore, tel. 510/455–4008) has the largest windsurfing school in the country, excellent for beginners. The site, on a lake about a half-hour's drive east of Oakland, is the perfect windsurfing location: The water and air temperatures hover in the 80s from April through October. The water is flat, with few waves, and the wind is light. The $95 beginners' course usually lasts two days and earns you the certification necessary for renting equipment at most shops. They guarantee that you will learn the sport, and will give you additional days of instruction for free if you need more help.

The **San Francisco School of Windsurfing** (Candlestick Park or Lake Merced, tel. 415/753–3235) specializes in increasing your skill level quickly. Beginners start at Lake Merced, but you soon learn to tackle the more popular bay. The school is renowned for dramatically improving intermediate students' abilities. The owner recommends that you not buy equipment until you've finished the entire course, since your beginning or intermediate board will become obsolete once you've improved. The two-day beginning course costs $95. Rentals cost $15 an hour, including wet suit, booties, and harness; a 10-hour pass is $100.

New windsurfing equipment is expensive—a grand, easy—so you may be forced to nickel and dime yourself with rentals. In addition to operating their main store, **Berkeley Boardsports** (843 Gilman St., Berkeley, tel. 510/527–7873) has set up shop next to the water at Alameda's Crown Beach and at Larkspur Landing in San Rafael. One hour on a board costs $10, but you can use the board all day for $40, including wet suit. If you're going to buy, it's prudent to look for secondhand equipment. Most windsurfing shops have a bulletin board and free magazines with ads for used gear.

WHERE TO WINDSURF

BEGINNER Alameda's **Crown Beach,** with easy access to shallow waters, offers the best conditions in the East Bay for learning the sport. Forces of nature work to the novice's advantage—

Smooth Sailing

San Francisco never seems as picturesque as when it's seen from sea level, but it isn't postcard scenery that draws sailors to the bay—it's the remarkably consistent west wind. The San Francisco Bay is one of the most challenging places in the country to sail. Even if you can't scrape up the dough for a yacht, you needn't remain a landlubber. A little charm and a tolerance for grunt work can earn you a job working crew on a boat. Crewing is the cheapest way to learn about sailing, and the water makes the best classroom. Post an ad at your local marina and talk to boaters, and your eagerness will likely win you a sailing invitation. The sailing magazine Latitude 38 (look for it in boating stores) is an excellent resource for finding used boats or placing an ad for a crew. They also print a schedule of races every March, just in time for the beginning of the season. The Berkeley Marina (end of University Ave.) is a great place to learn about sailing. Cal Sailing Club (tel. 510/287–5905), across from the marina, offers three months of unlimited lessons and equipment use for a membership cost of $45, $40 for U.C. students. You can sail to your heart's content on their 8- to 15-foot (not necessarily well-maintained) boats, but keep in mind that the students of today will be the instructors of tomorrow. To check out the club, take a free sail the first full weekend of each month from 1 to 4 PM—don't forget to wear something warm and waterproof.

Cal Adventures (Recreational Sports Facility, U.C. Berkeley, 2301 Bancroft Way, tel. 510/642–4000) offers equipment rental if you have the appropriate qualifications and reasonably priced classes if you don't. Also consider Olympic Circle Sailing Club (1 Spinnaker Way, Berkeley, near the marina, tel. 800/223–2984), whose courses are expensive but highly recommended by those in the know. If you can't afford a class, show up on a summer Wednesday for the 5:30 sunset sail. The two-hour ride (reservations required) costs $25 per person. Spinnaker Sailing/Rendezvous Charter (Pier 40, South Beach Harbor, San Francisco, tel. 415/543–7333) charters boats and teaches sailing in the city. If you prefer the passenger's seat, they also offer a two-hour sunset sail ($23) on Wednesday, Friday, or Saturday.

the wind is usually light and blows towards the shore, so if you zig when you should have zagged, you won't be lost at sea. To reach Crown Beach from downtown Oakland, take the Alameda Tunnel to Webster Street, turn right onto Central Avenue, turn left on McKay Avenue, and follow McKay to the beach.

Larkspur Landing, in Marin County, is good for a couple with unequal windsurfing abilities. The light wind close to shore accommodates beginners, while the more advanced windsurfer will be challenged farther out in the bay. Mornings are calmest and best for beginners; the wind picks up in the afternoon. The area is not without its weaknesses—parking your car, for example, is a major hassle. And when the wind is light, it's no fun to access the water: From a rocky shore, you have to paddle out into the bay while keeping a wary eye out for ferries. From U.S. 101 north, take the San Rafael/Richmond exit east, and continue a quarter-mile past the Larkspur Ferry Terminal.

INTERMEDIATE/ADVANCED The **Berkeley Marina,** at the end of University Avenue, requires intermediate to advanced skills. Access to the water is problematic, since you must launch off either the dock or the rocks. The windy and choppy conditions are tough on a beginner, but provide lots of wave-jumping opportunities for experienced windsurfers who like to spend time in the air. From I–80, take the University Avenue exit west to the end.

Crissy Field, in San Francisco's Presidio, should challenge advanced windsurfers. Beach access makes getting into the water easy, but with the strong tides and currents, getting out is a task. The current could easily sweep an unprepared windsurfer under the Golden Gate or across the bay to Treasure Island. In addition, boat and ship traffic make the water about as easy to navigate as the freeway at rush hour. If you're up to the challenge, you'll find Crissy Field just southeast of the Golden Gate Bridge (off Mason St.).

At **Candlestick Park** on the Peninsula, not everyone is going to the ball game. Flat water, strong winds, and easy access to the bay make Candlestick a favorite with windsurfers interested in speed. Winds average 19–25 mph, but they can get as high as 55 mph. You have to be an expert to handle the offshore winds, which carry you right out into the bay. If the wind dies, you'll be stranded out there; and if the Coast Guard has to rescue you because of your negligence, you'll pay at least $200. Think twice before windsurfing here on game days: Parking costs about $7 during baseball games and about $10 during football games.

The onshore wind and big chops make **Coyote Point,** near Candlestick, an advanced area. On the inside (close to shore), the wind is moderate, but on the outside (away from shore), it increases and the waves become choppy. The entrance fee for **Coyote Point Park** (tel. 415/573–2592) is $4, well worth it for the use of the hot showers. Follow U.S. 101 south past the airport to the Poplar Avenue exit, take Humboldt Street, turn right on Peninsula Avenue, go right across the overpass, and bear left onto Coyote Point Drive.

DAY AND WEEKEND TRIPS

By Julie Feinstein, Terence Priester, and Zak Smith

Whether you're looking for a day at the beach or a weekend in the mountains, a New Age healing session or an isolated cross-country ski trail, odds are good that you'll find what you want somewhere in the diverse and gorgeous country surrounding San Francisco. Perhaps more than any other major American city, San Francisco is distinguished by its proximity to dramatic natural terrain and interesting small towns. You could easily live here for a decade without exhausting your options for day and weekend trips. North of the city lies California's world-famous Wine Country; and to the south, Santa Cruz is a gathering point for surfers, New Agers, and neo-hippies. An afternoon's drive east will bring you to that most un-Californian phenomenon, snow, in the mountains surrounding Lake Tahoe, which are home to some of the country's best skiing. Although it helps to have a car, you can reach all these places on public transportation if you're patient.

The Wine Country

The Wine Country is only 60 miles northeast of San Francisco, an easy and highly recommended day trip if you have a car. You don't have to be a wine connoisseur to enjoy a visit to this region—even philistines appreciate the rustic beauty of the area and the opportunity to get a free buzz. Many of the wineries will pour you glass after glass of free samples. Choose carefully, though: A number of Napa Valley wineries charge a $2 or $3 tasting fee, which can add up if you're making the rounds. In some places, you may have to take a tour or watch a film before you can get to the tasting; but luckily, the tours are usually interesting (especially in the smaller wineries).

Most vineyards are concentrated in the Napa and Sonoma valleys, but the Wine Country actually stretches north to Santa Rosa and all the way into Lake and Mendocino counties. Vintners have been making wine here for well over 100 years, but it was only in 1976, when a cabernet sauvignon from Stag's Leap won a blind taste test in Paris, that Californians began boasting and people all over the world began buying. Since then, production has skyrocketed. Twenty-five years ago there were only about 25 wineries; now there are more than 200.

You'll undoubtedly be tempted to buy some of the wine you try, but don't buy in volume until you check the local supermarkets, which may have it for less.

Napa Valley has the greatest number, but its wineries are also the most expensive and pretentious. Once upon a time, visitors were greeted with open arms—and flowing bottles—by jolly vintners thankful for even a trickle of business. These days, unless you're wearing a sport

211

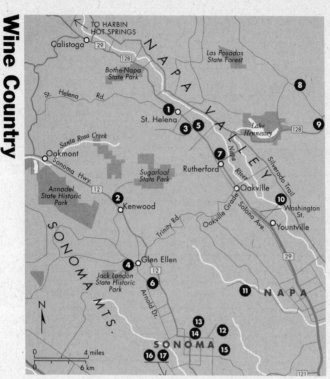

Wine Country

TO HARBIN
HOT SPRINGS
Calistoga
29
128
Bothe-Napa
State Park
St. Helena Rd.
Las Posadas
State Forest
St. Helena
Santa Rosa Creek
Oakmont
Sonoma Hwy.
Annadel
State Historic
Park
Sugarloaf
State Park
Rutherford
Lake
Hennessey
128
Napa River
Silverado Trail
12
Kenwood
Oakville
Washington St.
Solano Ave.
Oakville Grade
Trinity Rd.
Yountville
SONOMA MTS.
Glen Ellen
12
Jack London
State Historic
Park
Arnold Dr.
29
NAPA
N
SONOMA
0   4 miles
0   6 km
121

Beaulieu
Vineyards, **7**
Benziger, **4**
Beringer Winery, **1**
Buena Vista, **12**
Chateau St. Jean, **2**
Cline Cellars, **17**
Gundlach-
Bundschu, **15**
Hess Collection, **11**
Nichelini, **9**
Prager Winery, **3**
Ravenswood, **13**
Rustridge, **8**
S. Anderson, **10**
Schug, **16**
Sebastiani, **14**
Valley of
the Moon, **6**
V. Sattui, **5**

jacket and driving an expensive car, you may get a chilly reception. If so, hop in the car and make a beeline for the Sonoma Valley. While Sonoma has some big, impersonal wineries, it draws fewer tourists and is home to a greater share of rustic, unassuming vineyards. In both counties, the farther you stray from the main drag, the better off you'll be.

The best time to go is in autumn, during harvest season, when you'll see some real action in the wine cellars. In both spring and fall, wildflowers bloom amid the endless rows of manicured vines. Try to avoid the Wine Country in summer, though. The dry, dusty region becomes even drier and dustier, and the crowds can be suffocating—it sometimes feels as if each and every one of the 2.5 million annual visitors is backed up along Route 29, impatient for another glass of zinfandel. If you do go in summer, stay off Route 29 as much as possible and explore the less crowded and more scenic **Silverado Trail,** which runs parallel to Route 29 a mile to the east.

If you detest wine, you can luxuriate in the hot springs, mud baths, and mineral baths of Calistoga, loiter in the lovely Spanish mission and old adobes of Sonoma, or browse through the small museums devoted to former residents Jack London and Robert Louis Stevenson, both of whom wrote about the area. Be forewarned, though: An overnight stay in the Wine Country can take a monster-size bite out of your budget. Lodging tends to be even more expensive than in San Francisco, and food is pricey as well. You can survive cheaply by eating at roadside produce stands, drinking free wine, and sleeping in a state park. Otherwise, expect to pay through the nose.

VISITOR INFORMATION

Before you go (or once you arrive), you may want to call the **Napa Chamber of Commerce** (1556 1st St., Napa, tel. 707/226–7455), open weekdays 9–5, which can help you organize your trip and provide you with more maps than you'll ever need. The **Sonoma Valley Visitors' Bureau**

(453 1st St. E., Sonoma, tel. 707/996–1090), open daily 9–7 (until 5 in winter), offers friendly advice on what to see and do in the "other" valley. Additionally, most wineries carry the *California's Visitor's Review,* a free weekly that has maps and winery information.

COMING AND GOING

BY CAR Though traffic is heavy, the best way to reach the Wine Country is by car. Several different routes will get you there. From San Francisco, the best option is to take **U.S. 101** north over the Golden Gate Bridge and connect with **Route 37** east near Ignacio. From here, take **Route 121** north to **Route 12** north for Sonoma, or follow Route 121 as it curves east toward **Route 29** for Napa. Traffic is heaviest on weekends and during rush hours (7–9 AM, 4–6 PM), but even at the worst times it shouldn't take more than two hours.

Santa Rosa is less than an hour's drive from San Francisco straight up U.S. 101, but the trip can take twice as long during morning and evening rush hours. Instead, make the trek to Sonoma and then pick up Route 12 east toward Santa Rosa. It's a beautiful drive through green hills, cattle pastures, and quiet farms, and except for the occasional pickup or horse trailer, traffic shouldn't be a problem.

BY BUS **Golden Gate Transit** (tel. 415/332–6600 or 707/544–1323) provides bus service from San Francisco and Marin County to towns throughout Sonoma County. Bus 90 goes from San Francisco to Sonoma (1½ hrs, $4.50) two or three times a day. Bus 80 runs from S.F. to Santa Rosa (2 hrs, $4.50) frequently.

Greyhound has service from San Francisco (7th and Mission Sts., tel. 800/231–2222) to Napa (2½ hrs, $9.50 one-way, $18 round-trip) once daily, to Sonoma (2½–4 hrs, change in Vallejo or Santa Rosa, $13 one-way, $25 round-trip) twice each weekday, and to Santa Rosa (2 hrs, $11 one-way, $21 round-trip) twice a day. Tickets are usually cheaper if you buy them seven days in advance.

GETTING AROUND

Quaint and tempting as the **Napa Valley Wine Train** (1275 McKinstry St., Napa, tel. 707/253–2111) may sound, its scheduled stops are anything but comprehensive. In addition, it's expensive ($56 and up per person) and resented by the locals, because it pollutes the valley and brings too many tourists. For that kind of money, rent a car—you can't get drunk, but at least you have the liberty to stop when and where you want. Some people tour the Napa Valley by balloon, but this extravagance costs upwards of $150 per person.

BY CAR One of the most popular drives is unofficially known as the **Napa–Sonoma loop.** Start on Route 29 in Napa, head about 15 miles north to Oakville, and then take the scenic Oakville Grade/Trinity Road west to Glen Ellen, on Route 12 in the Sonoma Valley. The drive is spectacular and, without any stops, easily navigated in under two hours. Depending on your final destination, you may have to backtrack to take in Calistoga, St. Helena, or Santa Rosa, but all are easily accessed from Routes 12 or 29.

For the grand tour, take Route 29 north from Napa to Calistoga, head west for 12 miles toward Fulton and U.S. 101 on the Petrified Forest Trail, drive 4 miles south on U.S. 101 to Santa Rosa, and then take Route 12 south. Twenty-six miles later, you'll be in Sonoma. This semi-circular drive takes four hours without any stops, and it passes through the Wine Country's major towns and vineyards.

BY BUS If you can't afford to rent a car, there are ways to see the Wine Country by bus. It'll require some creativity on your part, but hey—that's half the fun. In particular, **Sonoma County Transit** (tel. 707/576–7433) connects all cities in Sonoma County. Buses run weekdays 6 AM–6:30 PM (some until 10 PM), and weekends 8–6. Fares are less than $2 to most places (ask for student and disabled discounts), and buses can get you within walking distance of a few wineries. **Napa Valley Transit** (tel. 707/255–7631) offers service between Napa and Yountville ($1, or 75¢ for students). **Santa Rosa City Bus** (tel. 707/524–5306) has bus service in and around Santa Rosa (85¢).

BY BIKE Biking is perhaps the best way to see the Wine Country. You may not want to make the long haul from Sonoma to St. Helena by bike, but within each region the wineries tend to be huddled close together, making them easy to see on two wheels. Bicyclists should stick to the Silverado Trail. Riding on Route 29 means a greater risk of being run over by tipsy drivers, especially on summer weekends. **Bike Tours of Napa Valley** (4080 Byway East, tel. 707/255–3380 or 800/707–BIKE), at the northern end of Napa, rents bikes starting at $6 per hour or $20 per day. In St. Helena, **St. Helena Cyclery** (1156 Main St., tel. 707/963–7736) charges $7 per hour, $25 per day, or $110 per week. The bikes at **Calistoga Bike Rentals** (1227 Lincoln Ave., tel. 707/942–0421), in downtown Calistoga, rent for $7 per hour or $25 per day. All these shops offer biking maps and tour suggestions, so squeeze as much information from them as possible before heading out.

A little-known and very scenic 17-mile loop will take you through the countryside and away from the traffic. It starts in Napa at Monticello Road (Rte. 121). Travel north to Vichy Avenue, then south to Hagen Road, where you head east to Third Avenue (just past the Napa Valley Country Club). Continue south along Third to Coombsville Road, which takes you west back to Route 121. Note: This is *not* a winery-tour trail.

Sonoma Valley

Although Napa Valley receives most of the hype, Sonoma Valley is the birthplace of California's wine industry, and it's a better bet than nearby Napa for budget travelers. For one thing, almost all the wineries in Sonoma offer free tasting; you can imbibe to your heart's content without spending a dime. In addition, most of the wineries are small, family-owned concerns, more relaxed and less crowded than those in Napa.

The town of **Sonoma** has recently grown into an upscale bedroom community for San Francisco commuters, so trendy restaurants and chic clothing boutiques are sprouting up. Sonoma has a rich history, though, and still retains some of the feel of old California. It was here that Father Junipero Serra built the last and northernmost of the California missions, **Mission San Francisco Solano** (1st and Spain Sts., tel. 707/938–1519), now a museum housing a collection of 19th-century watercolors by Chris Jorgenson. The missionaries planted the region's first vines here in 1823 to make wine for mass. Around the mission, many adobe buildings remain from the days of Spanish and Mexican rule, including the old army barracks and **Lachryma Montis**, the ornate home of the last Mexican governor, General Vallejo. Admission to the grounds, open daily 10–5, is $2.

The title of Jack London's book Valley of the Moon *has become an alternate name for the Sonoma Valley. The Native American word "sonoma" actually means "many moons."*

Nearby in **Glen Ellen,** north of Sonoma off Route 12, look for **Jack London State Historic Park.** Tired of drinking and brawling on the Oakland waterfront, London (1876–1916) came here to build his dream home, Wolf House. The house was torched by an arsonist before it was fin-

The Bear Flag Republic

For a short period in 1846, Sonoma belonged not to Mexico, Spain, or the United States, but to the lesser-known Bear Flag Republic. The republic was the brainchild of Captain John C. Frémont and a ragtag group of Yankee trappers, who decided to resolve tensions between the Mexican government and non-Mexican immigrants by throwing the Mexican commander in prison and creating their own country. The republic evaporated a few months later when the U.S. Navy arrived, but the bear remains on the California state flag.

ished, but the impressive stone foundations remain, along with the architects' drawings of what the house would have looked like. A shady half-mile walk through the oak trees takes you from the free Jack London Museum to his grave and the ruins of his home. Poison oak abounds, so stick to the road. *2400 London Ranch Rd., Glen Ellen, tel. 707/938–5216. Take Glen Ellen turnoff from Rte. 12 and follow signs. Parking: $5. Museum open daily 10–5.*

WINERIES Sonoma Valley is home to some 30 wineries and 6,000 acres of vineyards. It was here that California began its upstart drive to compete with old-world wineries, when Count Agoston Haraszthy planted the first European vines in 1857. You can easily spend a leisurely day driving up Route 12 through the 17-mile-long valley, stopping to sip a little wine, learn a little history, have a picnic, and laze around in the sun.

Benziger. You're encouraged to roam the beautiful grounds, enjoy the fragrant rose gardens, picnic in any spot you choose, and indulge in many a free taster. The employees at this winery (formerly called Glen Ellen) are knowledgeable, and you can take a guided or self-guided tour, though it's not required for tasting. *1883 London Ranch Rd., Glen Ellen, tel. 707/935–3000. Take Benziger turnoff from Rte. 12 and follow signs for Jack London State Park. Wheelchair access. Open daily 10–4:30.*

Buena Vista. Count Agoston Haraszthy, "the father of California wine," brought thousands of European grapevine cuttings to the United States in the mid-1800s to start this winery. The tour covers his colorful life as well as the history of the vineyard. Tastings (up to four wines, plus gewürztraminer grape juice) happen in the impressive, ivy-covered main building, and they're free. Definitely try the pinot noir and the Carneros Estate chardonnay. Also venture upstairs to see the artwork and meet the current resident artist. *18000 Old Winery Rd., Sonoma, tel. 800/926–1266. Take E. Napa St. east from the plaza, and turn left on Old Winery Rd. Open summer, daily 10:30–5; winter, daily 11–4:30.*

Chateau St. Jean. The palatial grounds include a fish pond, a fountain, and an observation tower from which you get a spectacular view of the vineyard and surrounding area. Though tasting is free, the room is crowded and the staff is too busy to be very helpful. For a more relaxed

A Rosé by Any Other Name . . .

In just one tasting session at a Napa or Sonoma winery, you'll be bombarded by as many as six or seven different varieties of wine. The tasting often starts with a sauvignon blanc or with chardonnay, a dry (not sweet) white wine that picks up a smooth, buttery taste when aged in oak barrels. If you prefer sweeter, fruitier wines, try the aromatic whites (Riesling, chenin blanc, muscat, and gewürztraminer). Muscats are rich, sweet dessert wines, tasting vaguely of honey—Benziger (see above) has a particularly good one. Gewürztraminer is slightly bubbly and a little spicy. Try one at Chateau St. Jean (see above). The reds come last at a tasting, because of their stronger flavor. The earthy cabernet sauvignon is a safe bet, essentially a higher-class version of the jug wine people drink around the campfire. To be bold, try the fuller, richer merlot. Cabernets and merlots both have a lot of tannins (pigments from grape skins that help preserve wines and allow red wines to improve with age). If these wines are too young, their tannic bitterness may make you pucker. Zinfandel (a low-alcohol, fruity red) and pinot noir are both lighter in tannins and meant to be drunk young. The zinfandel at Ravenswood (see below) is well worth a try, as is their merlot. Oh, and don't look for any "blush" or "California Chablis" at California's serious wineries—those are just fancy names marketers give cheap jug wines.

time, kick back with a bottle of their excellent gewürztraminer and have a picnic on the lawn. *8555 Rte. 12, Kenwood, tel. 707/833–4134. Just south of Sugarloaf State Park, at north end of the valley. Wheelchair access. Open daily 10–4:30.*

Cline Cellars. You pass through grapevines and roses on the way to the tasting room, in an old farmhouse dating from the mid-1800s. At the tasting bar, you can try four of the six wines, as well as homemade mustards, for free. Check out the bathhouse to the side, with original walls from the 1850s. You can picnic on the porch beside one of six ponds fed by neighboring hot springs. *24737 Arnold Dr. (Rte. 121), Sonoma, tel. 707/935–4310. On Rte. 121 btw Rtes. 12 and 37. Open daily 10–6.*

Gundlach-Bundschu. Someone at this 137-year-old, family-owned winery has a sense of humor. In the main building (surrounded by trellised wisteria), old photographs of the family and winery sit alongside a picture of Bacchus in shades. Then there are the corks, inscribed "Leave the kids the land and money—drink the wine yourself." Free tasters get you in the proper hedonistic mood. *2000 Denmark St., Sonoma, tel. 707/938–5277. Take E. Napa St. east from the plaza, right on E. 5th St., left on Denmark St., look for sign on the left. Wheelchair access. Open daily 11–4:30.*

Ravenswood. This small stone winery in the Sonoma hills has a relaxed, intimate feel. Better yet, the jovial staff does not seem to care how many wines you taste. Their motto is "No Wimpy Wines," and their merlots and zinfandels are definitely worth writing home about. If you didn't bring a picnic to savor on the terrace, try their barbecued chicken or ribs with bread, coleslaw, and potato salad ($6–$9), available on summer weekends only. *18701 Gehricke Rd., Sonoma, tel. 707/938–1960. From the plaza in downtown Sonoma, take Spain St. east to 4th St. E.; turn left, then right onto Lovall Valley Rd., then left on Gehricke Rd. Wheelchair access. Open daily 10–4:30.*

Schug. Walter Schug will pour you free tastes of his European-style wines at this mellow, family-run winery. Not many tourists get here, so the family members (who are viticultural experts) have plenty of time to answer your questions. They'll give you a tour if you're interested, and you can explore the rooms where the wines are aged and bottled. *602 Bonneau Rd., tel. 707/939–9363. Bonneau Rd. begins west of the intersection of Rtes. 116 and 121 south of Sonoma. Open daily 10–5.*

Sebastiani. This large, corporate-feeling winery was one of only seven California vineyards allowed to operate during Prohibition. These days, unless you like fighting yuppies and retirees for a spot at the counter (tasting is free), you should avoid Sebastiani, especially on summer weekends. *389 4th St. E., Sonoma, tel. 707/938–5532. Three blocks past Sonoma's central plaza, turn left on 4th St. E. and go 1 block. Wheelchair access. Open daily 10–5.*

Valley of the Moon. This intimate winery off the main drag is a breath of fresh air compared to the more crowded vineyards in the upper valley. The staff is friendly and helpful, and in that fine Sonoma Valley tradition, tasting is free. Especially good is the sémillon, a semi-sweet white wine. *777 Madrone Rd., Glen Ellen, tel. 707/996–6941. From Sonoma, take Rte. 12 north 6 mi to Madrone Rd. Wheelchair access. Open daily 10–5.*

WHERE TO SLEEP Beds don't come cheap in the Sonoma Valley. If you have a tent, your best bet is camping. Otherwise, you'll probably want to make the half-hour drive to Santa Rosa for an affordable room. Even at Sonoma's least expensive motel, the **El Pueblo Motel** (896 W. Napa St., on Rte. 12, tel. 707/996–3651 or 800/900–8844), a clean and generic double will run you a whopping $60 weekdays, $70 weekends ($52–$63 in winter). At least they have a great swimming pool, and the motel is close to the central square and several wineries.

You'll pay comparable prices at some of Sonoma's bed-and-breakfasts. **Hollyhock House** (1541 Denmark St., 2 mi southeast of Sonoma Plaza, tel. 707/938–1809) is an old two-story farmhouse on a quiet country road, with roosters, geese, rabbits, and a flower garden worthy of Monet. The three doubles cost $65–$100 on summer weekends ($50–$90 in winter), but you can lower the price of the cheapest room by staying more than one weekend night or coming on a weekday. Call at least a week in advance. The **Jack London Lodge** (13740 Arnold Dr., at London Ranch Rd., Glen Ellen, tel. 707/938–8510) offers comfortable doubles with antique decor at $70–$75 ($55–$60 Nov.–Apr.). The lodge has a pool and saloon, and a small continental breakfast is included on weekends and in summer. Reservations are strongly recommended, especially in summer. Skip their restaurant and go to the Sonoma Mountain Grill instead (see Food, below).

➤ **CAMPING** • **Sugarloaf State Park.** Only 8 miles north of Sonoma on Route 12, Sugarloaf has 50 campsites scattered around a large meadow (dry and uninviting in summer). There are 25 miles of trails for hiking, biking, and horseback riding. If you hike up the trail to your left as you enter the park, you're likely to see deer, especially around sunset, when they come out for early evening grazing. Campsites cost $14. Reserve through MISTIX (tel. 800/444–PARK) in summer and on weekends. *2605 Adobe Canyon Rd., Kenwood, tel. 707/833–5712. From Sonoma, take Rte. 12 north to Adobe Canyon Rd., which ends at the park. Flush toilets, running water.*

FOOD Sonoma is *the* place to get your fill of gourmet-this and roasted-goat-red-pepper-that. There are some options for those unable to lay out huge sums of cash, though. No-frills sandwiches ($5–$6) and ice cream are available at the **Old Sonoma Creamery** (400 1st St. E., on the central plaza, tel. 707/938–2938), open weekdays 9:30–5, weekends until 6. **Zino's on the Plaza** (420 1st St. E., tel. 707/935–0660), open daily 11–4 and 5–9, offers basic pasta entrees for under $10. This place is popular with the tourist crowds, though, and the staff can be less than cordial on busy summer evenings. Stop by **Murphy's Irish Pub** (464 1st St. E., tel. 707/935–0660) for homemade lamb stew served with mushy peas ($5.50) and a pint of stout ($3).

For the best breakfast deal in town, go to the **Feed Store Café and Bakery** (529 1st St. W., off the central plaza, tel. 707/938–2122). Weekdays 7–9 AM you can get a two-egg breakfast, fruity granola, oat bran pancakes, or orange-brandy French toast for $3 (on weekends it's $1–$2 more). At the **Sunnyside Coffee Club and Blues Bar** (140 E. Napa St., near the central square, tel. 707/935–0366), you can order the bittersweet-chocolate banana pancake with vanilla-bean whipped cream and piped Mexican churros ($6) for breakfast. At lunch, try the salad with soba noodles ($5). On Friday and Saturday nights, stop in for live jazz and blues until midnight. You'll find tasty Mexican food at the roadside **Cocina Cha Cha Cha** (897 W. Napa St., tel. 707/996–1735), open Sunday–Thursday 11–9 and Friday–Saturday until 10. A crisp taco with ground beef is only 99¢, and two people can easily split the enormous *burrito grande*, filled with the works and topped with a homemade spicy sauce ($6.75).

For an excellent sit-down meal, trek out to the one-street town of Glen Ellen, where you'll find the **Sonoma Mountain Grill** (13690 Arnold Dr., tel. 707/938–2370), open weekdays except Tuesday 11–9 and weekends 9–9. The fresh fish special, with a heaping salad, vegetables, and rice, is the most expensive thing on the menu ($12–$14), but it's well worth it—with an appetizer, it could feed two. Glen Ellen is so remote that you may find yourselves the only patrons on weeknights, though locals do stop by regularly for the pizza (12-inch with two toppings about $13), and they fill the place on summer weekends.

CHEAP THRILLS Wine isn't the only thing that's free in the Sonoma Valley. If you're watching the bucks, don't miss the free samples at the **Sonoma Cheese Factory** (2 Spain St., Sonoma, tel. 707/996–1931), where the popular Sonoma Jack cheese is made. At the mellower, family-owned **Vella Cheese Company** (315 2nd St. E., Sonoma, tel. 707/938–3232), you can watch the cheese being rolled by hand. The process happens Monday–Wednesday from noon to 2 PM. On Wednesday nights, the **Center of the Universe Café** at the Sonoma Community Center (276 Napa St. E., tel. 707/938–1641 or 707/938–4626) hosts music, poetry readings, and lectures. A donation is nice, but they're not strict about it. If you show up at 7 PM with a dish in hand, you can join the potluck dinner. At the nearby **Sonoma Historical Park,** in the central square downtown, you can throw a Frisbee or regress back to childhood on the swings and the slide. In summer, the **Sonoma Valley Jazz Society** offers free concerts. Call 707/996–7423 for information.

Napa Valley

While Sonoma is cheaper and more welcoming, it's Napa Valley, about a 20-minute drive east of Sonoma on Route 121, that lures most visitors to the Wine Country. It's clear from the traffic backed up on Route 29 that Napa Valley has become one of the biggest tourist attractions north of Fisherman's Wharf. The valley is still beautiful, the wine (in some cases) still free, the town of **Napa** still lined with attractive Victorian houses and California bungalows, but there's no doubt that Napa Valley is losing some of its old-time charm with each trampling tourist. The quiet town of **St. Helena,** 16 miles north of Napa on Route 29, has fewer tourists than the southern part of the valley. A few grocery stores and pharmacies and a no-frills rural appeal make this a good rest stop on your way up the valley.

WINERIES With literally hundreds of wineries crammed into the 35-mile-long Napa Valley, it's difficult to decide which ones to visit. Some, like **Sutter Home Winery** (277 Rte. 29, St. Helena, tel. 707/963–3104), right on the main drag, are packed with drunken revelers, while others, like **Trefethen Vineyards** (1160 Oak Knoll Ave., Napa, tel. 707/255–7700), draw a sedate crowd able to hold forth about a wine's bouquet and tannins. If you're irked by the idea of paying a $3 tasting fee, you'll have to choose carefully, but don't despair of finding free samples.

While wine tasting and mud bathing are both popular Wine Country activities, you won't want to indulge in both on the same day—unless you enjoy the pangs of a fierce headache.

In general, a good way to avoid crowds is to take the **Silverado Trail** (parallel to Rte. 29, 1 mi east), which passes through many vineyards without the hectic traffic of the main road. Exit Route 29 at any point between Napa and Calistoga and follow the Silverado Trail signs. Remember that it doesn't always work to just drop in at a winery, especially if you want to take a tour. At some of the smaller places, you may need an appointment.

How to Taste Like a Master

If you want to pass yourself off as a wine aficionado (as opposed to a freeloading swiller), you'll need to know some rules of tasting. First of all, move from light wines to dark, so as not to "clutter your palate," as a vintner might say. Begin by vigorously swirling an ounce of wine in your glass. Put your hand over the glass to hold in the aromas (as well as the wine, if you're new to the swirling business). Raise the glass to your nose and inhale deeply. In young wines, you smell only the grapes (for example, the smell of the pinot noir grape might remind you of black cherries); with aging, the wine becomes more complex, emitting a whole bouquet of aromas (in pinot, that can include violets, vanilla, a spicy pepper, or even leather). Next, take a sip—you're encouraged to slurp, because air helps you taste the wine. Swish the wine around in your mouth to pick up the more subtle flavors. Before downing the rest of your glass, notice the aftertaste (or "finish"), and then decide what you think. Try to identify the fruit and spice flavors in the wine. To make your tasting complete, look poised and self-assured and make some completely asinine summation. ("It's a cheeky little wine, reminiscent of running naked through verdant pastures.")

If you're seriously interested in wine tasting, you can take a course through U.C. Berkeley Extension's Wine Studies department. Offerings include Wines of California and Europe, California World-Class Wines, and others. The fees are steep ($125–$150 for a six-week course), but the courses are fun and incredibly informative. Contact U.C. Berkeley Extension (2223 Fulton St., Berkeley, CA 94720, tel. 510/642–4111) for more information.

Beaulieu Vineyards. Affectionately known as "BV," Beaulieu has supplied wine to President Eisenhower and Queen Elizabeth, among others. Yet this large winery is far from snooty. The staff greets you with a glass of wine at the door of the octagonal tasting room and encourages you to indulge in free samples. If you like dessert wine, be sure to taste their lovely muscat. Free, informative half-hour tours cover the wine-making process and BV's 100-year history. *1960 Rte. 29, Rutherford, tel. 707/963–2411. Wheelchair access. Open daily 10–5.*

Beringer Winery. Now owned by the controversial Nestlé chocolate company, Beringer has an interesting history: It's one of the few wineries to remain in continuous operation throughout the 20th century (since 1876, in fact). A government license to make sacramental wine kept Beringer in business during Prohibition, when most wineries were shut down. The half-hour tour takes you through the winery's hundred-year-old caves and beautiful grounds, and concludes with a free tasting (though the finer vintages are only available for a hefty $2–$4 per taste). Be prepared for that impersonal, corporate feel you get at most of the big wineries. Tours and tastings take place year-round, but reservations are advised on summer weekends. *2000 Main St. (Rte. 29), St. Helena, tel. 707/963– 7115. Open Nov.–May, daily 9:30–5; Apr.–Oct., daily 9:30–6.*

Hess Collection. Displaying a perpetually burning Underwood typewriter, this unique winery-cum-gallery gives you the chance to view contemporary European and American paintings, sculpture, and mixed-media works as you learn about wine. You can take a self-guided tour through the exhibits on the second and third floors and see various aspects of the wine-making process. Guided tours give more details about the art and artists. Skip the vaguely informative, semi-hokey audiovisual presentation. The only drawback is that it costs $2.50 to taste. Be sure to try the pinot noir, a new addition to the winery's line. *4411 Redwood Rd., tel. 707/255–1144. Exit Rte. 29 at Redwood Rd., and look for the sign on the left. Wheelchair access. Open daily 10–4.*

Nichelini. Napa's oldest continuously owned family winery lies 11 miles east of Rutherford and is worth every minute of the beautiful drive there. Outside, under the shade of walnut trees and next to an old Roman grape press (which looks like a giant garlic press), you can sample wines for free. Picnic to the strains of traditional Italian music, on a hill overlooking the countryside. *Rte. 128, St. Helena, tel. 707/963–0717. Open weekends 10–6.*

Prager Winery. Owner Jim Prager and the family dog Eno (short for "enology") know the meaning of hospitality, and will personally greet you. This rustic winery doesn't even produce enough cases a year to be classified as "small." ("That makes us 'tiny,'" quips Jim.) As you enjoy free tastes of port (their specialty) and perhaps a couple of other wines, Jim can explain the old-fashioned wine-making methods they employ. Prager ports are available only at the winery. The homey garden provides a quiet break from the Route 29 crowds. *1281 Lewelling Ln., St. Helena, tel. 707/963–PORT or 800/969–PORT. Look for the sign on Rte. 29 next to Sutter Home. Wheelchair access. Open daily 10:30–4:30, or whenever the last person leaves.*

Rustridge. While you're traipsing through Napa's backwoods, check out this winery, ranch, and B&B ($100 a night). You'll probably be the only visitor indulging in the free tasters, served in a converted barn. Someone might even have to run in from the fields to open the tasting room. You can picnic on the serene grounds of Catacula (Valley of the Oaks), as the native people once called this land. *2910 Lower Chiles Valley Rd., St. Helena, tel. 707/965–2871. From Rte. 29 north, take Rte. 128 east. Cross Silverado Trail, bear left at fork (look for Pope Valley sign), and make first right on Lower Chiles Valley Rd. Open daily 10–5.*

In the 1920s, European countries signed a treaty agreeing that only the French could use the name champagne. Those were Prohibition days in the United States, and since we were convinced we'd never again produce alcohol, we never signed the treaty. Thus, Americans can still legally make champagne, but many vintners play it safe and call their products "sparkling wines."

S. Anderson. Tours are given twice daily, frequently by John Anderson, son of the late Stan (as in "S.") Anderson. He does a wonderful job guiding you through his vineyards and candlelit stone wine caves, modeled after those in the Champagne region of France. The caves hold over 400,000 bottles of sparkling wine, awaiting their "turn" (champagne bottles are turned by hand in a labor-intensive riddling process to remove the yeast). The tour, with tasting, costs $3, but it's more than worth it. Plan for over an hour—John doesn't need much prompting to extend the visit. *1473 Yountville Crossroad (off Silverado Trail), tel. 707/944–8642 or 800/4–BUBBLY. Take the Madison exit off Rte. 29 in Yountville and follow signs to the Silverado Trail. Open daily 10–5, tours at 10:30 and 2:30.*

V. Sattui. Here's a mid-size version of Napa Valley's mega-wineries. Sattui is small enough that its wine is sold only on the premises, but this winery is neither mellow nor intimate. Hordes of people descend upon the free tasters and the attached gourmet deli, which offers a few free cheese and paté samples. The food is yuppie quality, so it doesn't come cheap, but a couple can get the fixings for a great picnic for under $10 and enjoy a meal on the winery's grounds. *1111 White Ln., St. Helena, tel. 707/963–7774. Opposite Beacon Gas on Rte. 29 just south of St. Helena. Open summer, daily 9–6; winter, daily 9–5.*

WHERE TO SLEEP Not surprisingly, the most expensive lodging in the Wine Country is here in the posh Napa Valley. If you're on a tight budget, don't even attempt to stay overnight unless you're camping. You may want to consider commuting from Santa Rosa (*see* Where to Sleep, in Santa Rosa, *below*). Otherwise, the cheapest place around is the **Silverado Motel** (500 Silverado Trail, tel. 707/253–0892), where a cheesy, cleanish double is $40 weekdays, $48 weekends ($30 weekdays and $35 weekends in winter). The **Napa Valley Budget Inn** (3380 Solano Ave., off Rte. 29 at Redwood Rd., tel. 707/257–6111) has bland but clean doubles starting at $46 ($66 on Friday or Saturday). The swimming pool is perfect after a long day at the wineries, many of which are within biking distance. At the **Wine Valley Lodge** (200 S. Coombs St., Napa, tel. 707/224–7911), comfy doubles cost $50 on weekdays, $75 on weekends, and one room is wheelchair accessible. Amenities include a pool and a barbecue in the courtyard. To reach the lodge, exit Route 29 south at Imola Avenue and turn left (east); after two stop lights, turn left onto South Coombs Street. No matter where you stay, call at least three weeks in advance in summer.

➢ **CAMPING** • Camping is your only budget option in Napa (and the Wine Country in general). Unfortunately, the campgrounds are usually way off the beaten path—good news for nature lovers, but bad news for those intent on visiting the wineries. To make matters worse, there isn't any public transportation to the campgrounds; unless you have a car, you'll have to hitchhike, walk, or bike back to civilization. If you're getting desperate and don't mind driving, head 20 miles east from Rutherford on Route 128 to Lake Berryessa. The lake is divided into seven campgrounds, including **Pleasure Cove** (tel. 707/966–2172) and **Spanish Flat** (tel. 707/966–7700). Altogether you'll find 225 tent sites near the water for around $15 a night. Crowds are not usually a problem; on the downside, the area around the lake is barren, dusty, and very hot during the summer—more of a place to crash cheaply for a night than to discover nature. Reservations are recommended for summer weekends.

Bothe-Napa State Park. This is the Wine Country's most attractive campground, situated in the Napa foothills amid redwoods, madrone, and tan oaks only 10 minutes north of St. Helena and its wineries. The sites are reasonably private, and the park is one of the few with a swimming pool ($3 separate fee), much used on hot summer days. The clean bathrooms have hot showers and flush toilets. The fee is $14 (half-price disabled camping pass available through MISTIX) and reservations are suggested in summer, especially on weekends. For reservations call MISTIX (tel. 800/444–PARK). *3801 St. Helena Hwy. N., Calistoga, tel. 707/942–4575. From St. Helena, go 5 mi north on Rte. 29. 48 sites. Wheelchair access, no cooking facilities.*

FOOD If wine tasting is Napa Valley's main attraction, gourmet cuisine runs a close second. The best way to eat well without losing your shirt, however, is to stock up at one of the area's makeshift farmers' markets (*see* Markets and Delicatessens, *below*), where you'll find a bevy of fresh produce at reasonable prices.

Chimney Rock Café. This tiny no-frills eatery isn't big on atmosphere (it's located on a golf course, after all), but it serves the cheapest three-egg omelets in the Wine Country (around

$4.25). The management is very friendly, and you get to watch the golfers tee off while you eat. *5320 Silverado Trail, tel. 707/258-2727. Open daily 6:30 AM–6 PM. Breakfast served until 1 PM.*

The Diner. Several good restaurants line Washington Street in Yountville, but this is the best for the price. You can get huge plates of American or Mexican food for lunch and dinner, or specialty eggs and pancakes for breakfast. Most meals are in the $7–$10 range, but portions are generous (couples should consider splitting an appetizer and a main course). *6476 Washington St., Yountville, tel. 707/944-2626. Open Tues.–Sun. 8–3 and 5:30–9.*

Many wineries provide picnic grounds at no cost. Pull over for a free wine-tasting session and follow it up with a leisurely lunch in the sun.

Green Valley Café and Trattoria. Remarkably unpretentious, the trattoria offers tasty pasta entrées like pesto pasta with green beans and potatoes ($9.25) or smoked salmon tortellini ($10.75). Locals come for the sandwiches (lunch only) at $5. It's hearty food for ordinary folks (as far as anyone in the Wine Country might be considered ordinary) in a casual, diner-like atmosphere. *1310 Main St., St. Helena, tel. 707/963-7088. Open Tues.–Thurs. 11:30–3 and 5:30–9, Fri.–Sat. until 10 PM.*

Red Hen Restaurant. Pull into the Red Hen for their popular fajitas ($22 for two people) and margaritas ($3), or one of the hefty "on the side" dishes, starting at about $3. Then take a seat on the large outdoor patio and watch people race by to wineries on nearby Route 29. *5091 St. Helena Hwy. (Rte. 29), tel. 707/255-8125. 5 mi north of Napa off Oak Knoll Rd. Open Sun.–Thurs. 11–10, Fri.–Sat. 11–10:30.*

➤ **MARKETS AND DELICATESSENS • Napa Valley Farmers' Market.** For fruits and veggies, cheese, eggs, honey, dressings, cut flowers, and baked goods, come to the market Tuesdays in Napa and Fridays in St. Helena. *Napa: Soscol Ave., btw 1st and Pearl Sts., tel. 707/963-7343. Next to Linedome Theatre (where you can park). Open May–Oct., Tues. 7:30 AM–noon. St. Helena: Old Railroad Depot, tel. 707/963-7343. East on Adams St. off Rte. 29, left at stop sign, and 1 block up on the right. Open May–Nov., Fri. 7:30 AM–11:30 AM.*

Pometta's Deli. This place is famous for its barbecued chicken platters ($7), but you can also get box lunches to go ($7–$12). Especially good is the vegetarian sandwich (about $4), stuffed with avocado, provolone, zucchini, and jalapeños. The restaurant offers indoor and outdoor seating and tournament horseshoe pits (free). Check for live music on Friday nights during summer. *Rte. 29 at Oakville Grade, Oakville, tel. 707/944-2365. Open Sat.–Thurs. 8–7, Fri. 8 AM–9 PM.*

Calistoga

Most tourists come to this offbeat town for mud and mineral baths, not as a last stop on the wine tour. The town's bubbling mineral spring became a spa in 1859, when entrepreneur Sam Brannan slurred together the word California with the name of New York's Saratoga Springs resort; and Calistoga has been attracting health seekers ever since. Unfortunately, most health seekers are loaded, and they're willing to pay up the wazoo to get their wazoo steam-wrapped. Prices at the spas are uniformly steep, varying by only a couple of dollars. **Nance's Hot Springs** (1614 Lincoln Ave., tel. 707/942-6211) is one of the cheaper places, offering "the works" (*see box, below*) for $62. Call ahead for reservations. Since Nance's mud baths are sex-segregated, heterosexual couples may prefer **Golden Haven Hot Springs** (1713 Lake St., tel. 707/942-6793), where a full treatment costs $64. Pick up 10%-off coupons at the **Calistoga Chamber of Commerce** (1458 Lincoln Ave., tel. 707/942-6333), open daily 10–5.

After your treatment, stroll past the funky shops on Lincoln Avenue, Calistoga's main drag. At the **Calistoga Bookstore** (1343 Lincoln Ave., tel. 707/942-4123), you'll find hundreds of titles on wine making, as well as New Age tomes and some erotica. For a more strenuous afternoon, **Jules Culver Bicycles** (1227F Lincoln Ave., behind Café Pacifico, tel. 800/564-0421) will rent you a bike ($6 per hour or $19 per day), recommend some great mountain-biking trails, and even arrange guided bike tours of the area.

While you're in Calistoga, you can also visit **Robert Louis Stevenson State Park** off Route 29, 9 miles northeast of Calistoga. Here you can hike to the bunkhouse of the Silverado Mine, where the impoverished author honeymooned with his wife, Fanny Osbourne, in the summer of 1880. The stay inspired Stevenson's *The Silverado Squatters.* The park is perched at the top of Mt. St. Helena, which is said to be the model for Spyglass Hill in *Treasure Island.* Its 3,000 acres are largely undeveloped, but picnicking is permitted.

WHERE TO SLEEP For $49 (second night $5 off), you can get a cabin for two at the **Triple S Ranch** (4600 Mt. Home Ranch Rd., tel. 707/942–6730). There's no phone or TV, but the complex does include a swimming pool and a pricey steakhouse. The ranch is north of Calistoga off Route 128; take Petrified Forest Road west for 2½ miles until you reach Mount Home Ranch Road. If you can't spend the night without a color TV, try the **Holiday House** (3514 Rte. 128, tel. 707/942–6174), 3 miles north of Calistoga; watch for the white picket fence. From the outside, it looks like you're pulling into a friend's house, but on the inside the three rooms ($55) are strictly Motel 6. If you want to stay on the main drag in town, the **Calistoga Inn** (1250 Lincoln Ave., tel. 707/942–4101) has clean, simple bed-and-breakfast rooms with shared baths and full-size beds for $49 ($60 Fri.–Sat.).

FOOD Lincoln Avenue is full of good delis like **Fellion's** (1359 Lincoln Ave., tel. 707/942–6144), where the spicy beef sandwich with chilis sells for $5.50. For quality Mexican food, walk to the west end of Lincoln, where it dead-ends into the **Calistoga Drive-In Taqueria** (1207 Foothill Blvd., tel. 707/942–0543). A veggie burrito here will run you $3.50, and the tortillas and chips are great. The restaurant is wheelchair accessible.

For a great, bottomless cup of coffee ($1) cruise down to the east end of town and visit the **Calistoga Roastery** (1631 Lincoln Ave., tel. 707/942–5757), open daily 7–6. The beans are roasted on the premises. The ice cream latte ($2.75) makes a great dessert. Or cool off with a homebrew in the shady garden at the **Calistoga Inn** (1250 Lincoln Ave., tel. 707/942–4101). Their award-winning ales and lagers are only $2 during happy hour. The California cuisine here is also excellent, and for once the portions are fair for the price. Try the grilled lemon chicken sausage with sauerkraut, roasted potatoes, and coleslaw ($7.25).

In Pursuit of Decadence

Though you'd normally hesitate to throw yourself in a roadside ditch and roll around in the muck, folks in the Wine Country believe that mud baths and sulfur springs heal all manner of ills. If you go for the top-of-the-line treatment at a sleek indoor establishment like Nance's (see above), you'll slide into a tub of hot volcanic mud, then shower and simmer in a bubbling mineral bath. Next you're swaddled in soft sheets and left to "set" like a human dumpling in preparation for your half-hour massage. The process is supposed to relieve tension and extract toxins from your skin and muscles.

A cheaper option is open-air bathing at rustic retreats like Harbin Hot Springs or White Sulphur Springs (see below). You won't get to play human mud pie at the outdoor spas, but you can bathe in natural springs and hike through rolling grounds far from the buzz of urbanity. Harbin's pools are clothing-optional, while White Sulphur's feature a high sulfur content—afterwards, you feel like you've just soaked in bleach.

If you're willing to drive a bit to soak in mineral baths, you can get a better deal at the spas listed below than in town. These hot springs offer many of the same amenities as the Calistoga spas, and an affordable room for the night to boot.

HARBIN HOT SPRINGS Near Middletown, this 1,200-acre community is run by the Heart Consciousness Church, a group that advocates holistic health and spiritual renewal. The retreat has three natural mineral pools, varying in temperature from tepid to very hot, and a cold, spring-fed "plunge" pool. There's also an acclaimed massage school, whose graduates would be happy to show you their stuff ($46 an hr, $60 for 90 min). A vegetarian restaurant serves breakfast (under $8) and dinner ($8–$12), and occasionally there are free movies (check the monthly calendar). To use the pools, you must pay $5 for a one-month membership or $15 for a year (only one member per group required), plus an additional day-use fee ($12 Mon.–Thurs., $17 Fri.–Sun.).

They say "clothing optional," but you're going to feel pretty out of place if you wear anything but a smile into the pools at Harbin Hot Springs. If you have the cash and the curiosity, get "watsu-ed"—an underwater shiatsu massage that's a house specialty.

Beds in the ramshackle dorm rooms start at $23 ($35 on weekends), and you have to provide your own sheets or sleeping bag. Private rooms with shared bath are $60. There are campsites along the creek and in nearby meadows, but at $14 per person ($23 Fri.–Sat., $17 Sun.), it's a lot to pay for a night in a tent, especially when the grounds are unkempt and the bathrooms few. Despite the cost, expect a crowd on weekends. *Tel. 707/987–2477 or 800/622–2477 (Northern California only). Take Rte. 29 north to Middletown, left at junction for Rte. 175, right on Barnes St., and go 1½ mi to Harbin Springs Rd. Greyhound runs daily from S.F. to Middletown, where a ride can be arranged. Wheelchair access.*

WHITE SULPHUR SPRINGS This St. Helena resort is actually a bargain, though it costs a few extra bucks. For $65, you get access to 300 acres of land, plenty of hiking and biking opportunities, a Jacuzzi, natural mineral baths, even a stand of redwoods; *and* you get a decent room for the night, either in the rustic, dormitory-style carriage house or in the inn, where each room has a half bath. It's a whole day's and night's decadence for the price of an hour or two at some of Calistoga's spas. A cheaper option is to stop by during the day and use the facilities for $15. If you only want to be there for an hour or two, the management will usually knock down the price—just ask. The pools are open until 1 AM, and you can even come by late at night (around 10 or 11) to use them. *3100 White Sulphur Springs Rd., St. Helena, tel. 707/963–8588. Take Spring St. west off Rte. 29 in St. Helena, and go 2.8 mi. Note: Don't take White Sulphur Springs Rd. from Rte. 29; it no longer goes all the way to the resort.*

Santa Rosa

When residents of Sonoma County refer to "the city," they no longer mean San Francisco. Once a small farming community, Santa Rosa has become one of California's fastest-growing suburban areas, with shopping malls, mini-marts, and housing tracts sprouting at an alarming rate. Most of old Santa Rosa was destroyed in the 1906 earthquake, but a section from about 6th to 3rd streets between Wilson and Davis called **Railroad Square** has been preserved. Today the square is the most happening part of town, home to the pleasant **Railroad Park,** as well as a battalion of cafés and restaurants. Four blocks farther east lie the 4th Street Mall and **Santa Rosa Plaza Shopping Center,** where every retail chain imaginable can be found. On weekdays, stop by the **Chamber of Commerce** (637 1st St., at Santa Rosa Ave., tel. 707/545–1414), open weekdays 8:30–5, for maps.

Daytime Santa Rosa is pretty slow, peopled almost exclusively by older folks, but the pace picks up with nightfall. Check out **A'Roma Roasters and Coffee House** (95 5th St., at Wilson St., tel. 707/576–7765) for café cuisine and live jazz, folk, and classical music Wednesday to Saturday. You can stop by weekdays 7 AM–midnight or weekends 8 AM–midnight, or call for a current schedule. It's a mellow place, popular with gays, lesbians, and straights alike. Another hip nighttime stop is **Café This** (122 4th St., tel. 707/576–8126) in Railroad Square, where the doors open at the owner's whim (early to late evening) and stay open as long as there are enough crazies to fill the place.

WHERE TO SLEEP Santa Rosa is a convenient base for day trips east to the Wine Country. Fortunately, staying here will cost less than lodging in Napa or Sonoma, if you plan ahead and reserve a space at one of the cheaper motels. **Motel 6** (3145 Cleveland Ave., tel. 707/525–9010) might be just right, with simple doubles ($34) and a pool, if the carpet deodorant doesn't kill you first. Pleasant doubles at the **Redwood Inn** (1670 Santa Rosa Ave., at Baker Ave., tel. 707/545–0474) are $35, $185 per week. The **Sandman Motel** (3421 Cleveland Ave., at Industrial Dr., tel. 707/544–8570) charges $54 for a boring but serviceable double.

The **Best Western Heritage Inn** (870 Hopper Ave., tel. 707/ 545–9000), off U.S. 101 at Mendocino Avenue, 2½ miles north of downtown, has muted '70s-chic rooms with carpeted walls and a heated swimming pool, and offers danishes and coffee in the morning. Rooms are $63 on weekdays, $69 weekends (off-season rates cheaper). If you're in town Sunday–Thursday, take advantage of the $49 special at the **Hotel La Rose** (308 Wilson St., tel. 707/579–3200) on Railroad Square. The rooms are beautifully decorated with antiques, and you get a free continental buffet in the morning. On the weekend, doubles cost $70–$95.

➤ **CAMPING** • **Spring Lake Park.** Though it's only a few miles from downtown Santa Rosa, the park is secluded and woodsy, with 31 campsites ($14) on a bluff overlooking Spring Lake (Site 14 has the best view). You can swim in the lagoon, row, or fish year-round. The road to the park winds through some new housing developments, but don't let that deter you. *5390 Montgomery Dr., tel. 707/539–8092. From downtown Santa Rosa, take U.S. 101 south to Rte. 12 east. Cross Summerfield Rd., go over hill, and turn left on Newanga Rd. Hot showers. Closed Mon.–Thurs. Labor Day–Memorial Day. Reservations advised.*

FOOD Unlike the rest of the Wine Country, Santa Rosa has plenty of restaurants that offer good food at affordable prices. On 4th Street, west of the freeway, something is bound to meet your fancy. **Mixx** (135 4th St., at Davis St., tel. 707/573–1344), serving such delicacies as grilled Cajun prawns ($9) and baked polenta ($7.50), makes a great splurge. The crème brûlée ($5) alone is worth the trek from San Francisco. **Omelette Express** is popular with locals for its 40 varieties of omelets, its burgers, and its sandwiches ($5–$9). Split the fabulous chicken emerald curry ($9.50) with your honey at **California Thai** (522 7th St., at B St., tel. 707/573–1441), and you'll forget about the bland suburban-mall atmosphere.

NEAR SANTA ROSA

PETALUMA If Petaluma looks eerily familiar, don't panic. The city was used as a backdrop for the films *American Graffiti* and *Peggy Sue Got Married*, and in a lot of ways it feels like every American small town. When you approach from the freeway, you first notice the tract homes, mini-markets, and gas stations on the outskirts of town. But once you reach Old Petaluma (concentrated in a six-block area along Petaluma Blvd. N.), where the streets are lined with Victorian houses and storefronts, it starts to feel like the town you always wanted to grow up in. The old houses look too cute to be real, and Disney himself couldn't have constructed a more classically American place than Petaluma's downtown.

The **Petaluma Area Chamber of Commerce** (215 Howard St., at Washington St., tel. 707/762–2785), open weekdays 9–5, sells maps ($1.50) that detail the city's historic buildings, including **McNear's Feed Mill** (now a café), the **Palace Theater,** and the stately homes along nearby Kentucky Street. Old Petaluma also includes interesting antique shops and bookstores. Grab a pint of homebrew from **Dempsey's Ale House** (50 E. Washington St., tel. 707/765–9694), at the back of the Golden Eagle Shopping Center. Peter, the proprietor, might give a tour to a group of eight or more if he's not busy brewing that day. You can enjoy a snack (roasted garlic with focaccia is $3) and sample the Red Rooster Ale on an outdoor patio overlooking the moss-green Petaluma River. For a hearty and healthy breakfast or lunch, stop in at **New Marvin's** (145 Kentucky St., downtown, tel. 707/765–2371), where four-egg omelets run $5–$7, homemade granola with yogurt and fruit is $3.75, and lunches (ranging from burgers and salads to brown rice and pasta) cost $5–$8. Marvin's is open weekdays 6:30 AM–3 PM, Saturdays 7–3, and Sundays 7:30–3.

If you feel the urge to stay the night, the only camping is at the korporate kampgrounds of **KOA** (20 Rainsville Rd., tel. 707/763–1492 or 800/922–CAMP), near U.S. 101 at the Old Redwood Highway exit. At their 300 cable-ready sites (tent sites $24, full hookup $29), you can "camp" without missing Geraldo. Tantalizing as this option may sound, the clean $38 doubles at **Motel 6** (5135 Montero Way, behind Quality Inn off U.S. 101's Old Redwood Highway exit, tel. 707/664–9090) are probably your best bet. If you don't mind sharing a bath, the historic **Cavanaugh Inn** (10 Keller St., tel. 707/765–4657) has two homey doubles at $55 and $65, which includes use of the kitchen and Billie's home-cooked gourmet breakfast. Any other option will run you at least $65.

If you're in Petaluma in mid-June, don't miss the Sonoma-Marin Fair, which advertises itself as an "escape back to those simple days of strong agricultural tradition." Get your entries ready for the Ugly Dog Contest (canines only), the special Fleischmann's Yeast Contest, and a mysterious event called the "Llama Extravaganza."

COTATI This funky farming community 8 miles south of Santa Rosa is a popular hangout with students from Sonoma State University—the sort of town that doesn't ever vote Republican. Come in June for the **Cotati Jazz Festival** (tel. 707/792–4600; tickets $12 a day) or in August for the **Cotati Accordian Festival.** For great down-home pancakes, homemade biscuits, and other breakfast and lunch staples ($3–$7), try **Mom's Boarding House** (8099 La Plaza St., tel. 707/795–3381). The veggie omelet ($5.50) is big enough for two, and there's a 10% student discount (be sure to ask for it when you order). **Señor Sol** (8197 La Plaza St., tel. 707/792–0807), on the west side of the central plaza, serves a wide variety of Mexican food ($1.60–$11.25) and 99¢ beers.

The Inn at the Beginning, billed as a café/pub-cum-bookstore, not only offers acoustic folk and blues music and poetry readings, but also has darts, a pool table, and a ton of history. Neil Young, Bo Diddley, and Jerry Garcia all played here between 1969 and 1982. Kick back with a pint of "Death and Taxes," a popular dark beer ($2.75), or sample the vegetarian chili ($3). Call for a schedule of events. *8201 Old Redwood Hwy., tel. 707/794-9453. Wheelchair access. Open weekdays 9 AM–midnight, weekends until 2 AM.*

Cotati's Inn at the Beginning specializes in trades—used books for lattes.

SEBASTOPOL Long famous for its Gravenstein apples, Sebastopol still has the look of a slow-moving agricultural town, despite its suburbanization in the last 10 years. Its proximity to Santa Rosa (only 7 miles west on Rte. 12) has turned it into a somewhat dull bedroom community, but you'll find a few cafés where cappuccinos are made with soy milk, bookstores that are havens for liberal thinkers, and restaurants worth a gander. For a taste of the local apples, come to the **Apple Blossom Parade** the last weekend in April or the **Gravenstein Apple Fair** in early August. If you don't mind branding yourself a tourist, you can visit one of the nearby commercial apple farms. Complete listings are available at the **Chamber of Commerce** (265 S. Main St., tel. 707/823–3032), open weekdays 9–5. The **Main Street Theatre** (104 N. Main St., tel. 707/823–0177) shows a number of plays in an intimate setting and hosts an annual Shakespeare Festival in August. Call ahead for a schedule and reservations. Tickets are $10; students pay $6 on Thursdays and on Sunday afternoons.

For food, try the trendy and tasty fare at the **East-West Café** (128 N. Main St., tel. 707/829–2822), open weekdays 7 AM–9 PM, Saturday 8 AM–9 PM, and Sunday until 8 PM. The menu offers adventures in tofu and egg for breakfast, and Asian and Mediterranean fare for $3–$8. **Copperfield's Café** (138 N. Main St., tel. 707/829–1286), open weekdays 8–6, Saturday 9–6, and Sunday 9–5, sells tempting sandwiches ($4–$5) named after authors like Jack Kerouac, Alice Walker, and Dr. Seuss. Next door, **Rosemary's Garden** (132 N. Main St., tel. 707/829–2539) has herbs, lotions, and women's books to fulfill your spiritual, homeopathic, or aromatherapy needs.

Coffee Catz (6761 Sebastopol Ave., at Gravenstein Station, tel. 707/829–6600) is a bit farther from the action, but it offers a different sandwich each day for $4 and live music Tuesday–

Saturday evenings at 8 PM. It's mostly jazz, except for Wednesday, which is an open-mike night with an occasional storytelling session. For summer fruit and berries, be on the lookout for come-and-go roadside stands, or stop by the local **farmers' market,** held Sundays June–October from 10 AM to 1 PM in the Park Plaza on McKinley Street, just behind Main Street.

Lake Tahoe

Straddling the border of California and Nevada on the northern flank of the Sierra Nevada range, Lake Tahoe is one of the West Coast's most popular outdoor playgrounds. During spring and summer, when temperatures hover in the 70s, the lake (about a 3½-hour drive east of San Francisco on I-80) offers boating, fishing, waterskiing, and jet skiing; and the mountains surrounding Tahoe Basin satiate the desires of even the most demanding hikers, bikers, equestrians, and anglers. In winter, attention shifts to downhill and cross-country skiing and the increasingly popular sport of snowboarding. The West Coast's number-one ski area, Tahoe has earned a worldwide reputation for its "extreme" conditions, provided by the sheer cliffs and steep faces of the Sierra Nevada.

Besides being deep and blue, Lake Tahoe is also damn cold. You can swim in it, but most visitors just dip their feet in and scamper back to shore. On the other hand, a quick dip is said by locals to be the best way to cure a hangover.

Given the array of pleasures, it's no wonder Lake Tahoe draws up to 100,000 tourists at peak periods. On weekends, the traffic on I-80 between the Bay Area and Lake Tahoe has to be seen to be believed. A common way to explore the lake is to drive around its 72-mile perimeter. On an average day, the trip takes about three hours, but plan on traffic slowing you down on summer weekends and holidays, and in winter, when there's snow on the roads. If the slow driving starts to annoy you, stop at a few scenic lookouts (especially Emerald Bay on the west shore) and disappear down a hiking path or two.

At regular intervals around the lake are a series of small towns—some charming, some tacky, all dependent on the tourist industry for their survival. Although it's a somewhat subjective division, the lake's locales are usually designated as belonging to either the north shore or the south shore. Thanks largely to the popularity of the ski resort at Squaw Valley, the north shore is the domain of Tahoe's young, energetic set, dedicated to spending as much time as possible exploring the great outdoors and as little time as possible in the restaurants, hotels, and upscale resorts where most of them find employment. The south shore, on the other hand, caters primarily to family vacationers who come to Tahoe to play on the lake in summer, on the ski slopes in the winter, and in the Vegas-style casinos on the Nevada side of the border all year round.

The north shore's largest town is **Truckee,** about 12 miles north of the lake, with a modern downtown area to the west and an Old Town (complete with board sidewalks, wood-frame storefronts, and an ancient railroad) to the east. Donner Pass Road connects the two sides of town and serves as the main commercial boulevard. **Tahoe City,** at the lake's northwestern corner, has a small-town warmth lacking in Truckee, and is home to many of Tahoe's younger residents. On the south shore, the city of **South Lake Tahoe** is packed to the gills with restaurants, motels, and rental shops. The pace never flags in summer, and in winter popular ski areas like Heavenly Valley keep the town jumping. Butting up against the east side of South Lake Tahoe is the imaginatively named town of **Stateline,** Nevada, offering a jumble of brightly lit casinos and tacky gift shops.

VISITOR INFORMATION

Lake Tahoe Forest Service Visitor Center. In addition to the usual tourist information, the center offers a great location, with beach access and self-guided nature trails. The staff will tell you all you want to know about the lake's natural and human history. This is also the place to pick up wilderness permits for the Desolation and Mokelumne wilderness areas. Depending on funding, they may be closed on certain days of the week. *Rte. 89, btw Emerald Bay and South Lake Tahoe, tel. 916/573–2674. Open summer, daily 8–5:30; closed winter.*

TO DONNER PASS

80

Truckee

Donner Lake

89

N

Northstar-at-Tahoe

267

CALIFORNIA

NEVADA

Toiyabe National Forest

431

Incline Village

Tahoe National Forest

Tahoe Vista

Crystal Bay

28

Truckee River

Kings Beach

28

Sand Harbor Beach

Squaw Valley

Tahoe City

i

Marlette Lake

Alpine Meadows

William Kent Campground

Kaspian Campground

89

Lake

50

Glenbrook

Homewood

Tahoe

50

Toiyabe National Forest

Sugar Pine Point State Park

Meeks Bay

89

Zephyr Cove

D. L. Bliss State Park

Nevada Beach

207

Eagle Point Campground

South Lake Tahoe

Stateline

Kingsbury Grade

Emerald Bay

Baldwin Beach

Desolation Wilderness

Bay View Campground

i

i

Heavenly

Campground by the Lake

NV

CA

Pope Baldwin Recreation Area

Fallen Leaf Lake

50

South Lake Tahoe Airport

Pioneer Trail

Eldorado National Forest

89

Eldorado National Forest

Upper Truckee River

KEY

i Tourist Information

0 ____ 6 miles

0 ____ 9 km

50

TO MOKELUMNE WILDERNESS

89

TO KIRKWOOD

Toiyabe National Forest

The **North Lake Tahoe Chamber of Commerce** (245 Rte. 89, Tahoe City, tel. 916/581–6900) lies between the Lucky supermarket and the Bank of America across from the Tahoe City "Y." You can also contact the **South Lake Tahoe Chamber of Commerce** (3066 U.S. 50, tel. 916/541–5255) or **Truckee-Donner Visitor Information** (Donner Pass Rd., Truckee, tel. 916/587–2757), at the Truckee Transit Depot in Old Town.

COMING AND GOING

BY CAR Both routes to Lake Tahoe from the Bay Area take 3–3½ hours when road and traffic conditions are at their best. To reach the north shore, follow I–80 east through Sacramento all the way to Truckee. For the south shore, take I–80 to Sacramento and turn onto U.S. 50 east, which leads directly to South Lake Tahoe. You won't be allowed into the mountains without chains if it snows; bring your own, or you'll have to pay inflated prices for a set near the CalTrans checkpoint. For road conditions, call CalTrans at 800/427–7623. On Friday and Sunday afternoons, especially during summer and on holiday weekends, traffic can be a nightmare. If you must drive to Tahoe on Friday, wait until 7 or 8 PM. Traffic is usually worst on I–80, so consider taking U.S. 50, even if you're headed for the north shore.

Finding your way around Lake Tahoe is no sweat. Three intersecting highways form a loop around the lake: **Route 89** (also known as **Emerald Bay Road**) skirts the western shore of the lake between Tahoe City and South Lake Tahoe; **U.S. 50** (a.k.a. **Lake Tahoe Boulevard**) intersects Route 89 in South Lake Tahoe and follows the lake's eastern shore; and **Route 28** (a.k.a. **North Lake Boulevard** and **Lake Shore Boulevard**) runs along the north part of the shore back into Tahoe City. The intersections of Routes 28 and 89 in Tahoe City and Route 89 and U.S. 50 in South Lake Tahoe are commonly referred to as the **Tahoe City "Y"** and the **South Lake Tahoe "Y,"** respectively.

BY BUS Greyhound (tel. 800/231–2222) runs four buses a day between San Francisco and Truckee (5–6 hrs, $30) and the same number between Truckee and Reno (1 hr, $9). If you're headed to the south shore, Greyhound makes the trip between San Francisco and South Lake Tahoe (5½ hrs, $37) three times a day. Both Amtrak and Greyhound use the **Transit Depot** in downtown Truckee (Donner Pass Rd., tel. 916/587–3822), a safe and comfortable place to wait for connections or pick up information at the tourist office. There are a few coin-operated lockers. In South Lake Tahoe, the Greyhound station (tel. 702/588–4645) is in back of **Harrah's Hotel and Casino,** on U.S. 50 1½ miles south of the South Lake Tahoe "Y."

Tahoe Area Regional Transit (TART) (tel. 916/581–6365 in CA, or 800/736–6365) has buses, most equipped with ski and bike racks, that serve the north and west shores of Lake Tahoe. Fare is $1. The **South Tahoe Area Ground Express (STAGE)** (tel. 916/573–2080) runs 24 hours within the city limits of South Lake Tahoe. Fare is $1.25.

Although the journey over the mountains can be painfully slow at times, the train ride between the Bay Area and Tahoe, especially the final climb up steep mountain passes, is filled with spectacular scenery.

BY TRAIN Amtrak (tel. 800/USA–RAIL) runs two train/bus routes a day between Emeryville and Truckee (transfer in Sacramento, 6 hrs, $50). If you're coming from San Francisco, take the free bus from the CalTrain Station at 4th and Townsend streets to the Emeryville Amtrak Station (5885 Landregan St., tel. 510/450–1180). Amtrak also has one train a day traveling the hour-long route between Truckee and Reno ($12 one way). All trains arrive at the Truckee Transit Depot (*see* Coming and Going by Bus, *above*).

BY PLANE You can reach the tiny **South Lake Tahoe Airport** (off Rte. 89, about 15 min south of South Lake Tahoe, tel. 916/541–4080) by air from San Francisco. **TWA** (tel. 800/221–2000) makes the trip for about $180 round-trip. Also check potentially cheaper flights into **Reno Cannon International Airport** (tel. 702/328–6499).

WHERE TO SLEEP

You face a mind-boggling number of options in choosing a place to stay in the Tahoe area. Hostels, motels, condos, cabins, and campgrounds abound everywhere you look. If you're just passing through for a night or two in summer and want to hang around the lake by day and gamble by night, a motel or campground on the south shore is the cheapest and most convenient alternative. But if you're coming up for a week in winter to ski with a group of friends, consider a condo or cabin on the north shore: It's more affordable than you might think. No matter when you come, reserve as far ahead as possible; in Tahoe, it's never too early to start hunting for a place to stay. On holidays and summer weekends everything is completely packed, despite the fact that most places raise their prices indiscriminately at these times.

HOTELS AND MOTELS In general, prices at all but the finest establishments on Lake Tahoe are flexible. Proprietors will charge whatever the traffic will bear, which means prices on popular weekends and holidays rise substantially. All prices in the following listing are for non-holiday periods. It can be tough to find a budget motel on the north shore. Instead, head to U.S. 50 between South Lake Tahoe and Stateline—just cruise the strip and keep your eyes open for the neon. As a last resort, look for cheap deals at the casinos on the Nevada side of the south shore.

➢ **SOUTH SHORE • El Nido Motel.** If you're seeking comfort at a reasonable price, the El Nido should end your search. Its excellent amenities include a hot tub; a "socializing" room with fireplace and cushy couches (used in winter only); and small, modern rooms with TV, VCR, and telephone. Flawlessly clean doubles start at $50 on weekdays, $60 on weekends. Call for details on winter ski packages. *2215 Lake Tahoe Blvd. (U.S. 50), tel. 916/541–2711. About 3½ mi west of the California-Nevada border. 21 rooms.*

Emerald Motel. The rooms are ordinary, but the motel is far enough away from the crowded downtown area to provide a sense of peace and quiet. Clean doubles with color TV start at $35 on weekdays and $45 on weekends; prices can drop as low as $25 and $35 in off-peak periods. For about $5 more you can have a small kitchenette. Ask for special rates (negotiable) for stays of four nights or more. *515 Emerald Bay Rd. (Rte. 89), tel. 916/544–5515. 1 mi north of the South Lake Tahoe "Y." 9 rooms.*

Pine Cone Acre Motel. Tucked away beneath the pines just off Route 89, this motel features clean (if not stylish) rooms, a pool, and a downright friendly manager. Doubles start at $55–$65 weekdays (depending on the time of year) and $65–$75 weekends. *735 Emerald Bay Rd. (Rte. 89), tel. 916/541–0375. About ½ mi northwest of the South Lake Tahoe "Y." 20 rooms. Wheelchair access.*

Trout Creek Motel. With shag carpet, lumpy beds, and small, dark rooms, this motel is basically a fleabag. But for just $30 per double on weekdays, who's complaining? At least there's a TV and showers. When the rates jump to $60 on weekends, it's time to look elsewhere. *2650 Lake Tahoe Blvd. (U.S. 50), tel. 916/542–2523. In South Lake Tahoe. 22 rooms. Wheelchair access.*

➢ **NORTH SHORE •** It's hard to find a budget motel on the north shore, especially in Truckee. The **Super 8 Lodge** (11506 Deerfield Dr., near I–80's Truckee/Squaw Valley exit, tel. 916/587–8888 or 800/843–1991) has the best rates in Truckee, but it's far from cheap: Doubles are $68 in winter, $56 in the off-season. For better prices, look in the smaller communities around the lakeshore.

Northwood Pines Motel. Yes, it's shabby and generic. But it's also priced right and centrally located (about 8 mi northeast of Tahoe City), especially if you're in Tahoe to explore the north shore's ski areas. The Northwood Pines offers standard, aging doubles for $40 on weekdays and $55 on weekends, as well as weekly rates starting at $160. *8489 Trout St., tel. 916/546–9829. Take North Lake Blvd. (Rte. 28) northeast, turn left on Bear St. and right on Trout St. 9 rooms.*

River Ranch Lodge. For a great splurge (especially in spring and fall, when prices are lowest), head to the classy River Ranch Lodge, beside the Truckee River between Truckee and Tahoe City. The River Ranch offers 21 frilly rooms, complete with flower-print curtains and bedspreads, tasteful wallpaper, and wooden furniture. About half have small decks overlooking the river. Doubles start at $50 on spring and fall weekdays ($75 on weekends), $75 on summer weekdays ($100 on weekends), and $90 on winter weekdays ($110 on weekends). Free continental breakfast is included. Several of the noisier rooms above the restaurant go for a slightly lower price, and there's also a special "small double"—nice, but not facing the river—for $40–$90, depending on the time of your stay. *Rte. 89 and Alpine Meadows Rd., tel. 916/583–4264 or 800/535–9900. 21 rooms.*

Tamarack Lodge Motel. About a mile north of downtown Tahoe City, the Tamarack offers wood-paneled, newly furnished doubles in a clearing surrounded by pines, within walking distance of the beach. Escape the crowds in a clean and comfortable double, starting at $45 weekdays and $50 weekends; for another $5 you get a room with kitchenette. *2311 North Lake Blvd. (Rte. 28), tel. 916/583–3350. 21 rooms.*

HOSTELS **Squaw Valley Hostel.** This privately run hostel, within walking distance of the Squaw Valley ski area, opens only during winter, usually from November 15 to April 15. During the week, a bed in a dormitory-style room runs $20; on weekends rates go up to $25. Since the hostel hosts groups during winter it's next to impossible to get a room on the weekend, but call well in advance and maybe you'll get lucky. *1900 Squaw Valley Rd., tel. 916/583–7771. From Truckee take Rte. 89 south, right on Squaw Valley Rd. 100 beds in 9 rooms.*

Star Hotel. The Star Hotel in Old Town Truckee has a dual identity. It's one part run-down hotel and one part run-down youth hostel, the only differences being the number of beds per room and the price. The hostel section has cramped dormitory-style rooms with lumpy bunk beds, not enough windows for the summer months, and not enough heat in winter. But at $15 per night, this private hostel is the cheapest place to bed down on the north shore, and access to a kitchen and common room are definite bonuses. Doubles in the Star's hotel section start at $45 off-season on weekdays and go up from there. *10015 West River St., at Rte. 267, tel. 916/587–3007. From Truckee, take Rte. 89 south and turn left on West River St. about ½ mi from downtown.*

WEEKLY/WEEKEND RENTALS If you're planning on spending a weekend or more in Tahoe, consider renting a condo, cabin, or house. It'll cost more than a motel room, but in most places you'll get a kitchen, a color TV, and a fireplace; and it's much easier to sneak six friends past the manager. You may even have access to a pool, a hot tub, a sauna, a weight room, or some combination thereof. Generally speaking, rental units are nearer to major ski areas than are motels, and they'll allow you to get away from the major roads.

Rental prices range dramatically, according to the season of your visit (summer is the most expensive), the length of your stay, which days of the week you choose, and where your unit is located. At the low end of the scale, you should be able to find a condo that sleeps two to four for about $75 a night or $425 a week in the off-season, with prices rising roughly 10% in summer. As a rule of thumb, the more people in your group and the longer you stay, the more affordable rentals become.

Literally hundreds of realty and property-management firms in the Lake Tahoe area vie to help you find a rental, so be sure to shop around before making a decision. A reservation or referral agency can help streamline the process. In the south shore area, the **Lake Tahoe Visitors' Authority** (1156 Ski Run Blvd., South Lake Tahoe, tel. 916/544–5050 or 800/AT–TAHOE) will direct you free of charge to a realtor tailored to your needs and price range. On the north shore, the **Tahoe North Visitors' and Convention Bureau** (tel. 916/583–3494 or 800/TAHOE–4U) will book reservations according to your requests for $5 or put you in touch with local rental agencies if you prefer. **R. RENT** (tel. 916/546–2549) specializes in north-shore budget rentals.

If you have the time and the inclination, you can save a few bucks by coming to the area and arranging a rental directly through a property owner. To find out what's available, check out the classified ads in the *Tahoe Daily Tribune* (with south-shore listings) and the *Tahoe World,* a north-shore paper that comes out each Thursday.

SEASONAL RENTALS Unless you just won the lottery, the only way to make a seasonal rental affordable is to join together with a group of friends and share a place. If you get together with 10 friends, rent a place for the winter for $4,000 (meaning you pay $400), and stay in it for 10 weekends, you can have yourself a comfortable Tahoe house, often with a hot tub, for the same price as 10 nights in an average motel—not a bad deal.

Be realistic about whether you'll use a seasonal rental enough to get your money's worth—many people fork over several hundred dollars for a place and end up making only one or two trips.

Things to keep in mind when looking for a seasonal rental include location, amenities, what utilities you'll be expected to pay, and, in winter, heating costs and the snow-clearing situation on nearby roads. Prices and availability of seasonal rentals fluctuate even more dramatically than for weekend or weekly rentals. In Tahoe, check the *Tahoe Daily Tribune* on the south shore or *Tahoe World* on the north shore for listings. Otherwise, contact any of the various visitors' bureaus or property management agencies (*see* Weekly/Weekend Rentals, *above*) to start your search.

CAMPING You can hardly drive half a mile in Lake Tahoe without bumping into a public or private campground, and almost all of them lie in beautiful pine forests. For obvious reasons, all campgrounds close in winter. The most conveniently located spot on the south shore is the **Campground by the Lake** (Rufus Allen Blvd. and U.S. 50, tel. 916/542–6096), a spacious spot with 170 sites shaded by young pines. Sites go for $17 and are surprisingly isolated, considering how close you are to downtown South Lake Tahoe (the campground lies between Stateline and the South Lake Tahoe "Y," where U.S. 50 meets the lake). Reservations are necessary only on holiday weekends.

Two inviting campgrounds are just south of Emerald Bay on Route 89. **Bay View Campground,** on the inland side of Route 89, has 12 primitive sites amid the pines, with picnic tables and fire pits but no running water. A stopping-off point for journeys into Desolation Wilderness, it imposes a two-night limit on stays; but for those two nights you'll sleep for free. If all the sites in Bay View are full, head just up the street to the beautiful **Eagle Point Campground** (Rte. 89, south of Emerald Bay, tel. 916/541–3030, for reservations 800/444–PARK). Here you'll find 100 well-spaced sites ($14)—all with fire pits, barbecues, picnic tables, food lockers, and access to bathrooms and showers—on a hillside covered with brush and pines. Some sites offer incredible views of Emerald Bay.

In the north-shore area, try **William Kent Campground** (off Rte. 89, tel. 916/573–2600 or 800/444–PARK for reservations), a 95-site national-forest campground set well off the highway 2 miles south of Tahoe City. Like most of the other campgrounds in Tahoe, William Kent lies in a moderately dense pine forest, within walking distance of the lake. Just down the road to the south, the **Kaspian Campground** is specially equipped for wheelchair travelers. For a complete listing of campgrounds, contact the Lake Tahoe Forest Service Visitor Center (*see* Visitor Information, *above*).

FOOD

Though the south shore is more noticeably jam-packed than the north, you'll find hundreds of restaurants all over Lake Tahoe, serving everything from fast food to lobster dinners. On the south shore, eateries are concentrated along U.S. 50 between South Lake Tahoe and Stateline, Nevada. In Stateline itself, you can get cheap (if generic) food at all-you-can-eat casino buffets. On the north shore, you'll find a heap of restaurants in downtown Truckee (especially on Donner Pass Rd.) and on Route 28 in Tahoe City. For fresh organic produce, bulk foods, and other eco-conscious grocery items, head to **Grass Roots** (2040 Dunlap Rd., at the South Lake Tahoe "Y," tel. 916/541–7788). If you're looking to splurge on local seafood, try **Fresh Ketch Lakeside Restaurant** (2433 Venice Dr. E., in the Tahoe Keys Marina, South Lake Tahoe, tel. 916/541–5683) on the south shore, or **Jake's on the Lake** (Boatworks Marina, near the Tahoe City "Y," tel. 916/583–0188) on the north shore. A meal at either will run you around $20.

SOUTH SHORE **Ernie's Coffee Shop.** A completely unpretentious greasy spoon serving breakfast and lunch only, Ernie's is popular among locals, some of whom keep their personalized coffee mugs hanging on the wall. Meals range from standard fare like the two-egg-and-toast breakfast ($4) to slightly adventurous creations like the tostada omelet ($6.50). *1146 Emerald Bay Rd. (Rte. 89), South Lake Tahoe, tel. 916/541–2161. ¼ mi south of the South Lake Tahoe "Y." Open daily 6 AM–2 PM.*

Los Tres Hombres Cantina. A typical Californianized Mexican restaurant with good, if not highly creative, food, Los Tres Hombres is popular with a south-shore crowd in their thirties. In part, the popularity is due to "fiesta hours," weekdays 4–6 PM, when pints of beer go for $1.75, double well drinks fetch just $3, and the chips and salsa are free. In addition to the standard burritos ($7.50) and fajitas ($11), Los Tres Hombres does offer a couple of specialties, including fish tacos ($8). *765 Emerald Bay Rd. (Rte. 89), tel. 916/544–1233. ½ mi northwest of the South Lake Tahoe "Y." Open daily 11–10.*

If you're broke and absolutely starving, try the cheap all-you-can-eat casino buffets in Stateline, Nevada.

Sprouts. South Lake Tahoe's vegetarian paradise features "food for health" and "energizing drinks." Feast on great veggie sandwiches ($4–$6), rice and vegetable plates ($4.25–$4.75), tempeh burgers ($4.50), and incredible fruit smoothies ($2.50–$3). They also have a wide selection of microbrewed beers ($2.25). The restaurant itself is a tiny affair, with a few wooden tables and a small outdoor patio. *3123 Harrison Ave. (U.S. 50), South Lake Tahoe, tel. 916/541–6969. Btw Stateline and the South Lake Tahoe "Y," just west of where U.S. 50 meets the lake. Open Mon.–Sat. 8 AM–9 PM, Sun. 8–7.*

NORTH SHORE **Blue Water Brewery.** Pretty much everything on the menu is made with beer, by people who love the stuff. So try the beer chili ($6) or the fish-and-chips in beer batter ($7.50) and, hey, have a beer ($3), brewed at an altitude of over 6,000 feet. There are also several vegetarian options, including vegan corn chowder ($5). *850 North Lake Blvd., behind Safeway, tel. 916/581–2583. Open daily 11 AM–midnight.*

Bridgetender Tavern and Grill. Housed in an old wooden cabin with high beam ceilings and trees growing through the roof, the Bridgetender is the north shore's best burgers-and-beer joint. Huge beef patties and tasty veggie burgers, both served with hearty french fries, go for $6. During the day you can sit on a patio overlooking the Truckee River; at night patrons come inside to sip beer and shoot pool. *30 Emerald Bay Rd. (Rte. 89), Tahoe City, tel. 916/583–3342. Next to the bridge at the Tahoe City "Y." Open daily 11–11.*

China Garden. Truckee's best Chinese restaurant serves up veggie dishes ($6–$6.50), seafood ($7.50–$9), and other Chinese standards in a typical red-carpet-and-Chinese-lanterns interior. Lunch specials, which come with soup, egg roll, fried rice, and your choice of entrée, run just $4.50–$5.50; dinner specials for two or more start at $8.50. *11361 Deerfield Dr., tel. 916/587–7625. In Crossroads Center, off Rte. 89 just south of the I–80 off-ramp. Open daily 11:30–3 and 5–9.*

Coyote's Mexican Grill. Whether you sit on the sun-drenched patio or in the tranquil southwestern dining room, you're bound to be pleased by the tasty grub at this woman-owned-and-operated, self-service Mexican eatery. Aside from the regular old burritos, tacos, and quesadillas—all under $6—Coyote's also features specialties like tequila-and-lime fajitas ($6.50) and mesquite chicken ($5). Sample the goods at the salsa bar before you sit down. *521 N. Lake Blvd. (Rte. 28), Tahoe City, tel. 916/583–6653. ½ mi east of the Tahoe City "Y." Open daily 10–10.*

AFTER DARK

Whether you're looking for a mellow patio to relax on or a rowdy bar at which to drink until all hours, Tahoe City is without a doubt the center of the lake's nightlife. Loud, crowded, and filled with hard-drinking youth scoping one another out, **Humpty's** (877 North Lake Blvd., 1 mi northeast of the Tahoe City "Y," tel. 916/583–4867) features the best live music in the area most nights (cover $2–$7). When Humpty's closes on Tuesday nights, the crowds head a few doors down to **Rosie's** (571 Rte. 28, tel. 916/583–8504), a large restaurant and bar housed in what was no doubt once a beautiful high-ceilinged cabin. Catering to a slightly less rowdy clientele, the **Naughty Dawg** (255 Rte. 28, ¼ mi east of the Tahoe City "Y," tel. 916/581–3294) has the best selection of high-quality beers in town, as well as surprisingly good salads and bar snacks. At the **Blue Water Brewery** (*see* Food, *above*) you can suck down microbrews and shoot a game of pool; live bands play Wednesday–Saturday nights.

With a large deck next to the Truckee River and a stylish indoor bar, the **River Ranch Lodge** (*see* Hotels and Motels, *above*) is an excellent place for a quiet drink. During summer, this place hosts an outdoor concert series with eclectic bookings ranging from jazz to hard rock (cover $5–$25). For the best coffee and desserts on the north shore, head to the **Truckee River Coffee Company** (11373 Deerfield Dr., Truckee, tel. 916/587–2583), in the Crossroads Center just south of the I–80/Route 89 junction. It's a homey café furnished with couches, a few small tables, and a piano. For a special treat, try the old-fashioned hot chocolate ($1.25) or the "coffee nut" ($4), made of hazelnut espresso, hazelnut syrup, and vanilla yogurt.

Considering the number of people on the streets by day, the south shore is surprisingly quiet by night. What limited action there is takes place on the Nevada side of the border in Stateline, where you'll find a number of casinos and the usual array of shows and "revues." Back in California, **Hoss Hogs** (2543 U.S. 50, tel. 916/541–8328) has an unbelievable collection of beer paraphernalia—labels, posters, hats, mirrors, etc.—and live music on a tiny stage several nights a week. Events on the south shore are covered in *Lake Tahoe Action,* a free weekly entertainment magazine put out by the *Tahoe Daily Tribune,* available at most motels.

Skiing

Whether you prefer downhill or cross-country, you can't go wrong in Lake Tahoe. Unbelievably sheer faces, narrow chutes, and huge cliffs have attracted a new breed of downhill skier bent on pushing the sport to new horizons. But don't be intimidated if you're just a novice. With over two dozen ski resorts, Tahoe offers ample opportunity for beginner and expert alike to tear up the slopes. Lately, Tahoe has also become a hot venue for snowboarding (*see box, below*). Associated with everything from surfing to grunge music, snowboarding is the hottest fad to hit the mountains in recent years.

The "Big Five" ski resorts—Squaw Valley, Alpine Meadows, Northstar-at-Tahoe, Heavenly Valley, and Kirkwood—all charge in the neighborhood of $40 a day, but if you're careful you can avoid ever paying these prices. For starters, buy multiple-day tickets, which will save you about $3–$7 per day. Also scour the local papers, motels, gas stations, and supermarkets for discounts and deals. Otherwise, consider skiing one of the smaller, less expensive resorts, many of which are quite good, especially if you're a beginning or intermediate skier. Some of the smaller places offer special discounts on mid-week skiing.

While the quality of food fluctuates from resort to resort, every mountain restaurant charges extortionate prices for the usual array of burgers, chili, and sandwiches. Plan ahead and pack your lunch.

WHAT TO PACK The type of gear you'll need depends in large part on the weather: Tahoe's temperatures can dictate several layers of sweaters or shorts and a T-shirt. Don't underestimate the danger of sunburn, even on a cold day (the sun is especially dangerous when it reflects off snow). In addition to skis, poles, and boots, required gear usually includes thermal underwear (preferably polypropylene), thin wool socks, gloves or mittens, a wool hat, sunglasses, goggles, a cotton or polypropylene turtleneck, a cotton or wool sweater, "powder" or "stretch" pants, and either a vinyl shell or a down jacket. Other things to think about, depending on the conditions, include sun block, glove and sock liners, ski masks, waterproof boots, and a visor or baseball cap.

EQUIPMENT RENTAL As a rule of thumb, the closer you get to the ski resorts the higher the cost of renting a pair of skis or a snowboard. On the other hand, the closer to the mountain you rent equipment, the easier it is to get an adjustment, repair, or replacement in the middle of your vacation. So rent at home only if you know exactly what you want and feel comfortable with the quality of the equipment.

Within Lake Tahoe, the same logic applies. You'll save money by renting from any of the hundreds of rental stores crowding the lake's major roads, but if you choose to rent from the higher-priced shops run by the ski resorts, you'll be able to get an adjustment midday. If you choose the former option, the best deal in town is the south shore's **Don Cheepo's** (3349 U.S. 50, about ¾ mi west of Heavenly, tel. 916/544–0356), which offers full downhill or cross-country rental packages (skis, boots, and poles) for $10, or the unbelievably low price of $7.60 if you produce a coupon (scattered around local motels and tourist information centers). Snowboards rent for $25, including boots—a very competitive price. **Porter's** on the north shore has low rates (full ski packages $14–$16, snowboards $20–$25), good equipment, and three locations, including one in Tahoe City (501 North Lake Blvd., just east of the Tahoe City "Y," tel. 916/583–2314) and one in Truckee (in the Crossroads Center on Rte. 89, just south of I–80, tel. 916/587–1500).

THE "BIG FIVE"

SQUAW VALLEY A vast resort with over 8,000 acres of open bowls, 2,850 vertical feet, and more than 25 chairlifts, Squaw Valley achieved international fame when it hosted the 1960 Winter Olympics. Today, it's unofficially known as the home of "extreme" skiing: The steep faces and 20- to 60-foot cliffs accessible off the **KT-22** and **Granite Chief** lifts provide plenty of challenges. But the beauty of Squaw is that it is truly an all-around ski area—70% of the mountain is suited to beginning and novice skiers, including much of the terrain at the highest elevations, where the views of the lake are best. On weekends, Squaw gets quite crowded, and a veritable small town—complete with shops, restaurants, bars, and two recreation centers—has sprung up at the mountain's base to serve visitors.

All-day lift tickets at Squaw are $40, with rental packages starting at $20 and first-time skier or snowboarder packages, including equipment and lessons, going for $49. Squaw makes snow along 80 acres at the bottom of the mountain; for an up-to-date snow report call 916/583–6955. To reach Squaw, take Route 89 south from Truckee for 8 miles and turn right on Squaw Valley Road.

Mountain Surfing

If you've always wanted to try surfing but feared getting tossed silly by the ocean, spend a day snowboarding. In the past few years, the practice of schussing down the mountain with your feet strapped to a board has overtaken Tahoe—and ski areas across the world—like a giant tidal wave. Requiring roughly the same fluidity and balance as surfing and skateboarding, snowboarding has been widely compared to these sports, both physically and culturally. Its devotees, generally young thrill seekers, initially met with resistance from major ski resorts, but by now most resorts have opened the slopes to boarders.

Snowboards generally rent for $22–$28 a day, including boots, and are available at most ski shops around Tahoe. If it's your first time out, follow these simple rules: Keep your weight back, steer with your rear foot, and maintain that no-pain, no-gain attitude no matter how many times you fall, because you're sure to ache from your feet to your buttocks when the day is over.

ALPINE MEADOWS Considering that it lies in the physical and figurative shadow of its better-known neighbor, Squaw Valley, the 2,000-acre Alpine Meadows resort has done quite well for itself, thank you. With a high base elevation of 7,000 feet (allowing for a longer season) and 12 lifts servicing over 100 runs, Alpine has built its reputation on the abundant snow and sunshine that grace its two mountains. Over half the runs on the front face and nearly all the runs on the back face of **Scott Peak** earn intermediate designations. But Alpine has also opened a handful of expert runs, notably **Palisades** and **Scott Chute,** two slopes that would make the average skier's hair stand on end for a month.

Most locals agree that Alpine Meadows is the best place to go for prime spring skiing.

At last look, full-day lift tickets at Alpine were going for $39, with half-day tickets (after 12:30) fetching $26. Rental packages from the ski shop in the main lodge are $19. Alpine Meadows is the home of the **Tahoe Handicapped Ski School** (tel. 916/581–4161), self-proclaimed "pioneer in ski programs for the mentally and physically challenged." To find out about snow and weather conditions at Alpine, dial 916/581–8374. Alpine Meadows is located off Route 89 about 2 miles south of Squaw Valley.

NORTHSTAR-AT-TAHOE With the best views of any north-shore ski area, extensive snowmaking capacity, great tree skiing, and two wind-protected bowls that get excellent powder after a snowstorm, Northstar-at-Tahoe has plenty to offer any skier. It certainly tries to be all things to all people, with a split of 25% beginner runs, 50% intermediate runs, and 25% advanced runs. Northstar is farther from the Bay Area than Squaw or Alpine, so it's not as popular. But it's definitely worth coming here for a day, if only for the incredible views of the basin from the top of the 8,610-foot **Mt. Pluto.**

In keeping with the other large ski resorts in the area, Northstar charges $39 for an all-day lift ticket, with half-day tickets (good after 1 PM) going for $27. Ski rentals run $18 a day, including boots and poles; snowboards are $25. For snow conditions, call Northstar's "Snowphone" at 916/562–1330. To get here from Truckee, take Route 267 south about 7 miles and follow signs.

HEAVENLY The only ski resort in Tahoe that straddles the California-Nevada border, Heavenly is officially the largest ski area in the United States. That means you'll find over 4,300 acres of skiable terrain, an incredible 3,500-foot vertical drop, and 25 lifts scattered over no less than nine peaks—a ski resort of Vegas-size proportions. And Heavenly's "upside-down" setup, with most of the expert runs toward the bottom of the mountain and many beginner and intermediate runs at the top of the 10,100-foot peak, means that less advanced skiers are afforded a rare opportunity to enjoy the area's best views. For experts, there's the 2,000-acre **Mott Canyon,** a boulder- and tree-filled canyon with steep faces and chutes aplenty. Making Heavenly that much more attractive is its snow-making capacity, the most extensive in Tahoe.

Heavenly has made a concerted effort to attract beginners. Among the various packages, the best deal is the full-day introductory lesson for $40, including four hours of instruction, a lift ticket good for novice lifts, and skis. Otherwise, regular tickets cost $40 per full day, $17 per half day (after 1). Ski-package rentals start at $18 a day, snowboards at $25. Heavenly's main entrance is off Lake Tahoe Boulevard (U.S. 50) in South Lake Tahoe, but lift lines are usually less severe at Heavenly's Nevada base, 3 miles up Kingsbury Grade from Lake Tahoe Boulevard. For a recorded report on snow conditions at Heavenly, call 916/541–7544.

KIRKWOOD With the highest base elevation of Tahoe's major ski resorts (7,800 ft), Kirkwood boasts the area's driest snow, which experienced skiers know means the best powder. And despite its relatively small size—10 lifts and 65 runs cover 2,000 acres—Kirkwood is the favored south-shore destination of advanced skiers, thanks to extreme runs like **Cliff Chute** and **Sisters Chute.** All told, 85% of Kirkwood's runs are designated intermediate or advanced. The resort's secluded location is beautiful, but it doesn't afford the spectacular views of the lake you'll find at the other major resorts. The payoff is a longer ski season than the other resorts, lasting well into late spring.

As with all of Tahoe's major resorts, lift tickets at Kirkwood are not discounted on weekdays; whenever you ski you'll pay $35 for a full day, $25 for a half day (9–noon). If you plan on skiing Kirkwood more than three times in the season, buy a Kirkwood Card for $15, good for $5 off every time you ski. Package deals include a "first-time only" special for $40, which buys you a pair of two-hour group lessons, equipment rental, and an all-day lift ticket valid only on designated lifts. For current snow conditions call 209/258-3000. From South Lake Tahoe, it's about a 30-minute drive to Kirkwood; take Route 89 south to Route 88 east.

THE BEST OF THE REST

Although Lake Tahoe's "Big Five" offer the best skiing, some of the region's other ski areas are cheaper and less crowded. If you're coming from the Bay Area, you can save 30–45 minutes driving time by skiing at any of the Donner Pass ski resorts—**Soda Springs, Sugar Bowl, Donner Ranch, Boreal,** or **Tahoe Donner.** Of these areas, Sugar Bowl, off the Soda Springs/Norden exit of I–80, is the largest and most beautiful. And with 50% of its runs designated advanced, including some of the best tree skiing in Tahoe, Sugar Bowl is especially attractive for experienced skiers. Lift tickets sell for $35, $25 for a half day (after 1 PM). For a snow report, call 916/426-3847. A few miles farther down the road, Donner Ranch, with lift tickets starting at just $10 on weekdays and $20 on weekends, is Tahoe's cheapest ski resort. It's not challenging enough to entice experts, but the five lifts and 360 acres provide plenty of thrills for beginning skiers and snowboarders. If you're planning a trip to Donner, though, try to rent your equipment before you reach the mountain—ski-rental packages start at $22 and snowboard packages at $30, some of the highest prices around. For a snow report, call 916/426-3635.

If you're in the area for a few days, definitely consider a day at the underrated 1,260-acre **Homewood.** On a steep peak that rises dramatically from the lake's west shore, Homewood offers outstanding views of the lake and a wide variety of terrain, from the bumpy slopes of **Exhibition** and **Double Trouble** to long cruises like **Miner's Delight.** A series of beginner lifts and T-bars provides plenty of room to learn the basics. Lift tickets go for $25 weekdays and $29 on weekends and holidays. Better still, Wednesday is two-for-one day, when you and a friend can ski for $12.50 each. Homewood is on Route 89, about halfway between Tahoe City and South Lake Tahoe. For snow conditions, call 916/525-2900.

CROSS-COUNTRY SKIING

Lake Tahoe is one of the best-known venues in the western United States for cross-country skiing. You'll have no problem finding a trail to suit your abilities at Tahoe's 13 cross-country ski areas, the most famous of which is the north shore's **Royal Gorge** (tel. 916/426-3871, take Soda Springs exit south from I–80), the largest cross-country ski resort in the United States. You can choose from 200 miles of trails running along a ridge above the north fork of the American River; fees are $16.50.

Strictly for skiers with at least some experience, **Eagle Mountain** (tel. 916/389-2254), dubbed "one of the area's best-kept secrets" by local authorities, offers incredible vistas along 45 miles of trails (fee $11). Highlights include the trails on Eagle Mountain itself, and the trails on **Cisco Butte,** which overlook Devil's Peak and the Royal Gorge. About an hour west of Truckee, Eagle is the closest to the Bay Area of Lake Tahoe's cross-country resorts. Take I–80 to the Yuba Gap exit and follow signs. Two other cross-country resorts on the north shore, **Northstar-at-Tahoe** (tel. 916/562-1330; $14) and **Squaw Creek** (tel. 916/583-6300; $10) are right next to downhill ski areas (*see above*), making them great choices for vacation groups with divided loyalties. Of the two, Northstar, with 40 miles of trails, is the more exciting destination.

On the south shore, only **Kirkwood** (*see above*; tel. 209/258-7248) offers both alpine and nordic ski trails, with over 50 miles of cross-country for skiers of all levels ($12). The award for best deal on the south shore, though, goes to **Hope Valley** (tel. 916/694-2266), located in a beautiful valley of the Toiyabe National Forest on the grounds of Sorenson's Resort. It offers 60 miles of trails for all levels, free. From South Lake Tahoe, take Route 89 south to Route 88 east.

Summary Activities

Lake Tahoe offers opportunities for just about every fair-weather sport imaginable. If you've done it, thought about doing it, always wanted to do it, or even heard a rumor that someone somewhere does it, chances are you can do whatever "it" is in Tahoe. An abbreviated list would include hiking, biking, fishing, sailing, waterskiing, jet skiing, rock climbing, hot-air ballooning, parasailing, horseback riding, and river rafting. The nearest tourist office (*see* Visitor Information, *above*) can load you up with armfuls of glossy brochures about all these sports. Of course, many of the more exotic adventures are pricey, but Tahoe is a great place to splurge.

If you're looking to rent equipment for just about any sport, **Don Cheepo's** (*see* Skiing, *above*) carries everything from waterskis to backpacks and other camping supplies. If you want to buy (or sell) equipment, **The Sport Exchange** (10095 W. River St., tel. 916/582–4510) in Old Town Truckee deals in used skis and fishing gear, as well as backpacking, camping, rock-climbing, and mountaineering equipment.

HIKING Almost every acre in the Lake Tahoe Basin is protected by some national, state, or local agency. **Tahoe National Forest** lies to the northwest, **Eldorado National Forest** to the southwest, and **Toiyabe National Forest** to the northeast and southeast. What this means for visitors is a whole lot of hiking trails, from easy scenic walks to strenuous climbs over mountain passes. For a complete list of day hikes, go to the Lake Tahoe Forest Service Visitor Center (*see* Visitor Information, *above*).

One of the most popular short walks is **Vikingsholm Trail,** a mile-long (one way) paved path leading from the parking lot on the north side of Emerald Bay to the shoreline and the 38-room Vikingsholm Castle. For something a little more woodsy, try the **Mt. Tallac Trail,** a half mile north of the visitor center (follow the marked asphalt road opposite Baldwin Beach to the trailhead parking lot). A moderate hike takes you 2 miles through a beautiful pine forest to Cathedral Lake. For a serious day-long trek (with no potable water along the way), continue on the trail another 3 miles as it climbs past a series of boulder fields to the peak of Mt. Tallac, the highest point in the basin at 9,735 feet. At the top, you'll find excellent views of the lake and Desolation Wilderness (*see below*). The trip up and back should take seven to eight hours.

If you're looking to do extensive backcountry camping, there are a number of options. Off the southwest corner of the lake, the 63,473-acre **Desolation Wilderness,** filled with granite peaks, glacial valleys, subalpine forests, and more than 80 lakes, is the most beautiful and popular backcountry destination in the area. South of the lake, **Mokelumne Wilderness,** straddling the border of Eldorado and Stanislaus national forests, has terrain similar to Desolation without the crowds. The region's other protected wilderness areas, **Mt. Rose** to the north and **Granite Chief** to the west, are less popular because they lack the beauty and accessibility of Desolation and Mokelumne. Before you enter any wilderness area, either for a day or for an extended visit, it's crucial to pick up a wilderness permit from the Lake Tahoe Forest Service Visitor Center (*see* Visitor Information, *above*)—if you don't you may actually be kicked off the trails.

If you suffer from hay fever, come to Tahoe prepared for battle. In the height of summer, pollen falls through the air like so many snowflakes.

BIKING A biker's paradise, Lake Tahoe has everything from mellow trails along the lake to steep fire roads and tricky single-track trails. Several paved, gently sloped paths skirt the lakeshore: Try the 3.4-mile **Pope Baldwin Bike Path** in South Lake Tahoe, less than a mile west of the entrance to Heavenly Valley; or the **West Shore Bike Path,** which extends about 10 miles south from Tahoe City to Sugar Pine Point State Park near the town of Tahoma. Also worthwhile are the bike path along the **Truckee River,** parallel to Route 89, which stretches from Alpine Meadows to Tahoe City, and the **U.S. Forest Service Bike Trail,** an 8½-mile paved path through pine forest and a rare aspen grove, which starts at Emerald Bay Road (just west of the South Lake Tahoe "Y") and ends at the lake.

Expert mountain bikers have a mind-boggling number of options. To start with, there's the famous **Flume Trail,** a 24-mile ride past several lakes and along a ridge with sensational views of Lake Tahoe. Strictly for experienced riders, the trail begins at the parking lot of Nevada State Park, just north of Spooner Junction on the lake's eastern shore (take Rte. 28 east from Tahoe City). A map is crucial. The **High Sierra Biking Map** ($6) and its accompanying book ($9) offer a detailed description of the Flume Trail (including a way to cut the ride in half for people with two cars), along with several dozen other excellent rides in the area.

If you like the idea of riding downhill all day, **Northstar-at-Tahoe** (*see* Skiing, *above*) opens a number of its ski runs for mountain biking June–September. An all-day ticket goes for $15 (bike rental $30, including helmet). **Squaw Valley** (*see* Skiing, *above*) allows mountain bikers to ride its tram up 2,000 feet, but will only permit you to come down a few of its ski runs. A single tram ride costs $17, unlimited rides $25; bikes rent for $17 per half day, $24 per full day (including helmet).

Dozens of shops around Tahoe rent mountain bikes, generally for about $4–$6 an hour, $15–$22 a day. On the south shore, try **Anderson's Bicycle Rental** (Rte. 89, at 13th St., 1 mi west of the South Lake Tahoe "Y," tel. 916/541–0500), conveniently located half a mile from the U.S. Forest Service Bike Trail, or, for slightly cheaper rates, **Don Cheepo's** (*see* Skiing, *above*), near the east end of the Pope Baldwin Bike Path. On the north shore, visit **Porter's Ski and Sport** (501 North Lake Blvd., just east of the Tahoe City "Y" on Rte. 28, tel. 916/583–2314).

BEACHES Dozens of beaches are scattered around the lake's shore, most charging $2–$5 for parking. Two of the best include **Chamber's Landing** near Tahoe City, a favorite of the north shore's young locals; and **Baldwin Beach,** a gorgeous and usually uncrowded sand beach between South Lake Tahoe and Emerald Bay. **Nevada Beach,** a more populated spot just across the Nevada border in Stateline, offers excellent views of the lake and its mountainous backdrop; and **Sand Harbor,** a crescent-shaped beach off Route 28 on the northeastern shore, is ideal for sunsets.

Despite Tahoe's wide range of outdoor activities, the well-known sport of sitting stagnantly on the beach, drinking a beer, and rising occasionally to take a dip in the lake's cold waters remains a popular pastime.

WATER SPORTS Lake Tahoe's often-frigid waters are home to many a rental outfit specializing in sailing, waterskiing, jet skiing, motorboating, windsurfing, kayaking, canoeing, sportfishing, and parasailing. Prices fluctuate a bit from shop to shop and according to the time of your visit, but in general sailboats go for $30–$35 per hour, $85–$95 per day; Jet Skis run $35–$70 per hour; Windsurfers rent for $10–$15 per hour, $30–$40 per half day; and canoes go for $10–$15 per hour, $30–$40 per half day. Parasailing rides, which usually last about 15 minutes, range from $35 to $50.

Shop around before you plunk down a sizable chunk of change. On the south shore, **South Shore Parasailing and Paradise Watercraft Rentals** (tel. 916/541–6166), with motorboats, canoes, kayaks, and other toys, is one of several shops operating out of **Ski Run Marina,** off U.S. 50 about a half mile west of the California-Nevada border. On the north shore, you'll find rental outfits in the **Sunnyside Marina,** about 2 miles south of Tahoe City on Route 89.

FISHING Like nearly everything in Tahoe, fishing options are abundant. The easiest and most obvious spot is (can you guess?) **Lake Tahoe,** stocked occasionally with rainbow trout by the folks at the Fish and Wildlife Service (to find the section of the lake most recently stocked, call 916/355–7040 or 916/351–0832). Also popular and easily accessible is the stretch of the **Truckee River** between Truckee and Tahoe City—just pick a spot and cast your line. To find the latest hot spots, ask around at local sporting-goods stores, many of which sport FISHING INFO HERE signs in their windows. At these stores, you'll also find fishing licenses, required by law ($9 a day, $24 a year).

For sportfishing on the lake, contact **Tahoe Sportfishing** (tel. 916/541–5448) in the Ski Run Marina or **Let's Go Fishing** (tel. 916/541–5566) in South Lake Tahoe. Half-day trips generally start at $50–$55, full-day trips at $70–$75.

Santa Cruz

Originally founded as a mission town, Santa Cruz has several identities. The old-time residents, many of Italian descent, still look askance at the liberal students and hippies who have been migrating to the town ever since the University of California opened its "alternative, no-stress" branch here in the 1960s. Although the students, hippies, and New Agers might not dominate this spectacular coastal community numerically, the lifestyles of these three overlapping groups have certainly defined Santa Cruz's cultural landscape. From Volkswagen buses to vegan (no meat, no dairy) restaurants, homeopathic healers to drum circles, Grateful Dead T-shirts to long-hairs smoking dope on the streets, you'll see signs of Santa Cruz's liberal attitude wherever you turn.

The carnival-like boardwalk is downtown Santa Cruz at its flashiest, drawing legions of hormone-crazed teenagers from Salinas and San Jose every weekend. The boardwalk's most popular attraction is the **Giant Dipper,** one of the oldest wooden roller coasters in the world. The harrowing ride affords you a brief panorama of Monterey Bay before plunging you down toward the beach. If your stomach's not quite up to such antics, head to Santa Cruz's stunning coast. The rocks off the craggy shore are favored perches for seals, the beaches are thronged by surfers and their retinue, and the hills surrounding the town fade into redwood forests ideal for hiking or musing.

Disaster struck Santa Cruz on October 17, 1989, when the 7.1-magnitude Loma Prieta earthquake destroyed the town's main shopping area, the Pacific Garden Mall. Squeaky new edifices have replaced the ruined buildings, and locals will tell you that the old-town charm is gone forever. But even if the mall is blander than before, Santa Cruz's sloppy individuality is still very much in place.

There's something gothic about Santa Cruz's version of the New Age—perhaps it's those sublime stands of redwoods brooding over the town like something from a Brothers Grimm story; perhaps it's the easy access to hallucinogens. According to some locals, Santa Cruz is the center of a powerful, undirected energy— resplendent and joyful on a good day, but positively sinister on a bad day.

BASICS

LAUNDRY **Ultramat,** the hippest laundromat around, eases the pain of doing laundry with the comfort of coffee and assorted noshes. Sip and munch while you watch your clothes dance. Each load in the washer costs $1.25, and dryers are 25¢ per 10 minutes. You can also take the easy way out and let the folks at Ultramat do all the work for 90¢ a pound (10-pound minimum). *501 Laurel St., at Washington St., tel. 408/426–9274. Open daily 7:30 AM–midnight; last wash at 10:30.*

LUGGAGE STORAGE Lockers are available at the **Greyhound** station for $1 a day ($3 for each additional day). *425 Front St., tel. 408/423–1800. Next to Metro Center. Open weekdays 7 AM–11 AM and 2 PM–8 PM, weekends 7–11, 3–4, and 6–7:45.*

MEDICAL AID **Westside Community Health Center** (1119 Pacific Ave., Suite 200, downtown above Logo's, tel. 408/425–5028) and the **Women's Health Center** (250 Locust St., tel. 408/427–3500) both offer general medical care at low cost, based on a sliding scale according to your ability to pay. Appointments are necessary at both clinics. Westside is open Monday, Thursday, and Friday 9–5; the Women's Health Center is open Monday and Wednesday–Friday 8–3:30, Tuesday noon–7, and Saturday 8:30–12:30.

VISITOR INFORMATION **Visitor Information Center.** A friendly staff has tons of free pamphlets, including the mediocre *California Coast* tourist magazine. They can't help with room reservations, however. Maps will set you back $1.50 each. *701 Front St., tel. 408/425–1234. 2 blocks north of Metro Center. Open Mon.–Sat. 9–5, Sun. 10–4.*

COMING AND GOING

BY CAR The most scenic route from either San Francisco, 1½ hours north, or Monterey, an hour south, is along **Route 1.** San Jose is about 45 minutes away on curvy **Route 17,** which

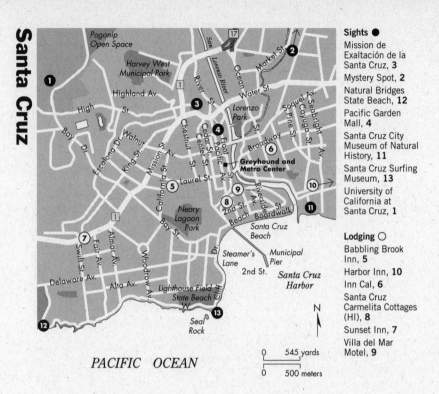

Sights ●

Mission de Exaltación de la Santa Cruz, **3**

Mystery Spot, **2**

Natural Bridges State Beach, **12**

Pacific Garden Mall, **4**

Santa Cruz City Museum of Natural History, **11**

Santa Cruz Surfing Museum, **13**

University of California at Santa Cruz, **1**

Lodging ○

Babbling Brook Inn, **5**

Harbor Inn, **10**

Inn Cal, **6**

Santa Cruz Carmelita Cottages (HI), **8**

Sunset Inn, **7**

Villa del Mar Motel, **9**

PACIFIC OCEAN

0 ——— 545 yards
0 ——— 500 meters

meets up with I–280, I–880, and U.S. 101 and is the faster drive to San Francisco and the East Bay. Avoid Route 17 on weekend mornings, when the entire Silicon Valley seems to head for the beaches, and at night, when the sharp curves of the road are difficult to see.

BY BUS **Green Tortoise** (tel. 408/462–6437), whose touring buses are known for their casual atmosphere, bunk beds, and "soft areas" made of foam pads and cotton pillows, travels from San Francisco to Los Angeles, stopping in Santa Cruz, once a week. Buses leave L.A. every Sunday night and arrive in the Safeway parking lot (2018 Mission St., north of downtown) in Santa Cruz on Monday morning (13 hrs, $30). Buses from San Francisco (3 hrs, $10) leave from 1st and Natoma streets, behind the Transbay Bus Terminal (see Getting In, Out, and Around by Bus, in Chapter 1), every Friday night at 8 PM, arriving in Santa Cruz around 11 PM. Reservations are recommended at least three days in advance, one week ahead in the summer.

Greyhound (425 Front St., tel. 408/423–1800) has direct service between Santa Cruz and San Francisco six times daily (2 hrs, $14). **Highway 17 Express Bus** (tel. 408/425–8600 or 408/688–8600) has hourly service, and is the cheapest way to travel between San Jose and Santa Cruz during the week ($2.25). Buses stop in Santa Cruz at the junction of Soquel Drive and Route 1, and in San Jose at the CalTrain station and at the corner of 3rd Street and San Fernando Avenue, one block from San Jose State University.

BY TRAIN You can't get to Santa Cruz directly by train, but **CalTrain** (tel. 800/660–4287) offers daily train service between San Francisco and San Jose (1½ hrs, $4.50). Trains run at least once an hour between 8 AM and 3 PM, more frequently during commute hours. From the San Jose CalTrain station (Cahill St. and W. San Fernando St.), take the **Santa Cruz CalTrain Connector** (tel. 408/425–8600) to the Metro Center (920 Pacific Ave.) in Santa Cruz. The bus leaves every two hours on weekdays, less often on weekends; it takes an hour and costs $5.

HITCHHIKING Depending on whom you talk to, Santa Cruz is either one of the mellowest or one of the most dangerous places to hitchhike in North America. If you want to give it a go, a good spot to catch a ride north out of town is at the corner of Swift Street and Route 1 (a.k.a. Mission St.) by the LITTER REMOVAL sign (no kidding). Hitching northeast along Route 17 toward San Jose or south along Route 1 is more difficult. Try standing at the Ocean Street on-ramp on 17. A less risky idea is the **UCSC rideboard** at Bay Tree Books, the college bookstore, in the center of campus. The availability of rides varies with the time of year, and some money to cover the cost of gas is appreciated, if not expected.

GETTING AROUND

Santa Cruz lies on the edge of Monterey Bay and is bisected by the San Lorenzo River. The town is full of crooked and confusing streets, so keep a sharp eye on a map. Route 1 becomes **Mission Street** when it enters Santa Cruz, and resumes its old identity on the way out of town. **Bay Street** and **High Street** both funnel into UCSC, while the boardwalk is on **Beach Street** just west of the river. The boardwalk, the pier, and downtown Santa Cruz (which centers around **Pacific Avenue** and **Front Street**) are all within comfortable walking distance of each other, and if you're feeling energetic the walk along **West Cliff Drive** from the boardwalk to the lighthouse is wonderfully scenic.

BY CAR Except on summer weekends, driving and parking are not difficult in Santa Cruz, even downtown. Free two-hour parking is available along Front and Cedar streets, and on weekends some parking lots are free all day. Possible parking spots include the **Santa Cruz County Building** (701 Ocean St.) and the **River Street Parking Garage** (River St.), which runs shuttles to the beach on weekends, when parking by the boardwalk gets difficult.

BY BUS Bus service is efficient and fairly easy to use. The Santa Cruz Metropolitan District Transit (SCMDT), also known as Metro, operates from the **Metro Center** adjoining the Greyhound Station. Any bus in town will eventually take you to the Metro Center, where you can pick up a copy of "Headways," a free pamphlet that lists all bus routes. The fare is $1, but you can purchase a special all-day pass for $3 on any bus or at the Metro Center. Exact change, in coins or one-dollar bills, is required; change machines are available at the Metro Center. A free shuttle runs between the Metro Center and the boardwalk in summer. *920 Pacific Ave., tel. 408/425–8600 or 408/688–8600. Open daily 7 AM–9 PM. Information booth in lobby open weekdays 8–5.*

BY BIKE Biking is the best way to get around Santa Cruz. Many streets have wide bike lanes and the weather is quite moderate, especially in spring and summer. Bring wheels from home if you can, since renting can be expensive. The imaginatively named **Bicycle Rental Center** (415 Pacific Ave., at Front St., tel. 408/426–8687), three blocks north of the boardwalk, has a competitive rate of $25 a day.

WHERE TO SLEEP

The price categories below refer to weekday rates, which often multiply as much as three times on weekends. Winter rates are about $10–$30 lower than in summer. The local youth hostel is probably the best deal around if you can get a room. Camping in the area is great, but campgrounds fill quickly in summer. If all the campgrounds listed below are full, Big Basin Redwoods State Park (*see* The South Bay in Chapter 2) is 30–45 minutes away.

Santa Cruz is a popular weekend trip for Bay Area residents, so be prepared for exponentially jacked-up weekend rates in motels.

Behind the boardwalk on 2nd Street, 3rd Street, and Riverside Avenue are some rather cheesy motels that rarely fill up, but you'll find comparably priced places clustered on Mission and Ocean streets that are much more comfortable, and equally convenient if you have a car. In particular, try the **Sunset Inn** (2424 Mission St., tel. 408/423–3471) for clean rooms in a pinch. Weekday rates range from $40 for a double to $85 for a suite that sleeps six. For a decadent treat, stay at one of several good B&Bs. At the downtown **Babbling Brook Inn** (1025 Laurel St., tel. 408/427–2437), rooms with country-French decor are surrounded by manicured gardens and a beautiful waterfall. Rooms come complete with private bath and a fireplace or Jacuzzi. The rates, which include a full breakfast, range from $85 to $150 per night for two.

> **UNDER $50** • **Harbor Inn.** In a residential neighborhood 10 minutes southeast of town, this inviting inn has large cathedral ceilings and doubles (starting at $45 in summer, $35 in the off-season) with a hodgepodge of old furniture and wooden beds. The antidote to characterless chain motels, the Harbor often fills in summer, so call ahead for reservations. Most rooms have kitchenettes, and larger groups can get a suite ($65–$85, depending on the season). *645 7th Ave., tel. 408/479–9731. From downtown, take Laurel St. across river, right on San Lorenzo Blvd., left on Murray St., left on 7th Ave. 19 rooms, most with bath. Wheelchair access.*

Inn Cal. The clean rooms are decorated à la chain motel, but the inn is only four blocks from the beach. A double goes for $45 during the week in summer, $55 on weekends; prices drop $10 during winter. Reservations are recommended. *370 Ocean St., at Broadway, tel. 408/458–9220. Take Bus 68 or 69 to cnr Ocean St. and Soquel Ave., then walk south along Ocean St. Wheelchair access.*

Villa del Mar Motel. Its location in downtown Santa Cruz makes the floral decor forgivable. Singles start as low as $38 and doubles at $42, jumping to $60 and $64, respectively, on summer weekends. *321 Riverside Ave., tel. 408/423–9449. 1 block from boardwalk. 23 rooms. Wheelchair access.*

HOSTEL **Santa Cruz Carmelita Cottages (HI).** The cottages are actually a couple of houses made hosteler-friendly. Located two blocks from the boardwalk on Beach Hill, these new accommodations cost $12 for members and $15 for nonmembers. Private doubles are $30, and "family" rooms (three to five people) cost $30–$40. It's just like living in a real house—with a bunch of strangers. Write (Box 1241, Santa Cruz 95061) or call ahead for reservations. *315 Main St., tel. 408/423–8304. From the boardwalk, walk up Main St. 25 beds. Curfew 11 PM, lockout 9–5. Reception open daily 7–9 AM and 5–10 PM. Lockers, sheets $1. Wheelchair access.*

STUDENT HOUSING The dorms at U.C. Santa Cruz's **College 8** accept guests from the end of June to the beginning of September, but rooms are plain, far from town, and expensive. A single runs $50, $65 with full board; a double is $40 per person, $55 with full board. The dorms are only open to those on "official" business, so you may want to say you're visiting the campus and sign up for a campus tour. *U.C. Santa Cruz Summer Housing, tel. 408/459–2611.*

CAMPING **Henry Cowell Redwoods State Park.** Fifteen miles north of Santa Cruz, this 111-site campground is buffered by a redwood forest and a stunning series of cliff faces. Things get a little out of hand during summer, when RVs and screaming teens overrun the place, but otherwise this is a camper's paradise. Reserve through MISTIX (tel. 800/444–PARK). Both tent and RV sites are $16 a night. *101 N. Big Trees Park Rd., Felton, tel. 408/335–4598 or 408/438–2396. Take Graham Hill Rd. from Rte. 1, or Bus 30 from Metro Center. Showers, toilets. Closed Dec.–Feb.*

New Brighton State Beaches. High above the ocean on a large cliff, this popular campground offers an incredible view of the coast from some sites. A steep path leads downhill to the soft beach below. Neither the tent nor the RV spaces have much privacy. Reservations—available through MISTIX (tel. 800/444–PARK)—are a must between May and September, when the place is filled almost every day. Sites go for $16 in summer, $14 in winter. *1500 Park Ave., tel. 408/475–4850. Bus 71 goes from Metro Center to cnr Soquel Ave. and Park Ave., but leaves you with a long walk.*

Sunset State Beach and **Manresa State Beach.** If New Brighton is booked, try these two scruffy beaches, both about 25 minutes south of Santa Cruz. Sunset has 90 campsites, all with fire rings, picnic tables, and hot showers. Spaces, reserved through MISTIX (tel. 800/444–PARK), are $16 in summer, $14 at other times, and go quickly on weekends. On the way to Sunset, you'll pass Manresa, which has 60 walk-in sites, with the same facilities, prices, and reservation system as Sunset. Sites are on a hill above the beach or set back in a sparse sprinkling of trees with little privacy. *San Andreas Rd. Sunset: tel. 408/724–1266. Manresa: tel. 408/761– 1795. Take Rte. 1 south to San Andreas Rd. exit, turn right at bottom of ramp, and right onto San Andreas Rd.*

ROUGHING IT Santa Cruz has a reputation as an easygoing town, but the police neverthe-less frown on people sleeping in public places. Lots of homeless people try it anyway, even though the cops periodically patrol the beaches and parks and issue waves of citations. If you're willing to take the risk, try one of the small beaches south of town, along Route 1. As long as you don't light a campfire or make a lot of noise, you may be left alone.

FOOD

To say that Santa Cruzians are health conscious is an understatement. Downtown, in the area bordered by Front Street, Pacific Avenue, and Cedar Street, reams of cafés, delis, and small restaurants offer health-oriented menus. For fresh produce, much of it organically grown, head to the **farmers' market,** held every Wednesday 2–6 on the corner of Pacific Avenue and Cath-cart Street; then trot over to Lorenzo Park (across River St. btw Water St. and Soquel Ave.) for a picnic.

Also look for the markets and fast-food chains along Mission Street. For a tasty slice of late-night pizza (until 11 PM most days, 1 AM Friday, and midnight Saturday), try **Uppercrust Pizza** (2415 Mission St., tel. 408/423–9010), on the west side of town near the Route 1 turnoff for Natural Bridges State Beach. At less than $2 a slice, Uppercrust is cheaper than **Pizza Amoré** (103 Cliff Dr., at Beach St. across from boardwalk, tel. 408/423–2336), open noon–10 daily, but the latter's pesto-ricotta slices ($3) are worth a try, and if you want a whole pie they'll deliver free of charge. For Mexican food, **Tacos Moreno** (1053 Water St., tel. 408/429–6095), a hole-in-the-wall about 5 minutes east of the downtown area, sells the cheapest (and some say the best) tacos ($2) and burritos ($3) in town daily 11–8. For sheer bulk, though, **Taqueria Vallarta** (608 Soquel Ave., tel. 408/457–8226) is the place to go. Enormous burritos ($3 vegetarian, $3.50 carnivore) are served up weekdays 10 AM–midnight and weekends 9 AM–midnight.

➤ **UNDER $5 • The Bagelry.** This deli warehouse specializes in wacky bagel spreads. If you're tired of dull bagels that pack no punch, try the homemade Pink Flamingo spread (cream cheese with lox and dill; $2.50) or the Luna spread (pesto, ricotta, and almonds; $2). A plain bagel with cream cheese costs $1.25, but plain bagels are for the timid only. If you're short on cash, try the "three-seed slug"—a flat, wide bagel without the hole (55¢). *320A Cedar St., tel. 408/429–8049. Other locations: 1636 Seabright Ave., tel. 408/425–8550; 4363 Soquel Dr., tel. 408/462–9888. All open weekdays 6:30 AM–5:30 PM, Sat. 7:30–5:30, Sun. 8–4.*

➤ **UNDER $10 • Dolphin Restaurant.** Work your way to the end of Santa Cruz's pier and grab an order of fish-and-chips ($5) from the outside window of the Dolphin. If you'd rather sit, head to the adjoining restaurant, where, in addition to fried fish, you'll find burgers ($5) and hearty clam chowder ($4.25 a bowl). *End of the pier, tel. 408/426–5830. Open summer, Sun.–Thurs. 8 AM–11 PM, Fri.–Sat. 8 AM–midnight; winter hours fluctuate, so call ahead.*

King Chwan. King Chwan has an amazing lunch deal—soup, salad, Chinese entrée, tea, and fortune cookie for $4. A slightly more elaborate combination dinner goes for $6.50. The light-ing is bright and the building looks like a large tract house, but for the money you can't com-plain. Even better, the food isn't half bad. *415 Ocean St., across bridge from Front St., tel. 408/429–5898, Wheelchair access. Open daily 11:30–10.*

Saturn Café. This is a great place to eat, read, and watch the spaced-out locals. If it's warmth you need, try the lentil chili ($3.50). For greens connoisseurs, the Titan salad ($6.50) is big and satisfying—enough for two to share. Better yet, indulge in the locally famous "Chocolate Madness" ($4.50), a huge conglomeration of chocolate cookies, chocolate ice cream, choco-late mousse, hot fudge, chocolate chips, and whipped cream. You can sip coffee here while your wash tumbles at the laundromat behind the café. *1230 Mission St., near Laurel St., tel. 408/429–8505. Open weekdays 11:30 AM–midnight, weekends noon–midnight.*

Zachary's. The basic breakfast—two eggs, potatoes, and your choice of homemade breads—sells for $3.50, but if you want something a little more elaborate, the huge stack of pancakes ($3.50) and the family-size omelets ($4 and up) are definitely worth the price. For the ultimate breakfast try Mike's Mess ($6): The pile of eggs, bacon, mushrooms, potatoes, cheese, sour cream, tomatoes, and green onions can easily feed two. The eating area is small and crowded, but the outstanding food is worth the wait (except maybe on weekends, when it can take up to an hour to get a table). *819 Pacific Ave., tel. 408/427-0646. Open Tues.–Sun. 7 AM–2:30 PM.*

DESSERT AND COFFEEHOUSES Because of the absence of nighttime diversions for the under-21 set in this town of over 15,000 college students, the café scene is an integral part of Santa Cruz's social life.

Caffe Pergolesi. In a big, rambling house downtown graced with a large outside deck, the Perg has all the trappings of a good café—potent house coffee ($1), double-potent espresso drinks ($1–$3), and a large selection of herbal teas (95¢). Try *chai*, a milky Indian spice tea ($2). The small food menu includes veggie lasagna ($5), quiche ($4.50), and sandwiches ($3), as well as the usual bagels ($2) and pastries ($1.50–$2). The crowd is somewhat eclectic, ranging from UCSC students to New Age–prophet types. This is definitely *the* place to play chess. *418A Cedar St., tel. 408/426-1775. Open daily 8 AM–midnight.*

True to the Santa Cruz health dogma, smoking is forbidden in many cafés.

Herland Book-Café. Although men are allowed at this bookstore/café, Herland was conceived as a safe haven for women. The books, grouped in categories like "Women of the Wild West" or "Women Respond to the Men's Movement," are all female-authored. The café offers coffee (75¢), tea (85¢), espresso drinks ($1.25–$2), and snacks ($1–$3). *902 Center St., at Union St., tel. 408/42-WOMEN. Follow Cedar St. toward Mission St., go left on Union St. and left on Center St. Open Tues.–Sat. 8 AM–10 PM, Sun.–Mon. 10–6.*

Jahva House. Located in a large warehouse, the Jahva House is open, airy, and comfortable. Big oriental rugs are strewn on the floors and ficus trees stand among the wood tables. The incredibly long coffee bar furnishes zillions of different coffees and teas, including organically grown varieties of both. For something extra-special, try a Mexican mocha ($2.50), a delicious mix of Mexican hot chocolate, espresso, and steamed milk. Excellent banana bread and slices of pie cost about $3. There's live music Monday nights. *120 Union St., tel. 408/459-9876. Walk down Cedar St. toward Mission St., turn left on Union St., and follow your nose. Open Mon.–Sat. 6 AM–midnight, Sun. 8–8.*

Santa Cruz Coffee Roasting Company. Although they've been known to play elevator music, this coffeehouse is still a great place to grab dessert ($2–$4). Enjoy the wonderful Snickers pie ($3) as you watch tourists and locals get wired. The coffee leans a little toward the upper end of the price spectrum. *1330 Pacific Ave., tel. 408/459-0100. Wheelchair access. Open weekdays 7 AM–11 PM, weekends until midnight.*

WORTH SEEING

Most of Santa Cruz's sights are downtown, within a walkable area. To explore the jagged coast, though, you'll definitely need a car or one heck of a mountain bike. Downtown, the **Pacific Garden Mall** is the center of the action, strewn with specialty stores, antique shops, restaurants, and cafés. Two worthwhile bookstores are **Bookshop Santa Cruz** (1520 Pacific Ave., tel. 408/423-0900), with a humongous selection of books, magazines, and international newspapers, and **Logo's** (1117 Pacific Ave., tel. 408/427-5100), Santa Cruz's premier used-book and music store. Also of interest is the **Mission de Exaltación de la Santa Cruz** (126 High St.), built between 1857 and 1931. The grounds are overrun with colorful gardens and fountains—the perfect place for a leisurely afternoon walk. On the beach near downtown lies the **Boardwalk,** a little Coney Island by the Pacific, with amusement-park rides, carnival games, kitschy shops, arcades, cotton candy, and plenty of teenage angst. Admission to the boardwalk is free, but the rides cost—usually $2–$3. If you do nothing else, ride the Giant Dipper ($3), a fabulous wooden roller coaster with a spectacular view.

UNIVERSITY OF CALIFORNIA AT SANTA CRUZ Take a quick tour of UCSC, in the thickly forested hills just north of downtown. The information center (tel. 408/459–0111) at the campus entrance is open weekdays 8–5 and has maps and tours. Be sure to investigate the spectacular **limestone quarry** near the campus bookstore, and take a self-guided tour of the organic growing system at the **Farm and Garden Project** (tel. 408/459–4140). If you park along Meder Avenue at the far west end of campus and catch the free shuttle at Bay and High streets, you can avoid the on-campus parking fee. You can also take Bus 41 from the Metro Center to the west entrance of campus.

SANTA CRUZ CITY MUSEUM OF NATURAL HISTORY You'll recognize this place by the huge replica of a whale out front. The museum is small but full of information about the Ohlone Native Americans, who originally populated the area, and the seals and sea lions that still do. If you're into honeybees, watch thousands encased under glass doing interesting apiarian things. The museum is on the east side of town, near Pleasure Point—a great place to watch the surfers do their thing. *1305 E. Cliff Dr., tel. 408/429–3773. From downtown, walk or drive down E. Cliff Dr. for 1½ mi. $2 donation requested. Open Tues.–Fri. 10–5, weekends 1–5.*

SANTA CRUZ SURFING MUSEUM At Lighthouse Point on West Cliff Drive, there's a tiny exhibit on surfing from its Hawaiian origins to the present, including an explanation of the modern wet suit. The museum is dedicated to the memory of an 18-year-old surfer who drowned in 1965. Also on display is a board bitten by a great white shark in 1987, testimony to the danger posed by sharks along the coast from Santa Cruz to Pigeon Point. Right outside the lighthouse, you can watch the surfers on Steamer's Lane, one of the best surf spots in California. Look a little farther out and you'll see Seal Rock, the summertime home of thousands of barking, shiny seals. *Mark Abbott Memorial Lighthouse, W. Cliff Dr., tel. 408/429–3429. Admission free. Open Mon., Wed.–Fri. noon–4, weekends noon–5.*

If you want some exercise, the path running parallel to West Cliff Drive from the boardwalk to Natural Bridges State Beach is a great place for a walk, jog, or bike ride. The 2-mile jaunt passes innumerable rocky coves and surfing points, and at least one nude beach.

NATURAL BRIDGES STATE BEACH Two miles west of town, the secluded and spectacular Natural Bridges State Beach is the perfect place to escape the overwhelming sensory stimulation of Santa Cruz. As its name implies, the beach features a series of bridge-like rock formations, as well as excellent tidal pools, picnic tables, barbecue pits, and plenty of soft, warm sand to stretch out on. Also on the grounds of the park is a **monarch butterfly colony,** one of the few places in the world where you can witness the amazing sight of thousands of brightly colored butterflies mating. The mating season usually lasts from mid-October to February, but call ahead for the latest, or to make a reservation for guided walks. *W. Cliff Dr., tel. 408/423–4609. From downtown, follow W. Cliff Dr. until you see the signs. Parking $6; or park on Delaware Ave. just east of the park entrance, and enter for free. Open daily 8 AM–sunset.*

Relaxing, Santa Cruz Style

If you're feeling battered from your journeys around California, Santa Cruz offers the perfect way to enter a state of total Zen relaxation. Head to Kiva (702 Water St., 1 block south of Market St., tel. 408/429–1142), a coed, clothing-optional spa favored by locals. For $10 you can spend as many hours as you like drifting into dreamy tranquility in hot tubs, saunas, and cold dips. The spa is open most days noon–11 PM and Fridays and Saturdays until midnight; the management reserves Sundays 9–noon for women only and gives women a two-for-one discount Monday through Wednesday.

MYSTERY SPOT If you abhor tourist attractions but feel a strange compulsion to "do" at least one, let this be it. This hilarious little place lies 3 miles north of Santa Cruz in the redwoods and, in the minds of true believers, is at the center of a mysterious force that makes people taller and compels balls to roll uphill. It's a tacky tourist trap, to be sure, but its gift shop is filled with one-of-a-kind souvenirs and kitschy knickknacks. Your $3 admission also buys you a Mystery Spot bumper sticker. *1953 Branciforte Dr., tel. 408/423–8897. From downtown drive east on Water St., turn left on Market St., go 2½ mi, and follow signs. Open daily 9:30–4:30.*

CHEAP THRILLS

Hiding in the redwoods, **Felton, Ben Lomond,** and **Boulder Creek** are small towns in a grand setting, definitely worth a day trip. All three get a bit crowded on weekends, particularly in summer, but they retain their mountain charm all the same. It will take only 30–45 minutes to travel through all three. On weekends, catch Bus 35 from the Metro Center or drive north along Route 9.

Along the coast about 5 miles southeast of Santa Cruz, the oceanside town of **Capitola** is popular for its wide, sandy beach, rickety wooden pier, and maze of artsy shops and seafood restaurants. After you're done window-shopping, head straight to **Mr. Toot's** (221 Esplanade, tel. 408/475–3679), a café full of old wood tables and comfortable couches, and have some chai ($2.25). If you need to grab a smoke, you can do so on the excellent deck, which has benches overlooking the beach. A few doors down is **Pizza My Heart** (209 Esplanade, tel. 408/475–5714), where you can get a big pesto slice ($2.50). Catch Bus 58 from the Metro Center, or take Route 1 south to the Capitola/Park Avenue exit and head toward the Pacific— you can't miss it.

For a groovy Santa Cruz experience, go to **It's Beach,** immediately west of the lighthouse, at sunset. Almost every day of the year, locals gather here to drum and dance as night falls. Also check out the numerous street performers on **Pacific Avenue** and the area surrounding the boardwalk.

FESTIVALS The **Cabrillo Music Festival,** usually held during the first week of August, has food, symphonic music, and other live entertainment. Call the Santa Cruz Civic Auditorium Box Office (tel. 408/429–3444) for more information. Tickets range from $6 to $25 depending on the performance and seating.

Shakespeare Santa Cruz is served up against a backdrop of beautiful redwoods during a six-week UCSC production of the Bard's works every mid-July–August on campus. Tickets start at $15 and peak at $21. For more information, call 408/459–2121.

Can you think of 1,001 things to do with fungus? You know, those little mushrooms that cover the forest floor during the rainy season? If you can't, the people at the **Fungus Fair** will be more than happy to assist you. The fair is held every January at the Santa Cruz City Museum of Natural History (*see* Worth Seeing, *above*). Entrance is $4.

AFTER DARK

Much of Santa Cruz's nocturnal activity takes place in the cafés and ends early. Nightlife in the traditional sense is decidedly lacking, and those establishments that do cater to the over-21 crowd check ID stringently. The journal *Good Times* (free at cafés and bookstores) comes out every Thursday with a listing of upcoming events. Look for happy hours and reduced cover charges, usually on Wednesday or Thursday nights.

Boulder Creek Brewing Company (13040 Rte. 9, tel. 408/338–7882), about 25 minutes north of Santa Cruz on Route 9, combines the best beer and the best live music in the area. Try their Ghost Rail Pale Ale ($3), Redwood Ale ($3), or, for heartier appetites, the Mudslide Stout ($2.75), "thick as a mudslide, twice as tasty." When live bands play there's usually a cover ($3 and up). Flamenco dancers, Middle Eastern musicians, and blues artists have all performed here. **Front Street Pub** (516 Front St., at Soquel Ave., tel. 408/429–8838), another microbrewery, has good ciders and its own Lighthouse Amber for $2.50. It tends to be an after-work stop off for those in their 20s and 30s.

The Catalyst (1011 Pacific Ave., tel. 408/423–1336), disparaged by some for its virtual monopoly of the Santa Cruz music scene, attracts a college crowd with local bands nightly and big names on occasion. Covers range from $1 on Thursday nights to $15 for major shows.

Poet and the Patriot Irish Pub (320 E. Cedar St., tel. 408/426–8620) has lots of smoke in the air (well, lots by Santa Cruz's standards), dart boards on the wall, and Irish beer on tap. For UCSC students and Santa Cruz's "artsy" crowd this is paradise, despite the pricey drinks. In the same building, the **Kuumbwa Jazz Center** (320 E. Cedar St., tel. 408/427–2227) offers jazz and blues shows randomly throughout the year. Call for tickets ($2–$14) and scheduling information.

The Red Room (1003 Cedar St., tel. 408/426–2994) is a UCSC institution, a darkly lit and run-down dive that's usually jammed with students. At night the adjacent restaurant becomes a venue for alternative music that ranges from grunge to punk. On some nights you pay a minimal cover. **The Blue Lagoon** (923 Pacific Ave., tel. 408/423–7117), across the street from the Metro Center, is the premier nighttime hangout for Santa Cruz's many gay and bisexual men and women. There's a $2 cover on weekends, but it's worth it for some of the best DJ dance music in town.

OUTDOOR ACTIVITIES

HIKING AND MOUNTAIN BIKING The redwood-filled hills surrounding Santa Cruz provide some of Northern California's best hiking and mountain-biking opportunities. Though a bit out of town, the prime spot for both is **Big Basin Redwoods State Park** (*see* The South Bay in Chapter 2). Closer to town, **Henry Cowell Redwoods State Park** (*see* Camping, *above*) has hundreds of miles of trails, many of which meander through virgin redwood forests. Bikes are allowed on designated fire and service roads, but not on hiking trails. Go to park headquarters for trail maps (75¢) and permits. To reach the park from downtown, follow Route 9 toward Felton. At the **Forest of Nisene Marks State Park** (Aptos Creek Rd. exit off Rte. 1, southwest of Santa Cruz, tel. 408/761–3487), you can view the ruins of a Chinese labor camp and hike to the epicenter of the 1989 Loma Prieta earthquake. Nisene Marks is also a favored locale of mountain bikers; inquire at park headquarters for trails where bikes are allowed. For bike rentals, *see* Getting Around, *above*.

SURFING Even though Southern California is reputed to be the state's surfing capital, many locals argue that Santa Cruz has the state's hottest surf spots, the most famous being **Steamer's Lane**, between the boardwalk and the lighthouse. If you don't consider surfing a spectator sport, the **Beach 'n' Bikini Surf Shop** (cnr Beach and Front Sts., near the boardwalk, tel. 408/427–2355) rents surfboards ($15), body boards ($10), and wet suits ($10) by the day.

FISHING If you want to throw in a line and try your luck on the pier, **Andy's Bait and Tackle** (end of pier, tel. 408/429–1925) will rent you a rod ($5, plus $25 deposit) and sell you bait ($3 and up). For deep-sea fishing, **Stagnaro Fishing Trips** (on the pier, tel. 408/427–2334 or 408/423–2010) runs day-long rock cod and salmon expeditions starting at $29.

The Central Coast

Simone de Beauvoir, Robinson Jeffers, Jack Kerouac, and Henry Miller number among those who've been inspired by Big Sur, the 90-mile stretch of coastline between Carmel and San Simeon. Luckily, Big Sur's dramatic and harsh geography, along with a core of adamantly protective locals, has precluded development; as a result the area is sparsely populated, with only a few gas stations and restaurants to disturb the serenity of the mountains. The only way to get to Big Sur is on Route 1—carved into the mountains by convict labor in 1937—which twists its way along jagged cliffs, past relentlessly pounding surf, and through ponderous redwood forests. The best way to enjoy it is to take it slowly, pausing at the many turnoffs to take in an awe-inspiring view, venture through foggy redwood forests, or lie in a meadow gazing at thousands of stars while sleep overtakes you.

The Big Sur coast is difficult to access by bus; most people have their own wheels, undoubtedly the best way to experience the grandeur of California's coastline. The traditional drive starts 48 miles south of Santa Cruz in Monterey, a heavily touristed and expensive coastal town. Heading south, you'll pass through the heart of Big Sur. At the southern fringe of Big Sur are San Simeon, home of the ornate Hearst Castle, and San Luis Obispo, a surprisingly lively college town 131 miles south of Monterey. Outside San Luis Obispo, Route 1 meets U.S. 101, continuing south to Santa Barbara and Los Angeles.

Outdoor types could easily spend a week in the region without getting bored, but the lack of budget motels and the dearth of transportation for travelers *sans* automobile can be a real hardship. If you just want to enjoy some coastal scenery and snap a few photos, you can easily get the idea in a long day, though two is preferable. In low season, the coastal drive takes less than six hours, but summer traffic on Route 1 can be a mess and will add a good two hours to your driving time. If you can, do the drive during the week or in late fall or early spring, when hotels and motels lop $5–$10 off their prices.

COMING AND GOING

BY CAR The best way to experience the 131-mile stretch of coastline between Monterey and San Luis Obispo is undoubtedly to drive it. It's nearly impossible to get lost—the only road is Route 1. To reach it from the north, take I-280 (from San Francisco) or U.S. 101 to Route 68 (from San Jose or the Peninsula). If you're coming from southern California, U.S. 101 meets the highway in San Luis Obispo.

If you don't have a car, think seriously about renting one. Many agencies will let you pick up a car in Monterey and drop it off in San Luis Obispo, or vice versa; of course, a "small" fee is charged. Deals pop up and disappear regularly. In Pacific Grove, near Monterey, try **Rent-a-Wreck** (95 Central Ave., Pacific Grove, tel. 408/373–3356); cars go for about $130 a week with 1,000 free miles, but you need to be over 25 if you don't want to pay $40 extra. At last look, **Hertz** (Monterey Peninsula Airport, tel. 800/654–3131) had a weekly rate of $160 for a compact with unlimited mileage and no drop-off fee.

BY BUS Traveling up and down the entire Central Coast on public transportation is impossible, but with some ingenuity and a lot of patience you can travel between a few towns. In the north, **Monterey-Salinas Transit** (tel. 408/899–2555) runs Bus 22 from Monterey to Nepenthe a few times a day (1½ hrs, $2.50). **Central Coast Area Transit** (tel. 805/541–2228) runs between San Simeon and San Luis Obispo ($2), but you'll have to transfer. Unfortunately, the San Simeon stop is 4 miles from Hearst Castle.

BY TRAIN Amtrak (tel. 800/USA–RAIL) runs the *Coast Starlight* line between the San Francisco Bay Area and San Luis Obispo (7 hrs, $52 one-way, $72–$104 round-trip). If you like rail travel, it's a cool thing to try; but though parts of the ride give a feel for the Central Coast's beauty, you'll be missing a whole lot of scenic turnoffs.

Monterey

This town at the south end of crescent-shaped Monterey Bay must once have been absolutely stunning. Unfortunately, its natural beauty and the publicity it received through John Steinbeck's novels have turned Monterey into a tourist trap, one of California's tackiest and most unabashedly commercial seaside resorts. Instead of small-town warmth and simplicity, you get the overpriced gift shops and lackluster restaurants of Cannery Row and Fisherman's Wharf, made famous by Steinbeck in *Cannery Row* and *Sweet Thursday*. If you're smart, you'll plan your trip so that you cruise into town in the morning, check out the top-notch aquarium and the coast (maybe including the 17-Mile Drive), and blow out of town that same afternoon, before the Disneyland-by-the-sea shtick begins to become oppressive.

During summer, the town plays host to the **Monterey Bay Theatrefest** (tel. 408/649–0340), with free outdoor performances on weekend afternoons in the Custom House Plaza. Call for schedules. The **Monterey Jazz Festival** (tel. 408/373–3366), a world-famous classic, takes place on the third weekend of September at the Monterey Fairgrounds. Tickets for the three-day festival start at around $110 and usually sell out about a month in advance. During the last week of June, look for big-name artists at the **Monterey Bay Blues Festival** (tel. 408/394–2652). Day tickets cost $20, but blues fans may want to pay the $50 to enjoy all three days.

Jimi Hendrix made rock-and-roll history at the Monterey Fairgrounds in 1969 when he burned his guitar in front of tens of thousands of awestruck fans.

COMING AND GOING Greyhound buses travel on U.S. 101 between San Francisco and Los Angeles, with regular service to Monterey via Salinas. The Monterey Greyhound depot (1024 Del Monte Ave., tel. 408/373–4735) is in a gas station on the eastern end of town. The trip to San Francisco takes about four hours ($19 one-way), and the journey to L.A. takes 12 hours ($44 one-way). Greyhound services are available at the station daily 7:30 AM–9 PM.

Monterey-Salinas Transit (tel. 408/899–2555) has regular connections to Carmel, Big Sur, and Salinas from Monterey. Fares range from $1 to $3. All buses depart from the downtown **Monterey Transit Plaza** (cnr Tyler and Pearl Sts.). For Big Sur, take Bus 22; it will get you as far as the Nepenthe restaurant on Route 1.

GETTING AROUND Getting around Monterey is not difficult. The bike/pedestrian path that parallels the shore runs from the historic downtown area to Fisherman's Wharf and Cannery Row. But because of summer tourism, both parking and crowds are a serious problem for drivers. The most reasonable parking garage in town charges $1 an hour and is located between Alvarado, Franklin, Washington, and Del Monte streets. A map that spotlights affordable public parking is available at the **Monterey Peninsula Chamber of Commerce** (380 Alvarado St., tel. 408/649–1770), open weekdays 8:30–5.

WHERE TO SLEEP Monterey is almost devoid of cheap lodging, but if you're persistent (or if you have a tent) you may be able to scare up something reasonable. A slew of motels on Fremont Street are accessible on Buses 9 and 10. The street is neither picturesque nor inviting, but it's pretty close to downtown (10 minutes by car). In a bind, there's always **Motel 6** (2124 Fremont St., tel. 408/646–8585), which has standard, sanitized-for-your-comfort rooms ($46) that sleep up to four. Across from Del Monte Beach in downtown Monterey, **Del Monte Beach Inn** (1110 Del Monte Ave., tel. 408/649–4410) is a small bed-and-breakfast offering rooms ($50–$75) tastefully decorated in the English countryside vein.

Lone Oak Motel. At this refreshingly tasteful, flawlessly clean motel, the price of a double— $48 weekdays, $82 (ouch!) weekends—includes unlimited access to a brand new Jacuzzi and sauna room, a great way to unwind after a hard day's traveling. Call ahead, as prices seem to fluctuate as quickly as you can count to three. *2221 Fremont St., tel. 408/372–4924. 46 rooms. Wheelchair access.*

Paramount Motel. Eight miles north of Monterey in the town of Marina, the Paramount is a clean and comfortable hotel with friendly managers who go out of their way to make you feel at home. For driving a bit and dealing with rooms that haven't been redecorated since the '50s, you'll get some of the cheapest doubles around ($33). No reservations are accepted; arrive in the morning and take your chances. *3298 Del Monte Ave., tel. 408/384–8674. Take Rte. 1 north to Del Monte Ave. and drive 5 min; or take Bus 12 to Beach Ave. and walk up Del Monte Ave.*

➤ **HOSTEL** • The **HI Monterey Youth Hostel** operates mid-June through August out of Monterey High School's gymnasium. Accommodations consist of foam mattresses on the gym floor, but it's hard to beat the price ($6 for HI members, $9 for nonmembers), and the staff is extremely helpful and friendly. *Tel. 408/649–0375. From the bay take Pacific St. south, right on Madison St., left on Larkin St. 75 beds. Curfew 11 PM, lockout 9:30–6. Reception open daily 7:30–9:30 AM and 6–11 PM. Sheets $1. Closed late Aug.–mid-June.*

➤ **CAMPING** • **Laguna Seca.** Most of the 185 campsites here have RV hookups, but a few undeveloped spaces are reserved for tent campers. Considering its location on the grounds of an auto-racing track—the site of various concerts and festivals in summer—the campground is surprisingly scenic, offering views of rolling hills and a long valley. Unfortunately, the sites themselves are pretty ugly and cost $15. Reservations, which must be made at least five days in advance, are advised during summer. *Rte. 68, tel. 408/755–4899 or 408/422–6138. 9 mi east of Monterey off Rte. 68 (follow signs).*

Veteran's Memorial Park Campground. Just five minutes from downtown, this first-come, first-served campground lies on a grassy knoll in a quiet valley—pleasant enough, but not quite the great outdoors. Forty primitive sites ($15), some shadier and more secluded than others, are packed tightly together. Showers are available, but bring your own food. *Via del Rey, tel. 408/646–3865. Take Rte. 68 west to Skyline Forest Dr., turn left at stop sign, and drive to bottom of hill; or take Bus 3 from Transit Plaza.*

FOOD Hearty seafood and health-food restaurants lie along Alvarado Street downtown, but unfortunately they're almost all overpriced. The **Bagel Bakery** (201 Lighthouse Blvd., tel. 408/ 649–1714), open daily 6:30–6, has the best deal in town for breakfast or lunch: Tasty bagels are 35¢–45¢, and you can add whatever toppings suit your fancy, including cream cheese (60¢), Jack or Swiss cheese (35¢), avocado (70¢), and sandwich meat ($1.50). **Rappa's** (end of Fisherman's Pier, tel. 408/372–7562) has a pleasant patio and a $7 lunch menu starring fish-and-chips. For picnic supplies, go to **Joseph's Patisserie** (435 Alvarado St., tel. 408/373–1108); sandwiches run $3–$5.

Fishwife. Among the best pasta and seafood restaurants on the peninsula, this casual place is a favorite with locals and travelers in the know. Fish dishes start at $9 and pastas are all less than $9. *1996½ Sunset Dr., Pacific Grove, tel. 408/375–7107. Near Asilomar Beach. Open Mon., Wed.–Sat. 11–10, Sun. 10–10.*

Papá Chano's. This taqueria offers tasty, large portions of Mexican basics. Tacos run $2–$3, and for a little more money a burrito ($3.50–$4.50) is a meal in itself. *462 Alvarado St., tel. 408/646–9587. Open daily 10 AM–11:30 PM.*

Toastie's Café. When you walk in you may feel trapped in a pink-lace dollhouse, but the fluffy yogurt-and-buckwheat pancakes ($4) and waffles smothered in blueberries ($4) should win you over. *702 Lighthouse Ave., Pacific Grove, tel. 408/373–7543. Open Mon.–Sat. 6 AM–3 PM and 5 PM–9 PM, Sun. 7 AM–2 PM.*

WORTH SEEING Monterey's main attraction is the world-famous **Monterey Bay Aquarium** (886 Cannery Row, tel. 408/648–4800), open daily 9:30–6, where you'll find sharks and sea otters in their natural habitat, a 28-foot kelp-forest aquarium, and screaming children running from their parents. Admission is $11.25 ($8.25 for students). From Route 1 south, take the Pacific Grove/Del Monte Avenue exit and follow signs for Cannery Row.

Dyed-in-the-wool Steinbeck fans will want to check out the bright-yellow **Kalisa's** (851 Cannery Row, tel. 408/372–3621), known in Steinbeck's time as the Laida Café—an "institution of commercialized love." Kalisa's has lost much of its charm since the '30s, but it's still an interesting place to grab a scoop of ice cream ($2). If you're over 21, you can visit one of Cannery Row's four wine-tasting rooms. **Bargetto Winery** (700 Cannery Row, tel. 408/373–4053) will let you sip chardonnay and merlot for free daily 10:30–6. Upstairs from Bargetto, **A Taste of Monterey** (700 Cannery Row, tel. 408/646–5446), also open daily 10:30–6, offers tasting of wine produced in Monterey County for a small charge. They also sell gourmet noshes.

The cash-strapped should head for **El Estero Park,** east of downtown at the intersection of Del Monte Avenue and Camino Estero. Here you can flop down on the banks of El Estero Lake, rent a pedal boat for $5 per half-hour from **El Estero Boating** (tel. 408/375–1484), and soak in the sun. For slightly more strenuous exercise, **Jack's Peak County Park** (tel. 408/647–7795), in the lightly forested hills south of Monterey, has mellow walks and picnic spots ($2 weekdays, $3 weekends). From the parking lot on the western end of the park, the mile-long **Skyline Trail** takes you past stunning views of Monterey Bay to Jack's Peak. To reach the park, drive 4 miles north on Route 68 and turn right on Olmstead Road.

Beach bums shouldn't waste time at Monterey State Beach, where the wind will make you wish you'd worn a sweater; it's nothing compared to the fabulous **Asilomar State Beach** (tel. 408/372–4076), 2 miles west of Monterey in the quiet town of **Pacific Grove.** Here, between October and March, you can glimpse thousands of monarch butterflies who make their winter homes in **Washington Park,** at the corner of Pine Avenue and Alder Street. If you're into dead butterflies, check out the excellent free exhibit at the **Pacific Grove Museum of Natural History** (165 Forest Ave., tel. 408/648–3116) Tuesday–Sunday 10–5. Finally, Pacific Grove is home to the **Point Pinos Light Station** (Ocean View Blvd., at Point Pinos, tel. 408/648–3116), the oldest continuously operating lighthouse on the West Coast. It's open weekends 1–4.

AFTER DARK Though Monterey's nightlife could hardly be called raging, there's no need to sit in your campground or motel room and clip your toenails. You'll find a load of gimmicky bars and clubs in the Cannery Row area, but if you prefer to mix with the locals, check out **Viva Monterey Cabaret Café** (414 Alvarado St., tel. 408/646–1415), where the hip set goes to toss down a few, watch local bands, or play pool, all under the scrutiny of a bartender with attitude. With a more laid-back atmosphere, the **Monterey Coffeehouse Bookshop** (472 Alvarado St., tel. 408/647–1822) is a great place to relax after a day at the beach. Browse through the latest literary offerings as you sip your java. They often have live music or poetry readings—pick up a copy of their *Book Page* newsletter for schedules.

OUTDOOR ACTIVITIES Not surprisingly, most of Monterey's sporting activities center around water. Cold, rocky Monterey Bay makes for a poor swimming hole, but it's a great place to fish, scuba dive, or grab a kayak and explore the coast.

➤ **BIKING AND MOPEDS** • **Monterey Moped Adventures** (1250 Del Monte Ave., tel. 408/373–2696) rents beach cruisers ($15 a day) and mopeds ($20 for the first hour, then $10 an hour; $50 a day). A driver's license and deposit are required. For $20 a day you can rent a mountain bike from **Bay Bikes** (640 Wave St., above Cannery Row, tel. 408/646–9090) and make tracks for the paved path that stretches from Asilomar State Beach past Lover's Point,

The Poor Man's 17-Mile Drive

Probably the most famous road on the Central Coast, the 17-Mile Drive takes you through Pebble Beach, with its immaculate golf courses, multimillion-dollar mansions, and incredibly scenic stretches of coast. You have to pay an utterly annoying $6.25 fee to drive the road, but if you enter by bike through the Pacific Grove gate (take Rte. 68 or Lighthouse Ave. west to Sunset Dr. and follow signs), you can avoid the fee and pedal past 8 miles of spectacular coast. Bay Bikes (see Outdoor Activities, above) has rentals for $20 a day; they even let you return the bike to their Carmel location (near the south end of the drive) for an extra $2.50. If you do decide to use your car, take advantage and explore the roads leading off the 17-Mile Drive. You might receive some less-than-friendly looks, but it's perfectly legal and you'll be treated to up-close views of some incredible mansions.

If the very idea of a fee road turns you off, there is another option. "The Poor Man's 17-Mile Drive," as locals like to call it, is really only 6 miles long, but it's nearly as dramatic as the real thing (and free). From Monterey, head west on Ocean View Drive (just west of Cannery Row) and follow the road as it bends southward past the spectacular Asilomar State Beach. Watch the sun set over wild sand dunes and the untamed Pacific; and look for Lover's Point, a grassy patch overlooking the ocean that's a popular daytime picnic area and nighttime make-out spot.

Cannery Row, and the wharf. Another great idea is to pedal down the 17-Mile Drive (*see box, The Poor Man's 17-Mile Drive, above*) for free, and on into Carmel or back to Monterey.

➤ **FISHING AND WHALE WATCHING** • Contact **Chris's Fishing Trips** (tel. 408/ 375–5951) or **Monterey Sport Fishing** (tel. 408/372–2203) on Fisherman's Wharf for half-day sportfishing trips. Both charge $25–$40, plus a small fee for equipment (tackle, poles, bait). Both also offer whale-watching trips ($12–$15) between December and March, when Monterey Bay is filled with migrating whales—a spectacular sight, to say the least. If ocean trips turn you a lovely shade of avocado green, head instead for **The Compass** (Wharf II, tel. 408/647–9222); pick up gear ($6 a day) and squid bait ($1.25), and cast off from Wharf II.

➤ **KAYAKING** • The folks at **Monterey Bay Kayaks** (693 Del Monte Ave., tel. 408/373– KELP) know everything there is to know about the sport and can recommend great takeoff points. Day-long rentals ($25) include kayak, oars, wet suit, and on-land instruction.

➤ **SCUBA DIVING AND SNORKELING** • Monterey Bay attracts divers from around the world with its vast kelp beds and magnificent underwater terrain. The bluffs and underwater caves off Ocean View Drive are the best scuba and snorkeling spots in the area. **Aquarius Dive Shop** (2240 Del Monte Ave., or 32 Cannery Row, tel. for both 408/375–1933) offers moderately priced equipment rentals for certified divers (about $70 the first day, $35 each additional day). A more feasible option for most people is snorkeling. Aquarius has gear for less than $30—not a high price, considering you'll need a wet suit, boots, gloves, and a hood to brave Monterey Bay's freezing waters. Snorkeling lessons and a tour will set you back $50 more.

Carmel

Perched on a rocky bluff 8 miles south of Monterey, this quiet, affluent beachfront town doubles as an artists' colony. Don't let the gorgeous coast and shady beaches fool you, however: Carmel is a strange place—an aloof bastion of conservatism known for its provincial attitudes and some of the most restrictive laws in the nation (high-heeled shoes are against the law, for example). Residents make every effort to preserve Carmel's small-town flavor. Downtown establishments do not have street addresses; and when the sun goes down, don't expect to find after-hours food or midnight revelry. No live entertainment is allowed in local drinking holes or restaurants. Instead, Carmel hosts its live shows at the bring-your-own-blanket **Outdoor Forest Theater Guild** (cnr Juniper St. and 2nd Ave., tel. 408/626–1681).

There are no sidewalks, no street lighting, and no mail delivery in residential Carmel-by-the-Sea. Locals enjoy this village setting and have chosen to pick up their mail at the post office, where they hang out and exchange gossip, just like in the old days.

Carmel fancies itself a small and private community, yet it's mercilessly invaded each day by tourists hopping from gift shop to art gallery to "quaint" café. Even more bizarre is the fact that Carmel elected Clint "Go ahead, make my day" Eastwood as its mayor. Above Clint's Hog's Breath Inn restaurant lies the **visitor center** (San Carlos St., btw 5th and 6th Sts., tel. 408/624–2522), open weekdays 9–5, Saturdays 10–5, and Sundays noon–4.

WHERE TO SLEEP Carmel is *not* cut out for those on a budget. Even the beat-up motels price their rooms as if they were lush suites in an upscale B&B. Your best bet is to camp— either in Carmel itself, north in Monterey, or south along the Big Sur coast. Otherwise, Monterey has a hostel and a few reasonably priced motels (*see above*).

The Homestead. Right in town, this place fits into the overdone country-inn category—a hotel that goes too far out of its way to be quaint and cozy. However, if you can afford to spend the money, the Homestead is awfully comfortable. Doubles start at $55 in winter, $65 in summer; four-person cottages are $95. Take a stroll in the well-kept gardens. *Lincoln St. and 8th Ave., tel. 408/624–4119. Exit Rte. 1 at Ocean Ave., follow to Lincoln St. and turn left. 8 rooms, 4 cottages, some with kitchen. Reservations advised.*

> **CAMPING** • **Saddle Mountain.** This well-groomed private campground is the only one within easy reach of Carmel. Fifty developed sites ($20 per night) lie on a terraced hillside. If you don't have camping gear, you can rent a cabin or nifty teepee for $32. The grounds are peaceful and the pool refreshing. *Schulte Rd., tel. 408/624–1617. Take Carmel Valley Rd. off Rte. 1, turn right at Schulte Rd. Showers available. Reservations advised.*

FOOD Unique and expensive are the norms here: Taverns, tearooms, al frescos, and broilers abound—everything except a McDonald's. If you'd rather picnic, go to the **Mediterranean Market** (Ocean Ave. and Mission St., tel. 408/624–2022), where you can create your own sandwich ($5), snack on tasty salads, or buy meats and imported cheeses by the pound. Head to the little park across the street to chow. The **Bagel Bakery** (173 Crossroads Blvd., junction of Rte. 1 and Carmel Valley Rd. 2 mi south of downtown, tel. 408/625–5180), a cousin of the Monterey shop (*see above*), is a bit out of the way but cheaper than anything you'll find downtown.

Friar Tucks. This friendly, pseudo-English place is down to earth compared to the rest of Carmel. Locals flock here for their morning brew. Burgers, salads, and sandwiches start at $5 and work their way up to $7. If you're in the breakfast mood, try one of the outstanding omelets ($6.50). *5th Ave. and Dolores St., tel. 408/624–4274. Open daily 6:30 AM–2 PM.*

WORTH SEEING Your first stop in Carmel will be the downtown area, easily accessed from Route 1, the only major thoroughfare for miles. Here you'll find a parade of pricey and often snobby gift shops, boutiques, restaurants, and art galleries. The **Carmel Art Association** (Dolores St., btw 5th and 6th Aves., tel. 408/624–6176) exhibits local works; if you've got a couple grand to blow, the pieces inside the small hall are for sale. You can pick up a map here that locates over 35 local galleries, many clustered on Dolores Street.

Carmel's **public beach,** at the end of Ocean Avenue, is the place to pick up a game of volleyball or nap in the sand, protected from the blistering sun and howling winds by cypress trees. For a more spectacular and less populated beach, head about a mile south along Scenic Road (off Ocean Ave. just above the public beach) until you come around the hairpin curve to **Carmel River State Beach,** known to locals as Oliver's Cove. When you see the view from here, you'll realize how poet Robinson Jeffers remained inspired for so many years—his home, known as the **Tor House** (26304 Oceanview Ave., 2 blocks from Scenic Rd., tel. 408/624–1813), is a stone's throw away. Jeffers, one of Carmel's most famous personalities, built Tor House and the adjacent Hawk Tower from rocks he carried up from the beach himself, creating one of California's most unique "natural" dwellings. Guided tours ($5 and worth it) are available by appointment Fridays and Saturdays 10–3. Otherwise, you get an excellent view of the house from Scenic Road.

The **Carmel Mission** (Rio Rd. and Lasuen Dr., tel. 408/624–3600), founded in 1770 by the busy Padre Serra (who is buried here), includes a stone church, museum, and gardens. It's open Monday–Saturday 9:30–4:30 and Sunday 10:30–4:30 in winter, daily until 7:30 in summer; and $1 donations are appreciated. Across the street is **Mission Trail Park,** where you can take a relaxing stroll; for serious hiking head to **Garland Ranch Regional Park** (*see* Outdoor Activities, *below*).

OUTDOOR ACTIVITIES

> **HIKING** • **Garland Ranch Regional Park** (Carmel Valley Rd., tel. 408/659–4488), 10 miles east of Carmel proper, is crisscrossed by dozens of rambling trails. If you've got strong legs and a few hours to spare, take the 5-mile **Lupine Loop** through the meadow and up, up, up on La Mesa and Sky Trail to Snively's Ridge. Besides a watchtower, you'll find one of the best 360° views on the Central Coast.

> **BIKING** • From Carmel you can take the 17-Mile Drive (*see box, above*) or pedal south on flat coastal roads for a few miles to Point Lobos. **Bay Bikes** (Lincoln St., btw 5th and 6th Aves., tel. 408/625–BIKE) rents hybrid bikes for $20 a day. If you're in good shape you can ride all the way to Monterey and drop off the bike at their other location for $2.50 (*see* Outdoor Activities, in Monterey, *above*). If you'd rather do your biking in the dirt, there are a few trails at Point Lobos State Reserve (*see* Near Carmel, *below*). Mountain bikers can also head to **Toro**

County Park (tel. 408/647–7799); take Carmel Valley Road past Garland Regional Park, go over the Laureles Grade, turn right on Route 68 toward Salinas, and follow signs.

NEAR CARMEL

POINT LOBOS STATE RESERVE Point Lobos State Reserve (Rte. 1, 4 mi south of Carmel, tel. 408/624–4909) is a day-use park where sea lions, harbor seals, and otters frolic. Whales pass by on their migration south from December to May. It's a great place to take a short nature walk: The **Cypress Grove Trail** loops past a rare species of cypress, the **Sea Lion Point Trail** leads to a magnificent series of sea coves, and the **South Shore Trail** takes you to Weston Beach, site of the reserve's best tidal pools. You can park for free across the street from the main entrance on Route 1; otherwise you pay $6 per vehicle. The park is open daily 9–4:30 in winter and until 6:30 in summer.

The reserve allows up to 15 teams on any given day to dive in **Whaler's Cove** among the otters, seals, and sea lions. Snorkelers and divers must pay a $6 fee; reserve for either activity through MISTIX (tel. 800/444–PARK). Proof of diver certification is required. To rent equipment, contact the Aquarius Dive Shop in Monterey (*see* Outdoor Activities, in Monterey, *above*).

Four and a half miles south of Point Lobos, **Garrapata State Beach** offers a series of loop trails perfect for those who don't like to sweat. **Soberanes Point,** a great place to watch otters playing on offshore rock formations, lies at the end of a short walk. A 1½-mile hike along a redwood-lined creek leads to **Soberanes Canyon. Rocky Ridge** slopes steeply on the 3-mile trek up but affords excellent coastal views. You can park along the road near the Soberanes Barn. The trailhead for the point is across the street from the beach; the ones for the canyon and ridge are behind the barn.

Big Sur

Roughly 8 miles south of Point Lobos, you'll find yourself in Big Sur, often described as more of a philosophy than a specific acreage. Every local defines Big Sur differently, but all agree that the region's precipitous cliffs, rocky beaches, and redwood forests make it one of the most dramatic stretches of coastline in the world. Save for tourists, the area is almost entirely unpopulated; only a couple of gas stations, a few inns, and the occasional exorbitantly priced restaurant break up the vast swath of nature.

Much of Big Sur lies within the 167,000-acre **Ventana Wilderness,** in Los Padres National Forest. Ventana's deep, wide valleys, waterfalls, hot springs, natural pools, perennial streams, and undisturbed wildlife (heaps of deer and more than a few bears) are enough to keep wilderness junkies on a perpetual high. Entrances can be found all along Route 1 between Bottcher's Gap (*see below*) and the town of Lucia. **Big Sur Station** (Rte. 1, just south of Pfeiffer Burns State Park, tel. 408/667–2315), open daily 8–6, is loaded with information on all of the surrounding wilderness.

WHERE TO SLEEP With more than 1,000 campsites up and down the coast, Big Sur is an ideal place to pitch a tent. If you want to sleep indoors, be prepared to pay handsomely for the privilege. If you don't have camping gear, your best option is to rent one of the tent cabins available at private campgrounds for $30–$40. One of the nicest is **Big Sur Campground and Cabins** (tel. 408/667–2322), a few miles south of Andrew Molera State Park on Route 1, where cabins sleeping two start at $40.

Deetjen's Big Sur Inn. This place, consisting of an inn and cabins secluded behind redwoods off Route 1, is rustic to the core, which means no phones, no TVs, thin walls, old bathrooms, and electricity that could blow out at any moment. Each room has its own name and is uniquely decorated with homey, personal stuff and a down comforter (you'll need it). The atmosphere and the people who run the place are both top-notch, and pleasant hiking trails lie behind the inn. Doubles start at $66, but all proceeds go to the non-profit Preservation Foundation, which runs the place. *Rte. 1, tel. 408/667–2377. 1 mi south of Nepenthe. 20 rooms, some with shared bath. Reservations a must.*

River Inn. The first place you hit coming south, the inn is comfortable and conveniently located near shops, a restaurant, and a gas station. The recently renovated rooms are clean, stylish, and typically expensive. Doubles start at $77 in the off-season and $88 in summer. *Rte. 1, tel. 408/667–2700 or 800/548–3610. 20 rooms. Reservations advised.*

➢ **CAMPING • Andrew Molera State Park.** Right off Route 1, about 10 miles south of Bottcher's Gap, Andrew Molera has more than 4,000 largely undeveloped acres with beach access and camping. Campers pay $3 per person and $1 per dog. Don't try to get by without putting your money in the self-payment box—a ranger *will* come around at 8 AM to collect the cash and hand out tickets to the weasels. The campsites are set against trees in a flat 10-acre meadow, half a mile from the parking area. Beware of staying here on summer weekends, when troops of Cub Scouts and pubescent preteens make life hell. The tents-only sites are first come, first served. Call Big Sur Station (*see above*) for more info.

Bottcher's Gap. If you want to kick it among the majestic madrones and oaks of the Ventana Wilderness, soaking up a view of a tremendous valley, you can trek to the 11 free first-come, first-served campsites in the gorge at Bottcher's Gap. There's no phone, no showers, and (at press time) no running water; but if you come on a weeknight, you'll have all the peace and solitude you could ever want. For the best info on the trails and the park, call Ranger Larry Born (tel. 408/625–5833). *8 mi east of Rte. 1 on Palo Colorado Rd., which is 5 mi south of Garrapata State Beach.*

Julia Pfeiffer Burns State Park. During summer, weekend warriors and car campers deluge the huge redwoods and shady oak trees of this popular park. There are two secluded environmental sites ($16) for hikers, bikers, and tent campers. Reservations through MISTIX (tel. 800/444–PARK) are advised. *Rte. 1, tel. 408/667–2315. 38 mi south of Carmel. Day-use fee $5.*

Pfeiffer Big Sur State Park. Although there are more than 300 RV and tent sites ($16) in this sprawling campground, the redwood groves and gurgling stream still make Pfeiffer one of the best places to sleep in Big Sur. For your convenience, there's a general store, a laundromat, and hot showers. It's crowded in summer, and sites should be reserved by calling MISTIX (tel. 800/444–PARK). If you're in the mood to ramble, head south along the river that meanders through the park; a semi-treacherous ¼ mile past the last campsite, you'll reach an unspeakably beautiful mountain pool surrounded by 200-foot cliff faces and rocky buttes. *Rte. 1, tel. 408/667–2315. Fire pits, picnic tables. Reservations advised.*

Plaskett Creek. In a big, grassy field on the east side of Route 1, Plaskett Creek offers 43 sites for $15. It's often empty during winter, but reservations through MISTIX (tel. 800/444–PARK) are advised in summer. Bring your own food. *Rte. 1, 9½ mi south of Lucia. No showers.*

FOOD There aren't many restaurants along the Big Sur coast, but you'll come across one or two good finds. The **Center Deli** (Rte. 1, next to Big Sur post office, tel. 408/667–2225) has groceries, a host of salads, and the cheapest sandwiches in the region ($3–$5), as well as fruit smoothies ($3) in summer. There's no seating, but you can grab a picnic lunch and eat at a nearby scenic overlook. The **Coast Gallery Café** (above Coast Art Gallery, Rte. 1, 33 mi south of Carmel, tel. 408/667–2301) is a casual deli with hot sandwiches ($6–$8) and a great view of the coast.

Café Kevah. Part of the Nepenthe restaurant complex, this café has daily brunch and lunch menus with interesting dishes like apple-bread pudding ($6.50) and spicy chicken brochettes ($6), as well as the most expensive espresso drinks this side of Paris ($3.50 and up) and a selection of scrumptious pastries ($2.50). The food is overpriced, but what you're really paying for is the fantastic view from the deck. If you want to splurge, head upstairs to the **Nepenthe** dining room, where pastas and seafood start at $12. *Rte. 1, tel. 408/667–2344. 29 mi south of Carmel. Open weekdays 9–4, weekends 10–5.*

EXPLORING BIG SUR Five miles south of Garrapata State Beach, Palo Colorado Road winds its way east from Route 1 through the Ventana Wilderness for 8 serpentine miles until it ends at **Bottcher's Gap.** From the parking lot, **Skinner's Ridge Trail** climbs 4 miles (roughly 3 hrs) to Devil's Peak, which affords incredible views of Ventana's dramatic wooded peaks and valleys. The eight-hour round-trip hike to **Pico Blanco**—a rugged mountain peak that the Esselen Native Americans thought of as the top of the world and the site of human creation—offers stunning views but winds through private property. The hike's not legal, but people do it anyway, trekking along the Boy Scout Service Road past the Boy Scout Camp and all the way up **Little Sur Trail.**

Back on Route 1, south of where Palo Colorado Road intersects the highway, look for the **Bixby Creek Bridge,** a 550-foot concrete span built in 1932. Just before the bridge, the circular **Old Coast Road** curves inland for 10 miles and meets back up with Route 1 opposite the entrance to Andrew Molera State Park. This is California at its rugged best—craggy cliffs, majestic redwoods, and views of Little Sur. If you're the four-wheeling type, you'll like the road's gravel- and mud-plagued inclines; a regular old car should be fine if it hasn't rained in the past few days.

Double back 1½ miles north of the road's base at Andrew Molera to check out the **Point Sur Light Station** (tel. 408/625–4419), built in 1889 to prevent shipwrecks along this foggy and rocky stretch of coast. Tours of the lighthouse are available on weekends for $2. Once the site of a Monterey Jack cheese factory and a dairy farm, **Andrew Molera State Park** offers more than 10 miles of hiking and mountain-biking trails. The strenuous hike on the **Ridge Trail** takes you through 2 miles of stunning coastal scenery to the top of a ridge. Take a deep breath and savor the spectacular view of the Pacific before you head down the **Panorama Trail** to the **Bluffs Trail,** which is especially striking in spring when the wildflowers are in bloom.

South of Andrew Molera, **Pfeiffer Big Sur State Park** (east side of Rte. 1, tel. 408/667–2315) is one of the most popular camping and hiking spots on the coast, especially during summer. Trails from the parking lot lead up to **Pfeiffer Ridge** and the 60-foot **Pfeiffer Falls,** at the end of a 20-minute hike through groves of huge redwoods. Just south of Pfeiffer on the same side of the highway, Big Sur Station (*see above*) is the starting point for the **Pine Ridge Trail,** a local favorite that leads into the Ventana Wilderness.

Sycamore Road, half a mile south of Big Sur Station, is unmarked save for a stop sign. If you can find it, brave the road for 2 miles and you'll land at **Pfeiffer Beach,** a violently turbulent, windswept cove with huge rock formations and an angry ocean that's definitely not suited for swimming. Five miles farther south lies **Nepenthe** (tel. 408/667–2345), an expensive restaurant with an extraordinary view (also the last stop of Bus 22 from Monterey). At the less expensive café next door (*see* Food, *above*), you can grab a coffee and watch the sun go down.

If you've filled your quota of stunning views and scenic overlooks for the day, head south a few miles from Nepenthe to the **Henry Miller Library** (Rte. 1, ¼ mile south of Nepenthe, tel. 408/ 667–2574), located in artist Emil White's home. The library displays the bohemian author's artifacts and has rotating exhibits on artists and writers associated with Miller or Big Sur. On summer weekends, stop by to soak up some aural vibes at afternoon concerts featuring anything from classical string quartets to folk and jazz. You'll pay a small cover; call ahead for details. The library is open Tuesday–Sunday 11–5 in summer, weekends only in winter.

Although not quite as spectacular as Pfeiffer Big Sur State Park, **Julia Pfeiffer Burns State Park** (tel. 408/667–2315) to the south has excellent and often less crowded hiking trails. But most

A Backpacker's Wet Dream

If you have two days and backpacking gear on your hands, think seriously about making the 10-mile hike to Sykes Hot Springs, one of the Central Coast's most enticing natural wonders. After a six- to seven-hour trek up steep ridges and along a river valley crowded with redwoods, you can soak your bones in the thermal spring and sleep under the stars before heading back the next day or continuing on into the depths of the Ventana Wilderness. The trail begins at the Big Sur Station parking lot; register and get a fire permit from the rangers here before heading out.

people pay the $6 entrance fee to see what was once the most spectacular sight in all of Big Sur, before parking lots, postcards, and crowds demystified some of its natural wonder: **McWay Falls,** which pours 70 feet down into the ocean. From the parking lot, a short half-mile walk leads to a bluff with an incredible view of the creek at the head of the falls. There are picnic tables here, and a few crooked trails lead down to the beach.

Three miles south of Julia Pfeiffer, a sign on the right side of the road reads: ESALEN INSTITUTE-RESERVATIONS ONLY. At the end of the road you'll find the world-famous **Esalen Institute** (tel. 408/667–3000), a one-time wacked-out hippie colony that specializes in the "exploration of human value and potentials." Locals tend to scoff, but the institute was one of the first places to introduce Gestalt therapy in the late '60s. Today, Esalen still attracts people from around the world to its skillfully run workshops and self-help sessions, although its gorgeous gardens, pool, and natural hot springs are now closed to the public during the day. To attend one of the outrageously expensive workshops, call the institute. Esalen occasionally rents out extra rooms for $65–$125; the price includes meals and access to the grounds.

Between 1 AM and 3:30 AM, you can relax naked in Esalen's natural hot springs, perched on a cliff overlooking the Pacific, for just $10—a pleasure that could run you ten times that much during the day.

OUTDOOR ACTIVITIES The main activity in Big Sur is hiking (*see* Exploring Big Sur, *above*), but to the dismay of many drivers, lots of people also bicycle along Route 1. Cyclists should be experienced and familiar with the narrowness of the highway and the lack of road shoulder. One benefit of pedaling the coast is that most of the state parks—including Pfeiffer and Julia Pfeiffer—offer cheap campsites (usually $3) to those on two rather than four wheels.

➤ **BIKING** • **Andrew Molera State Park** is the only Big Sur park with single-track trails for mountain biking. Mountain bikers in tip-top shape can take on the steep, overgrown **Ridge Trail,** which is over 2 miles long and has elevation gains of 1,200 feet. For a more relaxing ride, try the **River** and **Cottonwood trails,** both of which wind through the park's meadows and shrubbery, covering about 2 miles and taking only an hour of your time. All the trails start at the parking area or near Molera Point, about half a mile west of the parking area. Elsewhere in Big Sur, you'll have to stick to the fire and service roads, or risk a fine. One possibility is to head up **Naciemento Ferguson Road,** south of Lucia off Route 1. Bikes are not allowed to the left (where the Ventana Wilderness waits to swallow unwary cyclists), but off the right side of the road you'll see a few trails, most of which are quite steep in sections.

Index

259

Notes

Notes

Notes

Notes

Notes

Escape to ancient cities and exotic

islands  *with CNN Travel Guide, a*

wealth of valuable advice. Host Valerie Voss will take you

to all of your favorite destinations,

including those off the beaten path.

Tune into your passport to the world.

CNN TRAVEL GUIDE
SATURDAY 10:00 PMPT   SUNDAY 8:30 AMET

THE BERKELEY GUIDES
1995 "Big Bucks and a Backpack" Contest

**Four lucky winners will
receive $2,000*
cash and a Jansport®
World Tour backpack
to use on the trek
of a lifetime!**

HOW TO ENTER:

Complete the official entry form on the opposite page, or print your name, complete address, and telephone number on a 3" x 5" piece of paper and mail it, to be received by 1/15/96, to: "Big Bucks and a Backpack" Contest, PMI Station, P.O. Box 3562, Southbury, CT 06488-3562, USA. Entrants from the United Kingdom and the Republic of Ireland may mail their entries to: Berkeley Guides Backpack Contest, Random House Group, P.O. Box 1375, London SW1V 2SL, England.

You may enter as many times as you wish, but mail each entry separately.

* One Grand Prize — £1,000 and a Jansport® World Tour backpack — will also be awarded to entrants from the United Kingdom and the Republic of Ireland.

Prizes: On or about 2/1/96, Promotions Mechanics, Inc., an independent judging organization, will conduct a random drawing from among all eligible entries received, to award the following prizes:

(4) Grand Prizes—$2,000 cash and a Jansport® World Tour backpack, approximate retail value $2,180, will be awarded to entrants from the United States and Canada (except Quebec).

(1) One Grand Prize — £1,000 and a Jansport® World Tour backpack, approximate retail value £1,090, will be awarded to entrants from the United Kingdom and the Republic of Ireland.

Winners will be notified by mail. Due to Canadian contest laws, Canadian residents, in order to win, must first correctly answer a mathematical skill testing question administered by mail. Odds of winning will be determined from the number of entries received. Prize winners may request a statement showing how the odds of winning were determined and how winners were selected.

To receive a copy of these complete official rules, send a self-addressed, stamped envelope to be received by 12/15/95 to: "Big Bucks and a Backpack" Rules, PMI Station, P.O. Box 3569, Southbury, CT 06488-3569, USA.

Eligibility: No purchase necessary to enter or claim prize. Open to legal residents of the United States, Canada (except Quebec), the United Kingdom, and the Republic of Ireland who are 18 years of age or older. Employees of The Random House, Inc. Group, its subsidiaries, agencies, affiliates, participating retailers, and distributors and members of their families living in the same household are not eligible to enter. Void where prohibited.

General: Taxes on prizes are the sole responsibility of winners. By participating, entrants agree to these rules and to the decisions of judges, which shall be final in all respects. Winners must complete an Affidavit of Eligibility and Liability/Publicity Release, which must be returned within 15 days or prize may be forfeited. Each winner agrees to the use of his/her name and/or photograph for advertising and publicity purposes without additional compensation (except where prohibited by law). Sponsor is not responsible for late, lost, stolen, or misdirected mail. No prize transfer or substitution except by sponsor due to unavailability. All entries become the property of the sponsor. One prize per household.

Winners List: For a list of winners, send a self-addressed, stamped envelope to be received by 1/15/96 to: "Big Bucks and a Backpack" Winners, PMI Station, P.O. Box 750, Southbury, CT 06488-0750 ,USA.

Random House, Inc., 201 East 50th Street, New York, NY 10022

Complete this form and mail to:
"Big Bucks and a Backpack" Contest, PMI Station, P.O. Box 3562, Southbury, CT 06488-3562.
Entrants from the United Kingdom and the Republic of Ireland, mail to: Berkeley Guides Backpack Contest, Random House Group, P.O. Box 1375, London SW1V 2SL, England.

Mail coupon to be received by 1/15/96.

NAME

ADDRESS

COUNTRY   **TELEPHONE**

WHERE I BOUGHT THIS BOOK

A T-SHIRT FOR YOUR THOUGHTS . . .

After your trip, drop us a line and let us know how things went. People whose comments help us most improve future editions will receive our eternal thanks as well as a Berkeley Guides T-shirt. Just print your name and address clearly and send the completed survey to: The Berkeley Guides, 515 Eshleman Hall, U.C. Berkeley, Berkeley, CA 94720.

Your Name _____

Address _____

_____ Zip _____

Where did you buy this book? City _____ State _____

How long before your trip did you buy this book? _____

Which Berkeley Guide(s) did you buy? _____

Which other guides, if any, did you purchase for this trip? _____

Which other guides, if any, have you used before? (Please circle)
Fodor's   Let's Go   Real Guide   Frommer's   Birnbaum   Lonely Planet
Other _____

Why did you choose Berkeley? (Please circle as many as apply)
Budget information   More maps   Emphasis on outdoors/off-the-beaten-track
Design   Attitude   Other _____
_____

If you're employed: Occupation _____

If you're a student: Name of school _____ City & state _____

Age _____ Male _____ Female _____

How many weeks was your trip? (Please circle) 1 2 3 4 5 6 7 8 More than 8 weeks

After you arrived on your trip, how did you get around? (Please circle one or more)
Rental car   Personal car   Plane   Bus   Train   Hiking   Biking   Hitching
Other _____

When did you travel? _____

Where did you travel? _____
_____

The features/sections I used most were (please circle as many as apply):
Basics   Where to Sleep   Food   Coming and Going   Worth Seeing   Other

The information was (circle one):
Usually accurate   Sometimes accurate   Seldom accurate

I would _____ would not _____ buy another Berkeley Guide.

These books are brand new, and we'd really appreciate some feedback on how to improve them. Please also tell us about your latest find, a new scam, a budget deal, whatever—we want to hear about it.

For your comments:

_____

_____